MICROWAVE
Gourmet

BARBARA KAFKA

"IN THE MICROWAVE FIELD,
THIS WILL PROBABLY BE *THE* ONE TO BEAT
FOR SOME TIME."
Kirkus Reviews

"The book's
'Dictionary of Foods and Techniques' alone
makes it a must-have."
Susan Wyler, *Food & Wine* Magazine

"She comes up with intriguing methods,
such as using the microwave oven
to open oysters."
Cook's Magazine

"Kafka takes lots of the mystery out of
microwave ovens so that cooks
can discover new uses."
Booklist

"Wonderfully useful...highly recommended."
Library Journal

MICROWAVE
Gourmet

BARBARA KAFKA

AVON BOOKS ◆ NEW YORK

For My Father, James Beard, Robert Bak,
and Steven Spector
Men who lived with style and a
love of good food
In remembrance

AVON BOOKS
A division of
The Hearst Corporation
105 Madison Avenue
New York, New York 10016

Copyright © 1987 by Barbara Kafka
Illustrations by Lauren Jarrett
Published by arrangement with William Morrow and Company, Inc.
Library of Congress Catalog Card Number: 87-12764
ISBN: 0-380-71251-2

The William Morrow and Company edition contains the following Library
of Congress Cataloging in Publication Data:

Kafka, Barbara.
   Microwave gourmet.
1. Microwave cookery. I. Title.
TX832.K34   1987   641.5'882   87-12764

First Avon Books Printing: May 1991

AVON TRADEMARK REG. U.S. PAT. OFF. AND IN OTHER COUNTRIES, MARCA
REGISTRADA, HECHO EN U.S.A.

Printed in the U.S.A.

RA 10 9 8 7 6 5 4 3 2 1

ACKNOWLEDGMENTS

As a writer and cook, I have been extremely fortunate in the support I have received from professional friends, assistants and editors. It is probably impossible to distinguish between categories, but thanks are more than due. They are offered with my warm memories and chuckles of shared laughter and with recognition that without these people not only would my tasks have become chores, but they probably would have never gotten done. Affectionate thank you's to . . .

Ann Bramson, who has shepherded me through three books, worrying about my tardiness and defending me and my books at every turn, who thought I was only mildly crazy to write a microwave cookbook, who loyally learned to use an oven and now wants a second one, and who has elicited from me better books than I might otherwise have written.

Lois Bloom, who has worked with me for fifteen years without getting exasperated, but instead has offered warm support and much style.

Rebecca Marshall, who has worked with me on this and other projects for the last two years with enthusiasm, food knowledge, good hands, patience with both computer systems and boss, and a fine southern palate (her French isn't half bad, either).

Christopher Styler, who has worked with me for ten years off and on and helped with part of the testing for this book.

Rebecca Atwater, who sewed the pieces together and kept me in order when I seemed to be coming apart at the seams.

Joy Rosenberg, a recent recruit, who has transcribed recipes and tested valiantly.

Amy Schwartzman, Kathi Long anf Prudence Hillburn, who helped keep the financial books and the research books in order.

Elsa Tobar, who kept the house.

Leo Lerman, who made me write about food in the first place.

Alex Liberman, who brought me back to *Vogue*.

Edouard Cournand and Jacques Guerin, who first made me equate France and culture.

And Paula Wolfert, Joseph Baum, Amy Gross, Marion Asnes, Corby Kummer, Warren Picower, Carl Jerome, Margot Slade—all great supporters.

CONTENTS

INTRODUCTION

ONE of the most exciting things to happen in my culinary life in recent years has been my discovery of microwave cooking. The exquisite flesh of perfectly cooked fish, vegetables of intense color and full of vitamins without being soggy, Chicken in Red Wine ready just 20 minutes after I get home, perfect risottos without stirring and classic sauces are an easy part of my life. Efficiency and rapidity are only part of the story; better cooking and better eating are the true tale.

For many years, I was wrong about the microwave oven. I saw it abused in bad restaurants, and I thought that was the best it could do. I ate potatoes "baked" in it and rebelled at the lack of quality. I read the manuals that came with ovens and was repelled by the recipes I saw. I rejected the ovens along with their misuse. I was a microwave snob, as most of my chef and food-writing friends still are. When I finally announced, rather sheepishly, that I was writing a microwave cookbook, I felt I would have had a better reception had I announced my intention of going down to Times Square at 3:00 P.M. to take my clothes off.

I am a recent convert. I used to be wary of the microwave oven. I don't know if I was more frightened by what I (wrongly) thought was the danger of radiation or by having to learn a new technology. It took me a while to figure out how similar microwave cooking was to what I had always done, and just what the significant differences were.

I am still somewhat in awe of scientists and experts; therefore, as I learned, I was frequently astonished by the inaccuracies of the available information. I have had to puzzle out the truth for myself and combine it with what I already know of cooking to create a body of information and recipes on which I can rely. I am not willing to accept

1

food that is one bit less good from the microwave oven than I would serve at any time. The testing procedure was lengthy as I juggled ingredients, times and techniques to create equally valid recipes for different quantities of food and different powers of ovens.

I started out an aborigine scared of fire and ended up a computer-age person. I am not about to give up my copper pots, my cast-iron wood-burning stove or my barbecue; but I have a new friend in my kitchen, the microwave oven, and I use it more and more every day.

I hope you will come to enjoy it as I do. If you are a free-wheeling cook, you may feel cramped at the beginning. You must follow recipes exactly until you find out how the oven works. My best advise is to use it a great deal. The more you use recipes that work, where the food tastes good and suits the way you live, the more comfortable you will be with microwave cooking. It will no longer just be a way to reheat your coffee, defrost frozen dinners and make bacon. It can be an important aid in the way you cook every day. It can encourage you to try foods you thought were too hard or too time-consuming to make, or restore foods to your repertoire that you thought you no longer had time to cook: pâtés made in 11 minutes, broths that take 20 minutes, comforting soups that can be made in less time than it takes to set a table, stews and ragouts ready in under half an hour, sauces that even good restaurants don't take the time to make any more done in 10 minutes—all these are liberations from limitation and invitations to creativity.

The microwave oven makes it possible for all of us to cook and eat good homemade food again. We can return to entertaining without sacrificing our lives to it. If the microwave oven cooks something badly, I will be the first to tell you; but you will find that it cooks some things better than any other kind of cooking.

About the Recipes

These recipes are finicky about weights, measures, size of dishes and kinds of coverings. These elements influence microwave cooking fairly dramatically. Try to approximate them as closely as possible. You cannot simply multiply and divide microwave-cooking recipes; neither times nor ingredients work that way. To ease this problem, I have given several variations on very basic or much-used recipes. Use these prototype recipes as models for similar recipes that you are trying to develop, or turn to the Dictionary of Foods and Techniques in the back of the book for cooking times for different quantities.

All recipes were tested in large, full-power (650- to 700-watt) ovens. Where possible, I have supplied timings for different sizes and powers of ovens, both in the recipes and in the Dictionary. See page 9 for adapting recipes to different powers of ovens.

Compensating is something we have learned to do automatically when cooking in our regular ovens and on top of our regular stoves. We all know that our own stoves are just a little different from everybody else's. Our pots may be different, too. We adjust to these differences with hardly a thought. We will learn to do the same thing with microwave cooking. It just takes a little time.

Creating Or Adapting Your Own Recipes

When you are comfortable with your oven and these recipes, you may want to change them, or adapt other recipes that you know and love. Check similar recipes in the book to see what is done with the proportion of liquid to solids and to cooking times. Then try your own.

More aid is available from the Dictionary, which lists every food I worked with in the microwave oven and tells how it cooks, how long different quantities take to microwave-cook, how to adjust spices, herbs and wine in your recipes. It explains how much the food you buy by weight

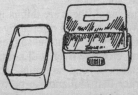

Scales are very useful;
food weight often
determines cooking time.

or pieces will measure in cups when it is cut up and when it is cooked. The Dictionary describes basic cooking techniques, as well as a few less common ones, to give you an idea of what does and does not work in the microwave oven. You will find, for instance, timings for defrosting or reducing a certain amount of liquid or sauce.

Uses of the Microwave Oven

Gradually, you will learn when and for what to use it. Rarely will you use it to make all the dishes in a meal unless some are make-ahead—desserts, pickles, relishes, sauces, a first course to be eaten cold. I seldom prepare foods and freeze them because it takes no longer to cook fresh than to defrost, and fresh is better.

Main courses, including meat and vegetables, casseroles, stews, plated meals, and the like, are good choices for microwave cooking. Once you have tried microwave-cooking fish, you may never cook it any other way unless you grill it outdoors. Most vegetables and fruits do well in the microwave oven, sometimes to cook fully, sometimes just for the first stage of their cooking before they are added to a pasta, soup or dessert. Many prepared components used in baking are made quickly and well in the microwave oven: caramel, custards, blanched or toasted nuts. The hotter the summer day, the greater its use. It doesn't heat up the kitchen—especially nice for preserving.

Polenta and risotto can now be everyday foods since you no longer have to stand stirring over a hot stove to the exclusion of all other activity. In fact, my prowess with risotto has converted more of my guests to microwave cooking than any promise of speed. Try the recipe on page 119; it will convert you, too.

On the other hand, there are things it cooks disastrously. I have followed every lead offered by overeager manufacturers and tried every solution suggested by overzealous writers. The microwave oven will not roast. It cannot make soufflés. Bread is beyond its limits. The suggestion of one blinkered writer that Hollandaise be made by opening the oven every 15 seconds in order to whisk vigorously would seem to be an advance backward. Do those things in the oven that it does well—precooking duck, for example. Finish it under the broiler while you cook the vegetable in the microwave oven. One modestly sized piece of equipment cannot be asked to do the work of a whole kitchen.

While testing ten microwave ovens of different manufacturers, sizes, control systems and powers, I kept in mind the reality that most of us are working with only one proud oven that efficiently cooks only one dish at a time. The day may come when we all lust for two microwave ovens—but not until we have learned that they are tools for cooking, not just as reheating and defrosting.

Learning Pleasant Truths And A New Cooking Style

The only real problem you may discover is that cooking in a microwave oven upsets your time sense, in the same way that a food processor or a computer does. You get used to the speed—in fact addicted to it. It is difficult to stop and allow time to bring large pots of water to a boil—in cooking pasta, for instance. You will be spoiled by the ease of cleanup. There are no baked-on, boiled-on messes; frequently, there are no cooking pots at all since many (or all) foods can be cooked right in their serving dishes or on individual plates.

Microwave cooking takes place in an enclosure, the oven, and cooking in that enclosed space takes a little getting used to. We all welcome the lack of heat, but we may miss the usual puttering—poking at the food, smelling it, reseasoning it. (Bakers are used to this, having few adjustments to make while the food cooks.) The virtues of microwave cooking—rapidity, simplicity and perfect results—will reconcile you to these changes. You will still enjoy delicious cooking odors; they just won't be as strong. You will create exceptional tastes. Most you will recognize; a few will be new, special and terrific.

I don't think I've ever had more fun working on a project. Do come along with me on the journey. I promise you'll taste some good food on the way.

THE OVEN

The Power

WHEN I first read about microwaves and how they cooked, it all seemed complicated and mysterious. Water molecules in food, it was explained, were set in motion by microwaves, causing friction that in turn caused heat. This made it all seem rather alien to me, unlike anything else I knew, until a more logical friend pointed out that this was the way most cooking procedures worked. (Just think of boiling water.) Then, when I discovered that the available information was distorted and that other matter (sugars and fats, for example) also danced around in the presence of microwaves, everything began to seem more orderly. I learned that a large piece of food was not cooked entirely by microwaves, but as in other kinds of cooking by internal conduction of heat.

"Microwave" means tiny (micro) waves. Other kinds of energy also travel in waves, but they are waves of longer lengths. Because microwaves are so short, they travel quickly, making most microwave cooking a rapid process. They slip quickly past the outer layer of a structure, so that the food rarely browns. In most cases, this isn't an overwhelming problem. Food cooks so quickly that it doesn't lose its juices and doesn't need the protection of a brown layer or crust. If you miss the browned look or flavor, simply sauté the food on top of the stove before cooking it in the oven, just as you do when making a pot roast. A lick of broiler heat at the last minute will gild rice puddings, cream-baked potatoes and cheese toppings.

The little rays quickly run out of energy, so food to be microwave-cooked is optimally cut into 3-inch pieces. Since the waves don't get trapped on the food's surface, within the sphere of their power they cook extremely evenly—no

6

fish with hard crusts and undercooked insides. The only problem occurs if the food being cooked is so small or so thin that it forces the waves to overlap in the middle of the food, burning it.

Because the microwaves really get the molecules jumping, food will stay very hot longer than if conventionally cooked, even though the surface may seem no hotter than usual. Remember that all foods, no matter how they are cooked, continue to cook after they are removed from heat—just think of scrambled eggs and roasts.

Fat seems to attract microwaves like a magnet, so there are advantages to cooking fatty foods in the microwave oven. Defatting ducks and short ribs is easy. Cooking marrow for classic sauces is a snap. Rendering chicken fat ceases to be a major event. The attraction of microwaves to sugar means easy, controllable caramelizing. Tight covering keeps steam washing down the walls of the containers, neatly avoiding untoward crystals.

All those jumping molecules mean *steam*. Some of it comes from the water content of the food itself; the juices of meat, the water in vegetables. Some of it may come from added broth, water, wine or other liquids; you don't need much to work up a head of steam. When it is held tightly in the container rather than allowed to escape, it helps cook the food quickly and evenly and keeps it moist. This also means you need to add less liquid. When liquid is heated in an uncovered container, rapid evaporation takes place, which is highly desirable for reducing sauces.

Because microwave cooking creates steam—pressure—within foods, a particular food with a relatively nongiving enclosure (a chestnut, for example) will explode from the steam pressure created as it cooks, like a soccer ball pumped too full of air. That is why it is suggested that you prick the skin of potatoes and sausages and the membrane encasing egg yolks and shad roe.

Other advantages of the microwave oven are that it will not heat up the kitchen (bliss in hot weather), and it uses relatively little energy.

The Features

If you are planning to buy a microwave oven, get one bigger than you think you need. You will soon discover how wonderfully useful it is. Tiny ovens are adequate if you mean never to do anything but reheat your coffee (ugh), defrost a lonely dinner, cook bacon, or cook very simply for only one or two. (Where it makes sense, I have given timings for these smaller quantities.)

Do not buy the space-age-control, multiuse (convection and broiling) oven to which you may be drawn. This suggestion comes from experience with washers and dryers: the simpler the appliance, the fewer repairs. In addition, there is an unsolved problem with multiuse ovens, which are metal-lined without any protective easy-to-clean plastic covering. Despite the introduction of fans, these ovens retain outrageous amounts of humidity, loosening the seal of plastic wrapping and distorting cooking results and times in other ways. Remember, most of these ovens do not cook two ways at once; you will be doing the procedures sequentially. The uncoated metal liners and shelves get so hot that you can easily burn yourself. Ordinary microwave ovens do not present this problem, and their plastic-lined interiors and glass liner at the bottom are also far easier to clean.

I don't like automatic cooking programs, defrosting programs, sensors and probes. They are too inaccurate to be reliable. In an orgy of proprietary paranoia, the oven manufacturers don't explain how their programs work, so you cannot adjust them or use standard recipes in them. The basic information to look for is how many watts the oven uses and what the settings such as "low" and "medium" mean as a percentage of full power. There are as yet no industry standards for such things.

In this book, most recipes call for *100%* power—"high" or "10" on some ovens—which is always the highest setting. A few recipes and defrosting instructions use a power of 30%; that can be called "low defrost," "medium low," "3," or "simmer" on ovens of different makes, which is frustrating. The power levels can also be erratic in some ovens. A little experimentation will probably straighten things out. You can try writing or calling the manufacturers; unfortunately, I have found that very unproductive. For most purposes, there is no reason to cook at anything less than 100%.

Most ovens have clocks; on some, the cooking timers can also function as general timers for your kitchen. Reconcile yourself to the irritating electronic beep the oven makes when it has accomplished its task. (With three or four beepers going off at any given time when I was testing this book, my kitchen was a zoo.)

There are two kinds of optional controls that are helpful. As with a clock, digital controls are more accurate than dials. Some ovens have a button you can touch for ''minute plus,'' which permits you to add a minute without turning the oven off and losing power if your food looks like it needs just a little more time.

Many of us are wary of microwaves, but anybody who can use a push-button telephone or set a digital clock should have no trouble using these machines—which are infinitely safer, in terms of radiation, than television sets. Different models have different opening devices, but they all are absolute controls: If the door is open, the power shuts off. Ovens that have a lever for opening instead of a handle are easier to use when your hands are full. All have doors that open from the right, so choose a place where you can open your oven fully without having to dance around the door.

Adjusting Recipes For Different Ovens

There is some variation between microwave ovens, but the differences are no more extreme than those between one make of stove and another. There are three main categories. Most full-sized ovens use between 650 and 700 watts of power (the standard of power for this book); cooking times in these ovens will be almost identical. Some smaller ovens use only 400 watts, while most medium ovens use 500 to 600 watts. There is no simple arithmetical way of calculating relative cooking times for ovens of different power. Cooking times in lower-wattage ovens will be longer, but the increase in time is mainly in the first part of the cooking. A small oven is like a car without much power; it will take longer to get up to 55 miles an hour, but once it is there, it will

cruise at speed as well as a more powerful car. On foods
that cook extremely quickly, such as wafer-thin cookies like
Florentines, allow another 30 seconds of cooking time in
less powerful ovens; for longer-cooking recipes, allow about
one and a half times the large-oven times: 15 minutes in a
small oven versus 10 in a large oven. If there is 1 cup or
more of liquid in the recipe, allow an extra 3 minutes of
cooking time.

Many small-scale recipes, usually variations for one or
two people, offer times for smaller ovens. Use the
Dictionary as a guide to small quantities when working out
your own recipes in small ovens. Only some of the baking
recipes have been working out for lower-power ovens. They
don't work well for baking large quantities.

Evenness Of Cooking

Microwaves are erratic; not even the oven manufacturers
can tell you exactly the pattern the waves will make in any
particular oven. This means hot spots and uneven cooking.
Some models have fans or other mechanical means of rotating the microwaves or the microwave-producing element.

Some ovens come with a carousel, a sort of lazy Susan
in the bottom that rotates the food as it cooks. If yours does
not have one, you can purchase an inexpensive one that
works like a windup toy, or you can remember to *rotate
foods that take a longer time to cook 45 degrees (a quarter
turn) after half the cooking time has elapsed*. The carousel
does slightly restrict the size of the dish that will fit in the

*You can cook directly on oven's glass liner. In
ovens with carousels, it is round (left); dishes
must fit on the carousel. If oven has no carousel,
buy a windup one (right).*

oven—14 inches with rounded corners is the maximum. I don't find that I need more than that, but you may. However, I find that much less rotating is necessary than commonly thought. Tight covering provides a mini-environment that evens out the cooking, and in recipes that call for stirring, the food is rotated without having to move the pan.

The Controls

Each make of oven, indeed each model, has controls that vary slightly. What you really need to discover is how to set a cooking time at 100% power, or "high," for a given time since almost all your cooking will be done in that mode. It is not hard.

Time on most ovens is set as it is on a digital clock: You press the number for the minutes, and then for the seconds. If you are setting for an even number of minutes, you must remember to press in two zeros for the seconds. To set a time of 3½ minutes, press in 3, then 3, then 0, for 3 minutes 30 seconds.

The Equipment

CONTAINERS. One of the saddest parts of cooking in the microwave oven is that your glorious copper pots will go unused. (Happily, you will not have to clean them.) This copper taboo extends to all metal pots. Don't get confused by Le Creuset and other enameled wares; they have a heart of metal. Do not use any ceramics decorated with gold or other metals. Be careful with all-over blue or orange-red glazes, as they may be metal-based. A little bit of these glazes in a decoration will not matter.

The problem with metal is that it absolutely blocks microwaves so your food can't cook. A lot of metal may also create an arc, or flash of light, in the oven; this won't kill your oven, but it is unpleasantly dramatic. A little bit of gold, silver or platinum in decoration may melt or discolor, not nice for the dishes.

Metal is sometimes used in special-purpose microwave dishes, such as browning dishes. Here it is perfectly fine, as is the limited use of aluminum foil to *shield* part of your food, like the thin tail part of a fish, and keep it from overcooking. It is called shielding because microwaves cannot pass through metal. Sometimes foil will be wrapped around dishes to keep the edges of the food from overcooking. Usually, the foil is removed at some time during the cooking to permit the shielded part to catch up.

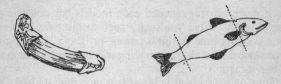

Shield banana (left) during ripening. Shield whole fish from either end to points indicated. If head and tail are removed, shield 1 inch of cut ends.

The containers and dishes you can use in the microwave oven may be quite different from what you usually think of as cookware (except for glass and ceramic soufflé dishes and those wonderful earthenware casseroles you bought but don't use because they seem to break in your oven). Large gratin pans, loaf pans, quiche pans, lasagne pans, pie pans, custard cups made from glass or ceramic, and the occasional all-glass cooking pans are all usable. One special pleasure of cooking with these pots or indeed irregular plates in the microwave oven is the ease of cleanup; no burned-on food—simple washing, no scrubbing, will do the trick.

Your cupboards will yield all kinds of surprising containers hitherto unused for cooking. You can use ceramic and glass bowls, pudding basins, coffee cups, teacups, glass measuring cups of all sizes (oversized with extra headroom is particularly useful), most of your plates and platters (including the best antique porcelains, as long as they don't have metal decoration, cracks or repairs), plastic storage containers marked "microwave-safe," vases, mugs, crocks, tureens, pitchers, undecorated paper towels and paper plates, and microwave-safe plastic bags and wrap. Despite the attractions of frugality and ecology, do not use recycled paper; it may, strangely enough, contain small metal particles, causing it to catch fire. If you must, go ahead and use special pans designed for the microwave oven in hideous plastic or conventional-looking glass and ceramic. I have found that Japanese lacquer bowls do very well. I was apprehensive about using them, but now it is a favorite way to heat a calming cup of soup without having the bowl get hot.

There is one dish specially made for the microwave oven that I highly recommend. It is $11'' \times 14'' \times 2''$ and has rounded corners so that it can fit on a carousel and still turn. It has the greatest capacity that is reasonable in a microwave oven, and I use it very often for everything from risotto to stew to cut-up duck.

It would be nice if those very useful plastic cooking bags came in more sizes. You cannot get an absolute seal (see page 21), but turning the end of the bag under or loosely knotting it will do quite well. (The largest bags may swell up too much to rotate freely on a carousel unless you shorten them slightly by knotting.) Often, you will be making your own bags by placing raw food on square pieces of microwave plastic wrap and then folding up the edges and sealing them tightly.

If the food is attractive, by all means cook it in glass; it shows it off, and, more important, you can see what is happening to it as it cooks. This is particularly helpful when you are reducing a sauce. A glass measure will let you see the reduction and measure it at the same time. When measuring cups are used to cook in, I always use glass.

Microwave-safe plastic has one important asset. It is invisible to microwaves. Using it instead of glass will shorten cooking times by 10 or more seconds, depending on the size of the dish—something to remember when cooking very sensitive foods. However, plastic tends to craze if transparent, and discolor with cooking over time. Worst of all, it is unattractive. Looks are more important in microwave-cooking containers than in other kitchen utensils, so try to save the plastic for storage and defrosting. Remember, much of the time the cooking dish, plate or platter will also be what you serve in or eat out of.

*Twist plastic bag containing food.
Knot to seal and shorten.*

*Place food on plastic square. Firmly
twist to seal; turn package onto seal.*

Use containers that approximate the shape and size suggested in the recipe. The size of the container (dish) and the way it lets you arrange the food influences the way food cooks and the timing. When devising your own recipes, use containers just large enough around to hold the food. Try to pick dishes deep enough to allow a little headroom so that sauces do not boil over, making a mess and loosening the covering. If you are using large dishes or platters, make sure they fit in the oven, and if you are using a carousel, make sure they have enough room to turn.

The size and shape of a cooking dish is an important variable when cooking in the microwave oven. When you reach for a dish described in a recipe, do not panic if you do not have one with precisely the same dimensions. Try to approximate it as closely as possible. The primary considerations in choosing a dish are volume, surface area, and depth (particularly if you are preparing a dish with a lot of liquid); the outline or form is really a secondary matter. As you can see from the illustrations below, 2-quart-capacity dishes can vary tremendously in shape.

Coffee cup   Ramekin   Demitasse cup

3" × 1½"   3½" × 1½"   3¾" × 2"

*These may all be used
interchangeably.*

4" × 2½" × 1¾"   6½" × 4½" × 1"   5" × 3½" × 1"

*Small ovals are good for baking
eggs, larger ones for single
portions of Macaroni and Cheese.*

6" × 2½"   7" × 3"   1½-quart

*Soufflé dishes come in all volumes.
Glass are best.*

5-quart to use
as a stock pot

2-quart   2-quart

*Use rimmed and rimless 2-quart dishes
interchangeably; use rimless dish for cakes.*

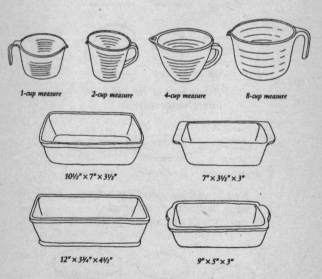

1-cup measure   2-cup measure   4-cup measure   8-cup measure

10½" × 7" × 3½"   7" × 3½" × 3"

12" × 3¾" × 4½"   9" × 5" × 3"

*Use loaf pan specified in recipe; different
shapes change cooking times even if the
volumes are the same.*

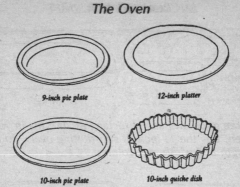

9-inch pie plate   12-inch platter

10-inch pie plate   10-inch quiche dish

Use only where flat dishes are called for; they do not hold stews.

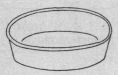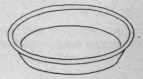

10" × 7¾" × 3" (2½-quart)   11" × 8½" × 2" (2½-quart)

Although dish on right has same volume, liquid in it will be lower than in that on left.

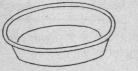

11" × 8½" × 3" (2-quart)   11" × 8" × 2" (1½-quart)

The flattened oval, though similar in dimension, cannot be substituted due to small volume.

Deep ovals can be used as same-volume soufflés. Use shallow ovals to replace similar-dimension rectangles. Measure volumes of all ovals.

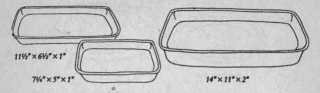

11½" × 6½" × 1"

7¼" × 5" × 1"

14" × 11" × 2"

Three good and useful rectangles; if it fits in your oven, buy the 14-inch. If substituting ovals, go by length and width, not volume.

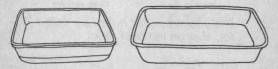

8-inch square (left); 10¾" × 7" × 2½" (right; can be used instead of 11½-inch rectangle or 11-inch oval)

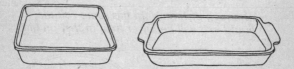

9-inch square (left); 13" × 9½" × 2" (right; can be used instead of 14-inch rectangle)

RACKS. There are helpful when you want to cook more than one dish of plated food at a time. They are ugly, but at least their legs fold so they don't take too much room to store. Be very sure when you open the legs that you snap them into place so that the rack does not collapse. If you are cooking two portions by cooking two platefuls at once, up the timing for two portions by 1 minute 30 seconds and exchange the position of the plates halfway through the cooking time. Some ovens come equipped with racks.

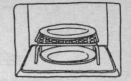

Rack with folding legs (left) fits in all ovens; two dishes cook at once (right).

BROWNING DISHES. These are dishes with metal surfaces or metalicized patterns applied to the bottom. These special surfaces absorb heat if preheated for about four minutes in the microwave oven. Just as when you brown in a skillet, you will need fat. You can, in this fashion, brown sandwiches, croutons or small pieces of food like sea scallops or chicken parts. They are not the most useful of pots. When not heated for use as browning dishes, they will work like ordinary microwave dishes. Check the manufacturer's instructions for preheating your dish. Remember that flat metal-lined dishes will require the same cleaning as conventional pots and pans.

9-inch round metal-lined browning dish; it gets as hot as any pot.

8-inch square browning dish with thin metal decal on bottom.

Covering Food

Rarely will the dishes that you are using come with a suitable lid. Be very careful of plastic containers designed for the microwave oven. Often the lids are marked, in nearly invisible letters, "not for use in the microwave oven"; they are just for storage. More important, lids almost never make a tight seal. Read on to see how important that is.

*Loosely cover dish with
doubled paper toweling.*

What you will use is paper toweling for loose covering and to avoid spatters, aluminum foil to shield parts of foods that you want to cook or defrost more slowly, and microwave-safe plastic wrap.

MAKING A TIGHT SEAL. I heartily recommend tight sealing with plastic. All the microwave-safe plastic wraps are usable, but polyvinyl chloride plastic wrap is by far the best. (Reynolds is the best-known brand.) It is not rigid when subjected to steam pressure; instead, it blows up like bubble gum. Don't be alarmed—nothing bad will happen. Indeed, good things will happen: Your food will cook more evenly. The held-in steam is one of your greatest cooking assets. Its pressure helps cook the food, keeps it from drying out, and creates a perfect mini-environment. Watching the plastic bubble swell when you have a good seal is a childlike pleasure.

*Bubble forms during
cooking if dish is tightly
sealed.*

Leave a large enough flap of wrap to extend well down the sides and under any handles of your container. If necessary, use two pieces of wrap with a good 2 inches of overlap. When lining a mold with wrap, use a big enough piece so that you can fold it back over the food in the mold. Individual fruits and vegetables or a modest amount of cut-up vegetables can be wrapped without using a dish. This is quick and avoids any washing up.

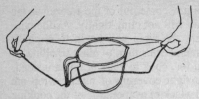

Place square of microwave plastic wrap diagonally over measure.

Carefully seal under pouring lip and around and under handle.

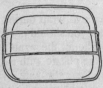

Overlap second piece of wrap by 2 inches if necessary to assure good coverage and tight seal.

Be careful when removing wrap from hot food. Pierce the plastic with the tip of a knife to release any steam, and peel off carefully. To uncover a measuring cup or baking dish, hold on to one corner of the plastic and pull it away from the container, lifting at the same time. It is no more dangerous than uncovering a steaming pot.

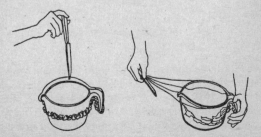

Prick small hole with point of sharp knife to release steam. Pull plastic up and away from container to release.

If your container has just come out of the freezer or the refrigerator, plastic wrap will not cling tightly. As the container heats in the oven, the wrap will begin to cling. It adheres less well to some plastics than to glass or china. If an airtight seal is called for, cook in glass or china instead.

The advantages of a tight covering of plastic wrap are more rapid cooking and a lack of evaporation of the cooking liquid or moisture in the food itself. Which leads to the correct thought that certain recipes or ingredients will benefit from cooking, *uncovered*, so that evaporation can take place.

If you need to remove wrap during cooking in order to stir or turn food over, you should not remove the food from the oven. You can take all the wrap off and replace it. Or you can simply slit the plastic with a knife while your dish is still in the oven, then stir with a wooden spoon. Just patch the hole with a fresh piece of plastic, or re-cover the dish right over the slit wrap.

If you don't prick the plastic, a strange thing may happen. As the steam cools, the plastic gets drawn down tightly onto the surface of the food; it looks shrink-wrapped. Don't worry; the minute you prick the plastic, the seal will release. The only time this is a problem is when your food is a fragile custard or timbale. That is why in such recipes I recommend pricking the plastic wrap even before removing the molds from the oven.

MICROWAVE BASICS

Planning Your Meal

BEFORE you start to cook, take your ingredients out of the refrigerator or freezer. Defrost what may need defrosting, following the information in the Dictionary under DEFROST-ING. In this book timings are based on the assumption that ingredients are at room temperature unless instructions are given for defrosting, or, as in the case of butter, melting. Depending on the amount of cold food that is added to a recipe, the cooking time can increase anywhere from fifteen seconds to a few minutes.

While you are getting used to the microwave oven, microwave-cook only one dish per meal, unless you can make the others ahead. The best way to time the main course is to figure out when your guests will get to it. Then count back for a starting time by the number of minutes the dish takes to cook. Often this means not putting food in the microwave until the guests are seated at the table, or have finished the previous course. Food cooked in the microwave oven will keep hot longer than foods cooked conventionally. Don't forget that if you are cooking an accompanying starch, you will need to start the water long before the main course goes in the oven.

Before You Begin to Cook

POT HOLDERS. These are a must when cooking in the microwave oven. Pots and dishes *do* get hot, no matter what you have heard to the contrary. They won't get so hot that you will burn yourself, just hot enough so that you might drop them.

STIRRING. Because the walls of plastic-lined ovens do not get hot, it is easy to stir things without removing them from the oven. By doing so, you conserve heat and shorten cooking times. Slit the plastic; insert a spoon in the slit and stir rapidly. Re-cover the dish or simply patch the plastic wrap with an overlapping sheet. The object is to move quickly so as to release as little retained heat from the oven and the food as possible. Be careful when cooking in a metal-lined microwave oven—its innards do get hot. Be very careful when you go back to regular cooking or you may burn yourself.

To stir, slit plastic wrap.　　　*Stir through slit in wrap.*

*Patch plastic wrap with fresh
square to make tight seal.*

SETTING THE TIMER. When you are going to stir or turn something in the oven, set the timer for the full cooking time and then remember when it is time to stir. (As you open the door, you automatically interrupt the cooking. To resume cooking, close the door and press the Start button.) Alternatively, set the timer for only the time until stirring, shaking or turning. To resume cooking, close the oven door and reset the controls for the remaining time.

Timings in this book are based on this rapid, in-oven manipulation. If you are more comfortable working a little more slowly and removing the cooking dish from the oven, add 30 seconds (one minute in less powerful ovens) to the cooking time in order to allow the heat to catch up with itself.

MICROWAVE OVENS "PREHEAT." You don't need to preheat ovens on purpose, but realize that the air in the oven, with its natural humidity, gets warm. This is important in two ways. First, successive batches of rapid-cooking foods—wafer cookies, for example—will cook more quickly (by about 15 seconds) than the first batch. Second, because this heat helps cook food, it is better not to remove the food from the oven in order to stir.

OVERALL PREPARATION AND COOKING TIMES have been given in the introduction to some of the recipes to give you an idea of how long you will actually be in the kitchen. (Compare microwave cooking times to longer, standard times!) Unfortunately, the microwave oven does not eliminate the need for peeling, cutting and chopping. If you do those things in a more leisurely fashion, allow a little extra time. Since you do not have to watch the pot, some preparation can be done while the food cooks. A food processor is often called for to speed up the cutting. If you do not have one, allow a little more time. Blenders are wonderful for some soups and sauces. Use a food mill when you want to purée and remove seeds and skins, or put the cooked mixture through a sieve.

Food mill with discs with
different-size holes

MULTIPLYING TIMES AND QUANTITIES. Microwave cooking is a funny business. You can't just multiply, divide or apply some other arithmetic formula to the business of increasing or decreasing recipes. Different multiples are involved for different basic ingredients. That is why there are so many variant recipes in this book: They ensure your success and give you models to follow for your own multiplication and division. Seasonings have to be changed when recipes are increased or decreased, since this change in size heralds a different cooking time. For example, the recipe for a briefly cooked food—say a fish fillet that is cooked for only 1 minute 30 seconds—pepped up with a smidgen of garlic and some dried herbs, will need ten times as much garlic but only four times as many herbs when the recipe is expanded for eight fillets that cook in 7 minutes. This, as you will see later in this chapter, has to do with the way garlic and dried herbs behave with longer microwave cooking.

Look ingredients up in the Dictionary to find out what special quirks they may have in microwave cooking, as well as additional cooking times.

Since microwave cooking frequently depends on a combination of steam cooking and the activity of different kinds of food molecules under the influence (sounds like Svengali) of microwaves, cooking times depend on the amount of liquid in the ingredients as well as the amounts of fat, sugar and protein.

When multiplying recipes, especially those that are cooked tightly covered, don't increase the amount of liquid arithmetically. Use as little liquid as is reasonable to achieve flavor. Liquid actually slows cooking. You can always add more at the end, or heat it separately and add it. With tight covering, almost no evaporation takes place. Indeed, liquid seems to appear from nowhere; it is drawn from the ingredients themselves. You may find that much less liquid is plenty.

Some examples of reduced liquid and reduced cooking time: Beef in Red Wine (page 240) microwave-cooks in 15 minutes with 1½ cups of liquid, as compared to conventional cooking, which takes 4 hours, with 3 cups of liquid for the same amount of beef; a pound of acorn squash cooks to moist perfection without any added liquid in 7 minutes in the microwave oven, versus 45 to 50 minutes if conventionally cooked with liquid added.

Liquid can be water, wine, broth, cream, juice, milk, liquid vegetables like tomatoes, or anything else that you add to moisten food. This liquid, as well as the liquid in the foods themselves—meat juices, the water content of vegetables—comes to a boil in the microwave oven and turns to steam, which either evaporates out of the dish if the food is uncovered, or helps to cook the food when the food is tightly covered.

When dividing recipes, it does not always follow that the liquid can be proportionally reduced. You may not leave enough to get up a good head of steam, and your food may take longer to cook. Adding a little water that will boil quickly and make steam is like priming the pump.

Size Of Food And Cooking Time

When possible, it is better to avoid large hunks of food and big, empty hollows like the space inside a whole chicken. You will be spending time heating that space. Since birds cannot be roasted successfully in any case, it is much better to cut them up before microwave-cooking them. Fairly large fish can be cooked whole; see FISH in the Dictionary. To get indications for the largest single piece of a given meat that can be cooked at one time—beef, for example—check the relevant recipe. If the largest quantity given is for 3 pounds, it is safe to assume that results with larger pieces of this meat have been unsatisfactory. See the section on cooking protein (page 30), for an explanation.

Relatively modest-size vegetables in the microwave oven will cook in roughly the same time whether cut up or whole (group cut-up pieces in a cup or bag).

You can slightly accelerate the cooking times of certain foods by cutting them into equal, optimal shapes and sizes and separating them in the dish to cook individually—fish medallions or meat loaves, for example. When you divide a recipe into individual containers for cooking, you may not be speeding the cooking process because each container will need to heat up. As plastic wrap doesn't need to heat up, directions for cooking a large quantity of cut-up vegetables may suggest wrapping them in individual plastic packages. It is also the reason to increase the dish size, rather than use several dishes at once.

As in Chinese cooking, pieces of the major ingredient(s) should be about the same size. Pieces about 3 inches cubed or discs 3 inches in diameter and 2 inches thick are optimal for rapid cooking. Food is best arranged so that large pieces do not touch; the microwaves can get at them better.

If a large piece of food is kept to a height dimension of around 3 inches and is not allowed to get much fatter (wider) than that—for example, a whole fish, a pâté or a slim piece of veal—its length will be less important.

The sizes into which secondary ingredients are cut does not matter much, unless they are disproportionately large (the vegetables should be smaller than the meat in a stew) or unless they are the major ingredient at some point in the cooking process (onions cooked first in butter before other ingredients are added). When a dish, a soup for instance, is composed of many different but equally important ingredients, they should be pretty much the same size.

Arranging Food

There is more to arranging food than using separate plastic-wrapped packages and separating roughly evenly shaped major ingredients. When cooking food on top of the stove, the center of the pot is the hottest. In a microwave oven, the food toward the outside of the dish cooks the most quickly. Arrange foods for microwave cooking either in a ring toward the outer perimeter of the cooking dish, with the quicker-cooking elements (such as vegetables) toward the center, or arrange food like the spokes of a wheel, with the thickest parts of the food toward the rim.

Because food cooks differently depending on where it is placed in the cooking dish, vegetables that normally need different cooking times can all be cooked at the same time. Place the long-cooking vegetables toward the outside of the dish and quick-cooking vegetables in the center. See VEGETABLES in the Dictionary for a list of long- and quick-cooking vegetables. Often, you can cook all the vegetables in the same time it would take to bring to a boil the water to cook just one vegetable. This permits you to cook a variety of vegetables even for one or two people.

The technique of arranging foods of different cooking times applies to more than vegetables. Follow the arrangement descriptions in the recipes, and refer to the illustrations that follow on page 29.

Petal arrangement, skinned and boned chicken breasts

Sections of foods (hubbard squash) arranged in dish and each covered

Long-cooking ingredients not touching, around quick-cooking ones

Pork chops with bones toward edge of dish

Arrange meat loaf or figs to hold shape or position.

Fish fillets folded, thicker (fold part) toward the edge of dish

Singly wrapped foods, here apples, arranged for even cooking

Pears or foods with thin ends (quick-cooking) toward center

How Different Kinds of Foods Cook

COOKING PROTEIN. You have only to cook an egg white—practically pure protein—to understand how rapidly proteins respond to microwaves. A few seconds too many and you achieve rubber. This rapid response is a fabulous benefit when cooking fish and chicken, foods that are not normally cooked in large quantities or for a long time. It is also a tremendous help in the cooking of broths, where extraction of bone gelatin, proteins and meat flavors occurs incredibly quickly. Using a protein-rich broth as a cooking liquid rather than water will actually shorten cooking times.

A small veal roast—a cut that toughens if really roasted—cooks sublimely well in the microwave oven. The rapidity makes it a joy to cook Ossobuco, Chicken in Red Wine or duck for one. Perhaps I should be content with these triumphs, but there are times when I crave a real stew or chili. There are problems with these dishes, as you will see; but I think, within limits, I have licked them. At least I can now eat these foods without having to spend half the day in the kitchen. See Lamb Stew (page 262), Chunky Beef Chili (page 237), and Sliced Beef Casserole (page 241).

Cooking large pieces of meat, or large quantities of meat that normally need to be stewed to be tender, is an iffy proposition. If the timing isn't correct, the meat will toughen up on you just when you think it is getting delightfully tender. Some microwave cooks solve the problem by cooking the meat at reduced power after it has been thoroughly heated at 100%. This seems logical; but I am not convinced. For one thing, the cooking time is sufficiently prolonged that it becomes a toss-up whether the meat might as well be cooked in the regular oven or on top of the stove. For another, I find the results unreliable.

When preparing meat dishes, do not try to increase quantities; the resulting increased cooking times will be disastrous. Only a limited group of beef stews improves with waiting, a process I call *mellowing* (see page 234). Otherwise, eat meats as soon as they are cooked. Reheating and defrosting can be problematic. You do not want to overcook. In addition, some foods take as long to defrost and reheat as to cook from scratch. See REHEATING and DEFROSTING in the Dictionary for guidelines.

COOKING SUGAR. Sugar by itself or with a little butter or water caramelizes well in the microwave oven. See entries for BROWNING, SUGAR and CARAMEL in the Dictionary. This feature is a bonanza for bakers and the makers of sweets, who no longer have to worry about burned pots of sugar crystals ruining their candy. Microwave techniques are fabulous for the making of syrups, jams and jellies: The sugar mixture gets dense (jells) before the fruit flavor dies. Onions will caramelize nicely, too, as they do on top of the stove when cooked long enough. This is good news for onion soup enthusiasts who don't want to stand over the stove stirring for an hour.

Meat will not caramelize or crust in the microwave oven. Colored glazes act only as concealments; they neither caramelize themselves nor affect the way meat cooks. Meat cannot be roasted or sautéed until brown in the microwave oven. On the other hand, I do not think it needs to be for stews—heresy!

COOKING WITH LIQUID. Use much less than normal; water takes a significant amount of time to come to a boil. Tight sealing will keep the food bathed in moisture. Most vegetables and fruits will cook wonderfully if tightly wrapped in microwave plastic wrap or in a plastic microwave bag—no liquid at all, no salt needed to keep the colors bright.

Vitamins are much less affected by rapid microwave cooking with very little liquid than they are by any other kind of cooking—a nice benefit for all of us.

FAT IN THE MICROWAVE OVEN. Fat is one of the things that cooks quickest in the microwave oven. It attracts the microwaves. This differential rapidity is useful when you want to render fat, particularly to separate it from another substance (like the flesh and skin of a duck) or from bone (to liberate marrow).

You have to add little fat when cooking with microwaves. Use it mainly for flavor or to coat something like rice (see Basic Risotto, page 119) to keep the pieces separate. You don't need it to keep food from sticking; it won't stick. You don't need it for sautéing; you cannot really sauté in the microwave oven anyhow. A little fat can accelerate the cooking process.

DEEP-FAT FRYING. Frying is possible in full-sized ovens in small quantities. See page 537.

STARCH. Whether in flour, potatoes or rice, starch can behave oddly or beautifully in the microwave oven. If the starch, such as *wheat flour*, is part gluten (the protein part, which stretches and lets baked goods rise), it will absorb great quantities of liquid and become gluey; cooked without liquid, it gets hard. The microwave successes you can have with wheat flour are extremely limited. Refer to BAKING in the Dictionary and page 409 for a fuller discussion. One nice sideline of flour's odd cooking properties is that you can make Brown Roux (page 338), so essential to New Orleans cooking, without danger of scorching.

Other starches also behave differently in the microwave. *Rice starch* absorbs great quantities of liquid slowly, hence the perfect risotto. On one hand, this tells us that rice as a side dish is just as quickly cooked on the stove. On the other hand, in the case of a dish like paella or pilaf, where you do not want the rice to overcook before the other ingredients are ready, the special properties of rice in microwave cooking are quite an asset.

Cornstarch behaves at its best in the microwave oven. It thickens sauces without lumps when added as a slurry, mixed until smooth with water or cooking liquid. It does not impart a raw taste; you do not need much of it; and it does not lose its binding power. It is also useful as a replacement for flour when baking cakes, as is potato starch.

Arrowroot behaves oddly. Since it is expensive, I have not worried about it much.

Vegetable starches absorb liquid, but less than they might in other kinds of cooking—a mixed bag of results. Potatoes cook, but they do not get mealy. This means you need to add more liquid when making mashed potatoes. It also means that potatoes cooked in stews and vegetable soups retain their shape, which is nice. Vegetables such as chayote, parsnips, sweet potatoes and even carrots, which tend to get watery when cooked conventionally, do fabulously in the microwave oven. Vegetable cooking times are given in the Dictionary.

FLAVORING AND SEASONING FOOD. Remember that microwave cooking tends to emphasize the inherent tastes of foods. If you want to gentle the flavor, as some people do with spinach and rhubarb, use more liquid, cook uncovered and lengthen the cooking time. In most cases, the added punch of natural flavor is a blessing. If you are in the habit of seasoning to compensate for bland ingredients, you may need to do less of this with microwave-cooked foods. If you have been seasoning to balance flavors, you may want to slightly increase seasoning amounts, but check the general indications for seasoning and entries for individual seasonings in the Dictionary.

Be careful with *salt*. Generally, you can use less than usual, as foods tend to absorb it and you will be using less liquid than is customary. Also, the better flavor of microwave-cooked vegetables requires almost no salt. Since food is hot when it comes from the oven, it can be salted then and still absorb the salt. The flavor of salt does not change in microwave cooking. However, if you are cooking foods uncovered, the liquid will reduce substantially and make the dish seem very salty. If you are cooking vegetables on their own with little or no liquid, do not add salt. It will draw liquid from the vegetable, leaving it with a wrinkled look.

Where canned broth can be substituted for homemade broth when you are in a hurry, the recipes say so. Never use it in a dish where the liquid is going to be substantially reduced. Sometimes you can adjust a recipe so that it can be made with canned broth by omitting salt until the final tasting. Other times this cannot be done, as in making glazes and many sauces. Fortunately, making broth is a speedy proposition with a microwave oven.

There are other ingredients that are often used canned. Always remember that salt is present in canned tomatoes, juices and tomato paste. Adjust recipes to suit your taste. If you are salt-sensitive, put up your own ingredients to replace those in cans. You can do it quickly with the microwave oven.

Black or white pepper should be used in tiny quantities.

It develops a terrific wallop in microwave cooking (though it does not get bitter as it does with prolonged stovetop cooking). If you are hesitant about controlling the punch of pepper, do not add it until the end of the cooking time, or until the food comes out of the oven.

Garlic, unless very briefly cooked or added at the end of the cooking time, should be used in quantities greater than you would imagine. It cooks to a soft sweetness in about seven minutes.

When making a stew, increase the proportion of wine or *alcohol* to broth. The flavors dissipate rapidly, as do those of vanilla, almond, lemon and orange when added as an extract, since it is alcohol-based.

Increase the warm *spices* such as cumin, coriander, cardamom, anise, caraway and allspice; they tend to become quite gentle. Be careful with the pungent spices such as cinnamon, nutmeg, dried ginger and five-spice powder; they will become more dominant. The hot spices—ground pepper, Szechuan peppercorns, dried chilies and ground mustard—must be sharply decreased or they will knock the socks off all but those with palates of asbestos. Decrease dry *herb* quantities, as all of their flavor will be reconstituted; increase fresh herb quantities or stir them in late in the game (their essential oils tend to volatilize). *Aromatics,* such as parsley, celery and carrots, can be increased slightly when used as flavorings rather than as major ingredients. Scallions and fresh ginger can be left at normal quantities, but should not be added too soon; they fade easily.

Additional Notes

1. Unless specified otherwise, all ingredients are used at room temperature.
2. Whenever adding cool liquids to hot ones, pour slowly, as the mixture may initially boil up. Never set a hot container on a wet surface.
3. Do not use cracked, chipped or repaired bowls or plates in the microwave oven.
4. Some microwave-oven manufacturers may not honor their warranty if you deep-fat fry in their ovens. Do not fry large amounts of food at one time or in any way differently from the method described.

FIRST COURSES

I DEARLY love first courses, and with the microwave oven I cook them up so speedily I sometimes have to stop myself, or there is just too much food. It is particularly rewarding to make pâtés. It is a matter of minutes to prepare one, instead of hours; and they can be ready and waiting when needed.

Besides the recipes for first courses in this chapter, there are many first courses that can be scooped out of cans and jars or be picked up at delis and take-out shops. More gala are little homemade composed salads with bits of leftovers tossed in, or cracklings, or freshly cooked mushrooms, or a few chicken livers still warm and sprinkled with vinegar.

Other ideas for first courses can be found in the vegetable and grains chapters. Garlic Custard (page 304), Asparagus Custard (page 303), Parsnip Flan (page 302), and many others make perfect first courses. Small portions of risotto and polenta are also good for starters, as are small portions of vegetable stew. Soups, hot or cold, are always welcome as an introduction to a meal where the main course is not too saucy. Some fish and seafood dishes can be served in half portions as first courses at a more formal meal.

Herewith, a group of recipes for foods really meant to be first courses. They also function splendidly as part of a buffet. From time to time I have tried to give an indication of how long the dish takes to make working at an efficient rate. Sometimes I even tell how long it used to take to make it pre-microwave.

Cold First Courses

One of the nice things about most cold, or cool, first courses is that they can be made ahead. They should be interesting enough to awaken the appetite, but not so aggressive as to satisfy or kill it.

STUFFED GRAPE LEAVES

Along the shores of the Mediterranean in Greece and Turkey they stuff young grape leaves and marinate them in olive oil and lemon juice. These make a super first course or hors d'oeuvre. Serve alone, or with some chunks of feta cheese, olives, and perhaps a few cold mussels as a first course. The stuffed leaves keep well for up to a week in the refrigerator. *Makes 2 dozen*

½ jar vine leaves (grape leaves in brine), or fresh grape leaves (see note)
¾ cup plus 2 tablespoons fruity olive oil
¼ cup chopped yellow onion
2 cloves garlic, smashed, peeled and minced
1 cup long-grain rice
1 cup chopped fresh dill
½ cup chopped fresh mint leaves
1 teaspoon kosher salt
¼ teaspoon freshly ground black pepper
2 tablespoons fresh lemon juice

1. Place grape leaves in a large bowl and rinse well with running water. Drain and set aside.

2. Heat ¾ cup olive oil in an 11″ × 9″ dish, uncovered, at 100% for 3 minutes. Add onions, garlic, rice, dill, and mint. Stir to coat. Cover tightly with microwave plastic wrap. Cook at 100% for 5 minutes.

3. Remove from oven. Uncover and let stand until cool. Add salt and pepper.

4. To stuff the grape leaves, place a leaf on a work surface with the rough side up and stem end closest to you. Place a teaspoonful of rice mixture at the stem end. Roll away from you, folding in both sides of the leaf as you go. Arrange stuffed leaves in two rows in a 11″ × 9″ dish (they should just touch each other). Pour 1½ cups water over leaves. Cover tightly with microwave plastic wrap. Cook at 100% for 12 minutes.

5. Remove from oven. Uncover and let stand until cool. Pour lemon juice and remaining 2 tablespoons olive oil over leaves. Cover tightly with microwave plastic wrap. Refrigerate for at least 6 hours, or up to a week. Serve at room temperature.

Note. If you have unsprayed fresh grape leaves, make a strong saltwater brine by boiling 1 cup kosher salt in 4 cups water in a 2-quart soufflé dish, uncovered, for 10 minutes at 100%. Put in 12 grape leaves. Cook uncovered for 2 minutes at 100%. Lift out leaves with a pancake turner or skimmer and place in ice water. Repeat with more leaves, if desired.

VARIATION

STUFFED GRAPE LEAVES WITH TOMATOES, RAISINS, OR NUTS To rice mixture, add one of the following ingredients, or any combination: ½ cup canned tomatoes, drained and crushed; ½ cup raisins; ½ cup pine nuts.

Spread the grape leaf flat and place a teaspoon of rice mixture in center. Fold in the edges of the leaf to enclose rice. Roll leaf away from you to make a neat package.

CLASSIC EGGPLANT APPETIZER

The meat of eggplant cooked in a microwave oven retains a beautiful green color, rather than taking on the dull brown of roasted eggplant. That gives these dips a fresh, appealing look and flavor that is delicious with raw vegetables or with warm pita bread. They are terrific for cocktail parties.

This wonderfully garlicky dish demands 1½ hours of baking in a conventional oven, but only 12 minutes in the microwave oven. *Makes 2 cups*

1 large eggplant (about
  1 pound), pricked
  several times with a
  fork
1 small onion, peeled
  and chopped (about
  ½ cup)
¼ cup chopped parsley

1 clove garlic, smashed,
  peeled and minced
1 teaspoon kosher salt
¼ teaspoon freshly
  ground black
  pepper
2 tablespoons olive oil
2 teaspoons fresh lemon
  juice

1. Place eggplant on a double thickness of paper toweling and cook, uncovered, at 100% for 12 minutes. Remove from oven. Let cool.

2. When eggplant is cool enough to handle, cut it in half lengthwise and scoop out flesh. Place in the workbowl of a food processor. Add onions, parsley, garlic, salt, and pepper and process just until mixture is coarsely chopped.

3. Transfer to a serving bowl. Stir in oil and lemon juice. Serve at room temperature.

VARIATIONS

RUSSIAN EGGPLANT ORIENTALE While waiting for eggplant to cool, stem, seed, and derib 1 green bell pepper; chop fine. Place in a 1-cup glass measure with 1 tablespoon olive oil. Cover tightly with microwave plastic wrap. Cook at 100% for 3 minutes. Remove from oven. Prepare eggplant mixture, stir in the pepper along with ½ cup Lightly Cooked Crushed Tomatoes (page 339) or chopped tomatoes, 3 tablespoons tomato paste, 2 tablespoons fresh lemon juice, and a pinch of cayenne pepper. Serve with lemon wedges.

EGGPLANT WITH ORIENTAL SEASONINGS Cook eggplant for Classic Eggplant Appetizer. Omit all seasonings except lemon juice and garlic. Add 2 chopped scallions, ¼ cup chopped fresh coriander, 1 tablespoon minced ginger, 2 teaspoons soy sauce, and 2 teaspoons sesame oil. Proceed as for Classic Eggplant Appetizer.

CALAMARI SALAD

It would be hard to think of a fresher-tasting or more quickly prepared salad. *Serves 4*

¾ pound medium squid, cleaned and sliced into rings (page 600)
3 center celery stalks with leaves, stalks strung and thinly sliced diagonally and leaves left whole
½ cup thinly sliced yellow onion

½ cup thinly sliced red bell pepper
2 tablespoons olive oil
2 tablespoons fresh lemon juice
1 teaspoon kosher salt
¼ teaspoon freshly ground black pepper
12 oil-cured black olives, pitted and coarsely chopped

1. Toss together squid, sliced celery, onions, and pepper in a 1-quart soufflé dish. Cover tightly with microwave plastic wrap. Cook at 100% for 2 minutes 30 seconds, shaking the dish once.

2. Remove from oven. Uncover and let cool slightly. When cool enough to handle, pour off liquid collected in bottom of dish. Add remaining ingredients and stir to coat. Serve at room temperature.

VARIATION

CALAMARI AND SEAFOOD SALAD Add 8 medium shrimp, peeled and cut in half, and 8 cleaned mussels to the ingredients for Calamari Salad; increase squid to 1 pound, bell pepper to ¾ cup. Arrange shrimp and mussels toward outside of a 2-quart soufflé dish; place vegetables and squid in center of dish. Cover tightly and cook for 5 minutes. Remove mussels from shells if desired. Proceed as for Calamari Salad, increasing lemon juice to 3 tablespoons. Taste to check seasonings. Serves 8.

GEFILTE FISH

This traditional Jewish dish for Passover makes a wonderful cold first course for anybody. It could also be served as a main course. Usually served with red and white horseradish, it could have a spicy rémoulade sauce or herb-rich mayonnaise instead. Always serve a little of the jelled broth and a few of the carrots with the fish. This must be made a day ahead. *Serves 12 as a first course, 6 as a luncheon dish*

FISH STOCK
- 3 pounds fish heads, skin and bones (from the fish you are using and other similar fish), well rinsed and gills removed.
- 1 medium carrot, trimmed, peeled and quartered
- 1 medium onion (about ½ pound), peeled and quartered
- ½ celery stalk, strung and quartered
- 1 bay leaf
- 4 cups water
- 1½ tablespoons kosher salt
- 3 medium carrots, trimmed, peeled and sliced crosswise ⅛ inch thick

FISH MIXTURE
- ½ pound whitefish fillets, skinned
- ½ pound carp fillets, skinned
- ½ pound pike fillets, skinned
- 2 medium onions, peeled and quartered
- 3 eggs
- ¾ cup matzo meal
- ¾ cup seltzer or club soda, chilled (for Passover, substitute cold water)
- 1 teaspoon kosher salt
  Large pinch freshly ground black pepper
- 1 teaspoon (½ envelope) unflavored gelatin, if necessary
  Red and white horseradish (optional)

1. To prepare the stock, place fish heads, skin, and bones, quartered carrot, onion, celery, bay leaf, water, and salt in an 8-cup glass measure. Cover tightly with microwave plastic wrap. Cook at 100% for 30 minutes.

2. Remove from oven. Uncover and strain.

3. Add sliced carrots. Cover tightly with microwave plastic wrap. Cook at 100% for 10 minutes. Remove from oven and set aside.

4. To prepare the fish mixture, place the fillets and onions in the workbowl of a food processor. Process until smooth. Add remaining ingredients except gelatin and horseradish and process just until combined. With damp hands, shape mixture into 12 ovals, 3½" × 2".

5. Arrange fish in a spoke around the edge of a 14" × 11" oval dish. Spoon carrot slices into center of dish and pour broth over all. Cover tightly with microwave plastic wrap, leaving a small vent in one corner. Cook at 100% for 12 minutes.

6. Place a small plate in the freezer (to test gel of finished stock).

7. Remove fish from oven. Uncover and turn each piece over. Let fish cool in the broth for 30 minutes.

8. Test the jelly by pouring a spoonful of broth onto the cold plate. Place the plate in the freezer for 1 minute. Broth should be firm. If it is not, place cooled broth in a bowl and sprinkle gelatin on top. Let stand for 2 minutes. Stir well and repeat test with chilled plate. If broth is still not firm, add rest of envelope of gelatin.

9. Place gefilte fish in the smallest deep container that can hold it in one layer. Cover with broth. Refrigerate overnight.

10. Serve gefilte fish chilled, with some of the jelled broth and carrots. Pass horseradish in a separate bowl, if desired.

Gefilte fish arranged, not touching, around carrots

Vegetables à la Grecque

The French have many delightful ways of preparing vegetables to be served cool. One is based on a Greek way of preparing artichokes, which are often then served with little onions and potatoes. The Greek version is usually flavored with dill or fresh or dried mint. The French version often has dried coriander seed, cardamom seed, and even mustard seed. The vegetables can be served singly, in an assortment, as part of a mixed hors d'oeuvre, or as an accompaniment to a pâté. The cooking liquid can be refrigerated for up to a month and reused for different vegetables. One nice thing about cooking artichokes this way is that much more of them, sometimes all, becomes edible with a knife and fork.

GLOBE ARTICHOKES
AND ONIONS Á LA GRECQUE

Large globe artichokes are more frequently cooked in Greece than the tiny ones described in the following recipe. If you plan to serve Scallions à la Grecque too, prepare the scallions first, and then add the additional ingredients to the broth and reuse for the artichokes.　*Serves 4 to 6 by itself, 8 to 16 as part of a mixed hors d'oeuvre*

4 globe artichokes (¾ pound each), leaf tips trimmed, quartered through stem and choke removed (see note)
8 small (1 to 1½-inch diameter) white onions, peeled
　Juice of 2 lemons, lemon shells reserved

2 cups Chicken Broth (page 331) or canned chicken broth
½ cup olive oil
1 tablespoon kosher salt
4 fresh dill sprigs
¼ cup chopped fresh mint or dill

1. Arrange artichokes, cut side down, in a 12″ × 7½″ × 2″ dish, with the fat stem ends toward the outside of the dish. Tuck onions and lemon shells among artichokes. Add broth, oil, salt, and dill sprigs. Cover tightly with microwave plastic wrap. Cook at 100% for 12 minutes.

2. Remove from oven. Uncover and turn artichokes over. Re-cover tightly and cook for 8 minutes more.

3. Remove from oven. Let stand, covered, until cool. Just before serving, stir in ¼ cup of the lemon juice, salt to taste, and sprinkle with mint or dill.

Note. Artichokes weighing ¾ to 1 pound should be quartered lengthwise; ½-pound artichokes should be cut in half lengthwise. If using ½-pound artichokes, use five and plan on serving at least one half artichoke per person.

VARIATIONS

LATE FALL ARTICHOKES À LA GRECQUE Add ½ teaspoon cardamom pods, crushed, and a pinch of dried oregano to the broth before cooking.

SCALLIONS À LA GRECQUE These scallions are more truly braised; they could be served hot as a side dish with Poached Chicken Breasts in Sauce Suprême or with a simple fish dish. Substitute 18 medium scallions (about 3 bunches), trimmed and cut into 5-inch lengths, for artichokes and onions. Reduce lemon juice to 1 tablespoon and reduce broth and oil by half. Omit lemon shells, dill, and mint. Proceed as for Globe Artichokes and Onions, cooking scallions in a 6″ × 2″ round dish for 6 minutes.

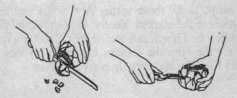

To trim artichokes, first cut off 1 inch from the top of the artichoke. Then, with scissors, clip the remaining leaf tips around artichoke bottom.

MINIATURE ARTICHOKES À LA GRECQUE

When very tiny artichokes are available, they can be cooked whole, and every bit is edible and delicious.   *Serves 6*

**1 pound baby artichokes
   (about 16), round
   bottom leaves and
   any really hard outer
   leaves removed and
   leaf tips trimmed by
   ½ inch
2 cups Chicken Broth
   (page 331) or canned
   chicken broth**

**¾ cup olive oil
3 cloves garlic, smashed
   and peeled
2 tablespoons fresh
   lemon juice
1 tablespoon kosher salt
¼ cup finely chopped
   fresh dill**

1. Place artichokes, broth, oil, and garlic in a 1½-quart soufflé dish. Cover tightly with microwave plastic wrap. Cook at 100% for 8 minutes.

2. Remove from oven. Uncover and turn artichokes over. Re-cover tightly and cook at 100% for 4 minutes more.

3. Remove from oven. Uncover and pour off all but 1 cup cooking liquid. Stir in lemon juice and salt. Sprinkle with dill just before serving.

BABY ARTICHOKES À LA GRECQUE

This recipe is for those spring days when you find small artichokes in the market. Ideally, they should be the pointy artichokes the French call *violets*, not globe artichokes. *Violets* are the ones the Italians flatten out to look like the flowers they are and then deep-fry.   *Serves 4*

8 baby artichokes (about
   2 ounces each),
   round bottom leaves
   removed and leaf
   tips trimmed, then
   cut in half
   lengthwise
¼ cup fresh lemon juice
⅔ cup Chicken Broth
   (page 331) or
   canned chicken
   broth

⅓ cup olive oil
 2 cloves garlic, smashed
   and peeled
½ teaspoon coriander
   seed
½ teaspoon crushed
   cardamom pods
¼ teaspoon mustard seed
   Kosher salt

1. Rub artichokes with lemon juice. Remove any inner leaves that have a reddish tinge at the edge.

2. Combine artichokes, any remaining lemon juice, broth, oil, garlic, spices, and salt in a 2-quart soufflé dish. Cover tightly with microwave plastic wrap. Cook at 100% for 10 minutes.

3. Remove from oven. Uncover and turn artichokes over. Re-cover and cook at 100% for 3 minutes more.

4. Remove from oven. Pierce plastic with the tip of a sharp knife. Let stand, covered, until cool.

ONIONS À LA MONÉGASQUE

This is one of those dishes that is nice to have in the refrigerator to serve as part of a mixed hors d'oeuvre. Allow onions to come to room temperature before using. They are also delicious with grilled fish or chicken, or nestled up to a pâté. Another nice side dish of onions is Onions in Barbecue Sauce (page 307). *Makes 1¼ cups; serves 6 in a mixed hors d'oeuvre, 8 to 10 with pâté*

½ pound pearl onions,
　　peeled (page 560)
2 tablespoon red wine
　　vinegar
2 tablespoons white wine
2 tablespoons olive oil
3 tablespoons tomato
　　paste
½ bay leaf
　Pinch dried oregano

½ cup dark raisins
2 tablespoons water
¼ teaspoon kosher salt
　Pinch freshly ground
　　black pepper
2 drops hot red-pepper
　　sauce
1 teaspoon granulated
　　sugar (optional)

1. Stir together onions, vinegar, wine, oil, tomato paste, bay leaf, oregano, and raisins in a 1-quart soufflé dish. Cover tightly with microwave plastic wrap. Cook at 100% for 10 minutes.

2. Remove from oven. Pierce plastic with the tip of a sharp knife. Uncover and stir in water, salt, pepper, pepper sauce, and sugar, if desired. Serve warm or cool. If you like it a little looser, add another tablespoon of water.

To double the recipe. Double all ingredients and cook for 15 minutes stirring once after 8 minutes.

VARIATION

SAFFRON ONIONS Omit tomato paste, bay leaf, oregano, and hot red-pepper sauce. Substitute white wine vinegar for red wine vinegar and 2 tablespoon yellow raisins for dark raisins. Increase sugar to 1 tablespoon. Add ¼ teaspoon ground cumin, ½ package powdered saffron or 1 vial of thread saffron mixed with wine, and a knife-point each of ground coriander and cardamom. Proceed as for Onions à la Monégasque, cooking for 8 minutes. Remove from oven and stir in 1 tablespoon water, ⅛ teaspoon salt, a pinch of black pepper, and an additional ½ teaspoon vinegar.

PEPPER SALAD

This is a very pretty cooked salad, light and easy to prepare. It is delightful when you want something before dinner that is not too filling. It is served at room temperature. *Serves 2*

1 yellow bell pepper,
   stemmed, seeded,
   deribbed, and
   julienned
1 green bell pepper,
   stemmed, seeded,
   deribbed, and
   julienned
1 red bell pepper,
   stemmed, seeded,
   deribbed, and
   julienned

1 tablespoon vegetable
   oil
½ teaspoon kosher salt
1 teaspoon fennel seed
½ teaspoon dried
   oregano
Large pinch freshly
   ground black
   pepper
1 tablespoon water

1. Arrange peppers in a 1-quart soufflé dish with yellow peppers on the bottom, green in the middle, and red on top.

2. Stir together remaining ingredients and pour over peppers. Cover tightly with microwave plastic wrap. Cook at 100% for 6 minutes.

3. Remove from oven. Uncover and serve warm or chilled.

CANNELLINI

These Italian favorites are available in cans. The canned beans are mushier than the freshly cooked beans, but they will do (see variation). *Makes 2½ cups*

1 cup dried cannellini
   beans
8 large cloves garlic,
   smashed and peeled
3 parsley sprigs
¼ cup olive oil
2 tablespoons chopped
   fresh basil

1 teaspoon kosher salt
   Pinch freshly ground
   black pepper
1 can (6½ ounces) water-
   packed tuna fish,
   drained (optional)
8 thin slices peeled red
   onion (optional)

1. Place cannellini in a 2-quart soufflé dish with 2 cups water. Cover tightly with microwave plastic wrap. Cook at 100% for 15 minutes.

2. Remove from oven. Pierce plastic with the tip of a sharp knife. Let stand for 5 minutes. Uncover and add 2 cups very hot tap water. Re-cover with a fresh piece of microwave plastic wrap. Let stand for 1 hour.

3. Uncover, drain, and rinse. Return to soufflé dish and add garlic, parsley, and 4 cups water. Cook, tightly covered, at 100% for 35 minutes.

4. Remove from oven. Let stand, covered, for 20 minutes.

5. Uncover, drain, and remove parsley. Let cool. Add oil, basil, salt, and pepper; stir well. Serve cold.

6. If desired, top with chunks of tuna and sliced red onions.

VARIATION

SALAD WITH CANNED CANNELLINI Drain and rinse 2 cans of cooked cannellini. Place in a 4-cup glass measure with ¼ cup water, garlic, and parsley. Cover tightly. Cook at 100% for 5 minutes. Continue as in step 5.

BRANDADE DE MORUE

Before the food processor and microwave oven, this took days of work. First the cod had to be soaked to soften and get rid of the excess salt. Then it had to be pounded into a purée, with or without potato, then sauced and seasoned. Now, it goes quickly and makes a good dip for vegetables or filling for salty pastry as an hors d'oeuvre. As a first course, serve in little ramekins with fried bread. You can also use it under Baked Eggs (page 67) instead of vegetable purée. *Makes 2 cups*

1 small (¼ pound) potato, pricked twice with a fork
½ pound salt cod fillet, washed in cold running water for 2 minutes

¾ cup Garlic Cream (page 348)
2 tablespoons fruity olive oil

1. Place potato on paper toweling in the oven. Cook at 100% for 6 minutes. When cool enough to handle, peel and pass through a ricer or the medium disc of a food mill. Set aside.

2. Place the fish in a 10″ × 3″ round dish and pour 3 cups cold water over it. Cover tightly with microwave plastic wrap. Cook at 100% for 5 minutes.

3. Remove from oven. Uncover and drain. Rinse fish with cold water and repeat the soaking process 2 more times.

4. Place fish in the workbowl of a food processor. Add Garlic Cream and process for 2 minutes. Add riced potato and oil. Process for 2 minutes longer, or until smooth and creamy.

SWORDFISH QUENELLES

This classic recipe, usually made with pike, is an excellent way to use trimmings from swordfish medallions (page 171). Serve with Watercress Sauce (page 369), Beurre Blanc (page 363), or Sauce Américaine (page 372). Other fish trimmings such as salmon can be substituted, or try shrimp or scallops.   *Serves 2 to 3*

½ pound skinned and boned swordfish, cut into 2-inch chunks	Pinch freshly ground black pepper
1 egg white	Pinch freshly grated nutmeg
1 teaspoon kosher salt	½ cup heavy cream, very cold

1. Place fish in the workbowl of a food processor. Process for 30 seconds. Add egg white and process for 30 seconds. Scrape down the sides of the workbowl. Add salt, pepper, and nutmeg, and process until mixture forms a ball (as for a dough). With machine running, add cream to mixture in a thin stream.

2. Remove bowl from food processor and refrigerate for 15 minutes.

3. Put 2 tablespoons of water in an 11″ × 8½″ × 2″ rectangular or oval dish. To form the quenelles, use two tablespoons to shape mixture into elongated ovals, or pipe mixture into 1″ × 2″ strips using a pastry bag fitted with a ½-inch tip. Place each quenelle as it is formed in the dish, arranging the quenelles around inside rim. Do not allow them to touch. Cover tightly with microwave plastic wrap. Cook at 100% for 2 minutes.

4. Remove from oven. Uncover and serve hot with sauce.

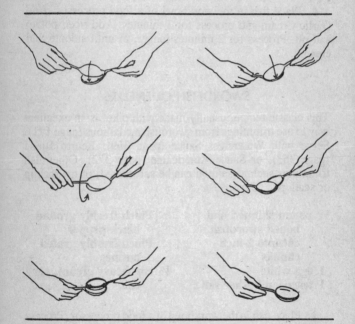

Scoop up a teaspoonful of quenelle mixture and shape, using two teaspoons. Scrape the mixture from spoon to spoon, working from the outside edge of the spoon toward the inside.

Pâtés

Cooking pâtés used to be an all-day affair with messy water baths. The microwave oven has virtually turned them into fast food. Make them the night before you want to use them, or several days before for the meat and liver pâtés.

With this ease of preparation, a totally pâté cocktail party or buffet with salad and cheese is easily in reach. Either prepare each pâté while the previous one is cooking or cook one a night for three or four nights, starting with the heavier pâtés and ending with the fish or chicken. As pâtés keep well for up to two weeks, you can have them on hand in case you want to invite people at the last minute.

After being removed from the oven and cooled, many pâtés need to be weighted in order to firm up their texture. To do so, cool the pâté to skin temperature (not cold). Cut a piece of cardboard to fit just inside the pâté mold or loaf pan. Wrap it in two layers of aluminum foil. Place it on top of the pâté and weight with a brick or two heavy cans. Place in refrigerator. If the mold is very full, set it on a plate before weighting to catch any spills.

Almost all the recipes on the pages that follow can be cooked in a standard glass loaf pan.

Line the mold with microwave plastic wrap, leaving excess plastic around the edge. Pour in pâté mixture and fold over excess plastic to enclose pâté. Place a piece of foil-covered cardboard on top of cooked, cooled pâté and weight with cans.

CHICKEN PÂTÉ

This is a beautiful pâté to look at, almost white and flecked with green. Full slices can be served on sprigs of parsley or on a pool of Red Pepper Purée (page 343). Little quarter-slices can be put on small, brown cocktail pumpernickel rounds as canapés for a party.

The pâté cooks for just 6 minutes and can be served warm (let it cool for 10 minutes after it comes out of the oven) or cold (it will need to be weighted in the refrigerator overnight). Serve it warm as a first course; it will be lighter as it is not weighted. Serve it chilled for a canapé; it will have a firmer texture. *Serves 8 to 10 as a first course, 20 for cocktails*

¾ pound boneless, skinless chicken breast, cut into 2-inch chunks
2¼ cups heavy cream
¾ cup (packed) minced watercress leaves, or ½ cup (packed) minced flat-leaf parsley and 2 tablespoons minced fresh tarragon

2 shallots, peeled and minced
1½ teaspoons kosher salt
⅛ teaspoon cayenne pepper
⅛ teaspoon freshly ground black pepper

1. Line a 7″ × 3½″ loaf pan with microwave plastic wrap, leaving a 4-inch overhang around top of pan.

2. Place chicken in the workbowl of a food processor and process until very finely chopped. With motor running, pour in 1¼ cups of the cream in a thin stream. Process until smooth.

3. Pass mixture through a sieve into a bowl. Stir in rest of cream and remaining ingredients. Pour into prepared pan and fold over plastic to enclose pâté. Cook at 100% for 6 minutes.

4. Remove from oven. To serve warm, uncover and let cool slightly before slicing in pan. To serve cold, uncover and let come to room temperature. Wrap tightly, weight, and refrigerate for 8 to 12 hours.

SMOOTH COUNTRY TERRINE

This pâté, while also smooth, is much more robust in flavor than the Scandinavian Liver Pâté (page 58). It would be very good before Chicken in Red Wine (page 215), with bread and cornichons or Onions à la Monégasque (page 45). *Serves 12 as a first course, up to 40 as part of a mixed hors d'oeuvre*

1 pound bulk sausage meat	½ teaspoon freshly ground black pepper
1 pound chicken livers, rinsed, and connective tissue removed	1 teaspoon Quatre-Épices (page 573)
½ pound cold unsalted butter, cut into ½-inch cubes	2 tablespoons Cognac or brandy
¾ cup white wine	1 bay leaf
1 tablespoon kosher salt	1½ cups Aspic (page 332) (optional)

1. Place sausage, livers, and butter in the workbowl of a food processor. Process until well combined. Stir in remaining ingredients, except bay leaf and Aspic, if using. Pass through a fine sieve and discard all gristle.

2. Pour mixture into a 1½-quart soufflé dish. Place bay leaf in center. Cover tightly with microwave plastic wrap. Cook at 100% for 18 minutes.

3. Remove from oven. Uncover and chill. Cover with Aspic if desired.

CHICKEN LIVER MOUSSE

While this seems very similar to other smooth pâtés, it is made differently. The chicken livers are gently cooked, then puréed, and the mold is not lined. It cannot be sliced; it must be spooned. Serve it with toasted white bread or sliced toasted brioche. *Makes 6 individual first course ramekins, or 1 large mousse to serve 18 with other hors d'oeuvres*

¾ pound unsalted butter, cut into small pieces

½ cup finely chopped onion

4 bruised juniper berries

2 cloves garlic, smashed and peeled

1 pound chicken livers, rinsed, and connective tissue removed

¼ cup dry vermouth

Large pinch freshly ground black pepper

2 teaspoons kosher salt

1 cup Aspic (page 332) (optional)

1. Place butter, onions, juniper berries, and garlic in an 11" × 8½" × 2" dish. Cook, uncovered, at 100% for 4 minutes.

2. Remove from oven. Add livers in a single layer. Cover tightly with microwave plastic wrap. Cook at 100% for 3 minutes, stirring once after 1 minute 30 seconds.

3. Remove from oven. Uncover and stir in remaining ingredient, except Aspic, if used. Pour into the workbowl of a food processor. Process until smooth. Pour mixture into six 4-inch ramekins, or a 1-quart soufflé dish. Chill for at least 1 hour. When chilled, cover each mousse with 3 tablespoons of Aspic, if desired.

VARIATION

DUCK LIVER MOUSSE Substitute equal weight duck livers, cleaned.

SHRIMP PÂTÉ

A simple and delicious first course. It is beautiful when its pale pink color is contrasted with the clear orange-yellow of Papaya Cumin Sauce (page 382) or the bright green of Watercress Sauce (page 369). Make a pool of the sauce on a serving plate, top with a slice of pâté, and sprinkle with glossy, black-brown papaya seeds or a sprig of watercress.

Shelling the shrimp takes about 15 minutes; if you are pressed for time, scallops are a good alternative. The entire pâté can be assembled and baked in just 8 minutes. Allow for an additional 20 minutes of standing time. Serve the pâté warm or cold. *Serves 8*

¾ **pound shrimp, shelled and deveined**	¾ **teaspoon kosher salt**
1½ **cups heavy cream**	⅛ **teaspoon cayenne pepper**
1 **tablespoon fresh lemon juice**	⅛ **teaspoon freshly ground black pepper**

1. Line a 7″ × 3½″ loaf pan with microwave plastic wrap, leaving a 4-inch overhang around top of pan.

2. Place the shrimp in the workbowl of a food processor. Process until coarsely puréed. Stop processor three or four times to scrape down sides of the workbowl.

3. Combine cream with remaining ingredients. With the processor motor running, add to shrimp purée in a thin stream. Stop the processor, scrape down sides, and continue processing until the cream is incorporated and the mixture is very smooth, about 1 minute. Do not overprocess or the cream will curdle.

4. Pour mixture into prepared pan. Fold over plastic wrap to enclose pâté. Cook at 100% for 4 minutes.

5. Remove from oven. Uncover the pâté, wrap in a kitchen towel, and let stand for 20 minutes. Unmold on a serving plate and serve warm or cool.

VARIATION

SCALLOP MOUSSE Substitute ¾ pound sea scallops for shrimp and 1 tablespoon white wine for lemon juice. Omit cayenne and add 2 tablespoons finely sliced fresh chives. Proceed as for Shrimp Pâté. Serve warm or cool.

SUMMER PÂTÉ WITH VEAL, SWEETBREADS AND SPINACH

This is a bit fancier and more work than some of the other pâtés, but it still can be put together and cooked in about 30 minutes. In 10 minutes, you can clean and trim your sweetbreads and vegetables (the vegetables can all go into the food processor). While the sweetbreads cook (16 minutes), you can make the pâté mixture. The assembled pâté cooks for only 10 minutes. If you want it simpler yet, eliminate the sweetbread; grind all pâté ingredients together and cook in about 15 minutes for a pretty, pale green pâté. Make these pâtés a day before they are served, as they need to cool and be weighted.

This is really three recipes in one. It is the best way to cook sweetbread that I know, and you get a wonderful dividend in the braised vegetables. Purée them in the blender for a sauce or thin the purée with 1 cup Chicken Broth to make a wonderful soup for two.   *Serves 10 to 12*

SWEETBREADS

- 3 tablespoons unsalted butter
- 2 carrots, trimmed, peeled and coarsely chopped
- 2 stalks celery, strung, trimmed and coarsely chopped
- ½ small onion, peeled and coarsely chopped
- 1¼ pounds sweetbreads, cleaned and trimmed (see note)
- 1 cup Chicken Broth (page 331) or canned chicken broth

FORCEMEAT

- 4 large shallots, peeled
- 2 pounds veal stew meat without fat, cubed
- 1¼ cups unsalted butter, cut into tablespoon-size chunks
- ½ teaspoon fresh rosemary
- 2 teaspoons freshly ground fennel seed
- ¼ teaspoon ground allspice
- 2 teaspoons kosher salt
- ¼ teaspoon freshly ground black pepper
- 4 cups spinach (about 1 pound), stemmed, well rinsed and dried

1. Line a 12″ × 4″ loaf pan with microwave plastic wrap, leaving a 4-inch overhang around top of pan.

2. To prepare the sweetbreads, heat butter in a 2-quart soufflé dish, uncovered, at 100% for 3 minutes. Add carrots, celery, and onions and stir to coat. Cook, uncovered, at 100% for 3 minutes.

3. Remove from oven. Arrange sweetbreads on top of vegetables and pour broth over all. Cover tightly with microwave plastic wrap. Cook at 100% for 5 minutes. Remove from oven. Uncover and turn sweetbreads over. Re-cover and cook for 5 minutes more.

4. Remove from oven. Uncover and set aside.

5. To prepare the forcemeat, place shallots and veal in the workbowl of a food processor. Process until veal is coarsely ground. Add remaining ingredients except spinach and process until combined.

6. Remove 2½ cups of veal mixture and set aside. Add spinach to remaining veal mixture in workbowl. Process until smooth.

7. To assemble the pâté, spread half the veal mixture without spinach in the bottom of prepared dish. Spread one third of spinach mixture on top. Arrange a strip of sweetbreads (if necessary cut sweetbreads in half lengthwise) down the length of the pan, leaving a ½-inch border on all sides. Cover sweetbreads with remaining spinach mixture. Spread remaining veal mixture on top. Fold overlapping edges of microwave plastic wrap over pâté to cover. Cook at 100% for 10 minutes.

8. Remove from oven. Let cook to room temperature. Weight and refrigerate for 12 to 24 hours. Unwrap, slice and serve.

Note. I have called for 1¼ pounds of sweetbreads since a pair usually weighs that much. If you can buy them by weight, you will need only ¾ pound. If you have leftover sweetbreads, or if you want to serve sweetbreads as a separate dish, remove them from the microwave oven after cooking; set aside on another plate and cover loosely while you purée the vegetables in a blender for a light and delicious sauce. Serve the sweetbreads sliced with the sauce to four people. The leftover ¾-pound quantity will feed two as a first course.

SCANDINAVIAN LIVER PÂTÉ

This creamy, mild-tasting liver pâté is a Scandinavian standard called Leverpostej. Ordinarily it requires an hour and a half of cooking time in a messy water bath. With my microwave method, it takes 25 minutes to prepare and exactly 12 minutes to cook. Like all pâtés, it does need to be made the night before you want to serve it. Unmolded and wrapped in foil and then in plastic, it will keep refrigerated for a week. Though it can be frozen, it hardly seems worthwhile when it is so quickly made. Sliced and served with bread and mustard, it makes an easy cold main course for a summer luncheon, and it is perfect for a cocktail party or when people stop by. *Serves 12 as a first course, 6 as lunch, and up to 40 for cocktails*

1 pound chicken or veal liver, rinsed, and connective tissue removed

¾ pound fresh pork fat, trimmed of any meat

1 small onion (about ¼ pound), peeled and quartered

1½ tablespoons anchovy paste

3 cups heavy cream

3 eggs

2 teaspoons kosher salt

¾ teaspoon freshly ground white pepper

½ teaspoon ground allspice

¼ teaspoon ground cloves

¾ pound fresh (unsalted) fatback, thinly sliced

1. Place liver, pork fat, onion, and anchovy paste in the workbowl of a food processor. Process until liquid. Add remaining ingredients except fatback. Process thoroughly. Pass mixture through a fine sieve.

2. Line a 9″ × 5″ × 3″ loaf pan with the fatback, making sure it does not overlap inside pan. Leave a 2-inch overhang around top of mold. Pour liver mixture into prepared mold and fold overhanging fatback over top of pâté. Cover loosely with paper toweling. Cook at 100% for 12 minutes.

3. Remove from oven. Uncover and let stand until cool. Cover tightly, weight top of pâté, and refrigerate for 8 to 12 hours.

To make a smaller pâté. Halve all ingredients and cook in a 7″ × 4″ × 4″ loaf pan for 8 minutes.

VARIATION

CHUNKY PÂTÉ Process liver coarsely and set aside. Process pork fat coarsely and combine with liver. Do not pass through sieve. Proceed as for Scandinavian Liver Pâté.

PÂTÉ WITH CHINESE BLACK BEANS

This is a classic pâté jazzed up with a few Chinese seasonings. Everybody seems to like it. If you are serving it as a first course, you can put a dollop of plum sauce in one corner of the plate, some Chinese mustard in another corner, and a short piece of scallion across the middle of each slice of pâté.

The French Pâté and Pâté with Walnuts variations go back to basics. Serve them with Dijon mustard, cornichons or sliced pickles, and good French bread.   *Serves 10 to 12 as a first course, 20 for cocktails*

¾ **pound chicken livers, rinsed, and connective tissue removed**

1 **small onion (about ¼ pound), peeled and quartered**

3 **cloves garlic, smashed and peeled**

¼ **cup Chinese salted black beans, soaked for 5 minutes and drained**

1½ **pounds pork shoulder, coarsely ground (by the butcher, if possible)**

⅓ **cup cooked, smoked ham, cut into ¼-inch dice**

¾ **pound plus 2 ounces unsalted (fresh) fatback, ⅓ cup cut into ¼-inch dice and the rest thinly sliced**

¾ **teaspoon dried oregano**

1½ **teaspoons dried thyme**

2 **teaspoons plus ¼ teaspoon mirin**

1½ **teaspoons Worcestershire sauce**

1½ **tablespoons tamari soy**

1 **teaspoon kosher salt**

½ **teaspoon freshly ground black pepper**

1. Place livers, onion, and garlic in the workbowl of a food processor. Process until coarsely chopped. Remove to a mixing bowl. Stir in remaining ingredients except fatback slices.

2. Test pâté for flavor: Wrap 1 tablespoon of mixture tightly in microwave plastic wrap. Cook at 100% for 2 minutes. Taste and adjust seasoning if necessary, and add more salt and pepper and garlic or herbs if desired.

3. Line a 9″ × 5″ × 3″ loaf pan with fatback, making sure it does not overlap inside pan. Leave a 2-inch overhang around top of mold. Pour liver mixture into prepared mold and fold fatback over top of pâté.

4. Cover loosely with paper toweling. Cook at 100% for 15 minutes.

5. Remove from oven. Uncover and let stand until cool. Cover tightly, weight top of pâté, and refrigerate for 8 to 12 hours. Slice and serve.

VARIATIONS

FRENCH PÂTÉ Omit Chinese black beans, mirin, and soy. Increase salt to 2 teaspoons, oregano to 1½ teaspoons, thyme to 3 teaspoons, and add 2 teaspoons Quatre-Épices (page 573) made from equal quantities of nutmeg, ginger, cinnamon, and cloves. Add 2 tablespoons brandy. Proceed as for Pâté with Chinese Black Beans.

PÂTÉ WITH WALNUTS Add 1 cup broken walnuts to liver and pork when chopping. Omit ham. Season as for French Pâté, using 3 tablespoons port instead of brandy. Garnish plate with walnut halves.

VEAL AND HAM PÂTÉ

This is most elegant looking, with rosy flecks of ham and darker mushroom flecks in a creamy-colored pâté. It has a robust flavor and is a good choice for almost any kind of meal. *Serves 10 as a first course, 20 to 40 as an hors d'oeuvre*

1 pound boiled ham, cut into 2-inch chunks
1 pound pork shoulder, cut into chunks
½ pound stewing veal
½ pound fresh (unsalted) fatback, cut into chunks
1 cup quartered mushrooms
½ bunch parsley, stemmed (flat-leaf if available)
1 tablespoon kosher salt
1 teaspoon freshly ground black pepper
1½ teaspoons crushed juniper berries
5 shallots (about 2½ ounces), peeled and quartered
¼ cup dry vermouth

1. Line a 9″ × 5″ loaf pan with microwave plastic wrap, leaving a 4-inch overhang around top of pan.

2. Place ½ pound of the ham and all of the pork, veal, and fatback in the workbowl of a food processor. Pulse on and off until coarsely ground and well combined. Remove mixture to a large bowl.

3. Place mushrooms, parsley, shallots, and remaining ham in processor. Pulse on and off until finely ground.

4. Combine with meat mixture and add vermouth, salt, pepper, and juniper berries, mixing well. Pack into prepared pan. Fold overlapping plastic over top to enclose completely. Cook at 100% for 20 minutes.

5. Remove from oven. Let cool to room temperature. Weight and refrigerate for 8 to 12 hours or overnight.

Hot First Courses

Many of the more substantial or elegant first courses—some hearty enough to be used as a main course—are served hot. That used to be a logistical problem that sometimes left me feeling like a general instead of a cook. Microwave cooking makes it easy to assemble or partly cook everything ahead and do the last-minute cooking while guests have a glass of wine. Clams Casino and Oysters Florentine can be finished while your guests are already sitting at the table.

SHRIMP BOIL

In Texas they have little hard-shelled shrimp that they cook in buckets of beer and shell with their fingers, washing them down with more cold beer. It's an ideal informal meal (or a start to one for solid eaters). Away from the Gulf, we have to make do with whatever shrimp is available. Either way, this dish is still a hands-on proposition best shared with good friends. It's not necessary, but a bowl of fresh Mayonnaise (page 382), for dipping, couldn't hurt anything except your outline. (If you do have access to real Gulf shrimp, add ½ cup beer and omit the lemon. Increase the initial cooking time to 3 minutes.)   *Serve 4 to 6 as a first course, 1 or 2 as a main course*

1 pound medium shrimp (24 to 26 shrimp)	**½ lemon, cut into quarters**
2 tablespoons Crab Boil (page 346), or store-bought crab boil mix	

Place shrimp in a 2-quart soufflé dish. Add Crab Boil and stir to coat. Add lemon. Cover tightly with microwave plastic wrap. Cook at 100% for 1 minute 30 seconds. Shake dish to redistribute shrimp. Cook for 1 minute 30 seconds longer.

CLAMS CASINO

This is one of those really good dishes that can still be found in old-fashioned Italian restaurants. It is quick to make using the microwave oven to open the clams and blanch the bacon. You can prepare this recipe without the salt; it just keeps the clams from tilting. The dish can be made entirely ahead and then tucked under the broiler after your guests sit down. Serve the clams on warm plates with little oyster forks or salad forks and plenty of Italian bread. Cold white wine, beer, or a not-too-refined red wine would all be good. *Serves 4 to 6*

24 littleneck clams, well
    scrubbed
⅓ cup (6 tablespoons)
    Snail Butter (page
    359)

Coarse salt (about 1
    cup), for broiling
    clams
2 slices bacon, cut into
    1½-inch pieces

1. Arrange clams, hinge end down, in a 2-inch-deep dish just large enough to hold them. Cover tightly with microwave plastic wrap. Cook at 100% for 7 minutes (any clams that do not open may be cooked for 1 additional minute; then discard any that remain closed).

2. Remove from oven. Uncover and remove clams from shells. Reserve clams and the deeper side of each shell. (Save clam broth for use in another recipe. It can be frozen.)

3. Heat a conventional broiler.

4. Melt Snail Butter in a 2-cup glass measure, uncovered, at 100% for 3 minutes.

5. Pour salt into a 10-inch round ovenproof dish to a depth of ½ inch. Arrange clam shells on salt. Divide melted Snail Butter evenly among shells. Place a clam in each and place a piece of bacon on top. Broil 5 inches from heat source for 2 minutes, until bacon is crisp.

To make 48 clams. Double all ingredients, cooking clams for 11 minutes to open. Proceed as for Clams Casino, but use a large cookie sheet with sides and about 2 cups salt for broiling.

Clams arranged, hinge end down, in a dish just large enough to hold them.

DIJON SNAILS

Far from the vineyard, snails come in cans, cooked and ready to be seasoned and reheated. Usually they are tucked into snail shells or covered with Snail Butter and grilled. It seems like a lot of useless labor to stuff them back into shells. Try this gentler version, served in individual soufflé dishes or small gratin dishes, or use the sauced snails as a topping for modest amounts of fine egg noodles. If you do not use noodles, serve with a spoon and bread for mopping up the sauce. *Serves 6*

1 cup heavy cream	1 tablespoon unsalted
1½ tablespoons Dijon	butter, cut into 4
mustard	pieces
1 tablespoon Snail	¼ cup white wine
Butter (page 359)	36 large snails (two 7½-
	ounce cans),
	drained and rinsed

1. Combine cream and mustard in a 4-cup glass measure. Cook, uncovered, at 100% for 5 minutes.

2. Remove from oven. Stir in Snail Butter and unsalted butter and keep warm.

3. Place wine and snails in a 1½-quart soufflé dish. Cover tightly with microwave plastic wrap. Cook at 100% for 1 minute 30 seconds.

4. Remove from oven. Uncover and drain. Stir snails into warm sauce.

VARIATIONS

SNAILS WITH DUXELLES Substitute 2 tablespoons Duxelles (page 340) for both Snail Butter and unsalted butter. Proceed as for Dijon Snails.

SNAILS IN SNAIL BUTTER Heat 6 tablespoons Snail Butter in a 4-cup glass measure, uncovered, at 100% for 2 minutes 30 seconds. Stir in snails and proceed as for Dijon Snails.

OYSTERS FLORENTINE

This Parisian dish is not too far removed from Clams Casino (page 62). Another member of the family is Oysters Rockefeller, of New Orleans origin, which I think is somewhat overrated. To make this recipe more like Oysters Rockefeller, add some mint and tarragon to the spinach when you are puréeing it. All these recipes can be made ahead, and grilled at the last minute. *Makes 12 oysters*

12 oysters (about 2 pounds), well scrubbed

½ pound spinach, cooked, rinsed, and squeezed (about ⅓ cup)

⅓ cup Thick Béchamel (page 365), nutmeg omitted

¼ teaspoon kosher salt
Freshly ground black pepper
Coarse salt (about 1 cup), for broiling oysters

½ cup Mornay (page 366)

1. Place oysters, hinge end down, in a 2-inch-deep dish just large enough to hold them. Cover tightly with microwave plastic wrap. Cook at 100% for 4 minutes. (Oysters will be just barely open. Any oysters that do not open may be cooked for 1 additional minute; then discard any that remain closed.)

2. Remove from oven. Uncover and pry oysters open with a blunt knife. Free oysters from shell. Set aside oysters and the deeper half of each shell. (Save and freeze liquid for use in another recipe.)

3. Place spinach, Béchamel, salt, and pepper in the workbowl of a food processor. Process until well combined; set aside.

4. Heat a conventional broiler.

5. Pour salt into a 10-inch ovenproof dish to a depth of ½ inch. Arrange oyster shells on salt. Place a tablespoon of spinach mixture in each shell and place an oyster on top. Cover each with 2 teaspoons Mornay. Broil 5 inches from heat source for 2 to 3 minutes, until browned and bubbly. Serve hot.

To make 24 oysters. Double all ingredients and cook oysters for 9 minutes to open. Broil on a large rimmed cookie sheet or in two batches.

STUFFED CALAMARI

The looks of some foods seem to dictate their destiny. The conical bodies of medium-size squid seem designed for stuffing. In this recipe, cooked stuffed squid are sliced into white-rimmed green circles and set on a sea of red. *Serves 4 as a first course, 2 as a main course*

1 pound fresh spinach with stems, well rinsed and drained

2 tablespoons olive oil

1½ pounds squid, bodies 5 to 6 inches long, cleaned, with tentacles chopped (page 600)

¼ cup chopped onion

¼ cup chopped celery

1 clove garlic, smashed and peeled

½ cup Breadcrumbs (page 354), coarsely ground

2 teaspoons kosher salt

2 teaspoons fresh lemon juice

½ cup diced, canned Italian plum tomatoes

2 tablespoons white wine

¼ teaspoon freshly ground black pepper

1. Place spinach in a 14″ × 11″ × 2″ dish and cook, uncovered, at 100% for 4 minutes.

2. Remove from oven. Squeeze spinach well to remove excess water. Roughly chop spinach and set aside.

3. Heat oil in a 4-cup glass measure, uncovered, at 100% for 2 minutes. Add chopped squid tentacles, onions, celery, and garlic. Cook, uncovered, for 2 minutes, stirring once.

4. Remove from oven and place in the workbowl of a food processor. Add spinach, Breadcrumbs, 1 teaspoon of the salt, and 1 teaspoon of the lemon juice. Process until finely chopped.

5. Divide the stuffing evenly among the squid bodies (use about 2 tablespoons, loosely packed, per squid).

6. Place tomatoes, wine, pepper, remaining 1 teaspoon salt, and 1 teaspoon lemon juice in a shallow 12-inch round dish. Arrange squid on top of sauce spoke-fashion with tails toward the center. Cook, uncovered, at 100% for 5 minutes.

7. Remove from oven and remove squid from dish. Cook sauce, uncovered, for 2 minutes longer.

8. Remove from oven. Spoon sauce onto serving plates. Slice squid, crosswise, into ½-inch slices and arrange, overlapping, on sauce.

BAKED EGGS

Now that eggs are no longer a daily breakfast occurrence, because of concern about cholesterol, maybe we can bring back some of the festive versions developed by the French. Eggs do not do uniformly well in the microwave oven; but what are variously called shirred or baked eggs do very well indeed if, once you break them into their cooking dishes, you take a knife with a very sharp tip and gently prick the yolk twice, breaking the membrane. This will keep the egg from exploding; strangely enough, the yolk will not run all over. I was scared to death the first time I tried this, but it works like a charm. *Serves 1*

¼ cup vegetable purée, such as Lightly Cooked Crushed Tomatoes (page 339), Duxelles (page 340) or Broccoli (page 293)

Pinch dried oregano (optional)
Kosher salt
1 egg
½ teaspoon unsalted butter, cut into bits
Freshly ground black pepper

1. Spread purée in bottom of a 3½″ × 2″ round ramekin. Stir in oregano, if desired, and a pinch of salt. Carefully break egg on top of purée and prick yolk twice with knife tip.

2. Scatter butter over egg and season lightly with pepper and salt.

3. Cover loosely with paper toweling. Cook at 100% for 1 minute. (In a small oven, cook for 1 minute 45 seconds.)

To multiply recipe. Place each egg in a separate ramekin and use ¼ cup purée for each. Place ramekins 4 inches apart and cover loosely with paper toweling. For 2 eggs, cook for 1 minute 45 seconds. For 4 eggs, cook for 3 minutes. For 6 eggs, cook for 5 minutes. (In a small oven, cook 2 eggs for 3 minutes 30 seconds, using a carousel.)

To bake 2 eggs in one gratin dish. Place ½ cup purée in a 4″ × 2″ glass or ceramic ramekin. Top with 2 eggs. Pierce yolks with knife tip. Top with 2 teaspoons butter cut in ¼-inch dice, sprinkle with salt and freshly ground black pepper. Cook at 100% for 1 minute 30 seconds. (In a small oven, cook for 3 minutes.)

VARIATIONS

HERB-BAKED EGGS WITH CREAM Place egg or eggs on the purée of your choice. Prick yolks. Top each egg with 1 teaspoon finely chopped fresh herbs—parsley, chervil, tarragon, chives and summer savory are all good, alone or in combination. Top each egg with 2 tablespoons heavy cream. Omit butter. Cook as for Baked Eggs.

EGGS WITH CREAMED SPINACH AND PERNOD Mix ½ teaspoon Pernod into each ¼ cup Creamed Spinach (page 300). Top each egg with 3 tablespoons Mornay (page 366) gently seasoned with hot red-pepper sauce, or with Fiery Pepper Sauce (page 344). Cook as for Baked Eggs.

EGGS WITH REFRIED BEANS, CHILIES AND CHEESE With the rim of the ramekin as a guide, cut 1 round slice of American cheese for each egg. Use ¼ cup Refried Beans (page 141) per egg, breaking egg on top of beans; sprinkle with a little chopped fresh chili, and cover with circle of cheese. Cook as for Baked Eggs.

BAKED HAM AND EGGS WITH MORNAY Cut rounds of ⅛-inch-thick ham slices. Place a ham slice in the bottom of each ramekin; top with an egg. Top each egg with 3 tablespoons Mornay (page 366). Cook as for Baked Eggs.

SHIRRED EGGS WITH MUSHROOMS For each egg, thinly slice ½ medium mushroom. Toss with 2 teaspoons melted butter, salt and ½ teaspoon chopped dill or other fresh herb. Place ¼ cup Duxelles (page 340) in bottom of each ramekin; top with an egg. Spoon sliced mushrooms, butter and seasonings over egg. Cook as for Baked Eggs.

POACHED EGGS IN SOUP Boil 3 cups Chicken Broth (page 331), canned chicken broth or any of the seasoned chicken broths (pages 83–84) in a wide 8-cup glass measure. Break 2 eggs onto a shallow saucer, prick the yolks and slide eggs into broth. Cook, uncovered, at 100% for 1 minute 30 seconds. (In a small oven, cook for 3 minutes.) Serves 2 as a soup.

EGGS IN RED WINE

This unlikely-sounding dish is a French classic and very good. It is usually served with triangular toast points stuck around it. *Serves 4*

¼ pound slab bacon, cut into lardoons (page 480)	½ bay leaf
	2 parsley sprigs
1 tablespoon chopped shallots	4 eggs
	2 teaspoons cornstarch dissolved in 2 tablespoons water
1 clove garlic, smashed, peeled and minced	
	1 teaspoon kosher salt
½ cup red wine	Freshly ground black pepper
½ cup water	

1. Place lardoons in a 10″ × 2″ round quiche dish. Cook, uncovered, at 100% for 2 minutes. Stir in shallots and garlic and cook, uncovered, for 2 minutes more. Add wine, water, bay leaf, and parsley. Cook, uncovered, at 100% for 8 minutes.

2. Remove from oven. Carefully break eggs into liquid and prick each yolk twice with the tip of a sharp knife. Cook, uncovered, at 100% for 1 minute 30 seconds.

3. Remove from oven. Remove eggs to a heated serving platter with a slotted spoon. Stir cornstarch mixture into wine mixture. Cook, uncovered, at 100% for 2 minutes 30 seconds.

4. Remove from oven. Remove bay leaf and parsley sprigs. Stir in salt and pepper and pour over eggs. Serve hot.

FRIED QUAIL

With frozen quail now fairly common in the supermarket, you can easily make this simple and festive first course. Your guests will have to use their hands, but since the birds are quartered, they are easy to eat. If you have questions about deep-frying in the microwave oven, see page 537 for more details. Do this only in a full-size oven. *Serves 4 as a first course, 8 as part of a mixed hors d'oeuvre*

3 cups vegetable oil	4 quail, fresh or
1½ tablespoons kosher	defrosted (page
salt	573), quartered
½ teaspoon cayenne	4 to 8 lemon wedges
pepper	Sprigs of fresh
	coriander, to garnish
	(optional)

1. Heat oil in a 2-quart nonplastic container measuring at least 3¼ inches high, uncovered, at 100% for 15 minutes.

2. Combine salt and cayenne and rub into skin of quail.

3. Place quail, 6 to 8 pieces at a time, in hot oil and cook, uncovered, at 100% for 1 minute. Drain on paper toweling. Cook successive batches in the same manner, heating oil 5 minutes between batches. Serve with lemon wedges and sprigs of fresh coriander, if desired.

VARIATION

MARINATED QUAIL Omit salt and cayenne pepper. Prepare quail as above and marinate in ⅓ cup tamari soy and 6 cloves garlic, smashed and peeled, for 15 minutes. Pat dry and proceed as for Fried Quail.

Stuffed Vegetables

In many countries, vegetables are stuffed at home and then taken to the baker to be slowly cooked after the day's breads have been taken out and the wood-fired heat has abated. In Turkey, one can still see children returning home just before mealtime, carrying pans filled with a tempting assortment of peppers, eggplants, and tomatoes. Oddly, the slow cooking of the dying oven produces results very similar to the magical speed of the microwave oven. The major difference is that the vegetables have better color and shape when cooked in the microwave oven.

For a lovely buffet or barely warm summer dinner, prepare an assortment of vegetables with a variety of stuffings—an inexpensive feast.

STUFFED BELL PEPPERS

Mix red and green peppers for more visual interest. This recipe may be doubled; just extend the cooking time to 30 minutes. *Serves 4 as a first course or side dish, 2 as a main course*

4 medium-to-large green or red bell peppers (about 2 pounds) Greek or Moroccan Stuffing (see following recipes)

½ cup water 2 tablespoons Basic Tomato Paste (page 340), or canned tomato paste ½ teaspoon kosher salt

1. Slice ½-inch "lids" off tops of peppers and set aside. Remove seeds from peppers and lids.

2. Divide stuffing evenly among peppers and replace their lids. Fit peppers, right side up, in a 10″ × 8″ oval dish.

3. To make cooking liquid, whisk together water, tomato paste, and salt until smooth. Pour mixture around peppers. Cover tightly with microwave plastic wrap. Cook at 100% for 20 minutes, until couscous or rice in stuffing is tender. Halfway through cooking, poke a small hole in plastic with the tip of a sharp knife.

4. Remove from oven. Uncover and let stand 5 minutes before serving.

Note. Peppers may be stuffed, then frozen uncooked. To cook, place frozen peppers in a 10″ × 8″ oval dish. Cover tightly with microwave plastic wrap. Cook with prepared cooking liquid at 100% for 30 minutes.

GREEK STUFFING

There was a time when this would have been made with lamb in Greece. Sadly, lamb is in short supply today, and imported beef is used instead. The flavors are fairly straightforward, much like those in Italian cooking.

¼ cup olive oil
1 large onion, peeled and minced (about 1½ cups)
6 ounces ground beef or lamb (about ⅔ cup)
1 can (14 ounces) Italian plum tomatoes, drained, coarsely chopped and liquid reserved

⅓ cup long-grain rice
2 teaspoons kosher salt
1 teaspoon dried thyme
1 teaspoon dried oregano
¼ teaspoon freshly ground black pepper

1. Heat oil in a 2-quart soufflé dish, uncovered, at 100% for 2 minutes. Stir in onions and beef. Continue cooking, uncovered, for 5 minutes, stirring once.

2. Remove from oven. Pour off all but ¼ cup drippings from pan. Place mixture in the workbowl of a food processor. Add tomatoes and process just until meat is finely chopped. Stir in remaining ingredients.

Note. Add 1 tablespoon fresh lemon juice to the cooking liquid for Stuffed Bell Peppers when using Greek Stuffing.

MOROCCAN STUFFING

This is less an authentic Moroccan dish than an evocation of characteristic Moroccan ingredients and flavors.

¼ cup olive oil
1 large onion, peeled and minced (about 1½ cups)
6 ounces ground lamb (about ⅔ cup)
2 cloves garlic, smashed and peeled
½ cup couscous or slightly undercooked rice

¼ cup raisins
2 tablespoons dried mint
2 tablespoons fresh lemon juice
1 teaspoon kosher salt
1 teaspoon ground cumin
¼ teaspoon freshly ground black pepper

1. Heat oil in a 2-quart soufflé dish, uncovered, at 100% for 2 minutes. Add onions, lamb, and garlic. Cook, uncovered, at 100% for 5 minutes, stirring once.

2. Remove from oven. Pour off all but ¼ cup drippings from dish. Place mixture in the workbowl of a food processor. Process until meat is finely chopped. Stir in remaining ingredients.

STUFFED EGGPLANT

Eggplants are perfect candidates for stuffing; but large ones provide altogether too much food for an attractive portion and have a nasty tendency to be bitter. Make this when smallish Japanese eggplants—the kinds that look like miniatures of our ordinary, large purple ones—are available, or use the long, thin Chinese or Middle Eastern eggplants in any shade from purple to almost white. The flesh gets combined with the stuffing to luscious effect. *Serves 6 as a first course or side dish, 12 as part of a mixed stuffed vegetable dish*

6 small purple eggplants
   (about 4 inches
   long) stemmed and
   cut in half
   lengthwise
Kosher salt
½ cup Duxelles (page
   340)
1 small onion (about ¼
   pound), peeled and
   quartered
3 tablespoons freshly
   grated Parmesan
   cheese
½ teaspoon ground
   cumin
   Freshly ground black
   pepper

3 tablespoons fresh
   lemon juice
1 tablespoon Chicken
   Broth (page 331),
   canned chicken
   broth or water

CRUMB MIXTURE
¾ cup fresh Bread-
   crumbs (page 354)
¼ cup coarsely chopped
   flat-leaf parsley
3 tablespoons freshly
   grated Parmesan
   cheese
2 to 3 tablespoons virgin
   olive oil

1. Scoop flesh out of each eggplant half, leaving a shell about ⅛ inch thick. Generously salt inside of shells and reserved flesh.

2. Place a sheet of paper toweling on a 9-inch pie plate. Arrange shells on paper toweling, cut side down, spoke-fashion with narrow ends toward center of dish. Place flesh in center of dish. Cover tightly with microwave plastic wrap. Cook at 100% for 3 minutes.

3. Remove from oven. Uncover and rinse both shells and flesh well. Pat dry with paper toweling, pressing on flesh to remove excess moisture. Set shells aside.

4. Place flesh and remaining ingredients in the workbowl of a food processor. Process until thoroughly combined and flesh is finely chopped.

5. Spoon mixture loosely into shells and arrange on the same platter, spoke-fashion, this time with narrow ends toward the outside of the dish. Cover with a sheet of paper toweling and then cover tightly with microwave plastic wrap. Cook at 100% for 4 minutes.

6. Remove from oven. Remove plastic, but leave paper toweling in place. Let stand for 3 minutes.

7. Heat a conventional broiler. Toss together ingredients for crumb mixture. Sprinkle 1 to 2 teaspoons of mixture over each eggplant half and broil until lightly browned. Serve immediately.

VARIATIONS

EGGPLANT STUFFED WITH GREEK OR MOROCCAN STUFFING Prepare eggplant shells and flesh as for Stuffed Eggplant through step 3. Do not make crumb mixture. Coarsely chop eggplant flesh and combine with a half recipe of either Greek or Moroccan stuffing (pages 72–73). Cook for 10 minutes, tightly covered, at 100%. Stuff eggplant shells. Continue as for Stuffed Eggplant, but without paper toweling.

ZUCCHINI STUFFED WITH GREEK OR MOROCCAN STUFFING Use young, 6-inch-long zucchini. Prepare and stuff as in first variation.

STUFFED ARTICHOKES

Stuffed artichokes are prepared somewhat differently from other stuffed vegetables, but they are equally delicious. Cooking artichokes this way permits you to easily obtain perfectly cooked artichoke bottoms for the many classic French recipes that use them. See the illustration for how to clean the bottom once the artichoke is cooked. *Serves 4 as a first course or side dish*

4 globe artichokes (about 8 ounces each), stems removed, 1 inch trimmed from top and leaf tips trimmed
1 lemon, cut in half

Salt Pork and Sage Stuffing, or Garlic and Parsley Stuffing (see following recipes)
2 tablespoons Chicken Broth (page 331) or canned chicken broth
1 tablespoon olive oil

1. Rub artichokes with lemon halves to keep them from discoloring. Wrap each artichoke tightly with microwave plastic wrap. Cook at 100% for 15 minutes, until the bottoms are tender.

2. Remove from oven. Pierce plastic with the tip of a sharp knife and let artichokes stand, wrapped, for 5 minutes.

3. Unwrap and remove purple-tipped leaves and chokes from the center of each. The artichokes may be prepared ahead up to this point. Keep them tightly wrapped and refrigerated for up to 1 day.

4. About 10 minutes before serving, divide the stuffing evenly among the artichokes, placing most of it in the cavity and sprinkling about 1 tablespoon between the leaves. Arrange artichokes in a 10″ × 8″ oval dish.

5. Stir together broth and oil and pour over artichokes. Cover tightly with microwave plastic wrap. Cook at 100% for 5 minutes.

6. Remove from oven, uncover, and serve hot.

SALT PORK AND SAGE STUFFING

Makes about 1 cup

6 ounces salt pork, cut into ½-inch cubes

1 small onion (about ¼ pound), peeled and quartered

¼ pound celery (about 1 stalk), trimmed, strung and cut into 2-inch lengths

½ teaspoon dried sage

½ cup fine dry Breadcrumbs (page 354) or unflavored store-bought breadcrumbs

3 tablespoons Chicken Broth (page 331) or canned chicken broth

¼ teaspoon freshly ground black pepper

1 tablespoon olive oil

1. Place salt in pork in a 10-inch pie plate and cook, uncovered, at 100% for 4 minutes. Remove from oven and set aside.

2. Place onion and celery in the workbowl of a food processor. Process until coarsely chopped.

3. Combine vegetables and salt pork and stir to coat. Cook, uncovered, at 100% for 2 minutes.

4. Remove from oven. Stir in remaining ingredients. Cook, uncovered, at 100% for 2 minutes.

5. Remove from oven and use to stuff artichokes.

Place trimmed artichoke (page 43) on wrap.

Gather ends of wrap tightly. Twist and pat down to seal tightly.

Spread leaves apart to expose choke and pale, inner, small leaves.

Remove small leaves by picking up and pinching.

Scrape out remaining choke with a metal spoon.

Trim artichoke—all leaves removed—for artichoke bottom.

GARLIC AND PARSLEY STUFFING

Makes about 1 cup

¼ cup olive oil
½ cup (loosely packed)
    flat-leaf parsley,
    finely chopped
2 cloves garlic, smashed,
    peeled and minced
¾ cup fine dry
    Breadcrumbs (page
    354) or unflavored
    store-bought
    breadcrumbs

1 tablespoon fresh
    lemon juice
1 teaspoon kosher salt
¼ teaspoon freshly
    ground black
    pepper

1. Heat oil in a 2-cup glass measure, uncovered, at 100% for 2 minutes. Add parsley and garlic. Cook, uncovered, at 100% for 4 minutes.

2. Remove from oven. Stir in remaining ingredients.

TOMATOES STUFFED WITH TABBOULEH

Since tomatoes retain their vivid color and do not burst when cooked in the microwave oven, it is ideal for cooking stuffed tomatoes. This dish, which is good hot or cold, has an intense tomato flavor. It is good as a vegetarian first course or as part of a stuffed vegetable main course (see Stuffed Kohlrabi, page 80, Stuffed Eggplant, page 73, and Broiled Stuffed Mushroom Caps, page 340) or as an accompaniment to grilled fish or roast lamb or chicken. The juice from the cooked tomatoes can become a vegetarian base for soup or, mixed with lemon juice and a minimum of olive oil, a light salad dressing. *Serves 6 to 8 as a first course or side dish*

8 small (2½ to 3-inch) or 6 medium (4-inch) tomatoes
Kosher salt
½ cup bulgur
2 cups tomato juice, fresh or canned
¼ cup plus 3 tablespoons olive oil
¼ cup chopped fresh mint leaves

1 tablespoon minced garlic
½ teaspoon hot red pepper flakes
½ cup chopped scallions (green and white parts)
Freshly ground black pepper
2 tablespoons fresh lemon juice

1. Cut a small slice from the top of each tomato. Scoop out inside of tomatoes, preferably with a silver spoon, leaving a shell ⅛ inch thick. Chop flesh and set aside together with seeds and juice.

2. Sprinkle salt inside each tomato. Prick the skin of each two or three times and rub with oil. Place tomatoes cut side down on paper toweling to drain.

3. Combine bulgur, tomato juice, oil, mint, garlic, pepper flakes, and scallions. Let stand 15 minutes.

4. Pour bulgur mixture into a sieve set over a bowl. Drain 20 minutes, stirring several times; reserve liquid. Pour mixture into a clean bowl and stir in pepper, lemon juice, salt to taste, and reserved tomato flesh, seeds, and juice.

5. Arrange tomato shells cut side up around the inside edge of a 9-inch pie plate. Fill shells with bulgur mixture, mounding it slightly. Pour reserved drained liquid around tomatoes. Cover tightly with microwave plastic wrap. Cook at 100% for 7 to 9 minutes, until tender when pricked with the tip of a sharp knife.

6. Remove from oven. Uncover and transfer tomatoes with a slotted spoon to serving plate. Save the tomato liquid to use as a base for soup or salad dressing.

STUFFED KOHLRABI

Briefly cooked in the microwave oven, kohlrabi is revealed to be a wholly new vegetable, elegant and pale jade green. Premicrowave, kohlrabi had to be cooked so long that it became white, watery, and fibrous.	*Serves 4 to 8*

8 small kohlrabi,	**1 tablespoon olive oil**
    trimmed and peeled	**½ cup cooked rice**
2 tablespoons anchovy	**Freshly ground black**
    paste	 **pepper**

1. Using a melon baller, remove the center of each kohlrabi and set aside. Place cored kohlrabi in a ring around the inside edge of a pie plate.

2. Finely chop reserved centers. Combine with remaining ingredients. You should have about 1 cup of stuffing.

3. Divide stuffing between kohlrabi, mounding slightly.

4. Pour 1 tablespoon water into center of pie plate. Cover dish tightly with microwave plastic wrap. Cook at 100% for 7 minutes. Serve.

To double the recipe. Double all ingredients. Use a 14″ × 11″ dish or oval platter and lengthen cooking time to 10 minutes.

To make 2 kohlrabi. Use 2 small kohlrabi, trimmed and peeled, 1½ teaspoons anchovy paste, ¾ teaspoon olive oil, 2 tablespoons cooked rice, and freshly ground black pepper to make about ¼ cup stuffing. Proceed as for 8 kohlrabi, using a small plate. Pour 1 teaspoon water into center of plate. Cook at 100% for 3 to 4 minutes.

STUFFED CHAYOTE

It is time for the northerners among us to become familiar with this southern and Caribbean specialty. It cooks fabulously in the microwave oven. Just broil it at the very end. This is rich.	*Serves 4 as a first course or side dish*

2 chayote, each pricked
    4 times with the tip
    of a sharp knife
4 tablespoons plus 2
    teaspoons unsalted
    butter
1 small onion, peeled
    and thinly sliced
1 clove garlic, smashed,
    peeled and minced
1 tablespoon minced
    parsley
½ teaspoon dried thyme

1 cup milk
½ teaspoon kosher salt
    Freshly ground black
    pepper
    Pinch cayenne pepper
1 cup freshly grated
    Gruyère cheese
½ cup fine dry
    Breadcrumbs (page
    354) or store-bought
    unflavored
    breadcrumbs

1. Place chayote in the oven and cook, uncovered, at 100% for 7 minutes. Remove from oven. When cool enough to handle, scoop out flesh and reserve flesh and shells.

2. Melt 4 tablespoons butter in a 10-inch quiche dish, uncovered, at 100% for 2 minutes. Add onion and garlic and stir to coat. Cook, uncovered, at 100% for 4 minutes. Add parsley, thyme, and reserved chayote flesh. Cook, uncovered, at 100% for 5 minutes, stirring twice.

3. Remove from oven. Add milk, stirring constantly until it is absorbed. Stir in salt, pepper, and cayenne. Cook, uncovered, at 100% for 2 minutes.

4. Preheat conventional broiler with rack in highest position.

5. Divide half the chayote mixture between the reserved shells. Using half the Gruyère, cover each layer of chayote mixture with a layer of cheese. Spread remaining chayote mixture over cheese and top with remaining cheese. (This dish may be prepared to this point up to one day in advance.).

6. Place stuffed chayote on a broiler pan. Sprinkle each with Breadcrumbs and dot with remaining butter. Broil until brown and bubbly.

SOUPS

SOUP restores me and gives me comfort. I like it hot or cold, thick or thin, as the preamble to a meal or as the meal itself. I find there are soups to entertain with and soups for personal pleasure. One of my greatest delights in microwave cooking is the possibility of making good soup every night if I wish.

Most soups are made with a meat-broth base, but many are made without broth at all and others are made with a vegetarian base. Look through the recipes on pages 330–336 for broths that can be made rapidly in the microwave oven and used as soups or the basis for soup. If your time is very limited, use a good canned chicken broth as the starting point. In that case, add salt carefully; canned broth is salted.

Soups can be clear or they can be thickened—with a purée, with cornstarch, with eggs, with a cooked potato, with cream, or with sour cream or yogurt.

Besides the soups in this chapter, there are others among the beans, grains, legumes, and vegetables purées; you can find them in the Index. Of course, you can create your own. Look in the Dictionary at the end of the book to see how to cook vegetables, grains, and purées that can be put together with broth in endless combinations to make new soups.

If you have any soup left over, reheat 1 cup in a 2-cup glass measure, uncovered, at 100% for 2 minutes; 2 cups in a 4-cup glass measure, uncovered, at 100% for 3 minutes; 4 cups in an 8-cup glass measure, uncovered, at 100% for 4 minutes.

CHICKEN BROTH &...

These variations on Chicken Broth are richly flavored and sustaining. The garlic becomes sweet and adds body, making it a soup version of Chicken and Rice (page 213). *Makes 2 cups*

2 cups Chicken Broth (page 331) or canned chicken broth	**2 tablespoons fresh lemon juice**
6 cloves garlic, smashed and peeled	**Kosher salt**
	Freshly ground black pepper

1. Place broth and garlic in a 4-cup glass measure.

2. Cover tightly with microwave plastic wrap and cook at 100% for 8 minutes.

3. Remove from oven. Pierce plastic to release steam. Uncover and stir in lemon juice. Correct seasonings.

To make 4 cups. Double all quantities in recipe or any variation and cook at 100% for 10 minutes.

VARIATIONS

EGG DROP SOUP Omit garlic. Make Chicken Broth & . . . Whisk 1 or 2 eggs. Remove plastic wrap, leaving soup in oven. Whisk in eggs. Cook, uncovered, at 100% for 2 minutes. Do not use lemon juice. Serve with grated Parmesan cheese, if desired.

HEALTH SOUP Reduce garlic to 2 cloves. In the workbowl of a food processor, chop leaves from 4 parsley sprigs with 5 spinach leaves and some watercress springs. Cook with Chicken Broth & . . . Omit lemon juice. Correct seasonings.

ESCAROLE SOUP Reduce garlic to 3 cloves. Cut 5 leaves of escarole (ideally leftovers from salad fixings) into thin strips across the veins. Put in measure with Chicken Broth &. . . . Add ¼ cup cooked or canned chickpeas, if available. Cook. Omit lemon juice. Correct seasonings.

HOT AND SPICY CHICKEN SOUP

This soup, inspired by a Thai soup, is one I like to make for myself, especially if I have a cold—it clears the nose. *Makes 2 cups*

2 cups Chicken Broth (page 331) or canned chicken broth
6 slices peeled fresh ginger, about ¼ inch thick
3 cloves garlic, smashed, peeled and sliced
⅛ teaspoon hot red-pepper flakes
1 teaspoon Worcestershire sauce
1 tablespoon fresh coriander leaves, cut into ribbons across the vein
2 tablespoons thinly sliced scallion greens
3 teaspoons light (low-salt) soy

1. In an 8-cup glass measure, combine broth, ginger, garlic, pepper flakes, and Worcestershire sauce. Cook, uncovered, at 100% for 8 minutes.

2. Remove from oven and stir in remaining ingredients. Serve hot.

NEW ENGLAND CLAM CHOWDER

This is the classic cream-based clam chowder. *Serves 4 to 5*

8 quahogs or large cherrystone clams, well scrubbed
2½ ounces bacon (about 3 slices, ¼ inch thick), cut into lardoons
1 cup finely chopped yellow onion (1 large onion)
1½ cups diced potatoes (about 3 medium potatoes)
1 tablespoon all-purpose flour
1 cup milk
1 cup heavy cream
Kosher salt
Freshly ground black pepper

1. Arrange clams, standing them on their hinge ends, in a 2-inch-deep dish. Cover tightly with microwave plastic wrap. Cook at 100% for 7 minutes.

2. Remove from oven and uncover. Remove clams from shells, reserving meat and any broth. Strain broth through a sieve lined with paper toweling and reserve (you will have about 1 cup). Chop clams coarsely and reserve with any juices they give off.

3. Put bacon in a 2½-quart soufflé dish. Cover loosely with paper toweling. Cook at 100% for 4 minutes.

4. Remove from oven. Stir in onions, potatoes, flour, and reserved broth. Cover tightly with microwave plastic wrap. Cook at 100% for 10 minutes. Remove from oven and set aside.

5. Combine milk and cream in a 4-cup glass measure. Heat, uncovered, at 100% for 4 minutes 30 seconds.

6. Remove from oven and stir into reserved vegetable mixture. Add clams and their juices. Stir well, add salt and pepper to taste, and serve hot.

To serve 12. Double all ingredients except bacon and onion. Increase bacon to 4 ounces and onion to 1½ cups. Cook clams as above for 20 minutes. Cook bacon as above for 8 minutes. Add onions, potatoes, flour, and reserved broth and cook, covered, for 20 minutes. Heat milk and cream in an 8-cup glass measure for 7 minutes. Combine all as above and heat, uncovered, for 3 minutes.

Arrange clams in a dish just large enough to hold them.

MANHATTAN CLAM CHOWDER

This is the other classic clam chowder, the one made with tomatoes. *Serves 10 or more*

16 quahogs or large cherrystone clams, well scrubbed

2 ounces slab bacon, cut into 2″ × ½″ × ½″ lardoons

3 medium carrots, trimmed, peeled and cut into 3-inch lengths

2 celery stalks, trimmed, strung and cut into 3-inch lengths

2 small yellow onions (about ¾ pound), peeled and quartered

4 cloves garlic, smashed and peeled

3 cups diced all-purpose potatoes (about 2½ pounds)

1 can (20 ounces) crushed tomatoes with juice

¼ teaspoon dried thyme

¼ teaspoon dried oregano

½ bay leaf

Freshly ground black pepper

Hot red-pepper sauce

1. Arrange clams standing on their hinge ends in a 14″ × 11″ × 2″ dish. Cover tightly with microwave plastic wrap. Cook at 100% for 20 minutes.

2. Remove from oven. Uncover and remove clams from shells, reserving meat and broth. Strain broth through cheesecloth or a paper filter and set aside. Chop clams coarsely and reserve with any juices they give off.

3. Place bacon, carrots, celery, onions, and garlic in the workbowl of a food processor. Process until coarsely chopped.

4. Place mixture in a 2-quart soufflé dish. Cook, uncovered, at 100% for 10 minutes, stirring twice. Add potatoes, tomatoes and their juice, thyme, oregano, and bay leaf. Cover tightly with microwave plastic wrap. Cook at 100% for 30 minutes.

5. Remove from oven. Pierce plastic to release steam and uncover. Measure reserved broth, add water if necessary to make 4 cups, and add to tomato mixture. Re-cover and let stand for 5 minutes.

6. Uncover, discard bay leaf, and stir in pepper, hot red pepper sauce, and clams and their juices. Serve immediately.

To serve 4 to 5. Halve all ingredients except carrots, potatoes and tomatoes. Use 1 carrot, 1 cup potatoes and 8 ounces tomatoes. Cook clams as above for 10 minutes. Cook chopped bacon, carrots, celery, onions and garlic, uncovered, for 6 minutes. Add potatoes, tomatoes and their juice, thyme, oregano and bay leaf. Cook, covered, for 20 minutes. Add reserved broth, re-cover and let stand for 5 minutes. Finish as above.

MUSSEL SOUP

Mussel soups are easy to make because cooked mussels give off a rich-tasting broth as they cook. The only real work is in cleaning the mussels. Discard any that feel strangely heavy; they may have gunk inside. The broth needs to be strained to remove any dirty bits and sand. Depending on how elegant you want dinner to be and how clean the hands of the eaters, you can serve the mussels in the shell or shelled. The cold variations are wonderful summer fare, but are always better with shelled mussels. *Serves 4 as a luncheon dish, 6 as a first course*

6 dozen mussels, scrubbed and beards removed	sliced, or 1 cup trimmed, strung and sliced celery
2½ cups white wine	1½ cups sliced yellow onion
12 whole peppercorns	
8 cloves garlic, smashed and peeled	3 cans (8¼ ounces each) crushed tomatoes with juice
2 medium fennel bulbs (about 1 pound), cored, quartered and	2 tablespoons kosher salt

1. Arrange mussels, hinge side down, in a single layer in a deep 14″ × 11″ × 2″ dish. Add 1½ cups of wine, the peppercorns, and the garlic. Cover tightly with microwave plastic wrap. Cook at 100% for 8 minutes.

2. Remove dish from oven and uncover. Holding mussels over dish to catch their liquid, remove meat from shells and set aside. Leave any unopened mussels in dish. Re-cover tightly with microwave plastic wrap. Cook at 100% for 3 to 4 minutes, until they open.

3. Remove remaining mussels from shells, discarding any unopened mussels. Strain cooking liquid through a sieve lined with a double thickness of cheesecloth. Reserve cooking liquid with mussels.

4. Combine fennel, onions, tomatoes, and remaining 1 cup wine in a 2-quart soufflé dish. Cover tightly with microwave plastic wrap. Cook at 100% for 13 minutes.

5. Remove from oven and uncover. Add reserved mussels with their cooking liquid, and salt. Stir well and serve hot.

VARIATIONS

BILLI BI Prepare as for Mussel Soup through step 4. In an 8-cup glass measure, whisk 1 cup cream with 1 cup Clam Broth (page 511) or Chicken Broth (page 331) and 4 egg yolks. Cover tightly with microwave plastic wrap and cook for 6 minutes at 100%. Remove from oven and uncover. Whisk into reserved mussel cooking liquid; add salt and pepper to taste. Refrigerate. When cold, stir in reserved mussels. Serves 6.

COLD CURRIED MUSSEL SOUP Cook as for Billi Bi, adding ½ teaspoon curry powder or Spice Powder I (page 345) to cream-broth mixture before cooking.

SHRIMP AND CORN CHOWDER

All chowders are not made with clams. Here is one festive enough for any party. *Serves 6*

1 red bell pepper, cored, seeded and finely chopped

1 green bell pepper, cored, seeded and finely chopped

2 cups Shrimp Cream (page 352) or heavy cream

2 cups Fish Broth (page 334), Clam Broth (page 511) or canned chicken broth

1 baking potato, peeled and diced

1 cup corn kernels, fresh or canned

¼ pound shrimp, peeled, deveined and cut into small pieces

¼ cup chopped celery leaves, taken from the center of the celery bunch, or ½ teaspoon celery seed

½ teaspoon dried thyme

2 teaspoons fresh lemon juice

1 teaspoon kosher salt

¼ teaspoon freshly ground black pepper

1. Combine peppers, Shrimp Cream, broth, and potato in a 2-quart soufflé dish. Cover with microwave plastic wrap. Cook at 100% for 12 minutes.

2. Remove from oven and uncover. Add remaining ingredients and stir well. Cook, uncovered, at 100% for 2 minutes. Serve hot.

TOMATO SOUP &...

These are some of my favorite, virtually instant soups. I always make and eat two cups. Then I feel happy. Sometimes I double the recipe to serve guests, and they seem to feel happy, too. *Makes 2 cups*

1 cup Chicken Broth (page 331) or canned chicken broth	4 leaves fresh basil (optional)
4 cloves garlic, smashed and peeled	1 tablespoon unsalted butter (optional)
1 can (8¼ ounces) plum tomatoes	Kosher salt
	Freshly ground black pepper

1. Put broth with garlic in a 4-cup glass measure.

2. Open can of tomatoes and cut through tomatoes in can until coarsely cut up. Add tomatoes and liquid to broth. Stir in basil, if desired.

3. Cover tightly with microwave plastic wrap. Cook at 100% for 7 minutes.

4. Remove from oven. Uncover and stir in butter, if desired. Taste and add salt and pepper, if needed. Serve hot.

To make 4 cups. Double all ingredients. Cook for 10 minutes.

VARIATIONS

TOMATO SOUP WITH COUSCOUS Substitute ¼ cup couscous for the garlic. Omit basil

TOMATO MINESTRONE Precook ¼ cup macaroni or small shells in salted boiling water on top of the stove. Measure out ¼ cup canned white cannellini beans and set aside. Add 1 pinch of dried oregano, 1 pinch of dried thyme, 1 tablespoon peeled and thinly sliced carrots, 1 tablespoon chopped onions, 1 tablespoon strung and thinly sliced celery, and 1 small mushroom, sliced, to the broth, tomatoes, garlic, and basil. Cover tightly; cook at 100% for 10 minutes. Remove from oven; uncover. Stir in drained macaroni and beans. Add more broth if you want a thinner soup. Add salt and pepper to taste. Serves 4.

CREAM OF TOMATO SOUP

There was a time when I could be satisfied with tomato soup out of a can—no more. I don't know if I have changed or the soup has. This makes me as happy as the canned soup used to. It is one good reason to make Chunky Tomato Sauce and keep it on hand, fresh or frozen. (Defrost frozen sauce before making soup.) *Makes 5 cups, serves 4 to 6*

1 cup Chunky Tomato
    Sauce (page 374)
2 cups Chicken Broth
    (page 331) or
    canned chicken
    broth
1 teaspoon granulated
    sugar

¼ teaspoon freshly
    ground black
    pepper
½ cup heavy cream
1 tablespoon thinly
    shredded fresh basil
    leaves or chopped
    fresh dill (both
    optional)

1. Place all ingredients except basil or dill in an 8-cup glass measure. Cook, uncovered, at 100% for 6 minutes.

2. Remove from oven and stir well. Serve hot, sprinkled with basil leaves or dill, if desired.

SIMPLE SEAFOOD STEW

This stew needs only a green salad and a bit of cheese afterward to make a meal of it. Put an extra bowl on the table for the empty shells. *Serves 4 as a main course, 6 as a substantial first course if extra mussels and clams are added*

2   small whole fish such
    as mackerel or red
    snapper (about 1½
    pounds each), gills
    and fins removed,
    head and tail
    discarded, cut
    across into 1½-
    inch slices
¾   cup sliced yellow
    onion (1 small
    onion)
2½ tablespoons good-
    quality olive oil
6   mussels, well
    scrubbed and
    beards removed
6   clams, well scrubbed
6   to 7 shrimp (about ¼
    pound), shelled
    and deveined
10 sea scallops, muscle
    removed, cut in
    half horizontally if
    very large
4   to 6 cloves garlic,
    smashed, peeled
    and thinly sliced

2   ripe tomatoes, cored
    and cut into
    chunks, or 4 whole
    canned tomatoes,
    squeezed to remove
    juice
    Large pinch saffron
    threads
1   tablespooon kosher
    salt
    Freshly ground
    black pepper
1½ cups Lightly Cooked
    Crushed Tomatoes
    (page 339) or
    whole canned
    American
    tomatoes, drained,
    squeezed and
    coarsely chopped
2   tablespoons Pernod
¾   cup Fish Broth (page
    317) or Clam
    Broth (page 511)
¾   cup white wine
    Fiery Pepper Sauce
    (page 344) or
    bottled hot red-
    pepper sauce
    (optional)
    Aïoli (page 383)
    (optional)

1. Arrange fish in a 2-quart soufflé dish with skin of fish against sides of dish. Place onions in center and drizzle with oil. Arrange mussels and clams around sides of dish on top of fish.

2. Arrange shrimp in a single layer on top of onions. Arrange scallops over shrimp. Scatter garlic and tomato chunks over top. Sprinkle with saffron, salt, and pepper.

Pour crushed tomatoes, Pernod, broth, and wine over all. Cover tightly with microwave plastic wrap. Cook at 100% for 15 to 17 minutes, just until clams open.

3. Remove from oven. Pierce plastic to release steam. Uncover, add pepper sauce, if desired, and stir. Serve with boiled potatoes, croutons, or rice, and pass Aïoli, if desired, in a separate dish.

ANISE SEAFOOD STEW

Anise is a licorice-tasting spice that goes very well with seafood and fish. It adds a little special oomph to this brightly colored stew. Serve some Aïoli (page 383) on the side, if you like. *Serves 3 to 4 as a main course, 6 as an ample first course*

Pinch saffron
½ cup white wine
6 large cherrystone clams, well scrubbed
1 can (14½ ounces) tomatoes, cut into chunks
6 cloves garlic, smashed and peeled
½ teaspoon freshly ground aniseed

Freshly ground black pepper
Pinch hot red-pepper flakes
½ pound cod fillets, cut into chunks
6 large shrimp (about ½ pound)
8 mussels, well scrubbed and beards removed

1. Stir saffron into white wine and let stand.

2. Arrange clams, hinge side down, in a 2-quart soufflé dish. Cover tightly with microwave plastic wrap. Cook at 100% for 3 minutes.

3. Remove from oven. Uncover and remove clams from their shells, reserving meat and any liquid.

4. Stir together tomatoes, garlic, aniseed, pepper, and red pepper flakes in a 2-quart soufflé dish. Place cod in center of dish. Arrange shrimp and mussels around cod. Cover tightly with microwave plastic wrap. Cook at 100% for 9 minutes 30 seconds, until mussels open.

5. Remove from oven. Gently stir in reserved saffron-wine mixture and clams with their broth. Reheat, if necessary, tightly covered, at 100% for 3 minutes.

FRENCH ONION SOUP

This is one of the most cheering of soups. Here it is made *blonde*, without browning (caramelizing) the onions. To make it *brune*, with the onions thoroughly caramelized, see Traditional French Onion Soup. The browned-onion version takes longer. You may want to serve the soup with a melted cheese crust on top (gratinéed). *Makes 5 cups, to serve 5, or 6 if croutons and cheese are added*

¼ pound unsalted butter
4 cups sliced yellow onion (2 pounds)
2 cups white wine or Champagne, not acid or sour

2 cups Chicken or Veal Broth (page 331) or canned chicken broth
Kosher salt
Freshly ground black pepper

1. Heat butter in a 14″ × 11″ × 2″ dish, uncovered, at 100% for 4 minutes. Stir in onions. Cook, uncovered, at 100% for 15 minutes, until onions are soft.

2. Add wine and broth. Continue cooking for 15 minutes longer.

3. Remove from oven. Season to taste with salt and pepper. Serve hot.

Note. If you are using canned broth, you will probably not need salt.

To make 2½ cups. Halve all ingredients. Heat butter in a 1-quart soufflé dish, uncovered, at 100% for 2 minutes. Add onions and cook for 10 minutes. Stir in wine and broth and cook for 10 minutes longer.

VARIATIONS

HEARTY ONION SOUP Prick 2 baking potatoes twice each with a fork. Place on a sheet of paper toweling and cook, uncovered, at 100% for 11 minutes. Remove from oven. When cool enough to handle, scoop out fresh and place in workbowl of a food processor. Add French Onion Soup and process until smooth. For half this quantity, cook 1 potato for 7 minutes and use only 2½ cups soup

TRADITIONAL FRENCH ONION SOUP Cook onions for 40 to 50 minutes, stirring 3 times, until golden brown. They will not have a uniform color. Continue as for French Onion Soup, preferably using Veal Broth. If desired, you may substitute ¼ cup port for that amount of wine. For a thinner soup, stir in 1 cup additional hot broth at the end of the cooking. Serves 6 to 8. To serve 3 to 4, halve ingredients; cook butter for 2 minutes; cook onions for 30 minutes; cook with broth and wine for 10 minutes.

GRATINÉED FRENCH ONION SOUP To gratiné, heat the broiler when you add the broth for French Onion Soup. Put a crouton (page 355) in the bottom of each of 6 ovenproof bowls. Divide soup among bowls. Sprinkle top of soup in each bowl with 1½ tablespoons (9 in all) grated Gruyère cheese. Place bowls on a cookie sheet. Place under broiler for 3 minutes, or until cheese melts.

CARIBBEAN FISH STEW

This is a substantial, mildly spicy, and unusual fish stew. It may require a little looking around for ingredients, but it is well worth the effort. *Serves 2 as a main course, 4 as a first course*

8 to 10 tomatillos, husked and cut into 6 wedges each (about 1½ cups)
½ cup seeded sliced serrano chilies or frying peppers with ¼ teaspoon hot red-pepper flakes
1 pound scrod or cod fillets, cut into chunks

Juice of 1 lemon
1 to 1½ cups water
¼ cup thinly sliced scallions (white and green parts)
1 tablespoon kosher salt
2 tablespoons olive oil
1½ teaspoons hot red-pepper flakes

1. Arrange tomatillos in a ring around inside edge of a 1½-quart soufflé dish. Scatter serrano chilies on top of tomatillos and place fish in center. Add lemon juice and water (1 cup for main course soup, 1½ cups for first course) and scatter scallions over all.

2. Cover tightly with microwave plastic wrap. Cook at 100% for 4 minutes.

3. Remove from oven and uncover. Stir carefully, leaving fish in center. Re-cover and cook at 100% for 2 to 3 minutes longer, and until fish is opaque.

4. Remove from oven and uncover. Add salt, oil, and pepper flakes; stir gently to mix. Serve immediately.

RUSSIAN STURGEON SOUP

The Russians have a kind of soup—really a meal—called solianka, which is at its best made with sturgeon. (Monkfish is a good substitute.) The broth turns a beautiful golden color and the fish does not dissolve, as so often happens in fish soups. The surprise is in the seasonings. Don't be afraid;

the pickles, olives and capers give emphatic flavor without spiciness. It is fresh-tasting, thinning, and very good. *Serves 4 as a main course, 8 as a first course*

2 pounds sturgeon bones and head, cleaned of all blood
4 cups water
2 tablespoons unsalted butter
½ cup finely chopped onion (¼ pound)
¼ pound mushrooms, cut into ¼-inch slices
2 pounds sturgeon fillet, cut into 6″ × 3″ pieces
5 shallots, peeled
1 carrot, trimmed, peeled and sliced in food processor
1 celery stalk, trimmed, strung and sliced across in food processor

1 leek, trimmed, well rinsed and sliced across in food processor
1 parsnip, peeled and sliced across in food processor
2 teaspoons Basic Tomato Paste (page 340) or canned tomato paste
2 teaspoons capers
1 tablespoon pitted and chopped Kalamata olives
3 sour pickles, chopped
Large pinch freshly ground black pepper
1 tablespoon kosher salt

1. Place fish bones, head, and water in a 2-quart soufflé dish. Cover tightly with microwave plastic wrap. Cook at 100% for 25 minutes. Strain broth and set aside (you will have about 4 cups).

2. Heat butter in a 14″ × 11″ × 2″ dish, uncovered, at 100% for 2 minutes. Stir in onion and mushrooms. Cook, uncovered, for 4 minutes longer.

3. Remove from oven. Arrange sturgeon on top of onion mixture in a single layer. Scatter shallots and sliced vegetables over fish. Pour reserved broth over all. Cover tightly with microwave plastic wrap. Cook at 100% for 18 minutes.

4 Remove from oven. Uncover and stir in remaining ingredients. Serve hot.

TRADITIONAL HOT BORSCHT

When winter comes on as it does very heavily in Russia, they make hot borscht that is thick with meat and vegetables. Wine-colored by beets and tomatoes, it is made sweet and sour by the vegetables, sugar and vinegar. It often makes a meal; but it could go before a light fish or chicken main course. The flavor of this soup improves with mellowing (see page 234).   *Serves 10 to 12 as a first course, 8 as a main course*

4 cups Light Beef or Veal Broth (page 331) or canned chicken broth

1½ pounds beets, scrubbed, 1 inch of stem left on

1 carrot, trimmed and peeled

6 cloves garlic, smashed and peeled

½ pound green cabbage, shredded as for fine coleslaw

1 pound fresh tomatoes, cored and coarsely chopped

1 pound beef chuck, cut into ½-inch cubes

6 tablespoons Basic Tomato Paste (page 342) or canned tomato paste

½ bay leaf

4 tablespoons red wine vinegar

2 tablespoons granulated sugar

2 teaspoons kosher salt Freshly ground black pepper

2 baking potatoes, cooked just prior to serving (page 571), peeled and quartered (optional)

½ cup chopped fresh dill, for serving

Sour cream, for serving

1. Combine broth and beets in a 3-quart soufflé dish. Cover tightly with microwave plastic wrap. Cook at 100% for 10 to 12 minutes (it will take less time if beets are small).

2. Remove from oven and uncover. Remove beets and reserve broth.

3. When beets are cool enough to handle, cut off stems and root ends and slip off their skins, holding them over the workbowl of a food processor to catch any liquid. Put medium grating disc in food processor. Grate beets and carrot.

4. Scrape grated vegetables into reserved broth. Stir in remaining ingredients except for potatoes, dill, and sour cream. Cover tightly with microwave plastic wrap. Cook at 100% for 8 minutes. Leaving dish in oven, uncover and stir well. Re-cover and cook for 8 minutes more.

5. Remove from oven. Soup may be mellowed at this point (page 234). Place a piece of potato in each soup bowl. Stir dill into soup just before serving. Ladle hot soup over potato. Top each serving with sour cream.

HOT BEET AND RED CABBAGE BORSCHT

The version of borscht is easily made from leftover Sweet and Sour Red Cabbage (page 311). If you don't have leftovers, make the Traditional Hot Borscht (page 98) instead. *Serves 4*

1 cup Sweet and Sour Red Cabbage (page 311)	2 teaspoons fresh lemon juice
1 beet (4 ounces), cooked (page 486), then grated	1 teaspoon kosher salt
2½ cups Chicken Broth (page 331) or canned chicken broth	2 tablespoons plus 2 teaspoons chopped fresh dill
	1 tablespoon sour cream, for serving

1. Combine cabbage, grated beet, and broth in a 4-cup glass measure. Stir in lemon juice, salt, and 2 tablespoons of the dill. Cover tightly with microwave plastic wrap. Cook at 100% for 4 minutes.

2. Remove from oven and uncover carefully. Serve each portion with a dollop of sour cream and ½ teaspoon of the remaining dill.

TOMATO AND CABBAGE SOUP

Make this soup in fall or winter when the whole world seems gray. *Serves 4*

1 can (14½ ounces) whole American tomatoes, with juice
½ cup coarsely chopped scallion greens
½ cup chopped flat-leaf parsley
2 tablespoons chopped fresh dill
2 cups (loosely packed) shredded white cabbage

1 small zucchini, trimmed and cut across into ¼-inch slices (about 1 cup)
⅛ teaspoon dried oregano
⅛ teaspoon dried thyme
1 tablespoon kosher salt
Freshly ground black pepper

1. Combine tomatoes, scallion greens, parsley, and dill in a 4-cup glass measure. Cover tightly with microwave plastic wrap. Cook at 100% for 5 minutes.

2. Remove from oven, uncover, and place in the workbowl of a food processor. Purée until smooth. Remove from food processor, leaving about ½ cup in workbowl. Set aside the rest.

3. Place cabbage and zucchini in a 4-cup glass measure. Cover tightly with microwave plastic wrap. Cook at 100% for 5 minutes.

4. Remove from oven, uncover, and place in workbowl of the food processor. Purée until smooth.

5. Combine cabbage and reserved tomato mixtures in 4-cup glass measure. Stir in oregano, thyme, salt, and pepper. Cover tightly with microwave plastic wrap. Cook at 100% for 5 minutes. Serve hot, or allow to come to room temperature and refrigerate for Cold Yogurt-Vegetable Soup.

VARIATIONS

COLD YOGURT-VEGETABLE SOUP For an extremely refreshing hot-weather soup, combine 2 cups chilled Tomato and Cabbage Soup with 1½ cups lowfat plain yogurt and

2 tablespoons water in a food processor or blender; blend well. Just before serving, stir ½ teaspoon chopped fresh dill into each portion. This will serve 4; repeat with remaining soup to serve 8.

STRAINED TOMATO VEGETABLE SOUP Place tomatoes in the workbowl of a food processor and purée. Scrape into an 8-cup glass measure. Add remaining vegetables and 1 cup water. Cook, covered, at 100% for 15 minutes. Add oregano, thyme, salt, and pepper to taste.

CREAMY CABBAGE SOUP

An unusual and surprisingly elegant soup.   *Serves 4*

1 large or 2 small baking potatoes (about 1 pound), washed, dried and pricked several times

1 small yellow onion, peeled and thinly sliced (about 1 loosely packed cup)

1 tablespoon unsalted butter, cut into bits

2 cups shredded green cabbage

1 cup Chicken Broth (page 331) or canned chicken broth

½ cup heavy cream Kosher salt Freshly ground black pepper Finely chopped parsley (optional)

1. Cook potato, uncovered, at 100% for 7 minutes. If cooking 2 potatoes, cook for 9 to 10 minutes. Remove from oven and set aside.

2. Place onions and butter in a 4-cup glass measure. Cover tightly with microwave plastic wrap. Cook at 100% for 3 minutes.

3. Remove from oven. Uncover and stir in cabbage. Re-cover and cook at 100% for 4 minutes.

4. Peel potato and cut into chunks. Place in the workbowl of a food processor. Add cabbage and broth to potato. Process until well combined but not completely smooth. Remove mixture to a bowl.

5. Stir in cream. Add salt and pepper to taste. Sprinkle individual servings with parsley, if desired.

WINTER VEGETABLE SOUP

A slightly unusual group of vegetables gives this a special taste. Quadratini are little squares of pasta. If you can't find them, substitute orzo. *Makes 4 cups*

3 carrots, trimmed, peeled and cut in half lengthwise
2 heads endive, trimmed
1½ medium turnips, trimmed, peeled and quartered
1½ cups thinly sliced leek, about 2 medium leeks (white part only)
1½ cups diced celery (about 6 stalks)

4 cups Chicken Broth (page 331) or canned chicken broth
½ clove garlic, smashed and peeled
⅓ cup quadratini
3 fresh basil leaves, ¼ teaspoon dried thyme, or 1 tablespoon chopped fresh dill
2 tablespoons unsalted butter, cut into bits
Kosher salt
Freshly ground black pepper

1. Put 2 cups of water on the stove to boil for the pasta.

2. Using a food processor fitted with the slicing disc, thinly slice carrots, endives, and turnips.

3. Place vegetables, broth, and garlic in a 2-quart soufflé dish. Cover tightly with microwave plastic wrap. Cook at 100% for 15 to 17 minutes, until carrots are tender.

4. Cook pasta for 5 minutes and drain.

5. Remove soup from oven and uncover. Add herbs, butter, salt, and pepper. Stir in pasta and serve hot.

GREEN LENTIL SOUP

Lentils make a wonderful, substantial soup. You can substitute other color lentils if they are easier to find.   *Serves
6 to 8*

1 cup dried green lentils
2 stalks celery, trimmed,
   strung and cut into
   2-inch lengths
1 leek, white part only,
   cut into 2-inch pieces
3 cloves garlic, smashed
   and peeled
2 medium carrots,
   trimmed, peeled and
   cut into 2-inch pieces

3 parsely sprigs
3 tablespoons olive oil
4 cups Chicken Broth
   (page 331), Lamb
   Broth (page 332) or
   canned chicken broth
1 tablespoon kosher salt
   Pinch freshly ground
   black pepper

1. Put lentils in a 2½-quart soufflé dish with 4 cups water.
Cover tightly with microwave plastic wrap. Cook at 100%
for 35 minutes.

2. Remove from oven. Let stand, covered, for 20 minutes. Uncover and drain lentils; you will have about 2½
cups. Set aside.

3. Place celery, leeks, garlic, carrots, and parsley in the
workbowl of a food processor. Process until finely chopped.

4. Add vegetables to reserved lentils. Stir in oil, broth,
salt, and pepper. Cover tightly with microwave plastic wrap.
Cook at 100% for 15 minutes.

5. Remove from oven and uncover. Purée about half the
soup in the food processor. Stir purée into remaining soup
and serve.

SPLIT PEA SOUP

This is usually family soup, but my version is so creamy and lovely I think you will be tempted to serve it for elegant winter dinners. With sausages, it can be an informal main course. I would add salad, cheese, and a spicy red wine like a zinfandel. *Serves 4*

1 cup green or yellow split peas
1½ cups Chicken Broth (page 331) or canned chicken broth

⅛ teaspoon ground or rubbed sage

1. Place peas and 2 cups water in a 2-quart soufflé dish. Cover tightly with microwave plastic wrap. Cook at 100% for 15 minutes.

2. Remove from oven. Pierce plastic with the tip of a sharp knife. Let stand for 5 minutes. Uncover and add 2 cups very hot tap water. Re-cover and let stand for 1 hour.

3. Uncover, drain, and rinse peas. Return to soufflé dish. Add 4 cups warm water. Cover tightly. Cook at 100% for 35 minutes.

4. Remove from oven. Let stand, covered, for 20 minutes. Uncover and place in a workbowl of a food processor. Process until smooth. Add broth and sage.

5. Return to soufflé dish. Heat, uncovered, at 100% for 4 minutes, stirring once.

6. Remove from oven. Serve hot.

VARIATION

YELLOW SPLIT PEA SOUP WITH KIELBASA Cook a smoked ham hock (page 338). Reserve cooking liquid and discard ham hock, or save for another use. Proceed as for Split Pea Soup, adding reserved ham hock cooking liquid with enough water to measure 4 cups. Add ⅓ pound kielbasa, cut into slices and each slice quartered, to soup before reheating. You could also use your choice of cooked sausage.

BLACK BEAN SOUP

This is a wonderful, heartwarming soup. You can stir 1 tablespoon of sherry into the finished soup and place a thin slice of hard-boiled egg on each portion instead of the sour cream and coriander. *Serves 6*

1 cup dried black beans
4 cups Chicken Broth (page 331) or canned chicken broth
1 tablespoon vegetable oil
1 medium yellow onion, peeled and finely chopped (about ¾ cup)
2 cloves garlic, smashed and peeled
1 leek, white part only, washed and chopped (about ½ cup)

½ celery stalk with leaves, strung and chopped (about ¼ cup)
1 bay leaf
1 whole clove
2 teaspoons kosher salt
Pinch freshly ground black pepper
Hot and Sweet Red Pepper Sauce (page 343) or Fiery Pepper Sauce (page 344) to taste
¼ cup sour cream, for serving
2 tablespoons chopped fresh coriander, for serving

1. Place beans in a 2½-quart soufflé dish. Add 2 cups water. Cover tightly with microwave plastic wrap. Cook at 100% for 15 minutes.

2. Remove from oven. Pierce plastic with the tip of a sharp knife. Let stand for 5 minutes. Uncover and add 2 cups very hot tap water. Re-cover tightly and let stand for 1 hour.

3. Uncover, drain, and rinse beans. Return to soufflé dish and add remaining ingredients except sour cream and coriander. Stir well. Cover tightly with 2 sheets of microwave plastic wrap. Cook at 100% for 35 minutes.

4. Remove from oven. Let stand, covered, for 20 minutes. Uncover and place in the workbowl of a food processor. Process until smooth. Stir in salt, pepper, and pepper sauce to taste. Serve with a dollop of sour cream and a sprinkle of coriander.

VARIATIONS

BLACK BEANS Make beans through step 3. Let stand as for Black Bean Soup. Do not process, simply drain and serve. Omit pepper sauce, sour cream, and coriander.

BLACK BEAN PURÉE Make beans as for Black Bean Soup. Drain, process until smooth, and serve. Omit pepper sauce, sour cream, and coriander.

CREAM OF CAULIFLOWER SOUP

This is a rich cream soup, a good choice to begin a light meal of filleted fish or roast chicken. Make the main course colorful. Any vegetable purée (pages 288–297) could be substituted for the cauliflower.   *Makes 5 cups; serves 6*

2½ cups Cauliflower Purée (page 295)	2 cups Chicken Broth (page 331) or canned chicken broth
1 cup Basic Béchamel (page 364)	Kosher salt
2 tablespoons unsalted butter	Freshly ground black pepper
	Fresh chives (optional)

1. In an 8-cup glass measure, whisk together Cauliflower Purée, Béchamel, butter, and broth. Cover loosely with paper toweling. Cook at 100% for 5 minutes.

2. Remove from oven. Stir well and season with salt and pepper. To serve, snip some fresh chives over each portion, if desired.

CARROT SOUP

This cream soup, a delightful orange-salmon in color, can be served hot or chilled. *Serves 2*

¾ pound carrots,
    trimmed, peeled
    and sliced in ¼-inch
    rounds
1 cup Chicken Broth
    (page 331) or
    canned chicken
    broth

2 tablespoons unsalted
    butter
½ teaspoon paprika
½ teaspoon kosher salt
¼ cup heavy cream
    Freshly grated
    nutmeg (for cold
    soup)

1. Arrange carrots in 2 or 3 layers in a dish just large enough to hold them. Cover tightly with microwave plastic wrap. Cook at 100% for 7 minutes.

2. Remove from oven. Uncover and place in the work-bowl of a food processor. Add broth, butter, paprika, and salt and process to a smooth purée. Pour into a 4-cup glass measure and stir in cream.

3. Cover tightly with microwave plastic wrap. Cook for 3 minutes.

4. Remove from oven. Serve hot, or allow to cool to room temperature and refrigerate. To serve chilled, dust each bowl of soup with grated nutmeg.

To serve 4. Double all ingredients. Cook carrots for 10 minutes. Purée in two batches, then stir in cream. Pour into an 8-cup glass measure and cover tightly with microwave plastic wrap. Cook at 100% for 5 minutes.

VARIATION

LIGHT CARROT SOUP Increase the broth to 1¼ cups and add 2 teaspoons cornstarch to carrots in food processor. Omit the cream. Increase final cooking time to 5 minutes.

LEEK AND POTATO SOUP

This is the French mother's equivalent of chicken soup. If you are cold and tired, try it. You'll feel a lot better soon. *Serves 4*

2 small all-purpose
    potatoes (⅜ pound),
    peeled and diced, or
    sliced with the
    French-fry cutter on
    food processor
1 cup diced leeks, about
    2 medium leeks
    (white part and 1
    inch of the green)

2 cups Chicken Broth
    (page 331) or canned
    chicken broth
1 cup heavy cream
2 tablespoons unsalted
    butter
Kosher salt
Freshly ground black
    pepper

1. Place potatoes, leeks, and 1 cup of the broth in an 8-cup glass measure. Cover tightly with microwave plastic wrap. Cook at 100% for 12 minutes.

2. Remove from oven. Uncover and pass through a food mill fitted with a medium disc or through a potato ricer. Stir in cream, butter, and remaining 1 cup broth. Season with salt and pepper. Heat in a 2-quart soufflé dish, covered tightly, for 5 minutes. Serve piping hot.

VARIATION

VICHYSSOISE Increase cream by ½ cup and stir in 2 teaspoons snipped fresh chives with cream, broth, and butter. Chill well and serve with additional chives sprinkled on top, if desired.

MUSHROOM SOUP

A few wild mushrooms added to the domestic ones will jazz up this soup no end. Russians, who love mushroom soup, would probably add a dollop of sour cream to each bowl when serving. It makes a robust vegetarian soup if you use Vegetable Broth.   *Serves 4*

2 tablespoons unsalted
  butter
1 pound mushrooms,
  stems trimmed,
  wiped clean and
  thinly sliced
1 celery stalk, trimmed,
  strung and finely
  chopped
1 small yellow onion,
  peeled and finely
  chopped

2 cups Chicken Broth
  (page 331), Vegetable
  Broth (page 335) or
  canned chicken broth
4 teaspoons cornstarch
½ cup heavy cream
2 teaspoons fresh lemon
  juice
2 tablespoons chopped
  fresh dill
1 teaspoon kosher salt
¼ teaspoon freshly
  ground black
  pepper

1. Heat butter in a 2-quart soufflé dish, uncovered, at 100% for 2 minutes. Stir in mushrooms, celery, and onions. Cover tightly with microwave plastic wrap. Cook at 100% for 6 minutes.

2. Remove from oven and uncover. Stir in ½ cup of the broth and let cool for 5 minutes.

3. Stir cornstarch into cream. Add to mushroom mixture and stir well. Add lemon juice, dill, salt, pepper, and remaining 1½ cups broth; stir. Cover tightly with microwave plastic wrap. Cook at 100% for 6 minutes. Serve hot.

To serve 8. Double all ingredients except butter. Cook mushroom mixture for 4 minutes. Cook an additional 8 minutes in step 3 after adding final ingredients.

DUXELLES SOUP

Duxelles is a kind of mushroom hash, finely chopped mushrooms sautéed in butter, that can be frozen or refrigerated for weeks. If you have some on hand, you can make a cup of mushroom soup in 5 minutes.   *Serves 1*

1 cup Chicken Broth (page 331) or canned chicken broth	**1 tablespoon heavy cream or sour cream**
1 teaspoon cornstarch	**2 drops hot red-pepper sauce**
¼ Duxelles (page 340), fresh or defrosted (page 489)	**Large pinch freshly ground black pepper**
	Chopped fresh dill (optional)

1. Combine broth, cornstarch, Duxelles, and cream in a 2-cup glass measure. Cover tightly with microwave plastic wrap. Cook at 100% for 5 minutes.

2. Remove from oven. Uncover and stir in hot red-pepper sauce and pepper. Sprinkle with fresh dill, if desired.

To serve 2. Double all ingredients. Place in a 4-cup glass measure and cook for 7 minutes.

To serve 4. Use 4 times the amount for all ingredients. Place in an 8-cup glass measure and cook for 10 minutes.

VARIATION

HEARTY MUSHROOM SOUP Make Duxelles Soup and place a quarter of a cooked baking potato, peeled, in each bowl.

VEGETABLE SOUP

This is a good, home-style vegetable soup. Add ½ cup cooked pasta if you want to make it heartier. *Makes 4 cups*

2 tablespoons unsalted butter or chicken fat
¼ pound yellow onions, peeled and chopped (about ½ cup)
2 medium or 3 small carrots, trimmed, peeled and chopped
2 celery stalks, trimmed, strung and chopped

Pinch dried thyme
1¼ cups tomato juice
2 cups Chicken Broth (page 331) or canned chicken broth
Kosher salt
Freshly ground black pepper

1. Heat butter in an 8-cup glass measure, uncovered, at 100% for 2 minutes. Add onions and cook for 3 minutes longer.

2. Add carrots and celery. (You will have about 2 cups of chopped vegetables.) Add thyme and ¼ cup of the tomato juice and cook, uncovered, at 100% for 10 minutes.

3. Remove from oven. Pour into the workbowl of a food processor and purée.

4. Return purée to an 8-cup glass measure. Add as much of the remaining tomato juice as needed to make 2 cups.

5. Add broth, and salt and pepper to taste. Cook, uncovered, at 100% for 2 minutes.

BEEF-BARLEY SOUP

There is no winter day so cold that you won't warm up with this home-style classic. Miraculously, the microwave oven cooks the beef perfectly in this tiny bit of time. Do remember to allow the time for the cooking of the barley. I sometimes make soup the day after I have made barley as a starch with dinner. The ideal leftover. *Serves 4*

2½ cups Creamy Barley
  (page 133)
3½ cups Chicken or
  Lamb Broth (pages
  331, 332) or
  canned chicken
  broth
¼ cup Italian dried
  mushrooms
  (Boletus, cèpes)
1 medium carrot,
  trimmed, peeled
  and sliced in thin
  rounds

2 cloves garlic, smashed
  and peeled
¼ bay leaf
¼ pound chuck, in ¼-
  inch cubes
¼ cup plus 1 tablespoon
  chopped fresh dill
Kosher salt
Freshly ground black
  pepper

1. Combine barley, 2 cups of the broth, mushrooms, carrots, garlic, bay leaf, and chuck in an 8-cup glass measure. Cover tightly with microwave plastic wrap. Cook at 100% for 14 minutes.

2. Remove from oven. Uncover and discard bay leaf. Add dill and remaining 1½ cups broth. Season with salt and pepper and serve hot.

ACORN SQUASH SOUP

Before the microwave oven, I would never have made this soup, because it took so long to cook acorn squash. Today, I make it frequently. The taste and golden color are sensational. It is elegant enough for even the most sophisticated dinner party. *Serves 4*

1 medium acorn
  squash (about 1
  pound), cut in half
  and seeded
3 cloves garlic,
  smashed and
  peeled
2½ cups Chicken Broth
  (page 331) or or
  canned chicken
  broth

1 tablespoon kosher salt
Pinch freshly ground
  black pepper
Scant ⅛ teaspoon
  ground cardamom
2 tablespoons unsalted
  butter, cut into small
  pieces (optional)

1. Tightly wrap squash halves in microwave plastic wrap. Cook at 100% for 7 minutes. Remove from oven and unwrap carefully. Scoop out flesh and purée with garlic in a food processor.

2. Combine the purée, broth, and seasonings in a 4-cup glass measure and stir well. Cover tightly with microwave plastic wrap. Cook at 100% for 10 minutes.

3. Remove from oven. Uncover and stir in butter, if desired.

To serve 8. Double all ingredients. Cook squash for 15 minutes. Use an 8-cup glass measure for step 2. Cook soup for 12 minutes.

ASPARAGUS SOUP

When asparagus have been in season for a while and all the hot and cold preparations, with vinaigrette, butter or Hollandaise, have begun to pall, then I make asparagus soup. I use only the trimmings, saving the tips for another dish. Asparagus soup made in the microwave oven is a delight, as it has a much clearer green color than soup made on the stove. It may be served hot or chilled.   *Serves 2*

Stalks and peelings from 1 pound asparagus, about ⅓ pound trimmings (cleaned tips saved for another use)
1½ cups Chicken Broth (page 331) or canned chicken broth

1 small onion, peeled and thinly sliced
2 teaspoons cornstarch
1 teaspoon fresh lemon juice
½ teaspoon kosher salt
⅛ teaspoon freshly ground black pepper

1. Place asparagus, broth, and onions in a 1½-quart soufflé dish. Cover tightly with microwave plastic wrap. Cook at 100% for 15 minutes.

2. Remove from oven. Uncover and pass through a food mill fitted with a fine disc.

3. Measure out ¼ cup of mixture; stir in cornstarch and blend well. Stir this back into remaining mixture. Add lemon juice, salt, and pepper. Cook, uncovered, at 100% for 6 minutes, until boiling and thickened. Serve hot or let cool to room temperature and refrigerate to serve chilled.

To serve 6. Multiply all ingredient quantities by 3 except lemon juice (double it). Cook asparagus with broth and onions in an 8-cup glass measure or soufflé dish for 20 minutes. Increase final cooking time to 10 minutes.

SORREL SOUP

Served cold, this is among the best of summer soups, lightly acid, refreshing, and smooth. In summer, I often keep a glass jar of it in the refrigerator. It can be thickened either with egg yolks or cornstarch. If substituting cornstarch use 2 tablespoons cornstarch and follow technique in 1-cup version. These basic ways of thickening are good to keep in mind for a host of cold summer soups.   *Makes 6 cups; serves 6*

4 tablespoons unsalted butter	**4 cups Chicken Broth (page 331) or canned chicken broth**
4 cups (medium-packed) chiffonade of sorrel (see note)	
1 tablespoon kosher salt	**6 egg yolks or 2 tablespoons cornstarch, to thicken**
Freshly ground black pepper	
½ cup heavy cream	

1. Combine butter, sorrel, salt, and pepper in a 2-quart soufflé dish. Cook, uncovered, at 100% for 3 minutes.

2. Remove from oven. Stir in cream and broth. Cook, uncovered, at 100% for 7 minutes.

3. Remove from oven. Whisk 1 cup of hot liquid into yolks and stir into remaining liquid. Cook, uncovered, at 100% for 2 minutes. Chill well before serving.

Note. To make a chiffonade, stack the sorrel leaves and cut into thin strips, ⅛ inch wide, across the central vein. This keeps the soup from getting stringy.

To make 1 cup. Combine 1 tablespoon butter, 1 cup sorrel, ¾ teaspoon salt, and pepper in a 4-cup glass measure. Cook, uncovered, at 100% for 2 minutes. Add 2 tablespoons cream, ¾ cup broth, and 1 teaspoon cornstarch dissolved in 2 teaspoons cold water. Cook, uncovered, at 100% for 1 minute 30 seconds. Chill before serving.

VARIATION

HEARTY SORREL SOUP Before making the 6-cup version of this soup, cook 2 baking potatoes for 11 minutes at 100%. While soup cooks for 7 minutes, peel potatoes and cut into ½-inch dice. Add to soup when adding egg yolks; extend final cooking time to 4 minutes. Serves 8.

COLD BEET BORSCHT

Borscht is one of the world's most beautiful and best-tasting soups. Frankly, it has always been a little bit of a hassle to make. Now that I know how to cook beets in the microwave oven, I cook them ahead, keep them on hand, and make this soup for family or friends whenever it seems appropriate.

There are varying views of how to serve it. I eat it plain, but if I am giving a party, I set out little bowls of scallions (both the green and white parts), chopped dill, sour cream, cooked peeled potato chunks (cold), and lemon wedges. *Serves 4*

2 cups water
2 tablespoons white vinegar
½ granulated sugar
1 cup peeled, grated cooked beets (page 486)

2 tablespoons fresh lemon juice or more, to taste
2 teaspoons kosher salt
½ cup heavy cream
¾ cup sour cream
4 teaspoons chopped fresh dill, for serving

1. Combine water, vinegar, and sugar in a 4-cup glass measure. Cover tightly with microwave plastic wrap. Cook at 100% for 5 minutes.

2. Remove from oven. Uncover and stir in beets. Let cool.

3. When cool, add lemon juice, salt, cream, and ½ cup of the sour cream. Stir to combine. Add more lemon juice, if desired, and chill. Garnish each serving with a tablespoon of remaining sour cream and a teaspoon of dill.

To serve 8. Double ingredients. Cook water mixture 10 minutes in an 8-cup glass measure. Continue as for Cold Beet Borscht.

COLD CURRIED TOMATO SOUP WITH YOGURT

Curried soups are somehow more cooling than other iced soups, as the British discovered in India more than a century ago. Make this ahead.   *Serves 4*

2 tablespoons vegetable oil

1 clove garlic, smashed and peeled

1 small yellow onion, peeled and sliced

1 tablespoon curry powder

1 cup Lightly Cooked Crushed Tomatoes (page 339)

3 cups Chicken Broth (page 331) or canned chicken broth

1 cup frozen peas, defrosted in a sieve under warm running water

1 cup plain yogurt

2 teaspoons fresh lemon juice

1. Heat oil in 2-quart soufflé dish, uncovered, at 100% for 2 minutes. Stir in garlic, onion, and curry powder. Cook, uncovered, at 100% for 8 minutes, stirring once.

2. Remove from oven. Add tomatoes, broth, and peas. Cover tightly with microwave plastic wrap. Cook at 100% for 5 minutes.

3. Remove from oven and let stand, covered, until tepid.

4. Uncover. Stir in yogurt and lemon juice, and chill before serving.

GOOD GRAINS, PASTA & ...

SOME of my favorite foods are starches. Now that the experts have told us all that we would be healthier if more of our daily diet came from such foods, I can feel virtuous as I indulge myself. While I sometimes eat these Italian style, as a first course, I like risottos, pastas, polentas, and other grains enough to make them the whole meal. Sometimes that meal is breakfast—oatmeal, farina, and the like.

Vegetarians, of course, do make starches the heart of the meal a lot of the time. While some vegetarians do not eat milk or eggs, it is a good idea to combine milk products and eggs in a restricted diet to be sure of getting a full array of proteins. Cheese is often combined with rice, pasta, and polenta in many lovely dishes. Cheese dishes are used as first courses when they are not being served as lunch or dinner.

Rice

I love rice. I love Sendak's *Chicken Soup with Rice*. I love risotto. I think pilafs are spiffy, rice pudding delish. I have been known to crave paella, lap up arroz con pollo, giggle over dirty rice. There, it's out: I make a fool of myself over rice.

If I am just making boiled or steamed rice to go with dinner or to put in soup, I probably won't make it in the microwave oven. It takes about the same time as it does on top of the stove: Of course, on top of the stove I have to allow time for the water to come to a boil. When it comes to the really good rice dishes, though, I turn to the microwave oven.

To identify different kinds of rice, learn more about them, and find out what substitutions you can make, see the entry on RICE in the Dictionary.

117

Risotto

If anything could convince the true cook, or even the ardent eater, that the microwave oven is a tool worth having, it would be that it makes risotto divinely, effortlessly, and relatively rapidly while the cook talks to the guests. From being a once-a-year treat, it can go to being an everyday delight.

Risotto is one of the great dishes that the Italians have given the world. It is rich and creamy in texture, much moister than ordinary rice without having the rice get over-cooked. Partly this is achieved by using a special kind of rice, arborio, grown in the Po Valley, and partly by a special cooking method that flourishes from Milan to Venice. Traditionally, the rice is cooked in a hot fat until it turns white and then slow-cooked and continuously stirred as hot broth is added, spoonful by spoonful, as the rice absorbs the liquid in the pot.

With the microwave oven, all that stirring is a thing of the past. The very idiosyncrasy of cooking that makes the microwave oven generally unacceptable for the cooking of floury dishes makes risotto work well. Starch absorbs liquid slowly in the microwave oven, and it also absorbs too much. That is exactly what you want the rice to do in a risotto.

The reason there are so many recipes in this section is not only to give a panoply of wonderful flavors, but to deal with the fact that these are recipes that cannot be simply multiplied or divided either by time or quantity. All the recipes are based on room-temperature broth. Cold or hot will change the cooking time. The cooking dish may seem large for the quantities; but that is essential to allow for sufficient evaporation. Risotto is never covered as it cooks. Since you will get so much evaporation, be careful with salt if you are using canned broth. You may even want to dilute it with one-quarter water. Arborio is the rice of choice in most of these recipes; but you can also use another Italian rice called ambra if you want a slightly less glutinous texture, as I did in the Shrimp and Spring Vegetable Risotto. You can cook American long-grain rice the same way; it will taste wonderful but the texture will be entirely different.

Vegetarians should feel free to substitute Vegetable Broth or Oriental Vegetable Broth (pages 335–336). Those who eat fish and seafood, but not meat, can use one of the fish broths or fumets (page 334). Liquid left from soaking dried wild mushrooms, vegetable juices (see Tomato Risotto) cooked vegetables, purées, herbs, spices and leftover cooked meats can all be included in risottos and in the pilafs that follow. One of my favorites is made with leftover cooked duck and Duck Broth (page 331), made with the carcasses.

For a creamier risotto, additional broth may be added at the outset of standing time. For 1 cup arborio rice, add ¼ cup broth; for ½ cup rice, add 2 tablespoons broth; for ¼ cup rice, add 1 tablespoon broth. The Venetians would add even more broth and eat their risotto with a spoon. In most cases—aside from seafood risottos—they would also sprinkle it liberally with freshly grated Parmesan cheese.

Risotto is one of the great dishes subject to many variations once the technique is mastered. Unfortunately, it has always been time-consuming and last-minute. Except for Saffron Risotto, which is served in Milan as a side dish with Ossobuco, risotto is always a first course in Italy. I like risotto best as a side dish with grilled foods; it is too creamy to be used with most sauced dishes. Some risottos, like the Shrimp and Spring Vegetable Risotto, make good light meals.

Risotto can be made ahead and reheated in the microwave oven. Make the risotto, but withhold one sixth of the liquid and stop cooking 2 minutes before the full time. Cover the partly cooked risotto loosely with paper toweling. When your guests sit down, stir in the remaining liquid and cook at 100% for 3 minutes 30 seconds.

BASIC RISOTTO

There are numerous kinds of risotto. This is the classic, the one to return to. It doesn't get much better than this. I have a friend who makes the whole recipe as a meal for one—admittedly, exceptional. *Serves 3 as a first course, 6 as a side dish*

2 tablespoons unsalted
    butter
2 tablespoons olive oil
½ cup minced yellow
    onion (about ¼
    pound)
1 cup arborio rice

3 cups Chicken Broth
    (page 331), canned
    chicken broth or
    any other broth (see
    pages 330–336)
2 teaspoons kosher salt
    Freshly ground black
    pepper
    Freshly grated
    Parmesan cheese
    (optional)

1. Heat butter and oil in a 10-inch quiche or deep pie dish, or 11″ × 8½″ × 2″ dish, uncovered, at 100% for 2 minutes. Add onions and stir to coat. Cook, uncovered, at 100% for 4 minutes. Add rice and stir to coat. Cook, uncovered, for 4 minutes more. (If using a small oven, cook onions for 7 minutes; add rice and cook for 7 minutes more.)

2. Stir in broth. Cook, uncovered, at 100% for 9 minutes. Stir well and cook for 9 minutes more. (If using a small oven, cook for 12 minutes, stir and cook for 12 minutes more.)

3. Remove from oven. Let stand, uncovered, for 5 minutes to let rice absorb remaining liquid, stirring several times. Stir in salt, pepper and Parmesan cheese, if desired.

To serve 6 as a first course, 10 to 12 as a side dish. Double all ingredients. Cook butter, oil and onions as in step 1, using a 14″ × 11″ × 2″ dish. Add rice and cook for 4 minutes. Add broth and cook, uncovered, for 12 minutes. Stir and cook for 12 minutes more. Finish as for Basic Risotto.

To serve 2 as a first course, 4 as a side dish. Halve all ingredients and use a 9-inch quiche dish or an 8-inch square dish. Cook onions for 2 minutes and rice for 2 minutes more. Finish as for Basic Risotto.

To serve 1 as a first course, 2 as a side dish. Reduce butter and oil to 2 teaspoons each, onions to 1 tablespoon, rice to

¼ cup, and broth to 1¼ cups. Heat butter and oil in a large soup plate or pie plate. Add onions and rice and cook for 2 minutes. Finish as for Basic Risotto, cooking for 12 minutes total. Let stand for 3 minutes.

RISOTTO WITH RADICCHIO AND RED VERMOUTH

In this country, we are becoming used to seeing the leaves of round, red radicchio in salad. In Italy, radicchio comes in many shapes and is eaten more often cooked than raw. It loses most of its beautiful red color, but it acquires a wonderful, slightly bitter taste. The flavor reminds me of aged red vermouth, so I have combined them.   *Serves 4 as a first course or side dish*

- 2 tablespoons unsalted butter
- 2 tablespoons olive oil
- ⅓ cup minced yellow onion
- 1 cup arborio rice
- 3 cups Veal or Chicken Broth (page 331) or canned chicken broth
- ¼ cup minced parsley
- 2 cups (packed) cored and shredded radicchio, any kind
- 2 tablespoons aged red Italian vermouth or other bitter vermouth
- 1½ teaspoons kosher salt
- Freshly ground black pepper
- ¼ cup freshly grated Parmesan cheese

1. Heat butter and oil in a 10-inch quiche dish or 11″ × 8½″ × 2″ dish, uncovered, at 100% for 2 minutes. Add onions and stir to coat. Cook, uncovered, at 100% for 2 minutes. Add rice and stir to coat. Cook for 2 minutes more.

2. Stir in broth and cook, uncovered, at 100% for 9 minutes. Stir in parsley and radicchio. Cook, uncovered, for 9 minutes more.

3. Remove from oven. Stir in vermouth, salt, and pepper. Let stand for 6 minutes. Stir in cheese and serve.

SAFFRON RISOTTO

This is the famous Milanese risotto that goes with Italian-Style Veal Shanks (page 260). Its Buddhist-monk's-robe color makes a great background for vegetable curries, casseroles and stews.   *Serves 1 as a first course, 2 as a side dish*

1 teaspoon unsalted butter	1 cup Chicken Broth (page 331) or canned chicken broth
1 teaspoon olive oil	
2 tablespoons minced onion	¼ cup white wine
1 clove garlic, smashed, peeled and minced (optional)	9 threads saffron Kosher salt Freshly ground black pepper
¼ cup arborio rice	

1. Heat butter and oil in a large soup plate or pie plate, uncovered, at 100% for 2 minutes.

2. Add onions, garlic, and rice; stir to coat,. Cook, uncovered, at 100% for 2 minutes.

3. Add broth, wine, and saffron. Cook, uncovered, for 6 minutes. Stir well and cook for 6 minutes more.

4. Remove from oven. Stir in salt and pepper and serve hot.

To serve 2 as a first course, 4 as a side dish. Increase saffron to 12 threads and double all other ingredients. Heat butter in a 9-inch quiche dish or 8-inch square dish. Continue as for single serving. Remove from oven and stir in salt and pepper.

To serve 3 as a first course, 6 as a side dish. Increase saffron to 16 threads and multiply all other ingredients by 4. Heat butter in an 11″ × 8½″ × 2″ dish or a 10-inch quiche dish. Cook onions for 4 minutes. Add rice and cook for 4 minutes more. Add broth and cook for 9 minutes. Stir and cook for 9 minutes more. Remove from oven and stir in salt and pepper.

TOMATO RISOTTO

This dish is one you can play with: add a few dried mushrooms when you add the broth, or stir in some chopped fresh herbs as soon as you take the risotto out of the microwave oven. Because of the thickness of the tomato mixture, you get somewhat crunchy rice at the indicated cooking time. If you like your rice a little creamier—more traditional—cook it 5 minutes longer. Add salt with discretion, as both canned broth and canned tomatoes can be salty. *Serves 3 as a first course, 6 as a side dish*

2 tablespoons unsalted butter

2 tablespoons olive oil

½ cup minced yellow onion (about ¼ pound)

1 tablespoon minced garlic (about 4 cloves)

1 cup arborio rice

2 cups canned Italian tomatoes, puréed with juice

1¼ cups Chicken Broth (page 331) or canned chicken broth

Freshly ground black pepper

⅓ cup freshly grated Parmesan cheese

Kosher salt (optional)

1. Heat butter and oil in a 10-inch quiche dish or 11″ × 8½″ × 2″ dish, uncovered, at 100% for 2 minutes.

2. Stir in onions and garlic. Cook, uncovered, at 100% for 4 minutes. Add rice and stir to coat. Cook for 4 minutes more.

3. Add tomatoes and broth. Cook, uncovered, at 100% for 9 minutes. Stir well and cook for 9 minutes more, 14 minutes for a thoroughly creamy risotto.

4. Remove from oven. Stir in pepper and cheese, add salt to taste, if desired, and serve hot.

To serve 6 as a first course, 10 as a side dish. Increase broth to 2¾ cups and double all other ingredients. Heat butter in a 14″ × 11″ × 2″ dish for 2 minutes. Add onions and garlic and cook for 3 minutes. Add rice and cook for 4 minutes more. Stir in tomatoes and broth and cook for 18 minutes. Stir and cook for 18 minutes more. Remove from oven. Stir in pepper, cheese, and salt to taste.

OLIVADA RISOTTO

This is an absolutely untraditional recipe. It is delicious and decorative, with a rich olive flavor and a lightly black color. It makes use of the jars of Italian olivada that can be bought in specialty shops. Don't add salt; the olivada is salty. *Serve 2 as a first course, 4 as a side dish*

1 tablespoons unsalted butter

1 tablespoon olive oil

2½ tablespoons minced garlic (about 3 cloves)

½ cup arborio rice

¾ cup canned crushed tomatoes with juice

1 cup Chicken Broth (page 331) or canned chicken broth

2 tablespoons olivada

2 tablespoons freshly grated Parmesan cheese

2 tablespoons (packed) shredded fresh basil leaves

Freshly ground black pepper

1. Place butter, oil, and 1½ teaspoons of the garlic in a 9-inch quiche dish or 8-inch square dish. Heat, uncovered, at 100% for 2 minutes. Add rice and stir to coat. Cook, uncovered, at 100% for 2 minutes.

2. Stir in tomatoes and broth. Cook, uncovered, at 100% for 8 minutes. Stir well and cook for 8 minutes more.

3. Stir in remaining 1 teaspoon garlic, the olivada, and the cheese. Cook, uncovered, at 100% for 2 minutes.

4. Remove from oven. Stir in basil and pepper. Serve hot.

To serve 4 as a first course, 8 as a side dish. Double all ingredients. Heat butter, oil, and 4 teaspoons minced garlic in an 11" × 8½" × 2" dish. Add rice and cook for 4 minutes. Add tomatoes and broth and cook for 18 minutes, stirring after 9 minutes. Finish as for Olivada Risotto.

CABBAGE RISOTTO

This unusual risotto is good on its own, but its combination with cabbage makes it a great vegetable dish. I never make small quantities of this because it hardly seems worth shredding the cabbage for a small amount. This risotto takes a little less than the usual amount of liquid because of the juice from the cabbage.   *Serves 3 as a first course, 6 as a side dish*

2 **tablespoons unsalted butter**
2 **tablespoons olive oil**
⅓ **cup minced yellow onion**
1 **cup arborio rice**
2¾ **cup Chicken Broth (page 331) or canned chicken broth**

1 **cup shredded cabbage**
¼ **cup (packed) chopped parsley**
2 **teaspoons kosher salt**
 Freshly ground black pepper
¼ **cup freshly grated Parmesan cheese**

1. Heat butter and oil in a 14″ × 11″ × 2″ dish, uncovered, at 100% for 2 minutes. Add onions and stir to coat. Cook, uncovered, at 100% for 2 minutes. Add rice and stir to coat. Cook, uncovered, for 2 minutes more.

2. Stir in broth. Cook, uncovered, at 100% for 9 minutes. Add cabbage and parsley and stir well. Cook, uncovered, for 9 minutes longer.

3. Remove from oven. Stir in salt, pepper, and cheese. Serve hot.

To serve 6 as a first course, 12 as a side dish. Increase broth to 3¾ cups and double all other ingredients. Cook onions for 3 minutes. Add rice and cook for 4 minutes more. Add broth and cook for 12 minutes. Stir and cook for 12 minutes more. Remove from oven and stir in salt, pepper, and cheese.

SHRIMP AND SPRING VEGETABLE RISOTTO

This dish is so beautiful that when *The New York Times* asked me to provide a microwave recipe that would be photographed for their entertaining issue, this is the one I chose. Italians use ambra rice rather than arborio in this recipe, both for its pale golden color and for its lighter, less glutinous consistency, but arborio can be substituted.
Serves 6 as a main course, 10 as a first course

3 tablespoons unsalted butter

3 tablespoons fruity olive oil

½ cup chopped scallion (white part only)

2 celery stalks, peeled and chopped

½ cup (packed) chopped flat-leaf parsley

2 cups ambra rice

4 cups Fish Broth (page 334), Clam Broth (page 511), Chicken Broth (page 331) or canned chicken broth

¾ pound asparagus, trimmed, peeled and cut into 2-inch lengths

1 pound medium shrimp, peeled, deveined and cut in half crosswise

¾ cup shelled fresh peas or frozen tiny peas, defrosted in a sieve under warm running water

1 to 2 teaspoons kosher salt

½ teaspoon freshly ground black pepper

¼ cup chopped scallion (green part only)

½ cup freshly grated Parmesan cheese

1. Heat butter and oil in a 14″ × 11″ × 2″ dish, uncovered, at 100% for 3 minutes. Add scallion whites, celery, parsley, and rice and stir to coat. Cook, uncovered, at 100% for 4 minutes.

2. Stir in broth and cook, uncovered, at 100% for 12 minutes. Add asparagus, shrimp, and peas and stir well. Cook, uncovered, for 12 minutes more.

3. Remove from oven. Stir in salt and pepper. Cover loosely with paper toweling and let stand for 8 to 10 minutes. Uncover, sprinkle with scallion greens and cheese, and serve.

WILD RICE

Wild rice is expensive. It is normally a nuisance to prepare because it requires a succession of soakings in fresh water. I find this microwave method infallible and rapid. Try it in a very festive meal.   *Serves 4 as a side dish*

1 cup wild rice	Kosher salt
2 cups cold water	Freshly ground black pepper

1. Combine rice and water in an 8-cup glass measure. Cover tightly with microwave plastic wrap. Cook at 100% for 12 minutes. (If using a small oven, cook for 20 minutes.)

2. Remove from oven, pierce plastic, and cover with a plate. Allow rice to stand for 15 minutes. Uncover. (If using a small oven, return to oven and cook, uncovered, at 100% for 10 minutes.) Drain. Add salt and pepper to taste and serve hot.

To serve 2. Combine ½ cup rice and 1 cup water in a 4-cup glass measure. Cook for 7 minutes. Finish as for Wild Rice.

To serve 8. Combine 1½ cups rice with 3 cups water in an 11″ × 8″ × 3″ oval dish. Cook for 18 minutes. Remove from oven, pierce plastic, and cover with a cookie sheet. Let stand for 15 minutes. Uncover and cook for 10 minutes more. Finish as for Wild Rice.

MUSHROOMS AND LIVERS WITH WILD RICE

This is a delicious dish with roasted birds. It can also be used as a stuffing with Grits (page 134). Use it, without the rice, in omelets. *Serves 8*

- **6 tablespoons unsalted butter**
- **1 small onion (about ¼ pound), peeled, cut in half lengthwise and sliced ⅛ inch thick**
- **3 ounces mushrooms, rinsed and cut into ¼-inch slices**
- **4 cloves garlic, smashed and peeled**
- **1 celery stalk, strung and cut on the diagonal into ¼-inch slices (about ½ cup)**
- **1 green apple (¼ pound), peeled, cored and cut into 1-inch chunks**
- **6 ounces livers from whatever bird you are using (chicken, duck, Cornish or Guinea hen, turkey, etc.), cleaned and cut into 1½-inch chunks**
- **1 teaspoon kosher salt**
- **¼ teaspoon freshly ground black pepper**
- **4 cups cooked Wild Rice (see preceding recipe)**

1. Heat butter in a 13″ × 9″ dish, uncovered, at 100% for 3 minutes. Add onions, mushrooms, garlic, celery, and apples and stir to coat. Cook, uncovered, at 100% for 4 minutes, stirring twice.

2. Remove from oven. Stir in remaining ingredients except rice. Cook, uncovered, at 100% for 2 minutes.

3. Remove from oven. Stir in Wild Rice and serve hot.

Pilaf

The Indians, the Turks, the Persians, and numerous peoples of Europe share a secret, the secret of pilaf. It's a good secret and, with the microwave oven, an easy one to unlock.

At first, a pilaf seems very much like risotto. The rice is cooked in fat with seasonings. Liquid is added for the final cooking. The difference is in the kind of rice used and in the covering of the rice for the final cooking with liquid. Less liquid is used, and the grains of rice remain separate and fairly dry. The long, thin grains of basmati rice are particularly suitable for pilaf, but you can use American long-grain rice, or, even better, parboiled (not instant) rice (see RICE in the Dictionary).

Pilaf is more often used as an accompanying starch than risotto. Since it is less creamy, pilaf is better at absorbing sauces. Yet it has enough texture to serve as a contrast to simple fish dishes. When deciding what kind of pilaf to make, pick one whose seasonings and color set off the main dish. Instead of Curried Pilaf with Curried Shrimp, for example, serve Tomato Pilaf or Coriander Pilaf. Use the Curried Pilaf as a surprising contrast to Veal Fricassee (page 256), or to go with Chicken Breasts Normande (page 207). With Irish Lamb Stew (page 262), try Basic Pilaf or Green Pilaf.

If you are making the main course in the microwave oven, you will probably make the pilaf first. If so, uncover the pilaf when removing from the oven. After the main course is cooked, sprinkle 1 tablespoon of water per portion over the pilaf. Cover tightly and heat for 2 minutes at 100% for four portions, 5 minutes for eight portions. That way, all parts of the meal will be hot.

Some pilafs serve as the main dish of a meal. These tend to be family meals rather than company meals. In main course pilafs, the kind with meat, seafood, or vegetables added to them, the same amount of rice serves fewer people than in side dish pilafs. This is true because people eat more pilaf when it is a main course. This means that if 1 cup of raw rice serves four people when cooked as a side dish, it will serve three when cooked in a main course combination.

BASIC PILAF

This can be made with any of the basic broths in the Savory Basics chapter, including the vegetarian broths. There is virtually no limit to the variations you can ring on this theme.   *Serves 4 as a side dish*

3 tablespoons unsalted butter	**1½ cups broth of choice**
1 cup basmati rice, parboiled, or Carolina rice	**Kosher salt**
	Freshly ground black pepper

1. Heat butter in a 2-quart soufflé dish at 100% for 4 minutes. Stir in rice. Cook, uncovered, at 100% for 4 minutes. (In a small oven, cook 7 minutes.)

2. Add broth. Stir. Cover tightly with microwave plastic wrap. Cook at 100% for 13 minutes. (If using a small oven, cook for 19 minutes.) Remove from oven and uncover; season to taste with salt and pepper.

To serve 8. Heat 4 tablespoons butter in a 14″ × 11″ × 2″ dish for 5 minutes. Add 2 cups rice and cook as for Basic Pilaf for 5 minutes. Add 3 cups broth and cook for 16 minutes more. Finish as for Basic Pilaf.

VARIATIONS

CORIANDER PILAF FOR 4 Proceed as for Basic Pilaf. Add 4 cloves smashed and peeled garlic to melted butter. Cook, uncovered, for 3 minutes. Add rice and cook. Add broth and cook. One minute before end of cooking time, remove plastic; stir in ⅓ cup chopped coriander and ⅓ cup peeled, seeded, and chopped cucumber. Re-cover with microwave plastic wrap and cook for 2 minutes 30 seconds. Season to taste with salt and pepper. Serve topped with yogurt.

CORIANDER PILAF FOR 8 Double quantities of rice and broth. Increase butter to 4 tablespoons. Use 10 cloves garlic, ½ cup coriander, and ⅔ cup cucumber. Proceed as for Basic Pilaf.

GREEN PILAF FOR 4 Proceed as for Basic Pilaf. At end, stir in ⅔ cup (loosely packed) washed, stemmed, and chopped spinach and ⅓ cup (loosely packed) chopped parsley. Cook, uncovered, 1 minute 30 seconds.

GREEN PILAF FOR 8 Proceed as for Basic Pilaf, stirring in ⅔ cup (loosely packed) parsley and 1⅓ cups (loosely packed) washed, stemmed, and chopped spinach at end. Increase final cooking time by 2 minutes.

TOMATO PILAF

This pilaf may seem to use more liquid than some others, but that is because puréed tomatoes are thicker, part solid, so you have to use more. The mustard seeds add a surprising little crunch.   *Serves 8 as a side dish*

4 tablespoons unsalted butter
1 tablespoon mustard seed
2 cups basmati rice or Carolina rice

1¼ cups Chicken Broth (page 331) or canned chicken broth
2 cups (14-ounce can) tomatoes with juice
Kosher salt
Freshly ground black pepper

1. Heat butter in a 14″ × 11″ × 2″ dish, uncovered, at 100% for 3 minutes. Stir in mustard seed and cook, uncovered, at 100% for 5 minutes. Add rice and stir to coat. Cook, uncovered, for 5 minutes longer.

2. Remove from oven. Stir in broth and tomatoes. Cover tightly with microwave plastic wrap. Cook at 100% for 16 minutes.

3. Remove from oven. Uncover and stir in salt and pepper to taste. Serve hot.

CURRIED PILAF

If this weren't so special, it could be Basic Pilaf. It isn't dinner; but I am willing to think up excuses for using it.   *Serves 4 as a side dish*

3 tablespoons unsalted butter	1½ cups Chicken Broth (page 331) or canned chicken broth
1 tablespoon Spice Powder III (page 346) or curry powder	½ cup frozen peas, defrosted in a sieve under warm running water, or any cooked vegetable
½ cup chopped onion (about ¼ pound)	
2 tablespoons raisins or slivered almonds	
3 cloves garlic, smashed, peeled and sliced	Kosher salt
1 cup basmati rice or Carolina rice	Freshly ground black pepper

1. Heat butter in a 2-quart soufflé dish uncovered, at 100% for 2 minutes. Stir in spice powder, onions, raisins, and garlic. Cook, uncovered, at 100% for 4 minutes. Add rice and stir to coat. Cook, uncovered, for 4 minutes more.

2. Pour broth over all. Stir. Cover tightly with microwave plastic wrap. Cook at 100% for 13 minutes.

3. Remove from oven. Uncover and stir in peas; add salt and pepper to taste. Serve hot.

To serve 8. Heat 4 tablespoons butter in a 14″ × 11″ × 2″ dish for 5 minutes. Add 2 tablespoons spice powder, ⅓ cup onions, ¼ cup raisins, and 5 cloves garlic; cook as for Curried Pilaf for 5 minutes. Add 2 cups rice and cook for 5 minutes more. Stir in 3 cups broth and cook, covered, for 16 minutes. Double remaining ingredients and finish as for Curried Pilaf.

VARIATIONS

VEGETARIAN CURRIED PILAF FOR 4 OR 8 For chicken broth, substitute half Coconut Milk (page 353) and half water. Proceed as for Curried Pilaf. For every 4 portions, stir in ⅓ cup shredded coconut with peas, salt, and pepper.

CURRIED PILAF WITH CHICKEN FOR 4 OR 8 Cook 3 chicken breasts to serve 4, cook 6 breasts for 8 (see page 504); cut into 1-inch cubes. Prepare Curried Pilaf. Stir in chicken with peas, salt, and pepper. Cover tightly with microwave plastic wrap. Cook at 100% for 2 minutes for smaller amount, 4 minutes for larger amount.

CURRIED PILAF WITH LAMB FOR 4 OR 8 Substitute Lamb Broth (page 332) for chicken broth. Make Curried Pilaf, adding ½ pound lamb for 4 servings, 1 pound lamb for 8 servings, cut into ¼-inch cubes, to rice. Add broth and cook, covered, for 15 minutes for smaller amount, 18 minutes for larger amount. Finish as for Curried Pilaf.

PILAF WITH HERBS AND LAMB FOR 4 OR 8 Eliminate spice powder. Cook as for Curried Pilaf. At end, stir in ¼ cup chopped fresh drill or mint for 4 servings, ½ cup for 8 servings.

CREAMY BARLEY

We tend to overlook barley as a side dish. I use it more conventionally as part of a soup, as in Beef Barley Soup (page 111). But barley can be cooked like rice for risotto; it is creamy and delicious, a wonderful side dish for roast meat.   *Serve 6 as a side dish*

2 tablespoons unsalted butter	3 cups Meat Broth (page 331) or canned chicken broth
2 tablespoons olive oil	
½ cup minced yellow onion (about ¼ pound)	2 teaspoons kosher salt Freshly ground black pepper
1 cup medium pearl barley	

   1. Heat butter and oil in an 11″ × 8½″ × 2″ dish, uncovered, at 100% for 2 minutes. Add onions and stir to coat. Cook, uncovered, at 100% for 4 minutes. (If using a small oven, cook for 7 minutes.) Add barley and stir to coat. Cook for 2 minutes more. (In a small oven, cook for 5 minutes.)
   2. Remove from oven. Stir in broth. Cook, uncovered, at 100% for 10 minutes. Stir well and cook for 15 minutes more. (If using a small oven, cook for 15 minutes, stir well, and cook for 23 minutes more.)

3. Remove from oven. Add salt and pepper and serve hot.

To serve 1 Heat 2 teaspoons each butter and oil in an 8″ × 6″ dish. Stir in 1 tablespoon minced onion and ¼ cup barley and cook at 100% for 2 minutes. Add 1¼ cups broth and finish as for Creamy Barley, cooking for 14 minutes total.

GRITS

Down South, grits can be a three-time-a-day habit. For breakfast, it may come with cream and sugar. Sometimes, bacon fat and crumbled bacon are substituted for the butter and salt. Grits can be seasoned like Soft Polenta (see following recipe). In the microwave oven, they don't lump. See page 541 for more information on grits. *Serves 4 to 6 as a side dish or for breakfast*

5 cups water	Freshly ground black
1 cup grits (not "quick-	pepper
cooking")	1 tablespoon unsalted
½ teaspoon kosher salt	butter

1. Combine water and grits in an 8-cup glass measure. Cook, uncovered, at 100% for 15 minutes. (If using a small oven, cook for 25 minutes.)

2. Remove from oven and whisk until smooth. Stir in salt, pepper, and butter and serve hot.

To serve 1. Combine 1 cup water and 3 tablespoons grits in a 4-cup glass measure and cook at 100% for 4 minutes. Stir in ½ teaspoon butter and a pinch of salt and pepper. Serve hot.

VARIATION

GRITS TO STUFF A LARGE BIRD Make a double quantity of Mushrooms and Livers with Wild Rice (page 128), using a 14″ × 11″ × 2″ dish. Double ingredient quantities and cook onion mixture for 7 minutes; add remaining ingredients and cook for 3 minutes 30 seconds. Substitute larger quantity of cooked grits (without butter) for wild rice in recipe. Use to stuff a 15-pound turkey or 2 to 3 roasting chickens.

SOFT POLENTA

The Italians are the most convincing thieves in the culinary business. They took our tomatoes and made us think they were as Italian as pasta. Then they took our cornmeal mush. and convinced us they knew more about it. They do grind corn differently than we do, coarser; but whether using Italian-grind polenta or American cornmeal, yellow or white, this is a wonderful accompaniment to all sorts of foods. You can serve it (with or without Gorgonzola cheese) drizzled with the pan juices of roasted meats or birds, with grilled fish or with rich stews.

I think polenta has been less popular than potatoes because, cooked on top of the stove, it demands long and constant stirring, and even then there are likely to be lumps. Also, it has always worked best in quantity: no polenta for one or two. With the microwave oven, the polenta is stirred only once during the entire cooking time; it is guaranteed lumpless, and it can be made for one or for a crowd. If you can cook this in a serving dish, choose one with a cover; it will prevent the polenta from forming a skin and will, at the same time, keep it hot. *Serves 8 as a side dish*

4 cups water	⅛ teaspoon freshly
¾ cup yellow or white	ground black
cornmeal	pepper
2 teaspoons kosher salt	¼ cup softened
3 tablespoons unsalted	Gorgonzola cheese
butter	or ¼ cup additional
	butter

1. Combine water, cornmeal, and salt in a 2-quart soufflé dish. Cook, uncovered, at 100% for 6 minutes. Stir well, cover loosely with paper toweling, and cook for 6 minutes more. (If using a small oven, cook uncovered for 9 minutes; cover loosely and cook for 9 minutes.)

2. Remove from oven. Uncover and stir in butter, pepper, and cheese (or additional butter). Let stand for 3 minutes. Serve hot.

To serve 1 or 2. Quarter all ingredients (use 3 tablespoons cornmeal). Proceed as for Soft Polenta, cooking in a soup bowl for 1 minute 30 seconds, uncovered, and then for another 1 minute 30 seconds, covered.

To serve 3 or 4. Combine 2½ cups water, ½ cup cornmeal, and 1 teaspoon salt in an 8-cup glass measure. Cook as for Soft Polenta for 5 minutes. Stir and continue cooking for 5 minutes longer. Finish as for Soft Polenta, stirring in 2 tablespoons butter and a pinch of pepper.

VARIATION

SPICY POLENTA Use Monterey Jack or fresh goat cheese instead of Gorgonzola and add 1 jalapeño pepper, stemmed, seeded, and chopped.

FIRM POLENTA

This is a firmer polenta. Usually it is chilled, sliced and fried or grilled. Serve fried or grilled slices plain as a side dish or top with Chicken Livers (page 507) or Mushrooms and Livers with Wild Rice (page 128); or top each slice with a slice of Fontina or mozzarella cheese and broil until melted and bubbly. Fried or grilled polenta is also delicious with Bitter Broccoli Sauce (page 148). *Serves 8 as part of a first course or as a side dish*

4 cups water	**4 tablespoons unsalted**
1½ cups yellow or white	**butter**
cornmeal	**⅛ teaspoon freshly**
2 teaspoons kosher salt	**ground black**
	pepper

1. Combine water, cornmeal, and salt in a 2-quart soufflé dish. Cook, uncovered, at 100% for 12 minutes, stirring once.

2. Remove from oven, stir in 3 tablespoons of the butter, and add the pepper. Let stand for 3 minutes.

3. Lightly grease a 7″ × 4″ × 2″ loaf pan with half the remaining butter. Pour polenta into pan and brush lightly with the last of the butter. Let stand until cool.

4. Cover and refrigerate until chilled. To serve, slice the polenta about ½ inch thick and fry or grill.

VARIATION

FRIED POLENTA Slice polenta ½ inch thick and set the slices on a wire rack to dry for about 20 minutes. Heat 2 tablespoons butter in a 10- inch square browning dish at 100% for 3 minutes. Preheat conventional oven to lowest setting. Arrange half the polenta slices in a single layer in the dish. Cook, uncovered, at 100% for 6 minutes, turning once, until golden brown and firm. Remove from oven. Place slices on a cookie sheet and place in conventional oven to keep warm. Repeat with remaining slices, using 1 tablespoon butter or more, if needed. Serve immediately.

GRILLED POLENTA Preheat broiler. Slice polenta ½ inch thick and let dry as for Fried Polenta. Brush with olive oil and grill until crusty, about 2 minutes on each side.

MILLET

Millet is a grain, small, round, and yellowish. It is unfamiliar to many of us, but before corn came to Italy, it was widely used, ground, for polenta. I like to cook it whole as I do risotto. It is quick, and it is an unusual side dish. Of course, a vegetarian broth can be used.   *Makes 8 cups*

¼ **pound unsalted butter**	1½ **teaspoons kosher salt**
2 **cups millet**	**Freshly ground black**
4 **cups Chicken Broth**	**pepper**
(page 331), canned	
chicken broth or	
Vegetable Broth	
(page 335)	

1. Heat butter in a 14″ × 11″ × 2″ dish, uncovered, at 100% for 2 minutes.

2. Add millet and stir to coat. Pour broth over all. Cook, uncovered, at 100% for 10 minutes.

3. Remove from oven. Stir in salt and pepper and serve hot.

COUSCOUS

Couscous is a pasta, although we seldom think of it that way. The traditional way to cook it calls for several steamings and rubbings. I like this as much, and it is much easier.   *Serves 10 to 12 as a side dish*

1 medium yellow onion,
    peeled and
    quartered
10 cloves garlic, smashed
    and peeled
¼ pound unsalted butter
3 tablespoons ground
    cumin, preferably
    freshly ground
1 tablespoon curry
    powder

2 cups couscous
4 cups Chicken Broth
    (page 331), canned
    chicken broth,
    Vegetable Broth
    (page 335), tomato
    juice or water
1½ teaspoons kosher salt
Freshly ground black
    pepper

1. Place onion, garlic, and butter in the workbowl of a food processor. Process until finely chopped. Scrape mixture into a 14″ × 11″ × 2″ dish. Cook, uncovered, at 100% for 2 minutes.

2. Stir in cumin and curry powder. Cook, uncovered, at 100% for 3 minutes.

3. Add couscous and stir to coat. Pour broth over all. Cook, uncovered, at 100% for 10 minutes.

4. Remove from oven. Stir in salt and pepper and serve.

To serve 5 or 6 as a side dish. Halve all ingredients. Cook onion mixture in a 2-quart soufflé dish for 2 minutes. Add cumin and curry powder and cook for 2 minutes more. Add couscous, stir to coat, and pour broth on top. Cook, uncovered, at 100% for 6 minutes. Stir in salt and pepper and serve.

To serve 3 as a side dish. Divide all ingredient quantities by 4. Cook onion mixture in a 7″ × 5″ oval or rectangular dish for 2 minutes. Add cumin and curry powder and cook for 2 minutes more. Add couscous, stir to coat, and add broth. Cook at 100% for 4 minutes. Season to taste with salt and pepper.

OLD-FASHIONED OATMEAL

When I was a child, every morning I was given cod liver oil, which I hated, hot cereal, which I loved, with butter melting on top, and a pitcher of heavy cream. That was good mothering. Maybe hot cereal will make a comeback because, with a microwave oven, it doesn't take too long at all. Cook oatmeal in a large container because it tends to boil over. Then sprinkle it with raw sugar or spoon honey on top. Maybe we can bring back family breakfast, especially on weekends. *Serves 1*

⅓ cup old-fashioned   Pinch kosher salt
   rolled oats (not   ¾ cup water
   "quick-cooking")

1. Combine all ingredients in a 2-cup glass measure. Cover tightly with microwave plastic wrap. Cook at 100% for 1 minute. Uncover and cook for 1 minute 30 seconds more. (If using a small oven, cook for 2 minutes, uncover and cook for 2 minutes more.)

2. Remove from oven. Let stand for 1 minute. Serve hot.

To serve 2 or 3. Double all ingredients. Combine in a 4-cup glass measure. Cover and cook at 100% for 2 minutes 30 seconds. Uncover and cook for 1 minute more. Remove from oven and let stand for 1 minute.

IRISH OATMEAL

These coarse-cut cereals permitted poor people to thrive. Today, they are the luxury version of oatmeal. *Serves 1*

1 cup water   Pinch kosher salt
¼ cup Irish or Scotch
   oatmeal

1. Combine water and oatmeal in an 8-cup glass measure. Cover tightly with microwave plastic wrap. Cook at 100% for 4 minutes and 30 seconds. Uncover and cook for 5 to 6 minutes more.

2. Remove from oven. Stir in salt and serve hot.

To serve 2 or 3. Combine 2 cups water with ½ cup oatmeal in an 8-cup glass measure. Cover tightly with microwave plastic wrap. Cook at 100% for 5 minutes. Uncover and cook for 5 minutes more. Stir and cook for 3 to 4 minutes more. Remove from oven, stir in salt to taste and serve hot.

FARINA

Another old-time breakfast food made easy, to enjoy with butter and cream and sweeteners if you want. I find the cream is enough. It makes me feel like a happy child again.   *Serves 4*

3 cups water	**1 teaspoon kosher salt**
½ cup farina	

1. Heat water in an 8-cup glass measure, uncovered, at 100% for 6 minutes. Add farina and salt and stir well. Cook, uncovered, at 100% for 3 minutes.

2. Remove from oven. Serve hot.

To serve 2. Halve all ingredients. Heat water in a 4-cup glass measure for 3 minutes 30 seconds. Add remaining ingredients and cook for 2 minutes.

To serve 1. Heat ¾ cup water in a 2-cup glass measure for 2 minutes. Add 2 tablespoons farina and ¼ teaspoon salt and cook for 1 minute.

CHILIED BEANS

My Chili (page 237) doesn't have beans in it, but I often serve beans on the side, as I do with many Mexican and Texan dishes, either straight up or as Refried Beans (see variation that follows). These, I think, are very tasty. *Serves 4*

1 cup dried pink, red, or black beans	**Pinch freshly ground black pepper**
1 medium onion, peeled and quartered	**1 teaspoon chili powder**
4 cloves garlic, smashed and peeled	**1 teaspoon ground cumin**
	1 bay leaf

1. Put beans in a 2½-quart soufflé dish and cover with 2 cups water. Cover tightly with microwave plastic wrap. Cook at 100% for 15 minutes.

2. Remove from oven. Pierce plastic with the tip of a sharp knife. Let stand for 5 minutes. Uncover and add 2 cups very hot tap water. Re-cover tightly and let stand for 1 hour.

3. Uncover beans, drain, and rinse. Return them to soufflé dish and add remaining ingredients. Stir to combine. Add 4 cups warm water. Cover tightly with two sheets of microwave plastic wrap. Cook at 100% for 35 minutes.

4. Remove from oven. Let stand, covered, for 20 minutes. Uncover, stir, and serve.

VARIATION

REFRIED BEANS Make Chilied Beans and pass through a food mill fitted with a medium disc. Reserve. Combine 2 tablespoons lard or vegetable oil and 2 tablespoons finely chopped onions in a 10-inch quiche pan or pie plate. Cook, uncovered, at 100% for 2 minutes. Remove from oven. Stir in Chilied Beans and 1 teaspoon kosher salt and spread mixture evenly in pan. Cook, uncovered, at 100%, for 4 minutes. Leaving pan in oven, stir and smooth mixture again. Cook for 3 minutes more.

BLACK-EYED PEAS

Despite their name, black-eyed peas are beans. They are much loved in the South and, in the guise of Hoppin' John, are traditional on New Year's Day. Accompanied by Pot Greens (page 572) and biscuits, they are often dinner. They are so filling that no extra meat is needed.   *Makes 3 cups*

1 smoked ham hock
    (about 8 ounces),
    split and washed
	1 cup black-eyed peas

1. Place hock in a 4-cup glass measure with 2 cups water. Cover tightly with 2 sheets of microwave plastic wrap. Cook at 100% for 35 minutes.

2. Remove from oven. Uncover and drain; reserve liquid and ham hock.

3. Place peas and 2 cups water in a 2-quart soufflé dish. Cover tightly with microwave plastic wrap. Cook at 100% for 15 minutes.

4. Remove from oven. Pierce plastic with the tip of a sharp knife. Let stand for 5 minutes. Uncover and add 2 cups very hot tap water. Re-cover with a fresh piece of microwave plastic wrap. Let stand for 1 hour.

5. Uncover, drain, and rinse peas. Return to soufflé dish and add reserved ham hock. Place reserved cooking liquid in a 4-cup glass measure and add enough water to measure 4 cups. Pour over peas and ham. Cook, tightly covered, at 100% for 35 minutes.

6. Remove from oven. Let stand, covered, for 20 minutes. Uncover and drain cooking liquid back into 4-cup measure. Cook, uncovered, at 100% for 16 minutes, until reduced to ¾ cup. Remove meat from ham hock and discard bone and skin. Place meat with beans.

7. Remove liquid from oven. Add to meat and beans; stir. Serve hot.

VARIATION

HOPPIN' JOHN Omit ham hock and prepare beans through step 4. Drain and rinse peas. Use all water instead of part ham hock cooking liquid. Cook 4 thick slices bacon in an 11″ × 8″ × 2″ dish, uncovered, at 100% for 3 minutes. Add ½ cup chopped onions and 1 cup long-grain rice. Cook, uncovered, at 100% for 4 minutes. Add 2 teaspoons salt, 2 cups water, and peas. Cover tightly with microwave plastic wrap. Cook at 100% for 20 minutes. Finish as for Black-Eyed Peas.

Potatoes

Here are a few very special recipes for potato dishes that fare exceptionally well in the microwave oven. Consult the Index and the Dictionary for more ways to cook potatoes.

GARLIC POTATOES

This is a microwave version of my favorite potato recipe. I find you can never have too many of these potatoes. They are good cold and they can be reheated. Serve them with roast meat, grilled chicken, or as good company to stewed vegetables.   *Serves 4 as side dish*

1 pound small new
    potatoes (about 10
    potatoes), scrubbed
    and patted dry
6 large cloves garlic,
    smashed and peeled

3 tablespoons good-
    quality olive oil
½ teaspoon kosher salt
    Freshly ground black
    pepper

1. Place potatoes in a 1½-quart soufflé dish. Add remaining ingredients and stir to coat potatoes. Cover tightly with microwave plastic wrap. Cook at 100% for 10 to 15 minutes (depending on size of potatoes), shaking dish once to redistribute potatoes. Potatoes are done when the tip of a small knife easily pierces the flesh to the center.

2. Remove from oven. Uncover and serve hot.

To serve 8 to 10. Combine 4 pounds potatoes, 15 cloves garlic, ¾ cup oil, 2 teaspoons salt, and pepper to taste in a 14″ × 11″ × 2″ dish. Cook at 100% for 20 minutes, shaking dish once to redistribute potatoes.

POTATO GALETTE

This is a thin little cake of crisply cooked potatoes such as you would find in any major French restaurant. Serve it with lightly sauced foods. The reason you have to arrange the potatoes beforehand is to be able to transfer them quickly to the preheated browning dish before it cools.   *Serves 1*

| 4 teaspoons unsalted butter | Kosher salt |
| 1 Maine potato (½ pound), peeled and very thinly sliced | Freshly ground black pepper |

1. Heat 2 teaspoons of the butter in a custard cup, uncovered, at 100% for 1 minute. Reserve.

2. Arrange potato slices to overlap in a circle on a dinner plate.

3. Heat remaining 2 teaspoons butter in an 8-inch square browning dish uncovered, at 100% for 2 minutes.

4. Remove from oven. With a wide metal spatula transfer potatoes to browning dish, being careful to keep them in a circle. Brush with reserved melted butter. Cook, uncovered, at 100% for 3 minutes. Carefully turn potatoes over and cook for 1 minute 30 seconds more.

5. Remove from oven. Season with salt and pepper and serve hot.

To serve 4. Increase butter to 3 tablespoons and use 4 potatoes (about 2 pounds). Proceed as for single serving, using a 10-inch square browning dish; arrange potato slices in four rows (1 potato per row). Heat second half of butter in the dish for 3 minutes and cook potatoes for 5 minutes. Turn and cook for 3 minutes more. Season and serve hot.

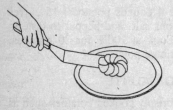

Arrange thinly sliced potatoes in a circle—for 1—transfer with spatula.

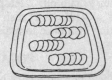

Arrange potatoes in lines—for 4—and transfer to browning dish.

SWEET POTATO PURÉE

This is a smooth creamy purée in the French style. Try it for a change at Thanksgiving.   *Serves 4 as a side dish*

2 **pounds sweet potatoes** (about 2 large potatoes), each pricked 3 or 4 times with a fork	1 **cup plus 2 tablespoons heavy cream** ¼ **pound unsalted butter** 2 **teaspoons kosher salt** **Freshly ground black pepper**

1. Cook potatoes, uncovered, at 100% for 13 to 15 minutes, until tender. Remove from oven and peel.

2. Pass potatoes through a ricer or the medium disc of a food mill. Add remaining ingredients and mix well. Serve hot.

To serve 8. Double all ingredients. Cook potatoes at 100% for 25 minutes.

Note. Mixture may be made in advance and kept, tightly covered and refrigerated, for up to 3 days. Then heat purée, uncovered, at 100% for 5 minutes before serving.

Pasta

I use the Italian word because it is the best known. Most parts of the world have at least one kind of noodle made with various kinds of grains and with or without eggs.

The nice thing about pasta is it permits you to invent endlessly and make something to eat when there is nothing in the house. You can chop up 2 cups of any vegetable mix that appeals to you—generally including some onion and garlic—and cook. Put 3 tablespoons of butter or olive oil in a 9″ × 13″ dish; cook for 3 minutes, uncovered, at 100%.

Stir in vegetables and 2 tablespoons of fresh chopped herbs, if you want. Cover tightly with microwave plastic wrap and cook for 5 minutes at 100%. Uncover. Add ⅓ cup heavy cream or Lightly Cooked Crushed Tomatoes (page 339). Cook, uncovered, for 3 minutes. Use to top 1 pound linguine, cooked.

See Savory Sauces (pages 360–364) for some pasta sauces. Fish and Seafood (pages 158–200) has some nice recipes for saucy clams and mussels. They are very good served over pasta.

The only thing to remember is that the water for the pasta must be started well before the sauce.

PASTA PRIMAVERA

While I tend to think that the flavor obtained by cooking the vegetables with sauce is best, in recent years many versions of Pasta Primavera, a dish made famous by Le Cirque restaurant in New York, have become popular. The problem has been that each vegetable needed to be separately cooked in its own pot of boiling salted water. The preparation was endless. Thanks to the way the microwave oven cooks differentially from the outside to the inside of a dish, all the vegetables can be cooked together quickly and come out as if each were lovingly and separately tended. You can bring the array of vegetables to the table in their cooking dish and toss them into the pasta that has previously been mixed with the two sauces—spectacular.	*Serves 8 to 10 as first course, 6 to 8 as main course*

4 tablespoons unsalted butter

2 tablespoons Chicken Broth (page 331) or canned chicken broth

½ cup heavy cream

2 cups Lightly Cooked Crushed Tomatoes (page 339)

3 tablespoons olive oil

2 cloves garlic, smashed, peeled and minced

1 tablespoon finely chopped fresh hot red or green chili peppers, or ½ teaspoon hot red-pepper flakes

¼ cup finely chopped parsley

4 cups broccoli florets (about 6 ounces)

¾ pound green beans, trimmed and cut into 1-inch lengths (about 1½ cups)

½ pound zucchini, trimmed and cut into 2″ × ½″ × ½″ strips

¾ cups snow peas, trimmed

4 asparagus spears, trimmed, peeled and cut into 2-inch lengths

½ cups green peas, fresh or frozen

2 cups thinly sliced mushrooms (about ½ pound)

⅓ cup pine nuts

1 tablespoon vegetable oil

1 pound spaghetti or spaghettini

⅔ cup freshly grated Parmesan cheese

2 tablespoons kosher salt

6 fresh basil leaves

1. Combine butter, broth, and cream in a 2-cup glass measure. Cook, uncovered, at 100% for 5 minutes. Reserve.

2. Combine tomatoes, olive oil, garlic, peppers, and parsley in a 4-cup glass measure. Cook, uncovered, at 100% for 5 minutes. Reserve.

3. Place a large pot of water on the stove to boil for the spaghetti.

4. In a 14″ × 11″ × 2″ dish, arrange the vegetables in concentric rings, with broccoli inside rim, then green beans, zucchini, snow peas, and asparagus. Mound green peas in center.

5. Toss mushroom slices and pine nuts in oil and sprinkle over vegetables. Cover tightly with microwave plastic wrap. Cook at 100% for 7 minutes.

6. Cook pasta in boiling water and drain.

7. Remove vegetables from oven and pierce plastic with the tip of a sharp knife.

8. Reheat reserved sauces at the same time, in their separate measures, uncovered, at 100% for 4 minutes.

9. Place drained pasta in a large ceramic dish that will fit into the microwave oven. While pasta is hot, toss with vegetables, cream sauce, and one half the tomato sauce.

10. Reheat pasta, uncovered, at 100% for 4 minutes.

11. Remove from oven and toss with Parmesan cheese, salt, and basil. To serve, spoon some of remaining tomato sauce over each portion.

Arrange vegetables in concentric rings with the slowest-cooking around the inside rim of dish and the quick-cooking vegetables in the center.

PASTA WITH BITTER BROCCOLI SAUCE

This is a simple, classic Italian pasta dish made with what is called broccoli di rape (see BROCCOLI DI RAPE in the Dictionary). It's a shame bitter broccoli isn't better known in this country. I often eat it without the pasta as a first course or with poached fish. Without pasta, but combined with the seasonings, it will serve four.   *Serves 8 as first course, 4 as a luncheon dish*

1 pound spaghetti
¾ cup olive oil
14 cloves garlic, smashed
    and peeled
½ teaspoon hot red-
    pepper flakes

1½ pounds broccoli di
    rape (2 bunches),
    cleaned and
    trimmed
2 teaspoons kosher salt
    Freshly grated
    Parmesan cheese

1. Bring a large pot of salted water to a boil for the pasta. When the water is boiling, add pasta and cook until al dente. Drain well.

2. Combine oil, garlic, and red pepper flakes in a 14″ × 11″ × 2″ dish. Heat, uncovered, at 100% for 4 minutes. Add broccoli and stir to coat. Cover tightly with microwave plastic wrap. Cook at 100% for 10 minutes.

3. Remove from oven. Uncover and stir well. Add drained pasta and salt and toss to combine. Serve hot with cheese passed on the side.

To serve 4 as a first course, 2 as a luncheon dish. Cook and drain ½ pound pasta. Heat ⅓ cup oil, 6 cloves garlic, and a pinch of red-pepper flakes in an 11″ × 8½″ × 2″ dish, uncovered, for 3 minutes. Add ¾ pound broccoli, cover, and cook for 7 minutes.

LASAGNE

Is there anybody who doesn't like lasagne? I don't think so. This one is made with meat sauce, but vegetarian versions can be made by substituting Duxelles (page 340) or Creamed Spinach (page 300) with some chopped basil for 2 cups of the Bolognese Sauce and using 1 cup of Chunky Tomato Sauce (page 374). Just make more layers. *Serves 8 as a main course*

5 sheets (about ½ pound)
    store-bought fresh
    lasagne noodles, 8″
    × 10″ (see note)
4 cups Salsa Bolognese
    (page 376)

3 cups Basic Béchamel
    (page 364)
3½ cups freshly grated
    Parmesan cheese

1. Bring a large pot of salted water to a boil.

2. Slip the pasta sheets, one at a time, into the boiling water. When the water returns to a boil, remove from heat. Drain immediately and refresh pasta under cold running water. Leave the pasta in cool water while you assemble the lasagne.

3. Cover the bottom of a 10″ × 8″ × 4″ dish with a thin layer of Bolognese Sauce. Lay a sheet of pasta on top. Pour about 1 cup of the sauce over the pasta, then spoon over it ½ cup of Béchamel. Sprinkle with ¾ cup of the cheese. Repeat these layers 3 times, ending with pasta. Spoon remaining Béchamel on top and sprinkle with remaining cheese. Cook, uncovered, at 100% for 15 minutes.

4. Remove from oven. Let stand for 5 to 10 minutes before serving.

Note. If fresh lasagne noodles are not available, use ½ pound dried noodles, cooking them for 5 minutes.

MACARONI AND CHEESE

Do you know people so sophisticated they won't admit to loving macaroni and cheese? I do. They are missing something very good. This is quicker than what you get in a package and a lot better. To make a more authentic brown and bubbly macaroni and cheese, run the dish under the broiler after cooking.   *Serves 1 as a main course, 2 as a side dish*

¾ cup milk
 1 tablespoon cornstarch
½ cup grated Cheddar
    cheese (about 1½
    ounces)
½ teaspoon kosher salt

1 teaspoon unsalted
    butter
Freshly ground black
    pepper
1 cup cooked macaroni
    (about ⅓ cup dry)

1. Combine milk and cornstarch in a 4-cup glass measure. Heat, uncovered, at 100% for 3 minutes.

2. Whisk in cheese, salt, butter, and pepper. Fold in cooked macaroni and pour mixture into a large soup bowl or serving dish. Cook, uncovered, at 100% for 3 minutes.

3. Remove from oven. Serve hot.

To serve 2 as a main course. Combine 1 cup milk and 2 tablespoon cornstarch in a 1-quart soufflé dish and cook for 3 minutes. Add ¾ cup cheese, 1½ teaspoons salt, 1 teaspoon butter, pepper, and 2½ cups cooked macaroni. Cook, uncovered, at 100% for 4 minutes.

To serve 4 as a main course. Combine 2 cups milk and 3 tablespoons cornstarch in a 10″ × 8″ dish and cook for 4 minutes. Add 1½ cups cheese, 2½ teaspoons salt, pepper, and 2 tablespoons butter. Fold in 5 cups cooked macaroni. Cook, uncovered, at 100% for 4 minutes 30 seconds.

Note. This dish may be frozen. Line the cooking dish with 2 layers of microwave plastic wrap; cook as instructed. Fold plastic over cooked macaroni and cheese. Let cool, then freeze. To defrost, heat at 100% for 3 minutes. Unwrap, replace in cooking dish, and broil until bubbly.

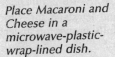

| *Place Macaroni and Cheese in a microwave-plastic-wrap-lined dish.* | *When food is cooked, close plastic. Cool; freeze; remove from dish.* | *Place back in dish to defrost. Unwrap and broil.* |

Cheese

Not every day needs meat, and cheese is a natural replacement. A nice thing about most cheese dishes, as you can see from Macaroni and Cheese (page 150) and Lasagne (page 149), is that they are equally appropriate as first and main courses.

QUICHE LORRAINE

When done right, this much-abused dish is simple and delicious. Here is a light, crustless version. If you want a crust, blind-bake it in standard fashion. Pour in quiche mixture after step 3 and continue with recipe.   *Serves 8 as a first course, 4 to 6 as a luncheon dish*

½ **pound baked ham,**
    cut into 1½-inch
    cubes
1 **small onion, diced**
    (about ½ cup)
2 **tablespoons unsalted**
    butter
5 **eggs**
1¼ **cups milk**

¾ **cup heavy cream**
½ **pound Swiss cheese,**
    grated
1½ **teaspoons kosher salt**
Pinch freshly ground
    black pepper
Pinch freshly ground
    nutmeg

1. Preheat conventional broiler.

2. Combine ham, onions, and butter in an 11″ × 8½″ × 2″ dish. Cook, uncovered, at 100% for 3 minutes.

3. Stir together remaining ingredients. Pour over ham mixture and stir to combine. Cook, uncovered, at 100% for 3 minutes. Stir well.

4. Cook, uncovered, for 3 minutes more. Cover tightly with microwave plastic wrap. Cook at 100% for 2 minutes.

5. Remove from oven. Uncover and let stand for 8 to 10 minutes. Just before serving, carefully brown top under the broiler.

GOUGÈRE

The citizens of Beaujolais and of Burgundy know how to down a glass of wine with the best of them. They also like a little something to eat as they drink. They invented the gougère, a small cheese-laden dollop of cream puff dough fried until crisp and eaten hot. If you want gougères that are mildly spicy, add cayenne. You can make the gougères early in the day and then reheat them on a paper towel, uncovered, in the microwave oven at 100% for 1 minute. Do this only in a full-sized oven. *Makes 15 gougères*

½ cup water	2 whole eggs
4 tablespoons unsalted butter	⅓ cup grated cheese (Gruyère, Parmesan or Cheddar)
½ cup all-purpose flour	
½ teaspoon kosher salt Pinch cayenne pepper (optional)	3 cups vegetable oil, for frying

1. Place water and butter in a 4-cup glass measure. Heat, uncovered, at 100% for 2 minutes 30 seconds.

2. Remove from oven. Place in the workbowl of a food processor. Add flour, salt, and cayenne, if desired. Process continuously for 1 minute 30 seconds.

3. With machine running, add eggs one at a time, processing for 30 seconds after adding each egg.

4. Add cheese and process just until mixed. At this point, the dough can be refrigerated, tightly covered, for up to 2 days.

5. When ready to cook, remove dough from refrigerator if prepared ahead. Heat oil in a 2-quart nonplastic container measuring at least 3¼ inches high, uncovered, at 100% for 15 minutes.

6. Drop 6 to 8 heaping teaspoonfuls of batter into oil. Cook, uncovered, for 1 minute. Leaving cup in oven, turn each gougère over with a slotted spoon. Cook for another 30 seconds.

7. Remove to paper toweling to drain.

8. Reheat oil for 5 minutes at 100%. Cook remaining dough.

GILDED CHEESE

A grilled cheese sandwich is probably the best use of browning dishes. A thin slice of ham may be added to each sandwich without changing the cooking time. Varying the cheese or adding a light coating of mustard will give you changes of pace. Consider removing the crusts from the bread and slicing each sandwich into 3 strips to make a hot hors d'oeuvre. Be careful: the cheese in these gets very hot. *Serves 1*

2 slices white bread	1 tablespoon unsalted
2 slices American cheese	butter, softened

1. Preheat a 10-inch round browning dish (preferably one with a metal cooking surface) at 100% for 5 minutes.

2. Put together the sandwich. Butter each side of the sandwich. Place in the browning dish and cook, uncovered, at 100% for 1 minute. Flip the sandwich over and cook for 1 minute more.

3. Remove from oven. Serve hot.

To serve 2. Double all ingredients and proceed as for single serving.

FONDUTA

Fonduce is Swiss. Just to Switzerland's south, over a mountain peak, Italy starts. Italians make a dish with melted cheese that I prefer to fondue called fonduta. In its most luxurious version, it is served without bread but with freshly shaved, beastly expensive white truffles and freshly ground black pepper on top.

Fontina cheese melts evenly and has a mildly nutty flavor. *Makes 4 cups, to serve 8 to 10 as a first course*

2 cups milk	Freshly ground black
½ pound Italian Fontina	pepper
cheese, grated	1 loaf country-style
4 tablespoons unsalted	Italian or sourdough
butter	bread (optional)
2 egg yolks	Italian white truffles,
Kosher salt	thinly shaved
	(optional)

1. Heat milk in an 8-cup glass measure, uncovered, for 4 minutes at 100%

2. Place cheese, butter, and egg yolks in the workbowl of a food processor. Quickly pour in hot milk. Process for 2 minutes.

3. Scrape mixture back into 8-cup measure. Cook, uncovered, for 3 minutes at 100%. Whisk. Cook for 3 minutes longer.

4. Return hot mixture to food processor. Process for 30 seconds. Season to taste with salt and pepper.

5. Serve in individual bowls or ramekins. Fonduta can be served with grilled pieces of country-style Italian bread. The ultimate luxury is to top the creamy cheese mixture with thin shavings of white truffle.

FONDUE

There was a time when fondue parties were all the thing, and every bride received a fondue set with a small burner to keep the fondue warm and long-handled forks to stick the chunks of bread on as they were stirred in the cheese. Ah, fickle America, the fondue sets got stashed in the closet, partly, I think, because the fondue had a nasty trick of coming apart just when you needed to serve it and there was no way of reheating it. Well, I think fondue is still good, and the microwave oven makes it fail-safe; it can even be reheated. So dust off the fondue set, but use a soufflé dish instead of the little pot. If you like, pass a bowl of toasted caraway seeds separately. Dip cheese-covered bread into seeds. Don't be tempted to experiment with the cheese: the natural Swiss cheeses work, while others often don't. *Makes 1 cup, to serve 4 as a light meal or first course*

1 cup dry white wine
2 cloves garlic, smashed and peeled
½ pound Swiss Gruyère or Emmentaler cheese
2 teaspoons kirsch

1 loaf country-style Swiss, Italian or sourdough bread, cut in 1½-inch cubes, each with some crust
Toasted caraway seeds (optional)

1. Put white wine and garlic in a 1-quart soufflé dish. Cook, uncovered, at 100% for 5 minutes.

2. Place cheese in the workbowl of a food processor. Pour in hot wine. Process for 2 minutes.

3. Return mixture to soufflé dish. Cook, uncovered, at 100% for 2 minutes; stir; cook for 2 minutes longer.

4. Put soufflé dish on heat source at the table. Stir in kirsch. Serve with bread chunks.

To reheat fondue. Fondue can be made ahead without risk, even a day ahead. The cooled fondue will congeal into a piece of rubber covered with liquid. Fear not; the microwave is here. Let fondue come to room temperature in the soufflé dish. Cook, uncovered, at 100% for 4 minutes. Remove from oven; whisk vigorously. Serve.

CHEDDAR CHEESE SAUCE

Just because we have learned to be fancy doesn't mean that we should ignore the homey pleasures of Cheddar Cheese Sauce. It can make a meal poured over toast and briefly broiled in the guise of Welsh Rabbit. Topped with a fried egg, it is a Golden Buck. Mixed with jalapeños and spread on tortilla chips and lightly broiled, it becomes nachos. Mixed with the same jalapeños but with the chips on the side, it is a dip. Use it as a topping for hamburgers, Old-Fashioned Meat Loaf (page 245), or broccoli.

One thing to beware of: if you want to add hot red-pepper sauce, Worcestershire sauce, bitters, or prepared mustard to spice up your cheese sauce or rabbits, follow the directions in the Welsh Rabbit variation or you will have a grainy mess.

This sauce stores, refrigerated, virtually forever. It can easily be reheated by placing it in the microwave oven for 2 minutes 30 seconds, uncovered, at 100%. Stir before serving.   *Makes 1¼ cups*

½ cup milk	Kosher salt
2½ cups grated Cheddar cheese (about ½ pound)	Freshly ground black pepper

1. Heat milk in a 2-cup glass measure, uncovered, at 100% for 1 minute.

2. Remove from oven. Add cheese and stir to moisten. Scrape mixture into a blender or food processor and purée until smooth.

3. Return to 2-cup measure. Heat, uncovered, at 100% for 30 seconds. Remove from oven and stir.

VARIATIONS

NACHO SAUCE Before heating cheese sauce for final 30 seconds, add 1 thinly sliced jalapeño pepper or 1 teaspoon Fiery Pepper Sauce (page 344).

WELSH RABBIT (RAREBIT) Prepare cheese sauce. Place in blender or food processor, add 1 teaspoon hot red-pepper sauce, Worcestershire sauce, or bitters, or a combination of the three, and purée for 30 seconds. Add 1 tablespoon cold unsalted butter and purée for another 30 seconds.

FISH AND SEAFOOD

ONE of the microwave oven's star turns is cooking seafood. It has become my preferred way to cook fish since the fish stays moist and cooks through absolutely evenly. It is no longer necessary to eat fish that verges on raw in the center in order to have fish that isn't dry and over-cooked on the outside.

While all the seafood first courses and main courses can be cooked in the microwave oven, it is the answer to a prayer when you are in a hurry to make dinner for one or two people. Simply plop the fish on one or two plates, with seasonings and a vegetable, if you wish; cover it tightly with microwave plastic wrap and cook. If you are cooking shellfish, use a soup bowl so as to catch all the delicious juices. For timings, see the recipes in this chapter and on pages 531–534.

Not all recipes can be adapted to a small oven. For those seafood recipes that are reasonable in a small oven, particularly recipes for one or two people, times are given. You can adapt the fish dishes yourself by consulting FISH in the Dictionary for timings. If you are cooking a recipe for two portions and wish to cook it on two plates, up the timing for two portions by 1½ minutes and switch the plates halfway through the cooking: put the plate on the microwave rack on the bottom of the oven and the plate on the bottom of the oven on the rack. Or you can cook each plate separately; the first will stay warm while the second cooks.

If you like fish and shellfish combinations, remember to time the cooking of the dish by the shellfish, which takes longer to cook. Always place the shellfish toward the edge of the dish. See Scrod with Clams Livornese (page 193) as an example. For soups and stews using combinations of fish and shellfish, see Soups, pages 82–116.

I often serve fish in small portions as a first course. Aside from portion size, I don't know too many other distinctions between a first course seafood dish and a main course one. If I am serving fish as a main course, I serve a soup or a vegetable dish first. Pâté would be good also.

Make sure that the flavors or sauce of one course don't interfere with the next. See Savory Sauces (pages 360–384) for wonderful embellishments for seafood.

Once you have gotten the hang of preparing fish in the microwave oven, I think you will do it often.

CLAMS POSILLIPO

One of the standards of old-style Italian-American cooking, this is too good to forget. It can be made even more quickly and easily by substituting bottled spaghetti sauce for the Lightly Cooked Crushed Tomatoes. Decrease the salt and seasonings if you use bottled sauce. Be sure to serve the clams with a large spoon and Italian bread to mop up every last trace of sauce. Have an empty bowl ready for the shells. This dish is also good on top of linguine; one-half pound of linguine, cooked, will serve four.

If you want to use more than 24 clams, don't try to increase the recipe. Instead, once everyone has sat down, put a second batch in the oven. Cook the parsley and garlic ahead. That way, the last clams served are as hot as the first ones. *Serves 1 to 2 as a main course, 2 to 3 as a first course*

3 tablespoons olive oil
⅓ cup parsley leaves, preferably flat-leaf parsley
3 large cloves garlic, smashed, peeled and sliced
2 tablespoons white wine
½ cup Lightly Cooked Crushed Tomatoes (page 339), canned crushed tomatoes, drained, or bottled spaghetti sauce

¾ teaspoon kosher salt
⅛ teaspoon dried oregano
⅛ teaspoon freshly ground black pepper
18 littleneck clams (about 2¼ pounds), well scrubbed and drained

1. Heat oil in a 2-quart soufflé dish, uncovered, at 100% for 3 minutes. Add parsley and garlic and cook, uncovered, for 3 minutes longer.

2. Remove from oven. Stir in wine, tomatoes or tomato sauce, salt, oregano, and pepper. Arrange clams on top, hinge ends down. Cover tightly with microwave plastic wrap. Cook at 100% for 7 minutes, until clams open.

3. Remove from oven. Uncover and serve hot.

To serve 2 to 3 as a main course. Use ½ cup parsley, increase garlic to 5 cloves and tomatoes or tomato sauce to ⅔ cup, and use 24 clams. Cook clams, covered, in a 14″ × 11″ × 2″ dish at 100% for 9 minutes.

VARIATION

MUSSELS POSILLIPO Substitute 2 pounds mussels for 24 clams and proceed as for Clams Posillipo for 2 to 3. Serves 2 to 3 as a main course, 6 as a first course.

MOULES MARINIÈRES

This is an addictive French classic. Fortunately, it is also easy to make. It is worthwhile paying a little extra for farmed mussels from Maine. They are very clean. Never judge mussels by their size: little shells often have better-tasting mussels. There will be more per pound, but the timing will be the same.

Serve with bread and spoons and put a bowl for shells on the table. If you want to serve more than 4 pounds, cook in two batches as for Clams Posillipo (page 159).   *Serves 2 as a main course, 3 to 4 as a first course*

2 pounds mussels (about 18 per pound), well scrubbed and beards removed
½ cup white wine
4 cloves garlic, smashed, peeled and cut in half

Freshly ground black pepper
¼ cup chopped parsley
⅓ cup heavy cream
Kosher salt

1. Combine mussels, wine, garlic, and pepper in a 2-quart soufflé dish. Cover tightly with microwave plastic wrap. Cook at 100% for 8 minutes.

2. Remove from oven. Uncover and remove mussels to a serving bowl. Strain liquid. Add parsley, cream, and salt. Cook, uncovered, at 100% for 1 minute.

3. Remove from oven. Pour liquid over mussels and serve hot.

To serve 4 as a main course. Double all ingredients. Divide ingredients equally between two 11″ × 8½″ dishes. Cook simultaneously, using a rack (page 18), for 14 minutes. Prepare sauce as for 2 servings and serve hot.

To serve 1 as a main course. Use 1 pound mussels. Halve remaining ingredients. Cook in a very large soup bowl or in a 1½-quart soufflé dish, tightly covered, for 3 minutes. Prepare sauce as for 2 servings and serve hot. (If using a small oven, cook for 6 minutes.)

VARIATIONS

MUSSELS WITH FENNEL Strew ½ pound thinly sliced fennel bulb over each 2 pounds of mussels; substitute 1 tablespoon finely chopped fennel tops for the parsley. Add a knife-point of powdered saffron to the white wine. Add 1 tablespoon Pernod, if you like. Cook as for Moules Marinières. Serve as is for a thinning version, or add the cream, or substitute 1 tablespoon olive oil for the cream.

MUSSELS WITH DILL Line the bottom of a 2-quart soufflé dish with 1 carrot, trimmed, peeled and sliced. Proceed as for Moules Marinières, covering 2 pounds of mussels with 8 large dill sprigs. Substitute 1 tablespoon fresh lemon juice for cream at end.

LINGUINE WITH MUSSELS, PESTO AND BELL PEPPER RELISH

Seafood can be a fabulous topping for pasta, especially mussels, which exude lots of rich-tasting liquid when cooked. In this beautiful dish, which can now be made in winter as well as summer, the black of the mussel shells, the brilliant colors of the pepper relish, and the green of the sauce combine for a delightful dish. *Serves 4 as a main course, 8 as a first course*

1 pound linguine
¼ cup white wine
4 cloves garlic, smashed,
   peeled and sliced
Bell Pepper Relish
   (page 164) made
   with flat-leaf parsley

1½ pounds mussels
   (about 18 mussels
   per pound), well
   scrubbed and
   beards removed
½ cup Pesto (page 383)
Kosher salt
Freshly ground black
   pepper

1. Put a large pot of salted water on to boil for the linguine. When it is boiling, add linguine and cook until al dente.

2. While the pasta cooks, combine wine and garlic in a 2-quart soufflé dish. Mound relish in the center of the dish. Arrange mussels around relish. Cover tightly with microwave plastic wrap. Cook at 100% for 6 minutes, until mussels open.

3. Drain pasta well.

4. Remove mussels from oven. Uncover and transfer mussels to a bowl. Stir Pesto, salt and pepper into relish mixture. Add drained pasta and stir to coat. Scatter mussels over all and serve warm.

SAUTÉ OF BAY SCALLOPS

A browning dish really comes into its own here. If you have gloriously good bay scallops, this is the simplest way to cook them. Serve them accompanied by nothing but a wedge of lemon. If bay scallops are unavailable, cut sea scallops in quarters. Scallops have a small, hard, shiny muscle running up the outside of the main muscle in a small strip. Remove these external muscles; they pull off easily. They may be saved to include in fish stock. *Serves 2 as a main course, 4 as a first course*

1 tablespoon unsalted butter, cut into bits	12 ounces bay scallops, external muscle removed, rinsed and patted dry

1. Heat a 9-inch round or 8-inch square browning dish at 100% for 4 minutes. Add butter and quickly swirl it around the dish. When butter is nearly melted, add scallops. Stir to coat with the butter and arrange in a single layer. Cook, uncovered, at 100% for 1 minute 30 seconds.

2. Remove from oven. Serve hot.

To serve 1. Cook ½ pound bay scallops with 1 tablespoon butter in a small oven as for Sauté of Bay Scallops for 2 minutes.

VARIATIONS

HERBED BAY SCALLOPS Add 2 tablespoons finely minced parsley, 1 finely minced shallot, and 1 tablespoon finely minced fresh herb—tarragon, basil, thyme, mint, or dill—to listed ingredients. Toss scallops with herbs and shallots before cooking. Serves 2 as a main course, 4 as a first course.

CURRIED BAY SCALLOPS Heat a 10-inch square browning dish for 4 minutes. Add 2 tablespoons butter and heat, uncovered, for 3 minutes. Add 1¼ pounds scallops and 1 tablespoon curry powder and stir well. Cook for 2 minutes. Remove scallops to a serving dish. Add 1 tablespoon fresh lemon juice and ¼ teaspoon salt to liquid and pour over scallops. Serves 4 as a main course, 8 as a first course.

SCALLOPS WITH BELL PEPPER RELISH

The fresh-tasting relish is used in Linguine with Mussels (page 162), but it would be good under any simple fish fillet. Timings would be as for fillets. *Serves 2*

½ **pound sea scallops, external muscle removed (see preceding recipe), rinsed and patted dry**
1 **teaspoon fresh lemon juice**
1 **teaspoon kosher salt**
⅛ **teaspoon freshly ground black pepper**

BELL PEPPER RELISH
¼ **cup diced red bell pepper, stemmed, seeded and deribbed**
¼ **cup diced green bell pepper, stemmed, seeded and deribbed**

¼ **cup canned corn kernels in water, drained**
¼ **cup canned tomatoes, diced, with liquid**
1 **scallion, trimmed and thinly sliced (green and white parts)**
1 **tablespoon coarsely chopped fresh coriander or flat-leaf parsley**
½ **teaspoon Fiery Pepper Sauce (page 344) or 1½ teaspoons roasted chili pepper, finely minced**

1. Stir together scallops, lemon juice, ½ teaspoon of the salt, and pepper. Set aside.

2. Combine relish ingredients. Spread in an even layer on a dinner plate. Arrange scallops in a single layer on top of relish. Cover tightly with microwave plastic wrap. Cook at 100% for 3 minutes.

3. Remove from oven. Let stand, covered, for 2 minutes. Prick plastic, uncover, add remaining salt and serve immediately.

To serve 4. Increase peppers, corn and tomatoes to ⅓ cup each and double remaining ingredients. Proceed as for 2 servings, cooking in a 2-quart soufflé dish for 7 minutes.

To serve 8. Increase peppers, corn and tomatoes to ⅔ cup each and double remaining ingredients. Proceed as for 2 servings, cooking in a 14″ × 11″ × 2″ dish for 11 minutes.

SHRIMP WITH ZUCCHINI

This is a pretty pink and green dish to have when you want to be nice to yourself or a cherished friend. If you are not having a first course, add some cooked rice or a large salad. If you cannot find large shrimp, substitute the same weight of medium shrimp. *Serves 1*

½ cup grated zucchini with skin (about 1 small zucchini)
1 teaspoon kosher salt
¼ teaspoon plus a pinch freshly ground black pepper
3 tablespoons Shrimp Cream (page 352)

½ teaspoon fresh lemon juice
⅛ teaspoon minced fresh tarragon
6 large shrimp (about ⅓ pound), peeled and deveined

1. Stir together zucchini, salt, and ¼ teaspoon pepper.

2. Combine Shrimp Cream, lemon juice, remaining pepper, and tarragon. Spread mixture on a dinner plate. Mound zucchini in center of plate and arrange shrimp in a circle around zucchini. Cover tightly with microwave plastic wrap. Cook at 100% for 1 minute 15 seconds. (If using a small oven, cook for 2 minutes 30 seconds.)

3. Remove from oven. Uncover and serve hot.

To serve 2. Double all ingredients. Proceed as for 1 serving, cooking shrimp and zucchini in a 10-inch quiche dish for 2 minutes 30 seconds, until shrimp are pink.

To serve 6. Multiply all ingredient quantities by 6. Proceed as for 1 serving, cooking shrimp and zucchini in a 14″ × 11″ × 2″ dish for 4 minutes. Slit plastic, stir, and re-cover. Cook for 3 minutes longer, until shrimp are pink.

SZECHUAN SHRIMP WITH CHILI PASTE

This is a simply prepared version of one of the hot and spicy dishes so popular today. *Serves 1 as a main course, 3 as a first course*

½ pound medium shrimp (20 to 24 per pound), shelled and deveined
1 scallion, thinly sliced
1 clove garlic, smashed and peeled

2 teaspoons Super Hot Chili Paste (page 344) or bottled paste
2 teaspoons soy sauce
1 teaspoon freshly grated ginger
1 teaspoon mirin or sherry

1. Toss together all ingredients until shrimp are evenly coated. Let stand for 5 minutes.

2. Arrange shrimp spoke-fashion, with tails in the center, on a dinner plate. Cover tightly with microwave plastic wrap. Cook at 100% for 2 minutes. (If using a small oven, cook for 3 minutes.)

3. Remove from oven. Uncover and serve hot.

To serve 3 as a main course. Double all ingredients. Proceed as for 1 serving, arranging shrimp in a 10-inch quiche dish and cooking for 3 minutes.

To serve 6 as a main course. Multiply all ingredient quantities by 4. Arrange shrimp in a 14″ × 11″ × 2″ dish. Cover and cook at 100% for 4 minutes. Slit plastic, stir, and re-cover. Cook for 3 minutes longer, until shrimp are pink.

SHRIMP CREOLE

Shrimp turned into a pretty, rich and fragrant concoction with vegetables, hot peppers and Louisiana's characteristic Brown Roux is a great American classic. The microwave oven turns the usually patience-trying Brown Roux into an easy success. The Shrimp Butter is a French touch worth trying. If you don't have time, substitute 2 tablespoons unsalted butter. *Serves 6 as a main course with rice*

4 tablespoons Shrimp Butter (page 351)

2 cups peeled and cubed yellow onions (about 1 pound)

5 cloves garlic, smashed and peeled

1½ cups cubed red bell pepper, stemmed, seeded and deribbed

1½ cups cubed green bell pepper, stemmed, seeded and deribbed

1¼ pounds medium shrimp (20 to 24 per pound), peeled and deveined (shells saved for Shrimp Butter)

1½ cups fresh Italian plum tomatoes, cored and quartered

1 teaspoon hot red-pepper sauce

Freshly ground black pepper

2 teaspoons kosher salt

4 tablespoons Brown Roux (page 338)

4 cups cooked white rice

1. Heat Shrimp Butter in a 2-quart soufflé dish, uncovered, at 100% for 1 minute. Add onions and garlic and stir to coat. Cook, uncovered, at 100% for 2 minutes. Stir in peppers. Cook, uncovered, for 3 minutes longer.

2. Remove dish from oven. Mound vegetables in center and arrange shrimp around vegetables. Scatter tomatoes over all. Cover tightly with microwave plastic wrap. Cook at 100% for 2 minutes. Uncover and stir well. Re-cover and cook for 2 minutes longer.

3. Remove from oven. Uncover and add pepper sauce, pepper, salt, and roux; combine well. Cover tightly and cook at 100% for 3 minutes. Serve over rice.

CURRIED SHRIMP

This is another recipe where shrimp lends its rich taste and light texture to a vibrantly flavored dish. Serve with Tomato Pilaf (page 131), made ahead and left covered, or steamed rice—white, brown, or saffron.

It's nice to know that you can feed so many people with 2 pounds of shrimp, considering what they cost. This is a great dish for a buffet.   *Serves 8 to 10*

 4 tablespoons unsalted butter

10 cloves garlic, smashed and peeled

 1 cup chopped onion

¼ cup fresh coriander leaves, coarsely chopped

1½ teaspoons Spice Powder III (page 346)

 2 red bell peppers, stemmed, seeded, deribbed, and cut into 2-inch chunks

 1 pound green apples, peeled and cut into 2-inch chunks (2 cups)

1½ cups cauliflower florets (about 1 pound)

 2 pounds medium shrimp (20 to 24 per pound), peeled and deveined

½ cup Coconut Cream (page 354) or canned unsweetened coconut cream

½ cup Chicken Broth (page 331) or canned chicken broth

¼ teaspoon Fiery Pepper Sauce (page 344)

 2 tablespoons fresh lime juice
   Kosher salt
   Freshly ground black pepper

1. Heat butter in a 14″ × 11″ × 2″ dish, uncovered, at 100% for 3 minutes. Stir in garlic, onions, coriander, and spice powder. Cook, uncovered, at 100% for 4 minutes.

2. Remove from oven. Add peppers, apples, and cauliflower and stir to coat. Cook, uncovered, at 100% for 5 minutes.

3. Remove from oven. Mound vegetables in center of dish. Arrange shrimp around inside rim of dish. Pour Coconut Cream and broth over all. Cover tightly with microwave plastic wrap. Cook at 100% for 4 minutes.

4. Uncover and stir well. Add pepper sauce. Cover tightly and cook at 100% for 4 minutes.

5. Remove from oven and uncover. Season with lime juice, salt, and pepper. Serve with rice.

STEAMED CRABS

I can't eat crabs. Sadly, I'm allergic to them. Everybody else in the kitchen had a feast the day we made these. We spread newspaper on the floor and everybody took turns whacking crabs with a hammer and picking out the meat. Purists eat them plain or with just a squeeze of lemon. For the others, make a bowl of Mayonnaise (page 382) and a bowl of Chunky Tomato Sauce (page 374) spiced up with some Fiery Pepper Sauce (page 344) or with commercial hot red-pepper sauce. On a hot day, steamed crabs are ideal for a picnic, with coleslaw, potato salad, or Corn Custard (page 306), and pitchers of cold beer. If you have a crowd, do two sets of crabs. They can be eaten cold or hot.

For other dishes, count on about ¾ cup picked meat from every 6 crabs. How much roe you get will depend on the number of she-crabs. *Makes 24 crabs*

24 live crabs (¼ to ⅓ pound each)

½ cup Crab Boil (page 346) or commercial crab boil mix

1 lemon, cut into wedges

1. Place all ingredients in a 14″ × 11″ × 2″ oval dish. Cover tightly with microwave plastic wrap. Cook at 100% for 25 minutes.

2. Remove from oven. Uncover and serve hot.

To steam 12 crabs. Halve all ingredients. Cook crabs in a 4-quart soufflé dish for 15 minutes.

To steam 6 crabs. Divide all ingredient quantities by 4. Cook crabs in a 9-inch square dish for 9 minutes.

FISH KABOBS

Into each life a cocktail party falls from time to time. These little kabobs are quick to make and perfect. Larger kabobs make an easy dinner and use up odds and ends of fish from making Harlequin of Fish Medallions (page 171).   *Makes 24 cocktail kabobs*

6 slices fresh ginger, peeled and sliced ⅛ inch thick
½ cup canned pineapple juice
3 tablespoons tamari soy
3 cloves garlic, smashed and peeled
¼ teaspoon hot red-pepper sauce

½ red bell pepper, stemmed, seeded, deribbed and cut into ½-inch pieces
2 scallions, cut into ½-inch pieces
6 ounces fish fillet (any fish is fine), cut into 24 cubes, ½ inch each

1. Combine ginger, pineapple juice, soy, garlic, and red-pepper sauce in a 12-inch quiche dish. Cook, uncovered, at 100% for 5 minutes.

2. Skewer pepper, scallions, and fish pieces on tooth-picks, alternating 2 pieces of fish with pepper and scallion on each. Roll each in prepared sauce. Arrange spoke-fashion around the inside rim of a 10-inch quiche dish. Cover tightly with microwave plastic wrap. Cook at 100% for 1 minute to 1 minute 30 seconds.

3. Remove from oven. Uncover and serve hot with sauce on the side.

Arrange skewers spoke-fashion.

To serve 2 as a main course. Prepare sauce; increase fish or chicken to ½ pound. Use 1 whole pepper and 4 scallions. Cut fillet and vegetables into 2-inch chunks and arrange on 8-inch wooden skewers. Proceed as for Fish Kabobs, cooking for 2 minutes 30 seconds. Serve over rice, if desired.

VARIATION

CHICKEN KABOBS Substitute 6 ounces boneless chicken breast for the fish fillet. Proceed as for Fish Kabobs.

HARLEQUIN OF FISH MEDALLIONS

This is one of the prettiest and best dishes I made while working on this book. The evenly shaped medallions cook perfectly and look attractive. They do, however, leave lots of fish trimmings. These can be used in Swordfish Quenelles (page 49) or in fish farce to stuff Paupiettes (page 174). The fish can be cut into 2-inch cubes; it will be a less striking dish, but there will be almost no odds and ends. Swordfish medallions are prettier with all three kinds of peppers; for salmon, use only the red and yellow. Tuna can be substituted, but it is less decorative than the others because of its color when cooked. *Serves 6 as a main course, 12 as a first course*

1½ cups Red Pepper Purée (page 343)
2½ pounds swordfish or salmon steaks (about 1½ inches thick), skinned, boned and cut into 12 medallions, 2 inches each (page 533)
Kosher salt
Freshly ground black pepper

¼ cup stemmed, seeded, deribbed and julienned red bell pepper, strips ¼ inch wide
¼ cup stemmed, seeded, deribbed and julienned yellow bell pepper, strips ¼ inch wide
¼ cup stemmed, seeded, deribbed and julienned green bell pepper, strips ¼ inch wide

1. Pour purée over the bottom of a 14″ × 11″ × 2″ dish to a depth of ¼ inch. Arrange medallions on top of purée, 1 inch apart, in a ring around inside edge of dish. Sprinkle with salt and pepper. Scatter pepper strips over fish and in center of dish. Cover tightly with microwave plastic wrap. Cook at 100% for 6 minutes.

2. Remove from oven. Uncover and serve hot.

To serve 1 as a main course. Pool 3 tablespoons purée on a dinner plate. Arrange 2 medallions (cut from ½ pound fish) on purée; scatter juliennes from ¼ pepper of each color on top. Cover and cook at 100% for 1 minute 30 seconds.

To serve 2 as a main course. Pool ⅓ cup purée on a 9-inch pie plate. Arrange 4 medallions (cut from 1 pound fish) on purée; scatter juliennes from ½ pepper of each color on top. Cover and cook at 100% for 2 minutes 30 seconds to 3 minutes.

To serve 3 as a main course. Pool ¾ cup purée in an 11″ × 8½″ × 2″ dish. Arrange 6 medallions (cut from 1½ pounds fish) on purée; scatter juliennes from ¾ pepper of each color on top. Cover and cook at 100% for 4 minutes.

VARIATION

HARLEQUIN OF FISH MEDALLIONS WITH WATER-CRESS SAUCE Substitute an equal amount of Watercress Sauce (page 369) for Red Pepper Purée.

Use a cooky cutter to cut fish steaks into medallions. Save scraps for another use.

SALMON MEDALLIONS

This is quick, simple, and good. Cod would be very good in this recipe in place of salmon. If you want a second vegetable, add spinach. For a slightly spicy dish, add 1 tablespoon Dijon mustard to marinade. (See Harlequin of Fish Medallions, page 171.) *Serves 3*

1 tablespoon olive oil	3 medium mushrooms
1½ teaspoons fresh	(about ¼ pound),
lemon juice	cut into ¼-inch
1 teaspoon kosher salt	slices
Large pinch freshly	1 small yellow onion,
ground black	peeled and cut into
pepper	⅛-inch slices
1½ pounds filleted	1½ pounds spinach,
salmon or cod (1½	stemmed, washed
inches thick), cut	and dried (optional)
into 6 medallions,	
2 inches each (page	
533)	

1. Combine oil, lemon juice, salt, and pepper in an 11″ × 8½″ × 2″ oval dish. Dip both sides of medallions in marinade to coat; let stand in marinade for 15 minutes.

2. Arrange 3 medallions along each short side of dish. Toss together mushrooms and onions and place in center of dish. Cover tightly with microwave plastic wrap. Cook at 100% for 4 minutes.

3. Remove from oven and pierce plastic with the tip of a sharp knife. Uncover and remove fish to a serving platter.

4. Return vegetables to oven. If spinach is used, make a circle of it around vegetables. Cook, uncovered, at 100% for 2 minutes longer.

5. Remove from oven. Pour remaining vegetables and cooking juices over fish and serve immediately.

To serve 1. Combine 2 medallions (cut from ½ pound of fish), 1 teaspoon oil, ½ teaspoon lemon juice, ¼ teaspoon salt, and pepper. Proceed as for 3 servings, using 1 mushroom and ⅓ small onion. Cook on a dinner plate, reducing time to 1 minute 30 seconds.

To serve 2. Combine 4 medallions (cut from 1 pound of fish), 2 teaspoons oil, 1 teaspoon lemon juice, ½ teaspoon salt, and pepper. Proceed as for 3 servings, using 2 mushrooms and ⅔ small onion. Cook on a 9-inch pie plate for 2 minutes 30 seconds to 3 minutes.

To serve 6. Double all ingredients. Proceed as for 3 servings, cooking medallions in a 14″ × 11″ × 2″ dish for 6 minutes.

*Arrange medallions
around the inside rim of
dish and place vegetables
in center.*

PAUPIETTES OF SOLE STUFFED WITH SALMON

This is the kind of food that people usually ate only in restaurants. With the advent of the microwave oven, paupiettes can be made easily at home. Yours will be better than the restaurant's because the stuffing will cook through without the fish getting overcooked. Paupiettes are usually served with a sauce, but it is no longer absolutely necessary since microwave-cooked fish stays moist. Use a Fish Velouté (page 367), Curry Velouté (page 367), Watercress Sauce (page 369), Shrimp Cream (page 352), or Beurre Blanc (page 363), if you like. Allow 3 tablespoons of sauce under each first course serving of a single paupiette, ⅓ cup under each main course portion. One butterflied shrimp for each paupiette is an elegant addition. Add 5 seconds to the cooking time for each shrimp added. *Serves 2 as a main course, 4 as a first course*

STUFFING

4 ounces skinless,
boneless salmon

2 tablespoons heavy
cream

½ teaspoon kosher salt
Large pinch freshly
ground black
pepper

½ teaspoon fresh lemon
juice

2 sole fillets (about 5
ounces each), each
cut in half
lengthwise

1. Place stuffing ingredients in the workbowl of a food processor. Process until smooth.

2. Place 2 tablespoons of the mixture on one end of fillet. Starting from that end, roll fillet lengthwise around mixture. Secure ends together. Repeat until all are done. You should have 4 white circles with pink centers. Arrange paupiettes in a circle around inside rim of a 9" × ½" round dish. Do not let them touch. Cover tightly with microwave plastic wrap. Cook at 100% for 3 minutes.

3. Remove from oven. Uncover carefully and serve hot with or without sauce.

To serve 4 as a main course, 8 as a first course. Double all ingredients. Proceed as for 2 servings, arranging paupiettes inside the rim of a 14" × 11" × 2" dish and cooking for 5 minutes.

VARIATIONS

PAUPIETTES STUFFED WITH DUXELLES Stuff fillets with ½ cup plus 1 tablespoon Duxelles (page 340) and cook as for Paupiettes of Sole Stuffed with Salmon.

PAUPIETTES WITH PROVENÇALE FISH FARCE Make a fish purée by grinding 6 ounces skinned and boned fatty fish in food processor. Add ¼ cup finely chopped red bell pepper, 1½ tablespoons pitted and chopped Niçoise olives, 1½ teaspoons chopped scallion, and freshly ground black pepper. Stir to combine. Stuff fillets with mixture and proceed as for Paupiettes of Sole Stuffed with Salmon.

SWORDFISH WITH TOMATO AND BASIL

This tastes as fresh as summer, and it is diet food as well.
There will be lots of nice sauce. Serve it with rice, couscous,
or millet if the diet isn't too strict.   *Serves 2 as a main
course*

3 large slices ripe tomato	**½ teaspoon olive oil**
4 large fresh basil leaves	**½ teaspoon fresh lemon juice**
¾ pound swordfish steak (1 inch thick)	**Kosher salt**
	Freshly ground black pepper

1. Arrange tomato slices in a single layer on a large
dinner plate. Place 2 basil leaves on top. Center swordfish
over tomatoes. Add oil, lemon juice, salt, and pepper. Place
remaining basil leaves on top of fish. Cover tightly with
microwave plastic wrap. Cook at 100% for 4 minutes.

2. Remove from oven. Pierce plastic with the tip of a
sharp knife and let stand, covered, for 2 minutes. Uncover
and serve hot.

To serve 3 to 4. Double all ingredients. Cook fish in an 11"
× 8½" × 2" dish for 5 minutes 30 seconds.

To serve 6 to 8. Multiply all ingredient quantities by 4.
Cook fish in a 14" × 11" × 2" dish for 9 minutes.

SALAD BAR DIET DELIGHT

For people on a hurry and cooking for themselves or a small
number of people, there is a new and convenient way to
shop abroad in the land. It is the salad bar, where you can
find an assortment of vegetables, washed, cut up, and ready
to use. For this recipe, there is no single group of vegetables
that you have to use. Make up an assortment that has color
and contrast. Put the slower-cooking vegetables around the
fish, the quicker-cooking vegetables on top. If you are using
cherry tomatoes, prick the skin once with the tip of a knife.
Do not use all the vegetables mentioned below, just an
attractive selection. For those not on a diet, serve with a
bowl of Watercress Sauce (page 369).   *Serves 1*

1 swordfish steak, ¾ inch thick (about ½ pound)

6 ounces assorted vegetables: some *slow-cooking*, such as peeled and sliced carrots, green beans, red cabbage, broccoli florets, cauliflower florets, peas, sugar snap peas, cherry tomatoes; some *quick-cooking*, such as asparagus, sliced red onion or scallions, sliced mushrooms, sliced green or yellow summer squash, sliced red and green bell peppers

Kosher salt

Freshly ground black pepper

1. Center fish on a dinner plate. Arrange slower-cooking vegetables around fish. Scatter remaining, quicker-cooking vegetables over all. Cover tightly with microwave plastic wrap. Cook at 100% for 4 minutes. (If using a small oven, cook for 5 or 6 minutes.)

2. Remove from oven. Uncover and sprinkle with salt and pepper to taste. Serve hot.

To serve 2. Double all ingredients. Divide ingredients equally between 2 dinner plates. Cook simultaneously, using a rack (page 18), for 8 minutes–10 minutes in a small oven.

Vegetables arranged on and around fish

JUST FOR THE HALIBUT

This is another simple, quickly prepared fish dish. To butterfly a shrimp, firmly hold it flat on a kitchen surface. Cut it in half from head to tail, leaving the tail intact.

Serves 1

1 teaspoon olive oil
½ pound halibut fillet
(about ½ inch thick)
4 medium shrimp in
shell, butterflied
4 sprigs fresh chervil,
fresh tarragon or
flat-leaf parsley

2 thin slices lemon, with
peel
1 tablespoon white wine
Kosher salt
Freshly ground black
pepper

1. Brush a large dinner plate with oil. Place fish in center and arrange 2 shrimp on either side. Sprinkle with herbs. Place lemon slices on top. Add wine, salt, and pepper. Cover tightly with microwave plastic wrap. Cook at 100% for 3 minutes. (If using a small oven, cook for 4 minutes 30 seconds.)

2. Remove from oven. Pierce plastic with the tip of a sharp knife. Let stand, covered, for 3 minutes. Uncover and serve hot.

To serve 2. Double all ingredients. Proceed as for single serving, cooking in a 10-inch quiche dish for 4 minutes 30 seconds.

To serve 4. Multiply all ingredient quantities by 4. Proceed as for single serving, cooking in a 13½″ × 9½″ × 2″ dish for 6 minutes.

To serve 6. Multiply all ingredient quantities, except shrimp, by 6. Use 12 shrimp. Proceed as for single serving, cooking in a 14″ × 11″ × 2″ dish for 8 minutes.

FISH WITH CURRIED CABBAGE

I invented this dish one day when I had salmon left from making the Harlequin of Fish Medallions on page 171. I liked it so much that I now make it on purpose with a wide variety of fish. Cod, swordfish, sea scallops, flounder, whiting, tuna, grouper, rockfish, and monkfish all work as well as salmon. If using monkfish, increase cooking time to 10 minutes. *Serves 3 to 4 as a main course.*

2 tablespoons unsalted
   butter
2 teaspoons curry
   powder
½ cup thinly sliced
   yellow onion
3 cups finely shredded
   green cabbage

¾ pound salmon fillet,
   skinned and cut into
   2-inch chunks
2 teaspoons kosher salt
Freshly ground black
   pepper
1 teaspoon fresh lemon
   juice

1. Heat butter in a 2-quart soufflé dish, uncovered, at 100% for 2 minutes. Add curry powder, onions, and cabbage and stir to coat.

2. Cover tightly with microwave plastic wrap and cook at 100% for 4 minutes. Remove from oven and stir.

3. Mound cabbage mixture in center of dish and arrange salmon around cabbage. Sprinkle salt, pepper, and lemon juice over all. Cover tightly with microwave plastic wrap and cook at 100% for 8 minutes.

4. Remove from oven. Uncover and stir. Re-cover dish and let stand for 3 minutes before serving.

BLUEFISH FILLETS WITH MUSTARD AND DILL

When bluefish are absolutely fresh they make for great eating. This extremely quick sauce is akin to the sauce served with gravlax. It lets the flavor of the bluefish shine through. If you are using frozen bluefish—those who fish often have a surplus—increase cooking time to 3 minutes 30 seconds. *Serves 1*

2 teaspoons Dijon
   mustard
2 teaspoons chopped
   fresh dill
¾ teaspoon fresh lemon
   juice
½ teaspoon vegetable oil
¼ teaspoon kosher salt
¼ teaspoon granulated
   sugar

¼ teaspoon freshly
   ground black
   pepper
1 piece bluefish fillet
   with skin (about ½
   pound)
4 thin slices tomato
4 thin slices zucchini,
   cut on the diagonal

1. Combine mustard, dill, lemon juice, oil, salt, sugar, and pepper and stir until smooth. Set aside one quarter of mustard mixture. Rub remaining mixture into fish.

2. Arrange fish on half of a dinner plate. Cover the other half of the plate with alternating, overlapping slices of tomato and zucchini. Spread remaining mustard mixture over vegetables. Cover tightly with microwave plastic wrap. Cook at 100% for 2 minutes. (If using a small oven, cook for 3 minutes 30 seconds.)

3. Remove from oven. Uncover and serve hot.

To serve 2. Double all ingredients. Divide ingredients equally between 2 dinner plates and arrange each as for single serving. Cook simultaneously, tightly covered, using a rack (page 18), for 4 minutes.

To serve 4. Multiply all ingredient quantities by 4. Proceed as for single serving, arranging fillets around the inside rim of a 11″ × 8½″ × 2″ dish and placing vegetables in the center. Cook, tightly covered, for 5 minutes.

BLUEFISH WITH FENNEL

Bluefish, which is slightly oily, pairs well with ingredients with a vigorous taste. Fennel is just about perfect and provides a little crunch as well.   *Serves 2*

1 tablespoon olive oil	bluefish fillets (¾
½ large fennel bulb,	pound)
split, cored and cut	½ teaspoon kosher salt
into ¼-inch slices;	Large pinch freshly
also use leaves	ground black
(about ¾ cup	pepper
together)	1 tablespoon Pernod

1. Place oil and fennel in an 8-inch square dish. Cook, uncovered, at 100% for 1 minute.

2. Remove from oven. Arrange fillets on top of fennel, head to tail. If the fillets are too long for the dish, tuck excess under the tail end. Sprinkle with salt and pepper; drizzle Pernod over all. Cover tightly with microwave plastic wrap. Cook at 100% for 3 minutes 30 seconds.

3. Remove from oven. Uncover and serve hot.

To serve 4. Double all ingredients. Cook fennel and oil in an 11″ × 8½″ × 2″ dish for 2 minutes. Add fillets, sprinkle with salt, pepper, and Pernod, cover, and cook at 100% for 5 minutes.

SCROD FILLETS WITH LINGUINE PESTO

Scrod is young cod. Sole, flounder, or snapper can also be used. *Serves 1*

2 ounces linguine	**1 scrod or cod fillet**
¼ cup Pesto (page 383)	**(about 6 ounces)**

1. Cook linguine until al dente. Drain well.

2. Toss three quarters of the Pesto with linguine while still warm. Arrange in a layer on a large dinner plate. Place fish on top of pasta. Drizzle remaining Pesto over all. Cover tightly with microwave plastic wrap. Cook at 100% for 4 minutes. (If using a small oven, cook for 6 to 7 minutes.)

3. Remove from oven. Uncover and serve hot.

To serve 2. Increase Pesto to ⅓ cup and double amounts of linguine and fish. Follow recipe for single serving, cooking in a 10-inch quiche dish for 6 minutes. You can also use 2 dinner plates: double all ingredients, divide them between the plates, and cook simultaneously, using a rack (page 18) and switching plates from top to bottom after 4 minutes, for a total of 7 to 8 minutes.

To serve 4. Increase Pesto to ⅔ cup and multiply quantities of linguine and fish by 4. Proceed as for single serving, cooking in an 11″ × 8½″ × 2″ dish for 8 minutes.

SLICED FRESH TUNA WITH BROCCOLI FLORETS

This recipe and the next one both use fish and broccoli. The results are very different due to variations in the seasoning, the fish, and the cooking method. In this recipe, the broccoli and tomato can be replaced with sugar snap peas and sliced mushrooms, cauliflower and summer squash, or green beans and 1 teaspoon Oriental sesame oil. *Serves 1*

1 tuna steak (4 ounces), cut across the grain into ½-inch-thick slices	2 teaspoons soy sauce
	1 teaspoon rice wine vinegar
½ cup broccoli florets	½ teaspoon grated fresh ginger
2 tablespoons finely diced fresh tomato	1 small clove garlic, smashed and peeled
1 scallion, trimmed and thinly sliced into rings	¼ teaspoon granulated sugar

1. Arrange tuna in a single layer to cover about half a dinner plate. Toss together broccoli and tomato and place on uncovered part of plate.

2. Combine remaining ingredients. Drizzle over tuna and broccoli. Cover tightly with microwave plastic wrap. Cook at 100% for 1 minute 30 seconds. (If using a small oven, cook for 3 minutes.)

3. Remove from oven. Uncover and serve hot.

To serve 2. Double all ingredients. Divide ingredients equally between 2 dinner plates and arrange each as for single serving. Cook simultaneously, tightly covered, using a rack (page 18), for 3 minutes, changing position of the plates after 1 minute 30 seconds.

To serve 4. Multiply all ingredient quantities by 4. Arrange tuna slices around the inside rim of an 11″ × 8½″ × 2″ dish and place vegetables in the center in the center. Cover and cook at 100% for 4 minutes.

FLOUNDER FILLETS WITH BROCCOLI FLORETS

This is a contemporary, 5-minutes fish version of an old favorite, chicken divan. It is pretty and festive. The cheese makes the sauce, but it could be a herbed goat cheese or one of those readily available cheeses that come in foil-wrapped packages. Any simple white fillet of fish can be used instead of flounder. *Serves 1*

1 skinned flounder or
   gray sole fillet (about
   5 ounces)
Kosher salt
Freshly ground black
   pepper
3 broccoli stalks with
   florets, stems no
   longer than 2 inches
2 tablespoon heavy
   cream

1 tablespoon soft garlic
   and herb cheese, at
   room temperature
1 tablespoon Fish Broth
   (page 334), Chicken
   Broth (page 331) or
   canned chicken
   broth
2 teaspoons minced
   shallots
¼ teaspoon cornstarch

1. Sprinkle the skin side of fillet with salt and pepper.
Fold fillet in half lengthwise, skin side in, and center on a
large dinner plate.

2. Arrange the broccoli stalks in spoke-fashion around
the fish, tucking the ends under the fillet, if necessary.

3. Stir together cream, cheese, broth, shallots, and cornstarch until blended. Pour mixture over fish and broccoli.
Cover tightly with microwave plastic wrap. Cook at 100%
for 2 minutes 30 seconds. If using a small oven, cook for
4 minutes.

4. Remove from oven. Uncover and serve hot.

To serve 2. Double all ingredients. Proceed as for single
serving, cooking fillets in an 11″ × 8½″ × 2″ dish for 3
minutes 30 seconds to 4 minutes.

To serve 4. Multiply ingredient quantities by 4. Proceed as
for single serving, cooking fillets in a 13½ × 9½″ × 2″
dish for 5 minutes.

*Fillet of fish with thin
end doubled over for
even cooking*

FILLET OF SOLE WITH ALMONDS

The French discovered long ago that almonds are perfect with sole. Many fish pass under the name of sole in the United States (see page 593). What you want for this recipe is a small, tightly grained piece of fish.   *Serves 1*

2 tablespoons unsalted
   butter
2 tablespoons blanched,
   sliced almonds
1 tablespoon chopped
   parsley, preferably
   flat-leaf parsley

1 tablespoon white wine
2 tablespoons Chicken
   Broth (page 331) or
   canned chicken broth
1 sole fillet (about 6
   ounces)

   1. Heat 1 tablespoon of the butter in an 8-inch square browning dish, uncovered, at 100% for 1 minute 30 seconds. Stir in almonds and parsley. Cook for 1 minute longer, stirring once.

   2. Remove from oven. Add wine and broth. Fold the fillet in half lengthwise and place in center of dish. Cover tightly with microwave plastic wrap. Cook at 100% for 2 minutes. (If using a small oven, cook for 3 minutes 30 seconds.)

   3. Remove from oven. Uncover and remove fillet to a serving plate. Whisk the remaining 1 tablespoon butter into the sauce and spoon over the fillet. Serve hot.

To serve 2. Use the same amount of butter and double remaining ingredients. Heat half the butter for 2 minutes and cook for 2 minutes with almonds and parsley. Proceed as for single serving, cooking fish for 2 minutes 30 seconds.

To serve 4. Increase butter to 4 tablespoons and broth to ½ cup. Multiply other ingredient quantities by 4. Heat half the butter in a 10-inch square browning dish for 4 minutes and cook for 2 minutes with almonds and parsley. Proceed as for single serving, cooking fish for 4 to 5 minutes.

MONKFISH IN GREEN SAUCE

Monkfish has only recently become popular in America, though it has long been highly esteemed in Europe. This recipe is a variation of a Basque way of cooking fish. Serve it with baking potatoes that have been cooked in the microwave oven, then peeled and cut in chunks or with steamed rice.

Monkfish takes longer to cook than most fish, as does sturgeon, which could easily be substituted here. If you wish to substitute hake or whiting, reduce cooking time for fish to 3 minutes for two pieces.

Sometimes this cooking liquid is thickened with a sort of scrambled egg-white mixture instead of cornstarch, as in the recipe to serve 6.   *Serves 2*

⅓ cup white wine
⅓ cup Chicken Broth (page 331) or canned chicken broth
⅓ cup Clam Broth (page 511), Fish Broth (page 334) or bottled clam juice
½ small Spanish onion, peeled and cut in half
⅓ cup parsley leaves, preferably flat-leaf parsley
1 large clove garlic, smashed and peeled

3 tablespoons good-quality olive oil
2 pieces monkfish fillet (about 5 ounces each), trimmed of outer membrane
Kosher salt
Freshly ground black pepper
1 teaspoon cornstarch
1 tablespoon water
½ cup frozen peas, defrosted in a sieve under warm running water
1 tablespoon fresh lemon juice

1. Combine wine, Chicken Broth, and Clam Broth in a 9-inch pie plate. Cook, uncovered, at 100% for 9 minutes.

2. Place onion, parsley, and garlic in the workbowl of a food processor. Process until finely chopped. Scrape into broth mixture. Add 1 tablespoon of the olive oil and stir to combine.

3. Rub fillets with remaining 2 tablespoons olive oil and sprinkle with salt and pepper. Place fillets petal-fashion on top of onion mixture with the wide ends toward the outside of the dish and the narrow ends toward the center. Cover tightly with microwave plastic wrap. Cook at 100% for 5 minutes.

4. Remove from oven. Uncover and remove fish to a serving platter; keep warm.

5. Mix cornstarch and water. Stir into onion mixture. Sprinkle peas around inside edge of dish. Cover tightly with microwave plastic wrap. Cook at 100% for 2 minutes.

6. Remove from oven. Uncover and add salt and pepper to taste. Spoon mixture onto 2 dinner plates and place a fillet on top of each. Drizzle each fillet with lemon juice and serve.

To serve 6. Combine ½ cup *each* wine, Chicken Broth, and Clam Broth in an 11″ × 8″ oval dish. Chop ½ pound Spanish onion, 1 cup parsley leaves, and 4 cloves garlic in the food processor. Add to wine and broth with ½ cup oil. Cook, uncovered, at 100% for 10 minutes. Prepare 6 pieces monk-fish fillets and arrange in sauce as in step 3. Cover and cook at 100% for 8 minutes. Remove fish to a serving platter. Beat together 4 egg whites with 2 tablespoons lemon juice; whisk into sauce, and add peas. Cover and cook at 100% for 4 minutes, stirring once with a fork after 3 minutes. Remove from oven and stir again. Pour over fish. This larger quantity can also be thickened with cornstarch instead of egg whites. In that case, reduce oil to 3 tablespoons and use 2 tablespoons cornstarch mixed with 4 tablespoons water to thicken.

CATFISH FILLET WITH CORNBREAD STUFFING

Catfish used to be an iffy business at best; it tended to have a muddy flavor. Today, the fish is being farmed in many parts of the South. The fillets are a pleasure to cook. They are small with firm flesh, and they can be substituted in recipes calling for small fillets of sole. Here, they are made with a thoroughly southern stuffing. *Serves 1*

½ cup Cornbread
   Stuffing (page 356)
1 catfish fillet (7 to 8
   ounces)
1 teaspoon fresh lemon
   juice

¼ teaspoon kosher salt
   Freshly ground black
   pepper
2 teaspoons unsalted
   butter

1. Mound stuffing in the center of a large dinner plate to a height of 1 inch. Encircle the stuffing with the fillet, leaving some stuffing exposed in the center. Sprinkle fillet with lemon juice, salt, and pepper and dot with butter. Cover tightly with microwave plastic wrap. Cook at 100% for 2 minutes 30 seconds. (If using a small oven, cook for 4 minutes).

2. Remove from oven. Uncover and serve hot.

To serve 2. Double all ingredients. Proceed as for single serving. Arrange stuffed fillets around inside rim of a 10-inch quiche dish and cook for 3 minutes.

To serve 4. Multiply ingredient quantities by 4. Proceed as for single serving. Arrange stuffed fillets, evenly spaced, around the inside rim of a 13½″ × 9½″ × 2″ dish and cook for 5 minutes 30 seconds.

FILLET OF SOLE OVER CELERY

In this recipe, the sole is cut into strips that curl up alluringly when cooked. The dish looks like spring, all white and pale green, and has a light but especially good flavor.

Serves 1

2 center stalks celery
   with leaves, strung
   and sliced across,
   leaves left whole
1 tablespoon Fish Broth
   (page 334), Chicken
   Broth (page 331) or
   canned chicken broth
2 teaspoons unsalted
   butter

1 teaspoon green
   peppercorns in
   brine, drained
¼ teaspoon kosher salt
1 sole fillet (about 6
   ounces), cut across
   width into 4 strips
½ teaspoon fresh lemon
   juice
¼ teaspoon celery seed

1. Place sliced celery, broth, butter, peppercorns, and salt on a dinner plate. Cover with microwave plastic wrap. Cook at 100% for 2 minutes.

2. Remove from oven. Uncover and scatter celery leaves over mixture. Place fish, evenly spaced, on top of celery. Sprinkle with lemon juice and celery seeds. Cover tightly with microwave plastic wrap. Cook at 100% for 1 minute. (If using a small oven, cook for 2 minutes.)

3. Remove from oven. Uncover and serve hot.

To serve 2. Double all ingredients. Divide ingredients equally between 2 dinner plates. Proceed as for single serving, heating broth mixture simultaneously, using a rack (see page 18), for 4 minutes. Cook fish as in step 2 for 2 minutes.

SALMON STEAKS OVER CURRIED RICE

This is a good party dish. To serve eight, double the quantity of rice. Prepare two separate portions for four, first cooking one and then the other. Serve at the same time.   *Serves 4*

1⅓ cups long-grain rice	2 scallions (white and green parts), thinly sliced into rings
1 tablespoon unsalted butter	
1 tablespoon vegetable oil	2 tablespoons plain yogurt
1 small onion, peeled and finely chopped	1 teaspoon fresh lemon juice
1 small carrot, trimmed, peeled and finely chopped	4 salmon steaks (about 9 ounces each), ¾ inch thick
2 teaspoons curry powder	2 tablespoons Fresh Mango Chutney (page 471) or store-bought chutney
2⅔ cups Chicken Broth (page 331) or canned chicken broth	1 tablespoon water

1. Cook rice conventionally on the stove. Heat butter and oil in a small heavy saucepan over medium heat; add onions, carrots, and curry powder and sauté until the onion is wilted, about 5 minutes. Add rice and stir until well coated. Pour in the broth and heat to boiling. Reduce the heat to a simmer, cover the pot, and cook just until rice is tender but firm, about 15 minutes.

2. Stir together scallions, yogurt, and lemon juice. Add the rice and stir to coat.

3. Spread rice in a single layer in an 11″ × 8½″ × 2″ oval dish. Arrange the steaks on top of the rice spoke-fashion, with tails toward the center of the dish.

4. Combine chutney and water and brush over the steaks. Cover tightly with microwave plastic wrap. Cook at 100% for 9 minutes.

5. Remove from oven. Uncover and serve hot

COD MEXICAN

This is spicy, pretty, and quick, especially when you have Hot Pepper Sauce in the refrigerator. If you are planning to make this dish for a party, make the sauce the day before. Slip the fish into the oven just as everybody sits down. *Serves 2*

¼ **cup Hot Pepper Sauce**
    (page 343)
1 **pound skinned cod**
    fillet, cut into four
    2″ × 2″ × 1½″
    chunks

8 **fresh coriander leaves**
1 **teaspoon fresh lime**
    juice

1. Place sauce in a 2-quart soufflé dish. Arrange fish chunks, skin side down, spoke-fashion inside the rim of dish, with the wide ends toward the center.

2. Place 2 coriander leaves on each chunk and sprinkle juice over all. Cover tightly with microwave plastic wrap. Cook at 100% for 2 minutes 30 seconds. (In a small oven, cook for 5 minutes.)

3. Remove from oven. Uncover and serve hot.

To serve 4. Double all ingredients. Pour sauce into an 11″ × 8½″ × 2″ oval dish and add fish chunks. Cook as for 2 servings for 4 minutes 30 seconds.

To serve 6. Pour 1 cup sauce into a 14″ × 11″ × 2″ dish. Add 12 fish chunks (cut from 2½ pounds), 1 tablespoon lime juice, and 24 coriander leaves. Cook as for 2 servings for 6 minutes.

POMPANO WITH LEEKS

Pompano is one of Florida's great gifts to American food. It has a firm texture and light flavor that should not be overwhelmed or hidden under heavy sauces. This way of cooking it is just perfect. Since it is so light, it is a good introduction to a meal.   *Serves 4 as a first course, 2 as a main course*

1 pompano (1½ to 2 pounds), skinned and filleted, each fillet cut in half along the center, head and bones cleaned and set aside	2 pieces lemon zest, 2 inches each
	Large pinch freshly ground black pepper
	2 medium leeks, rinsed well, trimmed and cut into ⅛-inch slices
½ bay leaf	1 tablespoon unsalted butter, cut into small bits
1 cup water	
½ cup white wine	
2 small yellow onions, peeled and quartered	2 teaspoons kosher salt

1. Place head, bones, and tail of fish, bay leaf, water, wine, onions, lemon zest, and pepper in a 4-cup glass measure. Cover tightly with microwave plastic wrap. Cook at 100% for 20 minutes.

2. Remove from oven. Uncover and strain. Reserve.

3. Arrange fillets around inside rim of a 10″ × 1½″ round dish. Place leeks in center and dot with butter. Pour reserved broth over fish and sprinkle salt over all. Cover tightly with microwave plastic wrap. Cook at 100% for 6 minutes.

4. Remove from oven. Uncover and remove fillets to a serving dish. Stir together leeks and liquid and let stand for 1 minute. Spoon over fish. Serve hot.

SHAD FILLET

Everybody seems to love shad roe, but they neglect the delectable fish from which it comes. Cooked in the microwave oven, shad has a melting tenderness, almost like a mousse. I find that you need somewhat less shad than you do other fish, because it is so rich. Make sure the fish is well boned when you buy it. I like Creamed Spinach (page 300) with shad. Cook the spinach first and leave covered while cooking the shad. Serve them together or make a bed of the spinach on a platter and place shad and sauce on top. If you serve the shad with roe, the amount of fish in this recipe will serve six. Serve each person a piece of fish and half a pair of roe. You can also serve the fish alone with the sorrel sauce I use for shad roe (see variation to following recipe). In that case, eliminate the dill.   *Serves 4*

1¼ pounds shad fillet	2 tablespoons fresh
2 tablespoons unsalted	lemon juice
butter, cut into ¼	Lemon wedges, for
inch bits	serving (optional)
2 tablespoons chopped	
fresh dill	

1. Lay the fillet, skin side down, in a 14″ × 11″ × 2″ dish. Lift up the two flaps of meat on either side of the fillet. Scatter half the butter and dill under flaps and the remaining butter and dill on top of flaps. Sprinkle with lemon juice. Cover tightly with microwave plastic wrap. Cook at 100% for 4 minutes.

2. Remove from oven. Uncover and serve hot with lemon wedges on the side, if desired.

To serve 6. Increase fish to 2 pounds. Cook for 6 minutes.

SHAD ROE

Shad roe is one of the pleasures of spring. Its rich flavor is frequently paired with the acid of sorrel. While shad roe is often broiled, that dries it out. You will be much happier with any of the cooking methods suggested below. If you are used to having your shad roe with bacon, prepare the bacon first (page 478). *Serves 1 as a main course (unless served with shad fillets), 2 as a first course*

¾ cup water	1 pair shad roe (7 or 8
1 tablespoon white	ounces), pricked 5
vinegar	times on each side
	with the tip of a
	sharp knife

1. Heat water and vinegar in a 9″ × 5″ × 3″ oval dish at 100% for 2 minutes 30 seconds. (If using a small oven, heat for 4 minutes.)

2. Add roe to liquid. Cover tightly with microwave plastic wrap. Cook at 100% for 2 minutes 45 seconds. (If using a small oven, cook for 5 minutes.)

3. Remove from oven. Uncover and serve hot.

To serve 2 as a main course, 4 as a first course. Double all ingredients in recipe or variations. Cook roe for 7 minutes.

To serve 4 as a main course, 8 as a first course. Multiply all ingredient quantities in recipe or variations by 4. Heat liquid in a 14″ × 11″ × 2″ dish for 5 minutes. Cook roe for 10 minutes.

VARIATIONS

SHAD ROE IN BUTTER Heat 12 tablespoons unsalted butter for 3 minutes. Add roe, cover with paper toweling, and cook at 100% for 2 minutes 45 seconds. Serve with fresh lemon juice and some of the butter spooned on top.

SHAD ROE WITH SORREL SAUCE For each pair of roe, stir together ¾ cup fine sorrel chiffonade (page 508), 1 tablespoon butter, and 2 minced shallots in the appropriate size dish. Cook, uncovered, for 2 minutes. Add roe, 3 tablespoons heavy cream, and ½ teaspoon salt. Cover tightly with microwave plastic wrap and cook at 100% for 2 minutes 45 seconds for 1 pair, 7 minutes for 2 pairs, and 10 minutes for 4 pairs.

SCROD WITH CLAMS LIVORNESE

I just love this dish. It is hard to get right in a conventional oven; the fish tends to overcook by the time the shellfish opens. In the microwave oven, it is fail-safe. When you prepare this recipe for more than a couple of people, use a whole fish like red snapper—it will be much more attractive. *Serves 1*

½ **pound scrod fillet (1
    inch thick)**
6 **littleneck clams, well
    scrubbed**
1 **tablespoon olive oil**
2 **teaspoons white wine**

Kosher salt
**Freshly ground black
    pepper**
1 **clove garlic, smashed,
    peeled and cut in
    three**

1. Place fillet in the center of a large dinner plate. Arrange clams, hinge side down, in sets of two around fillet.

2. Sprinkle oil, wine, salt, and pepper on fillet. Place garlic between clams. Cover tightly with microwave plastic wrap. Cook at 100% for 3 minutes 30 seconds.

3. Remove from oven. Uncover and serve hot.

To serve 2. Use 2 scrod fillets (about 1 pound) and 10 clams; double the remaining ingredients. Cook in a 12″ × 10¾″ × 3″ oval dish for 6 minutes. Let stand, covered, for 1 minute and serve hot.

VARIATIONS

SCROD WITH MUSSELS Substitute mussels, scrubbed and beards removed, for clams. Proceed as for Scrod with Clams Livornese, cooking single portion for 3 minutes, double portion for 5 minutes.

RED SNAPPER LIVORNESE This will generously serve 4 as a main course, 6 as a first course. Any other white-fleshed, firm fish can be substituted for snapper. Arrange a 2½-pound fish, head and tail on, diagonally in a 14″ × 11″ × 2″ dish. Sprinkle with ¼ cup white wine, 3 tablespoons olive oil, 1 teaspoon salt, and 2 grinds of black pepper. Cover tightly. Cook at 100% for 6 minutes. Add 20 clams, hinge side down, and 6 cloves smashed and peeled garlic in empty space around fish. Re-cover; cook for 10 minutes at 100%.

STEAMED WHOLE FISH

There are many times when I want to steam a whole fish to serve hot or cold. If you are serving it cold, be sure to remove the skin as soon as you can handle the fish; otherwise it tends to stick. The only limit to the amount of whole fish you can cook in the microwave oven is the length of the fish. That is why I have removed the head or both the head and the tail of larger fish. The fish steams in its own juice, which can be used to make a sauce such as Fish Velouté, Curry Velouté, Pesto, Chunky Tomato Sauce, Mayonnaise, Aïoli, Watercress Sauce, Béarnaise sauce, or Parsley Sauce. *Each ½ pound to ¾ pound of cooked fish feeds one person*

**1 whole fish, 1½ pounds
  with head and tail on**

Place fish on a 14″ × 8″ oval platter with a rim. Cover tightly with microwave plastic wrap. Cook at 100% for 8 minutes.

To steam a 2-pound fish, head and tail on. Arrange on a 14″ × 8″ oval platter. Cover tightly with microwave plastic wrap. Cook at 100% for 11 minutes. (To cook in a small oven, use an 11″ × 8″ dish, making sure to wrap tailpiece that juts out over edge. Cook for 14 minutes.)

To steam a 2½-pound fish, head and tail on. Arrange diagonally in an 11″ × 14″ × 2″ dish. Cover tightly with microwave plastic wrap. Cook 14 minutes at 100%.

To steam a 3-pound fish, head and tail on. Arrange in a 14″ × 11″ × 2″ dish, curling tail if necessary. Cover tightly with microwave plastic wrap. Cook at 100% for 16 minutes.

To steam a 6-pound fish, head removed, cooking weight 4½ pounds. Arrange diagonally in a 14″ × 11″ × 2″ dish. Cover tightly with microwave plastic wrap. Cook for 18 minutes at 100%.

To steam an 8-pound fish, head and tail removed, cooking weight 6 pounds. This can be done only in a full-size microwave oven without a carousel. Place fish on a 17-inch platter. Cover tightly with microwave plastic wrap. Place platter diagonally in oven. Cook for 22 minutes at 100%.

VARIATIONS

CHINESE STEAMED FISH Sprinkle each pound of fish with 1 piece of fresh ginger the size of a quarter, peeled and slivered, 1 clove garlic, smashed and peeled, 1 coriander sprig, 2 teaspoons salted Chinese black beans, 2 teaspoons Oriental sesame oil, 2 teaspoons rice wine vinegar, and 2 tablespoons tamari soy or hoisin sauce. A scallion, both green and white parts, cut in 1-inch lengths, may also be included. Cook as for plain Steamed Whole Fish.

VEGETABLE STEAMED FISH Sprinkle each pound of fish with 1 tablespoon peeled and chopped carrot, 1 tablespoon chopped onion, 1 tablespoon chopped strung celery, 1 tablespoon chopped parsley, ¼ teaspoon salt, and 2 tablespoons white wine. Cook as for Steamed Whole Fish. To serve, the vegetables can be poured over fish or they can be puréed in a blender with a little butter or cream to make a sauce.

HERB STEAMED FISH For each pound of fish, add 1 tablespoon of a chopped fresh herb or of a combination of herbs. Tarragon, lovage, or dill are good alone. Thyme goes well with savory and a tiny bit of oregano. If using rosemary, use only ½ tablespoon per pound. Place half the herbs in cavity of fish. Cook as for Steamed Whole Fish; sprinkle with remaining herbs. Season with salt and pepper to taste when cooking is finished.

MARINATED SARDINES

The wily Venetians discovered a way (in saor) to preserve sardines in hot weather. The sardines are cooked, then left to steep in a marinade for several days. This dish needs to be made and refrigerated at least two days before serving; it will keep for five days. Bring it to room temperature before serving. Two to three sardines make a main course with a salad. One sardine is enough for a first course, especially if accompanied by other hors d'oeuvres.   *Makes 8 sardines*

⅓ cup olive oil
1 small onion, peeled and minced
½ cup sliced celery (about 1 stalk)
2 carrots, peeled and cut into ¼-inch slices
⅔ cup white wine
⅔ cup white wine vinegar

3 fresh sage leaves or ½ teaspoon dried sage
2 bay leaves
1 teaspoon kosher salt
Freshly ground black pepper
3 tablespoons raisins
3 tablespoons pine nuts
8 fresh sardines (about ½ pound)

1. Place oil and onions in an 11″ × 7½″ × 2½″ dish and cook, uncovered, at 100% for 2 minutes. Add celery, carrots, wine, vinegar, sage, bay leaves, salt, and pepper. Cook, uncovered, at 100% for 8 minutes.

2. Stir in raisins and pine nuts. Cook, uncovered, at 100% for 2 minutes. Add sardines and cook, uncovered, at 100% for 1 minute 30 seconds.

3. Remove from oven. Remove fish to a storage container. Let liquid stand until cool. Pour over fish and refrigerate, tightly covered, for at least 2 days before serving.

To make 16 sardines. Use same amount of ingredients for marinade. Proceed as for 8 sardines. When first 8 sardines are cooked, remove from liquid. Reheat liquid, uncovered, at 100% for 2 minutes. Add remaining sardines and cook, uncovered, for 1 minute 30 seconds. Store all sardines covered with liquid in a single container.

FRIED SARDINES

Nothing is simpler or better than this. If you want more, make a second batch since it goes so quickly.   *Serves 4 as a main course, 8 as a first course*

8 fresh sardines (about ½ pound)	**Kosher salt**
2 cups vegetable oil	**Lemon wedges, for serving (optional)**

1. Heat oil in an 11″ × 8½″ × 2″ dish, uncovered, at 100% for 5 minutes. Place sardines in oil, arranging them head to tail. Cook, uncovered, at 100% for 1 minute.

2. Remove from oven. Turn fish over and let stand in oil for 1 minute. Remove to paper toweling and drain. Sprinkle with salt and serve with lemon wedges, if desired.

To make 16 sardines. Fry first 8 sardines. Strain oil and reheat for 5 minutes. Fry second 8 sardines.

WHOLE TROUT WITH LEMON BUTTER

I find a whole trout a luxurious dinner for myself alone or with a good friend. There are too many bones for a dinner party.

Most of the trout we get to eat are farm-raised. They are often frozen but can sometimes be bought fresh. When you find fresh trout, ask the fish man to butterfly a few, taking the bones out but leaving the two fillets attached at the back and the head and tail on. You can stuff these with Duxelles (page 340), wrap each one in microwave plastic wrap and freeze. Then they will be ready to cook when you want. Since trout freezes so well, this is an always at-hand luxury. All you need do is defrost them, still wrapped, at 100% for 2 minutes 30 seconds. Let stand for 10 minutes while you assemble the rest of dinner and then cook. *Serves 1*

1 whole brook, brown or rainbow trout (14 to 16 ounces), defrosted if frozen (page 521)	**Kosher salt**
	Freshly ground black pepper
2 teaspoons fresh lemon juice	**2 tablespoons unsalted butter, cut into 6 pieces**

1. Place fish on a large piece of microwave plastic wrap. Sprinkle the inside of fish with half the lemon juice, salt, and pepper. Tuck half the butter inside. Scatter remaining lemon juice and butter on top. Wrap tightly and place on a plate. Cook at 100% for 2 minutes, turning over once.

2. Remove from oven. Let stand, covered, for 1 minute. Unwrap and serve hot.

To serve 2. Double all ingredients. Divide ingredients equally between the fish. Arrange, head to tail, in an 11″ × 8½″ × 2″ dish; cover tightly with microwave plastic wrap; cook for 3 minutes 30 seconds, turning once. Remove from oven and let stand, covered, for 1 minute.

VARIATION

BUTTERFLIED TROUT WITH DUXELLES Substitute a whole butterflied trout for the whole trout. Halve butter and add 2 tablespoons Duxelles (page 340). Stuff fish with Duxelles and dot butter on top. Cook as for Whole Trout with Lemon Butter for 2 minutes 30 seconds.

TRUITE AU BLEU

This is a classic preparation for trout. The skin turns blue in the acid cooking liquid. I was happy to find that this dish, which can usually be made only with impeccably fresh trout, can be prepared with frozen trout in the microwave oven. *Serves 1 as a main course, 2 as a first course*

½ cup water
½ cup tarragon vinegar
1 teaspoon kosher salt
¼ teaspoon freshly
    ground black
    pepper

1 whole brook, brown or
    rainbow trout (14 to
    16 ounces), defrosted
    if frozen (page 521)

1. Combine water, vinegar, salt, and pepper in a 13½″ × 9½″ × 2″ dish. Cook, uncovered, at 100% for 8 minutes.

2. Remove from oven. Slip the trout into the hot liquid. Cover tightly with microwave plastic wrap. Cook at 100% for 2 minutes. Remove from oven, uncover, and carefully turn the fish over. Re-cover and cook for 2 minutes longer.

3. Remove from oven. Uncover and transfer fish with a wide metal spatula to a serving plate.

To serve 2. Increase water and vinegar to ¾ cup each and double remaining ingredients. Proceeding as for single serving, arrange fish head to tail in a 14″ × 11″ × 2″ dish and cook for 3 minutes. Turn both fish over, re-cover and cook for 3 minutes longer.

HERRING

Herring is the favorite fish of much of the world and sadly underused in this country. Made this way, it can be served hot with a Beurre Blanc (page 363) or cold. Allow it to cool in its cooking liquid.   *Serves 1 as a main course, 2 as a first course*

1 whole fresh herring
    (about ½ pound),
    scaled and gutted
½ cup sliced onions
    (about ¼ pound)
¼ cup trimmed, peeled,
    and thinly sliced
    young carrot

¾ cup white wine
½ teaspoon kosher salt
6 whole juniper berries
2 whole cloves
4 whole allspice berries
½ bay leaf

1. Place herring in an 11″ × 5″ dish. Add remaining ingredients. Cover tightly with microwave plastic wrap. Cook at 100% for 4 minutes.

2. Remove from oven. Let stand, covered, for 1 minute. Uncover; fillet and serve

To serve 4 as a main course, 8 as a first course. Use 4 herrings, 2 teaspoons salt, a large pinch freshly ground black pepper, and 6 cloves. Double remaining ingredients. Proceed as for 1 fish, cooking in a 14" × 11" × 2" dish for 10 minutes. Let stand for 2 minutes.

WHITING WITH PARSLEY SAUCE

Whiting *en colère* ("in a rage"), a fish arranged in a circle as if it were angrily biting its own tail, is a very good French standard served with a light parsley sauce.   *Serves 4*

1 whiting (2½ pounds)	½ cup (packed) finely
1 tablespoon plus 1	chopped parsley
teaspoon cornstarch	2 tablespoons thinly
⅔ cup milk	sliced chives
⅓ cup heavy cream	1 teaspoon salt

1. Arrange fish in a 2-quart soufflé dish or a round serving platter, spine up, with its head and tail touching.

2. Stir together cornstarch, milk, and cream and mix well. Stir in parsley, chives, and salt. Pour mixture over fish. Cover tightly with microwave plastic wrap. Cook at 100% for 7 minutes.

3. Remove from oven. Uncover and serve hot.

Place whiting in soufflé dish with the head and tail touching.

FAIR IS FOWL

I KNOW that puns are inexcusable; but this really expresses the way I feel about cooking birds in the microwave oven: good. Once you know how to cook skinned and boned chicken breasts alone, or with a sauce, or with a vegetable, there are countless variations you can try, including having the breasts on hand, individually wrapped and frozen, to cook directly with their accompaniments for yourself, or yourself and one other person. If you look at the Chicken Breasts with Sofrito recipe and its variations, you will know how to time the frozen chicken breasts. Then you can try them with any sauce or with any of the vegetable purées in this book. If you have questions about any cooking times or quantities, look up CHICKEN in the Dictionary.

Once you have tried a few of the stews that follow, have fun. Change the vegetables, change the cooking liquid, or change the seasonings. Almost anything goes as long as you keep the proportion of solid to liquid consistent. If you want to cut down on calories, remove the skin from chicken for stews, fricassees and the like. Don't remove the bones or you will lose flavor and gelatin. Don't try to cook a whole bird that isn't cut up. It doesn't work well. Don't think of any version of this as roasting. It isn't.

Duck is divine in the microwave oven. It is easy, and you really get rid of that fat. Turkey is more limited. A whole turkey really needs to go into a conventional oven; see page 134 for one of my stuffings. Little birds—a half, a whole, or several to an eater—do well in the microwave oven.

Remember, for most of these dishes you will want an accompanying starch (pages 117–157), or make plain rice or noodles. For some you will want a vegetable (see pages 273–329). Of course, a few contain their own rice or vegetables. Don't overdo it.

POACHED CHICKEN BREASTS

With this simple recipe, you can create an endless series of
dinners by adding different sauces or vegetables. This is
also the way to cook breast meat for chicken salads or to
substitute in Turkey à la King (page 224).

Poached chicken breasts are very good and elegant with
Braised Lettuce (page 287) and Sauce Suprême (page 368).
Plain rice and Velouté (page 366) work well. Think about
snipping some fresh herbs into the sauce. Allow ¼ cup
sauce for each half breast and 1 teaspoon minced herbs for
each ¼ cup sauce. If you are putting tarragon on the chicken,
add tarragon to the sauce. The lavish can top each half
breast with thin slices of black truffle and add some chopped
truffle to the sauce. Another possibility is to stir ½ teaspoon
tomato paste or 1 teaspoon Chunky Tomato Sauce (page
374) into each ¼ cup of Velouté for a gently pink dish that
can be sharpened with a few drops of fresh lemon juice and
hot red-pepper sauce. Parsley Sauce (page 369) and Watercress Sauce (page 369) provide nice color contrasts.

How many half breasts to prepare depends on individual
appetites and what else you are serving. If there is going
to be a first course, count on 1½ half breasts per person, 2
half breasts per person if there is no first course.   *Serves
4 to 8*

4 whole chicken breasts,	**3 sprigs fresh tarragon**
skinned, split and	**(optional)**
boned	**Sauce Suprême (page**
½ cup Chicken Broth	**368), for serving**
(page 331) or	
canned chicken	
broth	

1. Arrange chicken petal-fashion in a 12″ × 1½″ round
dish, with thin ends toward the center. Pour broth over
chicken and scatter tarragon on top.

2. Cover tightly with microwave plastic wrap. Cook at 100% for 8 minutes.

3. Remove from oven. Uncover and serve with sauce; you may stir a tablespoon or two of the cooking liquid into the sauce, if you like.

To make 1 half breast. Place breast on a small plate with ¼ cup broth and a sprig of tarragon, if desired. Cover and cook at 100% for 3 minutes.

To make 2 half breasts. Place half breasts, thin edges toward each other, on a dinner plate with ¼ cup broth and a sprig of tarragon, if desired. Cover and cook at 100% for 4 minutes.

To make 4 half breasts. Arrange half breasts spoke-fashion in a 9-inch quiche dish with the thick ends toward the outside of the dish. Add ¼ cup broth and 2 sprigs of tarragon, if desired. Cover and cook at 100% for 6 minutes.

To make 6 half breasts. Arrange half breasts spoke-fashion in a large round serving dish about 3 inches deep, with the thick ends toward the outside of the dish. Add ¼ cup broth and 3 sprigs of tarragon, if desired. Cover and cook at 100% for 7 minutes.

A whole, skinned, boneless chicken breast, cut in half, thick sides facing.

Split chicken breast cooked with the thick sides toward the edge of dish.

CHICKEN BREAST WITH DUXELLES

This simple dish makes a whole meal, super-easy if you have Duxelles in the freezer. Chicken, mushrooms, and spinach go together perfectly. The mushrooms add a richness here that really makes a half breast per person enough. If you want a sauce, add 1 tablespoon of Duxelles to ¼ cup Velouté (page 366) per person. Heat briefly, uncovered, in the microwave oven. *Serves 1*

1 half chicken breast,
    skinned and boned
2 tablespoons Duxelles
    (page 340)

1 cup (packed) stemmed
    spinach leaves,
    washed thoroughly
    and dried
Kosher salt
Freshly ground black
    pepper

1. Using your fingers, gently open up the pocket along the underside of the breast, being careful not to break the breast in two. Fill pocket loosely with Duxelles.

2. Arrange spinach in a layer on a dinner plate and center chicken on top. Cover tightly with microwave plastic wrap. Cook at 100% for 3 minutes.

3. Remove from oven. Let rest for 1 minute. Uncover. If there is too much liquid on the plate, carefully pour off; a little is fine. Season to taste with salt and pepper.

To serve 2. Double all ingredients. Proceed as for single serving, arranging on a large plate. Cover and cook at 100% for 4 minutes.

To serve 4. Multiply all ingredient quantities by 4. Proceed as for single serving, arranging chicken spoke-fashion in a 9-inch quiche dish. Cover and cook at 100% for 6 minutes.

CHICKEN CURRY

Everybody likes this. It can be made more of an event by serving it with little dishes of freshly grated coconut, raisins, chopped coriander, bananas sliced and dipped in lemon juice, toasted unsalted peanuts, and Fresh Mango Chutney (page 471). Add plain boiled rice or Tomato Pilaf (page 131).   *Serves 4*

3 tablespoons unsalted butter	1 tablespoon Coconut Milk (page 353) or 1 tablespoon milk
2 large yellow onions cut into 1½-inch square chunks (about 2 cups)	2 tablespoons Chicken Broth (page 331) or canned chicken broth
1 slightly underripe papaya, peeled and cut into 1½-inch square chunks	3½ teaspoons kosher salt
2 tablespoons Spice Powder III (page 346) or curry powder	2 teaspoons fresh lemon juice
1 pound chicken breasts (about 2 whole breasts), skinned, boned and cut into 2-inch chunks	¼ cup freshly grated coconut (see page 354 to open) or store-bought unsweetened coconut (optional)

1. Heat butter in a 2-quart soufflé dish, uncovered, at 100% for 3 minutes.

2. Remove from oven. Add onions, papaya, and Spice Powder III. Stir to coat well. Cook, uncovered, at 100% for 6 minutes.

3. Add chicken, Coconut Milk, and broth. Stir. Cover tightly with microwave plastic wrap. Cook at 100% for 6 minutes, shaking dish after 3 minutes to redistribute mixture.

4. Remove from oven. Uncover carefully. Stir in salt and lemon juice; sprinkle with coconut, if desired.

FROZEN CHICKEN BREASTS

When you come home tired and need a quick dinner for yourself or for friends and family, think of those tidy, individually wrapped, skinned and boned chicken breasts in the freezer. Here they are cooked on a bed of braised chopped vegetables, but you could use anything else you have around—maybe some Hispanic Sofrito or leftover vegetable purée or Chunky Tomato Sauce (page 374), just awaiting defrosting. Substitute your gleanings for Sofrito in the recipe. Refer to Poached Chicken Breasts (page 202) for additional ideas.　*Serves 2*

½ cup Sofrito (page 348)
2 frozen half chicken
　　breasts, skinned and
　　boned

½ cup Chicken Broth
　　(page 331) or
　　canned chicken
　　broth
Kosher salt
Freshly ground black
　　pepper

1. Put Sofrito in a 2-quart soufflé dish. Place chicken on top and add broth. Cover tightly with microwave plastic wrap. Cook at 100% for 5 minutes.

2. Remove from oven. Uncover and turn chicken over. Re-cover with fresh microwave plastic wrap. Cook at 100% for 5 minutes more.

3. Uncover and continue cooking for 2 minutes.

4. Remove from oven. Add salt and pepper to taste.

CHICKEN BREASTS NORMANDE

Normandy is too far north for grapes, but it is an ideal climate for apples. In fall, they make cider and from it a kind of applejack called Calvados. Normandy is rich in butter and cream, and its dishes are rich also—elegant for a party. This dish is very white. If you are serving a vegetable, try for color. Cut the peels of McIntosh apples into thin strips and scatter them on top, or sprinkle with finely minced parsley. Noodles and rice are good to sop up the sauce. *Serves 8*

3 tablespoons unsalted butter
2 pounds Granny Smith or McIntosh apples, peeled, cored and cut into 2-inch chunks (about 4 cups)
2½ tablespoons cornstarch
⅓ cup apple juice
1 cup Chicken Broth (page 331) or canned chicken broth
½ cup heavy cream
2 tablespoons Calvados
2 teaspoons kosher salt
Freshly ground black pepper
Pinch cayenne pepper
4 whole chicken breasts, skinned, split and boned

1. Heat butter in a 14″ × 11″ × 2″ dish, uncovered, at 100% for 1 minute.

2. Remove from oven. Add apples and stir to coat with butter. Cook, uncovered, at 100% for 5 minutes.

3. Stir cornstarch into apple juice. Remove apples from oven. Stir in cornstarch mixture and remaining ingredients except chicken. Cook, uncovered, at 100% for 8 minutes.

4. Remove from oven. Slip chicken into sauce, arranging with thick ends toward outside of dish. Cover tightly with microwave plastic wrap. Cook at 100% for 8 minutes.

5. Remove from oven. Uncover carefully and serve immediately.

CHICKEN DINNER IN TWENTY MINUTES

Serve this chicken dish over rice and with broccoli on the side. Boil water for the rice before doing anything else. Cook the rice (on top of the stove) and the chicken (in the microwave oven) at the same time. Cook the broccoli while you season the rice. Set out crusty French bread and chilled white wine, and you have a chicken dinner on the table in twenty minutes. *Serves 2 to 3*

2 whole chicken breasts, skinned, split and boned
1 small ripe tomato, cored and sliced ¼ inch thick
1 medium zucchini, trimmed and sliced ¼ inch thick
1 leek, trimmed and sliced ¼inch thick (including 1 inch of the green)

½ bunch flat-leaf parsley, coarsely chopped
3 tablespoons Chicken Broth (page 331) or canned chicken broth
1 tablespoon olive oil
1 teaspoon kosher salt
6 grinds fresh black pepper
1½ tablespoons fresh lemon juice

1. Arrange chicken pieces over half of a 12-inch round platter so that the pieces are fanned out but do not touch. Fan tomato slices opposite chicken and place zucchini in center. Scatter leeks and parsley over all.

2. Stir together remaining ingredients and drizzle over chicken and vegetables. Cover tightly with microwave plastic wrap. Cook at 100% for 9 minutes.

3. Remove from oven. Uncover and serve. Spoon the ample cooking juices over the rice and broccoli or whatever you are serving with the chicken.

CHICKEN WITH YELLOW BELL PEPPERS AND TOMATOES

This is a ravishingly fresh-tasting, late-summer dish when peppers and tomatoes are sweet and juicy. It produces its own sauce. Serve it with Rich, French Potato Purée (page

291) or just lots of crusty bread and a cold, dry white wine. At a party, I serve Chunky Pâté (page 59) first.   *Serves 4*

¼ cup fruity olive oil
1 cup sliced yellow
   onion (about 1 large
   onion)
2 yellow bell peppers,
   stemmed, seeded
   and cut into 1½-
   inch-wide strips

5 ripe plum tomatoes,
   cored and cut across
   into 4 slices each
1 teaspoon kosher salt
2 pinches freshly ground
   black pepper
2 whole chicken breasts,
   skinned, split and
   boned

1. Heat oil in a 14″ × 11″ × 2″ dish, uncovered, at 100% for 2 minutes. Add onions and stir to coat. Cook, uncovered, at 100% for 2 minutes.

2. Remove from oven. Add peppers, tomatoes, salt, and pepper. Stir to coat with oil. Mound vegetables in center of dish. Arrange chicken around vegetables, thinner sides facing the center. Cover tightly with microwave plastic wrap. Cook at 100% for 8 minutes.

3. Remove from oven. Uncover carefully and serve hot.

To serve 2. Halve all ingredients. Cook onions for 1 minute 30 seconds and chicken for 5 minutes.

CHICKEN SALAD

Make the chicken first and let it cool while the vegetables cook. Then assemble the salad. For cooking times for chicken, see Poached Chicken Breasts (page 202) or refer to the entry on CHICKEN in the Dictionary.   *Serves 4*

1 cup chopped fennel
   (about 1 medium
   bulb)
1 cup chopped yellow
   onion (1 large
   onion)
½ cup asparagus pieces,
   trimmed and cut
   into 1-inch lengths
   (3 to 4 ounces)

1 pound cooked chicken,
   cut into ½-inch
   chunks (about 3½
   cups)
⅓ cup thinly sliced
   scallion greens
¾ cup Mayonnaise (page
   382)

1. Put fennel in a 2-cup glass measure with 1 tablespoon water. Cover tightly with microwave plastic wrap. Cook at 100% for 1 minute.

2. Remove from oven. Drain and put into a mixing bowl. Cook onions and asparagus, separately, as for fennel in step 1.

3. Add chicken to vegetables and toss with remaining ingredients. Serve at room temperature.

CHICKEN LEGS WITH GARLIC CREAM

The lightly browned chicken combines wonderfully with the creamy, richness of the sauce. Serve with rice or noodles. Peas with Mint and Scallions (page 277) would be pretty and good with this. You may substitute any combination of thighs and drumsticks or thighs alone in this recipe.　*Serves 2*

2 teaspoons unsalted
　　butter
2 whole chicken legs, cut
　　into thighs and
　　drumsticks, each
　　drumstick cut to the
　　bone all the way
　　around the thin end
Kosher salt

Freshly ground black
　　pepper
⅓ cup Garlic Cream
　　(page 348)
2 tablespoons dry white
　　wine
1 teaspoon fresh lemon
　　juice

1. Place butter in a 9-inch square browning dish. Heat, uncovered, at 100% for 3 minutes.

2. Sprinkle chicken with salt and pepper. Place, skin side down, in the butter. Cook, uncovered, at 100% for 6 minutes, turning chicken over after 3 minutes.

3. Remove from oven. Pour off fat. Add Garlic Cream, wine, and lemon juice. Cook, uncovered, at 100% for 1 minute.

4. Remove from oven. Transfer chicken to a serving plate and keep warm. Stir the sauce well, scraping up the browned bits from the bottom of the dish. Adjust seasoning if necessary, and pour the sauce over the chicken.

To serve 4. Double all ingredients. Heat butter for 5 minutes in a 10-inch square or 10-inch round browning dish. Cook chicken for 10 minutes 30 seconds.

To serve 8. Multiply all ingredient quantities by 4. Cook the legs in 2 batches, 4 at a time, as for 4 servings.

Slit the skin and tendon on the drumsticks so the skin does not burst.

CHICKEN WITH BARBECUE SAUCE

No, this is not cooked on a grill. If you want a charred outside, shorten cooking time by 1 minute and place the chicken under a preheated broiler or on a grill just until browned.

You can substitute thighs or any combination of thighs and drumsticks for drumsticks. Arrange the chicken with the meatiest parts toward the outside of the dish.

Made with drumsticks, this is a good snack before an outdoor meal. Made with thighs or drumsticks and thighs, it is dinner. I like Mashed Potatoes (page 290) with it. Made with wings, it is an irresistible hors d'oeuvre; be sure to have plenty of paper napkins. *Serves 6 to 8 for hors d'oeuvres, 3 to 4 as a main course*

8 chicken drumsticks
     (about 1¾ pounds),
     each cut to the bone
     all the way around
     the thin end

1 recipe Mustard
     Barbecue Sauce
     (page 377) or ½
     recipe Red Barbecue
     Sauce (page 377)

1. Arrange legs spoke-fashion in a 13-inch round dish, with the thick ends toward the outside of the dish and the leg ends stacked one on top of another. Spoon enough sauce over chicken to coat well. Cover tightly with microwave plastic wrap. Cook at 100% for 12 minutes.

2. Remove from oven. Uncover and remove chicken to a serving plate.

3. Stir cooking juices into remaining sauce. Cover sauce tightly with microwave plastic wrap and cook at 100% for 5 minutes. Pass separately as a dipping sauce.

To make 2 drumsticks. Place drumsticks in a 6-inch round dish, cooking for 5 minutes.

To make 4 drumsticks. Place drumsticks in an 11″ × 6″ × 2″ rectangular dish, cooking for 7 minutes 30 seconds.

To make 6 chicken wings. Baste 6 wings, about 1 pound (split, tips removed and reserved for broth), with ⅓ cup sauce. Arrange in a single layer in a 9-inch pie plate. Cover and cook for 6 minutes. Proceed as for Chicken with Barbecue Sauce.

Arrange wings in a single layer in a 14″ × 11″ × 2″ dish. Alternate different sections, meatier side to edge of dish.

To make 12 chicken wings. Use 1½ cups sauce. Prepare and baste 12 wings, about 2 pounds, as for 6 wings, using about ½ cup sauce. Arrange in a 10″ × 8″ rectangular dish and cook for 10 minutes. Proceed as for Chicken with Barbecue Sauce.

To make 24 chicken wings. Use 1½ cups sauce. Prepare and baste 24 wings, about 4 pounds, as for 6 wings, using about ⅔ cup sauce. Arrange in a 14″ × 11″ × 2″ dish and cook for 14 minutes. Proceed as for Chicken with Barbecue Sauce.

CHICKEN AND RICE

This dish, or any of its variations (with lemon and eggs, with mint, with tomatoes), is just about as good as simplicity gets. It's the simplicity of a good black dress, right for any occasion. *Serves 4 to 6*

1 chicken (4½ pounds), cut into serving pieces	Freshly ground black pepper
2½ medium heads garlic, cloves smashed and peeled	1 cup long-grain rice
2½ cups Chicken Broth (page 331) or canned chicken broth	1 package tiny frozen peas, defrosted in a sieve under warm running water
	2 teaspoons kosher salt

1. Arrange chicken, skin side down, in a 2-quart soufflé dish: place breasts in center of dish, with legs, thighs, wings, and backs around them. Scatter garlic over and pour 1½ cups of the broth over all. Add 6 grinds pepper. Cover tightly with microwave plastic wrap. Cook at 100% for 20 minutes.

2. Remove from oven and uncover. Remove chicken and keep warm. Strain cooking liquid into a 2-cup glass measure and add broth to make 2 cups.

3. Bring cooking liquid and broth to a boil in a saucepan on top of the stove. Add rice and cook. When done, add peas, chicken, and salt, heat through, and serve.

VARIATIONS

AVGOLEMONO CHICKEN Cook chicken as for Chicken and Rice. Measure out 1½ cups cooking liquid, adding additional broth if necessary. Pour into a 4-cup glass measure and whisk in ¼ cup fresh lemon juice and 3 egg yolks. Cook, uncovered, at 100% for 2 minutes; whisk and cook for 2 minutes longer. Cook rice in additional broth. Add lemon sauce with peas and chicken.

CHICKEN WITH RICE AND MINT Add 1 teaspoon dried mint when cooking chicken, or add 2 tablespoons chopped fresh mint to rice after cooking.

CHICKEN WITH TOMATO AND BASIL Substitute 2 cups Lightly Cooked Crushed Tomatoes (page 339) for broth and increase salt to 1 tablespoon. Omit garlic, rice, and peas. Arrange a 2½-pound chicken in dish as for Chicken and Rice and season with salt and pepper. Scatter 1 cup fresh basil leaves over chicken and pour crushed tomatoes over all. Cook at 100% for 14 minutes. Remove from oven, uncover, and stir in 2 tablespoons cornstarch dissolved in 4 tablespoons cold water. Cook, uncovered, for 4 minutes, until sauce thickens. Stir. Cook rice separately with broth. Serves 3 to 4 as a main course.

CHICKEN WITH TOMATO, BASIL, AND GARLIC Arrange a 2½-pound chicken in dish as for Chicken and Rice. Substitute Lightly Cooked Crushed Tomatoes (page 339) for broth, increase salt, and omit rice and peas; reduce garlic to 8 cloves. Drizzle chicken with 2 tablespoons olive oil; cook and thicken sauce as in Chicken with Tomato and Basil.

A: *Breast halves*
B: *Drumsticks*
C: *Wings*
D: *Second joints*
E: *Back*

Arrange chicken pieces with the breast halves in the center, and legs and thighs around them. Drumsticks should have bone end pointing to center.

CHICKEN IN RED WINE

Early on in my love affair with the microwave oven, a gust of emotion overcame me when I realized that it was possible to come home tired and slightly lonely and 15 minutes later have made myself a deep-tasting, dark-sauced, authentic single portion of Chicken in Red Wine. Moreover, it would only take about 22 minutes to make the same thing for a group of friends, including the preparation time.

This is an absolutely splendid version of coq au vin. The chicken is perfectly tender when done, without being dried out, and the aromatic elements in the sauce retain their flavor. If you want to cut down on calories, skin the chicken, but leave the bones in for flavor and gelatin.

Before you start preparing your chicken, put salted water on to boil for rice, noodles, or new potatoes. When the chicken goes into the microwave oven, put the starch in to cook (wait a few minutes for noodles). Everything will be done at the same time. Choose a gutsy wine like zinfandel or Cahors for both cooking and drinking. Serve a green salad and a simple dessert, like Light Poached Pears (page 385), that can be made ahead or while you are eating.

While it would occur to few to prepare coq au vin for one, you can do that quickly and well in the microwave oven, and you can choose your favorite part of the chicken. *Serves 4*

¼ **pound slab bacon, cut into ¼″ × ¼″ × ½″ lardoons**

¼ **pound mushrooms, cleaned and sliced with stems attached**

¼ **pound pearl onions, peeled**

1 **chicken (2½ pounds), cut into serving pieces**

2 **tablespoons brandy**

2 **tablespoons Meat Glaze (page 337), preferably Chicken Glaze**

1 **tablespoon red wine vinegar**

2 **tablespoons Basic Tomato Paste (page 340) or canned tomato paste**

¼ **teaspoon dried thyme**

1 **bay leaf**

1 **tablespoon kosher salt**

8 **large cloves garlic, smashed and peeled**

½ **cup Chicken Broth (page 331) or canned chicken broth**

1 **cup good red wine**

2 **tablespoons cornstarch Freshly ground black pepper**

1. Put lardoons in a 2-quart soufflé dish. Cover loosely with paper toweling. Cook at 100% for 7 minutes.

2. Remove from oven. With a slotted spoon, remove lardoons and drain on paper toweling.

3. Add mushrooms to bacon fat and toss. Mound in the center of the dish. Place onions around inside edge of dish. Fit chicken breasts, skin side down, in center of dish on top of mushrooms. Put legs, thighs, wings, and the 2 meatiest pieces of the back around breasts, skin side down.

4. Pour brandy, Meat Glaze, vinegar, and tomato paste over chicken. Add thyme, bay leaf, and salt. Tuck garlic between chicken pieces. Pour broth and wine over chicken. Cover tightly with microwave plastic wrap. Cook at 100% for 15 minutes.

5. Remove from oven. Uncover carefully. Skim fat.

6. Stir cornstarch into 4 tablespoons of the cooking liquid. Stir into sauce, making sure to stir up liquid from bottom of dish. Add pepper to taste and scatter lardoons on top. Cook, uncovered, at 100% for 2 minutes.

7. Remove from oven. Stir well and serve.

To serve 1. Cut 1 thick slice bacon into ½" × 1" lardoons. Put lardoons in a 1-quart soufflé dish. Cook as for 4 servings for 4 minutes; skim out. Stir into fat 4 small mushrooms, quartered; 2 cloves garlic, smashed, peeled and cut in half lengthwise; and 6 peeled pearl onions or 2 small white onions, peeled and quartered; stir to coat. Add 1 chicken leg and thigh or a half breast with bone in, skin side down. Add ¼ cup broth, ¼ cup wine, 1 teaspoon brandy, 1 tablespoon Meat Glaze, ¼ teaspoon vinegar, 1½ teaspoons tomato paste, ¼ bay leaf, a pinch of thyme, ½ teaspoon salt, and pepper to taste. Cover and cook for 8 minutes. Dissolve 1 tablespoon cornstarch in 2 tablespoons cooking liquid; stir into sauce. Cook for 4 minutes. Remove from oven, turn chicken skin side up, and stir sauce thoroughly. Scatter lardoons on top and serve.

To serve 2. Use 2 slices bacon; cut and cook in a 2-quart soufflé dish as for single serving. Increase mushrooms to 8, pearl onions to 12, garlic to 6 cloves, red wine to ½ cup, brandy to 2 teaspoons, vinegar to ½ teaspoon, tomato paste to 1 tablespoon, and salt to 1 teaspoon; use ½ bay leaf, ½ chicken breast and 1 leg and thigh. Use same amount of broth, Meat Glaze, thyme, and cornstarch. Increase first cooking time of chicken to 10 minutes. Proceed as for single serving.

CHICKEN GUMBO

Although *gumbo* comes from an African word for okra, not all gumbos contain okra, nor do they have to have tomatoes and peppers. This gumbo is wonderful without any of them. Serve it with rice. It isn't wildly spicy; it is extra good. Since there are no tomatoes in the gumbo, you could add some to your salad.   *Serves 4 to 6*

¼ cup Brown Roux (page 338)

1 large yellow onion (about ¾ pound), peeled and cut into ½-inch wedges (leaving part of the core)

1½ cups sliced celery, cut ¼ inch thick on the diagonal

½ cup coarsely chopped celery leaves

8 cloves garlic, smashed and peeled

2 teaspoons filé powder, or ½ pound whole okra, trimmed (page 309)

2 cups Chicken Broth (page 331) or canned chicken broth

1 chicken (3 pounds), skinned and cut into serving pieces, wings split and breasts cut into each

1 tablespoon fresh lemon juice

2 teaspoons kosher salt

½ teaspoon freshly ground black pepper

½ teaspoon Fiery Pepper Sauce (page 344) or 1 teaspoon hot red-pepper sauce

1. Stir together roux, onions, celery, celery leaves, and garlic in an 11″ × 8″ × 3″ dish. Cook, uncovered, at 100% for 5 minutes.

2. Remove from oven. Stir in filé and broth. Arrange chicken with the meatiest pieces toward the outside of the dish. Cover tightly with microwave plastic wrap. Cook at 100% for 8 minutes.

3. Remove from oven. Uncover carefully and stir well. Cook, uncovered, at 100% for 7 minutes.

4. Remove from oven. Stir in lemon juice, salt, pepper, and pepper sauce.

CHICKEN PAPRIKÁS

This is a Hungarian classic. Serve it with boiled noodles or half a microwave-cooked baking potato, peeled, per person. It is worth searching out Hungarian paprika paste—it comes in tubes and jars—or making Hot and Sweet Red Pepper Sauce (page 343) in order to experience this dish at its best. *Serves 4*

2 tablespoons unsalted
butter
1¾ cups chopped onion
(about 2 large
onions)
2 cloves garlic,
smashed and
peeled
½ cup peeled, seeded
and finely chopped
tomatoes or
crushed and
drained canned
tomatoes
1 tablespoon plus 2
teaspoons paprika
powder
1 chicken (3 pounds),
cut into serving
pieces

1 cup Chicken Broth
(page 314) or
canned chicken
broth
2 tablespoons
cornstarch
1½ cups sour cream
1 tablespoon kosher
salt
2 tablespoons fresh
lemon juice
2 tablespoons Hot and
Sweet Red Pepper
Sauce (page 343)
or Hungarian
paprika paste

1. Heat butter in a 2-quart soufflé dish, uncovered, at 100% for 2 minutes. Add onions and garlic and stir to coat with butter. Cook, uncovered, at 100% for 1 minute.

2. Remove from oven. Stir in tomatoes and paprika powder. Add chicken, skin side down. Place breasts in center of dish and arrange remaining pieces around them, with the meatiest portions toward the outside of the dish. Pour broth over chicken. Cover tightly with microwave plastic wrap. Cook at 100% for 15 minutes.

3. Remove from oven. Uncover. Remove chicken to a serving platter and keep warm. Dissolve cornstarch in 4 tablespoons cooking liquid. Stir thoroughly into remaining cooking liquid; stir in sour cream. Cook, uncovered, at 100% for 5 to 7 minutes, until thickened.

4. Remove from oven. Adjust seasoning with salt and lemon juice. Whisk in pepper sauce. Return chicken to the sauce and cook, uncovered, at 100% for 3 minutes, until heated through.

CHICKEN FRICASSEE

This is a great American classic. It is as good a Sunday dinner as any you can imagine. It has vegetables in it, but you can throw in a handful of peas along with the carrots if you like. Serve the fricassee with rice. Put spoons on the table; the sauce is that good. *Serves 4 to 6*

2 tablespoons unsalted
    butter
1 medium onion (about
    ½ pound), peeled
    and sliced
1 carrot, trimmed,
    peeled and cut into
    1½-inch lengths
½ pound mushrooms,
    cleaned, trimmed
    and quartered
1 tablespoon lovage or
    celery leaves
1 bay leaf
1 chicken (4 pounds),
    trimmed of excess
    fat and cut into
    serving pieces,
    breasts cut in half
    across the bone

1½ cups Chicken Broth
    (page 331) or
    canned chicken
    broth
Kosher salt
Freshly ground black
    pepper
2 tablespoons
    cornstarch
½ cup heavy cream
3 egg yolks
2 tablespoons fresh
    lemon juice
3 tablespoons chopped
    parsley

1. Heat butter, uncovered, in a 2-quart soufflé dish at 100% for 2 minutes. Add onions, carrots, mushrooms, and lovage; stir to coat with butter. Add bay leaf. Arrange chicken, skin side down, on vegetables. Place breast pieces in center of dish and arrange remaining pieces around them, with the meatiest portions toward the outside of the dish. Add broth, salt, and pepper. Cover tightly with microwave plastic wrap. Cook at 100% for 18 minutes.

2. Remove from oven. Prick plastic. Let sit for 6 minutes. Uncover and skim fat. Stir cornstarch into ¼ cup of the cream. Stir in remaining cream and egg yolks, then add

¼ cup cooking liquid. Stir cream mixture thoroughly into stew. Cover tightly with microwave plastic wrap. Cook at 100% for 4 minutes.

3. Remove from oven. Uncover and stir in lemon juice and parsley. Taste and correct seasoning.

VARIATION

CHICKEN FRICASSEE WITH ANISE Substitute 1½ tablespoons aniseed or 1 teaspoon crushed anise for lovage or celery leaves.

CHICKEN LIVERS WITH MUSTARD AND CREAM

Microwave-cooked chicken livers are creamy and delicious, never tough and hard. You can serve them as a first course or as a main course with rice or an unsauced vegetable. Chicken livers are not expensive. Be sure to clean them well and remove all the connective tissue. When you buy a chicken, it comes with livers tucked inside. They are a dividend. (To freeze and defrost, see pages 520 and 521.) *Serves 1 as a main course, 2 as a first course*

½ **pound chicken livers, trimmed of connective tissue and cut in half**	2 **tablespoons heavy cream**
1 **tablespoon minced shallots**	2 **tablespoons Chicken Broth (page 331) or canned chicken broth**
½ **teaspoon kosher salt**	1 **tablespoon dry white wine**
Large pinch freshly ground black pepper	1 **tablespoon Dijon mustard**
	1 **tablespoon unsalted butter**

1. Toss livers with shallots, salt, and pepper. Whisk together cream, broth, wine, and mustard until well blended. Reserve.

2. Heat butter in a 9-inch square browning dish, uncovered, at 100% for 2 minutes 30 seconds. Shake dish once or twice, if necessary, to ensure that butter browns evenly. Add livers. Cook, uncovered, at 100% for 2 minutes, turning livers over once.

3. Remove from oven. Remove livers to a serving plate and keep warm. Pour cream mixture into browning dish and stir well. Cook, uncovered, at 100% for 2 minutes. The sauce should be slightly reduced and thickened.

4. Remove from oven. Return livers to the dish and toss to coat with sauce. Serve at once

To serve 2 as a main course, 4 as a first course. Double all ingredients. Heat butter in a 10-inch square or 10-inch round browning dish for 3 minutes. Cook livers for 3 minutes and reduce sauce for 3 minutes 30 seconds.

CORNISH GAME HEN WITH GRAPES

This makes a gala party meal. I find that people really don't want more than half a Cornish hen, especially the large ones most commonly available. Serving halves saves them embarrassment. It also is much easier to cut the birds. Rice, noodles, or Mashed Potatoes (page 290) go with this. A few asparagus spears never hurt anybody.   *Serves 2*

1 cup seedless green grapes (about 6 ounces)	**Large pinch kosher salt**
	1 Cornish game hen (1¾ pounds), split, backbone removed
¼ cup Chicken Broth (page 331) or canned chicken broth	

1. Place grapes and broth in a 10″ × 7″ × 4″ oval dish. Sprinkle with salt. Place split hen, skin side up, over grapes. Cover tightly with microwave plastic wrap. Cook at 100% for 8 minutes.

2. Remove from oven. Serve piping hot.

To serve 4. Double all ingredients. Use a 2-quart soufflé dish, arranging hens with legs toward outside of dish and breasts toward the center. Cook for 12 minutes.

To serve 6. Multiply all ingredient quantities by 3. Arrange hens as for 4 servings in a 12″ × 10″ × 2″ dish and cook for 15 minutes.

VARIATION

CORNISH GAME HEN WITH GRAPES IN CREAM SAUCE
Cook hen as for Cornish Game Hen with Grapes. Remove to a serving plate. Add 1 teaspoon kosher salt, 2 tablespoons heavy cream, a squeeze of fresh lemon juice, and a large pinch of cayenne pepper to grapes; stir well. Stir 1 teaspoon cornstarch into 2 tablespoons cooking liquid; add to sauce and stir to incorporate thoroughly. Cook, uncovered, at 100% for 1 minute. Remove from oven. Spoon hot sauce and grapes over hen.

COCOTTE OF CORNISH HENS

This simple dish is rich with herbs and vegetables. It is good with either Garlic Potatoes (page 143) or boiled new potatoes. *Serves 4*

2 large Cornish game hens (about 1¾ pounds each), fresh or defrosted, split and backbones removed

3 teaspoons kosher salt

¾ teaspoon freshly ground black pepper

1 package frozen peas, defrosted in a sieve under warm running water

12 spring onions or scallions, trimmed, leaving 2 inches of the green

2 medium carrots, trimmed, peeled and cut into 2″ × ¼″ lengths

2 teaspoons dried oregano

1 teaspoon dried thyme

2 tablespoons unsalted butter (optional)

1. Sprinkle hens lightly on both sides with salt and pepper. Toss together remaining ingredients except butter in a large bowl.

2. Put half of vegetable mixture in a 2-quart soufflé dish. Place the birds over the vegetables, with legs toward the outside of the dish and breasts toward the center. Cover with remaining vegetables. Cover dish tightly with microwave plastic wrap. Cook at 100% for 20 minutes; halfway through cooking time, uncover and turn hens over; re-cover.

3. Remove from oven. Uncover and remove birds to a serving platter. Stir butter into vegetables, if desired, and pour them over birds

TURKEY À LA KING

This dish got a bad reputation from endless committee and charity lunches, and the slices of canned pimento that were invariably tossed into it. It's too bad, because it's delicious. I think it's time to return Turkey à la King to its rightful place. It is a wonderful dish for leftover turkey or chicken. Since poultry is so quick to cook in the microwave oven, it is now easy to make it from scratch when there are no leftovers. Serve Turkey à la King with rice, mashed potatoes, or patty shells so that you can enjoy all of the lovely gravy. This is one dish that is really not at its best made with canned broth. *Serves 4*

4 tablespoons unsalted butter
2 tablespoons all-purpose flour
½ cup coarsely chopped celery
½ cup coarsely chopped onion
1 cup Chicken Broth (page 331)
½ cup heavy cream
½ cup frozen tiny peas, defrosted in a sieve under warm running water
1 teaspoon kosher salt
8 drops hot red-pepper sauce
2 cups cooked turkey or chicken (page 202 and page 503), cut into large chunks and kept warm, if possible

1. Heat 2 tablespoons of the butter in an 8-cup glass measure, uncovered, at 100% for 2 minutes. Remove from oven and whisk in flour.

2. Add celery and onions and cook, uncovered, at 100% for 3 minutes.

3. Remove from oven. Add ½ cup of the broth and whisk until smooth. Whisk in remaining broth and cream. Stir in peas. Cook, uncovered, at 100% for 8 minutes.

4. Remove from oven. Add salt, pepper sauce, and remaining 2 tablespoons butter, stirring until butter melts. Add turkey, stir, and serve.

Note. To make Turkey à la King from leftovers, use cold or room- temperature turkey and proceed as above. Stir an additional ¼ cup broth into final mixture. Cook, uncovered, at 100% for 2 minutes.

SQUAB WITH SEASONED BUTTER UNDER THE SKIN

In this country, squab refers to both small chickens and domestically raised pigeons. This recipe is really intended for the richer-tasting pigeons, but it can be made with squab broilers (chickens). It can also be made with small Cornish game hens.

This is a beautiful way to cook squab. The skin browns lightly, the flesh stays moist, and the flavors all blend together. Serve it on a bed of watercress. The butter and juices will wilt the cress a bit, and it will all taste delicious. Half of this bird satisfies me; but I suppose many will want the whole thing. *Serves 1*

2 tablespoons Seasoned   **1 squab (about 1 pound)**
     Butter (see following
     recipes)

1. Prepare the seasoned butter of your choice.

2. Carefully work your fingers between the skin and meat of the breast and legs of the squab. Place all but 2 teaspoons of the butter under the skin. Smear remaining butter over the skin.

3. Place the bird on a serving plate. Cook, uncovered, at 100% for 4 minutes.

To serve 2. Double all ingredients, cooking birds for 6 minutes.

To serve 4. Multiply all ingredient quantities by 4. Cook for 11 minutes in a 12″ × 8″ dish.

SEASONED BUTTERS

Makes 4 tablespoons, enough for 2 squabs

To make either of these compound butters, simply blend all ingredients well. Use at room temperature. Either recipe may be doubled.

SEASONED BUTTER 1

3 tablespoons unsalted butter
¼ cup (lightly packed) flat-leaf parsley leaves
1 teaspoon fresh lemon juice
½ teaspoon ground cumin
½ teaspoon kosher salt
⅛ teaspoon freshly ground pepper

SEASONED BUTTER 2

4 tablespoons unsalted butter
1 teaspoon Spice Powder 1 (page 345)
1 teaspoon fresh lemon juice
1 teaspoon soy sauce

CRISPIEST DUCK

This is the best and easiest way I have ever found for cooking duck. This recipe should turn duck from a rarely cooked company meal into an easy, frequent one. You can even make it just for one or two people without any problem.

Because fat cooks more quickly than protein in the microwave oven, the excess fat under the duck skin is rendered, leaving the meat tender, not dried out. The broth also helps protect the meat and keep it moist. Duck's rich taste welcomes spicy flavors and rich, slightly acid sauces. Any of the following sauces would be a treat: Blackberry

Sauce (page 381), Cranberry Sauce for Duck, Goose or Wild Turkey (page 379), or Cherry Sauce for Roast Birds (page 380). Allow ¼ cup of sauce for each portion of duck. *Serves 4 to 6*

1 duck, cut into serving pieces, legs, thighs, and breasts cut in half across the bone, wing tips removed and reserved for broth	1 to 1¼ cups Duck Broth (page 331), Chicken Broth (page 331) or canned chicken broth

1. Remove any loose fat from duck. Prick the skin of each piece of duck several times with a fork.

2. Heat the broiler of a conventional oven. Move rack to position closest to heat source.

3. Put duck, skin side up, in a 12″ × 8″ × 2″ dish. Add enough broth to cover meat and bone; leave skin and fat above the liquid. Cover loosely with paper toweling. Cook in the microwave oven at 100% for 17 minutes.

4. Remove from oven. Remove duck from dish and place on a broiler pan. Slash fat and skin crosshatch-fashion. Broil for 6 to 8 minutes, until browned and crisp.

To serve 1. Cut a duck breast in half across the bone; each piece will be approximately 3 to 4 inches square. Prick skin several times with a fork. Fit duck, skin side up, into a deep dish just large enough to hold the pieces. Add broth, ¼ to ½ cup, as for Crispiest Duck. Cook for 6 minutes, slash, and broil as for Crispiest Duck for 5 to 7 minutes.

To serve 2. Use about 1½ pounds of duck, cut in half across the bone, and about ½ cup broth. Prick skin several times with a fork. Cook as for Crispiest Duck in an 11″ × 8½″ × 3″ dish for 9 minutes. Broil for 5 to 7 minutes.

VARIATIONS

SPICE-RUBBED DUCK To make spice mixture, combine 1½ tablespoons freshly ground cumin, 2 teaspoons kosher salt, ¼ teaspoon freshly ground black pepper, and 2 tablespoons fresh lemon juice. Rub microwave-cooked duck pieces all over with spice mixture. Broil as for Crispiest Duck.

ORIENTAL GLAZED DUCK Cut 2 ducks into serving pieces; cut each breast, leg, and thigh into 2 or 3 pieces across the bone; remove wing tips (reserve for broth) and split wings.

Put wing tips, necks, giblets, and hearts in an 8-cup glass measure. Add 2 cups Chicken Broth (page 331) or canned chicken broth, 4 smashed, unpeeled cloves garlic, and ½ teaspoon ground cumin. Cover tightly with microwave plastic wrap. Cook at 100% for 20 minutes. Strain and skim; reserve.

Prick skin of each piece of duck several times with a fork. Arrange duck in a 14″ × 11″ × 2″ dish and proceed as for Crispiest Duck, using reserved duck broth. Remove from oven. Place duck on broiler pan and brush with Oriental Glaze (page 350). Heat broiler. When duck has marinated for 10 minutes, brush again with glaze and broil close to heat source for 8 minutes. Remove duck to a serving platter and keep warm. Deglaze broiling pan with a little of the reserved broth; serve as gravy with duck. Use reserved broth for soups. Serves 8.

DUCK GUMBO

This wonderful party fare is best partly cooked ahead, refrigerated overnight, skimmed, reheated with the vegetables and tasted for seasonings. If you are in a screaming hurry, you can serve this dish the day you make it. Skim very well after first cooking time; add vegetables. Reduce final cooking time to 10 minutes.

Serve the gumbo with a pilaf, such as Basic Pilaf (page 129), but substitute duck fat for butter and use chicken or duck broth for the liquid. This can be done while you are skimming the gumbo, before you start reheating. *Serves 10 to 12*

2 ducks, cut into
   serving pieces,
   breasts, thighs and
   legs cut across the
   bone into 2 or 3
   pieces, wing tips
   removed (reserve
   for broth) and
   wings split
1 large onion, peeled
   and cut into 2-inch
   chunks (about 1
   pound)
12 cloves garlic, smashed
   and peeled
2 teaspoons Fiery
   Pepper Sauce (page
   344)
3 cans (14 ounces each)
   tomatoes in juice,
   drained and
   crushed
1 tablespoon filé powder
1 cup Chicken Broth
   (page 331) or
   canned chicken
   broth

2 cups okra pods,
   trimmed (page 304)
   or 1 package frozen
   sliced okra, run
   under hot water
   until block of okra
   can be broken into
   4 pieces
½ pound carrots,
   trimmed, peeled
   and julienned
1 cup frozen peas
1 pound asparagus,
   trimmed and stems
   peeled and cut into
   1½-inch lengths
1 cup scallion pieces, cut
   on the diagonal into
   1-inch lengths (both
   white and green
   parts)
2 tablespoons fresh
   lemon juice
Kosher salt
Freshly ground black
   pepper
Fiery Pepper Sauce or
   Searing Pepper
   Sauce (page 344)

1. Combine duck, onions, garlic, pepper sauce, tomatoes, filé, and broth in a 14″ × 11″ × 2″ dish. Stir to combine well. Cover tightly with microwave plastic wrap. Cook at 100% for 20 minutes.

2. Remove from oven. Let come to room temperature, covered. Refrigerate overnight.

3. Uncover; skim and reserve fat. Add remaining ingredients except for lemon juice, salt, and pepper. Stir well. If using frozen okra, put each quarter of frozen block in a corner of the dish. Cook, uncovered, at 100% for 15 minutes, or until heated through, stirring once during cooking time. Break up frozen okra when stirring.

4. Remove from oven. Skim off any remaining surface fat. Add lemon juice, salt, pepper, and additional pepper sauce if desired. Serve with rice.

DUCK CONFIT

This is one of the few lengthy recipes in this book. It needs to be made at least two weeks before you want to use it; but then you have a store of duck in the refrigerator available as needed. Remove as much duck as you want from the fat. Scrape off excess fat and put it back in the storage container.

Use duck in any recipe calling for confit or broil it briefly and serve it with a vegetable purée (pages 288–300). Another possibility is to rub the duck with the spice mixture in Spice-Rubbed Duck (page 227) and broil. The duck is good sliced on top of a salad with chicory, duck cracklings (see entry on RENDERING in the Dictionary), and an onion vinaigrette.

When making confit, I start from Paula Wolfert's ideas in *The Cooking of Southwest France*.   *Makes 2 ducks*

6 large shallots, peeled
½ bunch parsley,
    preferably flat-leaf
    parsley
2 cloves garlic, smashed
    and peeled
6 tablespoons plus 2
    teaspoons kosher
    salt
2 teaspoons black
    peppercorns,
    coarsely ground
1 bay leaf, crumbled
  Pinch dried thyme

2 ducks (about 4 pounds
    each), cut into
    serving pieces, wing
    tips removed and
    saved for broth,
    extra skin and fat
    trimmed and
    reserved for
    rendered fat
4 to 6 cups rendered
    duck and pork fat
    (see note)

1. Place shallots, parsley, and garlic in the workbowl of a food processor and process until chopped. Stir in 6 tablespoons salt, ground peppercorns, bay leaf, and thyme. Rub mixture onto each piece of duck. Arrange seasoned duck pieces on a large tray in a single layer. Cover loosely with a kitchen towel or plastic wrap. Refrigerate for 24 hours.

2. Heat rendered fat in a 2-quart soufflé dish, loosely covered with paper toweling, at 100% for 10 minutes, until melted.

3. While melting fat, rinse duck pieces under cold running water. Dry. Fit legs and thighs into an 11″ × 8″ × 2″ dish in a single layer. Remove fat from oven and carefully ladle over duck until pieces are completely covered. Reserve remaining fat. Cover duck loosely with paper toweling. Cook at 100% for 15 to 18 minutes, until thigh meat is easily pierced with a toothpick.

4. Remove from oven. Allow duck to cool in fat for 30 minutes.

5. Choose a deep, narrow 2-quart ceramic or glass container to store confit, or 2 smaller, similarly shaped containers. Put a teaspoon of salt in bottom of container to absorb meat juices. Place legs and thighs in one container. Tent it with aluminum foil while preparing breasts and wings. Add fat from cooked leg pieces to reserved melted fat.

6. Fit breast pieces and wings into an 11″ × 8″ × 2″ dish. Ladle reserved fat to cover as before. Cover loosely with paper toweling. Cook at 100% for 10 to 12 minutes, until breast meat is easily pierced with a toothpick. Proceed as in steps 4 and 5, placing breasts and wings on top of leg pieces if container is large or into their own storage container if not, with 1 teaspoon salt sprinkled over the bottom.

7. Ladle fat through a fine sieve over duck. Let cool to room temperature. Cover tightly with plastic wrap and refrigerate overnight.

8. When duck has been refrigerated overnight, melt ½ pound rendered duck or pork fat in a 2-quart soufflé dish, lightly covered with paper toweling, at 100% for 2 minutes

30 seconds. Pour a ½-inch layer on top of the congealed fat that covers the duck. Cover with a double layer of plastic wrap. Tie it down: plastic wrap loosens when cold. Cover with doubled aluminum foil. Tie again. Store, refrigerated, for at least 2 weeks, and up to 4 months.

Note. For rendered fat, see entry on RENDERING in the Dictionary. Use reserved skin and fat from the ducks plus duck fat saved from cooking other ducks, such as Crispiest Duck or Duck Gumbo. Each piece of duck should have a covering of skin, but there are usually extra flaps between the leg and backbone and around the neck area. Render pork fat, allowing about 1 pound for every 1½ cups needed.

MINI-CHARTREUSE WITH SAUSAGE AND QUAIL

This is another ornate dish. Perfect for impressing a significant other or someone you hope will become a significant other. The French make this into an even fancier, molded dish, but I like it just like this with the flavors flowing together. It makes two portions from two quail—thrifty.   *Serves 2*

½ teaspoon dried thyme
1 celery stalk, trimmed and cut in half lengthwise
½ bay leaf
10 sprigs flat-leaf parsley
4 cups shredded white cabbage (about 1 pound)
1 carrot, trimmed, peeled and cut into 6 pieces

1 small onion, peeled and quartered
½ pound garlic sausage (kielbasa or any good smoked sausage)
2 cups Chicken Broth (page 331) or canned chicken broth
2 quail, cut in half
¼ pound smoked ham, sliced thick

   1. Make a bouquet garni: Sprinkle thyme over one piece of celery. Then arrange bay leaf and parsley over thyme and cover with the other piece of celery. Tie the bundle securely with kitchen twine.

2. In a 2-quart soufflé dish, toss together cabbage, carrots, onions, and bouquet garni. Tuck sausage into the vegetables and add broth. Cover tightly with microwave plastic wrap. Cook at 100% for 10 minutes.

3. Remove from oven. Uncover and tuck quail around the sides of the dish under the vegetables; place ham on top of vegetables. Re-cover tightly with fresh microwave plastic wrap. Cook at 100% for 3 minutes.

4. Remove from oven, uncover, and divide between 2 serving dishes.

PHEASANT WITH CURRANT CREAM

This is absolutely fabulous. It cannot be made very often since it uses fresh currants and pheasant. That makes it all the more special. This is the time for a big Burgundy wine. *Serves 2*

½ teaspoon dried oregano
½ bay leaf
1 pheasant (2¼ to 2½ pounds), fresh or defrosted, rinsed inside and out and patted dry

2 teaspoons unsalted butter, softened
Kosher salt
Freshly ground black pepper
½ pound fresh currants with stems
2 tablespoons heavy cream

1. Put oregano and bay leaf in pheasant cavity. Rub the skin with butter and sprinkle with salt and pepper. Place in the center of a shallow 12-inch oval dish. Arrange currants around the bird. Cook, uncovered, at 100% for 15 minutes.

2. Remove from oven. Let stand while you prepare the sauce. Drain cooking juices into a bowl and skim. Strain through a fine sieve into a clean bowl, and force currants through sieve into juices. Stir in the cream, and salt and pepper to taste.

3. Cut off the legs and place one on each of 2 serving plates. Slice the breasts, arrange on the plates, and spoon some of the sauce around the meat. Pass the remaining sauce separately.

MAINLY MEAT

THE microwave oven stews, braises, poaches, and steams meat to perfection. It cooks it in sauce splendidly. It does not roast or shallow-fry or sauté, so after much soul-searching and many failed attempts, I have decided to eliminate all such recipes. Those that are left are first-rate

Mellowing

If you have a little extra time, mellow your stews by cooking them ahead, and letting them cool to room temperature. Then either reheat immediately or refrigerate and reheat the next day. The stew will not overcook, not even the vegetables. (When you mellow, your meat will not overcook because it cools before simply being brought back to the appropriate temperature.)

Not all meats benefit from such treatment. For those that do, instructions appear at the end of the recipe. Food enough for eight will take 15 minutes to reheat at 100% and should be stirred once during the cooking time. It does not need to be covered. If it has not been refrigerated, reheat for 5 to 6 minutes.

Smaller quantities, leftovers for instance, will take less time to reheat for mellowing—let's say 3 minutes for a portion for one from refrigerated, 5 to 6 minutes for two, and 10 minutes for four. I would cover the portion for one; there is a greater chance of its getting too dry. If the food has not been refrigerated, it will take only 1 minute for a portion for one, 3 minutes for two, 5 minutes for four, and 8 minutes for six.

Stirring

In several of these recipes, you need to stir once or twice during the cooking time. You don't need to remove the dish from the oven; indeed, it is better not to. You can either carefully raise the plastic by pulling it away from the dish with a knife—releasing the seal, but keeping your hand away from the steam—or cut a slit in the plastic with a knife and stir through that. If you have cut a slit, patch it with an overlapping square of fresh microwave plastic wrap. If you have lifted the plastic, you can reseal it, or put on fresh microwave plastic wrap. You do not have to remove the old wrap.

To stir, slit plastic wrap.

Stir through slit in wrap.

Patch plastic wrap with fresh square to make tight seal.

You can remove the cooking dish from the oven each time you need to stir—but I wouldn't do it any more than I would take a roasting pan out of a conventional oven each time I needed to baste a roast. You lose moisture, steam, and heat.

Thanks to the microwave oven's ability to cook in serving dishes and attractive ceramic casseroles, you may want to cook many of the saucy dishes in a container that can come to the table. Keep it roughly the same size as the dish called for in the recipe.

Unless potatoes or another starch are called for in the recipe, you probably are going to want to make potatoes, rice, noodles, or another starch to go with these saucy dishes and sop up the good gravy. If you are cooking the starch in the microwave oven, make it before the meat and reheat it while the meat is mellowing or while you complete the seasoning. If you are making the starch on top of the stove, check your meat recipe and make sure you start the water for the starch early enough so it will be done at the same time as the main course. Of course, a crusty loaf of bread needs no cooking and will do the job just as well. For many of these homey, welcoming dishes, I give my guests a spoon. If they are a little timid at first, they quickly get into the spirit and use it to get up every last bit.

Beef

For these saucy dishes, stews, and pot roasts, the meat cooks better if marbled and aged. Use the cuts indicated. Do not use better cuts; you are likely to get dry meat.

HEART OF THE HOME BEEF STEW

This is basic eats, good solid food. Stir in some cooked potatoes, peeled and cubed, or serve with Mashed Potatoes (page 290) or Garlic Potatoes (page 143).   *Serves 6 to 8*

1 tablespoon vegetable oil

½ pound small white onions (about 1½ inches in diameter), peeled and quartered

6 cloves garlic, smashed and peeled

3 small carrots, trimmed, peeled and sliced ⅛ inch thick (about ¾ cup)

6 mushrooms, trimmed and quartered

½ cup parsley, chopped

3 tablespoons Basic Tomato Paste (page 340) or canned tomato paste

2 pounds stew beef (chuck), cut into 1-inch cubes

½ bay leaf

2 teaspoons dried marjoram

1 teaspoon dried oregano

1 teaspoon dried thyme

1 cup Veal Broth (page 331) or canned beef broth

1 tablespoon cornstarch dissolved in 2 tablespoons cold water

1½ tablespoons kosher salt

Freshly ground black pepper

1. Combine oil, onions, garlic, carrots, mushrooms, parsley, and tomato paste in a 2½-quart soufflé dish. Cook, uncovered, at 100% for 4 minutes.

2. Stir in remaining ingredients. Cover tightly with microwave plastic wrap. Cook at 100% for 10 minutes.

3. Stir well; re-cover. Cook at 100% for 5 minutes.

4. Stir again and re-cover. Cook for 3 minutes more.

5. Remove from oven. Mellow (page 234), if you wish. Serve hot.

CHUNKY BEEF CHILI

Fights have broken out, marriages broken up, and restaurants broken down over the proper recipe for chili. Serious chili people call for the beef or other meat to be cut into little cubes and say there should be no beans in the chili. Beans are served, if at all, on the side. The truly austere don't even include tomatoes. They say the red color should come only from the chili and other spices. I don't go that far. You can substitute other meat or game for beef—pork, lamb, venison, or buffalo, alone or in a combination. This chili can also be prepared with ground beef. If you like, serve Chilied Beans (page 140) on the side along with rice, sour cream, grated Monterey Jack or Cheddar cheese, chopped onions or scallions, and even shredded lettuce. *Serves 6 as a main course without beans or rice, 8 to 10 as a main course with beans and/or rice, or 8 to 10 as a first course on its own*

1 large onion (about ¾ pound), peeled and quartered

2 cloves garlic, smashed and peeled

2 tablespoons whole dried red peppers (each 1 inch long)

1 can (35 ounces) Italian plum tomatoes

1½ teaspoons ground cumin

1½ teaspoons ground coriander

2 teaspoons chili powder, or to taste

½ teaspoon dried oregano

½ teaspoon dried marjoram

¼ teaspoon cayenne pepper

1 piece (2 inches) cinnamon stick

2 pounds beef chuck, cut into ¼-inch cubes

½ cup coarsely chopped fresh coriander leaves

1 ounce unsweetened chocolate, chopped

2 tablespoons red wine vinegar

2½ teaspoons kosher salt Sour cream, for serving (optional) Grated Monterey Jack or Cheddar cheese, for serving (optional)

1. Place onions, garlic, and peppers in the workbowl of a food processor. Process until coarsely chopped. Drain tomatoes (reserving juice) and add them to food processor. Process until coarsely chopped.

2. Put reserved juice and tomato mixture in a 14″ × 11″ × 2″ dish. Stir in cumin, coriander, chili powder, oregano, marjoram, cayenne, and cinnamon. Cook, uncovered, at 100% for 9 minutes.

3. Stir in beef. Cover tightly with microwave plastic wrap. Cook at 100% for 15 minutes.

4. If mellowing or planning to reheat, do not add remaining ingredients until reheated. Otherwise, stir in coriander, chocolate, vinegar, and salt. Serve chili with sour cream and grated cheese, if desired.

VARIATION

CHILI WITH GROUND BEEF Substitute 2 pounds lean ground beef for cubed beef. Cook for only 5 minutes in step 3. If ground beef clumps together, whirl in food processor for a few pulses to break up.

TRADITIONAL POT ROAST

This takes 10 minutes to prepare and 1 hour to cook, longer than almost any other recipe in this book; but it is worth it, especially considering that top-of-the-stove cooking time is 3 to 4 hours. Serve with Mashed Potatoes (page 276) or noodles. *Serves 6 to 8*

2¼ pounds brisket of beef, trimmed
½ pound medium carrots, trimmed, peeled and cut into 2½-inch lengths
1 medium yellow onion (about ½ pound), peeled and quartered
½ bay leaf

4 cloves garlic, smashed and peeled
½ cup Veal or Chicken Broth (page 331) or canned chicken broth
2 teaspoons kosher salt
1 cup Lightly Cooked Crushed Tomatoes (page 339) or canned crushed tomatoes with purée

1. Place brisket, fat side down, in a 2-quart soufflé dish. Arrange carrots, onions, bay leaf, and garlic around brisket. Pour broth over vegetables and sprinkle salt over all. Pour crushed tomatoes over brisket. Cover tightly with microwave plastic wrap. Cook at 100% for 35 minutes.

2. Uncover and turn brisket over. Re-cover tightly. Cook at 100% for 25 minutes.

3. Remove from oven. Mellow (page 234) if time allows. Slice thin across the grain. Serve hot.

BEEF IN RED WINE

This dish, called boeuf bourguignon by the French, is like most traditional stews: it is better the day after it is made. Store, tightly covered, in the refrigerator overnight. To reheat, see Mellowing (page 234). *Serve 6*

2 ounces slab bacon, cut into 2″ × ¼″ × ¼″ lardoons

¼ pound small mushrooms, stems trimmed, wiped clean and quartered through stem

¼ pound small white onions, peeled and quartered

2 pounds boneless beef chuck, cut into 1½-inch cubes

2 teaspoons kosher salt
Freshly ground black pepper

½ cup red wine

½ cup Veal or Chicken Broth (page 331), or canned chicken broth

½ cup canned tomatoes, drained and crushed

3 tablespoons Basic Tomato Paste (page 340) or canned tomato paste

¼ teaspoon dried thyme

¼ teaspoon dried rosemary

¼ teaspoon dried tarragon

6 cloves garlic, smashed and peeled

1 tablespoon cornstarch dissolved in 2 tablespoons cold water

2 tablespoons Meat Glaze (page 337) (optional)

2 tablespoons Cognac or brandy

1. Place lardoons in a 2-quart soufflé dish. Cook, uncovered, at 100% for 4 minutes.

2. Remove from oven. Remove lardoons to paper toweling to drain and reserve.

3. Stir mushrooms and onions into hot fat. Cook, uncovered, at 100% for 4 minutes.

4. Sprinkle beef with salt and pepper. Stir into onion mixture and add remaining ingredients except cornstarch, glaze, Cognac, and reserved lardoons. Cover tightly with microwave plastic wrap. Cook at 100% for 15 minutes.

5. Uncover. Stir in cornstarch, glaze, Cognac, and reserved lardoons, stirring well to combine. Cook, uncovered, at 100% for 4 minutes.

6. Remove from oven. Allow the stew to mellow (page 234). Reheat and serve hot.

SLICED BEEF CASSEROLE

The French call this dish boeuf en daube. Elizabeth David, the post-World War II English guru of French cooking, devised a method of slicing the beef for daube to shorten the cooking time and allow it to become more thoroughly imbued with the flavors of the sauce. This works well in the microwave oven. You might consider it as a way of cooking other pot roasts. The traditional cooking time for boeuf en daube, even with sliced beef, is 4 to 6 hours. In the microwave oven, total cooking time is 15 minutes.   *Serves 6 to 8*

1 tablespoon unsalted butter

1 medium yellow onion, peeled and cut into ½-inch dice (about 1 cup)

4 medium carrots, trimmed, peeled and cut into ½-inch dice (about 1¼ cups)

½ teaspoon dried tangerine zest or dried orange zest, or 3 strips (3″ × ½″) fresh orange zest

¼ cup minced parsley leaves

8 cloves garlic, smashed and peeled

1 bay leaf

1 teaspoon dried thyme

2 teaspoons kosher salt

3 pounds chuck roast, sliced across the grain, ½ inch thick

½ cup Chicken Broth (page 331) or canned chicken broth

¾ cup red wine

¼ cup brandy

1 tablespoon Meat Glaze (page 337), preferably Veal Glaze (optional)

1 piece bacon rind (6″ × 2″)

1. In a 2½-quart soufflé dish, combine butter, onions, carrots, tangerine or orange zest, parsley, and garlic. Cook, uncovered, at 100% for 4 minutes.

2. Remove from oven. Stir in bay leaf, thyme, and salt. Arrange sliced beef overlapping in dish. Pour broth, wine, brandy, and glaze, if desired, on beef. Tuck bacon rind between meat slices. Cover tightly with microwave plastic wrap. Cook at 100% for 10 minutes.

3. Uncover and stir well, pushing meat from the top toward the bottom of the dish. Cook, uncovered, at 100% for 5 minutes.

4. Remove from oven. Mellow (page 234) daube, if desired. Serve hot.

LEONARD SCHWARTZ'S MEAT LOAF

A colleague at *Vogue* tasted this meat loaf at Leonard Schwartz's 72 Market Street restaurant in California. She loved it so much that we got, tested, and printed the recipe to applause. Here is a microwave version, which can't shorten the ingredient list or the chopping time, although you can chop in the food processor. It does shorten the cooking time. It is definitely good enough to be company meat loaf. *Serves 8*

1 medium white onion,
   peeled and cut into
   1-inch chunks
1 cup 1-inch lengths
   scallion, trimmed
   (white and some of
   the green parts)
¾ cup 2-inch pieces
   celery, strung
¾ cup 1-inch pieces
   peeled carrot
½ cup 1-inch chunks red
   bell pepper,
   stemmed, seeded
   and deribbed
½ cup 1-inch chunks
   green bell pepper,
   stemmed, seeded
   and deribbed
2 large cloves garlic,
   smashed and peeled
3 tablespoons unsalted
   butter
1 teaspoon kosher salt

¼ teaspoon cayenne
   pepper
1 teaspoon freshly
   ground black
   pepper
½ teaspoon freshly
   ground white
   pepper
½ teaspoon ground
   cumin
½ teaspoon freshly
   ground nutmeg
½ cup half-and-half
½ cup ketchup
1½ pounds lean ground
   beef
½ pound lean ground
   pork
3 eggs, beaten
¾ cup fine, dry
   Breadcrumbs (page
   354) or store-
   bought unflavored
   breadcrumbs

1. Place vegetables and garlic in the workbowl of a food processor. Process until minced. Reserve.

2. Heat butter in an 11″ × 8½″ × 2″ dish, uncovered, at 100% for 3 minutes. Add minced vegetables and stir to coat. Cover loosely with paper toweling. Cook at 100% for 8 minutes.

3. Remove from oven. Uncover and let stand for 2 minutes.

4. Combine remaining ingredients in a large bowl, mixing well to make sure seasoning are evenly distributed. Knead in cooled, cooked vegetables.

5. Divide the mixture into 8 balls. Shape each ball into a small, rounded, oval loaf, 5″ × 3½″ × 1″. Arrange loaves inside the rim of a 12-inch round platter. Cover tightly with microwave plastic wrap. Cook at 100% for 4 minutes. Uncover and cook for 4 minutes more.

6. Remove from oven. Remove meat loaves to a warm platter. Serve with cooking juices spooned over, if desired.

To serve 4. Halve all ingredients. Prepare mixture as for 8 servings. Pack prepared mixture into a 9-inch glass ring mold (loaf should be about 2½ inches thick). Cook, tightly covered with microwave plastic wrap, at 100% for 5 minutes; uncover and cook for 4 minutes longer.

To serve 2. Use ½ small onion, ¼ cup sliced scallions, scant ¼ cup sliced celery, scant ¼ cup sliced carrots, 2 tablespoons *each* chopped red and green bell pepper, ½ clove garlic, 2 teaspoons butter, ¼ teaspoon salt, a pinch of cayenne, ½ teaspoon black pepper, ⅛ teaspoon white pepper, ⅛ teaspoon cumin, ⅛ teaspoon nutmeg, 2 tablespoons *each* half-and-half and ketchup, 6 ounces ground beef, 2 ounces ground pork, 1 small egg and a scant ¼ cup Breadcrumbs. Prepare mixture as for 8 servings. Shape into a rounded loaf. Cook on a serving plate, covered, at 100% for 4 minutes; uncover and cook for 3 minutes longer.

To serve 1. Prepare mixture as for 4 servings. Shape prepared mixture into 4 loaves (½ pound each). If you wish, wrap and freeze 3 loaves. Cook each ½-pound loaf by itself, on a serving plate, tightly covered, at 100% for 3 minutes; uncover and continue cooking for 1 minute. To defrost a frozen ½-pound loaf, place it on a serving plate and cover tightly with microwave plastic wrap. Cook at 100% for 4 minutes 30 seconds; the meat loaf will be defrosted and ready to cook.

Cook meat loaf in a ring mold so that it cooks evenly.

OLD-FASHIONED MEAT LOAF

When I was a child, I loved—almost best of all—the meat loaf nights with slices of juicy meat loaf, swirls of Mashed Potatoes (page 290), and extra cooking juice from the meat loaf nestled into a back-of-the-spoon indent in the potatoes. Creamed Spinach (page 300) completed childhood bliss. It was the kind of food my parents told me not to play with; but the rivers of gravy that would flow out of my potato mountain were irresistible. This is a recipe that doesn't let memory down. I wish more people would serve me food like this when I come to dinner.

If I have extra, I pretend I'm a grown-up and serve it cold the next day as pâté.   *Serves 6 to 8*

1 celery stalk, trimmed,
    strung and broken
    into 3 pieces
1 small yellow onion,
    peeled
2 cups Lightly Cooked
    Crushed Tomatoes
    (page 339), or
    canned tomato purée
1 cup fresh breadcrumbs
  1 tablespoon coarse
    mustard

2 teaspoons Hot Pepper
    Sauce (page 343)
    or commercial hot
    red-pepper sauce
1 tablespoon
    Worcestershire
    sauce
1½ teaspoons kosher salt
    Freshly ground black
    pepper
2 pounds ground beef

1. Put all ingredients except beef in the workbowl of a food processor. Process until well mixed. Scrape mixture into a large bowl and, using your hands, combine with beef. Pack into a 9″ × 5″ × 3″ loaf pan. Cook, uncovered, at 100% for 12 minutes.

2. Remove from oven. Let stand for 10 minutes. Carefully drain off cooking juices. Serve hot or cold. Skim cooking juices. Use as a gravy over mashed potatoes, rice, or noodles.

SHORT RIBS OF BEEF

I love short ribs. They are a bit fatty, but succulent. The seasoning and sauce here are French, but the result is pure American. Short ribs take a little longer to cook in the microwave oven than other cuts of beef because of the bone. Have the butcher cut the ribs into pieces for you. Short ribs vary in weight. In the recipes that follow, you may substitute any number of ribs, keeping the total weight the same. *Serves 4*

2½ pounds beef short ribs (approximately 3 pieces, each cut across the bone into pieces 3″ × 2½″ each, making 6 pieces)
Kosher salt
Freshly ground black pepper
1 medium yellow onion, peeled and cut into ¼-inch dice (about 1 cup)
½ cup dry red wine
¼ cup Cognac
¼ cup fresh orange juice

12 cloves garlic, smashed and peeled
1 tablespoon Basic Tomato Paste (page 236) or canned tomato paste
3 strips (½″ × 3″) orange zest
1 tablespoon cornstarch
½ cup Niçoise olives, pitted or whole (optional)
¼ cup finely chopped parsley
1½ tablespoons fresh lemon juice

1. Sprinkle ribs with salt and pepper. Place in a single layer in a 2-quart soufflé dish. Add remaining ingredients except cornstarch, olives, parsley, and lemon juice. Cover tightly with microwave plastic wrap. Cook at 100% for 25 minutes, until tender.

2. Remove from oven and uncover. Take out ribs with a slotted spoon; keep warm. Skim fat from cooking liquid. Mix cornstarch with 2 tablespoons water and stir in a little of the cooking liquid. Stir back into cooking liquid. Stir in olives, if using, and parsley. Cook sauce, uncovered, at 100% for 2 minutes.

3. Season sauce with salt, pepper, and lemon juice. Mellow (page 234) ribs in sauce if time allows. Either return ribs to sauce if cooking dish is a serving dish or spoon sauce over ribs and serve.

To serve 2. Halve quantities of short ribs, onion, garlic, zest, cornstarch, olives, if using, and parsley. Use 3 tablespoons wine, 1½ tablespoons Cognac, 1½ tablespoons orange juice, 1½ teaspoons tomato paste, and a few drops of lemon juice. Cook as for Short Ribs of Beef in a 1-quart soufflé dish for 12 minutes. Proceed as in step 2, cooking for 1 minute 30 seconds after addition of cornstarch

To serve 8. Double quantities of short ribs, onions, tomatopaste, olives, if using, cornstarch, and lemon juice. Use ¾ cup wine, ⅓ cup Cognac, ⅓ cup orange juice, 18 cloves garlic, 5 strips orange zest, and ⅓ cup parsley. Cook as for Short Ribs of Beef in a 14″ × 11″ × 2″ dish for 35 minutes. Proceed as in step 2, cooking for 5 minutes after addition of cornstarch.

SHORT RIBS OF BEEF WITH MORELS

This terrific company dish for serious eaters contrasts down-home short ribs with the elegance of morels. *Serves 4*

½ cup dried morel mushrooms (about 1 ounce)

1 cup warm water

4 beef short ribs (about 1½ pounds), cut as in Short Ribs of Beef (see preceding recipe)

Kosher salt

Freshly ground black pepper

24 pearl or small pickling onions, peeled (page 560), or frozen onions, defrosted

½ teaspoon dried thyme

½ cup Veal Broth (page 331) or canned chicken broth

1. Place mushrooms and water in a 2-cup glass measure. Cover tightly with microwave plastic wrap. Cook at 100% for 3 minutes.

2. Remove from oven and let stand, covered, for 2 minutes. Uncover and drain mushrooms. Strain liquid through a double thickness of paper toweling and reserve. Rinse mushrooms under cool running water to remove grit and reserve.

3. Sprinkle ribs with salt and pepper. Place ribs, meaty side down, in a single layer in a 2-quart soufflé dish. Add reserved mushroom liquid, mushrooms, and remaining ingredients. Cover tightly with microwave plastic wrap. Cook at 100% for 25 minutes

4. Remove from oven and let stand, covered, for 1 minute. Uncover. Remove ribs, mushrooms, and onions to a serving plate and keep warm. Skim fat from sauce. Return sauce to oven and cook, uncovered, for 2 minutes.

5. Remove from oven and season with salt and pepper. Mellow (page 234) if time allows. Either return ribs to sauce if they were cooked in a serving dish or spoon sauce over ribs and serve.

To serve 2. Cook ½ ounce dried morels in ½ cup water, tightly covered, for 2 minutes; strain and reserve liquid and mushrooms as in Short Ribs of Beef with Morels. Halve quantities of short ribs, onions, and thyme. Use ¼ cup morel liquid and 3 tablespoons broth. Cook in a 1-quart soufflé dish for 12 minutes. Finish as in Short Ribs of Beef with Morels.

To Serve 8. Double quantities of short ribs, morels, onions, and thyme. Cook morels in 2 cups water, tightly covered, for 6 minutes; strain and reserve liquid and mushrooms as in Short Ribs of Beef with Morels. Use 1½ cups morel liquid and ¾ cup broth. Cook in a 14″ × 11″ × 2″ dish for 35 minutes. Finish as in Short Ribs of Beef with Morels.

BARBECUED SHORT RIBS

Nothing could be quicker or easier. If you don't have time to make my Red Barbecue Sauce (page 377), use your favorite brand of bottled tomato-based barbecue sauce. Biscuits, cornbread, mashed potatoes, or rice are indicated here. Bread and Butter Pickles (page 466) or Maple Corn Relish (page 465) would fit right in. The ribs can be placed on a hot charcoal grill just until marked, or lightly coated with sauce and run under a preheated broiler until lightly browned.   *Serves 4*

4 beef short ribs (about 1½ pounds), cut as in Short Ribs of Beef (page 246)	**6 tablespoons Red Barbecue Sauce (page 377) or bottled tomato-based barbecue sauce**
Kosher salt	**6 tablespoons beer**
Freshly ground black pepper	

1. Sprinkle ribs with salt and pepper. Place ribs, meaty side down, in a 2-quart soufflé dish. Beat sauce and beer together and pour over ribs. Cover tightly with microwave plastic wrap. Cook at 100% for 25 minutes.

2. Remove from oven. Let stand for 1 minute. Uncover. Transfer ribs to a serving plate and keep warm. Grill or broil as desired.

3. Skim fat from sauce. Season sauce to taste with salt and pepper. Pour over ribs and serve hot.

To serve 2. Use 2 short ribs, ¼ cup barbecue sauce, and ¼ cup beer. Cook as for Barbecued Short Ribs in a 1-quart soufflé dish for 12 minutes.

To serve 8. Use 8 short ribs and ½ cup plus 1 tablespoon each barbecue sauce and beer. Cook as for Barbecued Short Ribs in a 2-quart soufflé dish for 35 minutes.

Pork

Pork has been one of the great revelations of working on this book. I have always liked pork; but it rises to a new level of succulence with microwave cooking. It cooks through before it dries out. Even with the reduced fat content of today's pork, it bastes itself to perfection. Clearly, it doesn't brown. I think that is an improvement; the pork doesn't develop those nasty stringy bits. The only place where the browning seems important is in the Smothered Pork Roast (page 253). There, you broil the roast briefly after it is cooked, to crisp and brown the surface fat.

When cooking pork, it is important to make sure the meat is cooked through. The best way to tell is to use a small, instant-reading thermometer. Insert the thermometer halfway into the fleshiest part of the meat, not too close to the bone. Watch for a temperature of 140° F. to 145° F. The meat will keep cooking for a while after it comes out of the oven. All these recipes work for the time and temperature that are given, but your piece of meat may have a slightly different weight or shape. It is not critical; but it makes it worth using the thermometer.

PORK CHOPS WITH SAUERKRAUT

The Hungarians know a thing or two about food. One of the things they know is an extraordinary stew of pork and sauerkraut called Szekely Gulyas. This meatier version is made with pork chops.

I defy anybody to eat two of these pork chops and the savory sauerkraut that goes with them—too much. These are big chops. Steam some potatoes or butter some noodles. Drink icy beer or a white riesling wine.   *Serves 4*

2 tablespoons unsalted butter

1 large onion (about ¾ pound), peeled, thinly sliced and separated into rings

4 loin pork chops (1 to 1½ inches thick), 2 to 2½ pounds

3 pounds sauerkraut, drained and rinsed

1 tablespoon caraway seeds

6 cloves garlic, smashed and peeled

2 cups sour cream

2 to 3 tablespoons Hot and Sweet Red Pepper Sauce (page 343) or Hungarian paprika paste

1. Heat butter in a 14″ × 11″ × 2″ dish, uncovered, at 100% for 2 minutes. Stir in onions. Cook, uncovered, for 2 minutes more.

2. Remove from oven. Arrange pork chops on top of onions; place one in each corner of the dish with the bone against the side of the dish. Spread sauerkraut over chops and stir in caraway. Press garlic into sauerkraut. Cover tightly with microwave plastic wrap. Cook at 100% for 16 minutes.

3. Insert an instant-reading thermometer right through the plastic into the thickest part of a chop, without letting it touch the bone. If it reads 145° F., the chops are done. If it reads less than 145° F., patch the hole in the plastic with a small piece of wrap and cook at 100% for 1 to 2 minutes more.

4. Stir in sour cream and pepper sauce. Cover tightly with microwave plastic wrap. Cook at 100% for 2 minutes

5. Remove from oven. Uncover and serve hot.

6. This reheats and mellows (page 234) well. Add ½ cup water or broth when reheating.

PORK CHOPS IN TOMATO SAUCE

If there is a meal easier than this, I don't know it. No one will know that you make it using jarred spaghetti sauce. The only important thing is that it tastes good. This dish is meant to be served with spaghetti or linguine, with the sauce from the chops poured over the pasta. Since the chops are thin, they sop up a maximum of flavor. One chop and a portion of spaghetti and sauce feeds me; but I have known a small, if admittedly athletic, person to inhale 3 chops. You will have to be the judge. When you have figured it out, allow about 2 ounces of dry pasta per person. That makes 4 ounces if each person eats 3 chops, and 12 ounces if there are 6 eaters like me. I usually make about ½ pound of pasta and figure it will work out. Toss pasta with 1 tablespoon of olive oil before adding sauce. *Serves 6, 1 chop each*

6 **thin pork chops (½ to ¾ inch thick), about 2 pounds**
1 **cup bottled spaghetti sauce**
1 **tablespoon olive oil**
3 **large cloves garlic, smashed and peeled**

2 **tablespoons chopped parsley**
Large pinch dried thyme
Kosher salt
Freshly ground black pepper

1. Arrange chops in a 12-inch square dish with their bony sides against the sides of the dish.

Pork chops with bones toward edge of dish

2. Stir together spaghetti sauce, olive oil, garlic, parsley, and thyme and spoon over chops. Cover tightly with microwave plastic wrap. Cook at 100% for 8 minutes.

3. Insert an instant-reading thermometer right through the plastic into the thickest part of a chop, without touching the bone. If it reads 145° F., the chops are done. If it reads less than 145° F., patch plastic with a small piece of wrap and return to oven for 1 to 2 minutes more.

4. Remove from oven and uncover. Stir in salt and pepper to taste and serve.

To serve 1. Use 1 pork chop, ¼ cup sauce, 1 teaspoon oil, 1 small clove garlic, 2 teaspoons parsley, a small pinch of thyme, salt, and pepper. Center chop in a 6-inch round dish. Cover tightly with microwave plastic wrap. Cook as for Pork Chops in Tomato Sauce for 4 minutes.

To serve 12. Double all ingredients. Cook in 2 batches: spoon half the sauce over 6 chops and cook as for Pork Chops in Tomato Sauce. Serve the first 6 or keep them warm while preparing the rest.

SMOTHERED PORK ROAST

This is a cross between a pot roast and a real roast, and it is the best pork roast I have ever had, with the plus of a great vegetable. If you want to add something, it should be a simple, colorful vegetable like Glazed Carrots (page 278) or leaf spinach. Leftover meat is good cold in sandwiches or sliced and reheated with some of the vegetable purée. *Serves 6 to 8 as a main course*

3 baking potatoes, each pierced twice with a fork
3 tablespoons unsalted butter
4 cups sliced onions (about 1 pound)
1 cup strung, sliced celery (about ½ pound)

¼ cup minced parsley
1 boneless pork loin roast (3½ pounds, 4 inches in diameter)
2 teaspoons kosher salt
Freshly ground black pepper
½ teaspoon caraway seeds

1. Cook potatoes (page 571). Remove from oven. Cover with an inverted pot or two kitchen towels to keep warm.

2. Heat butter in an 11″ × 8″ × 2″ dish, uncovered, at 100% for 5 minutes. Stir in celery and parsley.

3. Sprinkle roast with salt, pepper, and caraway. Place in onion mixture, fat side down. Cover tightly with microwave plastic wrap. Cook at 100% for 10 minutes.

4. Uncover and turn roast over. Re-cover; cook for 10 minutes more.

5. Preheat conventional broiler.

6. Uncover roast and turn over again. Cook, uncovered, for 15 minutes.

7. Put roast in a pan that can go under the broiler. Broil until brown, if desired.

8. Scrape vegetables into a food processor. Peel and dice potatoes. Add to vegetables; purée until smooth. Serve with the roast.

SAUSAGE AND PEPPERS

This is super easy and very good. The spiciness of the dish will depend on the spiciness of the sausage you can find or want to use. If you cannot find fresh basil, substitute ½ teaspoon dried basil.   *Serves 3 to 4*

2 pounds fresh hot
   Italian sausage
   links, cut into 2-
   inch lengths
½ pound onion, peeled
   and cut into ½-inch
   cubes
1 green bell pepper,
   stemmed, seeded,
   deribbed and cut
   into 2-inch chunks

1 red bell pepper,
   stemmed, seeded,
   deribbed and cut
   into 2-inch chunks
¼ cup (tightly packed)
   fresh basil leaves
¼ cup store-bought
   marinara sauce
Kosher salt

1. Place sausage in an 11″ × 8″ × 2″ oval dish and cover loosely with paper toweling. Cook at 100% for 10 minutes, stirring twice.

2. Remove from oven. Uncover, drain well, and discard fat.

3. Add remaining ingredients except salt. Stir to coat. Cover tightly with microwave plastic wrap. Cook at 100% for 7 minutes.

4. Remove from oven. Uncover and sprinkle with salt. Serve with mashed potatoes or pasta, or on Italian bread.

VARIATION

SAUSAGE AND FENNEL Substitute ¾ cup bulb fennel cut into 2-inch chunks for green pepper and 1 teaspoon fennel seeds for basil. Serves 3 to 4.

BARBECUED SPARERIBS

Finish these out of doors on a grill or under your broiler. Eat hot or cold, as picnic food. Lamb riblets are particularly good for a cocktail party. The recipe gives you, as a dividend, 1 cup of cooking juices, which are delicious spooned over Mashed Potatoes (page 290) or used as the cooking liquid for Pot Greens (page 572). *Serves 3 to 4*

3½ pounds spareribs	**1 recipe Red Barbecue Sauce (page 377), made with minced garlic**

1. Arrange ribs in a single layer in a 14″ × 11″ × 2″ dish. Brush on one side with half of sauce. Cover tightly with microwave plastic wrap. Cook at 100% for 10 minutes.

2. If using broiler, preheat.

3. Remove meat from oven and uncover. Turn ribs over and brush with remaining sauce. Re-cover tightly with fresh microwave plastic wrap. Cook at 100% for 10 minutes.

4. Grill for 4 minutes, turning once, or broil, in broiler pan, 6 inches from heat source for 5 minutes, turning once. Serve hot.

VARIATIONS

ORIENTAL SPARERIBS Replace barbecue sauce with a sauce made by combining ¼ cup Chicken Broth (page 331) or canned chicken broth, ½ cup tamari soy, ⅓ cup sugar, ½ crushed star-anise pod or ½ teaspoon five-spice powder, 6 cloves smashed and peeled garlic, and 6 crushed red pepper pods in a 4-cup glass measure. Cover tightly with microwave plastic wrap. Cook at 100% for 3 minutes. Proceed as for Barbecued Spareribs.

BARBECUED LAMB RIBLETS Substitute an equal weight of lamb riblets for spareribs. Cook as for Barbecued Spareribs. Broil without turning. Serves 14 at cocktails.

Veal

Veal has become incredibly expensive. I don't like the quality of most of what is available and it's hard to get butchers to pay proper attention to it—separating it into individual muscles and so forth. Consequently, most of these recipes are for less expensive and less fussy cuts of veal. These are exactly the recipes that usually take a long time to cook, but not with a microwave oven.

Don't overcook veal: since it contains little fat, it dries out. Veal is pale in color. Pick colorful accompaniments—purées like Carrot and Potato (page 299) or Creamed Spinach (page 300)—or Wild Rice (page 127) to brighten the plate. Simply cooked veal can be accompanied by stuffed Vegetables (page 71–81), and it does well with a Mushroom Sauce (page 368), or Sauce Espagnole (page 371), or Sauce Poulette (page 368) made with veal broth.

VEAL FRICASSEE

This ivory-colored stew, the French blanquette de veau, is enlivened with a few nontraditional carrots. It is almost always served with plain rice. You could use Green Pilaf (page 130) instead, for a nice color contrast. Make the fricassee first. Let it mellow (page 234) before adding the egg-yolk mixture, while you cook the pilaf. Then reheat for 30 seconds more than the time given.   *Serves 4 to 6*

1 tablespoon unsalted
  butter
½ pound mushrooms,
  trimmed and
  quartered
½ pound pearl onions,
  peeled
2 carrots, trimmed,
  peeled and cut into
  2-inch lengths
2 pounds veal shoulder
  or leg, trimmed and
  cut into 2-inch
  cubes
2 cups Veal or Chicken
  Broth (page 331) or
  canned chicken
  broth

1 teaspoon dried thyme
½ bay leaf
1 clove garlic, smashed
  and peeled
2 tablespoons cornstarch
¾ cup heavy cream
3 egg yolks
Pinch freshly ground
  nutmeg
Kosher salt
Freshly ground black
  pepper
2 tablespoons fresh
  lemon juice

1. Heat butter in 2-quart soufflé dish, uncovered, at 100% for 30 seconds.

2. Toss mushrooms and onions in butter and mound in center of dish. Arrange carrots and veal in a circle around the onions.

3. Cover with broth. Add thyme, bay leaf, and garlic. Cover tightly with microwave plastic wrap. Cook at 100% for 15 minutes.

4. Remove from oven. Pierce plastic with the tip of a sharp knife. Remove plastic. Let stew stand for 10 minutes, to cool slightly so the eggs do not curdle when added.

5. Stir cornstarch into about 4 tablespoons of cream. Stir in remaining cream, egg yolks, and nutmeg and blend thoroughly. Add to stew and stir well. Cover tightly with microwave plastic wrap. Cook at 100% for 4 minutes.

6. Remove from oven. Uncover and stir. Taste and correct seasoning with salt, pepper, and lemon juice.

VARIATION

VEAL FRICASSEE WITH ANISE Add 1½ tablespoons aniseed or 1 teaspoon crushed anise when you add garlic.

LOIN OF VEAL

Admitted that veal is expensive, this is the way to get the maximum of what you pay for in the least possible amount of time with a minimum of fuss. The cooking takes all of 6 minutes. The meat doesn't shrink and stays white and tender. You can also serve it cold, thinly sliced, as a first course Italian-fashion (vitello tonnato), to an unexpectedly large group, or as a main course on a hot day, with a lettuce and tomato salad, cold white wine, and bread sticks. See page 384 for Tonnato Sauce. *Serves 4*

1 boneless loin of veal (1½ pounds)	**½ cup Veal or Chicken Broth (page 331) or canned chicken broth**

1. Put veal in a 9″ × 5″ × 3″ dish. Add broth and cover tightly with microwave plastic wrap. Cook at 100% for 6 minutes.

2. Insert an instant-reading thermometer right through the plastic into the center of the meat. At 145° F., the veal is done; it will be pale pink in the center. (For a loin cooked through, not at all pink, cook for 8 minutes.) If it is not done to your liking, patch plastic with a small piece of wrap and cook for 1 to 2 minutes longer.

VEAL STEW

This is an utterly delicious stew with an elegant sauce. Sauces today are seldom thickened with breadcrumbs the way this one is. It used to be commonplace and was called thickening with panade, a French word derived from *pain* (bread). The stew is rich, the sauce ample. Serve it with rice and it will serve more people than you might imagine. *Serves 6 to 8*

2 pounds veal shoulder or leg, trimmed and cut into 2-inch cubes

4 teaspoons kosher salt Freshly ground black pepper

2 cups Veal Broth (page 331)

1 celery stalk, trimmed, strung and cut into 3 pieces

1 carrot, trimmed, peeled and cut into 3 pieces

1 small onion (about ¼ pound), peeled and quartered

¼ cup (packed) parsley, preferably flat-leaf parsley

2 tablespoons unsalted butter Pinch dried thyme

2 cups fresh breadcrumbs

2 egg whites

1. Season veal with 2 teaspoons of the salt and the pepper. Put in a 2-quart soufflé dish and add 1½ cups of the broth. Cover tightly with microwave plastic wrap. Cook at 100% for 10 minutes.

2. Put celery, carrots, onions, and parsley in the workbowl of a food processor. Process until coarsely chopped. Scrape into an 8-cup glass measure. Add butter, thyme, remaining salt, and pepper to taste, and stir to combine.

3. Remove veal from oven and set aside. Cook chopped vegetables, uncovered, at 100% for 4 minutes.

4. Remove from oven. Whisk in breadcrumbs and egg whites. Add remaining broth and stir. Cover tightly with microwave plastic wrap. Cook at 100% for 5 minutes.

5. Remove from oven. Uncover veal and remove with a slotted spoon to a small container. Pour cooking liquid from veal into a blender. Add vegetable mixture and blend for 20 seconds. Return veal to soufflé dish and pour sauce over it.

ITALIAN-STYLE VEAL SHANKS

These veal shanks make a wonderful Italian winter dish called ossobuco. It is usually served with Saffron Risotto (page 122) and sprinkled on top with an attractive and sharp aromatic mix called gremolata. It used to take so long to make that it was only worth doing for a party. Now that it can be quickly made in the microwave oven, it is still good party fare, but is wonderfully heartwarming. Made in 12 minutes, it is a comfort to the soul. Some veal shanks made very large and meaty slices and will feed two. Give your guest demitasse spoons to scoop out the marrow from the center of the bone. It is a succulent, if not terribly healthy, prize. *Serve 4*

VEAL SHANKS
- 1 small onion, peeled and cut in half
- ¼ pound celery stalks, trimmed, strung and broken into 3 pieces each
- ¼ pound carrots, trimmed, peeled and cut into 2-inch lengths
- 4 pieces veal shank (about ¾ pound each), cut across the bone 2½ inches thick
- 2 tablespoons olive oil
- 3 cloves garlic, smashed and peeled
- 1 piece orange zest (3″ × ½″)
- 1 piece lemon zest (3″ × ½″)
- 1 teaspoon kosher salt
- ⅛ teaspoon freshly ground black pepper
- ¼ teaspoon dried thyme
- ½ bay leaf
- 3 parsley sprigs
- Pinch cayenne pepper
- ¼ cup canned tomatoes, drained and crushed
- 3 tablespoons Basic Tomato Paste (page 340) or canned tomato paste
- ¼ cup white wine
- ¼ cup Chicken Broth (page 331) or canned chicken broth
- 2 tablespoons Veal or Chicken Glaze (page 337)

GREMOLATA
- 5 cloves garlic, smashed and peeled
- 1 bunch parsley
- 5 pieces orange zest (3″ × ½″)
- 1 piece lemon zest (3″ × ½″)

1. Place onions, celery, and carrots in the workbowl of a food processor. Process until coarsely chopped.

2. On top of the stove, brown veal on all sides in oil; this will take about 10 minutes.

3. Put veal in an 11″ × 8″ × 2″ oval or rectangular dish. Scatter chopped vegetables over shanks. Tuck garlic and zests between shanks. Combine remaining ingredients for shanks and pour over. Cover tightly with microwave plastic wrap. Cook at 100% for 16 minutes.

4. Place ingredients for gremolata in food processor and process until finely chopped. Reserve.

5. Remove shanks from oven. Pierce plastic with the tip of a sharp knife. Let sit for 15 minutes before serving or mellow (page 234) for a longer time. Just before serving, top each shank with gremolata.

To serve 2. Halve all ingredients. Cook as for 4 servings in an 9½″ × 7″ × 1¾″ oval dish for 12 minutes.

To serve 6. Use 6 pieces veal shank as above, 3 tablespoons oil, 1 medium onion, about ¾ cup *each* chopped celery and carrots, 4 to 5 cloves garlic, 1½ pieces *each* orange and lemon zest, 1½ teaspoons salt, a scant ¼ teaspoon pepper, ½ teaspoon thyme, ¾ bay leaf, 5 parsley sprigs, large pinch cayenne, ¼ cup plus 2 tablespoons crushed tomatoes, 4½ tablespoons tomato paste, ¼ cup plus 2 tablespoons *each* wine and broth, and 3 tablespoons glaze. Prepare gremolata and proceed as for cooking shanks in a 14″ × 11″ × 2″ dish for 22 minutes.

Lamb

I don't know why, but we don't eat our fair share of lamb in this country. We raise some of the best. We have good, inexpensive lamb available to us, fresh and frozen, from New Zealand. We eat rack of lamb in fancy restaurants. We pretty much let it go at that, aside from an occasional chop. It's a shame. Lamb has wonderful flavor, it goes with a wide variety of seasonings, and it is relatively inexpensive. Lamb makes one of the best roasts, is terrific in curry, loves spinach, and goes with beans—fresh green French beans or dried flageolets (page 483).

When making lamb stew for close friends or family, buy lamb with the bone in. It will be more succulent. Neck and shoulder are good, inexpensive stew cuts. Sometimes lamb steaks, cut from the top of the leg, are available at a good price; they can be cut up for stew, as can regular lamb chops, if they are cheaply bought on special. For company, use stew meat that has been taken off the bone.

Lamb likes the stronger-tasting purées. Rutabaga Purée (page 297) or Winter Vegetable Purée (page 294), would both be good with stew. Szechuan Green Beans (page 308) and Chinese Stewed Tomatoes (page 310) are unusual partners for roast lamb.

LAMB STEW

Lamb stew is rich and full of flavor, even richer when made with bones. It can be a spring dish made with peas and green herbs or that midwinter classic, Irish Stew. The latter may sound plain, but I guarantee that it tastes terrific—ideal family fare. *Serves 4 to 6*

2 pounds lamb, bone in, cut into chunks no larger than 2½ inches square

3 cups Lamb Broth (page 332), Chicken Broth (page 331) or canned chicken broth

3 medium carrots, trimmed, peeled and cut into sticks 2″ × ¼″ × ¼″

½ pound onions, peeled and quartered

¼ cup strung, sliced celery

5 cloves garlic, smashed and peeled

1 tablespoon cornstarch

1 cup peas

½ cup finely chopped parsley

1½ tablespoons fresh mint leaves

2 tablespoons fresh lemon juice

Kosher salt

Freshly ground black pepper

1. Place lamb, broth, carrots, onions, celery, and garlic in a 2½-quart soufflé dish. Cover tightly with microwave plastic wrap. Cook at 100% for 15 minutes.

2. Uncover. Dissolve cornstarch in about 2 tablespoons cooking liquid. Add to lamb mixture and stir thoroughly. Add peas, parsley and mint. Recover tightly with fresh microwave plastic wrap. Cook at 100% for 2 minutes 30 seconds to 3 minutes, until sauce has thickened.

3. Remove from oven. Uncover and season to taste with lemon juice, salt, and pepper.

VARIATION

IRISH STEW Use 2 pounds lamb as for Lamb Stew; ½ pound peeled small white onions (not pearl); 1 pound peeled small white potatoes, cut in 2-inch chunks; ½ pound small turnips, about 2 inches in diameter, peeled and cut into ½-inch wedges; 1½ tablespoons kosher salt; freshly ground black pepper; and 1½ cups water. Omit other ingredients. Arrange lamb around inside edge of a 2-quart soufflé dish. Put vegetables in center. Dissolve salt in water and add with pepper to taste. Cover tightly with microwave plastic wrap and cook at 100% for 25 minutes.   Serves 4 to 6.

GREEN LAMB CURRY

Not all curries are yellow; a few of my favorites are green with herbs, like this one, which is a good dish for family or company. Don't be discouraged by the long list of ingredients. Most of them are spices.

The curry goes well with Tomato Pilaf (page 131). If you have a little time, or have it on hand, try Peach Chutney (page 470) or Fresh Mango Chutney (page 471). All the usual curry accompaniments (page 205) can be served.
Serves 4

2 teaspoons vegetable oil

1½ teaspoons sesame seed

½ teaspoon fennel seed

1½ teaspoons cumin seed

1½ teaspoons mustard seed

8 to 10 cloves garlic, smashed and peeled

1 cup (packed) parsley leaves

2 medium onions, peeled and quartered

1½ pounds lamb, cut into 1½-inch cubes (about 3 cups)

1 package frozen baby lima beans, defrosted in a sieve under warm running water

⅓ cup Lamb or Chicken Broth (page 331) or canned chicken broth plus any accumulated juices from lamb

1 pound spinach, thoroughly washed, stemmed and dried (about 1 packed cup)

1½ cups (lightly packed) dill sprigs

1 jalapeño pepper, stemmed, seeded, deribbed and cut into ½-inch pieces

1 tablespoon grated fresh ginger

⅛ teaspoon ground nutmeg

½ teaspoon dried thyme

1 bay leaf, broken in half

Kosher salt

1. Heat oil in a 2-quart soufflé dish, uncovered, at 100% for 2 minutes.

2. Add sesame, fennel, cumin, and mustard seeds. Cover loosely with a sheet of paper toweling. Cook at 100% for 4 minutes.

3. Put garlic and parsley in the workbowl of a food processor and process until finely chopped. Add onions and process until coarsely chopped.

4. Scrape mixture into soufflé dish, add lamb and toss to combine. Stir in lima beans and broth. Cover tightly with microwave plastic wrap. Cook at 100% for 4 minutes.

5. Put spinach, dill, jalapeño pepper, ginger, nutmeg and thyme in food processor. Process until finely chopped. Add this mixture and bay leaf to lamb and stir well. Re-cover tightly with microwave plastic wrap. Cook at 100% for 2 minutes.

6. Remove from oven and uncover. Stir in salt to taste and serve hot.

LEG OF LAMB

This is not a true microwave recipe, but it is a useful trick for which you can use the microwave oven. Since we sometimes buy leg of lamb already frozen or freeze it for storage, it is nice to be able to defrost and cook it in the same time or less than it would ordinarily take just to cook it. This makes leg of lamb good emergency rations to keep on hand for last-minute guests or to keep in a country house.

The meat is actually cooked at a very high temperature in a conventional oven, but since it heats somewhat during defrosting, the roasting time is reduced. The result is very good. For convenience's sake, defrost the lamb in a dish that can also go in the regular oven.   *Serves 8 to 10*

1 frozen 7-pound leg of lamb	1 teaspoon rosemary leaves, fresh or dried
4 cloves garlic, smashed, peeled and slivered	1½ cups Lamb Broth (page 332), canned chicken broth, red wine or a mixture of half wine and half broth
1 tablespoon kosher salt	
½ teaspoon freshly ground black pepper	

1. Preheat conventional oven to 500° F.

2. Place leg of lamb in a 14″ × 11″ × 2″ dish. Shield the shank of lamb with aluminum foil (page 12). Cover tightly with microwave plastic wrap. Cook at 100% for 14 minutes. Without removing from oven, uncover and remove foil shield. Re-cover and cook for 14 minutes more.

3. Remove from oven and uncover. Move roast to roasting pan, if necessary. Prick all over with a small knife and insert slivers of garlic in meat. Sprinkle all surfaces with salt, pepper, and rosemary.

4. Place in preheat oven. Cook for 20 minutes for rare, 25 to 27 minutes for medium rare.

5. Remove from oven. Put meat on a platter. Let stand for 15 minutes before carving. Pour fat out of cooking pan, leaving juices in pan.

6. If lamb was roasted in a microwavable dish, add broth or other liquids to dish. Place in microwave oven, uncovered, for 5 minutes at 100%. Remove and stir to dissolve all the meat juices in pan. Correct seasoning. Serve as gravy.

7. If meat was roasted in a metal pan, place on stove over high heat. Pour in broth or other liquids while scraping pan with a wooden spoon to dissolve all the meat juices. Cook for 3 minutes, stirring constantly. Season and serve.

VARIATION

ROAST LEG OF BABY NEW ZEALAND LAMB For a 4-pound frozen leg of lamb, use 3 cloves garlic, 1 teaspoon salt, ¼ teaspoon pepper, and 1 cup broth. Omit rosemary. Preheat oven as for Leg of Lamb. Place lamb in a 13½″ × 9½″ × 2″ dish and shield with foil. Cook, uncovered, at 100% for 15 minutes. Remove shield and cook for 6 minutes more. Remove from oven and stud with garlic as for Leg of Lamb. Roast in conventional oven for 20 minutes. Remove lamb to a serving platter. Pour fat out of the pan; add broth and deglaze, cooking for 3 minutes. Serves 6.

LAMB SHANKS WITH MINT

It would be nice to make the recipe for Lamb Shanks with Spinach (page 267) for eight, but it is impossible to get enough spinach into the pot. Instead try this entirely different recipe. It derives slightly from the idea of Greek lamb with mint, partly from the ubiquitous English mint sauce for lamb. *Serves 8*

4 lamb shanks (about 1½
    pounds each), each
    cut across the bone
    into 2 equal pieces
1 tablespoon kosher salt

4 tablespoons minced
    fresh mint
6 cloves garlic, smashed
    and peeled

1. Place shank pieces in a 12″ × 10″ × 3″ oval dish. Sprinkle with salt, half the mint, and all the garlic. Cover tightly with microwave plastic wrap. Cook at 100% for 22 minutes.

2. Remove from oven. Uncover and sprinkle with remaining mint. Serve hot or mellow (page 234), then reheat.

LAMB SHANKS WITH SPINACH

Lamb shanks make hearty eating, and they are inexpensive. All they require is a little work on the part of the eater to cut the meat off the bone. The only problem is deciding how many people they will serve. Lamb shanks vary in size and weight. This recipe is for ¾-pound shanks. The previous one is for larger shanks weighing 1½ pounds. A ¾-pound shank feeds one; a 1½-pound shank feeds two. The larger shank should be sawed in half across the bone to make serving easier. *Serves 4*

1 baking potato, peeled
    and cut into 1½-
    inch cubes
6 pounds spinach,
    stemmed, washed
    and squeezed of
    excess water,
    chopped in the food
    processor (about 6
    cups chopped)
4 lamb shanks, about ¾
    pound each

12 cloves garlic, smashed
    and peeled
2 teaspoons dried
    oregano
1 teaspoon dried thyme
8 ounces plain yogurt
1 tablespoon kosher
    salt
Freshly ground black
    pepper
1½ teaspoons ground
    cumin

1. Bring 1 quart lightly salted water to a boil on the stove. Add potato and cook until tender.

2. Spread half the spinach over the bottom of a 10″ × 8″ dish. Arrange shanks on the spinach. Sprinkle the meat with garlic, oregano and thyme. Cover with remaining spinach. Cover tightly with microwave plastic wrap. Cook at 100% for 30 minutes.

3. Remove from oven. Put shanks on a platter or plates and keep warm. Return dish with spinach to oven. Cook, uncovered, at 100% for 5 minutes. If mellowing (page 234) or making ahead, stop at this point. Then reheat.

4. Remove from oven. Stir in yogurt, salt, pepper to taste, and cumin. Drain potatoes and stir gently into spinach mixture. Arrange around shanks and serve hot.

To serve 2. Halve all ingredients. Proceed as for Lamb Shanks with Spinach, cooking shanks and spinach in a 2-quart soufflé dish for 22 minutes, then spinach alone for 3 minutes.

Other Meats

When we think of meat, we usually think of beef, pork, lamb and veal. Here, I have recipes for rabbit, tongue, and brains. They may not be everyday fare, but they are definitely worth trying in the microwave oven. To cook sweetbreads, see page 55.

RABBIT IN MUSTARD SAUCE

It is a commonplace that every time someone does not know how to describe a meat, from rattlesnake to alligator to frogs' legs, they say that it tastes like chicken. Well, rabbit does taste a bit like chicken, but better. Now that rabbits are available, frozen, in many supermarkets, you should give them a try. They are usually already cut into serving pieces. Serve with noodles, rice, or Potato Galette (page 143).
Serves 4 to 6

2 to 2½ pounds frozen
   rabbit, cut into
   serving pieces
2 cups milk
1 cup heavy cream
1 cup Dijon mustard

2 tablespoons fresh
   lemon juice
½ teaspoon kosher salt
½ teaspoon freshly
   ground black
   pepper

1. Arrange rabbit, bonier side up, in an 11″ × 8″ × 2″ oval dish.

2. Whisk together remaining ingredients. Pour over rabbit. Cover tightly with microwave plastic wrap. Cook at 30% (see page 9) for 15 minutes; halfway through cooking time, uncover dish and turn rabbit over.

3. Re-cover and increase power to 100% and cook for 17 minutes. Preheat conventional broiler.

4. Remove rabbit from oven. Uncover and remove rabbit to a broiling pan. Brush with some of the cooking liquid and broil 6 inches from the heat source for 2 to 3 minutes, until lightly browned. Serve with additional sauce.

SMOKED TONGUE

I love smoked tongue, both hot and cold, for sandwiches. The problem was that it took as long as 4 hours to cook it. In the microwave oven, it cooks perfectly in 20 minutes. If you do not want to serve it with cabbage, serve it with Creamed Spinach (page 300) and boiled potatoes. Put out some good mustard. Make sandwiches on rye bread with some Bread and Butter Pickles (page 466) on the side. Beer is the thing to drink with this—dark beer if you like. *Serves 8 to 10 as a main course*

1 smoked tongue (4
     pounds), trimmed
⅔ cups dark beer
1⅓ cups water

2 tablespoons brown
   sugar
2 cloves garlic, smashed
   and peeled
1 allspice berry

1. Shield 2½ inches of tip of tongue with aluminum foil (page 12). Place in a 2-quart soufflé dish. Combine remaining ingredients and pour over tongue. Cover tightly with microwave plastic wrap. Cook at 100% for 10 minutes.

2. Uncover, remove foil, and turn tongue over. Re-cover and cook for 10 minutes longer.

3. Remove from oven and uncover. Let cool slightly.

4. When tongue is cool enough to handle, peel it and cut off base end. Slice tongue thin. Store in cooking juices.

VARIATION

SMOKED TONGUE WITH CABBAGE Prepare tongue as for Smoked Tongue. When cooked, remove from dish and set aside. Cut a small cabbage (about 2 pounds) through the core into 3 to 4-inch wedges. Place in cooking juices from tongue and cover tightly with microwave plastic wrap. Cook at 100% for 10 to 12 minutes, until tender. Peel and slice tongue; serve with cabbage.

BRAINS

I once lost a boyfriend who saw me cleaning brains. I didn't find out what happened until many years later. Clearly, we were not fated for each other. Nevertheless, if I had had this recipe and a microwave oven then, he never would have had to see me doing that icky chore. The microwave oven miraculously eliminates the need for tedious preparation of brains. Brains are good hot with Browned Butter Sauce (page 361) or cold in a salad. *Serves 2 as a main course*

1 set brains, washed and
    medulla (connecting
    part in center)
    removed (about ¾
    pound)
½ cup water

2 tablespoons Sherry
    vinegar
Browned Butter Sauce
    (page 361) for
    serving (optional)

1. Place brains, rounded side up, in a 2-quart soufflé dish. Combine water and vinegar and pour over brains. Cover tightly with microwave plastic wrap. Cook at 100% for 4 minutes.

2. Without removing dish from oven, uncover and turn brains over. Recover and cook for 4 minutes more.

3. Remove from oven. Uncover, drain, and serve hot with Browned Butter Sauce, if desired.

VARIATION

BRAIN SALAD Prepare brains, substituting malt vinegar or white vinegar for Sherry vinegar. Drain and let stand until cool. Cut into ¼-inch slices and arrange on a bed of escarole or other bitter lettuce leaves. Combine 1 tablespoon tarragon vinegar, 3 tablespoons good-quality olive oil, 1 tablespoon minced fresh tarragon, ½ teaspoon salt, 1 hard-boiled egg (peeled, white minced and yolk forced through a sieve), and 1 tablespoon minced shallot. Pour over brains and serve with freshly ground black pepper. Serves 4 as a main course, 2 as a first course.

BRAISED BRAINS WITH TURNIP SAUCE

This dish tastes so good I hope you will be tempted to try it. It is very elegant. *Serves 4 as a main course*

1 cup diced turnips (about ¼ pound)
1 cup diced yellow onions (about ¼ pound)
⅓ cup strung, diced celery (1 to 2 stalks)
¼ cup minced plus ¼ cup finely chopped parsley
½ cup Chicken Broth (page 331) or canned chicken broth

2 sets brains (about 1¼ pounds), washed and medulla (center connecting part) removed
½ cup heavy cream
½ cup julienned cooked smoked tongue or boiled ham (optional)

1. Combine turnips, onions, celery, minced parsley, and broth in a 2-quart soufflé dish. Place brains on top, rounded side up. Cover tightly with microwave plastic wrap. Cook at 100% for 6 minutes.

2. Leaving dish in oven, uncover and turn brains over. Re-cover and cook for 6 minutes more.

3. Remove from oven. Uncover and remove brains to a warm dish. Place vegetables in the workbowl of a food processor. Add cream and process until smooth. Spoon some sauce onto each of 4 serving plates and place 1 piece of brain on top of each. Sprinkle with julienned smoked cooked tongue or boiled ham, if desired. Sprinkle with chopped parsley.

VEGETABLES

COOKING vegetables in the microwave oven is a pleasure, and not just because it is quick. They are better. They have much better color and flavor than vegetables cooked conventionally, and they retain more of their vitamins. They cook evenly, and their texture is better, no more waterlogged or stringy vegetables. They keep their shape better whether stuffed and cooked, cooked whole or in pieces, either on their own or in soups and stews.

Now that we are getting very good vegetables from our own warm states and from the Caribbean, Israel, Turkey, Central and South America, Australia, New Zealand and the Orient, where vegetables ripen in what seem to us strange seasons, we have harvest season year-round. The very best tomatoes, corn, peas, and lettuce still come from your own garden or nearby farms. These garden vegetables are the ones to eat raw or just briefly cooked. As you need barely any fat in microwave cooking, what you add is a very small amount, mainly for flavor.

To prepare vegetables in the microwave oven, consult the Dictionary at the end of the book. Under the name of the vegetable you want to cook, you will find how to prepare it and wrap it, and how long to cook it in large and small ovens. You will find how much you will get, raw and cooked, from the amount you buy or pick. You will also find some general information in the Dictionary about vegetables that may be new to you.

If you are using an oven with less than 650 to 700 watts, read page 9 to find out how to adapt the recipes. Information on wrapping vegetables or arranging them for microwave cooking can be found on pages 19–22 and 28–29. If you still have questions or need to defrost frozen vegetables, you should find the answers in the Dictionary.

273

Most of the recipes in this chapter are for fresh vegetables. With few exceptions, notably frozen tiny peas, which are better than all but fresh local peas, fresh vegetables are far better and cheaper than frozen or canned vegetables (except for tomatoes out of season). The microwave oven makes cooking vegetables so rapid and easy it seems a pity to cheat. Where you can, I have noted the fact. Remember, though, that vegetables that have been frozen have generally been blanched (lightly cooked). You have to shorten the cooking time or add them later in a recipe. Be careful. Since they often give off some of the water they were cooked in, you will need to drain them once they have been defrosted or to add less liquid when you cook them.

The recipes in this chapter go beyond basics. The chapter starts with the simplest recipes for the season's best and goes on to the kind that turn simple grilled fish or meat, poached fish, chicken, or veal into party fare. It ends with a few recipes meant to be whole meals. There are other vegetable recipes in this book, notably among the First Courses (pages 35–81). Starchy vegetables like potatoes and dried beans, as well as pastas and risottos with vegetables, are in the chapter beginning on page 117.

If you want to find a recipe for a sauce to serve with hot or cold vegetables, look in Savory Sauces (pages 360–384) or in the Index. Mornay (page 366), Cheddar Cheese Sauce (page 156), Parsley Sauce (page 369), Watercress Sauce (page 369), Chunky Tomato Sauce (page 374), and Mayonnaise (page 382) for cold vegetables are all good sauces to keep in mind. Several of the purées in this chapter can be thinned with cream or milk to make good and attractive sauces.

The number of people that I indicate a recipe will serve is based on one vegetable as a side dish. If you are preparing two vegetables, you can assume that each recipe will serve a third again as many people. If you are preparing three vegetables, double the number each recipe will serve.

When you are choosing a vegetable to go with a main course, the first rule of thumb is the saucier the main course, the simpler the vegetable. Vegetables should complement the main dish and each other in color, texture, and flavor, not repeat it or fight with it. A curried vegetable does not go with a curried main course, nor does Sweet and Sour Red Cabbage. The vegetable can give oomph to the main course when it is very simple, like poached fish or chicken, but it shouldn't overwhelm it. If you are serving more than one vegetable, do only one that is saucy. Combine it with a crisp vegetable or a puréed one.

If you are preparing the main course as well as the vegetables in the microwave oven, make the vegetables first and stick them back in for 1 or 2 minutes at 100% while you finish seasoning the main course. You can arrange the food on plates and put them in two by two, using a rack (see page 18) for 30 seconds to 1 minute to reheat.

I hope I will succeed in convincing you as you read this chapter to cook more vegetables and to make them a larger part of your diet, along with the grains and other starches I have given recipes for in other parts of the book. We all know it is a healthier way to eat. Let's make it a pleasure as well.

Simple Vegetables

Even non-vegetarians sometimes get a craving for a summery meal of vegetables. In the microwave oven, it can be quick, fresh, and easy. You can try a few of the recipes that follow; but, simpler yet, you could stop at a salad bar and pick up an assortment of already cleaned and cut-up vegetables (10 ounces per person). Arrange them on a dinner plate, with the quicker-cooking vegetables in the center and

Vegetables as in Pasta Primavera

Salad Bar Vegetable Dinner

Arrange long-cooking vegetables toward the rim, quick-cooking vegetables in the center.

the slower-cooking ones around them. See the Dictionary (page 611) for a list of which is which. Sprinkle with 1 tablespoon of fresh herbs and/or other seasonings, not salt. Add salt only after removing the plate from oven. Cover tightly with microwave plastic wrap and cook at 100% for 3 minutes 30 seconds. Voilà, Salad Bar Vegetable Dinner. If you want to add protein, top each portion with an egg after cooking 2 minutes. Prick the yolk twice with the tip of a very sharp knife and replace the dish, uncovered, in the oven for 2 minutes at 100%. Or serve the vegetables with Cheddar Cheese Sauce (page 156) or Mornay (page 366) or with an added starch. (Put any leftover cooked starch in the middle of the plate.) For more people, cook just the vegetables of Pasta Primavera (page 146) and serve with either of the cheese sauces or with Watercress Sauce (page 369).

BROCCOLI

I thought it might be interesting to take a vegetable like broccoli and follow it through this chapter, going from simple to complex recipes, especially to illustrate some of the basic ways to cook vegetables.

Broccoli is generally available all year-round. If you want to cook it so that it stays bright green, loses none of its vitamins and also has both stem and flowers perfectly cooked, this is the way. Serve with Cheddar Cheese Sauce (page 156) or one of the other sauces. You could top the broccoli with a Poached Chicken Breast (page 202); top that in turn with Mornay (page 366) and then pass the dish quickly under the broiler for Chicken Divan. If you season the broccoli with lemon juice, serve it immediately, or it will discolor. This is true for all vegetables seasoned with lemon juice. *Serves 4 to 6 as a side dish*

2½ pounds broccoli,
     trimmed of leaves
     and cut into 4- to
     5-inch stalks with
     florets

¼ cup water
Kosher salt
Fresh lemon juice

1. Arrange broccoli in a single layer, spoke-fashion with florets pointing toward the center of a 12-inch round platter. Pour water over broccoli. Cover tightly with microwave plastic wrap. Cook at 100% for 12 minutes.

2. Remove from oven. Uncover and add salt and lemon juice.

To make 1½ pounds broccoli. Trim 1 medium head broccoli (about 1½ pounds). Peel stalks. Cut off florets. Cut stem across into ¼-inch-thick coins. Divide broccoli florets and stems among 4 microwave-safe plastic bags; close tight. Arrange in a ring on microwave carousel or a large plate. Cook at 100% for 6 minutes. Add salt and lemon juice to taste.

To make ½ pound broccoli. Trim broccoli. Peel stalks. Cut off florets. Slice stem thin. Place florets and sliced stems in a 4-cup glass measure. You will have about 2 cups broccoli. Cover tightly. Cook at 100% for 4 minutes. Add salt and lemon juice to taste.

PEAS WITH MINT AND SCALLIONS

This is a classic way to prepare peas. There is none better when the peas are good. If you can get fresh local peas in summer, so much the better. If not, use the tiny frozen ones. They will be much more tender than old peas.   *Serves 4 to 6*

4 tablespoons unsalted
    butter
2 boxes (10 ounces each)
    frozen tiny peas,
    defrosted in a sieve
    under warm running
    water, or 2 cups
    shelled fresh peas
    (about 1½ pounds in
    the pod)

1 bunch scallions,
    trimmed and cut into
    1½-inch lengths, or 1
    cup frozen pearl
    onions
¼ cup fresh mint leaves,
    shredded, or 1
    teaspoon dried mint
Kosher salt
Freshly ground black
    pepper

1. Heat butter in a 1½-quart soufflé dish, uncovered, at 100% for 2 minutes. Stir in peas, scallions, and mint. Cover tightly with microwave plastic wrap. Cook at 100% for 3 minutes.

2. Remove from oven. Uncover and stir in salt and pepper. Serve hot.

To serve 2. Place ⅔ cup peas, ½ tablespoon butter, a pinch salt and a mint sprig in a 1-cup glass measure. Cover tightly with microwave plastic wrap. Cook for 3 minutes.

VARIATION

PEAS WITH MINT, SCALLIONS AND LETTUCE Stir in 1½ cups shredded Boston lettuce before final seasoning. Cook, uncovered, at 100% for 1 minute. Salt and pepper to taste. Serves 4 to 6.

GLAZED CARROTS

This recipe was devised for whole young carrots in their prime. It is not intended for those small things in bags that are dwarves. Occasionally, you will get dwarf carrots that are young. In that case, I apologize; but, generally, they are old carrots trying to look young by being genetically short. If you use larger carrots, peel them and cut them in quarters lengthwise and then into 2-inch lengths. If the carrots are very young, chop 1 tablespoon of the very tip leaves and sprinkle on top before cooking. *Serves 2*

6 small carrots, each about 6 inches long (½ pound), peeled and left whole with 1 inch of green stem	1 tablespoon unsalted butter, cut into bits 1 tablespoon granulated sugar

1. Arrange carrots, alternating tip and root ends in an 8½″ × 6½″ × 2″ oval dish. Scatter butter and sugar on top of carrots. Cover tightly with microwave plastic wrap. Cook at 100% for 8 minutes.

2. Remove from oven. Pierce plastic with the tip of a sharp knife and let stand for 1 to 2 minutes. Uncover, toss, and serve.

To serve 4. Double all ingredients. Cook in an 11" × 8½" × 2" dish for 12 minutes. Finish as for 2 servings.

FENNEL

Florence fennel, or bulb fennel, is a delicious vegetable that looks like round, white celery and tastes mildly like licorice. It is good cooked, and also raw, thinly sliced in salads with a lemon dressing. Except to Italians, fennel is less familiar than it should be, but it is becoming widely available. It makes a nice change. It goes well with fish, chicken, and veal. If the fennel is brown or stringy on the outside, go over it lightly with a potato peeler. Cut off the stems and just enough of the root end to make it tidy, but not so much that it falls apart. *Serves 4*

2 large bulbs fennel (about 3 inches across), cored, trimmed and cut into 6 wedges each
2 tablespoons finely chopped feathery tops of fennel (optional)

1 tablespoon unsalted butter, cut into small pieces
Kosher salt
Freshly ground black pepper

1. Place fennel in the center of a large piece of microwave plastic wrap. Top with fennel tops, if desired and available. Fold the plastic over the fennel to enclose it completely. Cook at 100% for 5 minutes.

2. Remove from oven. Let stand, covered, for 2 minutes. Unwrap and remove to a serving platter. Top or toss with remaining ingredients and serve hot.

To serve 1. Use 1 small or half a large bulb fennel and quarter the amount butter. Proceed as for 4 servings, cooking for 2 minutes 30 seconds. Let stand for 2 minutes.

To serve 2. Use 1 large bulb fennel and half the amount butter. Proceed as for 4 servings, cooking for 3 minutes 30 seconds. Let stand for 2 minutes.

VARIATIONS

FENNEL WITH LEMON BUTTER Proceed as for Fennel. Add 1 teaspoon fresh lemon juice with other seasonings.

FENNEL WITH OLIVE OIL AND LEMON Combine 1½ tablespoons olive oil, 1 tablespoon fresh lemon juice, ¾ teaspoon salt, and ¼ teaspoon pepper. Proceed as for Fennel. Add oil mixture instead of butter to warm fennel. Let stand until cool and serve at room temperature.

CREAMED ONIONS

This is one of the classics for Thanksgiving, so I give rather a large quantity. Try it at other times; it is delicious. It is very white, however; if it is not being served with an assortment of colorful foods, top the dish with 3 tablespoons finely chopped parsley.   *Makes 4 cups, serves 8 to 10*

4 tablespoons unsalted butter	**2 pounds small white onions (12 per pound), peeled**
2 tablespoons all-purpose flour	**Freshly ground black pepper**
1¾ cups milk	
1½ teaspoons kosher salt	

1. Heat 2 tablespoons of the butter in a 10-inch quiche dish, uncovered, at 100% for 1 minute. Whisk in flour and cook, uncovered, at 100% for 2 minutes more.

2. Remove from oven. Whisk in milk and salt, making sure there are no lumps. Add onions and stir to coat. Cover tightly with microwave plastic wrap. Cook at 100% for 10 minutes.

3. Remove from oven. Uncover and stir in remaining butter and pepper. Serve hot.

FRIED OKRA

In the South, they love okra dipped into cornmeal and deep-fried, and it is delicious. Other vegetables can be cooked the same way, as can clams and oysters. The seafood needs to be lightly dipped in flour first. You can make a main course from equal amounts of okra, asparagus, sweet potato (cut in slim fingers), and seafood, or serve it at cocktail parties, with a spicy tartar sauce or Mexican Chili Sauce (page 375) for dipping.

Fried okra makes a good first course. Of course, this would be right at home with catfish. Since the fried okra is very hot inside when it comes out of the fat, you don't have to worry about the first batch getting cold while the others cook. If you make it ahead, keep it warm on paper toweling in a conventional oven at a low setting, or you can put all of it back in the microwave oven on paper toweling for 1 minute at 100%, or just bring out the hot batches as they are done. Do not make this in a less than full-power oven. *Serves 6*

3 cups vegetable oil
1 cup yellow cornmeal
2 teaspoons kosher salt
½ teaspoon paprika
¼ teaspoon cayenne
    pepper
1 egg
1 cup milk
1 pound small okra pods
    (40 to 50 pods)

1. Heat oil in a 2-quart nonplastic container measuring at least 3¼ inches high, uncovered, at 100% for 15 minutes.

2. Stir together cornmeal, salt, paprika, and cayenne. In another bowl, combine egg and milk. Coat okra pods first in egg and milk mixture and then in cornmeal mixture.

3. Cook 8 to 10 coated pods at a time in hot oil, uncovered, at 100% for 1 minute. Remove and drain on paper toweling. Reheat oil for each successive batch for 5 minutes.

VARIATIONS

FRIED CLAMS OR OYSTERS Drain 24 shucked clams or oysters. Dip quickly in flour. Dust off. Proceed as for Fried Okra.

FRIED ASPARAGUS Cut 1 pound asparagus in 2-inch lengths. Proceed as for Fried Okra.

DEEP-FRIED SWEET POTATOES Cut 2 good-size sweet potatoes, cooked (page 571), cooled, and peeled, into finger-size pieces. Proceed as for Fried Okra.

HOT DILLED CUCUMBERS

Most of us think of cucumbers in salad and leave it at that. They make an interesting hot vegetable, whose smell freshens the air of the kitchen when they are being prepared and delights the dining room when they are served. These cooked cucumbers go very well with fish and chicken.
Serves 4

2½ pounds medium
    cucumbers (5 to 6),
    trimmed, peeled,
    quartered
    lengthwise and
    seeded, cut into 1-
    inch- to 1½-inch-
    long pieces

½ cup fresh dill, snipped
    into ¼-inch pieces
2 teaspoons cornstarch
2 tablespoons unsalted
    butter
2 teaspoons kosher salt

1. Combine cucumbers and dill in a 4-cup glass measure. Cover tightly with microwave plastic wrap. Cook at 100% for 6 minutes.

2. Remove from oven and uncover. Pour ¼ cup of the liquid into a small bowl. Stir in cornstarch and mix well; pour back over cucumbers. Add butter and salt and stir until butter melts. Cook, uncovered, at 100% for 4 minutes.

3. Remove from oven. Stir well and serve hot.

To serve 2. Halve all ingredients. Cook cucumbers for 4 minutes. Add cornstarch and cook for 4 minutes more.

ROASTED GARLIC

This is not an ordinary, everyday idea. You need to know your guests. They have to be adventurous eaters who are willing to use their hands since the way to eat the garlic is for them to pull off a clove with their fingers and, holding it by the root end, scrape the sweet and soft pulp out with their teeth. It is much like eating an artichoke. Everybody will be surprised. The garlic is not sharp—it is sweet and nutty. This can be a first course on its own, or can jazz up roast leg of lamb or roast chicken.   *Serves 4 as a side dish*

4 heads garlic, tips cut as illustrated below

⅓ cup Chicken Broth (page 331) or canned chicken broth

3 tablespoons olive oil

1. Place all ingredients in a 4-cup glass measure. Cover tightly with microwave plastic wrap. Cook at 100% for 6 to 8 minutes, cooking longer if bulbs are large.

2. Remove from oven. Let stand, covered, for 10 minutes.

To serve 2. Combine 2 heads garlic, ¼ cup broth and 2 tablespoons oil in a 4-cup glass measure. Cook, covered, for 5 minutes. Let stand for 5 to 10 minutes.

Cut tips off of entire head of garlic revealing cut cloves.

BRAISED LEEKS

This is one of my favorites. I often substitute it for creamed onions at holidays. It takes a long time to cook on top of the stove or in the oven, but in the microwave oven, it is so easy I will even make it for myself. Then I eat two large leeks. The recipe allows one large leek per person as a vegetable side dish. As a first course, hot or cold, serve two. Cold leeks can be drained and served with a mustard vinaigrette. Warm, they are special when made with Veal or Meat Broth and Glaze. It is easy to turn braised leeks into a main course with ham and Mornay.   *Serves 8*

8 leeks, white and 1
   inch of green,
   trimmed and well
   rinsed
1½ cups Chicken Broth
   (page 331), canned
   chicken broth or
   Meat Broth with
   Vegetables (page
   332)

3 tablespoons unsalted
   butter
2 ounces Veal Glaze
   (page 337) or Sauce
   Espagnole (page 371)
   (optional)
Kosher salt
Freshly ground black
   pepper

1. Arrange leeks alternating white and green ends in an
11″ × 8½″ × 2″ dish. Add broth, butter, glaze, if desired,
and salt. Cover tightly with microwave plastic wrap and
cook at 100% for 20 minutes.

2. Remove from oven. Uncover and turn leeks over. Re-
cover and cook at 100% for 20 minutes more.

3. Remove from oven. Uncover and add pepper. Serve
hot.

To serve 4. Combine 4 leeks, 1 cup broth, 2 tablespoons
butter and salt in a 9″ × 8″ × 2″ oval dish. Cook as for 8
servings for 15 minutes. Turn leeks and cook for 15 minutes
more. Finish as for 8 servings.

To serve 2. Combine 2 leeks, ⅓ cup broth, 1 tablespoon
butter and salt in a soup bowl. Cook as for 8 servings for
10 minutes. Turn leeks over and cook for 8 to 10 minutes
more. Finish as for 8 servings.

VARIATION

BRAISED LEEKS WITH HAM Preheat broiler. After the
leeks are cooked, remove in pairs to a lightly oiled broiler
pan. Cover each pair of leeks with 2 thin slices of ham.
Cover each leek and ham serving with ¼ cup Mornay (page
366). Place pan under broiler until sauce is lightly gilded.
Serve hot. Serves 4 as a main course.

MELTED LEEKS

This is a lovely vegetable recipe. Melted Leeks make a welcome addition to any main course, or can be used as an ingredient. Two tablespoons of it can be tucked under each fillet of fish or chicken before cooking without changing the timing but adding flavor. It is also good stirred into Velouté (page 366) and spooned over poached or steamed fish or chicken. *Serves 6*

1 **pound leeks, white and 1 inch of the green, trimmed, rinsed and sliced across ⅛ inch thick (about 6 leeks)**	2 **tablespoons unsalted butter** **Kosher salt**

1. Place leeks and butter in a 12″ × 7½″ × 3″ dish. Cook, uncovered, at 100% for 6 minutes 15 seconds.

2. Remove from oven. Stir and add salt to taste; serve hot.

To serve 3. Halve all ingredients, cooking in a 9″ × 8″ × 2″ oval dish for 4 minutes.

BRAISED ONIONS

This is a light and easy way to make onions. It would be good when you are serving Creamed Spinach (page 300). *Serves 4 to 6*

1½ **pounds yellow onion, peeled and sliced thin (about 6 cups)** 1 **tablespoon granulated sugar**	2 **tablespoons Chicken Broth (page 331) or canned chicken broth** 2 **teaspoons kosher salt** 4 **whole cloves**

1. Combine all ingredients in a 14″ × 11″ × 2″ dish. Cover tightly with microwave plastic wrap. Cook at 100% for 12 minutes.

2. Remove from oven. Uncover and serve hot.

BRAISED ENDIVE

Braised endives are not beautiful, but they look better cooked in the microwave oven than they do any other way. People go on cooking them because they taste so good. They have a faintly bittersweet quality that is terrific with roast veal, roast chicken, or grilled fish. They can be transformed into a main dish by treating them like the leeks in Braised Leeks with Ham (page 284). Braised Endive Oriental, one of the variations, is not a classic, but I am rather proud of it. It goes well with poached or steamed fish, giving a little extra flavor. *Serves 8 as a side dish*

8 heads Belgian endive, trimmed and well rinsed	¼ cup unsalted butter, cut into 4 pieces
⅔ cup Chicken Broth (page 331) or canned chicken broth	Kosher salt Freshly ground black pepper

1. Place endives in a 12″ × 7½″ × 3″ dish. Pour in broth and dot with butter. Sprinkle with a pinch of salt. Cover tightly with microwave plastic wrap. Cook at 100% for 8 minutes.

2. Remove from oven. Uncover and turn endives over. Cook, uncovered, for 8 minutes more.

3. Remove from oven. Add salt and pepper and serve hot.

To serve 2. Use 2 heads endive and halve all other ingredients. Cook as for 8 servings in a 9″ × 5″ × 3″ loaf pan for 6 minutes. Uncover and cook for 2 minutes more. Season and serve hot.

VARIATION

BRAISED ENDIVE ORIENTAL FOR 8 Increase broth to 1 cup, omit butter and add 4 teaspoons mirin, 8 teaspoons rice wine vinegar, 4 teaspoons Oriental sesame oil, and salt. Cook as for Braised Endive for 8 minutes. Turn endives over, re-cover and cook for 8 minutes more. Serves 8. To serve 2, quarter all ingredients in Braised Endive Oriental for 8, cooking in a 9″ × 5″ × 3″ dish for 6 minutes. Turn endives over, re-cover and cook for 2 minutes more.

BRAISED LETTUCE

This is another of those vegetables like cucumbers that Americans use mainly in salads. It is surprisingly good cooked, something the clever French have known for a long time. Here is a dish that looks and tastes to so much better made in the microwave oven than conventionally and is so much quicker that I really cannot imagine doing it any other way ever again. *Serves 8*

4 tablespoons unsalted butter	4 heads Boston lettuce (½ pound each), large outer leaves removed, washed and heads cut in half lengthwise
1 cup Chicken or Veal Broth (page 331) or canned chicken broth	
½ cup Sauce Espagnole (page 371) or Meat Glaze (page 337)	1 tablespoon cornstarch dissolved in 2 tablespoons cold water
1½ teaspoons kosher salt	

1. Heat butter and broth in a 14″ × 11″ × 2″ dish, uncovered, at 100% for 3 minutes. Stir in Sauce Espagnole and salt. Arrange lettuce halves with core ends pointing toward the outside of the dish. Cover tightly with microwave plastic wrap. Cook at 100% for 15 minutes.

2. Remove from oven. Uncover and remove lettuce to a warmed serving platter, folding ragged leaf edges under. Stir cornstarch into liquid in dish. Cook, uncovered, at 100% for 7 minutes.

3. Remove from oven. Spoon sauce over lettuce and serve immediately.

To serve 4. Halve all ingredients and omit cornstarch. Proceed, cooking lettuce in an 11″ × 8½″ × 2″ dish for 8 minutes. Finish cooking sauce for 4 minutes.

To serve 2. Quarter all ingredients and omit cornstarch. Proceed cooking lettuce in a 9½" × 7" × 1¾" oval dish for 5 minutes 30 seconds. Finish cooking sauce for 3 minutes.

The Purées

There was a time after everyone got a food processor and figured out how to use it when I thought I never wanted to see another purée. That time has passed. Purées are really delicious on their own, or thinned as sauces, and they are endlessly useful in soups, custards and timbales. I never mind having leftover purées for that reason. However, purées are a good way to use up leftover vegetables that were cooked simply.

The simplest purées are made from the cooked vegetables on its own. If you want, season the purée with butter, cream, salt, and spices, but you may find that microwave-cooked vegetables have such good flavor that a minimum of seasoning is needed. Microwave-cooked and peeled baking potatoes can be used to thicken purées of watery vegetables or to dilute the taste of strong vegetables. See the Dictionary for weights, preparation, cooking times, and puréed yield for individual vegetables.

Purée vegetables in a food processor or blender (with a little extra liquid) or with a food mill (see page 25 for illustration). The blender will give a somewhat silkier, more liquid result. The result with a food mill depends on which of its three discs you are using; it can go from slightly chunky to quite smooth. The food mill will separate the skin and seeds from vegetables such as tomatoes.

TO MAKE SOUPS FROM PURÉES. There are some recipes for puréed vegetable soups in the chapter on soups and as variations in this chapter. Almost any vegetable purée can be made into a soup by adding 3 cups of liquid to 1 cup of purée and heating it, covered. Do not overseason. The microwave-cooked vegetables have delightful flavors of their own. Even the most mundane vegetables like parsnips, carrots, rutabagas, and winter squash make surprisingly elegant soups; they can be served hot or cold. For soups, as well as purées and custards, watery vegetables do better when puréed with a cooked potato.

The liquid for a soup could be Chicken Broth, homemade (page 331) or canned, Vegetable Broth (page 335), Velouté (page 366), Sauce Suprême (page 368), Thin Béchamel (page 366), cream, milk, or a combination of broth and cream or milk. When reheating soups with milk, cream, or butter in them, use large containers and cook covered. They tend to boil over. It is better to use some cream, sour cream, or plain yogurt—lowfat is fine—in soups that will be cold. Whisk in the sour cream or yogurt after removing the soup from the oven and letting it cool somewhat; that way it is less likely to separate.

If additional thickening is called for after a hot soup is taken from the oven, you can swirl in a little butter or add some cornstarch—1 teaspoon per cup—mixed with cold water and cook, uncovered, at 100% for 3 to 4 minutes. You can also thicken soup with egg yolks as described on page 114. If you are using leftover butter-rich purées to make soup, reduce the amount of cream you add, and unless the purée contains potato, thicken the soup in one of the ways described.

TO MAKE VEGETABLE FLANS, CUSTARDS AND TIMBALES. To the cooked purée from ½ pound of vegetables (about ½ cup), add 4 whole eggs and ¾ cup heavy cream. Mix well. Taste for seasoning. Place ¼ cup of the mixture in each of 10 lightly greased 3-inch soufflé dishes or ramekins. Those with a bowl shape will cook more evenly. (See page 15 for illustrations.) Cover each tightly with microwave plastic wrap. Arrange in oven in a circle so they do not touch. Cook at 100% for 3 minutes 30 seconds. Prick plastic. Unmold onto individual plates atop 3 tablespoons of sauce, for a first course. Unmold onto a dinner plate, to serve as a side dish.

TO MAKE GRATINS FROM PURÉES. Take 2 cups of purée. If it is potato-thickened but has no butter or cream, add 2 tablespoons heavy cream and 2 lightly beaten whole eggs. Add ½ cup grated Parmesan, Swiss, or Gruyère cheese. If the purée is potato-thickened and has butter or cream, just add the eggs and cheese. If the purée is not already thickened and not made from a starchy vegetable, purée ½ of a microwave-cooked potato with the purée. Then follow rules for flans, custards and timbales. Preheat broiler. Smooth gratin mixture into an 11″ × 8 × 2″ dish that can go under the broiler. Cook gratin in microwave oven 2 minutes. Then put under broiler until lightly browned. If you like, sprinkle gratin with ¾ cup grated cheese before placing under broiler. If you don't care if the gratin browns, smooth purée about ½ inch deep into the dish; grate 2 tablespoons per ¼ cup of purée of Swiss cheese, Fontina or Doux de Montagne over purée. Cook, uncovered, for 4 minutes.

TO MAKE SAUCES FROM PURÉES. Purées without potatoes or starchy vegetables make better sauces than those with them. For cold sauces, thin with a little plain yogurt, broth, and a bit of olive oil, or mix with Mayonnaise (page 382). Season. For hot sauces, proceed as for soups, but add only ½ to 1 cup extra liquid to each cup of purée. Choose a liquid that goes with but does not repeat the food you are saucing. For instance, if you are making a sauce for a custard, make one without butter, cream, or eggs.

MASHED POTATOES

Mashed potatoes are really one kind of potato purée. They happen to be one of my favorite things in the world when I permit myself to indulge. I am capable of making dinner from a bowl of super mashed potatoes. Baking potatoes cooked in the microwave oven make superior baked potatoes for mashing or purée. They have more potato taste and no extra water. Potatoes cooked in water will give you a somewhat lighter, less fatty mashed potato. See the Dictionary for cooking times.

There are many different ways to make mashed potatoes: with cream, milk, butter, or any combination of the three. The potatoes can be mashed with a fork, put through a food mill, or riced. They should not be put in a food processor or blender unless they are being combined with another vegetable for a mixed purée: they tend to turn to glue. I prefer the ricer. *Makes 2 cups; serves 4*

2 baking potatoes (7 to 8 ounces each)	2 tablespoons unsalted butter
¾ cup milk	½ teaspoon kosher salt

1. Prick potatoes twice with a knife tip. Cook, uncovered, at 100% for 11 minutes. (In a small oven, cook for 18 minutes.)

2. Remove from oven with pot holder or towel. Holding it in same, carefully peel with a small knife. Cut in about 1-inch cubes. Put through ricer into a 4-cup glass measure. You will have just about 1¾ cups.

3. With a whisk, beat in milk, butter, and salt.

4. Place measuring cup, uncovered, in oven for 1 minute 30 seconds. (In small oven, cook for 3 minutes.)

5. Adjust seasoning as desired and serve hot.

VARIATION

LIGHT MASHED POTATOES Scrub and peel 2 all-purpose potatoes (7 to 8 ounces each). Cut in 1-inch chunks. Arrange in a circle around the rim of a 9-inch pie plate. Add ½ cup water. Cook, tightly covered, for 12 minutes. Drain, rice, and stir in ¾ cup milk, 2 tablespoons unsalted butter, and salt. Cook, uncovered, for 1 minute 30 seconds. Adjust seasoning as desired and serve hot.

RICH, FRENCH POTATO PURÉE

This is just a fancy version of mashed potatoes. It is the richest potato purée of all. It is much creamier than American-style mashed potatoes, almost a sauce. For your ultimate self-indulgence I give the recipe. I love it; but can't be responsible to your arteries.

The French would probably add even more milk at the end; they like the purée to be very silky. This must be beaten by hand. *Makes 1 cup; serves 2*

1 small baking potato (about 7 to 8 ounces)	¼ cup heavy cream
3 tablespoons unsalted butter, at room temperature, cut into chunks	1 tablespoon or more milk (optional)
	Kosher salt
	Fresh ground black pepper (optional)
¼ teaspoon kosher salt	

1. Prick potato twice with a knife tip. Cook, uncovered, at 100% for 7 minutes.

2. Remove from oven with pot holder or towel. Holding it in same, carefully peel with a small knife. Cut in about 1-inch cubes. Put through ricer into a 2-cup glass measure. You will have just under 1 cup.

3. With a fork or tiny whisk, beat in butter and salt. Potatoes will appear to shrink.

4. Place measuring cup, uncovered, in oven for 30 seconds at 100%.

5. Beat in cream, 1 tablespoon at a time. The purée absorbs more as it goes. If desired, beat in milk to thin and add more salt and pepper to taste.

6. Reheat for 30 seconds, covered with paper toweling.

VARIATION

CARROT AND POTATO PURÉE Cook 2 baking potatoes (7 ounces each). To make carrot purée, cook 1½ pounds carrots, cut into ⅛ to ¼-inch slices, in a dish large enough to hold them in 2 to 3 layers. Cover tightly with microwave plastic wrap and cook for 9 minutes 30 seconds. Remove from oven and purée in the workbowl of a food processor with peeled, sliced potatoes, 6 tablespoons unsalted butter, and salt and pepper to taste. Serve hot.   Serves 6.

BROCCOLI PURÉE

Here is our friend broccoli again. Use broccoli cooking instructions on page 276. *Makes 2¼ cups*

1½ pounds broccoli, stems and florets	**6 tablespoons unsalted butter**
	1 teaspoon kosher salt

1. Cook broccoli.

2. Remove from oven. Carefully open bags and remove broccoli to the workbowl of a food processor. Process to a coarse purée. Add butter and salt and process briefly to combine.

To make ½ cup. Wash and trim ½ pound broccoli. Cut into florets and thin-slice the stem. Place in a 4-cup glass measure. You will have about 2 cups of pieces. Cover tightly with microwave plastic wrap. Cook for 4 minutes at 100%. Purée in food processor. Use in Broccoli Timbale (page 301). For a rich purée to serve 2, add 3 tablespoons melted butter (2 minutes in microwave oven), 2 tablespoons heavy cream, and ¼ teaspoon salt; purée in blender.

CELERY ROOT PURÉE

This knobby, ugly, midwinter root vegetable is not used much in this country, though it is well loved in Europe. It is good shredded raw to make a salad with a mustard mayonnaise. It makes a subtle purée that needs no fat, unless you decide you want something richer. Combine this purée with a potato purée for variety. *Makes 1 cup*

1¼ pounds peeled and cubed celery root (about 2½ cups)	**2 tablespoons unsalted butter**
	½ teaspoon celery seed (optional)

1. Place celery root in a microwave-safe plastic bag and close tight. Cook at 100% for 9 minutes.

2. Remove from oven. Unwrap and place in the workbowl of a food processor with butter. Process until smooth.

3. Serve sprinkled with celery seeds, if desired.

VARIATIONS

CELERY ROOT AND POTATO PURÉE Cook celery root. Cook a 7-ounce baking potato. peel; purée with celery root, 2 tablespoons butter, and ¼ cup heavy cream. Add salt to taste. Makes 2 cups.

WINTER VEGETABLE PURÉE Combine Celery Root and Potato Purée with 1 cup Parsnip Purée (page 297). Season to taste. Makes 3 cups.

THREE-VEGETABLE WINTER CREAM SOUP Combine Winter Vegetable Puée with 2½ cups Chicken Broth (page 331) or canned chicken broth, ½ cup heavy cream, and 1 teaspoon kosher salt, Heat in an 8-cup glass measure, tightly covered, for 5 minutes at 100%. Serves 6.

CELERY PURÉE

This is a pale, pale green purée that is aromatic. *Makes 1½ cups*

1 pound celery, strung and cut across into ¼-inch pieces (2 cups)
2 tablespoons chopped celery leaves, if available

1 baking potato (7 ounces), cooked and riced
½ cup heavy cream
3 tablespoons unsalted butter
Kosher salt
Freshly ground black pepper

1. Place celery in a microwave-safe plastic bag with 1 tablespoon water and close tight. Cook at 100% for 5 to 6 minutes, until tender.

2. Remove from oven. Unwrap and place in the workbowl of a food processor. Process until smooth. Add remaining ingredients and process until well combined. Season to taste.

VARIATION

CELERY SOUP Add 1½ cups Chicken Broth (page 331) or canned chicken broth to finished purée. Stir to combine and serve hot. Serves 4.

CAULIFLOWER PURÉE

Cauliflower makes one of the most elegant purées. The potato version has more body, but is not necessarily better. Cauliflower cooks more evenly divided into florets. *Makes 2 cups (3 cups with potato added)*

1 small head cauliflower, cored, trimmed and florets removed	½ cup heavy cream Kosher salt
2 cooked baking potatoes (7 ounces each) (optional)	1 tablespoon packed, finely snipped or sliced chives (optional)

1. Place cauliflower florets in a rectangular dish just large enough to hold them in a single layer. Cover tightly with microwave plastic wrap. Cook at 100% for 7 minutes.

2. Remove from oven. Uncover and place in the workbowl of a food processor with peeled, sliced potato, if desired. Process until smooth with cream and salt to taste.

3. Sprinkle chives, if desired, on top or stir in.

ACORN SQUASH PURÉE

The winter squashes make silky-smooth purée of great elegance in varying shades of gold and yellow. They are quick and delicious, and they are easily transformed into party soups to serve hot or cold. If serving soup cold, make it one day ahead.   *Makes 2 to 2½ cups*

2 acorn squash, cut in half and seeded	Pinch cayenne pepper
1 cup heavy cream	1½ kosher salt
¼ pound unsalted butter	

1. Wrap each squash half tightly with microwave plastic wrap. Cook at 100% for 12 to 14 minutes, until flesh is easily pierced with a fork.

2. Remove from oven. Unwrap and scoop out flesh. Pass through a ricer or the medium disc of a food mill. Stir in remaining ingredients and serve hot.

VARIATIONS

BUTTERNUT SQUASH PURÉE Substitute 2½ pounds butternut squash for acorn squash. Proceed as for Acorn Squash Purée.

HUBBARD SQUASH PURÉE Substitute 2½ pounds hubbard squash for acorn squash. Cut into 4″ × 5″ pieces and wrap each piece in microwave plastic wrap. Proceed as for Acorn Squash Purée.

Hubbard squash pieces

WINTER SQUASH SOUP Combine any of the squash purées with 2 cups of Velouté (page 366). Season to taste with kosher salt, freshly ground white pepper, and a tiny pinch of nutmeg. Heat in an 8-cup glass measure for 5 minutes at 100%. Whisk and serve. Serves 4 to 5.

RUTABAGA PURÉE

Rutabaga is a strangely homely, strong tasting and old-fashioned vegetable generally overlooked in the search for the new. It makes a creamy, pale gold purée that would be wonderful with Heart of the Home Beef Stew (page 236) or Lamb Stew (page 262).   *Makes 3 cups*

1½ pounds rutabaga, trimmed, peeled and cut into ½-inch cubes
½ cup water
1 cup heavy cream

4 tablespoons unsalted butter
2 teaspoons kosher salt
Pinch cayenne pepper

1. Put rutabaga and water in an 8-cup glass measure. Cover tightly with microwave plastic wrap. Cook at 100% for 15 minutes.

2. Remove from oven. Uncover and place in the workbowl of a food processor. Process until smooth. Add remaining ingredients and process until well combined.

3. To reheat, if necessary, return to measure. Cook, uncovered, at 100% for 3 minutes. Stir well.

PARSNIP PURÉE

Parsnips are another old-fashion winter vegetable. They have a sweet and spicy taste.   *Makes 4 cups*

1 pound parsnips, trimmed, peeled and cut into 1½-inch chunks	4 tablespoons unsalted butter
1 cup water	1 to 1½ cups heavy cream
1 potato, baked, peeled and riced (page 571)	2 teaspoons kosher salt
	½ teaspoon freshly ground black pepper

1. Combine parsnips and water in a 4-cup glass measure. Cover tightly with microwave plastic wrap. Cook at 100% for 8 minutes.

2. Remove from oven. Uncover and place in the work-bowl of a food processor. Process until smooth. Add remaining ingredients and process until well combined.

VARIATION

UNSEASONED PARSNIP PURÉE Combine ½ pound peeled and cubed parsnips in a 4-cup glass measure with 1½ teaspoons butter and ½ cup Chicken Broth (page 331) or canned chicken broth. Cover tightly. Cook for 5 minutes. Purée. Makes 1 cup.

TURNIP PURÉE

Turnips are always around. They can be added to dinner any night. When people are served this purée, they will think they are getting mashed potatoes. The slight bite of turnips will come as a pleasant surprise. Think of this with Smothered Pork Roast (page 253), or with something as unexpected as Green Lamb Curry (page 263).   *Makes 1¼ cups*

| 1 pound turnips (about 4 turnips) trimmed, peeled and diced | 2 tablespoons unsalted butter |
| 1 potato, baked, peeled and riced (page 571) | ½ teaspoon kosher salt |

1. Place turnips in a 4-cup glass measure. Cover tightly with microwave plastic wrap. Cook at 100% for 6 minutes.

2. Remove from oven. Uncover and place in the workbowl of a food processor. Add remaining ingredients and process until smooth.

3. Return mixture to measure and reheat, uncovered, at 100% for 2 minutes.

4. Remove from oven. Uncover and serve hot.

BEET AND POTATO PURÉE

This is a luscious shade of pink. It would add color and interest to Poached Chicken Breasts (page 202) or steamed fish fillets. Without the potato, it makes an unusual sauce. *Makes 1¼ cups*

½ pound beets, rinsed
     and stems removed
1 small potato, baked,
     peeled and riced
     (about ½ cup) (page
     571)

6 tablespoons unsalted
     butter
1 teaspoon cider vinegar
¼ teaspoon kosher salt
     Freshly ground black
     pepper

1. Wrap beets individually in microwave plastic wrap. Arrange in a circle in the microwave oven. Cook at 100% for 8 minutes.

2. Remove from oven. Unwrap and drain beet juices into a bowl. Remove skins and place beets and juice in the workbowl of a food processor. Process until smooth.

3. Combine beets with remaining ingredients in a 4-cup glass measure. Heat, uncovered, at 100% for 4 minutes.

4. Remove from oven. Serve hot.

VARIATION

SWEET AND SOUR BEET SAUCE Cook beets as for Beet and Potato Purée. Purée in blender with all remaining ingredients except for potato purée. Taste and add a little sugar, if needed. Serve with other vegetables or with steamed fish.

CREAMED SPINACH

Most of us don't think of this as a purée, yet not only is it one of the best tasting, it is also one of the most versatile. It can be a base for spinach soufflé with the possible addition of grated cheese. It can be baked as a gratin. It also makes good soup that can be sharpened with the acid of sorrel in spring or the pepperiness of watercress in winter. *Makes 2½ cups*

2 pounds spinach, stemmed and rinsed	**1½ teaspoons kosher salt**
2 cups Thick Béchamel (page 366)	**Freshly ground black pepper**
	Freshly ground nutmeg

1. Place spinach in a microwave-safe plastic bag and close tight. Cook at 100% for 5 minutes 30 seconds. Remove from oven and unwrap. Rinse spinach in cold water. Drain well and squeeze out excess water.

2. Place spinach and remaining ingredients in the workbowl of a food processor. Process until well combined and smooth.

3. To reheat, place mixture in a 2-quart soufflé dish and cook, uncovered, at 100% for 4 minutes, stirring twice.

4. Remove from oven and serve hot.

VARIATIONS

CREAM OF SPINACH SOUP To Creamed Spinach add 2 cups Chicken Broth (page 331), canned chicken broth, or Vegetable Broth (page 335). Season to taste and heat in an 8-cup glass measure, tightly covered, at 100% for 4 minutes. To serve cold, chill in refrigerator overnight. Then whisk in ½ cup plain yogurt. Serves 4 to 5.

GREEN CREAM SOUP Make Creamed Spinach, substituting ½ pound sorrel, cut in thin strips across the center vein, or ½ pound watercress leaves, for ½ pound of the spinach. Cook with spinach. Proceed as for Cream of Spinach Soup.

Flans, Custards and Timbales

These are some of the most elegant of vegetable creations. Between the food processor and the microwave oven, they have become so easy I feel slightly guilty. A little leftover purée can show up in this disguise—½ cup of purée will make 10 servings (see pages 288–300).

These dishes are equally good as first courses and side dishes. For a first course, you serve them with a garnish or sauce (see pages 360–384 and the Index for a choice of sauces). When planning the vegetables for a meal, don't serve a purée with a flan or custard; the textures are too similiar. Pick an elegant stewed vegetable like Mushroom Ragout (page 316), or something simple like Glazed Carrots (page 278) or Peas with Mint and Scallions (page 277). Although these molds are rich, you probably would not serve a starch as well, so they don't make the meal heavy.

Individual servings can be baked in custard cups or as 3-inch soufflés; they do best in bowl-shaped ramekins (see illustration on page 15). You can use small teacups or demitasse cups instead. Point the handles to the center of the oven.

BROCCOLI TIMBALE

As a first course, this would look beautiful on Sweet and Sour Beet Sauce (page 299). Put a small, blanched broccoli floret on each plate. *Serves 10*

½ cup Broccoli Purée (½ cup variation, page 293)

4 eggs

¾ cup heavy cream

Kosher salt to taste

Vegetable oil for greasing molds

1. In a food processor or with a whisk, just combine all ingredients except oil.

2. Lightly oil 10 demitasse cups or small custard cups. Fill each with ¼ cup of broccoli mixture. Cover each tightly with microwave plastic wrap.

3. Place in microwave oven in a large ring, not touching. Cook at 100% for 3 minutes 30 seconds.

4. Pierce plastic. Remove from oven. Uncover. Unmold onto dinner plate, platter or first course plates with about 3 tablespoons of sauce on each.

PARSNIP FLAN

This is one of the best of the flans. As a first course it is sensational counterpointed by a thin slice of smoked salmon. *Serves 8*

Vegetable oil for greasing molds	**½ cup Chicken Broth (page 331) or canned chicken broth**
½ pound parsnips, trimmed, peeled and cut in chunks	**¼ cup heavy cream**
1 shallot, peeled	**2 egg yolks**
1½ teaspoons unsalted butter, cut into bits	**Kosher salt**
	Freshly ground black pepper

1. Lightly grease 8 ramekins (½-cup size) with oil. Set aside.

2. Place parsnips and shallot in a 2-quart soufflé dish. Add butter and broth. Cover tightly with microwave plastic wrap. Cook at 100% for 5 minutes.

3. Remove from oven. Place in the workbowl of a food processor. Process until smooth. Add cream and egg yolks. Process again until well combined. Stir in salt and pepper.

4. Pour ¼ cup of mixture into each prepared ramekin. Place ramekins in a 14″ × 11″ × 2″ dish and add water to a depth of 1 inch. Cover tightly with microwave plastic wrap. Cook at 100% for 8 minutes.

5. Pierce plastic with the tip of a sharp knife. Remove ramekins from oven. Let stand for 3 minutes. Uncover and unmold flans onto a serving platter or individual dishes. Serve immediately.

ASPARAGUS CUSTARD

This is terrific tasting, and luxury on the cheap as a little bit of asparagus feeds a lot of people. This is fine with fish. As a first course, serve the custard with a few lightly cooked asparagus. *Serves 10*

Vegetable oil for
  greasing molds
¾ pound asparagus, ends
  snapped off, peeled
  and cut into 2-inch
  lengths (½ pound
  trimmed)

2½ teaspoons kosher salt
1 tablespoon water
1 cup heavy cream
4 eggs
  Freshly ground black
  pepper

1. Lightly grease 10 ramekins (2½-inch size) with oil. Reserve.

2. Place asparagus pieces on a large piece of microwave plastic wrap. Sprinkle with ½ teaspoon of the salt dissolved in the water. Fold over plastic to enclose asparagus completely. Cook at 100% for 2 minutes 30 seconds. Remove from oven. Uncover and reserve.

3. Place cream in a 4-cup glass measure. Cook, uncovered, at 100% for 1 minute 30 seconds.

4. Place asparagus and eggs in the workbowl of a food processor. Process until smooth. With machine running, add hot cream in a thin stream until incorporated. Stir in remaining salt and pepper.

5. Pour ¼ cup of mixture into each prepared ramekin. Cover each tightly with microwave plastic wrap. Arrange ramekins around inside rim of a 12-inch platter or on carousel. Cook at 100% for 3 minutes 30 seconds.

6. Pierce plastic with the tip of a sharp knife. Remove from oven. Uncover and unmold onto a serving platter. Serve immediately.

GARLIC CUSTARD

These are fantastic. Your guests won't know what they are, only that they're good. The garlic is sweet and nutty, not sharp. The custard is smooth and creamy—just right with roast leg of lamb or roast chicken or grilled fish. They could be the centerpiece of a vegetable dinner with Curried Mushroom Caps with Peas (page 314), Szechuan Green Beans (page 308), and Chinese Stewed Tomatoes (page 310). As a first course, serve them on Red Pepper Purée (page 343), topped with a few strips of red pepper.   *Serves 8*

Vegetable oil for greasing molds	**2 tablespoons olive oil**
4 heads garlic, split into cloves and smashed	**1 cup heavy cream**
	3 eggs
¼ cup Chicken Broth (page 331) or canned chicken broth	**1 teaspoon kosher salt**

   1. Lightly grease 8 ramekins (2½-inch size) with oil. Set aside.

   2. Combine garlic, broth, olive oil, and cream in a 4-cup glass measure. Cover tightly with microwave plastic wrap. Cook at 100% for 10 minutes.

   3. Remove from oven. Uncover and pass through the medium disc of a food mill. Stir in eggs and salt.

   4. Pour ¼ cup of mixture into each prepared ramekin. Cover each tightly with microwave plastic wrap. Arrange around inside rim of a 12-inch platter or on carousel. Cook at 100% for 3 minutes 30 seconds.

   5. Pierce plastic with the tip of a sharp knife. Remove from oven. Uncover each and unmold onto a serving platter. Serve immediately.

RADICCHIO GRATIN

If we know radicchio at all, we know it as a salad ingredient, leaves peeled from a round, dark red vegetable that looks like a small cabbage. In its native Italy, radicchio is eaten as often cooked as raw, and there are many different varieties. It does lose most of its glorious color when cooked, but its slightly bitter, mysterious taste compensates for the loss. Try this gratin with a simple fish dish, Loin of Veal (page 258), Smothered Pork Roast (page 253), or a roast chicken. *Serves 4 to 6*

1 pound radicchio, well rinsed	**3 egg yolks**
1 teaspoon balsamic vinegar	**¼ cup heavy cream**
	Freshly ground black pepper
1 teaspoon kosher salt	
2 tablespoons unsalted butter	**2 tablespoons freshly grated Parmesan cheese**

1. Place radicchio in microwave-safe plastic bag and close tight. Cook at 100% for 5 minutes.

2. Remove from oven. Unwrap, and remove and discard cores. Place the rest in the workbowl of a food processor and process until smooth. Add remaining ingredients except cheese. Process until well combined.

3. Place mixture in an 8-inch square dish. Sprinkle with cheese. Cook, uncovered, at 100% for 14 minutes.

4. Remove from oven. Cover with a plate and let stand for 15 minutes. Serve warm.

To serve 8. Double all ingredients. Cook radicchio for 8 minutes. Proceed, cooking custard in a 10-inch square dish for 20 to 22 minutes, until firm. Let stand for 15 minutes.

CORN CUSTARD

An old southern favorite, this is a delight. It is light enough to serve with a simple main course, from fish to meat. It can stand on its own as an egg dish at a brunch or luncheon. You can spice it up, but try it this way at least once. *Serves 8 as a side dish, 4 to 6 as a brunch dish*

2 tablespoons unsalted
  butter
¼ cup chopped yellow
  onion (about ½
  small onion)
¼ cup sliced scallion
  greens
2 cups fresh corn
  kernels

4 eggs
1¼ cups milk
¾ cup heavy cream
2 teaspoons kosher salt
¼ teaspoon Fiery
  Pepper Sauce
  (page 344)

1. Preheat conventional broiler.

2. Combine butter, onions, scallions, and corn in an 11″ × 8″ × 2″ dish. Cook, uncovered, at 100% for 3 minutes. Remove from oven and stir well.

3. Whisk together remaining ingredients. Pour over corn mixture. Cook, uncovered, at 100% for 3 minutes. Stir well and cook for 3 minutes more.

4. Without removing dish from oven, cover tightly with microwave plastic wrap. Cook at 100% for 1 minute 30 seconds.

5. Remove from oven. Uncover and place under broiler 5 inches from heat source, until golden brown. Serve hot.

VARIATION

SOUTH OF THE BORDER CORN CUSTARD Add ½ cup peeled, seeded, and diced tomato (¼-inch pieces) and ¼ cup *each* green and red bell pepper, stemmed, seeded, deribbed, and diced, to the other vegetables in step 2. Increase cooking time to 4 minutes. Add ½ cup grated aged Cheddar cheese to the ingredients in step 3 and increase Fiery Pepper Sauce to 1 teaspoon. Cook as for Corn Custard.

Exciting Vegetables

These are spectacular vegetable dishes, the kind that make a dinner memorable no matter how simple. I hope they become as much a part of your repertoire as they have mine. You can cook one or two of these while the roast is in the oven. They can also be cooked before the main course and briefly reheated. Almost all of them can be served at room temperature. An assortment adds wonders to a buffet. I can imagine a whole buffet of vegetable dishes with a grain like Couscous (page 138) or a pilaf and with a green salad and a few cheeses. That would be great summer entertaining with no last-minute work.

ONIONS IN BARBECUE SAUCE

These are best in the early spring, when you can sometimes buy cipolline, small, flat Italian onions; but the recipe can be made with small white onions (not pearl size) and it is still sensational. The onions go with anything, can be eaten on their own, are good as a first course and simply terrific for cocktail onions. The only thing they do not go with is barbecue. To prepare them, you do need an assortment of vinegars and spices, but it is quickly done, especially if you start with bottled tomato sauce.   *Serves 8 as a side dish*

1½ pounds Italian flat onions (2½″ to 3¼″ × ½″), skinned and roots trimmed, or small round white onions (about 1½ inches in diameter)
½ cup white wine vinegar
¼ cup balsamic vinegar
¼ cup white wine
¾ cup Chunky Tomato Sauce (page 374) or store-bought tomato or spaghetti sauce

2 tablespoons olive oil
¼ teaspoon ground cumin
¼ teaspoon ground cardamom
¼ teaspoon dry mustard
½ teaspoon ground ginger
¼ teaspoon Searing Pepper Sauce (page 344) or commercial hot red-pepper sauce
2 tablespoons granulated sugar (optional)
Kosher salt (optional)

1. Combine all ingredients except sugar and salt in a 14″ × 11″ × 2″ dish. Pat the onions into a single layer, pushing larger onions to the outside of the dish. Cover tightly with microwave plastic wrap. Cook at 100% for 15 minutes. Uncover and cook 10 minutes more.

2. Remove from oven and stir well. Add sugar and salt, if desired.

SZECHUAN GREEN BEANS

This dish is a triumph. It takes only 1 tablespoon of oil for a pound of beans. There is no deep-frying. The color is good, the flavor delicious. Be careful if you make them ahead. They will disappear. People love to munch on them. I use them as a satisfying, low-calorie snack before dinner and as a picnic dish. *Makes 4 cups; serves 8 as a side dish*

6 cloves garlic, smashed and peeled

2 quarter-size slices fresh ginger, peeled

2 scallions, trimmed and cut into 2-inch lengths

1 tablespoon vegetable oil

1 teaspoon hot red-pepper flakes

1 tablespoon tamari soy

1 tablespoon rice wine vinegar

1 pound green beans, tipped and tailed

1. Place garlic, ginger and scallions in the workbowl of a food processor. Process until finely chopped. Remove to a 14″ × 11″ × 2″ dish. Add oil and pepper flakes. Cook, uncovered, at 100% for 3 minutes.

2. Remove from oven. Stir in remaining ingredients. Cook, uncovered, at 100% for 15 minutes, stirring 4 to 5 times.

3. Remove from oven. Stir and serve hot or cold.

STEWED OKRA

Even people who thought they didn't like okra will like this. It is just about perfect with fish or lamb or pork chops. Be sure to cut off the stems of the okra carefully, without cutting into the okra itself. As long as the okra isn't cut, it won't get slimy. *Serves 6 as a side dish*

¼ **pound sliced yellow onion (½ cup)**
4 **cloves garlic, smashed and peeled**
½ **teaspoon hot red-pepper flakes**
¼ **cup olive oil**
½ **pound okra, stems removed without cutting into the okra**

2 **cups crushed tomatoes with juice (1 can, 14½ ounces)**
1 **teaspoon kosher salt**
1 **tablespoon fresh lemon juice**
Freshly ground black pepper

1. Combine onions, garlic, red-pepper flakes and oil in an 8-inch square dish. Heat, uncovered at 100% for 3 minutes. Add okra and cook, uncovered, at 100% for 3 minutes.

2. Remove from oven. Stir in tomatoes. Cover tightly with microwave plastic wrap. Cook at 100% for 6 minutes.

3. Remove from oven. Uncover and stir in remaining ingredients. Serve hot.

VARIATION

CREOLE STEWED OKRA WITH SHRIMP Add 1 teaspoon filé powder and ¼ teaspoon hot red-pepper sauce to oil and onion mixture. Add 12 shrimp, peeled and deveined, or 2 boneless chicken breasts, cut in strips 1″ × 2½″, with tomatoes. Cook for an additional 2 minutes. Finish as for Stewed Okra. Serves 6 as a first course, 2 to 4 as a main course with rice.

CHINESE STEWED TOMATOES

Make all of this. You will never regret it. If there are leftovers, they are good in an omelet or with scrambled eggs. You can cook fish or chicken in them. Use this as a sauce for angel hair pasta. Serve some with a sandwich or sliced ham instead of coleslaw. Serve it as a vegetable with almost any main course that does not have tomatoes or sauce. Think of it as a relish with a robust pâté. You may have gathered that I like it. If you want to start small, there are directions for making less at the end of the recipe. *Serves 8 to 10 as a side dish*

6 cloves garlic, smashed and peeled
2 scallions, cut into 2-inch lengths
½ cup fresh coriander leaves and 2 inches of stems
1 tablespoon vegetable oil

3 pounds tomatoes, cored and cut into 8 wedges each
¼ cup dried Chinese black beans
2 tablespoons tamari soy
1 tablespoon rice wine vinegar
2 tablespoons cornstarch

1. Place garlic, scallions, and coriander in the workbowl of a food processor. Process until coarsely chopped. Scrape into a 14″ × 11″ × 2″ dish and add oil. Cook, uncovered, at 100% for 3 minutes.

2. Remove from oven. Add tomatoes and beans and stir to coat. Cover tightly with microwave plastic wrap. Cook at 100% for 10 minutes.

3. Combine tamari soy, vinegar, and cornstarch in a small bowl.

4. Remove tomato mixture from oven. Uncover and stir in cornstarch mixture. Cook, uncovered, at 100% for 3 minutes.

5. Remove from oven. Serve hot.

To serve 2. Chop ½ scallion (white only), 1 clove garlic, and 2 tablespoons coriander leaves in the food processor. Scrape into an 8-inch square dish with 1 teaspoon oil. Cook for 2 minutes. Add 2 tomatoes and 1 tablespoon beans. Cover and cook for 3 minutes. Combine 2 teaspoons tamari soy, 1 teaspoon vinegar, and 2 teaspoons cornstarch and stir in. Cook, uncovered, at 100% for 2 minutes.

SWEET AND SOUR RED CABBAGE

This has that warm, sweet and sour taste I like so much. It is good with boiled beef or Traditional Pot Roast (page 239). Leftovers can be made into Hot Beet and Red Cabbage Borscht (page 99). A dollop of sour cream and a sprinkling of finely chopped dill on each portion would not be amiss. *Serves 6*

1 medium onion, peeled and sliced thin (about 1½ cups)
2 tablespoons plus 1 teaspoon unsalted butter
1 medium head red cabbage(about 2½ pounds), washed, cored and shredded
¾ cup red wine vinegar
4 teaspoons granulated sugar
2 tablespoons (packed) dark brown sugar

1 teaspoon kosher salt
½ teaspoon freshly ground black pepper
6 cloves garlic, smashed and peeled
1 bay leaf
10 juniper berries
2 tablespoons fresh lemon juice
1 tablespoon light, unsulphured molasses

1. Place onions and 2 tablespoons of the butter in a 12″ × 10″ × 3″ dish. Cook, uncovered, at 100% for 2 minutes.

2. Remove from oven and stir in cabbage. Cover tightly with microwave plastic wrap. Cook at 100% for 8 minutes.

3. In a 4-cup measure, combine vinegar, granulated and brown sugar, salt, pepper, garlic, bay leaf, and juniper berries. Without removing cabbage from oven, uncover and pour vinegar mixture over all. Re-cover tightly and cook for 10 minutes more.

4. Remove from oven. Let stand, covered.

5. Combine lemon juice, molasses, and remaining butter in a 2-cup glass measure. Cook, uncovered, at 100% for 30 seconds.

6. Remove from oven. Uncover cabbage and stir in molasses mixture. Serve hot.

BOK CHOY

The leaves of large bok choy need to be cooked separately from the ribs. To separate them, hold the rib between the outstretched thumb and fingers of one hand. With the other hand, sharply pull off the green leaves. This recipe can be mixed into the following one for Bok Choy Ribs if you are serving it warm, but I prefer to keep them separate, serving the leaves with fish or seafood another day. If you get really beautiful little bok choy heads, no longer than 6 inches in all, cook them whole this way. You can cook up to six at a time, one per person. Increase cooking time by 2 minutes. *Serves 2 to 3*

2 tablespoons Oriental sesame oil
1 tablespoon sesame seeds
  Leaves from 2 heads bok choy (about 7 ounces), cut into ¼-inch chiffonade (about 7 cups)

2 tablespoons mirin
1 tablespoon low-sodium soy sauce
1 tablespoon Worcestershire sauce
2 teaspoons granulated sugar

1. Combine oil and seeds in a 14″ × 11″ × 2″ dish. Cover tightly with microwave plastic wrap. Cook at 100% for 3 minutes.

2. Remove from oven. Uncover and add bok choy. Stir well. Cover tightly with microwave plastic wrap. Cook at 100% for 4 minutes.

3. Remove from oven. Uncover and stir in remaining ingredients. Re-cover and cook for 2 minutes more.

4. Remove from oven. Uncover and serve.

BOK CHOY RIBS

The pale, white-green ribs of bok choy are slightly crunchy and mildly spicy. They can be served hot as a vegetable. They will also keep up to a week in the refrigerator and can be used as a pickle. See the recipe for Bok Choy for directions on how to separate the leaves from the ribs.
Serves 6

Ribs from 2 heads bok choy, cut into 2 to 3-inch lengths (about 8 cups)
1 tablespoon water
2 tablespoons cornstarch
⅓ cup vegetable oil

1 teaspoon small dried hot chilies
6 large cloves garlic, smashed and peeled
2 tablespoons granulated sugar
1 tablespoon kosher salt
¼ cup rice wine vinegar

1. Place bok choy in a 14″ × 11″ × 2″ dish. Sprinkle with water. Cover tightly with microwave plastic wrap. Cook at 100% for 6 minutes.

2. Remove from oven. Uncover, remove cooking juices to a small bowl and stir in cornstarch. Remove bok choy to a warm plate. Reserve liquid and bok choy.

3. Combine oil, chilies, and garlic in same dish. Cook, uncovered, at 100% for 4 minutes.

4. Remove from oven. Add reserved cornstarch mixture and stir well. Stir in sugar, salt, vinegar, and reserved bok choy. Cover tightly with microwave plastic wrap. Cook at 100% for 5 minutes.

5. Remove from oven. Uncover and serve hot.

CURRIED MUSHROOM CAPS WITH PEAS

This is a mild curry meant to go with American main courses. If you want it hotter, double the amount of Spice Powder; if using curry powder, double the amount and add ¼ teaspoon hot red-pepper sauce. This is good with hamburgers, roasts, or grilled chops of any kind.   *Serves 6*

1 tablespoon plus 1 teaspoon vegetable oil

2 teaspoons black or yellow mustard seeds

1 teaspoon Spice Powder III (page 346) or curry powder

1 clove garlic, smashed and peeled

½ teaspoon kosher salt

1 pound medium (1½-inch size) mushrooms, wiped clean and stems removed

¼ cup Chicken Broth (page 331) or canned chicken broth

½ cup tiny frozen peas, defrosted in a sieve under warm running water

⅓ cup Coconut Milk (page 353) or canned unsweetened coconut milk

1 teaspoon fresh lime juice

1. Heat 1 teaspoon of the oil in a 1½-quart soufflé dish, uncovered, at 100% for 2 minutes. Add the mustard seeds and cover loosely with paper toweling. Cook at 100% for 4 minutes, shaking dish once.

2. Remove from oven. Add remaining oil, spice powder, garlic, and salt. Add the mushroom caps and broth and stir to coat. Cover tightly with microwave plastic wrap. Cook at 100% for 12 minutes.

3. Remove from oven. Uncover and stir in remaining ingredients. Cook, uncovered, at 100% for 1 minute 30 seconds.

4. Remove from oven. Stir and serve hot or warm.

MUSHROOM CAPS WITH CUMIN
AND SOUR CREAM

This is almost the best vegetable there is with steak and Mashed Potatoes (page 290). It can also be served cold as a first course on some lettuce. If you want to cut down on calories, use plain lowfat yogurt instead of sour cream. *Serves 4*

2 tablespoons vegetable oil
1 teaspoon ground cumin
1 pound medium (1½-inch size) mushrooms, wiped clean and stems removed

½ teaspoon kosher salt
¼ cup sour cream
1 tablespoon minced flat parsley leaf
1 teaspoon fresh lemon juice
¼ teaspoon freshly ground black pepper

1. Heat oil and cumin in a 2-quart soufflé dish, uncovered, at 100% for 2 minutes. Add mushrooms and salt and stir to coat. Cover tightly with microwave plastic wrap. Cook at 100% for 12 minutes.

2. Remove from oven. Uncover and stir in sour cream, parsley, lemon juice, and pepper. Cook, uncovered, at 100% for 1 minute 30 seconds.

3. Remove from oven. Stir and serve hot.

MUSHROOM RAGOUT

No doubt about it, this is company food unless you feel like treating yourself to expensive dried mushrooms. If you have some wild mushrooms, freshly picked or store-bought, substitute cèpes (boletus) or chanterelles, cut in strips, for some or all of the store-bought mushrooms. Canned Chinese straw mushrooms can also be added. Stir it into Velouté (page 366) for a fabulous veal or chicken sauce serving 10 to 12 people. Save the soaking liquid from the dried morels to add to broth or sauces. It will do wonders for Vegetable Broth (page 335).

Serve the ragout with steak, veal, or chicken. You don't need much; it is rich. Add a green vegetable without sauce, like asparagus. Spoon the ragout into Puff Pastry Shells (page 443) as a first course. *Makes 2 cups; serves 6 as a side dish*

1 ounce dried morels (8 to 12 mushrooms)
1 pound fresh domestic mushrooms, sliced ¼ inch thick
2 teaspoons fresh lemon juice
1 ounce dried shiitake mushrooms
1 tablespoon minced shallot
2 tablespoons Meat Glaze (page 337) or Sauce Espagnole (page 371)

2 tablespoons red wine
1 tablespoon Cognac
2 tablespoons minced parsley
1 tablespoon unsalted butter
Kosher salt
Freshly ground black pepper
1 tablespoon (packed) finely chopped fresh dill (optional)
1 tablespoon Dijon mustard (optional)

1. Place morels in a 4-cup glass measure and cover with 1 cup cold water. Cover tightly with microwave plastic wrap. Cook at 100% for 3 minutes. Remove from oven and let stand, covered, for 3 minutes. Uncover and strain. Keep soaking liquid for another use. Use small morels whole. Slice large morels across into 2-inch pieces and reserve.

2. Combine sliced domestic mushrooms and lemon juice in a 9-inch quiche dish. Crumble dried shiitake mushrooms over mixture, discarding stems; stir. Cover tightly with microwave plastic wrap. Cook at 100% for 3 minutes.

3. Remove from oven. Uncover and stir in reserved morels. Add remaining ingredients except salt and pepper, dill, and mustard. Cook, uncovered, at 100% for 3 minutes.

4. Remove from oven. Stir in salt and pepper, dill and/or mustard, if desired. Serve hot.

VARIATIONS

CREAMY MUSHROOM RAGOUT Dissolve 2 teaspoons cornstarch in ½ cup heavy cream. Stir into mushrooms along with morels in step 3 and cook as for Mushroom Ragout. Finish, adding 1 tablespoon of the morel-soaking liquid and dill and/or mustard, if you like.

MUSHROOM RAGOUT WITH STRAW MUSHROOMS Add ¾ cup canned straw mushrooms, drained and rinsed, along with morels. Increase red wine and Meat Glaze *each* to 3 tablespoons. Cook for 4 minutes. If desired, finish as Creamy Mushroom Ragout, using 1 tablespoon cornstarch.

WILD MUSHROOM SAUCE Add cooked Mushroom Ragout to 1½ cups Velouté (page 366). Season with salt, a little pepper, and a pinch of cayenne. Reheat in an 8-cup glass measure, loosely covered with paper toweling, at 100% for 4 minutes.

EARLY SUMMER SQUASH

The quality of olive oil is particularly important in this dish. If you are not using one of the exceptionally fruity oils (which can also be exceptionally expensive), double the amount of oil and reduce cooking time by 1 minute. If small tomatoes (2 inches in diameter) are not available, core and quarter large tomatoes.

This combination was devised at the height of summer, when I returned from Vermont with a bounty of perfect produce. There are alternatives for some of the ingredients, but one item that is indispensable is fresh basil. Best of all was a version using half bush basil and half large leaf basil.

At once refreshing and comforting, this is one of my favorite recipes for a ripened garden on a warm day. The oil from the peppers is absorbed into all the other vegetables—delightful. It is also good over pasta. *Serves 8 as a first course or side dish*

1 pound very small yellow squash (about 8 to 10 squash, with flowers intact, if possible) or larger squash cut into 1″ × 1″ × 3″ pieces

4 medium Hungarian peppers or 4 medium frying peppers plus 1 teaspoon hot red-pepper flakes, crushed

1 pound small tomatoes, prickled 3 or 4 times each

¼ cup fresh basil leaves

2 tablespoons water

2 tablespoons fruity olive oil

1 teaspoon kosher salt

1. Arrange squash in a 2-quart soufflé dish spoke-fashion with flowers pointing toward the center. Place peppers in center and arrange tomatoes on top of squash. Tuck basil between vegetables. Pour water, oil, and salt over all. Cover dish tightly with microwave plastic wrap. Cook at 100% for 12 minutes 30 seconds, until vegetables are tender.

2. Remove from oven. Uncover and cut peppers in half. Serve hot or let cool to room temperature and serve with cold leftover meat or an omelet.

To serve 4. Use 3 Hungarian peppers or 3 frying peppers plus ¾ teaspoon hot red-pepper flakes. Halve all other ingredients. Arrange in a 6½″ × 3″ soufflé dish. Cover and cook for 9 minutes. Finish as for 8 servings.

To serve 2. Use 1 Hungarian pepper or 1 frying pepper plus ⅛ teaspoon hot red-pepper flakes and 2 teaspoons oil. Divide all other ingredient quantities by 4. Arrange in a large soup bowl. Cover and cook for 8 minutes. Finish as for 8 servings.

Main Course Vegetables

It isn't just vegetarians who from time to time relish making a meal out of vegetables. Dieters and delighters in the season's produce do so as well. The chapter on grains (page 117) has pasta and rice dishes that make good meatless main courses. Cook the vegetables for Pasta Primavera (page 146) and top with eggs as in Summer Vegetable Bonanza (page 328) or, even simpler, serve them with Watercress Sauce (page 369). You might want to pick three of your favorite vegetable recipes and serve them with a simple starch. Use one of the vegetable purées under Baked Eggs (page 67).

VEGETABLES FOR ONE

If you are cooking just for one, pick up already cleaned and sliced vegetables from a salad bar. There is no simpler way to satisfy a craving for a dish of crunchy, assorted fresh vegetables, with absolutely no work involved. *Serves 1*

8 to 10 ounces assorted vegetables, trimmed, peeled and sliced (see note)

2 tablespoons minced fresh herbs, such as basil, chives, dill, parsley or tarragon

Kosher salt

Freshly ground black pepper

1 tablespoon unsalted butter, cut into bits (optional)

1. Arrange vegetables on a plate with slower-cooking vegetables toward the outside. Sprinkle with herbs, salt, pepper, and butter, if desired. Cover tightly with microwave plastic wrap. Cook at 100% for 5 minutes.

2. Remove from oven. Uncover immediately.

Note. Slower-cooking vegetables include carrots, green beans, red cabbage, broccoli florets, cauliflower florets, peas, sugar snap peas, cherry tomatoes. Quick-cooking vegetables include asparagus, red onions or scallions, mushrooms, zucchini and summer squash, red and green bell peppers.

STUFFED CABBAGE LEAVES

There are people who can eat a piece of stuffed cabbage and live to eat their main course; I find it too filling. This recipe makes 8 to 10 stuffed leaves. You really have to know your guests' appetites to figure out how much to serve. One may be enough with a dollop of sour cream on top; but I have known grown people and growing boys to eat three.

Drink beer, or a cold red wine like Beaujolais. I would have a salad and relax. *Serves 4 to 8*

⅓ cup long-grain rice
1 head cabbage, broken
   outer leaves,
   removed and cored,
   leaving head whole
1 medium yellow onion,
   peeled and
   quartered (about ½
   pound)
1 clove garlic, smashed
   and peeled
2 quarter-size pieces
   fresh ginger, peeled
1 pound ground beef
1 tablespoon kosher salt
⅛ teaspoon nutmeg

SAUCE
2 cups canned tomatoes
   (1 can, 14½
   ounces), drained
   and crushed
¼ cup cider vinegar
½ cup brown sugar
1 tablespoon Meat Glaze
   (page 337) (optional)
2 tablespoons paprika, 2
   teaspoons paprika
   paste or 1 teaspoon
   Hot Pepper Sauce
   (page 343)
2 cloves garlic, smashed
   and peeled
½ cup raisins
½ cup sweet wine, like
   riesling or Tokay

1. Place rice in a 4-cup glass measure and cover with 1 cup cold water. Cover with microwave plastic wrap. Cook at 100% for 5 minutes. Drain, rinse, and reserve.

2. Place whole cabbage in center of oven and cook, uncovered, at 100% for 5 to 6 minutes. Remove from oven and let cool slightly. Peel back and remove 8 large or 10 small leaves.

3. Place onions, garlic, and ginger in the workbowl of a food processor. Process until finely chopped. Remove from processor and combine with ground beef, salt, nutmeg, and reserved rice.

4. Position a cabbage leaf, outside down, on a work surface. Fill with 2 tablespoons of meat mixture and fold sides of leaf over on both sides to enclose filling. Then roll up. Repeat with all leaves. Place stuffed cabbage roll, seam side down, in an 11" × 9" × 4" dish (see grape leaves, page 36).

5. Stir together sauce ingredients just to combine. Pour over prepared cabbage. Cover tightly with microwave plastic wrap. Cook at 100% for 15 minutes.

6. Remove from oven. Pierce plastic with the tip of a sharp knife. Uncover and remove cabbage to a warm serving dish. Return sauce to oven and cook, uncovered, at 100% for 5 minutes.

7. Remove from oven. Pour sauce over cabbage and serve.

GREEN CURRY OF SUMMER SQUASH

Served with a pilaf like Tomato Pilaf (page 131), this is enough for two to three as a main course. *Serves 4 as a side dish*

2 tablespoons vegetable oil

1 medium onion (about ½ pound), peeled and thinly sliced

1 clove garlic, smashed, peeled and minced

1 teaspoon Spice Powder I (page 345)

Large pinch cayenne pepper

4 cups stemmed and washed spinach (about 1 pound before cleaning)

3 scallions, trimmed and coarsely chopped

3 tablespoons chopped fresh dill

¼ cup Chicken Broth (page 331) or canned chicken broth

1 teaspoon kosher salt

2 medium zucchini (about ½ pound), trimmed, cut into 2-inch rounds and each round cut into eighths

2 small yellow squash (about ½ pound), trimmed, cut into 2-inch rounds and each round cut into eighths

1. Heat oil in a 2-quart soufflé dish, uncovered, at 100% for 2 minutes. Add onions, garlic, spice powder, and cayenne. Cook, uncovered, at 100% for 4 minutes.

2. Remove from oven. Add remaining ingredients except zucchini and yellow squash. Cover tightly with microwave plastic wrap. Cook at 100% for 5 minutes. Uncover and stir in squash. Re-cover and cook for 5 minutes more, stirring once.

3. Remove from oven. Uncover and let stand 3 minutes before serving.

VEGETABLE CURRY

This makes for a wonderful meal with plain rice or a pilaf, or as an accompaniment to broiled chicken, fish, lamb, or beef. Here, making your own spice powder really pays off. If you like things spicy, double the amount of Spice Powder or curry.

This curry is very good cold. Reduce the final cooking period to 10 minutes; let stand covered until cool. Refrigerate until ready to serve.   *Serves 8 as a main dish, 12 to 16 as a side dish*

1 large baking potato (about 10 ounces), peeled and thinly sliced in a food processor

¼ cup Clarified Butter (page 494) or unsalted butter

1 large onion, peeled, quartered and thinly sliced in a food processor

3 cloves garlic, smashed and peeled

1 tablespoon Spice Powder III (page 346) or curry powder

2 cups Chicken Broth (page 331) or canned chicken broth

1 cup Lightly Cooked Crushed Tomatoes (page 339)

2 cups cauliflower florets

2 large carrots, trimmed, peeled and thinly sliced in a food processor

1 large red bell pepper, stemmed, seeded, deribbed, and cut in 1-inch dice

2 cups broccoli florets (about 3 ounces)

¼ pound green beans, trimmed and cut in half (1 cup)

2 tablespoons fresh lime juice

2 tablespoons chopped fresh coriander

Kosher salt

Freshly ground black pepper

1. Put a pot of salted water on to blanch potatoes. When it is boiling, add potatoes and blanch for 5 minutes. Drain and reserve.

2. Heat butter in a 2-quart soufflé dish, uncovered, at 100% for 3 minutes. Add the onions, garlic, and spice or curry powder. Cook, uncovered, at 100% for 8 minutes, stirring once.

3. Add broth, crushed tomatoes, cauliflower, carrots, and reserved potatoes. Cover tightly with microwave plastic wrap. Cook at 100% for 12 minutes.

4. Uncover and stir in peppers, broccoli, and beans. Re-cover and cook at 100% for 12 minutes.

5. Remove from oven. Let stand covered for 2 minutes. Uncover and stir in lime juice and coriander; add salt and pepper to taste.

To serve 4. Blanch 1 small potato. Heat 3 tablespoons butter in a 1½-quart soufflé dish. Add 1 large sliced onion, 2 cloves garlic, and 2 teaspoons spice powder and cook for 6 minutes. Halve quantities of broth, crushed tomatoes, cauliflower, and carrots and cook as for 8 servings for 10 minutes. Uncover and add 1 pepper, 1 cup broccoli, and ⅔ cup beans. Cover and cook for 10 minutes more. Halve remaining ingredients and finish as for 8 servings, letting the curry stand for 2 minutes. To serve cold, reduce final cooking time to 8 minutes. Taste to see if it requires more lime juice or a little bit of vegetable oil.

To serve 2. Blanch 1 small potato. Heat 2 tablespoons butter in a 1-quart soufflé dish. To butter add 1 small sliced onion, 1 clove garlic, and 1 teaspoon spice powder and cook for 6 minutes. Add 1 small pepper, ½ cup broccoli, and ⅓ cup beans. Cook for 6 minutes more. Finish as for 8 servings, adding 2 teaspoons lime juice and 2 teaspoons coriander with the salt and pepper at end. To serve cold, reduce final cooking time to 5 minutes.

EGGPLANT, TOMATO AND FENNEL

This is a sensational first course, major vegetable course or vegetarian main dish that could not be made anywhere as well as in the microwave oven, which permits the vegetables to stay whole and still blend their juices. *Serves 4 as a first course, 2 as a main course*

4 small Japanese
    eggplants (about 3½
    inches long), each
    pricked 4 times with
    a fork
4 large plum tomatoes
    (about ⅔ pound),
    each pricked 4 times
    with a fork
½ bulb fennel, cored and
    quartered
    lengthwise

4 large cloves garlic,
    smashed and peeled
3 sprigs fresh basil
¼ teaspoon fresh thyme
2 tablespoons olive oil
1 tablespoon water
1 tablespoon kosher salt
    Freshly ground black
    pepper

1. Arrange eggplants spoke-fashion, stems toward the center, around the inside rim of a 2-quart soufflé dish. Place tomatoes in center. Scatter fennel on top of eggplant. Tuck garlic, basil, and thyme between vegetables. Pour oil, water, salt, and pepper over all. Cover tightly with microwave plastic wrap. Cook at 100% for 15 minutes.

2. Remove from oven. Uncover and let stand for 3 minutes before serving.

ORIENTAL GREEN VEGETABLE CASSEROLE

Who would believe these everyday vegetables would taste so special when brought together with rather simple seasonings? Tasting is believing. *Serves 2 as a main course with rice, 4 as a side dish*

1 small green bell
  pepper, stemmed,
  seeded, deribbed
  and cut into 2-inch
  strips
6 scallions, trimmed,
  whites cut into 3-
  inch lengths and
  greens cut into ¼-
  inch rounds
¼ pound zucchini,
  trimmed, cut in half
  lengthwise, then cut
  into 2-inch pieces

¼ pound snow peas,
  strung
¼ cup fresh coriander
  leaves
2 tablespoons tamari
  soy
1½ tablespoons rice wine
  vinegar
6 thin slices fresh
  ginger, peeled
2 teaspoons vegetable
  oil

1. Toss together all ingredients in a 1-quart casserole. Cover tightly with microwave plastic wrap. Cook at 100% for 6 minutes.

2. Remove from oven. Uncover and stir well once or twice before serving.

SPICY VEGETABLE RAGOUT

This stew is meant to be ladled over a heap of Couscous (page 138) in a soup bowl. It is not authentic couscous, but no one will mind, or miss the meat. It is a great dish for a party with a sliced roast and a salad. It makes a good buffet dish, kept warm in a chafing dish or on a hot plate. In that scenario it would serve a small army.

The flavors are spicy, but they don't shout. The surprise comes from the cinnamon, which gives a hint of sweetness that is typical of Moroccan cooking. It will take you about half an hour to prepare all the vegetables, but the ragout cooks quickly, so you can entertain without fuss. Make the Couscous ahead and reheat it, covered, for 3 minutes at 100%. The vegetables will stay hot. With so many vegetables and the tomato-based sauce, it's a pretty dish.
Serves 6 to 8 as a main course

COOKING LIQUID
- 4 cups tomato juice
- 12 cloves garlic, smashed and peeled
- 2 teaspoons aniseed
- 1 tablespoon ground cumin
- 2 teaspoons ground coriander
- 2 teaspoons ground ginger
- ½ teaspoon ground allspice
- ¼ teaspoon freshly grated nutmeg
- 1 teaspoon hot red-pepper flakes
- 1 teaspoon ground cardamom
- ¾ teaspoon ground cinnamon
- 1 teaspoon Fiery Pepper Sauce (page 344) or 1 teaspoon *each* sambal olek and harissa
- 2 tablespoons olive oil

VEGETABLES
- 1 cup canned chick-peas, drained and rinsed
- 1 box (10 ounces) frozen artichoke hearts or 8 fresh baby artichokes, trimmed and cut in half lengthwise
- 2 medium carrots, trimmed, peeled and cut into 1-inch rounds, or 4 small turnips, trimmed, peeled and cut into 1½-inch chunks
- 1 package (10 ounces) frozen okra pods, or 12 fresh okra pods or 1 pound cauliflower florets
- 1 can (14 ounces) baby corn, drained and rinsed
- 1½ pounds tomatoes, cored and cut into 1½-inch wedges
- 1½ pounds eggplant, cut into 1-inch cubes
- 1 pound small onions, peeled and quartered, or 1 box (10 ounces) frozen pearl onions
- 1 pound asparagus spears, trimmed and cut in 2-inch lengths

- 1 tablespoon kosher salt
- ½ cup shredded fresh coriander leaves and stems
- 2 tablespoons fresh lemon juice
- 1 tablespoon fresh lime juice
- Couscous (page 138)

1. Combine cooking liquid ingredients in a 14″ × 11″ × 2″ dish. Add all vegetables and salt. Stir to coat. Cover tightly with microwave plastic wrap. Cook at 100% for 20 minutes.

2. Remove from oven. Uncover and cook at 100% for 10 minutes.

3. Remove from oven and stir in coriander, lemon juice, and lime juice. Serve over Couscous.

SUMMER VEGETABLE BONANZA

This is terrific in early summer when the first of the vegetables start coming on. Serve it with Garlic Potatoes (page 143) or BURGUR (see entry in the Dictionary). You can add eggs or stir in ¾ pound feta cheese or tofu, rinsed and cut in ½-inch cubes, at the last minute. Serve lots of chunky bread, please.   *Serves 12 as a side dish or first course, 6 as a vegetarian main course*

2 pounds baby eggplants (4½ to 5 inches long), Chinese eggplants (5 to 6 inches long), each pricked 4 times with a fork, or 2 pounds of larger eggplants cut in 2″ × 2″ × 3″ pieces

½ pound baby zucchini (3 to 4 inches long), trimmed, or larger zucchini cut in 1″ × 1″ × 3″ pieces

½ pound baby yellow squash (3 to 4 inches long), trimmed, or larger squash cut in 1″ × 1″ × 3″ pieces

2 pounds plum tomatoes (about 12), cored, each pricked 4 times with a fork

12 cloves garlic, smashed and peeled

1 cup (tightly packed) fresh basil leaves

1 tablespoon kosher salt

1 tablespoon dried thyme

8 grinds fresh black pepper

6 tablespoons olive oil
Extra sprigs of basil, for serving (optional)

1. Arrange eggplants around the inside rim of a 14″ × 11″ × 2″ dish. Place zucchini and squash in center and arrange tomatoes in a ring on top. Tuck garlic and basil between the vegetables. Sprinkle salt, thyme, pepper, and oil over all. Cover tightly with microwave plastic wrap. Cook at 100% for 20 minutes.

2. Remove from oven. Uncover and let stand for 3 minutes. Serve with extra basil sprigs on top, if desired.

VARIATION

SUMMER VEGETABLE BONANZA WITH EGGS For a vegetarian meal for a hungry troop, break one egg per person on top of the cooked vegetables in a ring around the edge. Prick each yolk twice with the tip of a very sharp knife. Re-cover and cook at 100% for 2 minutes longer. Serve with bulgur. Serves 6.

SAVORY BASICS

COOKING, particularly microwave cooking, takes little time. It's usually the assembling of the ingredients, particularly the cooked ones, that takes so long. This is when the microwave oven is of incalculable aid. If you need some cooked vegetables for a soup, a sauce, or a purée, if you need melted chocolate or butter, look in the Dictionary and you'll be able to whip them out in good order. If you need to blanch nuts or defrost meat, look in the Dictionary. You will find other basics in the sections on Savory Sauces, Sweet Basics, Sweet Sauces. That still leaves you with lots of other things you will need to prepare as parts of a recipe. Perhaps the most frequently called for are broths (stocks), which can be found in this chapter. The other recipes included here are good for unregenerate, top-of-the-stove cooks. They may even end up getting attached to their microwave ovens.

MEAT BROTHS

You will have better broth if you chop the bones into small pieces (or, much better, get the butcher to do it for you). When buying meat, even if you are buying it boned, ask for the bones and freeze them until you have enough to make broth. Broth can be made with or without vegetables; it is a matter of taste and depends, too, on what sort of recipe you are going to use the broth in. I tend to use vegetables in making broth for fricassees and clear soups, and not to use them in broths for vegetable soups. When making Chicken Broth, you may add hearts and gizzards to the bones, but do not add chicken livers.

It is a good habit to ask for the bones when buying filleted chicken or fish. When removing wing tips to prepare chicken wings in Chicken with Barbecue Sauce (page 211), save those as well. When you roast a chicken, save the gizzards if you are not using them for Chicken Gravy (page 333). Pop your gleanings into a freezer container and make broth when you have enough bones and other good stuff.

If you want an absolutely clear broth, as for Aspic, clarify. See CLARIFYING in the Dictionary. *Makes 4 cups*

2 pounds chicken, duck, veal, beef marrow or lamb bones (see following instructions)	**4 cups water**

1. Place bones and water in a 2-quart soufflé dish. Cover tightly with microwave plastic wrap. Cook at 100% for 30 minutes, or 40 minutes for a broth that will jell.

2. Remove from oven. Let stand, covered, until liquid stops bubbling. Uncover carefully and strain through a fine sieve. Cool. Store, tightly covered, in the refrigerator or freezer. Remove fat.

To make 2 cups broth. Use 1 pound bones and 2 cups water. Cook for 20 minutes.

Chicken Broth. Use bones, necks, backs, and even giblets (gizzards and hearts, not liver); cut into 2-inch to 3-inch pieces

Duck Broth. Chop bones into 3-inch to 4-inch pieces. You may substitute Chicken Broth or canned chicken broth for the water. Do not use canned broth if you are planning to make Duck Glaze; it will be too salty.

To make 7 cups: Make Duck Broth and transfer hot broth and bones to a 3-quart soufflé dish. Add 3 cups Chicken Broth or canned chicken broth (not if planning to make Glaze), and ¾ pound raw duck bones, chopped. Cover and cook at 100% for 30 additional minutes.

Veal Broth. Use veal knuckles sawed across the bone to expose the marrow and hacked into 2-inch pieces.

To make 8 cups: Use 5 pounds raw veal knuckles and 8 cups water. Cook for 45 minutes.

Light Beef Broth. Use beef marrow bones. Add 1 small onion, quartered, and 1 small carrot, trimmed, peeled and quartered.

Lamb Broth. Hack 1 pound lamb bones into 1-inch pieces. Substitute Chicken Broth or canned chicken broth for the water. Cook for only 20 minutes.

To make 2 cups: Halve ingredients and cook for only 15 minutes.

Aspic. Clarify (see CLARIFYING in the Dictionary) 4 cups broth. If your broth will not jell, sprinkle one package of gelatin on top of warm, clarified broth; return to the oven and heat at 100% for 5 minutes.

MEAT BROTH WITH VEGETABLES

Makes 4 cups

2 pounds chicken bones and giblets, or veal bones or shin bones of beef, or a combination	¼ pound celery, cut into 3-inch lengths
	½ pound tomatoes, cored and halved
½ pound onions, peeled and quartered	¼ pound carrots, cut into 3-inch lengths
	3 parsley sprigs
	4 cups water

1. Preheat broiler.

2. Chop bones as for Meat Broths (page 330). Spread bones and vegetables in a single layer in a roasting pan. Broil 6 inches from the heat source for 40 minutes, shaking the pan occasionally, until well browned.

3. Remove bones and vegetables to an 8-cup glass measure. Pour water over solids and cover tightly with microwave plastic wrap. Cook at 100% for 30 minutes.

4. Remove from oven and pierce plastic with the tip of a sharp knife to release steam. Uncover and strain broth through a fine sieve. Cool. Store, tightly covered, in the refrigerator or freezer. Remove fat.

VARIATIONS

LIGHT VEGETABLE AND CHICKEN SOUP Use the same ingredients plus 1 clove garlic, smashed and peeled, and 3 fresh dill sprigs. Do not brown bones and vegetables first.

RICH AND MEATY SOUP This really goes beyond soup if you serve the sliced beef in the soup with vegetables. Add some cooked noodles and you have a lovely dinner for 6.

Make Meat Broth with Vegetables using veal knuckles. Strain and skim off fat. Place in a 2-quart soufflé dish with 1 pound beef shank meat cut across the grain into ¼-inch-thick slices. Cover tightly and cook at 100% for 10 minutes. Remove from oven. Remove meat with a slotted spoon. If using broth for a thick soup, do not strain. If you want a clear broth, line a sieve with a wet cloth and pour the broth through. You will have 4 cups of enriched broth, which can be used in any recipe after skimming off fat and, if desired, clarifying.

To use as a whole meal, do not strain soup. Reserve meat. Add to broth 1 small carrot, peeled and thinly sliced, ½ bay leaf, a pinch of thyme, 1 cup peas, 1 small turnip, peeled and thinly sliced, 1 tablespoon finely chopped parsley, and, if desired, 1 small parsnip, peeled and thinly sliced. Cover tightly and cook for 4 minutes at 100%. Remove soup from oven; season to taste with salt and pepper. Add meat and cooked noodles or cooked cubed potatoes. Pass horseradish sauce and mustard.

CHICKEN GRAVY Break chicken neck in half. Place in a 4-cup glass measure with all the giblets (not the liver), 3 cloves garlic, 2 parsley sprigs, ½ small peeled onion, ½ bay leaf, and 1 small peeled carrot cut into 1-inch lengths. Cover with 1 to 1½ cups Chicken Soup, a version of meat broth with vegetables, or canned chicken broth. Cover tightly with microwave plastic wrap. Cook for 20 minutes at 100%. Strain and skim stock. Cut giblets into small pieces. If you have the patience, pick the meat off the neck bones, discarding the bones. (If making gravy for a roast chicken, deglaze the roasting pan with the skimmed stock.) In any case, whisk 2 tablespoons Roux (page 337) into hot broth. Return sliced giblets and neck meat to thickened stock. Cook, uncovered, for 2 minutes at 100%. Season to taste with salt and pepper and chopped dill, parsley, lovage, or tarragon, if desired.

You can quickly poach 6 halves of skinned and boned chicken breasts in the Chicken Gravy for 7 minutes. The gravy won't need its last 2 minutes of cooking, because it will get that while the chicken cooks. Serve with noodles, rice, broccoli, or spinach.

FISH BROTH

Fish broth should not be made with the bones of flatfish— sole, flounder and the like—or the broth will be bitter. Blood will do the same thing. For basic fish broth, use the bones of white-fleshed fish. Salmon and sturgeon bones give a flavorful and beautifully colored broth—pale gold for sturgeon, pale salmon for salmon—but they are too definite in flavor to use with other kinds of fish. If you want a broth that will jell, increase cooking time to 40 minutes.　*Makes 4¼ cups*

2 pounds whole fish heads and bones, broken into 2-inch to 3-inch pieces	**4 cups water**

1. Remove gills. Wash heads and bones thoroughly to rinse away all traces of blood. Use a small knife to open any sealed pockets of blood, as it will make the broth bitter. Cut head in half and bones into 2-inch pieces.

2. Place heads, bones, and water in a 2-quart soufflé dish. Cover tightly with microwave plastic wrap. Cook at 100% for 20 minutes.

3. Remove from oven. Leave covered until bubbling stops, about 3 minutes. Uncover carefully and strain through a fine sieve lined with a single layer of cheesecloth. Cool and skim. Store, tightly covered, in the refrigerator or freezer.

VARIATIONS

SEAFOOD FUMET Use 1¾ pounds shrimp shells and 2 pounds fish heads and fish bones, cleaned. Use 2½ cups water and 2½ cups white wine instead of all water. Proceed as for Fish Broth, cooking for 12 minutes. Makes 5 cups.

FISH FUMET Use 2 pounds fish heads and bones, 1 celery stalk cut into 2-inch lengths, 1 small peeled carrot cut into 1-inch lenghts, 3 parsley springs, ½ bay leaf, 1 whole leek or medium-size onion, peeled and cut into chunks, 2½ cups water, 2½ cups white wine, and a pinch *each* of dried thyme and savory. Proceed as for Fish Broth. Makes 5 cups.

VEGETABLE BROTH

This basic vegetarian broth is good to have on hand for everyday cooking if you are a vegetarian, or for when you are having vegetarians as guests. It is cloudy when finished and is best used for bean soups, vegetable soups, and legume soups (lentils, for instance). This broth has no salt or pepper; if you want, add to taste. You can also use the cooking liquid reserved from making Tomatoes Stuffed with Tabbouleh (page 78) or strained Tomato and Cabbage Soup (page 100) for a vegetarian broth with a strong tomato flavor. *Makes 3 cups*

4 cloves garlic, smashed and peeled
1 small onion, peeled and halved
   Stems from 1 bunch parsley
1 medium carrot, trimmed, peeled and cut into 1-inch lengths
2 celery stalks, trimmed, strung and cut into 1-inch lengths

1 baking potato (1 pound), scrubbed and cut into 1-inch chunks
4 cups water, part replaced with strained liquid from soaking dried mushrooms, if available
1 bay leaf
   Pinch dried thyme
   Pinch dried oregano

1. Put vegetables into the workbowl of a food processor and process until coarsely chopped.

2. Scrape into a 2-quart soufflé dish. Add water, bay leaf, thyme, and oregano. Cover tightly with microwave plastic wrap. Cook at 100% for 25 minutes.

3. Remove from oven. Uncover and strain through a fine sieve, pressing on vegetables to extract all the broth.

Additional vegetables. To change the flavor and color of this broth, add 1 large cored tomato, or 1 packed cup washed spinach leaves, or ½ cup mushroom peelings and stems.

ORIENTAL VEGETABLE BROTH

This is a clear broth with a zing of flavor. It is only mildly salty so increase the amount of soy sauce if you wish.   *Makes 4 cups*

4 cups water	**¼ cup thinly sliced onion**
6 quarter-size slices fresh	**or leftover scallion**
ginger, peeled	**greens**
1 cup fresh coriander	**1 teaspoon hot red-**
stems and leaves	**pepper flakes**
6 cloves garlic, smashed	**2 tablespoons tamari soy**
and peeled	

1. Put all ingredients in an 8-cup glass measure. Cover tightly with microwave plastic wrap. Cook at 100% for 15 minutes.

2. Remove from oven. Uncover and strain through a fine sieve, pressing on vegetables to extract all the broth.

Nearly endless additions. Add 1 sheet of nori (shredded), or 1 tablespoon dashi, or ½ cup thinly sliced cabbage, or 1 tablespoon lemongrass powder (sereh) or two 6-inch pieces lemongrass, bruised with the handle of a knife. If you don't need a clear broth, add 1 teaspoon Oriental sesame oil.

MEAT OR FISH GLAZES

Classic French cooking makes use of highly reduced, concentrated essences of various kinds of meat and fish broths and stocks to enrich sauces or to use as the basis of sauces. Glace de viande, for example, is made from a stock based on gelatin-rich veal bones and intensely flavored with beef. Sometimes vegetables are included in the making of glaze, bringing the mixture close to a demi-glace or a reduced Sauce Espagnole (page 371).

Once you discover how easy it is to make a concentrate in the microwave oven, without the bother of filthy pans or ruinous scorching, you will, as I do, make a quantity and freeze it. It keeps virtually forever. Salt is never added to a broth for concentrate, as the reduction would make it overly intense.

Place your unsalted broth in a glass measuring cup at least half again as large as the amount of broth. Cook, uncovered, at 100% until the liquid visible in the cup is reduced to the quantity you want. You usually want a 4-to-1 reduction. That is, 1 cup broth will give you ¼ cup glaze.

ROUX

Although flour generally cooks oddly in the microwave oven, a good amount of roux—fat and flour cooked together—does well. Keep it on hand to make Basic Béchamel (page 364). Roux can also be stirred into cooked food in the same way that beurre manié is in classic French cooking. Do not try to use beurre manié, however; it won't work.

The Creoles of New Orleans have a rich-tasting, special Brown Roux that ordinarily cooks slowly on top of the stove, requires constant stirring, and risks burning. None of this happens when Brown Roux is prepared in the microwave oven. Make a quantity and then whip up your Gumbos and Shrimp Creole quickly and easily.

Roux keeps, refrigerated, virtually indefinitely. *Makes ⅓ cup*

4 tablespoons unsalted butter	4 tablespoons all-purpose flour

1. Heat butter in a 1-quart soufflé dish, uncovered, at 100% for 3 minutes.

2. Remove from oven. Thoroughly whisk in flour. Cook, uncovered, at 100% for 3 minutes

To make 3 tablespoons. Reduce butter and flour to 2 tablespoons each. Heat butter in a 4-cup glass measure for 2 minutes and cook with flour for 2 minutes.

To make ⅛ cup. Increase butter and flour to 8 tablespoons each. Heat butter for 4 minutes and cook with flour for 3 minutes.

VARIATION

BROWN ROUX Prepare Roux; cook after addition of flour for 8 minutes, stirring twice. To make 1⅓ cups, increase butter and flour to 1 cup each. Heat butter for 4 minutes. Add flour and cook for 15 minutes, stirring three or four times.

HAM HOCKS

There are numerous southern recipes that call for ham hocks and use their cooking liquid. I find it easier and better to precook the ham hock so as not to overcook the other elements in the recipe.

Check frequently, every 10 minutes or so, to make sure the plastic keeps a tight seal; if it does not, replace with fresh microwave plastic wrap. *Makes 1 ham hock and ¾ cup cooking liquid*

1 meaty, smoked ham hock, about 8 ounces, washed and split in half	2 cups water

1. Put ham hock and water in a 4-cup glass measure. Cover tightly with 2 sheets of microwave plastic wrap. Cook at 100% for 35 minutes.

2. Remove from oven. Pierce plastic with the tip of a sharp knife and uncover carefully.

To make 3 ham hocks. Arrange 3 split hocks (about 1½ pounds), cut sides down, in a 2-quart soufflé dish. Add 2½ cups water. Cover and cook at 100% for 35 minutes.

LIGHTLY COOKED CRUSHED TOMATOES

Make the best of off-season tomatoes with this cooked-down concentrate, or profit from an abundance of fresh tomatoes in season. There is virtually no limit to its uses. Freeze in 1-cup and 2-cup portions for making sauces or soups, or freeze in smaller, ice cube-size portions to add intense tomato flavor to a dish. See DEFROSTING in the Dictionary.   *Makes about 4 cups*

12 medium tomatoes
    (about 4 pounds)

1. Core and cut a deep X across the bottom of each tomato. Place in a 2½-quart soufflé dish. Cook, uncovered, at 100% for 20 minutes, stirring once.

2. Remove from oven. Pass through a food mill fitted with a medium disc. There should be about 8 cups cooked tomatoes.

3. Return tomatoes to soufflé dish. Cook, uncovered, at 100% until almost all liquid has evaporated; this will take about 45 minutes.

4. Remove from oven. Let cool completely. Store, tightly covered, in the refrigerator or freezer (freeze in small quantities).

To make 2 cups. Use 6 tomatoes (about 2½ pounds). Cook for 12 minutes and pass through food mill; there will be about 4 cups tomatoes. Return to oven and cook until almost all liquid has evaporated, about 20 minutes.

BASIC TOMATO PASTE

I still buy commercial tomato paste, preferably the kind in tubes, but if I want to indulge myself and my food, I make my own. I never did it pre-microwave because it took 6 hours. Now I do it once or twice a year because it is so much better and takes only 1½ hours. Freeze in very small quantities, 1 to 2 tablespoons—just what will be needed for a recipe.

Caution: Just because this is cooked in a microwave oven does not mean the tomatoes will not burn. Stirring is important to guard against over-cooking in "hot spots."
Makes 1½ cups

**4 pounds plum tomatoes,
washed and cored**

1. Place tomatoes in a 2-quart soufflé dish. Cook, uncovered, at 100% for 20 minutes.

2. Remove from oven. Pass through a food mill fitted with a fine disc.

3. Return tomatoes to soufflé dish. Cook, uncovered, at 100% until paste is of desired thickness, stirring occasionally; this will take from 1 hour to 1 hour 15 minutes.

4. Remove from oven. Cool. Store, tightly covered, in the refrigerator or freezer.

DUXELLES

Duxelles, cooked chopped mushrooms and shallots, is one of the best secrets of French cooking. A little bit enriches a sauce, more makes a soup, more still a stuffing for fish. Use 2 tablespoons or so to fill an omelet. Substitute Duxelles for meat in Lasagne (page 149) for a vegetarian dish of singular complexity of taste. If you have Duxelles around, it makes a handy hors d'oeuvre, as in Broiled Stuffed Mushroom Caps: Fill clean, medium mushroom caps with 1 tablespoon Duxelles each. Sprinkle each with ½ teaspoon freshly grated Parmesan cheese. Place on a baking sheet under a preheated broiler and cook about 30 seconds, or until the cheese melts.

When cooking Duxelles, you may see a little butter in the mixture at the end of the cooking time, but there should be no mushroom liquid left. If there is, continue to cook, uncovered, in 1- to 2-minute increments until it has evaporated. The cooking time varies, depending on the size of the chopped mushrooms; the larger the mushroom pieces, the shorter the cooking time.

Freeze some Duxelles in ice cube trays, then store in plastic bags, for days when you want to toss just one or two cubes into a Béchamel or pasta sauce. Freeze in larger quantities for use as a stuffing. *Makes 1½ to 2 cups, depending on the wateriness of the mushrooms*

¼ pound unsalted butter	½ cup (tightly packed)
1 pound mushrooms or	parsley leaves
mushroom stems,	2 teaspoons kosher salt
wiped clean and	½ teaspoon freshly
finely chopped	ground black
¼ pound shallots, peeled	pepper
(about 5 shallots)	

1. Heat butter in a 1-quart soufflé dish, uncovered, at 100% for 2 minutes, until melted. Add mushrooms and stir to coat. Cook, uncovered, at 100% for 5 minutes.

2. Put shallots and parsley in the workbowl of a food processor and process until finely chopped.

3. Remove mushrooms from oven. Stir in shallots, parsley, salt, and pepper. Cook, uncovered, at 100% for 8 minutes.

4. Remove from oven.

To make ¾ cup. Halve all ingredients. Proceed as for Duxelles, cooking mushrooms for 4 minutes. Add shallots, parsley, salt, and pepper and cook for 5 minutes.

Pepper Purées

Columbus may have been dismayed that his new route did not take him to the haunts of the spice trade. Nevertheless, it is hard to see how the cooks of the world got on before he found the land from which hot chili peppers came. They quickly turned up in food from Africa, Asia, Arabia, Egypt and Europe. I don't think the English in Australia use hot pepper, but Malaysia is virtually pickled in them. Hot peppers are available green and red, fresh, dried, and smoked. They are related to the sweet pod peppers: bell peppers, gypsy peppers, pimentos, Hungarian peppers, and Italian frying peppers.

All of these peppers are good for cooking, and make wonderful sauces when puréed. Some purées are suitable for use on their own. Others are sauces in the sense that the pepper sauces you buy in bottles are. You use them in small quantities to season foods. Hotness and thickness will vary depending on the proportion of hot to sweet peppers, whether you remove the seeds from the hot peppers, and how you purée them. A food mill will remove most of the skin and seeds. A blender or food processor will pulverize them.

In addition to hotness and texture, it is nice to keep color in mind. If possible, use all green, all red, yellow and green, or yellow and red peppers together. The result will be beautiful clear colors, not muddy ones.

When working with hot peppers, fresh or dried, you may want to wear rubber kitchen gloves; the oil in the flesh of the peppers and their seeds can be extremely irritating to the skin. Never touch your face with your hands while working with hot peppers.

These peppers are cooked in microwave-safe plastic bags. (If you don't have any, all of these recipes, except that using 2½ pounds of bell peppers, can be cooked in a 2-quart soufflé dish tightly covered with microwave plastic wrap. The bag does a slightly better job, however.) If you are using an oven with a carousel, the bag must be closed in such a way that, when it fills with steam, it won't interfere with the turning of the carousel. When opening the bag (or the wrap), be very careful if hot peppers are enclosed because the steam carries some of the hot oils. Use a long knife to puncture the plastic and release the steam, and avert your face.

RED PEPPER PURÉE

This elegant, mild sauce has a fresh taste and a glorious color. It could be made equally well with yellow bell peppers. Either version could be the base of a cold soup if mixed with cornstarch-thickened chicken broth and a little yogurt. Warm, it is a terrific sauce for ravioli or tortellini. Try it under one of the vegetable timbales (page 301). I also use it when steaming fish (page 194). *Makes 3 cups*

2½ pounds red bell
    peppers, stemmed
    and seeded (about
    5 very large
    peppers)

1. Put peppers in a microwave-safe plastic bag and close tight. Cook at 100% for 15 minutes.

2. Remove from oven and carefully open the bag. Put peppers through a food mill fitted with a medium disc.

To make 1 cup. Use ¾ pound red bell peppers, cooking for 6 minutes.

VARIATIONS

HOT AND SWEET RED PEPPER SAUCE Use ¾ pound red bell peppers and 2 ounces jalapeño or other small hot peppers, cored, quartered, and seeded. Proceed as for Red Pepper Purée, cooking for 6 minutes. Add 1 teaspoon kosher salt to puréed sauce. Makes 1 cup. For 2 cups, double ingredients and cook for 15 minutes

HOT PEPPER SAUCE Use this sauce in place of Louisiana and Caribbean green pepper sauces that are usually shaken from bottles. Use ¾ pound green bell peppers (about 2 peppers) and 1¼ pounds green hot peppers, stemmed and seeded. Proceed as for Red Pepper Purée, cooking for 18 minutes. Pass through a food mill fitted with a fine disc. Stir in 1 teaspoon kosher salt and 2 tablespoons fresh lime juice. Store in a tightly covered glass jar. Makes 1¼ cups.

FIERY PEPPER SAUCE Use in place of the hottest red pepper sauces from Louisiana or Thailand. You may make this with variously colored peppers, but the resulting sauce will be muddy. For a sauce as brilliant as it is strong, use hot peppers of the same color, all red or all green.

Use 1 pound hot peppers, stemmed, seeded, and deribbed. Proceed as for Red Pepper Purée, cooking for 12 minutes. Pass through a food mill fitted with a fine disc. Store in the refrigerator in a tightly covered glass jar or bottle. Makes ½ cup

SEARING PEPPER SAUCE Make Fiery Pepper Sauce, but do not remove seeds or ribs from peppers. This sauce is slightly thicker than the other hot sauces—spoon, don't shake—and so strong that you can substitute it for the hottest pepper sauce you can buy and use only half the amount called for.

CHINESE CHILI SAUCE Make Hot Pepper Sauce, using red bell peppers and red hot peppers and adding ½ ounce dried, hot, red chili peppers. Five minutes before the end of the cooking time, carefully open the bag—away from your face, as pepper steam can burn—and add 8 smashed and peeled garlic cloves; reclose the bag and complete cooking and puréeing. Use rice wine vinegar instead of lime juice. Add salt. Keep in a tightly closed jar in the refrigerator. Makes 1⅓ cups.

SUPER HOT CHILI PASTE Stir 2 ounces dried chilies into 1 cup water in a 4-cup glass measure. Cover tightly with microwave plastic wrap. Cook at 100% for 8 minutes. Purée in blender. Makes ½ cup.

CHILI OIL

Muskier tasting than the purées, Chili Oil is frequently used in small amounts in Chinese cooking to jazz things up. It can be quickly made in the microwave oven. Make it at least 2 days before you plan to use it. *Makes ½ cup*

5 dried, small, hot red peppers, or 2 tablespoons hot red-pepper flakes	½ cup vegetable oil

1. Put peppers and oil in a blender or food processor and process until well combined. Scrape into a 2-cup glass measure and cover tightly with microwave plastic wrap. Cook at 100% for 3 minutes.

2. Remove from oven. Pierce plastic with the tip of a sharp knife and let cool.

3. Uncover and pour into a clean jar or bottle. Store, tightly covered, away from heat or light.

Spice Powders

One of my favorite cookbooks was published some time ago in India. It advises the housewife to send her spices to the spice mill only in the care of a family member or trusted servant, so that the valuable spices won't be stolen. She is also enjoined to mix her spices when they come back warm from the spice mill, or to put them in the raging sun to toast.

I do not frequent a spice mill whose crushing stones warm the spices as they grind them, nor do I live in a land of scorching sun. So the microwave oven has become my mundane sun, an electric coffee mill my mill stones—not exotic, but very effective. An endless group of spice powders and curries can be made. Here are a few that I have found useful. Don't make too much at a time.

SPICE POWDER I (A MILD, WARM BLEND)

Makes ¼ cup

2 tablespoons coriander seed	2 teaspoons fennel seed
2 tablespoons mustard seed	½ teaspoon crushed red pepper
2 teaspoons cumin seed	

1. Spread all ingredients in an even layer in a flat dish. Cook, uncovered, at 100% for 6 minutes, shaking pan once.

2. Remove from oven. Let cool completely. Grind to a fine powder in a spice grinder or clean electric coffee mill. Store in an airtight container at room temperature.

To make 1½ tablespoons. Halve all ingredients, cooking for 6 minutes.

VARIATIONS

SPICE POWDER II Add 1 teaspoon celery seed and 4 pinches ground cloves to ingredients for Spice Powder I, cooking for 6 minutes. This is good in vegetable dishes.

SPICE POWDER III Add 1 teaspoon ground mace and 1 teaspoon ground turmeric to ingredients for Spice Powder I, cooking for 6 minutes. Use in place of commercially prepared curry powders.

CRAB BOIL

In Maryland and Baltimore, they make spicy mixtures for seasoning crabs and other seafoods as they cook. While they can be bought in packages, I prefer this homemade blend. Try it on shrimp. *Makes ¼ cup, enough for 24 crabs*

1 tablespoon chili powder	1 teaspoon celery seed
1 tablespoon kosher salt	1 teaspoon cumin seed
½ bay leaf	1 teaspoon oregano
1 tablespoon mustard seed	1 teaspoon cayenne pepper
1 tablespoon dry mustard powder	1 teaspoon paprika

Combine all ingredients. Sprinkle over crabs or other shell-fish such as shrimp and cook as directed.

Basic Vegetables Braise

French recipes for a braise or a stew often call for the inclusion of a mirepoix, a mixture of herbs and chopped vegetables that has been briefly cooked ("sweated"). This can be quickly done in the microwave oven. The Italians have a similar preparation, called Soffrito, with which the main ingredient of a recipe is cooked to imbue it with flavor before final cooking. Spanish and Spanish-derived cuisines use a mixture called, almost identically, Sofrito, for the same purpose. It is nice to be able to reclaim these important culinary elements without too much work. Feel free to chop all the vegetables and herbs together in a food processor.

MIREPOIX

Makes about 1 cup

3 tablespoons unsalted butter

2 carrots, trimmed, peeled and coarsely chopped

2 celery stalks, trimmed, strung and coarsely chopped

½ small onion, peeled and coarsely chopped, or the well-washed white of 1 leek, coarsely chopped

1 tablespoon finely chopped parsley (optional)

Pinch dried thyme (optional)

1 clove garlic, smashed, peeled and chopped (optional)

1. Heat butter in a 2-quart soufflé dish, uncovered, at 100% for 3 minutes.

2. Remove from oven. Add vegetables and parsley, thyme, and garlic. Stir to coat. Cook, uncovered, at 100% for 3 minutes.

VARIATIONS

SOFFRITO The Italian version uses the same vegetables as the French, without the thyme. The major difference is that olive oil, pancetta, or lard is substituted for the butter, though even in Italian cooking butter is sometimes used. A Soffrito is a very personal thing, with each cook changing the proportion of the vegetables and adding herbs and even, from time to time, some peeled, seeded, and chopped tomato or prosciutto. Proceed as for Mirepoix.

SOFRITO This is as prominent in Spanish cooking as the previous two are in their cuisines. It varies enormously from region to region in Spain. Olive oil is always the fat. It may be as simple as ½ cup sliced onions, 4 minced garlic cloves, and ¾ cup peeled, seeded, and coarsely chopped tomato, which you should cook for 5 minutes. A fancy Sofrito might contain olive oil, onions (finely chopped), garlic, and tomatoes, plus 1 small green or red bell pepper—stemmed, seeded, deribbed and finely chopped, ⅓ cup finely diced ham, a bay leaf, 2 tablespoons finely chopped parsley, and even some chopped chorizo (2 ounces). Cook for 6 minutes. This is good with eggs or shrimp.

GARLIC CREAM

For those who like garlic, this makes a terrific sauce for fish, broiled chicken, or roast leg of lamb. It is gentle and mellow, thickened by the thoroughly cooked garlic. Cook chicken and rabbit in it. Mash potatoes with it. Use it in Brandade de Morue (page 48). *Makes 1¼ cups*

2 heads garlic
1 cup heavy cream
½ cup Chicken Broth
     (page 331) or
     canned chicken
     broth
½ teaspoon kosher salt
¼ teaspoon freshly
     ground black
     pepper

1. Place garlic on a flat, hard surface and cover with a cloth. Whack once or twice with a heavy saucepan. Remove the cloth; separate the cloves, discarding any loose, papery skin. (There is no need to peel each garlic clove.)

2. Combine all ingredients in an 8-cup glass measure. Cook, uncovered, at 100% for 10 minutes.

3. Remove from oven. Pass through a food mill, fitted with a fine disc, into a 1-quart soufflé dish. Cook, uncovered, at 100% for 8 minutes. The cream should be thick enough to lightly coat a spoon.

To make 2½ cups. Double all ingredients, cooking for 15 minutes.

To make ¼ cup. Divide all ingredients quantities by 4, cooking for 7 minutes. You may substitute 1½ teaspoons Chicken Glaze (page 337) for broth.

VARIATIONS

GARLIC-CREAM MASHED POTATOES Mix ¼ cup Garlic Cream with each mashed, microwave-cooked baking potato.

COLD CREAM OF GARLIC SOUP Mash 1 cooked baking potato and blend with ¼ cup Garlic Cream and ¾ cup Chicken Broth (page 331) or canned chicken broth until perfectly smooth. Season with kosher salt and freshly ground black pepper. Serve well chilled.

TAMARI GLAZE

There are times when a flavorful glaze adds a little extra something to a simple piece of fish and seals the surface. This is an easy one for salmon or swordfish steaks (¾ inch thick), or 1-inch fillets of halibut, cod, monkfish, etc., or shelled shrimp. Be sure to cook glaze in a 4-cup glass measure, though it may seem large—the ingredients boil up furiously and could otherwise make a huge, sticky mess. Oriental Barbecue Sauce (page 255) makes a good glaze too. *Makes ½ cup, enough for 4 fish steaks or fillets, or 5 pounds shelled shrimp*

1 cup tamari soy   **¼ cup light corn syrup**

1. Combine tamari soy and corn syrup in a 4-cup glass measure. Cook, uncovered, at 100% for 10 to 12 minutes, until reduced to ½ cup.

2. Remove from oven.

For fish steaks or 1-inch-thick fillets. Brush both sides with glaze. Let marinate for 5 minutes. Brush each side again. Cook, uncovered, at 100% for appropriate times listed in the Dictionary; halfway through cooking time, turn fish over and brush with glaze. When done, remove from oven and let stand, lightly covered with a sheet of paper toweling, for 2 minutes.

For 1 pound shelled shrimp. Toss with 1½ tablespoons glaze. Place in a 2-quart soufflé dish with 2 thin slices peeled, fresh ginger and 1 lemon, quartered. Covered tightly with microwave plastic wrap. Cook at 100% for 2 to 3 minutes, until shrimp are pink; halfway through cooking time, shake dish to redistribute shrimp for even cooking. See Dictionary for cooking times for other quantities of shrimp, and adjust amounts of glaze, ginger, and lemon accordingly.

VARIATION

SPICY TAMARI GLAZE Add 3 quarter-size pieces peeled, fresh ginger, 1 tablespoon Oriental sesame oil, 1 large pinch hot red-pepper flakes, and 3 garlic cloves, smashed and peeled, to glaze before cooking. Cook; strain and use.

ORIENTAL GLAZE

This glaze is delicious on Crispiest Duck (page 226). Glaze duck with it before broiling. Then remove duck to a warm platter and combine remaining glaze with liquid in pan. Serve on the side as gravy. This glaze can be used on pork—chops or roasts—veal, and chicken. *Makes enough for 1 duck*

⅓ cup tamari soy
6 cloves garlic, smashed
   and peeled
2 tablespoons grated
   fresh ginger

1 cup Chicken Broth
   (page 331, with 4
   cloves garlic,
   smashed and peeled,
   and ½ teaspoon
   ground cumin added
   to the bones), or
   canned chicken broth
1 tablespoon granulated
   sugar

Combine tamari, garlic and ginger in a 4-cup glass measure. Cover tightly with microwave plastic wrap. Cook at 100% for 5 minutes. Stir in broth and sugar.

SHRIMP BUTTER

Shrimp shells are full of flavor, so instead of throwing them out, make this butter. It can be used as part of the butter in a Beurre Blanc (page 363), in the Roux for Basic Béchamel (page 364), to cook shrimp or vegetables that are to be served with shrimp, or stirred at the last minute into a sauce for shrimp. Like all butters, it freezes well. *Makes 1½ cups*

1 pound unsalted butter   **Shells from 4 pounds shrimp**

1. Put butter and shells into the workbowl of a food processor. Process until shells are coarsely chopped.

2. Scrape mixture into a 2-quart soufflé dish. Cook, uncovered, at 100% for 15 minutes, stirring twice.

3. Remove from oven. Strain through a fine sieve, pressing on shells to extract as much butter as possible. Shrimp butter, tightly covered, keeps for 2 weeks in the refrigerator or for 2 months in the freezer.

To make ½ cup. Use 12 tablespoons unsalted butter and shells from 1 pound shrimp, cooking for 10 minutes.

SHRIMP CREAM

Here is another use for shrimp shells, one that is slightly less rich than Shrimp Butter. Seasoned, it makes a sauce all on its own for fish, possibly fish steamed with a few shrimp. It can be used as the liquid in Basic Béchamel (page 364). Add a few chopped shrimp during the last 30 seconds of cooking time along with some finely cut chives and, if desired, a few spoonfuls of Duxelles (page 340) for an elegant sauce. *Makes 1 cup*

1 cup heavy cream	**Shells from 1 pound shrimp**

1. Combine cream and shrimp shells in a 1-quart soufflé dish. Cover tightly with microwave plastic wrap. Cook at 100% for 5 minutes.

2. Remove from oven. Let stand, covered, for 5 minutes.

3. Uncover and strain through a fine sieve, pressing on shells to extract as much liquid as possible. Store tightly covered. Shrimp Cream will keep for 4 days in the refrigerator or for a few months in the freezer.

TEMPURA

When I discovered that it was possible to deep-fry in the microwave oven and that it was easy, it became important to find batters and coatings that would work well. Batters most successful for the microwave oven are somewhat different from standard batters. One of the best is the classic Japanese tempura batter made with rice flour. Don't try to make this ahead; it gets too thick. *Serves 4 to 6 as a first course*

½ cup water	3 cups vegetable oil, for
½ teaspoon paprika	frying
¾ cup beer	2 pounds fish fillets or
1 cup plus 2 tablespoons rice flour	vegetables, cut into 2½″ × 1″ pieces, or
1 egg	whole, peeled shrimp
	Kosher salt

1. Combine water and paprika in a 1-cup glass measure and heat, uncovered, at 100% for 2 minutes.

2. Remove from oven and pour into the workbowl of a food processor. Add beer, flour, and egg and process just until blended.

3. Pour oil into a 2-quart nonplastic container measuring at least 3¼ inches high, and heat, uncovered, at 100% for 15 minutes.

4. Dip fish or vegetables into batter and then carefully drop into hot oil, 4 to 6 pieces at a time. Cook, uncovered, at 100% for 1 minute, until golden. Remove with a slotted spoon and place on paper toweling to drain. Sprinkle with kosher salt.

5. Reheat oil, uncovered, at 100% for 5 minutes between successive batches.

COCONUT MILK

This may not be a standard ingredient of American and European cooking, but it certainly is used all over India, Southeast Asia, and the islands of the Pacific. It smooths curries—I use it in Chicken Curry (page 205) and Curried Shrimp (page 168). It keeps well and freezes. I'm sure you will find many more uses for it.

This is a better coconut milk, or cream, than I can make in conventional ways. It is also better than the canned kinds. To tell the truth, I never used to make it because it was just too much work. Now that opening coconuts is easy, I keep Coconut Milk on hand. It can also be made with packaged, shredded coconut from the supermarket, but be sure not to get the sweetened kind.

The leftover coconut can be dried or toasted. If you want rich coconut cream, make the coconut milk a day ahead to give the cream time to form.   *Makes 1¼ cups*

To open a coconut. Using a hammer and nail, drive holes through each of the three eyes of a 2-pound coconut. Make sure these holes pierce to the center of the coconut; they allow steam to escape. Drain the liquid from the coconut into a bowl and set aside. Place the whole coconut in a microwave-safe plastic bag and close tight. Cook at 100%

for 6 minutes 30 seconds. Remove from oven and open plastic bag, being careful of steam. Add the liquid collected in the bag to the reserved coconut liquid. The coconut will be cracked in several places; simply remove the hairy shell.

With a vegetable peeler, remove the papery brown skin from the coconut and cut the flesh into several pieces. Grate in a food processor; you will have 2 to 2½ cups.

2 cups grated fresh coconut	**⅓ cup reserved coconut liquid**
	1 cup milk

1. Combine all ingredients in an 8-cup glass measure. Cover tightly with microwave plastic wrap. Cook, uncovered, at 100% for 7 minutes.

2. Remove from oven. Uncover and strain through a sieve lined with cheesecloth, pressing on the coconut to extract as much liquid as possible.

VARIATION

COCONUT CREAM Cook and strain Coconut Milk. Cover tightly with plastic and refrigerate overnight. Coconut cream will rise to the top and may be skimmed; you will have about ⅓ cup. Remaining milk is excellent.

DRIED OR TOASTED COCONUT

Use coconut on everything from layer cakes to curry. Toasting crisps the coconut and emphasizes the nutty flavor. Open and prepare the coconut as for Coconut Milk (page 353).

Spread the grated flesh of a 2-pound coconut in a 12-inch round dish. For dried coconut, cook, uncovered, at 100% for 5 minutes, stirring twice; for toasted coconut, cook for 10 minutes, stirring three or four times.

BREADCRUMBS

It annoys me to pay for dry breadcrumbs when I always have leftover bread around. Dried and lightly toasted in the microwave oven, breadcrumbs are thrifty and perfect. If making crumbs from French or Italian bread, allow for a little more weight of bread since the crusts are thicker. Crumbs can be made successfully from darker-grained breads like pumpernickel and rye bread. They add a little variety to life. *Makes 1½ cups*

1 loaf (1 pound) white
    bread

1. Trim crust from bread. Crumble bread in food processor.

2. Spread crumbs in a thin layer in a 13″ × 9″ oval or rectangular dish. Cook, uncovered, at 100% for 8 minutes, stirring twice during cooking.

3. Remove from oven. Cool. For very fine crumbs, crumble again in food processor. Store tightly covered.

VARIATION

PUMPERNICKEL CRUMBS Use 1 pound trimmed pumpernickel bread, cooking crumbs 2 cups at a time for 4 minutes. Makes 8 cups fairly coarse crumbs.

CROUTONS

You really need a carousel for this—hot spots in your oven will cause uneven browning. *Makes 2 cups*

¼ pound unsalted butter   **4 cups ½-inch cubes**
                                        white bread (crusts
                                        trimmed)

1. Heat butter in a 14″ × 11″ × 2″ dish, uncovered, at 100% for 4 minutes. Add bread and stir to coat. Cook, uncovered, at 100% for 5 minutes.

2. Remove from oven and stir thoroughly. Cook, uncovered, at 100% for 5 minutes longer.

3. Remove from oven and let cool. Store tightly covered.

VARIATIONS

DEEP-FRIED CROUTONS Omit butter. Heat 3 cups vegetable oil in a 2-quart nonplastic container measuring at least 3¼ inches high, uncovered, for 15 minutes. Add 2 cups bread cubes and cook, uncovered, for 1 minute. Remove with a slotted spoon to drain on paper toweling. Heat oil for 5 minutes and cook second batch of bread cubes.

TOAST POINTS Trim crusts from 6 slices white bread. Cut each slice diagonally to form 4 triangles. Heat ⅓ cup olive oil in a 14″ × 11″ × 2″ dish, uncovered, at 100% for 2 minutes. Arrange bread in a single layer in dish. Cook, uncovered, at 100% for 3 minutes, turning once. Drain on a double thickness of paper toweling.

CORNBREAD STUFFING

Stuffing is fun, it tastes good, and it stretches the meat dollar. This version doctors up commercial cornbread stuffing. If you have leftover cornbread, use it and dry as for Breadcrumbs (page 354). *Makes 3 cups, enough for 6 catfish fillets or 6 pork chops*

1 red or green bell pepper, stemmed, seeded, deribbed and cut into 3-inch pieces
1 medium onion, peeled and quartered
1 celery stalk, trimmed, strung and cut into 3-inch pieces
4 tablespoons unsalted butter

2 cups packaged cornbread stuffing mix
¾ cup Chicken Broth (page 331) or canned chicken broth
½ cup corn kernels (fresh or canned)
1 teaspoon kosher salt
¼ teaspoon freshly ground black pepper

1. Place pepper, onion, and celery in the workbowl of a food processor. Process until finely chopped.

2. Heat butter in a shallow, 1-quart soufflé dish, uncovered, at 100% for 4 minutes. Stir in pepper, onion, and celery. Cook, uncovered, at 100% for 8 minutes, stirring once.

3. Remove from oven. Scrape mixture into a large mixing bowl. Stir in remaining ingredients. Let stand for 5 minutes; taste for seasoning before using.

GOAT CHEESE CROUTONS

These are wonderful with a salad. You can use any kind of goat cheese (chèvre) as long as it isn't too dry. You can cook the bread before dinner and top with the cheese. Pop into the oven while you are tossing your salad. The croutons will be ready when you are. Put one on each salad plate or pass a plate of them. They also make a good hors d'oeuvre. *Serves 10*

10 slices (¼ inch thick) French bread cut on the diagonal
 3 tablespoons olive oil
⅓ pound goat cheese, preferably 2-inch diameter small log, without cinders

Finely minced chives, or freshly ground black pepper (optional)

1. Arrange bread slices in a ring around inside edge of a 10-inch platter. Brush lightly with olive oil.

2. Cook, uncovered, at 100% for 4 minutes.

3. Slice cheese into 10 pieces, each ¼ inch thick.

4. Turn croutons over. Top each with a slice of cheese. Sprinkle with chives or pepper, if desired. Brush with remaining olive oil.

5. Cook, uncovered, at 100% for 1 minute.

CREAM PUFF DOUGH

This basic dough makes impressive little pastry puffs that are astoundingly useful. It is also just about mindlessly easy to make, in the microwave oven. The puffs can be deep-fried with great success (see Beignets, page 428, and Gougères, page 153). The dough can be baked in a conventional oven, for uses both sweet and savory: split and filled as hors d'oeuvres—with a spoonful of Duxelles (page 340) or Fresh Mango Chutney (page 471) or a snail in Snail Butter (page 359)—as part of the classic French dessert croquembouche, and as miniature cream puffs filled with Pastry Cream (page 439) and topped with Chocolate Sauce (page 437).   *Makes 12 to 15 small puffs*

½ cup water	½ cup all-purpose flour
4 tablespoons unsalted butter	½ teaspoon kosher salt
	2 whole eggs

1. Place water and butter in a 4-cup glass measure and heat, uncovered, at 100% for 4 minutes, until mixture boils.

2. Remove from oven and pour into the workbowl of a food processor. Add flour and salt and process for 1 minute 30 seconds.

3. Add eggs, one at a time, processing 30 seconds after each addition. Batter should just hold a soft shape. (Recipe may be prepared in advance to this point; batter will keep, tightly covered and refrigerated, for 2 days.)

4. Bake conventionally, as per traditional recipes.

SNAIL BUTTER

Quick to make, easy to store, and very useful. Form this butter into a roll; refrigerate or freeze; then slice off pieces to use as needed. It is a good topping for steamed fish or chicken, freshly cooked vegetables, rice, and mashed potatoes. Obviously, it gets used with snails (page 64), and is a standard part of Clams Casino (page 62). *Makes ½ pound*

---

4 cloves garlic, smashed and peeled
1 bunch parsley, washed and stemmed (reserve stems for soup)

2 tablespoons white wine
1 teaspoon kosher salt
½ pound unsalted butter

1. Put garlic and parsley in the workbowl of a food processor. Process until finely chopped. Add remaining ingredients and process until well blended and pale green in color.

2. Scrape mixture onto a sheet of waxed paper or plastic wrap and shape into a log. Wrap tightly in plastic and refrigerate. Snail Butter will keep for 2 to 3 weeks refrigerated, for 2 months frozen.

SAVORY SAUCES

No matter what the nouvelle cuisine and "plain" cooks tell you, a good sauce has been the making of many a meal. The trouble with most sauces, however, was that they took so long to make. That's no longer true. Even the great broth-based classics of French cooking are simplified with broths, that cook in half an hour in the microwave oven. Equally, the tomato-based sauces of Italian cooking can be zipped through.

I give recipes for sauces from scratch, but I am not above a little cheating. I identify those sauces that will not be damaged by a canned broth, canned tomatoes, or even jarred tomato sauces.

One thing about sauces is that they pretty much need to hang together. That means they are usually bound in some way, with what the French call a liaison. All this means is that you don't want puddles of fat in your sauce or to be able to see too clearly the ingredients from which it is made.

The deglazing sauces are nothing more than pan juices dissolved in water, broth, and/or wine. After your meat has cooked, usually roasted, simply pour off the fat. If you have roasted in a pan that can go into the microwave oven, add your broth or wine to the pan. Stir. Cook, uncovered, at 100% for 2 minutes. Stir, scraping the bottom of the pan. Correct the seasonings and serve as is, or swirl in 1 to 2 tablespoons butter, or thicken the sauce. To thicken, make a slurry of 1 tablespoon cornstarch in 2 tablespoon cold water for each cup of sauce to be thickened. Whisk into sauce and cook, uncovered, for 3 minutes at 100%. You could also thicken the sauce with Roux (page 337).

Other sauces are thickened with egg yolks, or they are emulsions held together by forcing oil or butter to marry with egg yolks or an acid reduction or lots of gelatin, as provided by the bones in very rich stocks.

By the way, there are sauces that I do not suggest that you make in the microwave oven—Béarnaise, for example. You can make the reduction for a Béarnaise in the microwave oven and melt the butter for it; but don't try to whisk it in the oven.

DRAWN BUTTER SAUCE

This is what you are supposed to get with boiled lobster and hot artichokes. It is nothing other than our old friend Clarified Butter (page 494). If you want, add some strained lemon juice. You can also cook fresh herbs (1 tablespoon finely chopped for each ¼ pound butter) or spices like cumin or chili powder (1 teaspoon for each ¼ pound) along with the butter.

BROWNED BUTTER SAUCE

Browned Butter Sauce is exquisite for brains, ray, and all manner of other fish. Cooked Brains (page 270) or fish are warmed briefly in the sauce. (Consult the Dictionary for cooking times for fish fillets.) Small quantities of the thinner fillets may be entirely cooked in the sauce below. The only difficulty in making this sauce has been getting the butter brown without burning it. This microwave technique makes it easy. *Makes ½ cup, enough for 4 generous servings*

¼ **pound unsalted butter**	**Kosher salt**
2 **tablespoons drained and rinsed capers**	**Freshly ground black pepper**
1 **tablespoon fresh lemon juice**	

1. Place butter in a 4-cup glass measure. Cover lightly with a sheet of paper toweling. Cook at 100% for 8 minutes.

2. Remove from oven. Strain through a sieve lined with a sheet of paper toweling. Pour into an 11″ × 8½″ × 2″ dish and add remaining sauce ingredients. Cook, uncovered, at 100% for 1 minute.

ALMOND BUTTER SAUCE

This is a simple, quick, classic sauce for fish or chicken. Cook the sauce first, then cook the main ingredient and reheat the sauce for 30 seconds if it seems cold. *Makes ⅔ cup*

¼ pound unsalted butter	6 tablespoons Chicken
½ cup blanched almonds	Broth (page 331),
¼ cup chopped parsley	Fish Broth (page
2 tablespoons white wine	334), or canned
	chicken broth

1. Heat butter in an 11″ × 8″ × 3″ oval dish, uncovered, at 100% for 4 minutes.

2. Remove from oven. Stir in remaining ingredients. Cook, uncovered, at 100% for 5 minutes 30 seconds, until almonds are golden brown.

BEURRE BLANC REDUCTION

Keep this sauce base in the freezer. Simply defrost and whisk up with butter as needed. Use 2 tablespoons strained reduction for every ¼ pound unsalted butter. This is also the base for Béarnaise sauce. Use in any good standard recipe. Melt your butter in a large measuring cup lightly covered with paper toweling in the microwave oven. *Makes 1½ cups*

3 cups dry white wine	¾ cup chopped fresh
3 cups white wine	parsley
vinegar	3 tablespoons dried
¾ cup chopped shallots	tarragon or ⅓ cup
(about ¼ pound)	fresh tarragon

1. Put all ingredients in a 14″ × 11″ × 2″ dish. Cook, uncovered, at 100% for 40 minutes.

2. Remove from oven. Let cool before freezing or straining through a fine sieve, pushing firmly and freezing strained liquid.

To make 1 cup. Halve ingredients, cooking in a 13" × 9" rectangular or oval dish for 25 minutes.

BEURRE BLANC

If you don't have Beurre Blanc Reduction handy (page 362), you can make this complete sauce quickly, to be used for steamed or poached fish and for chicken. If you have fresh tarragon, use double the quantity of dried. Some people strain their reduction. It makes a lighter, more elegant, but slightly less savory sauce. If you add 2 tablespoons of heavy cream to the reduction after it is cooked, your sauce will be more stable. It does not, however, reheat well. You can put it in a warmed thermos and then use when you are ready.

Beurre Blanc can be varied; but it won't be *blanc* (white) anymore. In whatever version, it holds together because of the high amount of acid in the reduction.

If you have made a quantity of Beurre Blanc Reduction, make sauce with 1½ tablespoons unstrained reduction or 1 tablespoon strained reduction and ¼ pound of butter. *Makes ½ cup*

¼ cup dry white wine
2 tablespoons tarragon
  vinegar
2 tablespoons minced
  gray shallots
½ teaspoon dried
  tarragon or 1
  teaspoon chopped
  fresh tarragon

¼ pound unsalted butter,
  cut into 8
  tablespoons, at
  room temperature
Kosher salt
Freshly ground black
  pepper

1. Combine wine, vinegar, shallots, and tarragon in a 1-cup glass measure. Cook, uncovered, at 100% for 8 minutes.

2. Remove from oven. The liquid should have evaporated, leaving only moistened shallots; if mixture is still quite liquid, return to oven and cook at 100% for 1 to 2 minutes longer.

3. Uncover. Whisk in butter, 2 pieces at a time. Season with salt and pepper. Serve at once.

VARIATIONS

BEURRE ROUGE Substitute pink-purple shallots for the gray ones. Substitute red wine and red wine vinegar for the wine and vinegar. Proceed as for Beurre Blanc.

SAFFRON BEURRE BLANC This is a nice color. It is good with steamed scallops or steamed fish fillets. Make Beurre Blanc, omitting dried tarragon. You may substitute white wine vinegar for the tarragon vinegar. After your reduction has been made, put through a fine sieve. Place in a clean pot—not aluminum—and add 8 threads saffron or a knife-point of saffron powder and 2 tablespoons heavy cream. Over lowest heat on top of the stove, whisk in butter. Taste for salt and pepper and perhaps a dash of lemon juice and hot red-pepper sauce.

MUSTARD CREAM SAUCE

Mustard holds this cream sauce together and thickens it. Since it is so important, use a good kind. It won't work with coarsely ground—grainy—mustard. The sauce is good on veal, rabbit, and chicken. *Makes 2 cups*

1 cup milk	¼ teaspoon kosher salt
½ cup heavy cream	¼ teaspoon freshly
½ cup Dijon mustard	ground black
1 tablespoon lemon juice	pepper

1. Combine all ingredients in an 8-cup glass measure. Cook, uncovered, at 100% for 12 minutes.

2. Remove from oven.

BASIC BÉCHAMEL

This standard white sauce of French and Italian cooking can taste like glue if not cooked long enough, and have lumps if not made properly. The method here is close to infallible.

Thick Béchamel will be needed to make Creamed Spinach (page 300). Thin Béchamel can be varied with different chopped fresh herbs (about ¼ cup) mixed in at the end, or with various spices (about 2 teaspoons) cooked with the flour and butter.

If you have Roux (page 337) on hand, you can omit the first two steps of the recipe. You can also bind Béchamel with cornstarch. See Parsley Sauce (page 369) for method. *Makes 2 cups*

4 tablespoons cold, unsalted butter, in one piece	2 cups milk
	1½ teaspoons kosher salt
4 tablespoons all-purpose flour	Freshly ground black pepper

1. Heat butter in a 4-cup glass measure, lightly covered with a sheet of paper toweling, at 100% for 3 minutes.

2. Remove from oven. Uncover and thoroughly whisk in flour. Cook, uncovered, at 100% for 3 minutes (2 minutes if using a combination, convection-microwave oven).

3. Remove from oven and whisk in milk. Cook, uncovered, for 3 minutes at 100%. Whisk to remove lumps, and cook for 3 minutes longer.

4. Remove from oven. Whisk thoroughly and season with salt and pepper.

To make 1 cup. Halve all ingredients. Heat butter for 2 minutes; cook butter and flour for 2 minutes. Whisk in milk and cook for 2 minutes. Whisk and cook for 2 minutes longer. Season.

To make 1 quart. Double quantities of butter, flour, and milk; increase salt to 2 teaspoons. Heat butter in an 8-cup glass measure for 4 minutes; cook butter and flour for 3 minutes. Whisk in milk and cook for 4 minutes. Whisk to remove any lumps and cook for 2 minutes; whisk again and cook for 2 minutes longer. Season.

VARIATIONS

THICK BÉCHAMEL Increase butter and flour to 6 tablespoons each and cook as for Basic Béchamel.

THIN BÉCHAMEL Decrease butter and flour to 2 tablespoons each and cook as for Basic Béchamel.

MORNAY

Mornay is a Béchamel or white sauce with cheese. It is good with vegetables, eggs, and fish. *Makes 1 cup*

2 tablespoons cold, unsalted butter, in one piece	½ teaspoon kosher salt Pinch freshly ground black pepper
2 tablespoons all-purpose flour	¼ cup freshly grated Parmesan cheese
1 cup milk	

1. Heat butter in a 4-cup glass measure, uncovered, at 100% for 2 minutes.

2. Remove from oven. Thoroughly whisk in flour. Cook, uncovered, at 100% for 2 minutes (1 minute in a combination, convection-microwave oven).

3. Remove from oven. Add milk and whisk until mixture is smooth. Cook, uncovered, at 100% for 3 minutes 30 seconds.

4. Remove from oven. Add salt, pepper, and cheese and whisk until smooth. Cook, uncovered, at 100% for 3 minutes.

To make 2 cups. Double all ingredients. Heat butter for 3 minutes; cook butter and flour for 3 minutes. Whisk in milk and cook for 6 minutes; add cheese, whisk, and cook for 4 minutes.

VELOUTÉ

Velouté is a somewhat more elegant version of Béchamel. There are people who claim that this was the real Béchamel, and only later did milk substitute for broth. The sauce can be lightened by using all broth instead of a broth and cream mixture. It can be made with prepared Roux (page 337). It can also have herbs stirred in; but don't get too jazzy—this is an elegant sauce that should let the broth flavor sing through.

Velouté makes a good base for soup. Stir in 1 cup vegetable purée and thin with 1 cup broth, if necessary. Season. Makes about 4 servings of soup. *Makes 2 cups*

2 tablespoons unsalted butter	1 cup Chicken Broth (page 331) or canned chicken broth
2 tablespoons all-purpose flour	Kosher salt
1 cup heavy cream	Freshly ground black pepper

1. Heat butter in an 8-cup glass measure, uncovered, at 100% for 2 minutes.

2. Remove from oven. Thoroughly whisk in flour. Cook, uncovered, at 100% for 2 minutes.

3. Remove from oven. Whisk in cream and broth. Cook, uncovered, at 100% 2 minutes; stir and cook for 3 minutes more.

4. Remove from oven. Add salt and pepper and whisk until smooth.

VARIATIONS

FISH VELOUTÉ Halve butter and flour. Omit cream and substitute ½ cup Fish Broth (page 334) for broth. Heat butter in a 4-cup glass measure, uncovered, at 100% for 1 minute. Stir in flour, 1 tablespoon *each* minced carrot, minced celery, and minced yellow onion, and 1 parsley sprig, minced. Cook, uncovered, at 100% for 3 minutes. Remove from oven and whisk in broth, salt, and pepper. Cook, uncovered, at 100% for 2 minutes. Makes ½ cup.

CURRY VELOUTÉ Add 1 tablespoon Spice Powder III or curry powder when adding flour. Proceed as for Velouté.

MUSHROOM SAUCE Increase butter to 4 tablespoons. Add flour and cook as for Velouté. Add ¼ pound cleaned and sliced mushrooms (you may substitute dried mushrooms for part of the fresh mushrooms) and a squeeze of fresh lemon juice, a knife-point of cayenne pepper, and 2 tablespoons finely chopped fresh dill (optional). Cook, uncovered, at 100% for 3 minutes. Finish as for Velouté.

SAUCE POULETTE A versatile sauce to accompany mussels, veal, or vegetables. Substitute 1 cup appropriate cooking liquid for broth and milk for cream. Proceed as for Velouté, cooking for 3 minutes after addition of liquid. Whisk ¼ cup of hot mixture into 3 egg yolks; whisk back into mixture. Cook, uncovered, at 100% for 1 minute. Remove from oven and whisk in 1 tablespoon fresh lemon juice and salt and pepper to taste. Makes 2 cups.

SAUCE SUPRÊME

This luscious sauce is so good I like to eat it by the spoonful. It's not as heavy as the amount of flour would seem to indicate. The flour gets absorbed by the vegetables and the prolonged cooking. *Makes 2 cups*

7 tablespoons unsalted butter	2 tablespoons finely chopped celery
3 tablespoons all-purpose flour	1 cup Chicken Broth or Veal Broth (page 331)
2 tablespoons finely chopped carrot	1 cup heavy cream
2 tablespoons finely chopped onion	1 teaspoon kosher salt Freshly ground black pepper

1. Heat 3 tablespoons of the butter in an 8-cup glass measure, uncovered, at 100% for 2 minutes.

2. Stir in flour and vegetables. Cook, uncovered, at 100% for 3 minutes.

3. Remove from oven. Whisk in broth and cream. Cook, uncovered, at 100% for 7 minutes, until reduced by one third.

4. Remove from oven and season with salt and pepper. Add remaining butter, stirring until melted. Strain sauce through a fine sieve.

VARIATION

SAUCE IVOIRE Prepare Sauce Suprême and whisk 2 teaspoons Chicken or Veal Glaze (page 337) into the finished sauce.

PARSLEY SAUCE

This is basically a cornstarch-thickened Béchamel flavored with herbs. If you prefer this method, you can make all your white sauces this way, rather than thickening them with a flour and butter roux.

Parsley Sauce is traditional with fish. *Makes 1 cup*

½ cup finely chopped parsley leaves
2 tablespoons thinly sliced chives
1 tablespoon plus 1 teaspoon cornstarch

⅔ cup milk or Fish Broth (page 334)
⅓ cup heavy cream
1 teaspoon kosher salt

Combine all ingredients in a 4-cup measure. Cover tightly with microwave plastic wrap. Cook at 100% for 5 minutes.

WATERCRESS SAUCE

This is another cornstarch-bound sauce; but it is the most incredible brilliant green. Once you have made this, I think you will find a dozen ways to use it. Try it under vegetable flans or custards (pages 301–306), with salmon or other fish fillets, with chicken breasts, and with Loin of Veal, hot or cold (page 258). *Makes 1¾ cups*

1½ cups watercress sprigs
1¼ cups Chicken Broth (page 331) or canned chicken broth

2 tablespoons cornstarch
½ cup heavy cream
Kosher salt
Freshly ground black pepper

1. Put watercress and 1 cup of the broth into the workbowl of a food processor. Process for 1 minute. Pour into a 4-cup glass measure.

2. Stir cornstarch into remaining broth to make a smooth slurry. Stir thoroughly into watercress mixture. Cover tightly with microwave plastic wrap. Cook at 100% for 4 minutes.

3. Remove from oven. Uncover and stir in cream, salt, and pepper.

MARCHAND DU VIN SAUCE

This is a quick and easy red wine sauce to accompany grilled and roasted meat. *Makes 1½ cups*

¼ cup chopped shallots
(about 5 medium
shallots)
1 clove garlic, smashed,
peeled and minced
2 cups red wine
1 cup Chicken, Duck or
Veal Broth (page
331)

1 tablespoon Chicken,
Duck or Veal Glaze
(page 337)
2 teaspoons cornstarch
dissolved in 3
teaspoons cold water
(optional)
Freshly ground black
pepper

1. Put shallots, garlic, wine, and ½ cup of the broth in an 8-cup glass measure. Cook, uncovered, at 100% for 20 minutes, until reduced by one half.

2. Remove from oven. Stir in glaze and remaining ½ cup broth. If using Marchand du Vin with a roast or sauté, deglaze cooking pan with this mixture; cook on top of the stove until slightly thickened, and season to taste. If using to sauce grilled meats, briskly stir in cornstarch slurry. Cook, uncovered, at 100% for 2 minutes. Season to taste.

VARIATION

SAUCE BORDELAISE Prepare Marchand du Vin Sauce. Prepare marrow (page 552) and slice into ¼-inch rounds. Spoon sauce over filet or other meat, and arrange 2 or 3 slices of marrow on top of each serving.

SAUCE ESPAGNOLE

This is the ultimate, classic French brown sauce. It is hardly instantaneous in the microwave oven, but it can be made in one afternoon instead of three days the old-fashioned way. I make it and freeze it. To defrost, see page 519.
Makes 3 cups

1 small onion, peeled and halved

2 carrots, trimmed, peeled and cut into 3-inch lengths

½ pound boiled ham, trimmed if necessary and cut into 2-inch chunks

1 teaspoon dried thyme

1 bay leaf

½ cup white wine

10 cups Veal Broth (page 331)

4 tablespoons unsalted butter

4 tablespoons all-purpose flour

1 cup Lightly Cooked Crushed Tomatoes (page 339)

1. Place onions, carrots, ham, thyme, and bay leaf in the workbowl of a food processor. Process until well chopped.

2. Scrape mixture into a 4-cup glass measure and add wine. Cook, uncovered, at 100% for 15 minutes. Add 4 cups of the broth and cook, uncovered, for 20 minutes.

3. Remove from oven and set aside. Heat butter in an 8-cup glass measure, uncovered, at 100% for 3 minutes. Remove from oven and whisk in flour until smooth. Cook, uncovered, at 100% for 3 minutes.

4. Remove from oven and whisk in vegetable mixture. Cook, uncovered, at 100% for 40 minutes, stirring 3 or 4 times, until reduced to 2 cups.

5. Add remaining 6 cups broth and stir well. Cook, uncovered, at 100% for 20 minutes. Stir, and cook for 20 minutes more.

6. Remove from oven and stir in crushed tomatoes. Cook, uncovered, at 100% for 20 minutes.

7. Wet a 2-foot square of cheesecloth with cold water and wring out. Place a double thickness of cheesecloth in a sieve. Strain sauce into a clean bowl.

SAUCE AMÉRICAINE

This is a perfect sauce. It is served with lobster, scallops, or shrimp, or even on filleted fish or skinned and boned chicken breasts; but I am happy putting it on rice or Mashed Potatoes (page 290). The truly spiffy can put it under a warm Shrimp Pâté (page 54).

Scallops or shelled shrimp can be cooked directly in the sauce. Precook the other foods and serve topped with sauce. *Makes 1¾ to 2 cups*

½ pound tomatoes, cored and coarsely chopped
½ cup Shrimp Butter (page 351)
2 tablespoons olive oil
1 cup Cognac
1 cup white wine (somewhat sweet, if possible)
1 cup Fish Broth or Clam Broth (page 334)
2 tablespoons Veal Glaze (page 331)

2 tablespoons minced shallots
¼ teaspoon Quatre-Épices (page 573)
Pinch cayenne pepper
Pinch dried tarragon
4 drops hot red-pepper sauce
1 tablespoon fresh lemon juice
Kosher salt
Freshly ground black pepper

1. Combine all ingredients except pepper sauce, lemon juice, salt, and pepper in an 11″ × 8″ × 3″ oval dish. Cook, uncovered, at 100% for 30 minutes, until mixture is reduced by two thirds.

2. Remove from oven. Pass through a food mill fitted with a fine disc. Return mixture to dish. Cook, uncovered, at 100% for 4 minutes.

3. Remove from oven. Stir in pepper sauce and lemon juice, and season to taste. Sauce may be put through a fine sieve if you are a perfectionist. I prefer the tiny lumps.

VARIATION

SCALLOPS OR SHRIMP À L'AMÉRICAINE Use 2 pounds medium scallops or shrimp. Stir into finished sauce. Cook, uncovered, at 100% for 5 minutes, stirring once. If using bay scallops, cook for only 3 minutes. Taste and add lemon juice, cayenne, and 1 tablespoon extra Shrimp Butter, if desired.

TOMATO SAUCE FROM A JAR, MADE DELICIOUS

You can substitute the same quantity of Lightly Cooked Crushed Tomatoes (page 339) for jarred sauce. Add 1 teaspoon dried thyme and ½ teaspoon dried oregano to the tomatoes. *Makes 4 cups*

¼ cup olive oil
¾ cup sliced yellow onion
5 cloves garlic, smashed and peeled
¾ cup sliced red bell pepper (1 medium pepper), stemmed, seeded and deribbed
¾ cup sliced yellow bell pepper (1 medium pepper), stemmed, seeded and deribbed

½ cup finely chopped parsley
¾ cup thinly sliced young zucchini (about 1½ zucchini)
1 jar (14 ounces) marinara sauce
¼ teaspoon dried thyme
Kosher salt
Freshly ground black pepper

1. Heat oil in an 11″ × 8½″ × 2″ dish, uncovered, for 2 minutes. Stir in onions and garlic and cook for 4 minutes.

2. Remove from oven. Add remaining ingredients and cover tightly with microwave plastic wrap. Cook at 100% for 5 minutes.

CHUNKY TOMATO SAUCE

This is the perfect Italian tomato sauce with a good fresh taste. It is a basic sauce capable of many variations. Allow about 1 cup of sauce for each ½ pound cooked pasta. I generally make the larger quantity and freeze it in ½ cup portions. See Dictionary for DEFROSTING.   *Makes 4 cups*

1 medium onion, peeled and quartered	4 cups Lightly Cooked Crushed Tomatoes (page 339)
¼ cup parsley leaves	
3 cloves garlic, smashed and peeled	2 teaspoons kosher salt
⅓ cup vegetable oil (a good olive oil is best)	¼ teaspoon freshly ground black pepper

1. Put onions, parsley, and garlic in the workbowl of a food processor and process until finely chopped.

2. Heat oil in a 2-quart soufflé dish, uncovered, at 100% for 2 minutes. Stir in onion mixture. Cook, uncovered, at 100% for 8 minutes, stirring once.

3. Remove from oven. Stir in crushed tomatoes, salt, and pepper. Cook at 100% for 6 minutes.

4. Remove from oven. Taste and adjust seasoning.

To make 2 cups. Use a small onion and 2 small garlic cloves; halve all other ingredients. Proceed as for Chunky Tomato Sauce, cooking onion mixture for 6 minutes. Add crushed tomatoes and cook for 4 minutes.

VARIATIONS

TOMATO CREAM SAUCE Prepare 2 cups Chunky Tomato Sauce. Add 1 cup heavy cream, 2 teaspoons fresh lemon juice, and a large dash of hot red-pepper sauce. Cook, uncovered, at 100% for 4 minutes. Adjust seasonings to taste. Makes about 3 cups.

FRESH TOMATO SAUCE WITH BASIL This sauce uses Lightly Cooked Crushed Tomatoes straight from the refrigerator; if using freshly cooked tomatoes that are still warm, shorten cooking time to 8 minutes. Omit parsley. Add ¼ packed cup whole basil leaves. Increase garlic to 8 cloves; omit salt. Combine in a 1-quart soufflé dish. Cook, uncovered, at 100% for 10 minutes.

SALSA PUTTANESCA Heat 2 tablespoons olive oil in a 4-cup glass measure, uncovered, for 2 minutes. Stir in 1 small onion, peeled and minced; cook, uncovered, for 3 minutes. Add 1½ cups Chunky Tomato Sauce, ¼ cup tuna packed in olive oil (drained), 1 tablespoon anchovy paste, 2 tablespoons *each* red wine, chopped oil-cured olives, and chopped capers, and freshly ground black pepper to taste. Cook, uncovered, at 100% for 4 minutes. Makes 2 cups.

MEXICAN CHILI SAUCE Heat 1 tablespoon vegetable oil in a 4-cup glass measure, uncovered, for 2 minutes. Stir in 1 minced scallion, 2 tablespoons coriander leaves, and 1 seeded, minced jalapeño pepper. Cook, uncovered, at 100% for 4 minutes. Stir in 2 cups Chunky Tomato Sauce. Cook, uncovered, at 100% for 5 minutes. Remove from oven and let stand until room temperature. Stir in 2 teaspoons fresh lime juice and kosher salt to taste. Makes 2 cups.

TOMATO SAUCE WITH BASIL

This is a quick sauce based on canned tomatoes. It's perfectly respectable and delicious.   *Makes 3 cups*

2 cans (14 ounces each) crushed tomatoes, Italian plum preferred	2 teaspoons kosher salt Freshly ground black pepper
3 tablespoons olive oil	2 tablespoons shredded fresh basil leaves
5 cloves garlic, smashed, peeled and minced	1 tablespoon tomato paste

1. Place tomatoes, oil, garlic, salt, and pepper in a 2-quart soufflé dish. Cook, uncovered, at 100% for 6 minutes.

2. Remove from oven. Stir in basil and tomato paste. Cook, uncovered, at 100% for 3 minutes.

SALSA BOLOGNESE

This is a terrific version of Italian meat sauce for pasta. Just tumble it onto cooked spaghetti or ziti, use in Lasagne (page 149), and over Fried Polenta (page 137).   *Makes 4 cups*

¼ cup dried porcini (about ½ ounce)
1 small carrot, trimmed, peeled and cut into 3-inch lengths
1 small onion, peeled and quartered
1 stalk celery, trimmed, strung and cut into 3-inch lengths
2 ounces pancetta, cut into 1″ × ⅛″ × ⅛″ juliennes

½ pound ground pork
½ pound ground beef
¼ pound ground veal
1 can (35 ounces) Italian plum tomatoes, coarsely chopped, with liquid
2 teaspoons kosher salt
¼ teaspoon freshly ground black pepper

1. Place mushrooms in a small bowl and pour water over to cover. Heat, uncovered, at 100% for 1 minute.

2. Remove from oven. Let stand at room temperature for 10 minutes. Drain mushrooms, rinse thoroughly under cool running water, and squeeze dry. Mince.

3. Place carrots, onions, and celery in the workbowl of a food processor and process until finely chopped. Set aside.

4. Place pancetta in a 2-quart soufflé dish. Cook, uncovered, at 100% until pancetta is lightly browned and has begun to render its fat, about 4 minutes. Set aside.

5. Combine ground meats with reserved vegetables and mushrooms. Add to pancetta. Cook, uncovered, at 100% until lightly browned and cooked through, about 20 minutes, stirring 4 times.

6. Remove from oven. Drain liquid from pan. Stir in tomatoes, salt, and pepper. Cook, uncovered, at 100% for 35 minutes, stirring 4 times. The sauce will be very thick.

MUSTARD BARBECUE SAUCE

Use one quarter cup of this sauce to baste 6 split chicken wings. To use the rest as a dipping sauce, put in a 2-cup glass measure and cover tightly with microwave plastic wrap; cook at 100% for 5 minutes. *Makes ¾ cup*

5 ounces spicy brown mustard (1 small jar)
⅓ cup dark corn syrup
4 cloves garlic, smashed and peeled

¼ teaspoon Searing Pepper Sauce (page 344) or ½ teaspoon hot red-pepper sauce

Thoroughly combine all ingredients.

RED BARBECUE SAUCE

Use half this uncooked sauce to coat chicken wings before cooking them (see Dictionary for cooking times). To use the remaining sauce for dipping cooked wings, put in a 2-cup glass measure and cover tightly with microwave plastic wrap; cook at 100% for 5 minutes. This recipe makes enough sauce to cook and accompany 12 split wings, or a rack of spareribs (see Dictionary). *Makes 1⅓ cups*

1 cup ketchup
⅓ cup dark brown sugar
4 cloves garlic, smashed and peeled
2 tablespoons cider vinegar

½ teaspoon kosher salt
Freshly ground black pepper
½ teaspoon hot red-pepper sauce

Thoroughly combine all ingredients.

SATAY SAUCE

Use this piquant dipping sauce for the marinated chicken below. Pass coriander and scallions in separate bowls.
Makes 1¾ cups

¼ cup Chicken Broth (page 331) or canned chicken broth
½ cup tamari soy
⅓ cup granulated sugar
½ star-anise pod or ½ teaspoon five-spice powder
6 cloves garlic, smashed and peeled

6 red pepper pods, crushed (about 2 teaspoons)
⅓ cup smooth peanut butter
2 tablespoons fresh lime juice
Fresh coriander leaves, for serving
Thinly sliced scallions, for serving

1. Combine broth, tamari soy, sugar, anise, garlic, and red pepper in a 4-cup glass measure. Cover tightly with microwave plastic wrap. Cook at 100% for 3 minutes.

2. Remove from oven. Pierce plastic and let cool for 5 minutes.

3. Uncover. Whisk in peanut butter and lime juice. Serve with cooked, marinated chicken.

SATAY MARINADE

Makes enough to marinate 4 pounds chicken parts

3 tablespoons tamari soy
2 tablespoons fresh lime juice
12 cloves garlic, smashed and peeled

½ teaspoon ground cumin
8 slices quarter-size fresh ginger, peeled

Combine all ingredients in a dish large enough to hold chicken. Add chicken and marinate, tightly covered, for at least several hours, or overnight if desired. Cook for times in Dictionary.

CRANBERRY SAUCE FOR DUCK, GOOSE OR WILD TURKEY

Frankly, at Christmas, I often use cranberry sauce right out of a can, or I chunk up an uncooked relish in the food processor. This is another kind of sauce altogether, a superbly elegant one for the most festive of company dinners. *Makes 1 cup*

4 tablespoons unsalted butter (1 tablespoon cut into bits)
¼ cup granulated sugar
2 tablespoons fresh orange juice
1 cup fresh cranberries or frozen, defrosted, cranberries
1 teaspoon dark rum
Freshly ground black pepper

1 teaspoon Veal Glaze (page 337)
4 teaspoon skimmed pan juices (from the roasted bird) or Chicken Broth (page 331)
4 drops hot red-pepper sauce
1 teaspoon kosher salt

1. Heat 3 tablespoons of the butter in an 8-inch square dish, uncovered, at 100% for 2 minutes.

2. Remove from oven. Add sugar, orange juice, and cranberries. Cover tightly with microwave plastic wrap. Cook at 100% for 3 to 4 minutes, until most of the cranberries have popped.

3. Remove from oven. Uncover and whisk in remaining ingredients.

To make 2 cups. Double all ingredients, cooking sauce for 5 to 6 minutes.

CHERRY SAUCE FOR ROAST BIRDS

I have the prettiest little cherry tree. If I'm lucky, I get to the cherries before the birds. In season, you can buy pie cherries. This is the kind of sauce, called Montmorency, that was always meant to go with duck, not that heavy, thickly sweet stuff with Bing cherries.

If you roast your chicken or grill your Crispiest Duck in a pan that can go in the microwave oven, the pan can be deglazed in the oven instead of on top of the stove. See the introduction to this chapter for instructions.　*Makes 2½ cups*

Roast chicken, 2½ to 3
　　pounds, or Crispiest
　　Duck (page 226)

THE SAUCE
2 cups sour cherries,
　　stemmed and pitted
18 shallots, peeled
¼ cup Chicken or Duck
　　Broth (page 331) or
　　canned chicken
　　broth

3 tablespoons red wine
1 teaspoon brandy or
　　kirsch
3 tablespoons granulated
　　sugar
1 teaspoon kosher salt
½ teaspoon freshly
　　ground black
　　pepper
2 tablespoons cornstarch
　　dissolved in ¼ cup
　　cold water

1. Roast chicken in conventional oven, or cook Crispiest Duck. Keep warm.

2. Combine sauce ingredients except cornstarch in a 4-cup glass measure. Cover tightly with microwave plastic wrap. Cook at 100% for 5 minutes.

3. Remove from oven. With the tip of a sharp knife, puncture plastic to allow steam to escape. Uncover and strain through a fine sieve. Reserve strained sauce and cherries.

4. Remove chicken or duck to a serving platter. Warm meat juices in the roasting pan over high heat on top of the stove. When juices are bubbling, add strained cherry sauce. Continue to cook, stirring to incorporate any browned bits from the pan into the sauce.

5. Briskly stir in cornstarch slurry. If sauce is in a microwavable dish, cook, uncovered, at 100% for 3 minutes 30 seconds. Otherwise, cook over the stove just until thickened. Taste and correct seasoning with salt and pepper.

6. Stir in cherries and serve in a sauceboat.

BLACKBERRY SAUCE

This is fabulous with Crispiest Duck (page 226). Make the berry purée ahead. Prepare duck, skim cooking juices, and finish sauce while duck is broiling. Garnish with a few whole blackberries and a blackberry leaf, if possible. Serve with mountains of Mashed Potatoes (page 290) topped with butter. This makes a highly unusual sauce for venison, too. *Makes 2 cups*

1 pint blackberries or black raspberries	¼ cup raspberry vinegar
¾ cup granulated sugar	1 teaspoon freshly ground black pepper
4 cloves garlic, smashed and peeled	1 teaspoon fresh lemon juice
¼ cup Duck Broth (page 331) or pan juices from duck	

1. Combine berries, sugar, and garlic in a 4-cup glass measure. Cover tightly with microwave plastic wrap. Cook at 100% for 4 minutes.

2. Remove from oven and uncover carefully. Remove garlic from berry mixture and set aside. Place mixture in a blender or food processor and purée. Strain mixture through a fine sieve. There should be about 1½ cups.

3. Return mixture to 4-cup measure. Add broth, vinegar, and reserved garlic. Cover tightly with microwave plastic wrap. Cook at 100% for 5 minutes.

4. Remove from oven. Add pepper and lemon juice. Taste and correct seasoning, if necessary.

PAPAYA CUMIN SAUCE

A cooling, tart, and mildly spiced sauce that is as good with Scallop Mousse (page 55) as it is with Crispiest Duck (page 226). The papaya seeds are edible, with an astringent flavor, and can be used to garnish the food you are saucing. Place the seeds in a sieve and rinse to remove pulp. Drain on paper toweling. *Makes 1¼ cups*

1 ripe papaya (about 1 pound), halved lengthwise and seeded	¾ teaspoon ground cumin
½ cup Chicken Broth (page 331)	½ teaspoon kosher salt
1 tablespoon plus 2 teaspoons fresh lemon juice	⅛ teaspoon freshly ground black pepper
	Pinch cayenne pepper

1. Spoon papaya flesh into a 4-cup glass measure. Add remaining ingredients except for 1 tablespoon of the lemon juice. Cover tightly with microwave plastic wrap. Cook at 100% for 10 minutes.

2. Remove from oven. Let stand for 3 minutes.

3. Purée mixture in a blender or food processor. Beat in remaining 1 tablespoon lemon juice.

MAYONNAISE

No, I don't make it in the microwave oven; but every cookbook needs one. *Makes 1 cup*

3 egg yolks	½ cup vegetable oil
2 teaspoons fresh lemon juice	Kosher salt
½ cup olive oil	Freshly ground black pepper

1. Place yolks and lemon juice in the workbowl of a food processor and process until well blended.

2. With the machine running, add oils in a thin stream and process until thoroughly incorporated and mixture is smooth. Season to taste with salt and pepper.

AÏOLI

This is a garlicky mayonnaise often used in fish soups and stews. *Makes ⅔ cup*

2 eggs
4 teaspoons fresh lemon
  juice
12 drops hot red-pepper
  sauce
2 teaspoons kosher salt

¼ teaspoon freshly
  ground black
  pepper
½ cup light olive oil
6 to 8 cloves garlic,
  smashed and peeled

1. Place eggs, lemon juice, hot red-pepper sauce, salt, and pepper in the workbowl of a food processor. Process until well blended.

2. With the machine running, add oil in a thin stream until thoroughly incorporated and the mixture is smooth.

3. Add garlic and process until smooth.

PESTO

No, this doesn't get made in the microwave oven, either, but it is a useful basic sauce.

If you wish to freeze Pesto, do not add the cheese. Beat in the cheese after defrosting, and serve at room temperature. *Makes 1 cup*

Leaves from 1 large
  bunch basil (about 1
  cup, packed) or
  parsley
2 cloves garlic, smashed
  and peeled
¾ cup olive oil
¼ cup pine nuts or
  walnuts

¼ cup freshly grated
  Parmesan cheese or
  crumbled
  Gorgonzola
¾ teaspoon kosher salt
¼ teaspoon freshly
  ground black
  pepper

1. Put basil and garlic in the workbowl of a food processor and process until coarsely chopped. With the motor running, add oil in a thin stream.

2. Add nuts, cheese, salt, and pepper. Process until nuts are finely chopped.

TONNATO SAUCE

This is so good with the Loin of Veal (page 258) that I had to include it. It is also good with vegetable flans and custards (pages 301–306)—not white ones.   *Makes 1½ cups*

1 can (6½ ounces) tuna, drained
2 anchovy fillets
1½ tablespoons drained capers
⅔ cup Mayonnaise (page 382)
1½ tablespoons olive oil
1½ tablespoons Veal Broth (page 331) or broth used to poach the loin
1½ tablespoons fresh lemon juice
2 tablespoons chopped parsley
Kosher salt

1. Put tuna, anchovies, and capers in the workbowl of a food processor. Process until mixture is smooth. Add Mayonnaise and process until smooth. With the machine running, add oil, then broth, in a thin stream.

2. Add lemon juice, parsley, and salt to taste. Process briefly to mix. Taste and add more lemon juice or salt if desired. Refrigerate, tightly covered.

DESSERTS

I AM an odd duck. Even in great restaurants, I have frequently been known to order a green salad while everybody else is having dessert. At home, I am ordinarily more than satisfied with a piece of fruit and some cheese. There are times, though, when even I want something sweet, something self-indulgent.

Fruit Desserts

Cooking fruits, fresh and dried, is one of the microwave oven's triumphs. To poach fresh fruits, see individual fruits in the Dictionary. Use in all sorts of combinations or with poached dried fruits. See Dictionary also for small-oven timings.

Herewith a few desserts that take fruit a few marvelous, fresh-tasting steps further. They start out taking almost no time at all to prepare, and go on to take just a little more. Simple as they are, they are good enough to end any meal, and each one is as pretty as the fruit from which it is made.

LIGHT POACHED PEARS

This delicious, easily prepared dessert can be eaten cold or warm. It is a dieter's delight because no sugar is added. The pears cook absolutely evenly and have more flavor than conventionally poached pears since they lose none of it to the poaching liquid. Serve plain, with heavy cream, Crème Anglaise (page 438), or with Blueberry Sauce (page 386). A very nice accompaniment to the pears are crisp Florentines (page 424) or Ginger Lace Cookies filled with ginger cream (page 425). *Serves 6*

6 Bosc pears, peeled and cored	6 pieces lemon zest, each 2 inches long
2 tablespoons fresh lemon juice	6 pieces orange zest, each 2 inches long
	6 whole cloves

1. Rub pears with juice to prevent discoloring. Place 1 piece lemon zest and 1 piece orange zest inside each core cavity. Stick a clove in side of each pear.

2. Set each pear in center of an 8-inch square sheet of microwave plastic wrap. Twist ends together at top to seal tightly.

3. Place wrapped pears in a ring inside rim of a 10-inch round dish. Cook at 100% for 8 minutes.

4. Remove from oven. Open hot pear packages carefully over a bowl to catch juices for Blueberry Sauce, if desired.

5. Serve warm or cold, either plain or centered on a dessert plate in a pool of Blueberry Sauce or heavy cream.

To poach other quantities. Divide ingredient quantities accordingly, cooking 1 pear for 3 minutes, 2 pears for 4 minutes 30 seconds, 4 pears for 7 minutes.

VARIATION

PEARS IN PARCHMENT Wrap a single pear, prepared as for Light Poached Pears, in an 8-inch square of parchment paper. Cook at 100% for 4 minutes. Serve in untwisted paper as in a pastry shell.

BLUEBERRY SAUCE

This delicious sauce goes particularly well with Light Poached Pears. Try it also under Puff Pastry (page 443) feuilletés split and layered with fresh blueberries and Pastry Cream (page 439).   *Makes 1½ cups*

1 pint blueberries
3 tablespoons granulated
   sugar

6 tablespoons pear juice,
   from Light Poached
   Pears (page 385)
⅛ teaspoon ground
   cinnamon

1. Pick over berries, discarding any that are overripe, green, or discolored. Put into a 4-cup glass measure.

2. Sprinkle with sugar. Cover tightly with microwave plastic wrap. Cook at 100% for 3 minutes.

3. Remove from oven. Uncover, pour into the workbowl of a food processor and purée. Pass through a fine sieve.

4. Add pear juice and cinnamon. If serving with Light Poached Pears, allow ¼ cup sauce for each portion.

PEARS IN RED WINE

If you want the traditional pears poached in French fashion in red wine, the microwave oven cooks the red wine syrup in short order and the pears even more quickly. I don't like the pears too sweet, but you can increase the sugar to 2 cups. (This poaching syrup can be used for other fruits, such as peaches). The pears will darken in color the longer they are allowed to sit in the syrup. I have allowed ½ pear per person, thinking you might want to serve each portion with some cinnamon ice cream, or with some Crème Anglaise (page 438). The 1-cup version of sauce should be enough for four. *Serves 4*

POACHING SYRUP

1 cup granulated sugar
2 cups red wine
1 piece cinnamon stick,
   1½ inches long
4 whole allspice berries
   Pinch freshly grated
   nutmeg

1 cardamom pod,
   crushed
2 whole cloves
2 Bosc pears (7 to 8
   ounces each), peeled,
   cored and halved

1. Combine all ingredients except pears in an 8-cup glass measure. Cook, uncovered, at 100% for 3 minutes. Stir well. Cover tightly with microwave plastic wrap. Cook at 100% for 5 minutes longer.

2. Remove from oven. Arrange pears in an 8½″ × 7″ × 2½″ dish, cored side up, alternating wide and narrow ends. Pour liquid over pears. Cover tightly with microwave plastic wrap. Cook at 100% for 12 minutes.

3. Remove from oven and pierce plastic with the tip of a sharp knife. Cool pears in syrup. Serve pears with a little of the syrup.

To poach 1 pear. Halve all ingredients, cooking syrup for 2 minutes 30 seconds; cook pears in syrup for 3 minutes.

To poach 4 pears. Double all ingredients, cooking syrup for 4 minutes; cook pears in syrup for 17 minutes.

POACHED RED PLUMS

These plums are a good compote on their own, or are good in a mixed compote contributing a little of their syrup. I make this at the end of summer when pears are too hard. Greengages can be poached the same way. Add 2 minutes to each poaching time. Leftover syrup can be refrigerated and reused. The nicely colored syrup from the red plums can be refrigerated and added, 2 tablespoons at a time, to inexpensive sparkling wine to make a beautiful and festive drink.   *Makes 6 plums*

POACHING SYRUP
2 cups water
2 cups granulated sugar
1 piece cinnamon stick, 1 inch long

1 tablespoon vanilla extract
3 pieces lemon zest, 3″ × 1″
6 firm red plums (about 1 pound)

1. Combine water, sugar, and cinnamon in a 2-quart soufflé dish. Cook, uncovered, at 100% for 3 minutes. Remove from oven and stir well. Cover tightly with microwave plastic wrap. Cook at 100% for 6 minutes.

2. Remove from oven. Uncover and stir in vanilla and zest. Add plums. Cover tightly with microwave plastic wrap. Cook at 100% for 8 minutes.

3. Remove from oven. Pierce plastic with the tip of a sharp knife. Uncover and store, tightly covered in the refrigerator.

To poach 10 plums. Cook in the same quantity of syrup for 10 minutes.

To poach 16 plums. Cook in two batches in the same quantity of syrup; six plums for 8 minutes, ten plums for 10 minutes.

BOURBON PEACHES

These peaches are more than a dessert, they are the song of the South. I make them when peaches are in season and use them all winter. While one can be served to each guest as a dessert with some plain whipped cream and a crisp cookie, or with vanilla ice cream, a half peach would be delicious with baked ham or a roast loin of pork. Consider using the extra syrup in a bourbon old-fashioned instead of simple syrup. These peaches will keep, covered with syrup and refrigerated, for a good year. *Makes 15 peaches*

1 cup water
2 cups granulated
    sugar
2¼ pounds very small
    hard peaches
    (about 15), each
    pricked once
½ orange, squeezed and
    shell reserved

½ lemon, squeezed and
    shell reserved
4 whole cloves
3 whole allspice berries
½ teaspoon ground
    ginger
1 cup Kentucky sour
    mash bourbon

1. Combine water and sugar in an 8-cup glass measure. Cover tightly with microwave plastic wrap. Cook at 100% for 15 minutes. Stir twice during cooking, making sure to reseal plastic tightly after opening.

2. Remove from oven. Uncover and add peaches. Stir in remaining ingredients except bourbon. Cover tightly with microwave plastic wrap. Cook at 100% for 5 minutes.

3. Remove from oven. Uncover and let cool slightly. When peaches are cool enough to handle, slip off their skins. Pack peaches into a tall, narrow container.

4. Strain poaching syrup through cheesecloth. Stir in bourbon and pour over peaches to cover. Cover tightly and refrigerate until ready to use.

RUMMY BANANAS

If it weren't for the rum, this would make a cozy children's dessert. On the other hand, I have served it as a party dessert, to a chorus of contented sighs. Sometimes I make a small version for myself—an ideal self-indulgence and comfort food. You can serve this with Florentines (page 424) and ice cream, but it's good enough all on its own.   *Serves 6*

¾ cup dark rum
½ cup dark brown sugar
2 tablespoons unsalted
   butter
1 piece (2 inches) vanilla
   bean or ½ teaspoon
   vanilla extract

2 tablespoons fresh
   lemon juice
Zest of ½ lemon, cut
   into julienne strips
2 thin slices fresh ginger
6 bananas (2½ to 3
   pounds)

1. Combine rum, sugar, butter, vanilla bean, lemon juice, zest, and ginger in a 4-cup glass measure. (If using vanilla extract, do not add it until step 2.) Cover tightly with microwave plastic wrap. Cook at 100% for 3 minutes.

2. Remove from oven. Uncover and stir. (Add vanilla extract if you are using it.) Set aside.

3. Peel bananas and remove ½ inch from each end. Arrange pinwheel-fashion in a 10-inch round dish. Pour rum mixture over bananas. Cover tightly with microwave plastic wrap. Cook at 100% for 5 minutes 30 seconds.

To serve 2. Use ⅓ cup rum, 2 bananas, and halve remaining ingredients. Fit bananas into a dish just large enough to hold them, cooking for 3 minutes.

Arrange bananas pinwheel-fashion in a 10-inch round dish. Other longish foods such as quartered artichokes can be arranged in the same way with the thicker end toward the outside of the dish.

MAPLE SYRUP-BAKED APPLES

Baking apples in the microwave oven is so quick that I even am willing to make one for my own dinner. The apple skins are edible and the apples are evenly cooked all the way through. Also, the apples don't explode into a disorderly mess. You can certainly use other apple varieties in this recipe, but check the Dictionary for cooking times. Check it also if you're using a very small (400 to 450 watts) oven. · *Serves 6*

6 Granny Smith or
  Greening apples (8 to
  9 ounces each),
  cored, with a 1½-
  inch collar peeled
  from top of apple
1 tablespoon dried
  currants

3 tablespoons chopped
  walnuts
  Grated zest of 1
  orange
2 tablespoons fresh
  orange juice
3 tablespoons fresh
  lemon juice
¾ cup maple syrup

1. Arrange apples in a 12″ × 9½″ × 2½″ oval dish so that they don't touch each other or the sides of the dish. Divide currants, walnuts, and zest evenly among apple cavities.

2. Combine juices and syrup and pour around apples. Cover with microwave plastic wrap, airtight but loose enough so that plastic isn't stretched over tops of apples if they stand higher than sides of dish. Cook at 100% for 9 minutes.

3. Remove from oven. Puncture plastic with the tip of a sharp knife and let stand for 5 minutes (apples will continue to steam).

4. Uncover and serve warm with some of the syrup.

To bake other quantities. Divide ingredient quantities accordingly. See Dictionary for cooking times.

PEACH CRISP

This is an easy dessert for summer days when peaches are plentiful and ripe. The brown streusel topping made with dark pumpernickel breadcrumbs is good enough to make in extra quantity and have on hand for another time, hence this recipe gives you about twice the quantity you need for the peaches. The chocolate richness is a perfect contrast to the fresh fruit taste. This could also be made with nectarines, apricots, or peeled apple slices that have been tossed in a little lemon juice. *Serves 4, and makes 1 cup streusel*

STREUSEL
¼ cup blanched almonds
½ ounce good-quality
   semisweet chocolate
¼ cup granulated sugar
1 cup breadcrumbs from
   stale, dark Russian
   pumpernickel,
   trimmed

4 tablespoons unsalted
   butter
1 pound peaches, peeled
   and sliced into 8
   wedges each (about 4
   peaches)

1. Place almonds, chocolate, and sugar in the workbowl of a food processor. Process until finely ground. Stir in breadcrumbs.

2. Heat butter in a 4-cup glass measure, uncovered, at 100% for 2 minutes. Remove from oven and add crumb mixture. Stir to moisten crumbs with butter. (This streusel mixture may be made in advance and kept, tightly covered and frozen, until needed.)

3. Layer peach slices in a 1-quart soufflé dish, Sprinkle with ½ cup streusel mixture. (Freeze remaining streusel mixture.) Cook, uncovered, at 100% for 6 minutes.

4. Serve hot, with cream or ice cream.

To serve 1. Peel and slice a peach. Put in a ½-cup ramekin and sprinkle with 2 tablespoons streusel mixture. Cook for 2 minutes.

To serve 2. Peel and slice 2 peaches. Put in a 2-cup soufflé dish and sprinkle with 3 tablespoons streusel mixture. Cook for 4 minutes.

FIGS IN RED WINE

A ripe, sun-warmed fig is sweet and voluptuous whether eaten out of hand or paired with lightly salty prosciutto. Sometimes figs aren't perfectly ripe, or you just want another kind of dessert. That's when this poached fig dessert comes into its own. The ring mold helps to hold the figs upright in an arrangement that permits them to cook evenly. Serve cold or warm. This is good with heavy cream or Crème Anglaise (page 438). *Serves 6*

8 teaspoons granulated sugar	**⅛ teaspoon freshly ground black pepper**
½ cup Marsala or port wine	**1 piece (2 inches) vanilla bean, split lengthwise**
¼ teaspoon ground allspice	
⅛ teaspoon ground cloves	**12 ripe figs, preferably black**

1. Combine sugar, wine, allspice, cloves, pepper, and vanilla bean in a 10 inch glass ring mold. Arrange figs evenly around mold.

2. Cover tightly with microwave plastic wrap. Cook at 100% for 5 minutes.

3. Remove from oven. Serve figs warm with their poaching liquid.

To serve 1. Substitute ½ teaspoon vanilla extract for vanilla bean, and divide all other ingredients quantities by 4; combine all ingredients in a 2-cup ramekin, cover, and cook for 1 minute 30 seconds to 2 minutes.

To serve 3. Halve all ingredients except vanilla bean; arrange figs in an 8-inch glass ring mold, cover and cook for 3 minutes.

APPLE CHARLOTTE

Charlottes are old-fashioned desserts, made either with a contrast of buttery crisped bread and meltingly fruity acid apple filling topped with whipped cream or as a cupcake (the kind that was sold on the streets of New York around the turn of the century). Our elegant version is part of the classic French repertoire. Don't try to make a smaller version, as the apples will burn before the charlotte cooks. *Serves 4 to 6*

4 tablespoons unsalted butter	4 pounds Granny Smith apples, peeled, cored and thinly sliced (about 8 cups)
10 slices firm white bread, crusts removed	2 tablespoons fresh lemon juice
½ cup plus 2 tablespoons granulated sugar	1 cup heavy cream, whipped, for serving

1. Heat butter in a 2-cup glass measure, uncovered, at 100% for 1 minute 30 seconds. Set aside.

2. Preheat conventional oven to 350° F.

3. Trim bread to line a 1½-quart soufflé dish: using a 2-inch round cookie cutter, cut out enough bread rounds to cover bottom of dish, overlapping slightly; cut enough 1″ × 2″ pieces to fit, overlapping, around sides of dish.

4. Place bread shapes on a cookie sheet. Brush on one side with melted butter. Toast in conventional oven until lightly brown.

5. Generously butter dish and dust with 2 tablespoons of the sugar.

6. Remove toast from oven. Arrange overlapping rounds, golden side down, over bottom of soufflé dish. Arrange overlapping rectangles around sides. Reserve any extra pieces.

7. Toss apple slices with remaining ½ cup sugar and lemon juice. Layer slices in lined dish. Arrange any remaining toast on top of apples.

8. Cover tightly with microwave plastic wrap. Cook at 100% 5 minutes.

9. Uncover and cook for 8 to 10 minutes longer, until set.

10. Remove charlotte from oven. If apple mixture has reduced dramatically during cooking, you may want to trim edges even with top of filling. Set a plate over top of dish (charlotte will continue to steam) and let stand until cool enough to handle.

11. Unmold charlotte onto a serving plate. Serve warm or cold. Slice with a serrated knife, and serve with whipped cream.

KEY LIME PIE

Once upon a time, the Florida Keys had a large crop of small, dark green limes that yielded small quantities of a wonderfully aromatic, flowery tasting juice that was often made into diaphanous pies topped with a cloud of whipped cream—no longer. Today when Key limes are available, they come from Mexico during a short winter season. Fortunately, the juice freezes well so we can have Key Lime Pie whenever we want. This is not a thick, heavy meringue pie. It is a chiffon pie, light as foam, that needs to be made a morning or day ahead. Substitute fresh lemon juice for the lime juice for lemon chiffon pie. *Makes one 9-inch pie*

1½ cups milk	¼ cup water
3 whole eggs, separated	¾ cup heavy cream
½ cup granulated sugar	Sweet Tart Pastry
½ cup Key lime juice, squeezed from 12 Key limes or 3 to 4 regular limes	(page 442), cooked and left in its pie plate
1 envelope unflavored gelatin	2 tablespoons confectioners sugar

1. Heat milk in a 4-cup glass measure, uncovered, at 100% for 2 minutes.

2. Whisk together egg yolks and granulated sugar. Whisk in hot milk. Return mixture to 4-cup measure. Cook, uncovered, at 100% for 2 minutes. Remove from oven and stir in lime juice.

3. Combine gelatin and water in a 1-cup glass measure. Heat, uncovered, at 100% for 45 seconds. Remove from oven and stir into lime mixture. Place mixture in the refrigerator and chill, stirring occasionally, until it begins to set.

4. Whip cream to soft peaks and fold into lime mixture. Pour into tart shell and refrigerate for 2 hours.

5. When pie is set, beat egg whites to soft peaks. Continue beating, adding remaining sugar by teaspoonful, until whites are stiff.

6. Heat conventional broiler. Spread meringue over pie, making sure to cover lime filling completely. Place pie under broiler and brown lightly. Refrigerate if not eating immediately.

Puddings and Custards

There is some part of my soul that remains forever a child. No dessert pleases that side of me as much as puddings and custards. I even cool my puddings uncovered in the refrigerator so that my spoon breaks a skin, making a hole into which to pour heavy cream. Grown-ups will want to loosely cover the desserts before cooling so that no skin develops. Such desserts are closely related to custard sauces and pastry creams. Indeed, a flavored Crème Anglaise (page 438) can be served with almost any of these desserts as an added decadence.

CHOCOLATE PUDDING

This lovely dessert is adapted from a recipe of Larry Forgione's. He is the chef-owner of An American Place in New York. In the microwave oven it is as easy and as rapid as any mix, but how different! I will put it up against a French pot de crème or mousse any time. Use very good chocolate; it's worth it. Don't worry about making eight portions when there are only four people eating. These delights will keep up to a week, loosely covered, in the refrigerator. I promise they will disappear.   *Serves 8*

2 cups milk	2 tablespoons water
½ cup granulated sugar	2 eggs
5 ounces good-quality semisweet chocolate, grated	4 egg yolks
	2 tablespoons unsalted butter
2 tablespoons cornstarch	1 tablespoon dark rum
2 tablespoons unsweetened cocoa powder	2 tablespoons vanilla extract

1. Place milk, sugar, and chocolate in an 8-cup glass measure. Cook, uncovered, at 100% for 4 minutes, stirring twice during cooking. Remove from oven and set aside.

2. Sift together cornstarch and cocoa powder. Add water to make a smooth slurry.

3. Stir slurry into chocolate mixture. Whisk in whole eggs and yolks. Cook, uncovered, at 100% for 2 minutes. Remove from oven, stir thoroughly, and cook for 2 minutes more.

4. Remove from oven and pour mixture into the work-bowl of a food processor. Add butter, rum, and vanilla and process until smooth. Pour into individual cups or an 8-cup serving bowl and chill.

BUTTERSCOTCH PUDDING

A nice discovery of working with the microwave oven has been to find out how easy it is to make caramel, the base for butterscotch—no scorched pans, scorched sugar, or disastrous crystals. See Dictionary for notes on CARAMEL.
Serves 8

1 cup granulated sugar	6 ounces unsalted butter
¼ cup water	2 eggs
1 cup heavy cream	4 egg yolks
2 tablespoons cornstarch	2 teaspoons vanilla
1 cup milk	extract

1. Combine sugar and water in an 8-cup glass measure. Cover tightly with microwave plastic wrap. Cook at 100% for 8 minutes, until light and gold.

2. Uncover carefully and stir in cream. Cook, uncovered, at 100% for 3 minutes.

3. Remove from oven. Make a slurry of cornstarch and ¼ cup of the milk. Add to caramel mixture.

4. Stir in remaining ¾ cup milk, butter, eggs, and yolks. Cook, uncovered, at 100% for 2 minutes.

5. Remove from oven and stir until smooth. Cook, uncovered, at 100% for 2 minutes longer.

6. Remove from oven and pour into the workbowl of a food processor. Add vanilla and process until smooth. Pour into individual cups and chill for at least 1 hour before serving.

POLENTA PUDDING WITH RASPBERRIES

Most of us think of polenta as that lush Italian version of cornmeal mush that is eaten instead of potatoes or rice, or that is fried to make a wonderful base for sauces as a first course. The very clever northern Italians, however, came up with another, less expected polenta dish, a creamy yellow dessert with fresh fruit, served with a sauce of the same fruit. If you want it to be yet more magnificent, serve with Crème Anglaise (page 438). This would be luscious after a light main course such as a fish with vegetables.

If this is more dessert than you need for your dinner, don't worry; you will finish it happily the next day.
Serves 8

1 pint fresh raspberries	**Grated zest of 1 lemon**
⅔ cup plus ¼ cup granulated sugar	**1 teaspoon vanilla extract**
4 cups water	**¼ teaspoon kosher salt**
¾ cup yellow cornmeal	**Unsalted butter, for the mold**

1. Toss together raspberries and ¼ cup of the sugar in a small, shallow dish. Cook, uncovered, at 100% for 4 minutes. Remove from oven and reserve.

2. Combine water, cornmeal, zest, and remaining ⅔ cup sugar in an 8-cup glass measure. Cook, uncovered, at 100% for 12 minutes, stirring twice.

3. Remove from oven and let stand for 10 minutes, stirring once or twice. Stir in vanilla and salt.

4. Set aside 1 cup of the raspberry mixture. Place remaining mixture in the workbowl of a food processor and process until smooth, adding water if necessary to make a thin sauce. Reserve.

5. Stir raspberry mixture that was set aside (not sauce) into the polenta just until marbled—don't completely incorporate it. Pour into a buttered 9″ × 4″ bowl or 4-cup pudding basin. Chill for 4 hours, until firm.

6. Unmold onto a serving dish and serve with the reserved sauce.

CRÈME BRÛLÉE

There is a territorial dispute as to whether this great classic dessert originated at English universities—the most common notion—or was a Spanish recipe, brought to England by a chef. Whatever, it has become wildly popular in America's top restaurants in the last years. It is a shallow pool of thin custard alluringly topped with a thin, hard, translucent golden brown sugar glaze that must be rapped sharply with the back of a spoon in order to fracture it before the dessert is eaten. The glazing must be done under a conventional broiler, but making the custard is simplified by the microwave oven.

You should make the custards at least 6 hours before you intend to glaze them. The custards may be variously flavored although it is not traditional.   *Serves 4*

1½ cups milk	1 teaspoon vanilla extract
3 eggs	6 tablespoons light brown
3 tablespoons	sugar, to caramelize
granulated sugar	tops of custards

1. Heat milk in a 4-cup glass measure, uncovered, at 100% for 4 minutes.

2. Remove from oven. Whisk together eggs, sugar, and vanilla until well combined. Whisking constantly, add hot milk in a thin stream. Divide mixture evenly among four ½-cup ramekins.

3. Place ramekins in a shallow ceramic dish just large enough to hold them without touching. Pour water around them to a depth of 1 inch. Cook, uncovered, at 100% for 5 to 6 minutes. Do not overcook—custards will still be wet at center.

4. Remove from oven and set ramekins on a cooling rack. When completely cool, refrigerate for at least 6 hours.

5. Preheat conventional broiler.

6. Sift 1½ tablespoons brown sugar over each custard, completely covering the top. Fit ramekins into a metal pan. Fill gaps between ramekins with ice and add water to a depth of ½ inch.

7. Broil just until sugar melts, about 4 minutes. Watch carefully to avoid burning. Remove from oven and rub each caramel crust with ice for 30 seconds, to harden it.

Note. Do not refrigerate Crème Brûlées once their tops have been broiled, as caramel crust will soften and liquefy.

To serve 6. Use 2 cups milk, 4 eggs, 4½ tablespoons granulated sugar, 2 teaspoons vanilla, and ½ cup plus 1 tablespoon brown sugar. Heat milk in a 4-cup glass measure for 5 minutes; cook custards for 6 minutes.

To serve 8. Double quantities of milk, eggs, and granulated sugar; use 1 tablespoon vanilla and ¾ cup brown sugar. Heat milk in a 8-cup glass measure for 7 minutes; cook custards for 8 minutes.

Space ramekins evenly around dish to ensure even cooking.

VARIATION

FLAVORED CRÈME BRÛLÉE This can be produced by flavoring the milk with anything you choose.

Coffee Crème Brûlée: Stir 2 teaspoons instant coffee or espresso into milk for 4 servings.

Ginger Crème Brûlée: Stir ½ teaspoon freshly grated ginger or 1 teaspoon dried ginger into milk for 4 servings.

Orange Crème Brûlée: Stir 2 teaspoons triple sec and ½ teaspoon grated orange zest into milk for 4 servings.

BREAD PUDDING

There is nothing homelier or better than a bread pudding. If you have stale bread—which is how this dessert originated, as did French toast—use it. Do not toast as in step 2; instead melt butter for 3 minutes at 100%, then toss in bread and proceed. This is another recipe with many possible variations. Stir in ¼ cup chocolate morsels, or add ¼ cup ¼-inch cubes of peeled apple stirred with ¼ teaspoon ground cinnamon. Substitute fresh raspberries turned in 2 tablespoons poire (pear brandy) for the raisins. As long as you respect the proportions, the pan size, and the cooking time, you can give your imagination free rein.   *Serves 4*

¼ cup raisins
½ cup warm water or
    bourbon
3 cups ½-inch cubes
    white bread, crusts
    trimmed
4 tablespoons unsalted
    butter

2 tablespoons granulated
    sugar
3 egg yolks
1 cup heavy cream
2 teaspoons vanilla
    extract

1. Soak raisins in water for 10 minutes.

2. Place bread in a 9½″ × 7″ × 2″ oval dish and cook, uncovered, at 100% for 4 minutes, stirring once. Remove from oven and set aside.

3. Drain raisins and set aside.

4. Heat butter in a 2-cup glass measure, uncovered, at 100% for 2 minutes. Remove from oven. Drizzle half the melted butter over bread and stir to coat.

5. Whisk together sugar, egg yolks, cream, and vanilla. Whisk in remaining melted butter and stir in raisins. Pour mixture over bread and cook, uncovered, at 100% for 3 minutes.

6. Remove from oven. Cover dish with a plate and let stand for 5 minutes. Serve warm.

RICE PUDDING

What is the matter with Mary Jane?
. . . It's lovely rice pudding for dinner again!
                                        A. A. MILNE

I would be delighted with rice pudding again; but then I am not a Victorian child subjected to it with startling frequency.

For those who like their rice pudding with a baked topping, pour finished pudding into four individual gratin dishes. Heat broiler. Combine ½ cup sugar with 1 tablespoon ground cinnamon. Sift over puddings to coat. Place dishes on a cookie sheet. Put under broiler about 2 minutes, or until the puddings glaze. Allow to cool; refrigerate or serve warm. *Serves 4*

½ cup raisins	1 vanilla bean, split
1 cup rice, parboiled,	lengthwise
not instant	2 cups heavy cream
2 cups milk	2 egg yolks
¼ cup granulated sugar	

1. Combine raisins, rice, milk, sugar, and vanilla bean in a 2-quart soufflé dish. Cook, uncovered, at 100% for 10 minutes. Stir, and cook for 10 minutes longer.

2. Remove from oven. Whisk together cream and egg yolks, and stir into rice mixture.

3. Cook, uncovered, for 1 minute. Stir, and cook for 1 minute longer.

4. Remove from oven and stir. Let sit for 5 minutes before serving. Serve with additional heavy cream, Tart Apricot Purée (page 445) or Fresh Strawberry Sauce (page 438).

TAPIOCA PUDDING

As a child, I hated what we called "fish eyes and glue." As a grown-up cook, I couldn't understand the French haute cuisine penchant for thickening with tapioca. Tapioca really gets magnificently cooked in the microwave oven; I am a convert to these creamy and delicious desserts that are even good warm.   *Serves 5 to 6*

2 cups milk	**Pinch kosher salt**
3 tablespoons tapioca (instant type)	**1 egg**
3 tablespoons granulated sugar	**1 teaspoon vanilla extract or 1 teaspoon almond extract**

1. Stir together milk, tapioca, sugar, and salt in an 8-cup glass measure. Cover tightly with microwave plastic wrap. Cook at 100% for 5 minutes. Uncover and stir well. Cook, uncovered, for 4 minutes more.

2. Remove from oven. Stir well. Beat together egg and vanilla. Stirring constantly, pour ½ cup tapioca into egg and then pour mixture back into tapioca. Cook, uncovered, at 100% for 1 minute.

3. Remove from oven. Stir well and cover with microwave plastic wrap, placing plastic directly on pudding to prevent a skin from forming. Serve warm or chilled.

To Serve 10 to 12. Double all ingredients. Cook as for Tapioca Pudding in a 2½-to-3-quart soufflé dish for 8 minutes. Stir and cook, uncovered, for 5 minutes more. Add eggs and vanilla as for Tapioca Pudding and cook for 1 minute more. Serve in soufflé dish or pour into ½-cup ramekins and chill.

Chocolate Tapioca for 5 or 10. Proceed as for Tapioca Pudding. After final cooking and while pudding is still hot, whisk in 2 ounces grated unsweetened chocolate (for smaller portion) or 4 ounces chocolate (for larger portion). Finish and serve as for Tapioca Pudding.

Steamed Puddings

It occurred to me forcibly as I was laboring to make decent cakes in the microwave oven that exactly the things that were causing me problems with the cakes would help make perfect steamed puddings. This didn't make me any happier about the cakes, but when I did get around to trying steamed puddings, I was happy to find my suspicions were right.

I love steamed puddings and their moist texture somewhere between cake and pudding. Until the microwave oven, I made them infrequently, as they required long steaming in a hot water bath that needed to be constantly checked and have water added. Now they are no more difficult or time-consuming than any other dessert.

Most of them would welcome a topping of unsweetened whipped cream, or Ginger Cream (page 425). Under the Queen, they would have served hard sauce, but these days that's a lot of butter (even for me).

THANKSGIVING PUDDING

I'm afraid I have gotten rather satiated with the rich, traditional pies associated with thanksgiving—pumpkin, pecan and mincemeat. Wanting something equally good but a little less heavy, I devised this steamed pudding. Pumpkin can replace the acorn squash, if you like. Place ¾ pound of 1-inch cubes of pumpkin flesh (2 cups) in a large measure and cook, tightly covered with microwave plastic wrap, for 8 minutes. *Serves 8*

¼ **pound plus 2 tablespoons unsalted butter**
1 **acorn squash (about 1 pound), halved and seeded**
1 **cup (packed) dark brown sugar**
5 **eggs**
½ **cup heavy cream**
⅓ **cup cake flour, sifted**
1 **teaspoon vanilla extract**

¾ **teaspoon ground cinnamon**
¼ **teaspoon ground allspice**
Candied orange peel, for garnish (optional)
2 **tablespoons pomegranate seeds, for garnish**
Heavy cream, for serving (optional)

1. Butter a 9″ × 4″ ceramic bowl or a 4-cup pudding basin with 2 tablespoons of the butter.

2. Wrap squash halves tightly in microwave plastic wrap. Cook at 100% for 8 minutes.

3. Remove from oven. Because of steam, unwrap carefully. Let cool to room temperature.

4. Put sugar and remaining ¼ pound butter, cut into 1-tablespoon pieces, in the workbowl of a food processor and blend.

5. Scrape the cooked squash from its shell into the processor. Add remaining ingredients except garnishes and cream and blend to a smooth mixture.

6. Pour into prepared bowl. Cover tightly with microwave plastic wrap. Cook at 100% for 9 minutes, until set; if pudding looks moist in the center, that is fine.

7. Remove from oven. Pierce plastic with the tip of a sharp knife and cover top of bowl with a heavy plate; this will keep the pudding hot. Let stand for 15 minutes.

8. Unmold pudding onto a serving plate. Garnish with candied orange peel and pomegranate seeds. Serve warm with whipped cream, if desired.

To make individual puddings. Cook in 2 batches of four ½-cup ramekins each for 2 minutes.

To make a single, smaller pudding. Halve the ingredients and halve the cooking time; cook in a smaller bowl (7″ × 4″) or 3-cup pudding basin. From this quantity you can, of course prepare 1 batch of individual puddings.

STEAMED CHOCOLATE PUDDING

Even if you have never tried a steamed pudding, you must try this rich and moist one, a dessert to dream about. *Serves 8*

¼ pound plus 2 tablespoons unsalted butter
8 ounces semisweet chocolate
½ cup (packed) light brown sugar
1 teaspoon vanilla extract
½ cup heavy cream
⅓ cup cake flour, sifted
½ teaspoon baking powder
3 eggs
Heavy cream, for serving (optional)

1. Butter a 9″ × 4″ ceramic bowl or a 4-cup pudding basin with 2 tablespoons of the butter.

2. Grate chocolate in a food processor. Add remaining ¼ pound butter, cut into 1-tablespoon pieces, and sugar. Process until thoroughly combined.

3. Add remaining ingredients, except cream for serving, and process to a smooth mixture.

4. Pour into prepared bowl. Cover tightly with microwave plastic wrap. Cook at 100% for 5 minutes, until set.

5. Remove from oven. Pierce plastic with the tip of a sharp knife and cover top of bowl with a heavy plate; this will keep the pudding hot. Let stand for 10 minutes.

6. Unmold pudding onto a serving plate. Serve warm or cold, with whipped cream if desired.

To make individual puddings. Cook in 2 batches of four ½-cup ramekins each for 1 minute 30 seconds.

To make a single, smaller pudding. Halve all ingredients and halve cooking time; cook in a smaller bowl (7″ × 4″) or 3-cup pudding basin. From this quantity you can, of course, prepare 1 batch of individual puddings.

STEAMED PEAR PUDDING

Unlike the other steamed puddings, this is pale in color. The strong, but somehow mysterious flavor and perfume of pears comes as a pleasant surprise. *Serves 8*

¼ **pound plus 2 tablespoons unsalted butter**
1½ **pounds ripe Bosc pears (about 3 pears)**
¼ **cup fresh lemon juice**
1 **cup granulated sugar**
5 **eggs**
½ **cup heavy cream**
⅓ **cup cake flour, sifted**
1 **teaspoon vanilla extract**
½ **teaspoon ground cinnamon**
½ **teaspoon ground ginger**
¼ **teaspoon ground cloves**

1. Butter a 9″ × 4″ ceramic bowl or a 4-cup pudding basin with 2 tablespoons of the butter.

2. Peel, halve, and core pears. Rub with lemon juice to prevent discoloration. Set in a 4-cup glass measure or soufflé dish and cover tightly with microwave plastic wrap. Cook at 100% for 3 minutes.

3. Put remaining ingredients, including ¼ pound butter cut into pieces, in the workbowl of a food processor. Remove pears from oven and add them to processor. Blend to a smooth mixture.

4. Pour into prepared bowl. Cover tightly with microwave plastic wrap. Cook at 100% for 9 minutes, until set.

5. Remove from oven. Pierce plastic with the tip of a sharp knife and cover top of bowl with a heavy plate; this will keep the pudding hot. Let stand for 15 minutes.

6. Unmold pudding onto a serving plate. Serve warm.

To make individual puddings. Cook in 2 batches of four ½-cup ramekins each for 2 minutes.

To make a single, smaller pudding. Halve the ingredients and halve the cooking time; cook in a smaller bowl (7″ × 4″) or 3-cup pudding basin. From this quantity you can, of course, prepare 1 batch of individual puddings.

STEAMED PAPAYA PUDDING

As steamed puddings go, this is rather exotic; but my, it is good, especially when other fruit desserts are in seasonally short supply. *Serves 8*

1 pound papaya, peeled, seeded and cut into 2-inch pieces	½ cup sour cream
	6 tablespoons cake flour, sifted
¼ pound plus 2 tablespoons unsalted butter	1 teaspoon vanilla extract
1 cup granulated sugar	1 teaspoon ground cardamon
6 eggs	

1. Place papaya in a 4-cup glass measure. Cover tightly with microwave plastic wrap. Cook at 100% for 4 minutes.

2. Butter a 9″ × 4″ bowl or a 4-cup pudding basin with 2 tablespoons of the butter.

3. Remove papaya from oven. Place in the workbowl of a food processor with remaining ingredients, including ¼ pound butter cut into small pieces, and blend to a smooth mixture.

4. Pour into prepared bowl. Cover tightly with microwave plastic wrap. Cook at 100% for 9 minutes, until pudding is set.

5. Remove pudding from oven. Pierce plastic with the tip of a sharp knife and cover top of bowl with a heavy plate; this will keep the pudding hot. Let stand for 15 minutes.

6. Unmold pudding onto a serving plate. Serve warm, with additional sour cream if desired.

To make individual puddings. Cook in 2 batches of four ½-cup ramekins each for 2 minutes.

To make a single, smaller pudding. Halve the ingredients and halve the cooking time; cook in a smaller bowl (7″ × 4″) or 3-cup pudding basin. From this quantity you can, of course, prepare 1 batch of individual puddings.

Cakes and Cookies

I AM about to tell you with hideous honesty the severe limitations of baking in the microwave oven. Before I do, I want to boast and tell you that the recipes I have included are terrific. You can make any of them with a perfect assurance of success, a success and a rapidity far beyond that possible in a conventional oven.

In addition, the confirmed baker will find that many elements of baking—component parts of recipes—are quickly and well accomplished in the microwave oven: Pastry Cream, Melting Chocolate, Blanching Nuts, Toasting Nuts, Praline Powder and Paste, Apricot Glaze, Ganache, Chocolate Glaze, White Mountain Icing, Melting Butter, and many more.

Now we must go on to the unfortunate limitations of excellence. This is a touchy subject because so many baking recipes have been written for the microwave oven. If you like them, by all means use them. I find that most are unsuccessful (including most that I tried to develop myself).

I will not give you recipes that I do not consider as good as any to be made.

One of the troubles with baking arises from the odd way that the starches in wheat flour—particularly gluten, which is in fact a protein—absorb liquid in the microwave oven; they tend to turn gluey. Rather than creating a pleasant crumb, you get a wet and soggy layer. Where I have lined cake pans with paper toweling, it is to encourage a dry surface. Additionally, flour does not brown in baking, so flour-based cakes stay a ghastly color. The baking problem is compounded by the tendency of eggs to become rubbery quickly in the microwave oven. As if all of this were not enough, the very size and shape of cakes mean that they cook unevenly in the microwave oven. Where I have shielded the outside of the pan with aluminum foil, it is to prevent the outside of the cake from cooking before the center.

The more "gluten-dependent" doughs for bread are a disaster. You will either get wet cardboard (tasting as if one of those clever people who puts sawdust into commercial products to lower the calories and up the fiber had sabotaged your kitchen in the night) or a heavy sodden mass that looks and weighs the same as one's child's first attempt at bread baking. You can, however, raise yeasts and doughs splendidly.

Similar, if less intense, problems arise for pastry. High sugar content doughs such as Sweet Tart Pastry (page 442) will brown only slightly. Puff Pastry (page 443) cooked in small batches is sufficiently spectacular—rising higher than any I have baked conventionally—to make it worth putting up with its pale color (you can always glaze it briefly under the broiler). Almost all other pastries toughen before they cook through.

Cakes such as tortes and cookies that are almost or totally flour-free, using nuts or chocolate to hold them together, can be extraordinarily good. There are several of them in this chapter. Substituting ground oats or rice flour for wheat flour where appropriate works well; but these flours have no gluten and cannot be used in risen cakes. Substituting cake flour, whole wheat flour, or wheat germ for part of all-purpose flour helps, but results are far from perfect. Note that in the Sponge Cake, the American Chocolate Layer Cake, and the Apricot Tea Cake, cornstarch has been substituted for all or part of the flour. Potato starch can be substituted in equal quantities in all recipes where cornstarch is used. If you love to bake and want to experiment, this is a direction that might well be worth following. Please, let me know what happens.

I have tried hundreds of recipes, most of them discarded as total disasters or less than marvelous. Here are the very worthy survivors.

Cakes

All of these recipes were developed and tested in full-power ovens: 650 to 700 watts. In a medium-power oven (around 500 watts) they take about half again as long. Some recipes have been tested for lower wattages. For the others, I am sorry, but you are on your own. In some cases you cannot make a full-size layer in a small oven.

If you have never baked cakes in the microwave oven before, there are things I should warn you about so you are not surprised. As they cook, egg-risen cakes will look like soufflés that are about to spill over, but actually they will deflate instead. When taken from the oven or the pan, they will not look entirely familiar. Many cakes will shrink more from the sides of the pans than conventional cakes. There is no surface browning, and they may seem slightly moist. This extra moisture will generally be absorbed as the layer sits. When you turn the layer out, if it seems gelatinous on the bottom, put it back in the oven, as is, for 1 minute at 100%. If cake layers are not frosted immediately, they should be tightly wrapped in microwave plastic wrap, since they have formed no protective crust to keep in the moisture. This open texture is perfect for icing.

Soufflé dishes or molds vary in thickness and in the structure of their upper edge. If possible, use glass soufflé dishes. They heat more quickly and cool off more quickly than ceramic. Since the glass soufflé dishes often come in nests, you will have all the sizes you may need.

Pans are prepared in a number of ways to permit the cakes to rise and/or cook properly. Pans should be prepared as indicated for best results. Sometimes the outside—not the bottom—of the pan is wrapped in aluminum foil. This helps certain cakes to cook through before the edges get overcooked. Some pans are prepared by being buttered and then coated with sugar to keep the cakes moist and to help them rise. This may leave a moist layer on the bottom of the cake. We find that as the cake sits unmolded, the moisture absorbs. If you dislike the moisture, try lining the mold with paper toweling as for Sponge Cake (page 413).

APRICOT TEA CAKE

This is a light and lovely moist cake to serve plain with good tea or, at the end of a meal, with espresso. Its appearance will be like that of the Sponge Cake, but it will have orange-colored flakes. Use leftovers to make a trifle. *Serves 8*

1 tablespoon unsalted butter	Pinch kosher salt
½ cup plus 2 tablespoons granulated sugar	½ cup cornstarch, sifted
6 eggs, separated	1 tablespoon vanilla extract
¼ cup Sweet Apricot Purée (page 445)	Apricot Glaze (page 444) (optional)

1. Heat butter in a 2-quart soufflé dish, uncovered, at 100% for 1 minute. Remove from oven and spread melted butter around dish to coat. Coat bottom and sides of dish with 2 tablespoons sugar.

2. Beat egg yolks and remaining ½ cup sugar until light and lemon-colored, about 2 minutes. Fold in apricot purée, salt, cornstarch, and vanilla.

3. In a clean bowl, beat egg whites to soft peaks. Fold one third of whites into yolk mixture and combine well. Fold in remaining whites. Pour into prepared soufflé dish. Cook, uncovered, at 100% for 7 minutes.

4. Remove from oven. Let cool for 5 minutes. Turn out carefully onto a serving plate. Glaze with Apricot Glaze, if desired. If not serving immediately, store tightly wrapped in two layers of plastic.

To make a half-size cake in a small oven. Halve all ingredients. Cook in a 1½-quart soufflé dish for 9 minutes 30 seconds, using a carousel.

SPONGE CAKE

This is a tremendously useful cake. Served as a whole cake, confectioners sugar can be sifted over it using a paper doily as a pattern—charming for tea. As layers, it can be made into a Big City Strawberry Shortcake (page 414) or the all-time favorites for which variations follow. *Makes 1 cake, or 2 layers*

7 eggs, separated	1 teaspoon vanilla
1 cup plus 1 tablespoon granulated sugar	extract
	½ cup cake flour
1 tablespoon boiling water	½ cup cornstarch

1. Line bottom and sides of a 2-quart soufflé dish with paper toweling cut to fit. Cut a 4-inch-wide strip of parchment long enough to encircle the dish; secure to outside of dish with string to form a 1-inch collar above rim.

2. Beat egg yolks for 30 seconds, until eggs begin to thicken. Gradually beat in 1 cup of the sugar and continue beating until very thick, about 2 minutes.

3. Stir in water and vanilla extract. Sift together flour and cornstarch and gently fold into batter, about a third at a time.

4. In a clean bowl, beat egg whites until frothy. Add remaining 1 tablespoon sugar and beat until soft peaks form. Stir about one quarter of the whites into batter, then fold in remaining whites.

5. Pour batter into prepared dish. Cook, uncovered, at 100% for 5 minutes 30 seconds or just until set. Do not overcook or the cake will toughen.

6. Remove from oven and let cool on a wire rack for 10 minutes. Turn cake out onto rack; gently peel off paper towel; let cool completely.

7. If desired, cut horizontally into 2 equal layers using a bread knife or serrated metal spatula.

To make a half-size cake in a small oven. Use 4 eggs and halve remaining ingredients. Cook in a 1½-quart soufflé dish for 8 minutes, using a carousel.

VARIATIONS

CHOCOLATE-HAZELNUT LAYER CAKE Split cake into 2 layers. Spread bottom layer with Hazelnut Cream (page 423). Replace top layer. Coat with Ganache (page 447).

LEMON LAYER CAKE Add 1 teaspoon grated lemon zest to the cake batter before baking. Split into layers. Spread bottom layer with Lemon Curd (page 446). Replace top layer. Glaze with Apricot-Lemon Glaze (page 444).

CHOCOLATE TRUFFLE LAYER CAKE Split cake into 2 layers. Make a double quantity of Ganache (page 447). Into one half of the warm Ganache, beat until smooth 4 tablespoons unsalted butter and 1 tablespoon brandy. Spread Ganache with added butter on bottom layer. Replace top layer. Pour on remaining, plain Ganache. When Ganache is set, top cake with shaved bittersweet chocolate.

BIG CITY STRAWBERRY SHORTCAKE

When I was growing up in New York City, the original Lindy's restaurant, domain of Leo Lindy himself, was going strong. There they served the most glorious of strawberry shortcakes. It wasn't until I was older that I found out that my beloved cake wasn't a real strawberry shortcake at all. Strawberry shortcake, I learned, is made with big baking powder biscuits, split and served with a sauce of strawberries mashed with sugar. The top of the biscuit is lavished with whipped cream and more strawberry sauce.

No matter how wise I might get, first love remained true love. I was driven to re-create my Big City Strawberry Shortcake. Variations with other berries are given, but nothing quite matches the grandeur of the layers separated and topped with oversize whole strawberries. *Serves 6 to 8*

1 tablespoon plus 1 teaspoon unflavored gelatin	¼ cup granulated sugar
¼ cup cold water	1 Sponge Cake (page 413)
3 cups heavy cream	2 pints strawberries, washed and hulled

1. In a 1-cup glass measure, sprinkle gelatin over water. Heat, uncovered, at 100% for 1 minute.

2. Remove from oven and let cool (do not allow to harden).

3. Whip cream until nearly doubled in bulk. Beat in sugar. Gradually beat in gelatin and continue beating until stiff. Refrigerate for 15 minutes before using.

4. Split cake into 2 layers. Place bottom layer, cut side up, on a serving plate. Spread with a ½-inch layer of cream. Arrange a layer of berries, bottoms down, over the cream. Cover with more cream to make an even layer. Top with second cake layer, and spread top and sides with more cream. Cover top densely with a layer of beautiful strawberries.

VARIATIONS

BLUEBERRY BASH Replace each strawberry layer with a solid layer of blueberries. This will take two 1-pint boxes. Drizzle some Blueberry Sauce (page 386) over all and pass additional sauce in a pitcher.

PERFECT PEAR SHORTCAKE Make 2 Sponge Cakes, split each into 2 layers, and brush top of each layer with a glaze of ⅓ cup apple jelly warmed with 1 tablespoon water. Replace strawberries with 6 poached pears (see Dictionary), cut lengthwise into thin slices. Add 2 to 3 tablespoons poire (pear brandy) to cream mixture when adding sugar. Drizzle Raspberry Sauce (page 438) over top and on dish around base of cake.

AMERICAN CHOCOLATE LAYER CAKE

Nothing caused as much dispute in the kitchen as whether this cake or the two basic variations was best. The American Chocolate Layer Cake was defended by an American purist who felt that the open texture and medium chocolate intensity produced the most authentic version. The Truffled Layer Cake has more chocolate and rises higher. And the European Dark Chocolate Cake is broader and flatter, and has a moister, more intense chocolate flavor than either of the other two. It was the crowd pleaser, even though it seemed to me more like a torte than the American idea of a layer cake.

What is shown by comparing the recipes is how relatively minor changes in the proportions of ingredients totally alter the way cakes bake in the microwave oven. It is not just a change in taste, but a change in texture and even dimension. *Makes one 7" × 4½" cake that can be cut into two 7" × 2¼" layers; fill to serve 6 to 8*

1 tablespoon unsalted butter	6 eggs, separated
	Pinch kosher salt
½ cup plus 2 tablespoons granulated sugar	½ cup cornstarch, sifted
	1 tablespoon vanilla
4 ounces good-quality semisweet chocolate	extract

1. Heat butter in a 2-quart soufflé dish, uncovered, at 100% for 1 minute. Remove from oven and spread melted butter around inside of dish to coat. Coat bottom and sides of dish with 2 tablespoons of the sugar. Set aside.

2. Place chocolate in a 4-cup glass measure. Cover tightly with microwave plastic wrap. Cook at 100% for 2 minutes (1 minute 30 seconds in a combination convection-microwave oven).

3. Remove from oven. Beat together egg yolks, salt, and remaining ½ cup sugar until light, about 2 minutes. Stir in melted chocolate, cornstarch, and vanilla.

4. In a clean bowl, beat egg whites to soft peaks. Fold one third of the whites into chocolate mixture and stir gently to combine. Fold in remaining whites. Pour mixture into prepared dish. Cook, uncovered, at 100% for 6 minutes.

5. Remove from oven and let stand for 5 minutes. Turn out onto a serving platter. When cool, slice cake crosswise into 2 layers. Fill and frost with Chocolate Fudge Frosting (page 418). If not frosting cake immediately, wrap tightly in plastic.

To make a half-size cake in a small oven. Halve all ingredients. Cook in a 1-quart soufflé dish for 7 minutes, using a carousel.

VARIATIONS

TRUFFLED LAYER CAKE Double the quantity of chocolate and heat for 3 minutes 30 seconds (2 minutes to 2 minutes 30 seconds in a combination convection-microwave oven). Proceed as for American Chocolate Layer Cake, cooking cake for 8 minutes. Cake will be 7″ × 5″. Split into 3 layers, 7″ × ¾″ each. Fill between layers with Chocolate Truffle mixture (page 434) and glaze with Ganache (page 447). (To make a half-size cake in a small oven, halve all ingredients and cook in a 1-quart soufflé dish for 8 minutes, using a carousel.)

EUROPEAN DARK CHOCOLATE CAKE Double the quantity of chocolate and heat for 3 minutes 30 seconds (2 minutes to 2 minutes 30 seconds in a combination convection-microwave oven). Use 5 eggs and reduce cornstarch to ⅓ cup. Proceed as for American Chocolate Layer Cake, cooking cake for 6 minutes. Cake will be 7″ × 2½″. Leave whole or split into 2 layers. Fill with Chocolate Truffle mixture (page 434) and glaze with Ganache (page 447). (To make a half-size cake in a small oven, halve all ingredients and cook in a 1-quart soufflé dish for 8 minutes 30 seconds, using a carousel.)

ORANGE CHOCOLATE CAKE To European Dark Chocolate Cake add grated zest of 1 orange to batter and 1 tablespoon orange liqueur to frosting.

MOCHA CAKE To any of the three basic cakes, add 1 tablespoon instant espresso powder to batter and 1 tablespoon coffee liqueur to frosting.

SACHERTORTE Spread bottom layer of European Dark Chocolate Cake with raspberry jam and add 1 tablespoon raspberry liqueur to frosting.

CHOCOLATE FUDGE FROSTING

I have never felt that I had to invent the wheel. One of my favorite chocolate frostings is in *Joy of Cooking*. I have adapted it for microwave cooking. *Makes enough to fill and frost one 7-inch 2-layer cake*

1 cup granulated sugar	½ teaspoon vanilla
½ cup heavy cream	extract
2 ounces semisweet	2 tablespoon unsalted
chocolate, cut into	butter
1-inch pieces	

1. Stir together sugar and cream in a 4-cup glass measure. Cover tightly with microwave plastic wrap. Cook at 100% for 4 minutes.

2. Remove from oven and pierce plastic with the tip of a sharp knife. Uncover and add chocolate and vanilla, stirring well until chocolate is melted. Let cool to room temperature.

3. When chocolate mixture has cooled, beat in butter. Continue beating until mixture is of spreading consistency, about 5 minutes. If frosting is slightly warm, refrigerate for 15 minutes until slightly thickened.

REINE DE SABA

An Americanized version of a classic French cake adapted for the microwave oven—flour is changed to cornstarch— this is about as rich and elegant as a simple chocolate layer cake can get. It will last for several days if you want to make it ahead and if you can keep people from nibbling at it. *Serves 6*

¼ pound plus 2	⅔ cup granulated sugar
teaspoons unsalted	3 eggs, separated
butter	⅓ cup cornstarch, sifted
¼ cup currants	⅓ cup finely ground
2 tablespoons bourbon	blanched almonds
4 ounces semisweet	Ganache (page 447),
chocolate	for glazing

1. Butter the bottom of a round 8″ × 2″ dish using 2 teaspoons of the butter, and cover bottom with waxed or parchment paper cut to fit. Shield sides of dish: Cut a strip of aluminum foil 3 inches wide and long enough to encircle dish; wrap foil around outside of dish and secure by folding excess inch over rim.

2. Put currants in a 2-cup glass measure and pour bourbon over. Heat, loosely covered with paper toweling, at 100% for 2 minutes. Remove from oven and reserve.

3. Place chocolate in a clean 2-cup glass measure and heat, uncovered, at 100% for 2 minutes (1 minute 30 seconds in a combination convection-microwave oven).

4. In an electric mixer, cream remaining butter and sugar for 2 minutes, until light.

5. Add egg yolks one at a time, incorporating each thoroughly before adding the next. Stir in chocolate, cornstarch, almonds, and currants.

6. In a clean bowl, beat egg whites until stiff. Fold into yolk mixture until just incorporated.

7. Pour into prepared dish. Cook, uncovered, at 100% for 3 minutes. Leaving cake in oven, remove foil shield; cook for 2 minutes longer. (If using a small oven, cook, uncovered, for 5 minutes, using a carousel. Remove foil shield; cook 4 minutes longer.)

8. Remove cake from oven, cover with a plate, and let sit for 10 minutes.

9. Turn out onto a cooling rack. When completely cool, glaze with Ganache.

ITALIAN CHOCOLATE CAKE

As I looked for a virtually flourless cake, I remembered Edda Servi Machlin's Egg-White Chocolate Cake from her book, *Classic Cuisine of the Italian Jews*. With her kind permission, I have adapted it to the microwave oven.
Makes one 7-inch cake

8 egg whites
½ cup unsweetened cocoa powder, sifted
1 cup granulated sugar
3 tablespoons vegetable oil
⅓ cup hazelnuts, toasted, skins removed and coarsely chopped
⅓ cup almonds, blanched, toasted and coarsely chopped
⅓ cup walnuts, toasted and coarsely chopped
½ teaspoon kosher salt
Confectioners sugar, for dusting cake

1. Shield the sides of an 8″ × 3″ round glass or ceramic dish: Cut a strip of aluminum foil 4 inches wide and long enough to encircle dish; wrap outside of dish and secure by folding excess inch over rim.

2. Stir together 2 of the egg whites, cocoa powder, sugar, and oil until combined. Stir in nuts and set aside.

3. Beat remaining 6 egg whites and salt to stiff peaks.

4. Fold one third of whites into nut mixture until well incorporated. Gently fold in remaining whites and pour mixture into prepared dish.

5. Cover dish loosely with paper toweling and cook at 100% for 2 minutes. (If using a small oven, cook for 4 minutes, using a carousel.)

6. Remove from oven and cover dish with a plate. Allow cake to stand, covered, for 5 minutes (cake will continue to cook).

7. Turn cake onto a serving plate and dust with confectioners sugar. Serve when cool.

PUMPERNICKEL TORTE

This torte is made in two layers, cooked successively in the same pan. It will be easiest, therefore, to keep microwave plastic wrap and cooling racks handy when making it.
Serves 10 to 12

½ cup blanched almonds
1 ounce good-quality semisweet or bittersweet chocolate
2 cups fine, dry Pumpernickel Crumbs (page 355)

¾ cup granulated sugar
6 whole eggs, separated
1 cup raspberry preserves
Ganache (page 447), to glaze cake (optional)

1. Line a 10-inch quiche dish with microwave plastic wrap, leaving a 2-inch overhang around the top of the dish.

2. Place almonds and chocolate in the workbowl of a food processor. Process until finely ground (do not over-process). Add to crumbs and stir to combine.

3. Beat together ½ cup of sugar and egg yolks until light and lemon-colored, about 2 minutes.

4. Beat egg whites to soft peaks. Beating constantly, add remaining sugar by the tablespoon until incorporated and whites hold stiff peaks. Fold one third of whites into yolk mixture. Fold in half of crumb mixture, then fold in remaining whites and crumb mixture.

5. Pour one half of batter into prepared dish. Cook, uncovered, at 100% for 4 minutes.

6. Remove from oven. Gently lift out cake layer and place on a rack to cool. Line dish again with microwave plastic wrap. Pour remaining batter into prepared dish. Cook as above.

7. Remove from oven. Remove layer to a rack to cool as in step 6. Let layers stand for 5 minutes. Wrap each tightly in 2 sheets of plastic wrap until ready to use. (Cake may be prepared to this point up to 1 day in advance.)

8. Assemble the cake: Sandwich layers together with preserves and brush sides of cake with preserves. Glaze with Ganache, if desired.

NUT CAKE WITH HAZELNUT CREAM

The Austrians love their nut cakes almost as much as they do their strudel. This recipe was developed from a turn-of-the-century Viennese cookbook; it needed almost no modification. The luxury-loving Viennese never were very keen on flour in their tortes.

The Hazelnuts Cream and the Coffee Glaze are splendid recipes for other uses. The cream could go between Sponge Cake layers, the glaze on simple cookies.   *Serves 8 to 10 (it is very rich)*

Unsalted butter, for the dish	½ cup fine, dry Breadcrumbs (page
¾ cup granulated sugar	354) or store-
6 eggs, separated	bought,
1½ cups finely ground walnuts	unseasoned breadcrumbs
	Hazelnut Cream (see following recipe)
	Coffee Glaze (see following recipe)

1. Butter a 12″ × 2″ round dish and coat with 2 teaspoons of sugar.

2. Beat together egg yolks and remaining sugar until lemon-colored.

3. In a clean bowl, beat egg whites until stiff. Fold one third of the whites into yolk mixture. Fold in walnuts and Breadcrumbs. Fold in remaining whites.

4. Pour into prepared dish and cover loosely with paper toweling. Cook at 100% for 6 minutes (top will look moist).

5. Remove from oven. Allow to cool in dish for 8 to 10 minutes. Turn out onto cooling rack.

6. Prepare Hazelnut Cream.

7. Using a serrated knife, slice cake in half horizontally to make 2 layers. Spread Hazelnut Cream on bottom layer and place second layer over the first. Cover tightly and refrigerate while preparing Coffee Glaze. (You may prepare the cake to this point up to 1 day in advance.)

8. Prepare Coffee Glaze. As soon as it is ready, pour it over top of cake. Do not spread glaze; simply tilt cake to distribute glaze over top. Let cool to room temperature.

HAZELNUT CREAM

½ **pound unsalted butter**	**2 tablespoons strong**
¼ **cup granulated sugar**	**coffee**
½ **cup hazelnut Praline**	
Powder (page 448)	

1. Cream butter and sugar until light. Beat in Praline Powder. Add coffee and beat until creamy.

2. If not using immediately, store in a cool, not refrigerated, place.

COFFEE GLAZE

1 cup confectioners sugar	**2 tablespoons strong**
	coffee

1. Combine sugar and coffee in a 2-cup glass measure. Cover tightly with microwave plastic wrap. Cook at 100% for 3 to 4 minutes.

2. Use hot glaze immediately.

Cookies

Most snack cookies should be made in a conventional oven. But, strangely, the more elegant and difficult cookies—thin lacy Florentines, Ginger Lace Cookies, and Tuiles—are easy and rapid in the microwave oven, which caramelizes them just enough without risk of scorching. These are typically the finishing touches served with homemade sorbets, ice creams, and poached fruits. For the "more is never enough" crowd, they can even be served with Bavarian creams and custards. If only a few cookies are needed to go with a dessert, extra batter can be refrigerated or even frozen. The batter is so rich that it will defrost rapidly at room temperature.

Do not substitute plastic measures for glass in these recipes. The batters will cook rapidly.

FLORENTINES

These may be the most elegant of the thin, crisp accompaniment cookies. They are studded with the fresh zests of lemons and tangerines and redolent of sliced almonds.

I like these cookies left plain, but it is always possible to gild the lily. They can be spread on the bottom with melted chocolate. Unglazed, these cookies will last for several days in a tightly closed tin.   *Makes 2½ to 3 dozen*

¼ pound unsalted butter
¼ cup sour cream
½ cup granulated sugar
¼ cup honey
1 tablespoon finely grated tangerine zest
1 tablespoon finely grated lemon zest
½ cup blanched, sliced almonds
¼ cup all-purpose flour, sifted
Vegetable oil, for the cooking platter
Bittersweet chocolate (optional)

1. Heat butter in a 2-cup glass measure, loosely covered with paper toweling, at 100% for 2 minutes.

2. Stir together butter, sour cream, sugar, honey, zests, and almonds until well blended. Stir in flour just enough to mix.

3. Lightly coat a 12-inch round flat platter with oil. Drop teaspoonfuls of mixture in a ring inside rim of platter, with 2 inches between each cookie (cook 6 to 8 at a time). Cook, uncovered, at 100% for 3 minutes.

4. As oven heats with successive batches, cooking time will shorten to 2 minutes 30 seconds. Allow each batch to cool for 2 minutes after baking, then remove with a metal spatula to cooling rack.

5. When completely cool, spread flat side of each cookie with melted chocolate, if desired.

GINGER LACE COOKIES

A classic teatime treat from before Mrs. Beeton right up to the present. *Makes 2½ dozen.*

4 tablespoons unsalted butter	1 teaspoon fresh lemon juice
¼ cup (packed) dark brown sugar	Vegetable oil, for the cooking platter
4 tablespoons light corn syrup	2 cups heavy cream (optional)
½ teaspoon ground ginger	⅓ cup diced crystallized ginger (optional)
½ cup cake flour, sifted	

1. Combine butter, sugar, corn syrup, and ground ginger in a 4-cup glass measure and cook, uncovered, at 100% for 4 minutes.

2. Remove from oven and briskly stir in flour and lemon juice.

3. Lightly coat a 12-inch round platter with vegetable oil. Drop teaspoonfuls of batter in a ring inside rim of platter, with 2 inches between each cookie (cook about 6 cookies per batch). Cook, uncovered, at 100% for 2 minutes 30 seconds.

4. As oven heats with successive batches, cooking times will shorten to 2 minutes. Allow each batch to cool for 1 minute after baking.

5. Oil the handle of a wooden spoon. With a metal spatula, carefully lift each cookie off platter and gently wrap it around handle. As each cookie is shaped, transfer it to cooling rack.

6. If desired, just before serving, make Ginger Cream: Whip cream to soft peaks. fold in diced ginger. Using a pastry bag fitted with a large star tip, pipe cream into both ends of each cookie.

Note. Cookies may be left flat and served without cream, as for Florentines (page 424).

TUILES

These are the most common of the thin and crisp French
dessert cookies. They get their name from their supposed
resemblance to the classic terracotta tiles on the roofs (*tuiles*)
of certain French houses.

As with Ginger Lace Cookies, the oven will heat up with
successive batches. The same precautions apply.   *Makes 2
to 3 dozen*

4 tablespoons unsalted butter	2 egg whites 1 egg yolk

¾ cup finely ground
    almonds or walnuts
	1 teaspoon vanilla extract
	    Vegetable oil, for the

½ cup granulated sugar	cooking platter

1. Heat butter in a 2-cup glass measure, uncovered, at
100% for 2 minutes.

2. Place remaining ingredients except oil in the workbowl of a food processor and process until well combined.
With the motor running, pour in melted butter in a thin
stream.

3. Generously grease a 12-inch round platter. Drop batter
by teaspoonfuls 2 inches apart (make about 4 cookies per
batch). Cook, uncovered, at 100% for 2 minutes 30 seconds
to 3 minutes. (As the oven heats with successive batches,
cooking time will be shorter.)

4. Remove from oven. Lift cookies off platter with a
metal spatula and drape over the handle of a wooden spoon
to cool.

OATMEAL CRISPS

With her kind permission, I have adapted this recipe of Maida Heatter's from *Great American Cookies* for the microwave oven. These delicious wafers give a sensation of instant health. They would be good with coffee or caramel ice cream or Bourbon Peaches (page 389).   *Makes 6 dozen cookies*

2 tablespoons unsalted
   butter
3 eggs
¾ teaspoon ground
   cinnamon
1 teaspoon vanilla
   extract
½ teaspoon kosher salt
1½ cups granulated sugar

4 teaspoons baking
   powder
3½ cups quick-cooking
   oats
⅓ cup all-purpose flour,
   sifted
Vegetable oil, for the
   cooking platter

1. Heat butter in a 1-cup glass measure, uncovered, at 100% for 1 minute 30 seconds. Reserve.

2. Beat eggs until foamy. Add cinnamon, vanilla, salt, and sugar and beat until well mixed, about 2 minutes.

3. Add melted butter and remaining ingredients except vegetable oil and blend well.

4. Lightly coat a 12-inch round, flat platter with vegetable oil. Drop the batter by ½ teaspoonfuls onto the platter in a ring around the inside rim. (Make about 6 cookies per batch.) Cook, uncovered, at 100% for 3 minutes, just until cookies are golden at center.

5. As oven heats with successive batches, cooking time will shorten to 2 minutes 30 seconds. With a metal spatula, remove cookies to a rack to cool. Store in an airtight container for up to a week.

Note. Batter can be made a day in advance and kept, tightly covered, in the refrigerator.

BEIGNETS

These are light, delicious, deep-fried morsels made from cream puff dough—sort of very fluffy doughnut holes. In New Orleans, they eat them for breakfast. I like them warm with fruit sorbets. See Chocolate Sauce (page 437). They can be rewarmed by placing on paper toweling, uncovered, at 100% for 1 minute. Do not attempt to make these in a less than full-power oven.   *Makes 12 to 15 cookies*

½ cup water	2 eggs
4 tablespoons unsalted butter	3 cups vegetable oil, for frying beignets
½ cup all-purpose flour	Confectioners sugar,
½ teaspoon kosher salt	for dusting beignets

1. Place water and butter in a 4-cup glass measure and heat, uncovered, at 100% for 2 minutes 30 seconds, until mixture boils.

2. Remove from oven and pour into the workbowl of a food processor. Add flour and salt and process continuously for 1 minute 30 seconds. Add eggs, one at a time, processing for 30 seconds after each addition. Batter should just hold a soft shape. (Recipe may be prepared in advance to this point; batter will keep, tightly covered and refrigerated, for 2 days.)

3. Heat oil in an 8-cup glass measure, uncovered, at 100% for 15 minutes. Drop teaspoonfuls of batter into hot oil (6 to 8 beignets at a time) and cook, uncovered, at 100% for 1 minute. Open oven door and turn beignets over, using a slotted spoon or wire skimmer. Continue cooking for 1 minute to 1 minute 30 seconds, until golden brown.

4. Remove beignets to paper toweling to drain. Reheat oil for 5 minutes between batches. Dust with confectioners sugar before serving.

FUDGY BROWNIES

Everybody has his or her own notion of what makes the perfect brownie. I like the fudgy ones thick with nuts and raisins. Make these in small batches. They cook so quickly you can have them fresh whenever you want. It takes about 5 minutes to whip them up and 8 minutes to cook them. You don't have to shield them; the tight covering helps them to cook evenly. *Makes 16 brownies*

¼ pound unsalted butter
2 ounces unsweetened chocolate
1 ounce semisweet chocolate
¼ cup granulated sugar
1 cup (packed) light brown sugar

2 eggs
1 teaspoon vanilla extract
Pinch kosher salt
¼ teaspoon baking powder
¾ cup cake flour, sifted

1. Place butter and all chocolate in an 8-cup glass measure. Cover tightly with microwave plastic wrap. Cook at 100% for 2 minutes.

2. Remove from oven. Uncover and whisk until combined. Whisk in all sugar and then eggs, one at a time. Stir in vanilla.

3. Sift together salt, baking powder, and flour. Fold into chocolate mixture. Pour into an 8-inch square or oval dish. Cover tightly with microwave plastic wrap. Cook at 100% for 4 minutes. Uncover and cook for 2 minutes longer.

4. Remove from oven. Cut into squares and let stand until cool.

VARIATIONS

CHUNKY FUDGY BROWNIES When folding in dry ingredients, stir in ⅓ cup raisins and ⅓ cup coarsely chopped walnuts. Cook as for Fudgy Brownies

REBECCA'S RASPBERRY BROWNIES Substitute ¼ cup Raspberry Jam (page 454) for ¼ cup granulated sugar and omit raisins and walnuts. Proceed as for Fudgy Brownies.

CAKEY BROWNIES Omit semisweet chocolate, ¼ cup granulated sugar, vanilla, raisins, and walnuts. Decrease flour to ⅔ cup and increase baking powder to ½ teaspoon. For the sugar, you can use either light brown or granulated sugar. Proceed as for Fudgy Brownies, cooking, covered, for 3 minutes. Uncover and cook for 2 minutes longer.

THE ORIGINAL CHOCOLATE SANDWICH COOKIE

One day for pure escapism, I was reading *A Thousand Ways to Please a Husband, with Bettina's Best Recipes,* by Louise Bennett Weaver and Helen Cowles Le Cron, published in 1917, a morally edifying text based on the notion that good cooking and prudent housekeeping would render a marriage not only happy, but endlessly romantic in a vine-covered cottage. It was filled with marvelous cautionary tales about good wives and bad wives who were rescued by Bettina's smarmy example. Oh, for simpler times. Among the recipes, I found one for dry chocolate cookies to be sandwiched together with White Mountain Frosting. Eureka! The prototype Oreo.

They keep for a long time and would be nice with a cup of coffee or a glass of milk. (I don't know if Bettina would approve of the caffeine.)   *Makes 12 cookies*

1½ ounces semisweet chocolate	½ cup fine, dry Breadcrumbs (page 354) or unseasoned, store-bought breadcrumbs
2 tablespoons unsalted butter	
¼ cup granulated sugar	
1 egg	½ teaspoon vanilla extract
	White Mountain Frosting (see following recipe)

1. Place chocolate in a 2-cup glass measure. Heat, uncovered, at 100% for 1 minute 30 seconds to 2 minutes, until melted.

2. Remove from oven and set aside. Cream butter and sugar until light. Beat in egg. Stir in Breadcrumbs, vanilla, and melted chocolate.

3. Line a 12-inch round platter with parchment or waxed paper, cut to fit. Spread batter in a thin layer over entire platter. Cook, uncovered, at 100% for 3 to 4 minutes, just until firm.

4. Remove from oven and allow to cool. Gently turn cookie circle out onto a clean surface. Peel parchment from bottom. Cut out 24 cookies using a 1½-inch round cookie cutter.

5. Sandwich two cookies together with White Mountain Frosting (see following recipe) or butter cream as filling.

WHITE MOUNTAIN FROSTING

This frosting is normally made for cakes, not just for sandwiching cookies. It's a sort of marshmallow event. If you want to fill as well as frost the cake, you will need 3 cups. *Makes 1½ cups, enough to frost but not to also fill a cake*

1 cup granulated sugar	1 egg white
⅛ teaspoon cream of tartar	½ teaspoon vanilla extract
¼ cup water	

1. Combine sugar, cream of tartar, and water in a 4-cup glass measure. Cover tightly with microwave plastic wrap. Cook at 100% for 5 to 6 minutes, until syrup registers 238° F. on a candy thermometer (soft ball stage).

2. Beat egg white until foamy.

3. Remove syrup from oven. Beating constantly, add sugar syrup to white in a thin stream until incorporated. Continue to beat until cool (mixture will thicken as it cools). Beat in vanilla.

4. If not using immediately, cover bowl with a damp towel for up to 30 minutes.

To make 3 cups. Double ingredients, cooking sugar mixture for 7 minutes 30 seconds.

VARIATION

COCONUT FROSTING Dry 1½ cups unsweetened grated coconut (page 354). Fold into 3 cups White Mountain Frosting. Fill and frost a 2-layer cake. Sprinkle ½ cup more grated coconut on top and sides.

ALMOND SHORTBREAD

The usually abstemious Scots make a dry cake, shortbread, so rich in butter that it is a concealed sin. This almond version may just go it one better. Make ahead to keep on hand for unexpected guests. Good with tea.   *Makes two 9-inch round shortbreads*

1½ cups cake flour	¼ pound unsalted butter,
1 cup cornstarch	cut into ½-inch
2 cups ground, toasted	pieces
almonds	2 to 3 tablespoons water
1 cup granulated sugar	

1. Combine flour, cornstarch, almonds, and sugar in the workbowl of a food processor. Process briefly to combine. Add butter, pulsing on and off, just until mixture is crumbly. Add water and pulse twice, or just until mixture pulls together into a mass.

2. Divide dough in half. Shape each half into an 8-inch patty on 12-inch squares of microwave plastic wrap.

3. Transfer one patty on its plastic to a 12-inch flat platter. Cook, uncovered, at 100% for 2 minutes 30 seconds to 3 minutes, just until set.

4. Remove from oven. Pick up the corners of the plastic and carefully transfer the fragile shortbread to a flat surface to cool. Score the shortbread lightly into 8 wedges. Cook and score the second patty.

5. Let shortbreads cool completely. Store in a tightly covered tin.

Note. To toast 2 cups blanched, sliced almonds, place in a 14″ × 11″ × 2″ dish and cook, uncovered, at 100% for 10 minutes, stirring twice.

ALMONDS PRALINES

These pralines are hard with caramel—not chewy. This is a very festive treat to serve as candy, or as an accompaniment to ice cream or poached fruit. Best of all, this usually hard-to-make delicacy is quick and easy thanks to the microwave oven's winning ways with sugar. Follow cooking times; the caramel will continue to darken after being taken from the oven. *Makes ½ pound, 12 to 18 pieces*

1 cup blanched almonds   **Vegetable or safflower**
1 cup granulated sugar   **oil, for the cookie sheet**
¼ cup water

1. Place almonds in a single layer on a plate. Cook, uncovered, at 100% for 5 minutes, until golden. Lightly oil a cookie sheet.

2. Combine sugar and water in an 8-cup glass measure. Stir thoroughly to dissolve completely. Cover tightly with microwave plastic wrap. Cook at 100% for 4 minutes.

3. Without taking measure from oven, uncover very carefully. Continue cooking, uncovered, 4 to 5 minutes longer, until golden brown. Do not stir.

4. Remove from oven. Add almonds to hot syrup and stir to coat. Working quickly, scoop up 2 to 3 coated almonds at a time with an oiled fork and drop onto oiled sheet. Allow to harden. If praline becomes too hard to scoop, return to oven, uncovered, for 1 minute to soften.

Note. To clean measure, fill with cold water and heat, uncovered, at 100% for 12 to 15 minutes. Remove from oven and pour off water. Repeat if there is still undissolved caramel stuck on measure.

PEANUT BRITTLE

This is a childhood delight that cooks quickly and without risk in the microwave oven. Don't eat it with weak teeth. Don't expect to keep it for long, either; it just seems to vanish.   *Makes 1½ pounds*

1 cup granulated sugar	1½ cups raw peanuts,
½ cup light corn syrup	blanched or
½ cup water	unblanched
	Vegetable oil, for the
	baking sheet

1. Combine sugar, corn syrup, and water in an 8-cup glass measure. Cook, uncovered, at 100% for 3 minutes.

2. Remove from oven and stir thoroughly. Add peanuts; stir again. Cover tightly with microwave plastic wrap. Cook at 100% for 15 minutes.

3. Lightly coat a spatula and a large baking sheet or 16″ × 12″ marble slab with vegetable oil. Remove syrup from oven. Pierce plastic with the tip of a sharp knife and uncover carefully. Pour mixture onto oiled surface. With the oiled spatula, spread peanuts to distribute them evenly through cooling syrup. Let harden.

4. When brittle is cool, break into chunks with a wooden mallet or rolling pin. Store in an airtight container.

CHOCOLATE TRUFFLES

Everybody seems to love truffles. There are truffles made without the butter, but I prefer these richer ones. I also prefer truffles that are rolled in unsweetened cocoa; but there are those who think they are eating a truffle only if it has been dipped in chocolate. To dip in chocolate, melt 3 ounces bittersweet chocolate (page 509). Allow to cool to room temperature. Dip cold formed truffles (using a toothpick if you want), one by one, into melted chocolate. Set on a cake rack over a cookie sheet. When all truffles have been dipped, place in refrigerator.   *Makes about 30 truffles*

2 cups Ganache (page
    447), at room
    temperature
4 tablespoons unsalted
    butter

1 tablespoon Cognac
1 cup Dutch process
    cocoa powder, sifted,
    for coating truffles

1. Beat together all ingredients, except cocoa, until well combined. Pour into a 1-quart soufflé dish. Chill for 2 hours.

2. When thoroughly chilled, scoop up balls of truffle mixture with a melon baller, dipped in warm water between scoops. Roll each truffle in cocoa powder. Store, tightly covered, refrigerated, in additional cocoa powder.

VARIATIONS

ORANGE TRUFFLES Replace Cognac with triple sec. Place cocoa for coating in food processor with three strips of candied orange peel, and process until peel is finely chopped.

MOCHA TRUFFLES Replace Cognac with 1 tablespoon triple-strength coffee. Mix 1 tablespoon powdered instant espresso with cocoa for coating.

Sweet Sauces

There are times when the difference between a ho-hum dessert and a gala one is a good sauce. This little group is quickly made in the microwave oven and can bless everything from ice cream to simple cake to custards and pastry.

CHUNKY BLUEBERRY SAUCE

This luscious sauce is simply perfect over pancakes or ice cream or with shortcake. For a more elegant version to serve with desserts, add 2 tablespoons poire (pear brandy) or triple sec to cooked berries and strain through a sieve. See also the Blueberry Sauce that accompanies Light Poached Pears (page 385). *Makes 1½ cups*

1 pint blueberries

3 tablespoons granulated
    sugar

1. Pick over berries, discarding any that are overripe, green, or discolored. Put into a 4-cup glass measure.

2. Sprinkle with sugar. Cover tightly with microwave plastic wrap. Cook at 100% for 3 minutes.

CARAMEL SAUCE

Serve this quick and easy sauce warm with Apple Charlotte (page 394), under a square of Puff Pastry (page 443) that has been split in half and filled with Pastry Cream (page 439), or poured over ice cream. *Makes 1 cup*

½ cup granulated sugar
2 tablespoons cold water

½ cup heavy cream
1 tablespoon unsalted butter

1. Combine sugar and water in a 4-cup glass measure. Cover tightly with microwave plastic wrap. Cook at 100% for 4 to 5 minutes, until syrup just begins to turn light gold.

2. Remove from oven, uncover carefully, and slowly pour in cream. Stir in butter. Cook, uncovered, at 100% for 1 minute to 1 minute 30 seconds, until dark gold.

BUTTERSCOTCH SAUCE

The major difference between this and Caramel Sauce is that this is much richer. It is the classic sauce for ice cream sundaes. I don't know anybody sophisticated enough to resist its wiles. *Makes 2 cups*

¼ pound unsalted butter
1 cup light brown sugar
½ cup light corn syrup
2 tablespoons heavy cream

½ teaspoon kosher salt
½ teaspoon vanilla extract

1. Put 4 tablespoons of the butter and the sugar, corn syrup, cream, and salt in an 8-cup glass measure. Cover tightly with microwave plastic wrap. Cook at 100% for 5 minutes.

2. Remove from oven. Uncover and whisk in vanilla extract and remaining 4 tablespoons butter. Serve warm or at room temperature.

3. To store, let cool to room temperature and cover tightly; it will keep in the refrigerator for up to 4 months. Reheat for 1 minute, uncovered, at 100%; stir and serve.

CHOCOLATE SAUCE

Imagine a warm dark pool of this under freshly fried Beignets (page 428) dusted with confectioners sugar. It is also surprisingly good with Light Poached Pears (page 385). *Makes 1½ cups*

4 ounces good-quality semisweet chocolate, broken into 1½-inch pieces	2 tablespoons unsalted butter
	2 tablespoons heavy cream
¼ cup strong coffee	2 tablespoons dark rum

1. Place all ingredients in an 8-cup glass measure. Cover tightly with microwave plastic wrap. Cook at 100% for 5 minutes.

2. Remove from oven. Uncover and whisk sauce until smooth. Serve warm or at room temperature.

Note. This sauce will keep very well refrigerated, in a tightly covered glass jar, for a week or more. Reheat for 1 minute, uncovered, at 100%; stir and serve.

NESSELRODE SAUCE

There was a time when eating ice cream meant a trip to an ice cream parlor. Eating was done on little marble-topped tables or at a grand Victorian soda fountain. Those were the days of Nesselrode Sauce, too good to be forgotten. *Makes 3 cups*

1 jar (6 ounces)
   maraschino cherries,
   drained and coarsely
   chopped (juice
   reserved)
1 container (3½ ounces)
   candied mixed fruits

1 cup orange
   marmalade
½ cup coarsely chopped
   candied ginger
1 cup roasted, unsalted
   mixed nuts, coarsely
   chopped
½ cup dark rum

1. Put all ingredients in an 8-cup glass measure. Stir in one half of the reserved maraschino juice.

2. Cook, uncovered, at 100% for 5 minutes.

3. Remove from oven and stir well. Let sauce ripen stored in a tightly covered jar in the refrigerator for at least 2 days. Serve over vanilla ice cream.

Note. The sauce will keep, tightly covered, for months.

FRESH STRAWBERRY SAUCE

This sauce owes nothing to microwave cooking; but it will be good with many of your microwave-prepared desserts, particularly Big City Strawberry Shortcake (page 414). Serve on the side in a pitcher. Raspberry Sauce can be made by substituting raspberries for the strawberries and whirring in a food processor or blender. Strain, if desired. *Makes 1 cup*

1 pint strawberries,
   hulled and mashed
   with a silver fork

½ teaspoon fresh lemon
   juice
2 tablespoons granulated
   sugar

Combine all ingredients well and allow to macerate for at least 5 minutes before serving.

CRÉME ANGLAISE

I could call this Custard Sauce, but it seems so French to me that it would be in disguise in English. A little Créme Anglaise seems to go with every dessert that isn't frozen.

Poached fruit—pears, plums, and peaches—chocolate mousse and un-iced cakes all enjoy this pairing. The flavor can be varied by substituting rum, triple sec, or another alcohol for the vanilla extract. *Makes 2½ cups*

2 cups milk	**¼ cup granulated sugar**
6 egg yolks	**1 teaspoon vanilla extract**

1. Heat milk in a 4-cup glass measure, uncovered, at 100% for 3 minutes. Remove from oven.

2. Whisk together egg yolks and sugar. Gradually whisk hot milk into egg mixture. Return mixture to 4-cup measure. Cook, uncovered, at 100% for 2 minutes.

3. Remove from oven and whisk vigorously for 30 seconds. Return to oven and cook for 1 minute longer.

4. Remove from oven. Whisk in vanilla extract. Strain sauce through a fine sieve into a clean bowl. Refrigerate, tightly covered, until ready to use.

To make 1 cup. Halve all ingredients, cooking milk and egg mixture for only 1 minute 30 seconds. Remove from oven, whisk in vanilla extract, strain, and cover.

Sweet Basics

There are some sweet things that are not desserts on their own, or accompaniments to desserts. They are parts of desserts. Quick and easy to make in the microwave oven, they permit you to invent your own combinations. See the Index for additional icings, fillings, glazes, toppings and syrups.

PASTRY CREAM

Filling cream puffs, or forming a thin layer under fruit in large or individual tarts, Pastry Cream is widely used. See Sweet Tart Pastry (page 442) and Apricot Glaze (page 444), which is used to brush the raw fruit. It can be flavored by flavoring the milk as it heats, as in the variations that follow.

Do not try to freeze and defrost. It takes longer to defrost than to make from scratch. Also, Pastry Cream made with cornstarch loses some thickening when frozen and defrosted. *Makes 2½ cups*

2 cups milk	6 egg yolks
6 tablespoons granulated sugar	2 teaspoons vanilla extract
2 tablespoons cornstarch	

1. Heat milk in a 4-cup glass measure, uncovered, at 100% for 4 minutes. Remove from oven and set aside.

2. Sift together sugar and cornstarch. Whisk into egg yolks. Gradually whisk in hot milk. Return mixture to 4-cup measure and cook, uncovered, at 100% for 2 minutes.

3. Remove from oven and whisk vigorously. Return to oven and cook for 1 minute longer.

4. Remove from oven and whisk in vanilla extract. Strain through a fine sieve into a clean bowl. Refrigerate, tightly covered, until ready to use.

VARIATIONS

CHOCOLATE PASTRY CREAM When whisking in vanilla, also whisk in 3 ounces of chopped bittersweet chocolate.

COFFEE PASTRY CREAM When heating milk, add 1½ tablespoons instant coffee or espresso.

RASPBERRY CREAM Instead of whisking in vanilla, stir in 3 tablespoons good raspberry jam and 2 tablespoons framboise (raspberry brandy).

ORANGE PASTRY CREAM Use only 1½ cups milk. When whisking milk into egg-yolk mixture, add ½ cup orange juice. For vanilla, substitute 2 tablespoons triple sec and the grated zest of 1 large orange.

ALMOND PASTRY CREAM Substitute an equal quantity of amaretto or almond extract for the vanilla. At the same time, stir in ¼ cup Praline Powder (page 448).

CRUMB CRUSTS

Most crusts do not cook well in the microwave oven—they do not color and are heavy—but crumb crust, which implies precooked flour, does just fine. Fill with your favorite mixtures, or with Lemon Curd (page 446). If filling with a precooked mixture, first cook Crumb Crust, uncovered, at 100% for 2 minutes; let it cool completely before filling. *Makes 1½ cups, enough for one 8-inch or 9-inch crust*

PUMPERNICKEL CRUST

1 cup fine, dry dark Pumpernickel Crumbs (page 355)
¼ cup coarsely ground almonds
½ ounce bittersweet chocolate, grated
¼ cup granulated sugar
4 tablespoons unsalted butter, melted

MELBA TOAST CRUST

1 cup melba toast crumbs
¼ cup granulated sugar
Grated zest of ½ orange

Grated zest of ½ lemon
4 tablespoons unsalted butter, melted

GRAHAM CRACKER CRUST

1 cup graham cracker crumbs
¼ cup granulated sugar
Grated zest of 1 orange
¼ teaspoon ground ginger
4 tablespoons unsalted butter, melted

Combine ingredients and mix well. Press firmly over bottom and on sides of an 8-inch to 9-inch glass pie plate.

SWEET TART PASTRY

Because of the high proportion of sugar, this crust cooks well and will tan, if not brown. It is a classic tart shell to fill with a Pastry Cream (page 441), a layer of fruit, and a light topping of Apricot Glaze (page 444).

If you want to roll out several at one time, do. Then freeze in disposable pie tins. Stack when frozen. When needed, remove frozen crust to microwave-safe pie plate. Bake frozen exactly as for fresh crust. *Makes enough pastry for one 9-inch tart shell or four 4½ inch tartlets*

2 cups all-purpose flour	Grated zest of 1 lemon
¾ cup granulated sugar	2 eggs, lightly beaten
Pinch kosher salt	1 tablespoon ice water
10 tablespoons unsalted butter, cut into ½-inch pieces	2 tablespoons milk (optional)

1. Sift together flour, sugar, and salt. Cut in butter until mixture is mealy, or process briefly in a food processor with on/off pulses until mixture is like oatmeal.

2. Add zest, eggs, and water and stir just until dough can be gathered into a ball. Do not overmix. Wrap in plastic and chill 30 minutes before using.

3. Lightly flour work surface. Roll pastry ⅛ inch thick. Fit into tart mold—try to avoid stretching dough as you work with it. Chill dough in mold for 15 minutes. If desired, brush with milk. The finished crust will have more shine, but may be a little tougher.

4. Cook, uncovered, at 100% until pastry looks quite dry, about 4 minutes for a 9-inch tart, or 2 minutes to 2 minutes 30 seconds for 4 tartlets.

5. Remove from oven. Let cool 2 minutes. Remove from mold(s) and let cool completely on a wire rack.

PUFF PASTRY

Microwave-baked puff pastry will not brown and therefore should be served in conjunction with brightly colored fruits and vegetables. It does rise impressively high whether you make it yourself or, in haste, use store-bought. Don't over-cook or it will crumble on you. There are so many books with wonderful, if long, recipes for puff pastry that one is not included here. What follows are instructions for baking squares and shells made from defrosted frozen puff pastry. *Serves 4*

4 squares (3″ × ⅛″)
    defrosted frozen puff
    pastry, each square
    pricked 5 times with
    a fork

1. Place pastry squares evenly spaced around the inside rim of a 12-inch round platter. Cook, uncovered, at 100% for 6 minutes. If you are using a small oven, cook for 9 minutes.

2. Remove from oven. Split crosswise and serve warm or at room temperature with Pastry Cream (page 439) and fresh raspberries.

To make 8 squares. Prick 8 squares and place around the inside rim of a 12″ × 10″ × ½″ platter. Cook for 8 minutes.

To make 2 squares. Prick 2 squares and place on a 10-inch pie plate. Cook for 2 minutes 30 seconds. (If you are using a small oven, cook for 4 minutes 30 seconds.)

VARIATION

PUFF PASTRY SHELLS Place 4 frozen puff pastry shells around the inside rim of a 12-inch platter. Cook, uncovered, at 100% for 8 minutes. (If you are using a small oven, place shells on a 10-inch pie plate and cook for 14 minutes.) To make 2 shells, place shells on a 10-inch pie plate and cook at 100% for 3 minutes 30 seconds. (If you are using a small oven, cook for 5 minutes 30 seconds.)

APRICOT GLAZE

While apricot jam can be briefly heated in the microwave oven and then put through a sieve, homemade glaze is better. The kitchen smells wonderful while it is cooking.   *Makes 1½ cups*

1 pound ripe apricots (about 7), halved and pitted

2 tablespoons fresh lemon juice
1 cup granulated sugar
¼ cup water

1. Place apricots in an 8-cup glass measure. Stir in lemon juice, sugar, and water. Cover tightly with microwave plastic wrap. Cook at 100% for 10 minutes.

2. Remove from oven and pierce plastic with the tip of a sharp knife. Uncover and pass through medium disc of food mill. Place a fine sieve over a clean 8-cup glass measure and pass purée through sieve. Cook, uncovered, at 100% for 12 minutes more.

3. Remove from oven. Uncover and let stand until cool. Pour into a jar with a lid and refrigerate tightly covered. To use, heat, uncovered, at 100% for 2 minutes.

VARIATION

APRICOT-LEMON GLAZE Increase lemon juice by ¼ cup, increase sugar by 2 tablespoons, and omit water.

See also Coffee Glaze (page 423).

TART APRICOT PURÉE

Use this tart purée to make Danish and other sweet pastries, or stir 1 cup into the base mixture for 1 quart of vanilla ice cream and freeze. *Makes 1½ cups purée*

8 ounces dried apricots (about 1½ cups)
1½ cups water
1 piece (2 inches) vanilla bean

2 tablespoons granulated sugar
2 tablespoons fresh lemon juice

1. Combine apricots, water, vanilla bean, and sugar in a 4-cup glass measure. Cover tightly with microwave plastic wrap. Cook at 100% for 7 minutes.

2. Remove from oven. Uncover, drain apricots, and discard vanilla bean.

3. Pour into the workbowl of a food processor, add lemon juice, and purée until smooth, about 1 minute.

SWEET APRICOT PURÉE

This easy-to-make purée can be kept on hand for use as a soufflé base, Bavarian cream flavoring, or filling between cake layers. Try ½ cup stirred into Pastry Cream (page 439). See Apricot Tea Cake (page 412). This purée is even good as jam. *Makes ¾ cup*

3 ounces dried apricots (about ½ cup)
½ cup water
¼ cup granulated sugar
1 piece (2 inches) vanilla bean

2 tablespoons fresh lemon juice
2 teaspoons grated lemon zest

1. Combine all ingredients in a 2-cup glass measure. Cover tightly with microwave plastic wrap. Cook at 100% for 6 minutes.

2. Remove from oven. Uncover and discard vanilla bean.

3. Pour into the workbowl of a food processor and purée.

VARIATION

SPICY AND CHUNKY APRICOT JAM Add 3 quarter-size pieces of peeled fresh ginger to apricots as they cook. Remove along with vanilla bean. After removing from food processor, stir in ¼ cup chopped blanched almonds or macadamia nuts.

LEMON CURD

Serve with berries, pound cake, toast, or a Crumb Crust (page 441), where it can be topped with meringue and briefly broiled to make a superior lemon meringue pie. Use as filling in Lemon Layer Cake (page 414). Put into tartlets made with Sweet Tart Pastry (page 442) and top with sliced berries. *Makes 1 cup*

¼ pound unsalted butter	**Grated zest of 1 lemon**
½ cup granulated sugar	**3 eggs**
4 tablespoons fresh lemon juice	

1. Place butter, sugar, juice, and zest together in a 4-cup glass measure. Cover tightly with microwave plastic wrap. Cook at 100% for 4 minutes.

2. Remove from oven, uncover and stir well.

3. Whisk ¼ cup of lemon mixture into the eggs to warm them. Whisking constantly, pour egg mixture back into remaining lemon mixture.

4. Cook, uncovered, at 100% for 2 minutes. Remove from oven and whisk until smooth. Cook for 2 minutes longer.

5. Remove from oven and immediately pour into the workbowl of a food processor. Process for 30 seconds until smooth. Cool before serving.

GANACHE

This is the classic, smooth chocolate that glazes cakes in the best French tradition. The cake is placed on a cooling rack over a large plate and the glaze is poured over it and allowed to flow down the sides. It is important to remember not to touch it once it is poured on the cake, or it will not stay shiny. Many of the chocolate truffles in the world are simply leftover Ganache, chilled and formed with a melon baller before being rolled in cocoa. See Chocolate Truffles (page 434) for another version. *Makes 2 cups*

1 cup heavy cream

8 ounces good-quality semisweet chocolate, grated (about 1¼ cups)

1. Heat cream in a 4-cup glass measure, uncovered, at 100% for 2 minutes 30 seconds.

2. Remove from oven. Add chocolate, stirring until melted and mixture is smooth.

CARAMEL

This is the hard-crack caramel that is often allowed to harden in a thin transparent disc on an oiled cookie sheet. This thin disc is scored into pie wedges before it cools and the wedges arranged on top of cakes like dobosh torte. *Makes ½ cup*

½ cup granulated sugar **¼ cup water**

1. Combine sugar and water in a 4-cup glass measure. Cover tightly with microwave plastic wrap. Cook at 100% for 5 minutes 30 seconds.

2. Remove from oven and pierce plastic with the tip of a sharp knife. Uncover carefully and use.

To make 1 cup. Use twice the amount of sugar and water, cooking caramel for 8 minutes.

PRALINE POWDER

Makes 8 ounces, about 1 cup

1 cup blanched almonds   ¼ **cup water**
    or hazelnuts   **Vegetable or safflower**
1 cup granulated sugar   **oil, for the cookie**
                               sheet

1. Place almonds in a single layer on a plate. Cook, uncovered, at 100% for 5 minutes, until golden. Set aside.

2. Combine sugar and water in an 8-cup glass measure. Stir thoroughly to dissolve completely. Cover tightly with microwave plastic wrap. Cook at 100% for 4 minutes.

3. Without taking measure from oven, uncover very carefully. Continue cooking, uncovered, 4 to 5 minutes longer, until golden brown. Do not stir.

4. Remove from oven. Lightly oil a cookie sheet. Add almonds to hot syrup and stir to coat. Pour onto oiled sheet all at once.

5. Allow to cool. When cool to the touch and hard, break praline into 1-inch to 2-inch pieces.

6. Put praline pieces in the workbowl of a food processor. Process only to a fine powder; do not overprocess, or powder will become a dense paste.

Note. To clean glass measure, fill with cold water and heat, uncovered, at 100% for 12 to 15 minutes. Remove from oven, pour off water. Repeat if there is still undissolved caramel stuck on measure.

VARIATION

PRALINE PASTE Continue to process Praline Powder until it becomes a dense paste. For a smoother paste, add 1 tablespoon cocoa butter and process until thoroughly incorporated.

JAMS & . . .

THESE are the grace notes, the added flourishes that I sometimes remember after the song has faded. They are jams, jellies, preserves, salsas, relishes, fruit butters, chutneys, applesauce, pickles, mustards, and the like, friends to have in the cupboard or refrigerator and to pull out as needed. They are the makings of breakfast, brunch, and afternoon tea. If I were Pennsylvania Dutch, there would be more of them; no meal would be deemed adequate without the traditional seven sweets and seven sours.

While preserves can be made out of season, it seems to me to miss the whole point—and they cost more. If you are smitten by the preserving urge in fall or winter, work with cranberries or dried fruit. Try the Fresh Mango Chutney (page 471). Make mustards and Kimchi (page 467). Wait until spring for rhubarb and strawberries, until summer for raspberries, blackberries, sour cherries, and corn.

These are not foods you need, except perhaps at Thanksgiving, Christmas, Passover, Easter. On the other hand, they are a nice afternoon's project. They make welcome hostess presents; they don't demand immediate eating. Before you start, make sure you have enough jars on hand. They might as well be attractive; that way they can go right on the table, or be lovely when the gift wrapping is torn away.

I go one step further and wrap each kind in a different bright color of tissue—Strawberry Jam in clear red, Cranberry Jelly in maroon, Peach Chutney in apricot, for example—so that when it comes time to give a gift, they are color-coded. I can pick an assortment, put them in a colorful shopping bag or into a basket, tie with a ribbon, and I am ready to go. Since I also make flavored vinegars, like raspberry, I usually include a bottle of that as well. Jars of

Spiced Mixed Nuts (page 558) are nice in the assortment, along with some of your own Chunky Tomato Sauce (page 374) or Mexican Chili Sauce (page 375).

Sterilizing jars in the microwave oven is unsatisfactory, I am told by the health experts. This is one time when I listen. I sterilize the jars on top of the stove while I am cooking. I proceed to put up in classic fashion following the instructions of the jar manufacturers.

Jellies and Preserves

I may have fantasies about being an old-fashioned cook making everything from scratch; but, sadly, they just are not true. My breads are more often bought than baked, and I resort to cans and jars more than I might like. I grow herbs and vegetables, but I cannot bear to raise chickens. I am redeemed from my own obloquy by rows of translucent jars lined up in a shallow, nineteenth-century jelly cupboard. They contain summer's fruits, some from my own trees, some bought. I make jams, jellies, preserves, fruit syrups to pour over pancakes and waffles, and dense, spicy apple, peach, and apricot butters.

Technically, preserves are everything you put up for keeping. I use the word in its other sense, as a preparation that retains the shape of the whole fruit. In a jam, the fruit is squashed. In a jelly, you really don't sense the fruit except as a flavor. Fruit butters are thick and savory, but they don't jell. Syrups pour.

I find I don't need to make huge quantities. This way I can put up the fruit as it ripens or gets picked. Making preserves becomes a little bit of cooking rather than a major chore. By the time the last bits of fall fruit have been added—a few jars made here, a few jars made there—it adds up to a handsome collection and gives more variety. I use small jars, 4 to 6 ounces. That way I don't have to eat the same preserve every day or risk having them go bad once opened. Small jars also make more charming presents in an assortment.

If opened or unopened preserves crystallize, open the jar and put it in the microwave oven for 1 minute at 100% and it will smooth out.

Chunky Blueberry Sauce (page 435) is somewhere between a preserve and syrup (sauce). It is worth putting up. Your own favorite recipes can also be adapted for the microwave oven by following the recipes with respect to cooking times and proportions of fruit to sugar.

Jellies and preserves are made quickly and cleanly in the microwave oven. I don't use any pectin because I don't like preserves to be too hard, and all the ones I tried jelled satisfactorily when cooked according to these recipes. I find that using a thermometer does not tell much. Instead, I have a simple test. To check jelly for the proper consistency, place a small amount on a plate and put in the freezer until well chilled. If a spoon pulled through the jelly leaves a wide track, it is ready. If it is not yet jelled, put it back, uncovered, in the microwave oven for 5 minutes at a time, testing after each 5 minutes. Place in sterilized jars and seal according to jar manufacturer's instructions, or refrigerate. If you want to seal your jelly with paraffin, it must be melted in the conventional oven or on top of the stove in a double boiler; microwaves pass right through it.

Many people don't like or cannot digest the tiny seeds in berries. They will be happier making the jams that have been put through a food mill. Some may want to go so far as to put the jam through a fine sieve after it comes out of the food mill.

The amounts of sugar and lemon juice in the recipes are not absolute. They will depend on the sweetness of the fruit and your palate. Don't play around too much, or you may upset the jelling. I don't like my jams and preserves too sweet. Europeans tend to like them sweeter than Americans. If you like them very sweet, add ¼ cup sugar for each 1 cup used below.

Because of the heat and steam in cooking jam, be sure to use large enough pieces of plastic wrap to cover. On 14″ × 11″ × 2″ dishes, use 2 pieces of overlapping wrap, lengthwise. To stir, use the technique of cutting a slit with the tip of a sharp knife through the plastic; stir with a wooden spoon, making sure to scrape the bottom of the dish to get any undissolved sugar. Patch with a piece of plastic that amply overlaps the slit. If you remove plastic, be careful, because the sugar-steam is hot. Re-cover as above.

To stir, slit plastic wrap.　　Stir through slit in wrap.

Patch plastic wrap with
fresh square to make
tight seal.

STRAWBERRY PRESERVES

Wait until you smell these preserves some cold winter's morning. You will become a preserving convert. Strawberry Preserves should be made in season from fully ripe fruit that is not huge. Berries that are 1 inch or smaller are best; don't use bad or mushy berries. I prefer the dark Fairfax berries, which are very fragrant. You get less preserves from the same amount of strawberries as raspberries—there is more air in a box of strawberries and strawberries contain more water. *Makes 1½ cups*

4 cups strawberries,
　wiped clean,
　stemmed and hulled

1 to 1¼ cups granulated
　sugar
2 teaspoons fresh lemon
　juice

1. Toss together berries and sugar in a 2-quart soufflé dish. Let stand for 5 minutes. Cover tightly with microwave plastic wrap. Cook at 100% for 10 minutes. Uncover and stir well. Re-cover and cook at 100% for 10 to 15 minutes longer, until very thick.

2. Remove from oven. Uncover and stir in lemon juice. Divide preserves among sterilized jars. Seal with ⅛ inch of melted paraffin, if desired.

To make 3 cups. Double quantities of ingredients. Cook in a 14″ × 11″ × 2″ dish. Cook 15 minutes; stir; cook 15 minutes; uncover; stir; cook 20 minutes, or until very thick.

VARIATION

STRAWBERRY JAM Make preserves. After final cooking, pass the mixture through a food mill fitted with the medium disc. Finish as for preserves.

Use a food mill when making jams to remove seeds, skin and pits from the fruit.

RHUBARB-STRAWBERRY JAM

I like this tarter version of Strawberry Jam. The strawberry flavor still dominates, and the jam is a little lighter in color. Don't worry about stringing the rhubarb. Just remove any strings that really get in your way while slicing. If the jam seems stringy once it's cooked, pass through a food mill fitted with a medium disc. This can be made into a very good pie filling (see variation). *Makes 4 cups*

1 pound rhubarb, washed, trimmed and cut into ¼-inch diagonal slices	1 pint strawberries, wiped clean, stemmed and hulled
	2½ cups granulated sugar

1. Combine all ingredients in a 2½-quart soufflé dish. Cover tightly with microwave plastic wrap. If your oven does not have a carousel, place soufflé dish on a large plate. Cook at 100% for 10 minutes. Uncover and cook for 10 minutes longer. If any liquid bubbles out of the dish during cooking, simply scrape off of carousel or plate back into dish at end of cooking.

2. Remove from oven. Divide jam among sterilized jars. Seal with ⅛ inch of melted paraffin, if desired.

VARIATION

RHUBARB-STRAWBERRY PIE FILLING Make jam, reducing final cooking time to 6 minutes uncovered. Add 2½ tablespoons tapioca, cover tightly, and cook for 4 minutes longer. Pour into baked Sweet Tart Pastry (page 442) or a Crumb Crust (page 441). Cover with meringue or whipped cream, if desired.

RED RASPBERRY JAM

Raspberries are too fragile to really hold their shape when cooked, and so can't be made into preserves. I don't put the jam through a food mill, but most people like at least some of the seeds removed, so I tell you to put it through a food mill. If you really want to get all the seeds out, you will then have to put it through a fine sieve.

The smaller amount of sugar produces a fairly tart jam. If you like yours sweeter, use the larger amount.

Raspberry jam is useful for baking as well as for breakfast. It is a wonderful clear red. To melt for baking, open a 6-ounce jar of raspberry jam that has been strained. Stir in 2 teaspoons framboise or triple sec or water. Place open jar in center of microwave oven. Heat at 100% for 30 seconds. Stir and use.

Black raspberries hold their shape better than red raspberries and so can be made into preserves. Follow the variation for Black Raspberry Jam, but do not put it through the food mill. This will be less tart than Red Raspberry Jam. *Makes 4 cups*

8 cups red raspberries   **2 to 2½ cups granulated sugar**

1. Combine berries and sugar in a $14'' \times 11'' \times 2''$ dish. Cover tightly with microwave plastic wrap. Cook at 100% for 15 minutes. Uncover and stir well. Re-cover and cook for 15 minutes longer. Uncover and stir once more. Cook, uncovered, for 15 minutes longer.

2. Remove from oven. Pass through the fine disc of a food mill. Divide among sterilized jars. Seal with ⅛ inch of melted paraffin, if desired.

To make 2 cups. Halve all ingredients. Combine berries and sugar in a 2-quart soufflé dish and let stand for 5 minutes. Cook for 10 minutes. Uncover and cook for 8 to 10 minutes longer, until thick.

VARIATION

BLACK RASPBERRY JAM Substitute an equal amount black raspberries for red raspberries and proceed as for Red Raspberry jam. Stir in 4 teaspoons fresh lemon juice after final cooking. To make 1½ cups, proceed as for 2 cups Red Raspberry Jam, using black raspberries instead of red raspberries. Add 2 teaspoons fresh lemon juice after final cooking.

SOUR CHERRY PRESERVES

I have two dwarf cherry trees with perfectly round crowns. Studded with pink-white blooms in the spring and round, light red fruits in early summer, they look like a child's drawing. My only problem is that the birds usually decide that the fruit is ripe just before I do. I have had to resort to shrouding at least one tree in bird netting and crawling up under the net to pick. Fortunately, there is lots of fruit and it is easy to pick.

This is the kind of preserve you can't buy. It is made with whole Montmorency cherries. I often bottle it with the pits in. Then, it is a pink-red jelly with glints of orange, with the fruit trapped in it. It is very beautiful. I don't mind spitting the pits out as I eat; but this is not for everyone. If you put it through a food mill, you will get a smaller amount of a cross between jam and jelly. It won't be clear, but is still beautiful.

The tart-sweet flavor is good with cheese. Try a mild, soft goat cheese instead of cream cheese. *Makes 2 to 2½ cups*

4 cups sour cherries	**2 tablespoons fresh**
1 cup granulated sugar	**lemon juice**

1. Combine cherries and sugar in an 8-cup glass measure. Cover tightly with microwave plastic wrap. Cook at 100% for 10 minutes. Uncover and stir well. Re-cover and cook for 10 minutes longer.

2. Remove from oven. Uncover and skim. Test consistency (page 451). When jelled, stir in lemon juice.

3. Divide preserves among sterilized jars. Seal with ⅛ inch of melted paraffin, if desired.

VARIATION

SOUR CHERRY JELLY Make Sour Cherry Preserves. After final cooking, pass through the medium disc of a food mill. If the jelly is still not as clear as you like it, pass through a sieve. You will have about 1¾ cups after passing through the food mill, and 1¼ cups after passing through the sieve.

CURRANT JELLY

The red stuff you buy in jars never seems to taste like currants, but rather like sugar and pectin tinted red, which is how I suspect it is made. It's a shame. Currants have a delicious, fresh, acid flavor. If you can buy them in season, or have a few bushes, you can keep that flavor in a brilliant jelly that is traditionally served with meat, particularly game, as well as with toast or in baked goods.

The most tedious part of cooking or serving currants is stripping the tiny berries from their tiny stems. With this method you don't need to. You cook the berries in bunches. All you have to do is rinse them first. Currants are hard to pick, but even I can manage a quart. *Makes 2 cups*

4 cups fresh currants, with stems	1¼ cups granulated sugar

1. Combine currants and sugar in an 8-cup glass measure. Cover tightly with microwave plastic wrap. Cook at 100% for 5 minutes. Without taking dish from oven, uncover and stir, wiping down insides with a damp cloth to prevent sugar from crystallizing. Cook, uncovered, at 100% for 10 minutes longer. Test consistency (page 451).

2. Pass jelly through the fine disc of a food mill to remove stems and seeds. If you like a clearer jelly, pass through a double thickness of dampened cheesecloth.

3. Divide among sterilized jars. Seal with ⅛ inch of melted paraffin, if desired.

APPLE JELLY

This is a beautiful, clear, naturally red jelly. It makes the perfect base for Hot Pepper Jelly or Apple Mint Jelly. For the latter, you will use green-skinned apples instead of red for a more appropriate color. Mint jelly is traditional with roast lamb. Hot Pepper Jelly has become popular because of the southwestern food craze. I like it with toast and cream cheese, but I think most people use it with meat.

At the end, you will have a nice dividend of 3 cups of applesauce. *Makes 2 cups*

3 pounds McIntosh or other tart red apples, quartered	3 cups granulated sugar 1 lemon, quartered and seeds removed

1. Combine all ingredients in a 9½″ × 5½″ round dish. Cover tightly with microwave plastic wrap. Cook at 100% for 20 minutes.

2. Remove from oven. Uncover and pass through the fine disc of a food mill. Strain jelly through a double thickness of dampened cheesecloth. Reserve pulp and use as applesauce (you will have about 3 cups). Place jelly in a clean 3-quart dish. Cook, uncovered, at 100% for 25 minutes, or until jelled.

3. Remove from oven. Divide among sterilized jars and seal with ⅛ inch of melted paraffin, if desired.

VARIATIONS

HOT PEPPER JELLY Make Apple Jelly, adding 15 dried hot chili peppers for the final 5 minutes of cooking time. Strain through a sieve.

APPLE MINT JELLY Substitute equal amount Greening or Granny Smith apples for McIntosh apples. Add ⅔ cup (packed) coarsely chopped mint leaves for final 3 minutes of cooking time. Strain through a sieve.

PLUM JAM

I am surprised people don't make more Plum Jam because it is delicious. To quarter the plums, cut all the way around the circumference to the pit, them twist apart. Cook with pits, which add natural pectin and flavor. They will separate out in the food mill.

The color and flavor of the jam will depend on the plums used. Dark-skinned plums will give you a bright red, prune plums a softer rose color. Greengage jam will be green. If you find those little gold-yellow plums called mirabelles, cook them for 12 minutes. The jam will be a wonderful golden color and smell like honey. *Makes 2 cups*

1½ pounds red plums, washed and quartered	¾ cup granulated sugar

1. Combine plums and sugar in an 8-cup glass measure. Cover tightly with microwave plastic wrap. Cook at 100% for 10 minutes.

2. Remove from oven. Uncover and stir, scraping the bottom of the measure to get any undissolved sugar.

3. Pass plums through a food mill fitted with a medium disc. Return to glass measure. Cook, uncovered, at 100% for 3 minutes.

4. Remove from oven. Divide among sterilized jars. Seal with ⅛ inch of melted paraffin, if desired.

APPLESAUCE

Applesauce can be a dessert. It can also go on potato pancakes or make a side dish with roast loin of pork. Fresh is so much better than canned or jarred. Make it as you need it. Made with red-skinned apples, it will have a lovely rosy color. There are two other easy ways to come by Applesauce: as a variation of Apple Butter (see following recipe) and as a dividend in making Apple Jelly (page 457).

One reason to use this recipe is that you don't add the sugar until step 4. That lets you taste and use less sugar if you want. You could even use a sugar substitute. To make Applesauce with other apple varieties, see timings in Dictionary. *Makes 3 cups*

6 **Granny Smith or McIntosh apples**	**Pinch ground nutmeg**
Fresh lemon juice, for rubbing apples	**Pinch ground allspice**
1 **cup granulated sugar**	2 **tablespoons unsalted butter**

1. Core the apples and peel a 1½-inch strip around the top. Rub cut surfaces with lemon juice. Wrap each apple loosely in a square of microwave plastic wrap, twisting the ends to make a tight seal. Arrange in a ring on a platter and cook at 100% for 9 minutes.

2. Remove from oven. Pierce plastic with the tip of a sharp knife and drape apples with a clean towel. Let stand for 5 minutes.

3. Unwrap apples over the workbowl of a food processor, to catch any juices. Process until smooth.

4. Scrape into a 4-cup glass measure and add remaining ingredients. Cook, uncovered, at 100% for 2 minutes.

5. Remove from oven. Let stand until cool. Store, tightly covered and refrigerated, for up to a week.

To make 1½ cups. Halve ingredients. Cook apples for 4 minutes. Cook applesauce for 1 minute.

VARIATION

HORSERADISH APPLESAUCE Make 1½ cups Applesauce. Do not add seasonings or butter. When sweetened applesauce is cold, stir in ¼ cup bottled horseradish sauce. Serve chilled with boiled beef or Smoked Tongue (page 269).

*Wrap each apple
individually and arrange
in a ring for even
cooking.*

APPLE BUTTER

I remember making apple butter on Indian day at summer camp. It was a long process and there was always the risk of scorching the apple butter as it reduced itself to a dark brown pulp. To be authentic, we used maple syrup because the Indians didn't have refined sugar. I didn't like it much and I was discouraged by the amount of stirring required.

The microwave oven changes all that—almost no stirring and it is quickly done. I substitute sugar, part white and part light brown, for the maple syrup. It gives it more apple flavor. If you want to be authentic, use ¾ cup maple syrup instead of the sugars, but it will be sweeter.

Apple Butter has a pleasant spiciness, and it can be used as a relish with pork or venison.   *Makes 2 cups*

1½ pounds McIntosh or Greening apples, quartered	½ cinnamon stick or ½ teaspoon ground cinnamon
½ cup (lightly packed) dark brown sugar	3 whole allspice berries
½ cup granulated sugar	3 whole cloves
	Pinch freshly ground nutmeg

1. Combine all ingredients in an 11″ × 8½″ × 4″ dish. Cover tightly with microwave plastic wrap. Cook at 100% for 15 minutes.

2. Remove from oven. Uncover and pass through the medium disc of a food mill. Return to dish. Cook, uncovered, at 100% for 10 minutes longer.

3. Remove from oven. If you want a smoother butter, pass through the fine disc of a food mill.

4. Pack in sterile jars, or let stand until cool and store, tightly covered and refrigerated, for up to 2 months.

To make 4 cups. Double amount of apples and sugar. Use 1 stick cinnamon or ¼ teaspoon ground cinnamon, 6 allspice berries, 5 cloves, and ¼ teaspoon nutmeg. Cook in a 14″ × 11″ × 2″ dish for 20 minutes. Pass through food mill and cook for 10 minutes longer.

VARIATION

APPLESAUCE Use all granulated sugar instead of half dark brown sugar. Do not cook for the final time after passing through the food mill. You will have a little more Applesauce than you would have Apple Butter.

PEACH BUTTER

Lighter in color and more sophisticated than the Apple Butter, this can be served as a jam, or used as a relish with grilled fish or chicken. *Makes 2 cups*

1½ pounds peaches, washed, pitted and quartered	1 cup granulated sugar
	½ teaspoon cinnamon
	4 whole cloves
½ cup water	¼ teaspoon mace
1 tablespoon cider vinegar	1 piece (2 inches) vanilla bean

1. Combine all ingredients in a 2-quart soufflé dish. Cover tightly with microwave plastic wrap. Cook at 100% for 10 minutes.

2. Remove from oven. Uncover and pass through the fine disc of a food mill. Return to soufflé dish. Cook, uncovered, at 100% for 5 minutes.

3. Remove from oven. Let stand until cool. Store, tightly covered and refrigerated, for up to 2 months.

To make 4 cups. Double all ingredients, cooking in a 14″ × 11″ × 2″ dish for 15 minutes. Pass through food mill and cook, uncovered, for 7 minutes 30 seconds longer.

QUINCE PASTE

A Viennese specialty called Quittenkase, this is a translucent sweet that jells hard enough to mold and then slice. It is usually served as dessert, like the South American guava paste that is made the same way. Small slices can accompany cream cheese or a mild goat cheese, and it's a nice addition to brunch. Almost all ordinary preserves made with quinces turn a light reddish-pink. This cooks so quickly in the microwave oven that it stays gold. If you store it, tightly wrapped in two layers of plastic wrap and refrigerated, it will change color with time. *Makes 4 cups*

2½ pounds quinces, washed and quartered	½ lemon, cut into wedges
	2 cups granulated sugar

1. Combine quinces and lemon in an 8-cup glass measure. Cover tightly with microwave plastic wrap. Cook at 100% for 10 minutes.

2. Remove from oven. Uncover and remove all pieces of quince that can be easily pierced with the tip of a sharp knife. Re-cover dish and cook for 5 minutes longer.

3. Remove from oven. Uncover and stir in sugar. Pass through the fine disc of a food mill.

4. Scrape mixture into an 11″ × 8½″ × 2″ dish. Cook, uncovered, at 100% for 15 minutes, stirring once or twice.

5. Remove from oven. Pour into one or more glass or ceramic molds or bowls. Let stand until cool. Store, tightly covered and refrigerated, for up to 2 months.

VARIATION

GUAVA PASTE Substitute an equal quantity of guavas for quinces and proceed as for Quince Paste.

Relishes &...

Relishes, pickles, savory jellies, and chutneys are meant to introduce a meal or go with the main course. They are not breakfast food. Often they are quite chunky or contain whole fruits or vegetables. Almost every cuisine seems to have characteristic dishes like this. Think of ketchup. Today, it is smooth tomato stuff out of a bottle, but there used to be mushroom ketchups, walnut, and the like.

Pickled black walnuts, cornichons, and many other kinds of standard pickles can be made if you have access to the ingredients. I didn't. Onions à la Monégasque (page 45), Onions in Barbecue Sauce (page 307), and Saffron Onions (page 46) can be put up and eaten as relishes.

BEET AND APPLE RELISH

This quickly made relish has crunch from the apples and color and sweetness from the beets. It is good with fish or pork. *Makes 4 cups*

¾ pound beets, rinsed and stems removed

½ Granny Smith or Greening apple, peeled, cored, and cut into ¼-inch to ½-inch dice

⅓ cup chopped yellow onion

2 tablespoons cider vinegar

½ teaspoon kosher salt

1 tablespoon granulated sugar

Pinch freshly ground black pepper

1. Wrap beets individually in microwave plastic wrap. Arrange in a circle in oven. Cook at 100% for 10 minutes.

2. Remove from oven. Unwrap over a bowl to catch juices. Slip off beet skins and cut into ¼-inch to ½-inch cubes.

3. Combine beets with remaining ingredients in a 4-cup glass measure. Cover tightly with microwave plastic wrap. Cook at 100% for 4 minutes.

4. Remove from oven. Uncover and divide among sterilized jars, or let stand until cool and store, tightly covered. Refrigerate for up to 2 months.

CRANBERRY SAUCE

Come Thanksgiving, I need a surefire recipe for a glistening cranberry mold. They don't get better, quicker, or easier than this one. *Makes 2 cups*

1 bag (12 ounces) fresh or frozen cranberries

1 cup granulated sugar

½ cup cranberry juice

Pinch kosher salt

1. Combine all ingredients in an 8-cup glass measure. Cook, uncovered, at 100% for 10 minutes.

2. Remove from oven. Rinse a 2-quart soufflé dish with cold water. Pour Cranberry Sauce into dish. Refrigerate, loosely covered, for 4 to 6 hours, until firm. Run a knife around edge of dish and unmold onto a serving platter.

VARIATION

CHUNKY CRANBERRY NUT SAUCE Add ½ cup coarsely chopped pecans and segments from 1 orange zest and pith removed, cooking for 12 minutes.

MAPLE CORN RELISH

I can eat this by the spoonful; but it really is made to go with hamburgers, grilled steak, meat loaf, ribs, broiled fish, or fried chicken, the picnic and barbecue foods. While it is by far best with fresh corn, if you run out in winter and crave a batch, it can be made with vacuum-packed canned corn niblets. In spite of the hot peppers, this is only mildly spiced. *Makes 4 cups*

1½ cups fresh corn kernels (from 3 ears) or canned niblets in water, drained

½ small green cabbage, cut into ¼-inch cubes (1½ cups)

½ cup finely chopped onion (1 small onion)

½ cup diced red bell pepper, stemmed, seeded and deribbed

½ cup diced green bell pepper, stemmed, seeded and deribbed

1 tablespoon Dijon mustard

1 cup cider vinegar

½ cup maple syrup

1½ teaspoons dry mustard

1 tablespoon kosher salt

2 teaspoons crushed hot red peppers, or 10 small dried red peppers

1 tablespoon finely chopped fresh ginger (about 6 quarter-size pieces, peeled)

4 large cloves garlic, smashed, peeled and minced

1. Combine all ingredients in a 2-quart soufflé dish (if you are using canned corn, do not add it now). Cover tightly with microwave plastic wrap. Cook at 100% for 5 minutes. Uncover; add canned corn if you are using it. Cook, uncovered, at 100% for 3 minutes longer.

2. Remove from oven. Divide among sterilized jars. Seal.

BREAD AND BUTTER PICKLES

I usually like my pickles sour, but these crunchy, sweet and sour slices are a pretty and worthwhile exception. Unlike many pickles, these can be eaten as soon as they are made. I refrigerate them because they taste better cold and crisp. *Makes 4 cups*

3 pounds small, unwaxed cucumbers (Kirbys if possible), washed, trimmed and cut into ¼-inch slices (in food processor if you want)

¾ cup sliced onions (about 1 medium onion)

1 large clove garlic, smashed and peeled

3 tablespoons kosher salt

2¼ cups granulated sugar

¾ teaspoon turmeric

¾ teaspoon celery seed

1 tablespoon mustard seed

1½ cups white vinegar

1. Combine cucumbers, onions, garlic, and salt in a large bowl. Cover with 2 trays of ice cubes or crushed ice and stir well. Let stand for 3 hours.

2. Drain cucumbers and discard liquid. Set aside.

3. Combine remaining ingredients in a 9½″ × 5½″ round dish. Cook uncovered, at 100% for 6 minutes. Add reserved cucumber mixture. Cover tightly with microwave plastic wrap. Cook at 100% for 12 minutes.

4. Remove from oven. Uncover and divide among sterilized jars. Seal.

KIMCHI

I've never had a Korean meal that didn't include these pickled winter vegetables. Sometimes the Kimchi is red in color. I prefer this pale, not overly spicy version. In Korea, they used to bury the crocks of Kimchi in the ground to keep it cold while it fermented. This recipe is not that authentic, but it smells a lot better. I like it with French foods like pâté, with cold sliced meat, or as part of a mixed hors d'oeuvre. You have to start this the day before you put it up to let the cabbage soak and wilt.   *Makes 4 cups*

1½ pounds Chinese
 turnip (daikon
 radish may be
 substituted), peeled
¼ cup kosher salt
1 cup water
1½ pounds Chinese
 cabbage, washed
 and cut across the
 vein into 1½-inch
 slices

4 large scallions, cut
 into 2-inch lengths
4 large cloves garlic,
 smashed and peeled
3 slices peeled fresh
 ginger, julienned
10 whole small dried
 chilies

1. Cut turnip across into ⅛-inch slices, using the slicing disc on the food processor.

2. Combine salt and water in a deep, non-metal dish; a medium-size crock would be perfect. Add turnip and cabbage and cover tightly with microwave plastic wrap. Let stand overnight, stirring occasionally.

3. Drain vegetables and reserve salted water.

4. Place scallions, garlic, and ginger in the workbowl of a food processor. Process until finely chopped. Add to drained vegetables and mix well.

5. Pour reserved water back into a 4-cup glass measure and cook, uncovered, at 100% for 5 minutes.

6. Remove from oven. Divide vegetables among sterilized jars. Add chilies and pour liquid over vegetables to within ½ inch of top of jar. Store, tightly covered and refrigerated, for at least 2 days before serving.

DILLY CARROTS

I'm not so fond of dilled string beans; I don't like the color they turn. Carrots, on the other hand, stay a beautiful orange and remain crisp. This is an ideal low-calorie cocktail snack. You can reuse the brine. *Makes 4 pints*

3 pounds small fresh carrots, trimmed, peeled and cut into sticks ¼″ × ¼″ across and 1 inch shorter than height of jar
1 bunch fresh dill

8 cloves garlic, smashed and peeled
1½ teaspoons hot red-pepper flakes
1½ teaspoons dried dill seed
2 cups cider vinegar
2 cups water
¼ cup kosher salt

1. Fit carrots, standing up, around the inside rim of sterilized jars, leaving a space in the center. Place 2 large dill sprigs and 1 clove garlic into the center of each jar. Set aside.

2. Combine remaining ingredients in an 8-cup glass measure. Cook, uncovered, at 100% for 6 minutes.

3. Remove from oven. Pour liquid over carrots to within ½ inch of top of jar. Set aside any extra liquid. Arrange filled jars in an evenly spaced circle—not touching— around inside rim of carousel or around inside edge of oven. Cook, uncovered, at 100% for 10 minutes.

4. Remove from oven. Pour reserved liquid into jars to cover carrots, if necessary. Store, tightly covered and refrigerated, for up to 2 months.

PICKLED PEACH RELISH

This relish has the prettiest colors, and is good and spicy, a surprise with cold meats, chicken, or fish.   *Makes 3 cups*

¼ cup cider vinegar
¼ cup granulated sugar
 2 cups peeled, chopped
    peaches (5 to 6 large
    peaches)— firm to
    medium ripe

1 cup chopped red bell
    peppers (about 1
    large pepper),
    stemmed, seeded
    and deribbed
1 fresh hot pepper,
    seeded and chopped
1 teaspoon grated peeled
    fresh ginger

   1. Stir together vinegar and sugar in an 8-cup glass measure. Cover tightly with microwave plastic wrap. Cook at 100% for 3 minutes.
   2. Remove from oven. Uncover and stir in peaches, peppers, and ginger. Cook, uncovered, at 100% for 4 to 6 minutes, until peaches are tender.
   3. Remove from oven. Pack in sterilized jars, or let stand until cool and store, tightly covered and refrigerated, for up to 2 weeks.

PEACH CHUTNEY

This is a wonderful and unusual summer chutney that is best if allowed to mature for at least one day before eating. Serve it with baked ham or roast chicken as well as curry. I also like it on a plate with tuna fish salad or egg salad and sliced tomato. *Makes 4 cups*

1 lemon, cut into ¼-inch slices, each slice quartered and seeds discarded

3 cloves garlic, smashed, peeled and quartered

1½ cups granulated sugar

½ cup raisins

½ cup whole almonds, blanched

4 slices peeled fresh ginger, cut into matchsticks

6 cardamom pods, crushed and hulls discarded

½ teaspoon hot red-pepper flakes

⅓ pound shallots, peeled

¾ cup cider vinegar

1 teaspoon black mustard seed

1 teaspoon cumin seed

1 teaspoon kosher salt

1½ pounds peaches—firm to medium ripe—trimmed, pitted and cut into 2-inch chunks

½ pound celery, trimmed, strung and sliced on the diagonal

1. Combine all ingredients except peaches and celery in a 2-quart soufflé dish. Cook, uncovered, at 100% for 5 minutes.

2. Add peaches and stir well. Cover tightly with microwave plastic wrap. Cook at 100% for 5 minutes.

3. Remove from oven. Uncover and stir in celery. Place in sterile bottles and seal, or let stand until cool and store, tightly covered and refrigerated, for up to 2 months.

FRESH MANGO CHUTNEY

This chutney can be made in midwinter. It is a classic, and good to keep on hand to go with curries, ham sandwiches, simply cooked fish, and scrambled eggs. A slightly under-ripe papaya can be substituted for the mango. Mango chutney that you can buy has so little fruit these days that it's worth making your own.   *Makes 2 cups*

1 large ripe mango, peeled and cut into ½-inch-thick slices
1 tablespoon Spice Powder III (page 346) or curry powder
¼ teaspoon celery seed
Pinch ground cloves
1 jalapeño pepper, roasted, peeled and sliced
1 teaspoon kosher salt
1 tablespoon vegetable oil

6 thin slices peeled fresh ginger
½ cup brown sugar
½ cup tomato juice
½ cup water
2 teaspoons cornstarch dissolved in ¼ cup water
2 teaspoons fresh lemon juice
1 tablespoon chopped fresh coriander
1 tablespoon chopped fresh mint

1. Stir together all ingredients except lemon juice, coriander, and mint in a 2-quart soufflé dish. Cook, uncovered, at 100% for 5 minutes. Stir well. Cook for 5 minutes longer.

2. Remove from oven. Stir in remaining ingredients. Store, tightly covered and refrigerated, for up to 2 months.

VARIATION

FRESH SPICY MANGO CHUTNEY Add 1 small yellow onion, diced; 1 small tomato, seeded and diced; 3 cloves garlic, smashed, peeled and sliced; ¼ cup slivered almonds; ¼ cup raisins, and an additional ½ tablespoon mint. Increase lemon juice to 1 tablespoon. Decrease sugar to 2 tablespoons and cornstarch to 1 teaspoon. Omit celery seed, cloves, jalapeño, tomato juice, and coriander.

DICTIONARY OF FOODS AND TECHNIQUES

COOKING in the microwave oven is different from other kinds of cooking. If you read the first chapters of this book, you will see exactly how. It is not just that cooking times are different, but also that they are dependent on the weight and dimensions of the foods. Buying a small scale and learning to use it makes a valuable ally. The way the food cooks also depends on the way you wrap it, the size of the plate (the kind you eat from) or dish (the kind you use in the microwave oven) and the amount of liquid (see pages 31–32), assorted vegetables or other ingredients cooked with the food. How it cooks even depends on the amount of fat protein, sugar, fat and water in the food.

All this will seem unfamiliar at first. If you think of it in baking terms, it may be easier to understand and accept. When you read a cake recipe, you don't begin by changing the size of the pan, the cooking time or the cooking temperature. You know that would change the results and might create disaster.

In researching the basic information for this book, I have tested as many possible basic variations for the cooking of a certain kind of food as possible. I am sharing the results with you in this Dictionary, food by food and technique by technique. These are not recipes. They are results of tests that tell you how things work.

My hope is that this Dictionary will make it possible for you to really cook in the microwave oven, not just follow recipes. I wish I had had it when I started this book. Now I have it, and I use it almost every time I cook in the microwave oven. If I want to change a recipe or make it for fewer or more people I look in the Dictionary.

For instance, if a recipe calls for 4 halves of cooked, split and boned chicken breasts, and you want to cook 8 halves of split and boned breasts, look up CHICKEN; you will find out the cooking time and what kind of container to use. Go on from there. As you can see, you can't cook the breast as you would on top of the stove for the same amount of time but in a larger container, nor can you just multiply the cooking time by two. You need the information in the Dictionary.

If you want to cook more than 8 halves, you will find there is no cooking time given. That means a larger quantity was tried but didn't cook well. *When a technique or quantity does not work, it has been omitted.* Since the cooking time for the 8 halves is only 8 minutes, do it twice for 16 half breasts. If you have a small oven and know that most of the recipes were tested in a large oven, look to page 18 to see how to modify the recipe, or look in the Dictionary. Alternate cooking times are given for small quantities of chicken in the small ovens, but no times for large quantities. This means that larger quantities are not realistic in a small oven. You can always try if you want.

When you want to make chicken stew, but none of the recipes in the book is exactly what you want, look at CHICKEN again. You will see that for a 4-pound bird you can include 1 pound of vegetables and 2 cups of liquid, that you cook in a 2-quart soufflé dish, cover tightly with microwave plastic wrap and cook at 100% for 22 minutes. You might decide to use onions, carrots and mushrooms and 1½ cups chicken broth and ½ cup cream. If you're still confused because you don't know how much the vegetables weigh, look up CARROT. Under "Yield," you will see that ½ pound of carrots equals 1½ cups of peeled, sliced raw carrots cut across into ¼-inch-thick round slices. That means you can still add ¼ pound of mushrooms and ¼ pound of onions, which the Dictionary says is ½ cup chopped.

Season as you want. If you have a question about how those seasonings will act in the microwave oven, look them up as well. If the stew is too thin when it has finished cooking, look up THICKENING or CORNSTARCH and find out what to do.

Now, I don't really have to do all that anymore. Some of it I remember; some of it I can figure out. But I probably will look up CHICKEN all the same.

More simply, let's say I want to cook artichokes for a crowd. That's not a recipe; that's a simple Dictionary cooking time and technique. I just look up ARTICHOKE and I'm in business. If there are any questions about what some of the words like "tightly wrap" mean, look in the Index for a reference, or check the general information chapters in the front of the book, complete with clear illustrations.

Cooking in the microwave oven is different, but it is well worth learning. The more you do, the less you will have to look up. If you're at all like me, this Dictionary will stay useful.

Cross-references to other entries in this Dictionary appear in SMALL CAPITAL LETTERS. Recipe titles are capitalized. All cooking times are for large ovens unless specifically stated.

A

ACORN SQUASH This delicious winter squash is better cooked in the microwave oven than any other way. The resulting squash is smooth, not fibrous. Because it cooks so rapidly in the microwave oven, you will be able to prepare it more often.

Cooked acorn squash can be a wonderful component of soups, purées and even desserts. See Acorn Squash Soup, Acorn Squash Purée and Thanksgiving Pudding. For cooking times, see SQUASH, WINTER.

ALCOHOL Many flavors used in cooking are carried in alcohol, ranging from red wine to vanilla and the other extracts, from brandy or Cognac to pastis. Alcohol, and hence the flavors it carries, volatilizes much more quickly in microwave cooking than by other means. It is therefore unnecessary to flame such high-proof alcohols as brandy when adding them to food to be cooked in the microwave oven; if this eliminates a measure of drama from cooking, it certainly adds safety. The percentage of liquor in any given recipe should be increased by one half if cooked for a short time, and doubled if cooked for more than 7 or 8 minutes.

ALLSPICE See SPICES.

ALMOND These nuts can be bought in the shell, shelled (with the skin left on) or blanched (with skin removed). They are often blanched and ground into a fine powder or paste for use in baking, curries and old recipes for soup. To grind, use a nut grater (which looks much like a rotary cheese grater) or grind in a food processor. Use a blender to make paste.

Almonds often require some preparation, such as toasting, before they can be used in a recipe, and in this the microwave oven is an invaluable helper. Seasoned, toasted almonds make a good snack with drinks. For blanching, salting, spicing and toasting, see NUTS. See also Pralines, Praline Paste and Praline Powder.

ANISEED These small seeds taste like a subtle version of licorice and are often used to flavor liquors. They are sadly underused in seasoning food. Try toasting them whole and sprinkling on chicken or veal stew or powdering them in an electric coffee mill (1 ounce of whole aniseeds will yield 4 tablespoons ground seed). See GRINDING and TOASTING.

APPLE The microwave oven bakes apples beautifully, keeping the skin a good color. It also quickly prepares apple purée,

with or without additions of butter or sugar for applesauce. See Maple-Syrup-Baked Apples.

Remember that apples will not caramelize when they are baked, but stay pale in color. They will darken with the longer cooking of Apple Butter.

COOKING TIMES FOR APPLES

Times are the same for large and medium ovens. For small ovens, add 1 minute per apple to cooking time. Core apples; peel top 1½ inches; rub cut sides with lemon; wrap, individually, airtight but loosely in microwave plastic wrap; put in a dish at least ½ inch deep.

Granny Smith apples 8 to 9 oz. each. See illustration page 34.

1 apple	*3 min. (rest, wrapped, 5 min.)*
2 apples	*3 min. 30 sec. (rest 5 min.)*
4 apples	*5 min. 15 sec. (rest 5 min.)*
6 apples	*9 min. (rest 5 min., puncture wrap and drape apples with a towel)*

McIntosh apples About 7 oz. each.

1 apple	*1 min. 45 sec.*
4 apples	*4 min.*

Rome Beauty apples About 10 oz. each.

1 apple	*2 min. 30 sec.*
4 apples	*4 min. 45 sec.*

Yields

| 4 lb. Granny Smiths | 8 c. thinly sliced apples |
| 1½ lb. apples | 2½ c. applesauce |

APRICOT The brief season for these glorious, sweet little fruits is one of early summer's delights. The rest of the year we can enjoy them dried. The dried fruit makes good jam, much used as a glaze in baking, and is the base for wonderful purées to be used in desserts like soufflés and in sauces, sweet or savory. To plump dried apricots, see SOAKING, dried fruit. See also Sweet Apricot Purée, Tart Apricot Purée and Apricot Sauce.

ARROWROOT This starch is expensive and doesn't work well for last-minute thickening in the microwave oven; replace with CORNSTARCH, BEURRE MANIE or ROUX.

ARTICHOKE Artichokes are the flowers of one of the desirable thistles; on the stem, allowed to go to seed and dried, they make spectacular dried arrangements. Globe artichokes are big, roundish, green and mature in the summer season of the area in which they are planted—July in California, December in Chile. There is another kind of artichoke, small, pointed and slightly purplish in color, that is meant to be eaten whole. See Baby Artichokes à la Grecque.

The microwave oven is a blessing for cooking artichokes. It eliminates the need for water, time (as much as half an hour), the messiness of flour in the water to minimize discoloration, the tricky business of balancing a plate on the artichokes to keep them submerged, and the dangers and mess of dealing with a large pot of boiling water when you are done with it. It turns out artichokes that are rich in vitamins, never soggy and so green that some guests may have trouble believing they are cooked. It even means that fancy recipes calling for artichoke bottoms become feasible once again. Simply let the cooked artichokes cool; pull off the leaves; scrape off the chokes with a silver spoon and rub the cleaned bottom with a cut lemon.

The procedure for cooking globe artichokes is simple. Trim the artichokes (most easily done with a serrated knife): Cut each stem flush with the bottom of the artichoke; cut 1 inch off the top of the artichoke. Neatly trim off other prickly leaf tips. Pull off any browned bottom leaves. As you work, rub all cut surfaces with lemon to keep them from discoloring. See illustration page 43.

Place each artichoke in a microwave-safe plastic bag, closing it tightly, or on a sheet of microwave plastic wrap. Fold the plastic over the artichokes to enclose them completely, and make a tight seal. Use additional sheets of microwave plastic wrap if necessary. Place in a circle on the carousel or on a large plate. Cook at 100%. With a fingernail, press the bottom of an artichoke; it should give. Remove from the oven. Let stand 5 minutes. Prick the plastic with a knife to release steam. Unwrap carefully.

4 artichokes	15 min.
6 artichokes	19 min.

Yields

8 oz. artichoke	1 oz. heart
6 average hearts	6½ oz.
6½ oz. hearts	6½ oz. purée

COOKING TIMES FOR ARTICHOKES

Baby artichokes ¾ oz. each, about 18 per lb. Remove round bottom leaves; trim leaf tips; cover tightly.

1 lb. artichokes with 2 c. broth and ¾ c. olive oil, turned once (1½-qt. soufflé)	12 min.

Small artichokes 2 oz. each. Trim as baby artichokes; cover tightly.

4 artichokes	10 min.
8 artichokes	11 min.
16 artichokes	14 min.
8 artichokes with 1¼ c. liquid, turned once (2-qt. soufflé)	13 min.

Large (globe) artichokes 8 to 12 oz. each. Wrap individually; arrange in circle on large dish.

1 artichoke	7 min.
1 artichoke	12 min. (small oven)
2 artichokes	10 min.
2 artichokes	20 min. (small oven, with carousel

ASPARAGUS Another vegetable that cooks quickly and well in the microwave oven without any water—no tying in little bunches—and that keeps its color.

Trim the asparagus by snapping off the woody ends. Peel, if desired, from just below the tip to the end with a vegetable peeler. When cooking whole spears, lay them two to three deep (pointing in the same direction) in a rectangular baking dish or on a plate. Cover tightly with microwave plastic wrap and cook at 100%.

Tips or short pieces to be cooked before incorporation in another dish should be placed, in ½-pound batches, in tightly closed microwave-safe plastic bags. Place bags in oven in a circle so that they do not touch.

However you cook asparagus, carefully unwrap it as soon as it comes out of the oven; wrapped, the asparagus will continue to steam and can overcook very quickly. If you are using the asparagus tips or pieces in a dish where they will be reheated, place them in a sieve immediately after cooking and run cold water over them to keep them firm.

COOKING TIMES FOR ASPARAGUS

Whole stalks Trim. Arrange 2 or 3 deep in a dish just large enough to hold them; cover tightly.

¼ lb.	4 min. (small oven)
½ lb.	2 min. 30 sec.
½ lb.	5 min. (small oven)
1 lb.	4 min. 15 sec.
2 lb.	7 min.

Tips and/or stalks 1″ to 2″ lengths. Put ½-lb. quantities in microwave-safe plastic bags.

½ lb.	3 min.
1 lb.	4 min. 30 sec.

Yields

1 lb. aspar-agus	3½ c. (1″ to 2″ lengths)
3½ c.	2 c. purée

AVOCADO I really don't like cooked avocados. I buy them ripe, preferably the Haas variety, and use them raw in salads and dips. If fate has brought you a hard avocado and you absolutely must use it, cut it in half lengthwise and remove the pit. Wrap each half in microwave plastic wrap and cook together in the microwave oven for 1 minute. Remove immediately from the oven; run under cold water and unwrap. The avocado will be softer, edible—but not my choice.

B

BACON Making bacon in the microwave oven is a trick most people seem to have learned, and it certainly beats cooking it in hot fat in a frying pan. The timing depends on the thickness and number of slices and how crisp you want them. Bacon made in the microwave oven stays flat—great for sandwiches—and the clean-up is minimal. Be careful; remember that you are dealing with hot fat. The fat in the meat permits browning.

Do not let the slices overlap or they will not cook properly. If cooking 2 slices, place 2 sheets of paper toweling under them on a plate. Cover loosely with another sheet. To cook 4 to 8 slices, arrange on 4 sheets of paper toweling. Cover loosely with 1 sheet. Cooking bacon is an instance where oven size and power make a big difference.

Sometimes you may need, as for Clams Casino, to blanch bacon, meaning to partially cook it in water (which also eliminates salt). To blanch sliced bacon, whole strips or pieces of any size, place in a shallow container and add water to cover. Cook, uncovered, at

100%. It is a simple matter to cut raw bacon into pieces if the strips are cold and you use a sharp knife or scissors. Defrosting softens bacon, making it easy to separate frozen strips.

BLANCHING TIMES
FOR BACON

Whole strips Arrange in a single layer in a shallow container, uncovered.

8 slices bacon with 1 c. water	2 min. 30 sec.

COOKING TIMES FOR BACON

Sliced bacon In large microwave oven, arrange as above.

2 slices bacon	2 min. for moist bacon 3 min. for crisp bacon
4 slices bacon	2 min. 30 sec., moist 3 min. 30 sec., crisp
6 slices bacon	4 min., moist 4 min. 45 sec., crisp
8 slices bacon	6 min., moist 6 min. 45 sec., crisp

Sliced bacon In medium or small microwave oven, arrange as above.

2 slices bacon	2 min. 30 sec. for moist bacon 4 min. for crisp bacon
4 slices bacon	3 min., moist 5 min. 30 sec., crisp
6 slices bacon	4 min. 45 sec., moist 6 min. 30 sec., crisp
8 slices bacon	Ovens too small

Country-style bacon ¼″ thick. In any oven, arrange as above.

2 slices bacon	4 min.
4 slices bacon	5 min. 30 sec.
6 slices bacon	6 min. 30 sec.
8 slices bacon	7 min. (large oven only)

Canadian bacon In any oven, arrange on a single sheet of paper toweling, uncovered.

2 slices bacon	1 min.
4 slices bacon	1 min. 45 sec.
6 slices bacon	2 min. 15 sec.

DEFROSTING TIMES
FOR BACON

Sliced bacon   In unopened package, heat at 100%.

1 lb.   *1 min.*

LARDOONS

These thick match-shaped strips of bacon are cooked or "rendered" and used as a classic garnish for Chicken in Red Wine and other kinds of stews. Buy slab bacon of the thickness your recipe requires. When cooked, remove lardoons from grease with a slotted spoon. Save the grease for the recipe if needed. The lardoons can be reheated briefly by placing them on a piece of paper toweling in the microwave oven and heating at 100% for 30 seconds.

COOKING TIMES FOR
LARDOONS

Slab bacon lardoons   Cut ¼" or ½" slices bacon into strips 2" long and ¼" or ½" thick. Place in a single layer; cover loosely with a sheet of paper toweling.

¼ lb. bacon   *7 min.*

Yields

*5 slices slab   ¼ lb.
 bacon
¼ lb.   ⅓ c. lardoons*

BAKING   Technically, baking is anything done in an oven, usually without added liquid, or even in an enclosed pot on top of the stove without liquid.

Cakes, pies, cookies and breads, even soufflés, are what most of us consider to be baking. To tell you the truth, this is not where the microwave oven shines. You can't use your usual baking recipes and expect them to work. Soufflés won't work no matter what you do.

I have developed some fabulous baking recipes (see Cakes and Cookies, pages 409–435). If you read the introduction to that section and the introduction to Cakes, you will see what the problems are and how you can avoid them.

Baking problems involve the protein gluten (the stretchy part of starch in wheat flour and to a lesser extent in other starches) and the way it absorbs water. Avoiding wheat flour is the best solution; otherwise you will have an overly wet, unpleasant food. However, yeast, baking powder and baking soda need gluten to accomplish the magic of rising.

Egg-risen mixtures have problems of their own. They tend to rise too fast and then collapse, tough and unpleasant, which is what happens to soufflés. However, if the eggs are carefully balanced against a nongluten starch like cornstarch, the whole thing can be made to work. Try my recipes before plunging in to adapt your own. They may give you some guidelines.

Nonsweet, nonbread-baking works very well in the microwave oven, the kind of baking that used to be done in the bread-baker's oven after the bread came out: stuffed vegetables, baked (not roasted) meats such as pot roasts and short ribs, and casseroles (excluding cassoulet, which needs to form a crust). The difference between my results and those of the bread oven is that my method doesn't take overnight, only minutes.

Proofing or rising dough works well in the microwave oven. See RAISING.

BAKING POWDER The microwave oven has very little effect on the way this works; but because most flour baking is unsatisfactory in the microwave oven, you will not be using much of it. When you do use it, remember that it only has about a 4-month shelf life once opened. It's too bad no one packages it in more reasonable sizes; but, as it's cheap, it's worth the trouble of replacing.

BAKING SODA We use this not so much as a leavening agent, but to counteract the acidity of buttermilk or other ingredients in some recipes.

BALSAMIC VINEGAR See VINEGAR.

BANANA North Americans tend to eat one kind of banana, the large, yellow, sweet ones, mostly raw. The future will probably bring a broader knowledge of various plantains, many of them intended mainly for cooking. Even the ubiquitous banana makes a wonderful dessert when cooked. See Rummy Bananas.

We have become accustomed to bananas that are picked so very green that not only are they still green by the time we buy them, but they remain green in our fruit baskets. The microwave oven can—and here it is tempting to say "magically"—ripen this fruit for you. This is better for feeding babies than hard, under-ripe fruit.

Shield a banana in its skin for 1 inch at either end with doubled aluminum foil (see illustration page 12). Cook 1 minute at 100% in a large or medium microwave oven, for 1 minute 30 seconds in a small oven.

Yields

scant ½ lb.	1 large banana
1 large banana	½ c. purée
2½ lb.	6 large bananas
6 large bananas	2¾ c. purée

BARLEY One of the first grains man cultivated. At one time it was the principle grain used in peasant bread-making. Today, sadly, it has declined in culinary popularity, although vast quantities of it are used in the production of liquor. It is a nice change from rice and potatoes both as a side dish (see Creamy Barley) and as a soup ingredient (see Mushroom Barley Soup).

In cooking, we generally use pearl barley, which is husked,

cooks rapidly and has a pleasant texture. If you have had the barley on the shelf for a long time, it is liable to be very hard and dry. Add 5 minutes to the cooking times below and add more liquid if needed.

COOKING TIMES FOR MEDIUM PEARL BARLEY

Risotto technique Uncovered.

¼ c. barley with 1 c. broth (8" × 6" flat oval dish)	16 min.
1 c. barley with 3 c. broth (12" × 9" × 2" flat oval dish)	27 min.
1 c. barley as above	43 min. (small oven)

Boiled Cook in a 2½-qt. soufflé; cover tightly with 2 sheets microwave plastic wrap; omit resting time.

1 c. barley with 4 c. water	30 min.
2 c. barley with 6 c. water	30 min.

BASIL I use this loveliest of herbs frequently, and I am delighted that it is now available fresh, year-round, in many supermarkets. There are two basic varieties, the large-leaf French basil and the smaller-leaf bush basil, which is generally used to make pesto in the Genoan style. Bush basil is more peppery and aromatic. Look for crisp leaves without any black spots. Wash thoroughly and, if cutting, cut across the veins in the leaves. Often, basil leaves are nicest when used whole. They make a wonderful addition to salads. See DRYING, herbs.

BASS OR STRIPED BASS One of the world's best eating fish, with flesh that is white and firm without being chewy. Unfortunately, this means that it is often expensive. Rockfish from the West Coast and red snapper can be substituted; this is important to know since recently bass supplies have often been restricted due to overfishing and pollution. I look forward to the day when aquaculturists figure out that they can farm bass. See FISH for cooking times. See also SEA BASS.

BATTER Batter-based breads, cakes and pancakes are almost useless in microwave cooking; batters to coat food for frying are useful. See Tempura and FRYING.

BAY LEAF Even more than with the other dried herbs, be careful with this one or you will get a bitter flavor. If in doubt, use less. Most recipes call for too much bay leaf in any case. Consider adding it only for the last 4 to 5 minutes of the cooking time. Remember to remove any leaves before serving or reheating a dish; people can choke on them.

BEAN CURD See SOY.

BEANS When I first started using the microwave oven, I was so infatuated with its speed that I dismissed any usage that wasn't super-quick. After I calmed down a little, I realized that the reduced time involved in soaking dried beans and cooking them the microwave way was the difference between almost never cooking them from scratch and feeling free to use them as an ingredient.

Some legumes cook as beans do. See LEGUMES or specific kind of legume.

Canned beans are obviously no problem; you are just re-heating.

FRESH BEANS

GREEN, WAX, HARICOT VERT, YARD-LONG BEANS and other fresh pole and bush beans are quick, not watery, and retain their color in the microwave oven. Top, tail and string as necessary. If the beans are very large, or if the recipe calls for it, cut either into lengths or halve (French) lengthwise. Cooking times are by weight, tight wrapped in microwave plastic wrap or microwave-safe plastic bags.

BROAD BEANS

Dried BROAD, FAVA and LIMA BEANS do not cook to best advantage in the microwave oven. You blanch them to make shelling easier. Cook them on top of the stove.

DRIED BEANS

Dried-bean cooking times are determined by the size of the beans. It seems odd, but smaller beans take slightly longer to cook because there are more of them to the pound. The cooking times for these beans follow.

Never salt the beans before cooking, as it toughens the skin. All dried beans must be soaked before cooking.

Large dried beans: black beans, black-eyed peas, cannellini, kidney beans, red beans, pink beans, pinto beans.

Small dried beans: flageolets, navy beans, white beans.

Legumes: broad (fava) beans, chick-peas, lentils, lima beans, split peas.

SOAKING DRIED BEANS AND LEGUMES

To soak 1 or 2 cups dried beans of any size or legumes, place in a 2-quart soufflé dish with 2 cups water. Cover tightly with microwave plastic wrap. Cook at 100% for 15 minutes. Remove from oven and let stand, covered, for 5 minutes. Uncover and add 2 cups very hot water. Re-cover and let stand for 1 hour. Drain.

COOKING TIMES FOR LARGE DRIED BEANS

Put *presoaked* beans in 2-qt. soufflé; cover tightly with 2 sheets   microwave   plastic wrap.

| 1 c. beans with 4 c. warm water | 35 min. (rest 20 min.) |
| 2 c. beans with 6 c. warm water | 45 min. (rest 20 min.) |

Yields

6¼ oz., dried	1 c., dried
1 c., dried	2½ c., cooked
2½ c., cooked	2½ c. purée

COOKING TIMES FOR SMALL DRIED BEANS

Put *presoaked* beans in a 2-qt. soufflé; cover tightly with 2 sheets microwave plastic wrap.

| 1 or 2 c. beans with 4 c. warm water | 40 min. (rest 30 min.) |

Yields

| 1 c., dried | 3 c., cooked |
| 3 c., cooked | 3 c. purée |

COOKING TIMES FOR FRESH BEANS

Whole green and wax beans, trimmed Wrap tightly in ¼-lb. amounts sprinkled with water.

¼ lb. beans	3 min. 30 sec. to 4 min.
¼ lb. beans	5 min. (small oven)
½ lb. beans	4 min. to 4 min. 30 sec.
½ lb. beans	6 min. (small oven)
1 lb.	6 to 8 min.

Yields

| 1 lb. | 5 c., raw |
| 5 c., raw | 4 c., cooked |

Whole haricots verts and yard-long beans, trimmed Arrange in a single layer; cover tightly.

| ¼ lb. beans with 1 c. water (4-c. measure) | 6 min. |
| 1 lb. beans with 3 c. water (14" × 11" × 2" dish) | 15 min. |

BEEF This may still be America's favorite food, no matter what we have learned about limiting its ingestion for our health's sake. When it comes to cooking those most favorite cuts of all, the steaks and roasts, the microwave oven is of no earthly use at all; no amount of browning mixture or glaze will conceal the fact that these cuts would have cooked better in a conventional oven, on a grill, in a sauté pan or under a broiler. Use the microwave oven for DEFROSTING.

It also has limitations in cooking pot roast and stew. If you wish to brown the meat before cooking, do so on top of the stove; browning pans are inadequate. Prolonged microwave cooking has a tendency to toughen meat; do not exceed recipe times. Do not use too much liquid: It is inefficient, boils the meat and makes a less good sauce. Follow the timings and proportions below or in recipes selected from the Index.

Such foods can be eaten when ready or reheated, which mellows the flavors (see MELLOWING).

The recipes I have worked out are very good, and they certainly save time. They are not fancy. They are the kind of homey food I relish at parties as well as on my own.

Dishes made with ground meat such as meat loaf, chili and pasta sauces can be very successful. See Leonard Schwartz's Meat Loaf, Chunky Beef Chili, and Salsa Bolognese.

COOKING TIMES FOR BEEF

Brisket Cover tightly.

2¼ lb. with 1½ c. liquid and 1 lb. vegetables, turned once (2-qt. soufflé)	60 min.

Chuck Cover tightly.

2 lb., ¼" cubes, with about 4 c. liquid and ¾ lb. vegetables (14" × 11" × 2" dish)	15 min.
2 lb., 1" cubes, with 1 c. liquid and 1 lb. vegetables (2½ qt. soufflé)	18 min.
3 lb., ½" thick slices, with 1½ c. liquid and 1 lb. vegetables (2-qt. soufflé)	15 min.

Ground beef Cover tightly.

2 lb. with about 4 c. liquid and ¾ lb. vegetables (14" × 11" × 2" dish)	5 min.

Meat Loaf

2 lb. ground beef with 2 c. thick liquid, uncovered (9" × 5" × 3" pan)	12 min., stand 10 min.
3 lb. ground meat with 3 eggs and ¾ lb. vegetables, shaped as below and covered tightly for half of cooking time:	
½-lb. loaf (on a serving plate)	4 min.
1-lb. loaf (on a serving plate)	7 min.
8 half-lb. loaves (12" round platter)	8 min.
2-lb. loaf (9" ring mold)	9 min.

Short ribs of beef Cut into 3" × 2½" pieces. Cover tightly.

1¼ lb. with 6 to 8 tbsp. liquid (1-qt. soufflé)	12 min.
2½ lb. with ¾ to 1 c. liquid (2-qt. soufflé)	25 min.

Short ribs of beef (cont.)

5 lb. with 1½ to 2¼　35 min.
c. liquid (14" ×
11" × 2" dish)

BEEF BROTH See Meat Broths.

BEEF GLAZE See Meat Glazes.

BEEF LIVER This is rarely sold by its rightful name. I think much of the calves liver sold is actually beef liver (just as much of the veal sold is simply undercolored beef—just look at the size of the legs). At times I have bought frozen beef liver that was being sold as pet food.

Beef liver is particularly good in pâtés, where its strong taste has a contribution to make. If you can buy it, it should be considerably cheaper than other livers. Substitute it happily in Country Pâté and Pâté with Chinese Black Beans, but not in Scandinavian Liver Pâté, where its taste would be overwhelming. It is really not worth cooking on its own.

BEET Often sold precooked in European markets to be sliced into salads, combined with potatoes in purées or included in soups and stews. When baked, beets retain a maximum of color and flavor. Microwave cooking achieves the same effect rapidly and with almost no mess.

Trim the beet greens down to within 1 inch of the beets. (If they are small, save them for

POT GREENS.) Scrub beets well. Wrap each beet tightly in microwave plastic wrap. Arrange in a circle on a dish or microwave carousel. Cook as below. If using immediately, cool slightly, trim the tops and slip off their skins. (You can then clean your hands with some lemon if you don't wish to be mistaken for Lady Macbeth.)

If you unwrap the beets over a bowl, you can catch the juices for adding to soups and to beet purée. Precooked beets will last, well wrapped and refrigerated, for over a week and are worth keeping on hand. See Cold Beet Borscht and Beet and Potato Purée.

COOKING TIMES FOR BEETS

Small beets 2 oz. each. Put in a dish at least ½" deep and large enough to hold them in a single layer; cover tightly.

½ lb.	*8 min.*
½ lb.	*12 min. (small oven)*
1 lb.	*12 min.*
1½ lb.	*16 min.*

Large beets Wrap individually in microwave plastic wrap; turn once.

1 beet, 11 oz.	*20 min.*
6 beets, 2½ lb.	*25 to 30 min.*

Yields

4 small beets	*½ lb.*
½ lb.	*⅔ c. purée*

BEET GREENS One of those dividends known to the South and often thrown away in ignorance up North. They are best when young and small. They achieve Nirvana as POT GREENS.

BEURRE MANIÉ This standard of the French repertoire is simply made of equal quantities of flour and butter worked together to form a smooth paste. It is easily done in the food processor. You can make a quantity ahead and roll it up in plastic wrap to use as needed. About 1 tablespoon of beurre manié thickens 1 cup of sauce. It must be stirred into your stew or other saucy item about 5 minutes before the end of cooking time. Generally, I have found CORNSTARCH or ROUX to be better last-minute thickeners.

BLACK BEAN For cooking times, see BEANS. Chinese black beans require no presoaking if the recipe requires 3 minutes or more cooking time. If not, barely cover with water in a glass measure. Cover tightly with microwave plastic wrap. Heat at 100% for 1 minute 30 seconds.

BLACKBERRY Both the fat, cultivated varieties and the firmer, seedier wild ones are some of the most aromatic and delicious of berries. Substitute equal weights in Black Raspberry Jam and Big City Strawberry Shortcake.

BLACK-EYED PEA Despite its name, this is a bean. For cooking times, see BEANS, dried.

BLACK RASPBERRY These blackberry look-alikes have a more mysterious flavor. Substitute equal weights of black raspberries in Big City Strawberry Shortcake.

BLANCHING *VEGETABLES* are blanched—usually in copious, salted water—to precook them briefly so they hold their color and flavor for more prolonged cooking. This is usually unnecessary in microwave cooking since vegetables cook so quickly and retain their color so well. (Cook spinach and watercress, for example, directly in butter or liquid such as broth for terrific results.)

Most vegetables are blanched before freezing. Cook in water for half the normal times given for individual vegetables in this Dictionary. (Since water takes time to come to a boil, the vegetables will be less than halfway cooked.) Run cold water over blanched vegetables to stop the cooking process. Freeze.

Certain *NUTS* and *LEGUMES,* fresh and dried, are blanched to remove their skins. I find that the skins are much more easily removed after microwave cooking than any other method. See BEANS, NUTS and LEGUMES.

You will sometimes need to blanch *BACON* before using in certain recipes. See BACON.

BLOWFISH An Atlantic fish more genteely sold as sea squab, blowfish are only distantly related to the frightening and potentially poisonous fugu of Japan. Cook in a little melted butter with chopped fresh herbs. See FISH (follow cooking times for filleted fish according to weight).

BLUEBERRY This is one berry that cooks not only more quickly but also infinitely better in the microwave oven, making richly flavored sauces for pancakes and desserts. Blueberry sauces are worth making in quantity when the berries are in season; store them in sterile jars or freeze the sauce in small (2-ounce) quantities. Defrost in a plastic-topped glass or a microwave-safe plastic bag at 100% for 2 minutes. See Blueberry Sauce.

BLUEFISH Essentially a summer catch, this strongly flavored fish is vastly underrated. It does very well with white wine, mustard sauces, onions, fennel and other strong-tasting accompaniments. Allow ¼ cup sauce or thinly sliced vegetables to each 8-ounce portion of fish and you will not have to change the cooking time. For example, for one person, thinly slice enough fennel to make ½ cup. Strew in a single layer on a dinner plate or glass pie dish. Cover with a piece of fillet about ½ pound and 1 inch thick; sprinkle with salt and pepper, the juice of ½ lemon and 1 tablespoon olive oil. Cover tightly with microwave plastic wrap. Cook at 100% for 2 minutes 30 seconds. Serve immediately. See FISH for other preparations and cooking times.

BOILING Most of the time you don't want to boil foods in a great deal of liquid. It slows things down. There are times when you do want to bring some liquid to a boil—a soup, perhaps, or some liquid to add to a stew or to a purée to make a soup. One cup of liquid in a 2-cup glass measure, tightly covered, takes between 2 minutes 30 seconds and 3 minutes 30 seconds at 100%. The lowest time is for water, wine and tomato juice. Three minutes covers broth, cold cream, sugar water and heavily salted water. The longest time is needed for refrigerated milk.

BOK CHOY The name is very confusing. The long, rather white-leafed cabbage that used to go by this name in the Northeast (and still does in Cantonese communities) is now called NAPA CABBAGE, to avoid confusion with the Mandarin bok choy that looks like a dark-leafed escarole with fleshy white bottoms and ribs. Both kinds of bok choy are very low in calories and delicious if not overcooked. The leaves and stalks are often separately cooked. See CABBAGE for other varieties. See also Bok Choy Ribs.

COOKING TIMES FOR BOK CHOY

2 medium heads bok choy 1½ lb. each. Cook in a 14" × 11" × 2" dish; cover tightly.

Ribs, cut into 2" to 3" lengths with ½ c. liquid	*11 min.*
Leaves, cut into ¼" chiffonade with 6 tbsp. liquid	*6 min.*

Yields from whole heads

⅓ lb. bok choy	*1 c. shredded, raw*
½ lb. bok choy	*2 c. shredded, raw*
2 c. shredded, raw	*¾ c., cooked*
7 c. shredded, raw	*1¼ c., cooked*
1 large head bok choy	*2 lb.*
2 lb. whole	*10 c. shredded, raw*
10 c. shredded, raw	*3½ c., cooked*

BOLETUS   EDULIS   See
CEPE.

BOURBON This strongly flavored liquor is hard to use subtly in cooking. It is a little easier with the microwave oven because of the rapid volatilization. Bourbon is also the name of the best Mexican vanilla. See ALCOHOL.

BRAISING   Normally means slow, moist cooking in a tightly closed environment. Tight covering with microwave plastic wrap mimics perfectly the pots closed with a dough seal of earlier times. Braising gradually breaks down the fibers of meats and vegetables, making them tender, and it produces marvelous gravies by extracting the flavors and gelatinous qualities of the foods and integrating them. It is like stewing, but with less liquid; and because of the rapidity of microwave cooking, it is a more successful method. Care must be taken when braising meats not to overcook them and toughen them. See Braised Leeks, Ossobuco and Chicken Fricassee.

BRAINS These are something we are all delighted to have, but few of us eat, which is a shame. Brains are highly esteemed as food in other parts of the world. They cook wonderfully in the microwave oven, either as an ingredient for a first-course cold dish (see Brain Salad) or with a nutty brown butter enlivened by capers, lemon or vinegar. Try heating them (1 set, tightly covered with microwave plastic wrap) with 1 tablespoon butter, a little ham (¼ pound, slivered), 2 sliced mushrooms and ½ cup cooked or defrosted green peas, enriched with ¾ cup Sauce Espagnole or 2 tablespoons Meat Glaze if you have it on hand. This will serve four as a first course, two as a main course.

COOKING TIMES FOR BRAINS

Trimmed With ½ cup liquid; cover tightly.

1 set brains (1-qt. soufflé)	8 min.
1 set brains with 2½ c. chopped vegetables (2-qt. soufflé)	12 min.

BRAN The husk of wheat or other grain. Comes under the heading of what's good for you. A small amount can be sprinkled into muffins and breads without changing the cooking times. Try a tablespoon sprinkled over a cup of cooked carrots.

BRANDY The generic name for fruit alcohols, grape included. Only those made from grapes in the Cognac region of France are called Cognac. See ALCOHOL.

BREAD Shares the difficulties of all things made with wheat flour (see BAKING, problems). Although many authors give bread recipes for the microwave oven, I find that classic breads raised with yeast are always better made in a conventional oven, especially considering the time and energy spent kneading. In the microwave oven, raised breads become a wet, spongy mess. Steamed breads, however, work wonderfully well, cooking in less than one quarter of the normal, messy time spent in a hot water bath.

Moist breads raised with baking soda or powder (banana and nut, for example) also work well. Quick breads and muffins respond very erratically, and since they take so little time in a conventional oven, I see no benefit to making them in the microwave oven. Use the microwave oven to speed the proofing and raising of yeast doughs if you like. See RAISING and REHEATING.

BREADCRUMBS Frequently used dried or buttered. See Breadcrumbs recipe.

BREADING This never works in the microwave oven. All you get is a gluey mess.

BROAD BEAN This bean does not cook well in the microwave oven. See BEANS.

BROCCOLI One of those foods that seems to cook miraculously in the microwave oven. No longer do we risk soggy tops when the stems are cooked through or nasty fibrous stems when the florets are perfect. Our broccoli stays radiantly green and healthy. Salt is better added just after cooking, but it can be dissolved in the tiny amount of water sprinkled on before cooking. It can be served cold by placing it under cold running water immediately after removing from the oven; do not sauce until just prior to eating or it will discolor. Hot, cooked broccoli makes a lovely purée to serve with any roast or grilled meat or fish. It also is a perfect base for a hot or cold soup.

Do not try to cook whole heads—too uneven. If cooking a large quantity, arrange flower tops toward the center of the dish with stalks pointing outward. Just a few stalks can be lined up. Florets can be cooked in 1-cup quantities in microwave-safe plastic bags. Peeled and sliced stems, good when cold in chicken salad, can also be cooked in plastic bags. When cooking in more than two bags at a time, arrange bags in a circle. One medium head will generously serve two people.

COOKING TIMES FOR BROCCOLI

Longer times are for old broccoli, or for medium or small ovens.

Stalks separated In a single layer in a dish just large enough to hold them; cover tightly.

½ lb. with 1 Tbs. water	4 to 6 min.
1 lb. with 1½ Tbs. water	6 to 8 min. 30 sec.
2 lb. with 3 Tbs. water	8 to 10 min.
2½ lb. with ¼ c. water	12 min.

Florets or ¼″ coins Put ½-c. amounts in microwave-safe plastic bags arranged in a circle or in a dish just large enough to hold them in a single layer; cover tightly.

6 oz.	2 min.
14 oz.	3 min. 15 sec.
1 lb.	4 min.

Yields

1 medium head broccoli	1¼ lb., untrimmed 15 oz., trimmed
6 oz. florets, raw	4 c., raw
4 c. florets, raw	2 c., cooked
2 c. cooked florets	1 c. purée
8 oz. stems	2 c., raw (peeled ¼″ coins)
2 c. raw coins	1 c., cooked
1 c. cooked coins	⅔ c. purée

BROCCOLI DI RAPE More stem than floret, it has a pleasant bitter taste and is frequently used in Italian cooking. Serve as a first course, as a vegetable or over pasta. See Spaghetti with Bitter Broccoli Sauce.

COOKING TIMES FOR BROCCOLI DI RAPE

Cut into 2″ pieces Cover tightly.

¾ lb. broccoli di rape with ⅓ cup olive oil heated for 3 min. (11″ × 8½″ × 2″ dish)	7 min.

Broccoli di rape (cont.)

1½ lb. broccoli di rape with ¾ cup olive oil heated for 4 min. (14" × 11" × 2" dish)	10 min.

Yields

2 bunches	1½ lb., untrimmed
1½ lb.	1¼ lb., trimmed
1¼ lb.	12 c. (tightly packed), cut into 2" pieces

BROWNING In traditional cooking, *meats* are often sautéed before stewing or braising in order to sear them, sealing in their juices. In microwave cooking, that process is not necessary, since cooking proceeds so quickly that there is no excessive loss of juice. You will need much less fat than in conventional cooking; fats are used only for their flavor. I don't think you'll miss the browning in the finished flavor.

Meat browns when it roasts in the conventional way. This does not happen in the microwave oven, and all the colored glazes in the world cannot disguise this fact: This lack of sealing, or searing, is one reason meat does not truly roast in the microwave oven. See ROASTING. If you wish a browned outer surface, sauté the food briefly on top of the stove; then complete cooking in the microwave oven, as in Ossobuco. When there are darkly colored sauces, as in Chicken in Red Wine, you will not miss the dark color of the pieces of meat that you would have if they had first been browned.

Browning of *FATS* does take place in the microwave oven. See BACON and BUTTER.

Browning of *SUGARS*—caramelization—is an important aspect of working with sweets. It is brilliantly easy and fabulously good in the microwave oven. See CARAMEL and Pralines. Many vegetables and fruits have high sugar contents that will caramelize. See Classic French Onion Soup and Apple Butter.

Surface browning of *CHEESES, GRATINS* and *CASSEROLES* cannot be done in the microwave oven. The surface of the food cooks no differently than the inside does. Where a browned *CRUST* or *SKIN* is desired, the best solution is to virtually complete the cooking in the microwave oven, and then brown briefly under a broiler. See Macaroni and Cheese and Crispiest Duck.

Of course, you can also glaze foods as long as you realize you are not roasting them. See Barbecued Chicken Legs and Barbecued Short Ribs of Beef.

BRUSSELS SPROUTS
These miniature cabbages grow decoratively up the plant's stem, hiding under leaves. Traditional at Thanksgiving, com-

bine with one third their weight in blanched chestnuts and toss with butter. Don't overcook them, as they easily become mushy. Oven size does make a difference in cooking times.

COOKING TIMES FOR BRUSSELS SPROUTS

Large and medium ovens
Trim bottoms; rinse; in a single layer in a dish just large enough to hold them; cover tightly.

½ pt. (6 oz.)	2 min.
1 pt. (12 oz.)	3 min.
1½ pt. (18 oz.)	4 min. 45 sec.
2 pt. (24 oz.)	6 min. 45 sec.

Small oven Prepare as above.

½ pt.	4 min.
1 pt.	6 min.
1½ pt.	Oven too small

BULGUR Cracked wheat. It is a wonderful grain to serve with dishes prepared in the microwave oven since it requires little attention and tastes good hot or cold. You must remember to allow time for the water or broth to come to a boil and for the bulgur to steep, or your main dish will be ready before the bulgur. To serve bulgur piping hot, after steeping and just before serving, cover tightly with microwave plastic wrap and heat in the microwave oven for 4 minutes.

For basic bulgur to serve 6 to 8 people, combine 1½ cups bulgur with 7 cups boiling water; let stand 25 minutes. Drain if necessary.

Sliced mushrooms, onions or garlic, and herbs and/or spices may be cooked in the microwave oven in a little melted butter and added to the bulgur: Heat 6 tablespoons butter at 100% for 3 minutes; stir in ½ pound sliced mushrooms, 2 teaspoons ground cumin, 2 tablespoons finely minced parsley and 3 cloves finely minced garlic. Cook, uncovered, at 100% for 5 minutes. Stir into steeped bulgur with salt and pepper to taste just before reheating in the microwave oven.

BUTTER In this book I always use unsalted so that it will contain less water and be fresher. In a day when we all have freezers, there is no reason for salted butter. See Index for butter sauce recipes and compound butters like Snail Butter (no snails in it) that can be used for various recipes. See also FATS and SOFTENING.

Butter contains varying amounts of water. If it contains a great deal of water, you may hear the butter pop when it is being melted. This can also happen in metal-lined multiuse ovens if condensing moisture drops back into the butter; the butter may spit and mess up the oven. Always melt butter in a fairly large container. If spitting continues to haunt you, loosely cover the container with paper toweling.

CLARIFIED BUTTER

This removes the water and remaining milk solids that tend to burn during high-heat cooking. Sometimes it is aged to make GHEE for Indian cooking. I tend to be lazy about clarifying butter, but here is how it is done: Cut the butter into tablespoon-size pieces. Heat, loosely covered with paper toweling, at 100% to melt. Skim solids from surface of liquid and discard. Pour off clear liquid carefully, leaving the milky solids behind.

MELTING TIMES FOR BUTTER

Cut into tablespoon-size pieces. Cover loosely with paper toweling; cook at 100%.

¼ lb. or less butter (2-c. measure)	2 min.
½ lb. butter (4-c. measure)	2 min. 30 sec.
1 lb. butter (8-c. measure)	4 min.

Yields

¼ lb. butter	⅓ c. clarified butter
½ lb. butter	¾ c. clarified butter
1 lb. butter	1⅔ c. clarified butter

BROWNED BUTTER

Browned butter has a rather different flavor. Strain through a sieve lined with paper toweling.

BROWNING TIMES FOR BUTTER

Cut into tablespoon-size pieces. Cover loosely with paper toweling; cook at 100%.

¼ lb. butter (4-c. measure)	8 min.
½ lb. butter (4-c. measure)	10 min.

Yields

¼ lb. butter	½ c. browned butter
½ lb. butter	1 c. browned butter

BUTTERFISH These small (at least one per person) but very tasty oval fish are quite bony and hence lack popularity. Either get someone to fillet them for you or serve only to intrepid friends. They are delicious served on a bed of onions that have been cooked in butter or oil (¼ cup thinly sliced onions in 1 teaspoon fat for each fish). Top with a little white wine, freshly ground black pepper and ¼ teaspoon anchovy paste per fish. For cooking times, see FISH.

BUTTERMILK Today's buttermilk—the liquid left after the butter is churned—tastes little like the thick clabbered stuff I remember from my childhood. It is thin and innocuous, drunk by some and used by others to give a tart edge to the taste of baking powder biscuits and other baked goods, where its acid is generally offset with a little baking soda.

BUTTERNUT These odd New England nuts must be one year old before they can be cracked, and even then opening them is difficult. The yield is delicious, if small. See NUTS, toasting.

BUTTERNUT SQUASH Cut this squash in half, scoop out fibers and seeds, and tightly wrap each half in microwave plastic wrap. For cooking times, see SQUASH, winter.

C

CABBAGE Great green cabbage got a terrible reputation during the many years that it was virtually the only green, nonroot vegetable to last through the winter. It was generally old, overcooked and smelly. Let us not give up on this wonderful family of vegetables that has taken such a bad rap. Young cabbage shredded and wilted (melted) in butter with seasonings is good as a vegetable dish, or as part of a recipe.

To cook in wedges: Remove any shabby outer leaves, core cabbage and cut into wedges. To blanch whole leaves as containers for stuffings: Remove unattractive outer leaves; core deeply; cook the cabbage head whole. If leaves are still difficult to pull away intact, cook 1 minute more.

See also BOK CHOY, BRUSSELS SPROUTS, NAPA CABBAGE, RED CABBAGE and SAVOY CABBAGE.

COOKING TIMES FOR GREEN OR WHITE CABBAGE

Shredded cabbage Cover tightly; season fat or liquid if desired.

2 c. (4-c. measure)	4 min.
2 c. (4-c. measure)	6 min. (small oven)
3 c. with 1 Tbs. liquid or 2 Tbs. fat (2-qt. soufflé dish)	12 min.
8 c. with 1 Tbs. water or 3 Tbs. fat (2-qt soufflé dish)	12 to 14 min.

Whole leaves Use cabbage whole, deeply cored, set uncovered on carousel or plate.

2½ lb. cabbage	5 min.

Wedges Cut each wedge 4 to 5 oz., about 2½″ to 3½″ at the widest part. Arrange in a shallow dish in a ring, petal-fashion, with core edge toward outside of dish; cover tightly.

2 wedges (8″ plate)	8 min.
2 wedges (8″ plate)	12 min. (small oven)
4 wedges (10″ plate)	12 min.
6 wedges (12″ round dish)	16 min.

COOKING TIMES FOR RED CABBAGE

Shredded Cover tightly.

| 9 c. with 7 tsp. butter and 1½ c. onion; ¾ c. liquid added after 8 min. (12″ × 10″ × 3″ dish) | 18 min. |

Yields

½ lb. raw	2 c., shredded
2 c. shredded	1 c., cooked
1 lb., cored, raw	4 c., shredded (lightly packed)

CALAMARI See SQUID.

CALF'S LIVER The liver of very young veal is delicate in taste and texture. It should not be overcooked. I think it is best sautéed or broiled. In this book it is used to make Scandinavian Liver Pâté. Ask for kosher calf's liver; because of the way the animals are killed, the liver is more delicate. Make sure the butcher has removed the external membrane and the big veins.

CANNELLINI See BEANS for cooking times.

CANNING See PRESERVING.

CAPER Salted, preserved flower buds that make a nice addition to Browned Butter Sauce and give an edge to the flavor of some of the blander meats such as veal scallops and brains. Oddly, the smaller buds are considered choicer than the larger ones. Taste capers for saltiness before using them. If unpleasantly salty, run them under cold water in a small sieve. Be stingy when adding salt or acid to a dish or sauce containing them.

CAPON A bird that is born male but grows up neutered. Do not attempt to roast in a microwave oven (see ROASTING). Capon may be steamed for use in salads or sauced dishes. For timing and method, see CHICKEN, whole bird.

CARAMEL Thanks to the way sugar cooks in the microwave oven, making caramel of different colors and hardnesses is easy, rapid and reliable. Tight wrapping causes condensation from steam to continually wash the insides of the cooking container, eliminating problems of crystallization; and cooking in a glass measure permits you to see exactly the color the caramel is turning and to stop it if it is becoming too dark. Pots used for making caramel on top of the stove are frequently ruined or hard to clean. This is no problem in the microwave oven.

Caramel is nothing but cooked sugar that has browned from the heat. As a sweet, the sugar has been sufficiently cooked, usually with a small amount of water, so that it liquifies. This sweet caramel may vary in color from pale gold to very dark brown, and from reasonably soft—employable in chewy candies—to the hard-crack stage used in nut brittles and as a rich stained-glass covering for cakes and other desserts.

I must emphasize how important a tight seal is here. If you don't get one, the sugar will cook unevenly and will crystallize. Use a large enough piece of microwave plastic wrap to extend 3 inches down the sides of the cup and wrap the handle, and to have enough give so that it attaches firmly to the glass above and below the handle as well as below the spout.

Avoid stirring, as this may cloud the caramel. If stirring is absolutely necessary, use a metal spoon lightly coated with a vegetable oil. The less hard stages of caramel will be very lightly colored. The caramel—hard in particular—continues to darken after it comes out of the oven. Be very careful when removing the plastic from hot sugar mixtures as the steam is

very hot. Prick the plastic to release the steam; pull an edge of the plastic away from the measuring cup and lift.

Other kinds of foods caramelize as well, so that when we roast a bird or piece of meat to a rich brown exterior in a conventional oven, we would also call this caramelization. Onions, with their high sugar content, caramelize as they cook and their liquid is driven off. See French Onion Soup (page 94).

See also SUGAR, SIMPLE SYRUP, Pralines, Caramel Sauce and Peanut Brittle.

COOKING TIMES FOR SUGAR AND CARAMEL

To make 1 cup, stir together 1 cup sugar with ⅓ cup warm water to remove any lumps. Place in a 4-cup glass measure. Cook tightly covered at 100% in a large oven. Prick plastic immediately after removing from oven.

Soft ball	5 min.
Hard ball	6 min.
Hard crack	7 min. 30 sec.
Caramel, colored and hard	9 min.
Caramel, colored and hard	16 to 17 min. (small oven)

CARAWAY If these tasty seeds have been sitting around your kitchen for some time getting musty just waiting for you to sprinkle them on buttered noodles, they may benefit from a brief but rejuvenating toast. See TOASTING, small seeds and GRINDING.

Yield

1 Tbs., whole	¾ Tbs., ground

CARDAMOM Often a component of curry powder, this otherwise underused spice can be bought ground or in its seed pod, which is a papery husk containing many small seeds. While whole pods can be cooked in broths that are to be strained, I generally crumble the pods between my fingers to remove the husks and separate the seeds before using them. See GRINDING and TOASTING, whole spices. See also Steamed Papaya Pudding.

CARP Long-lived freshwater fish that grow to great size and are related to the decorative goldfish in the bowl, carp can be either light, clean, medium-soft-fleshed, or it can be nasty if coming from muddy waters. It can be cooked as any white-fleshed, mild-tasting fish (see FISH for cooking times) and is a traditional component of Gefilte Fish.

CARROT These basic vegetables cook rapidly in the microwave oven without getting mushy. This means that they can be added to a stew or soup right at the beginning of the cooking time and emerge as recognizable pieces of carrot, not orange slime.

Try to avoid buying those huge roots known as chefs' specials because some chefs buy them to minimize peeling time. These monsters have thick cores and tend to be bitter. When buying small carrots, check to see if they are real babies, or midgets or dwarves. The two latter kinds are genetically small but full-grown; peel and cook as other carrots. True baby carrots, about ¾ inch wide at the top and from 3 inches to 5 inches long, may not even need peeling, especially if they have just been pulled from the garden.

Scrub carrots with a hard brush, and peel if the skin has any gritty texture or bitter taste. Cooking in butter and a little bit of sugar and salt is particularly nice. Arrange with the thin tips toward the center of a dish or place in a microwave-safe plastic bag. Season and add butter. Seal. Cook at 100%. Oven size does affect cooking times.

COOKING TIMES FOR CARROTS

Times are the same in large and medium ovens. In small ovens, add 2 minutes to cooking time. For standard carrots, peel and cut in juliennes or crosswise into ¼-inch or ⅛-inch rounds; for baby carrots, peel, leaving ½ inch green tops; arrange in 2 or 3 layers in a dish just large enough to hold them; cover tightly.

Plain carrots Peel and cut in juliennes or into rounds; cover tightly.

¼ lb.	4 min. 30 sec.
½ lb.	6 min. 30 sec.
¾ lb.	7 min.
1 lb.	8 min.
2 lb.	11 min.

Glazed whole, small carrots About 12 per lb. Peel; arrange in a dish just large enough to hold them; cover tightly.

½ lb. with 1 Tbs. each butter and sugar	8 min.

Yields

½ lb.	1½ c. ¼″ slices, raw
1½ c., raw	1 c., cooked
1 c., cooked	⅔ c. purée
3 c., cooked	2 c. purée

CASHEW I know people ruthless enough to pick these marvelously rich and expensive nuts out of nut mixtures, leaving the shattered peanuts for me. In addition to being gobbled solo, they are sometimes added to curries and curried salads. You may want to toast them lightly before using. See NUTS, toasting.

CATFISH Small, bottom-dwelling pond fish, very popular in the South, they are now farmed and sold extensively, frozen, usually as fillets, all over the country. The farmed fish avoid the worst problem of catfish: a muddy taste. Do not attempt to bread catfish in traditional fashion when cooking in the microwave oven; you will only achieve glue. They can be cooked as any other small, relatively firm but nonfatty fish (sole, for instance). See FISH for cooking times.

CAULIFLOWER If you need a large whole head, bring a pot of water to a boil and proceed in traditional fashion; it will be too big to cook evenly in a microwave oven. Small heads, under 1½ pounds with the leaves, and florets, those small rounded tips about 2 inches long and 2 inches across at their widest, cook quickly and well in a microwave oven, either alone (to toss with a little butter or top with Mornay) or in soups and purées (see Cream of Cauliflower Soup).

COOKING TIMES FOR CAULIFLOWER

Florets Cook in a single layer in a dish just large enough to hold them; cover tightly.

½ lb. florets	4 min.
½ lb. florets	6 min. (small oven)
1 lb. florets	7 min.
1 lb. florets	10 min. (small oven)
1½ lb. florets	9 min.

Whole head Core and trim; cook in a dish just large enough to hold it; cover tightly.

Cauliflower (cont.)

1 small head,	*7 min.*
1½ lb. with leaves,	
or 1 lb. 2 oz. cored	
and trimmed	

Yields

1 small head	*5 c. florets,*
	raw
5 c. florets,	*4½ c. florets,*
raw	*cooked*
4½ c.,	*2 c. purée*
cooked	

CAVIAR At their very best, these salted fish eggs should be left alone except for the spoon (bone, shell or tortoise shell if possible) that conveys them to your mouth. In any case, don't cook caviar. Stir into a cooked dish like scrambled eggs after the food is cooked.

CAYENNE A spicy red pepper pod usually bought dried and ground. See CHILI.

CELERY This lovely vegetable, traditionally an herb, is massively ignored except for inclusion in chicken soup or chicken or tuna fish salad, or for display in a cut-glass bowl with olives. Even there it tends to be misused. Celery needs to be well washed and then strung thoroughly by peeling with a vegetable peeler.

Try cooked celery, leaves included, mixed with Basic Béchamel, Mornay or Sauce Suprême. Brown under the broiler. Try adding 1 cup cooked celery to 2 cups cooked potatoes before mashing them. For a spectacular soup, puréed or not, combine 1 cup cooked celery, 1½ cups Chicken Broth and either 1 cup cubed, cooked potatoes or 1 cup Sauce Suprême. A touch of cream would not be amiss. Salt and pepper to taste.

COOKING TIMES FOR
CELERY

Trim, string and slice ¼" thick.

To steam celery Cook in tightly sealed microwave-safe plastic bags in ½-c. quantities.

1 c. celery with	*2 to 3 min.*
½ Tbs. water	
2 c. celery with	*5 to 6 min.*
1 Tbs. water	

To sweat celery Cook in a 4-c. glass measure with butter melted at 100% for 2 min.; cover tightly.

½ c. celery	*4 min.*
with 2 tsp.	
butter	
1 c. celery with	*6 min. 15*
1 Tbs. butter	*sec.*

Yields

2 stalks cel-	*¼ lb.*
ery	
¼ lb.	*½ c., raw,*
	¼" slices
½ c. raw	*¼ c., cooked*
1 c. raw	*½ c., cooked*

CELERY ROOT This knobby root, once peeled, is delicious raw; it is also excellent cooked in soup or puréed with potatoes—1 part celery root to 3 parts potato.

COOKING TIMES FOR CELERY ROOT

Trim, peel and cut into ½-inch dice. Cook in tightly sealed microwave-safe plastic bags in ¾-cup amounts. Add 1 minute 30 seconds to cooking times for quantities of less than 1½ pounds in small ovens.

¾ lb. celery root	*6 min.*
1¼ lb. celery root	*9 min.*
2½ lb. celery root	*15 min.*

Yields

1 celery root, 11 oz.	*1¼ c. ½" dice, raw*
1¼ c., raw	*¾ c., cooked*
¾ c., cooked	*½ c. purée*
1¼ lb. celery root	*2½ c. ½" dice, raw*
2½ c., raw	*1½ c., cooked*
1½ c., cooked	*1 c. purée*

CELERY SEED The seeds of this spice are so small that they sometimes get caught in the teeth. They do a lot for a chicken or tuna fish salad. They cook in the microwave oven much as they do any other way. See TOASTING, small seeds.

CÈPE The generic name for this wonderful, fleshy wild mushroom is Boletus edulis. Cèpes is the French name. The Italians call them porcini, the Germans steinpilz ("stone mushroom") or herrenpilz ("master mushroom") and the Russians belyi grïb. The cèpe has a large fleshy cap whose underside looks like a sponge, with all-over pores that have no discernible arrangement. The somewhat more fibrous stem is shaped like a baluster and is almost as thick in the middle as the cap itself is wide.

Cèpes are picked in late summer and fall. When fresh, they are usually grilled whole or vigorously cooked in olive oil (done better on top of the stove). Sliced, both fresh and dried, they are a wonderful component of sauces, soups, stews and grain dishes, darkening and intensifying the taste. They will do wonders added to dishes made with common, fresh store-bought mushrooms. An ounce of dried cèpes added to risotto during the final cooking time makes a lovely dish. See SOAKING, cèpes, and DRYING, mushrooms.

CEREAL See GRAINS.

CHANTERELLE This heavenly golden-yellow, trumpet-shaped wild mushroom is increasingly available in stores. If you pick chanterelles, as I do, you can begin to look for them in late spring and on into early summer. Store-bought ones may come from different climates and be available into fall and early winter. They are best cooked in hot butter or olive oil, and they like garlic and fresh herbs. A few added to your Duxelles or Mushroom Soup can make a vast improvement. They are German favorites called Schwarzwalder ("Black Forest") pfifferlinge.

CHAYOTE This is the Southwest's name for New Orleans's beloved mirliton, the Caribbean's christophine and the more prosaic vegetable pear. Now becoming widely available across the country, this squash is shaped like an avocado, has a waxy yellowish skin, a large pit and subtle, aromatic flavor. I strongly prefer cooking it in the microwave oven, where it doesn't get waterlogged and keeps its delicate pale green color.

COOKING TIMES FOR
CHAYOTE

Prick whole vegetable 4 times; set on paper toweling, uncovered.

1 chayote	*6 min.*
2 chayotes	*9 min. 30 sec.*
4 chayotes	*15 min.*

Yields

1 chayote	*½ lb.*
½ lb.	*⅓ to ½ c. cooked pulp (2 oz.) and 2 shells*

CHEESE It will not make a nice brown crust in the microwave oven. It will do other things very well: melt without separating, recover from the re-

frigerator or even from that dread malady, unripeness. See Index for recipes.

Yield

1 lb. hard cheese	*5½ c., grated*

CHERRY Fresh and raw are the best ways to enjoy Bing, Queen Anne and other "table" cherries. Sour cherries and pie cherries, such as Montmorency, do well in sauces and pie fillings. They also make a terrific tart preserve (see Sour Cherry Jelly). See Cherry Sauce for Roast Birds.

CHESTNUT The microwave oven can blanch and cook chestnuts very well, but it doesn't give them a roasted flavor. It does make peeling them wonderfully simple. Cut an X with a sharp knife into the flat side of each one. Cook for the appropriate time, then peel as soon as they are cool enough to handle; return any difficult ones to the oven for 1 additional minute. Cook peeled chestnuts for the additional time indicated before using them in a recipe. Add to Brussels sprouts, desserts, stuffings and purées.

COOKING TIMES FOR
CHESTNUTS

Raw, unshelled chestnuts Cut as above; arrange in a single layer in a shallow dish just large enough to hold them, uncovered.

½ lb.	6 min.
1 lb.	8 min.
1½ lb.	11 min.

Shelled chestnuts Cook and peel as above. Arrange in a single layer in a shallow dish just large enough to hold them, uncovered.

½ lb.	4 min.
1 lb.	6 min.
1½ lb.	8 min.

CHICKEN Chicken can be poached, stewed, steamed and braised perfectly in the microwave oven. It cooks rapidly, staying moist and cooking evenly. You cannot roast in a microwave oven. The birds cook best cut into pieces, whether skinned and boned or not.

CHICKEN PIECES

Chickens, depending on their size and your recipe, may be quartered, or jointed. One jointed chicken yields 2 half breasts, 2 thighs and 2 drumsticks, as well as backbone, wings and neck. Use the last three in the dish or use for stock. When cooking breasts from very large birds, you may cut them crosswise into 2 pieces. Use pieces whole, skinned or skinned and boned. Skinning reduces calories; boning shortens cooking time and reduces the flavor but makes for more elegant eating when it comes to a saucy dish or stew.

Many traditional chicken recipes call for browning the pieces as a first step. Microwave cooking does not require this, nor does it do it well. You can lightly brown small quantities in a browning dish (see page 19). I have found, as in the Chicken in Red Wine, that richly flavored preparations do not require browning. If the unbrowned skin will offend you, remove it before cooking. If you insist on the classic browning of a number of chicken pieces before putting them in to stew, do it on top of the stove.

A flavored butter or stuffing under the skin will flavor and baste the meat and color the cooked skin.

Chicken with the bone in is best cooked in liquid in the microwave oven. Look at the Index for recipes for tomato sauces, broths, barbecue sauces and marinades.

Skinned and boned chicken pieces can be cooked individually wrapped in microwave plastic wrap if you want them neutral. Flavor by cooking in broth, or premarinate, or sprinkle with herbs and spices before wrapping.

While skin-on and bone-in pieces can overlap slightly, they will cook more evenly in one layer. Follow dish indications in recipes. See also illustration of arrangement of chicken pieces, page 215.

Microwave cooking of boneless parts is a quick way to cook chicken for salad, hash, or any of the Mexican recipes that use precooked chicken.

Cooking times are given for chicken in various pieces, with the skin and bone, without the skin and bone and in different quantities of liquid and/or vegetables. Since the time will vary depending on what is cooked with the chicken, this permits you to develop your own recipes.

Know the appetites of the eaters and the size of the meal you are planning before deciding how many pieces of chicken to allow per person. If cooking 2 servings on 2 separate plates, see page 18 for timing information. If you want to serve seconds and feel that you need more than the maximum number of chicken pieces given below, do not attempt to multiply the number of pieces. Make 2 batches; that way the chicken will be hot and ready when your guests are ready for a second serving.

See also browning dishes (page 19), adjusting cooking times for oven size (page 9), arranging foods in microwave (page 28) and microwave oven racks (page 18).

COOKING TIMES FOR CHICKEN BREASTS

Breasts, skinned and boned Split into 2 half breasts about ¼ lb. each; cover tightly.

half breast (6″ plate)	2 min. 30 sec.
half breast as above	3 min. (small oven)
whole breast (dinner plate)	3 min. 30 sec.
	4 min. (small oven)
2 whole breasts (10″ round dish)	5 min.
2 whole breasts, with 1½ c. vegetables (2-qt. soufflé)	9 min.
2 whole breasts as above	6 min. (small oven)
4 whole breasts, about 3 lb., with ¼ c. broth (14″ × 11″ × 2″ dish, or 12″ round dish)	8 min.

Breasts, skin and bone left on Split; cover tightly.

half breast stuffed under the skin, accompanied by 1 portion cooked vegetable (dinner plate)	2 min. 45 sec. 4 min. 30 sec. (small oven)
half breast as stew, with ¾ c. liquid and ½ c. raw vegetables (large soup plate)	12 min.
whole breast steamed	5 min. 30 sec.

in ¼ c. broth (8" round dish)	
2 whole breasts steamed in ¼ c. broth (8" × 10" oval dish)	7 min. 30 sec.

COOKING TIMES FOR CHICKEN LEGS AND LEG PIECES

Each leg is composed of a drumstick and a thigh piece. A complete leg, 2 thighs or 2 drumsticks cook in the same amount of time. On average, each piece will weigh just under ¼ pound. A whole leg, therefore, will weigh just under ½ pound.

Before cooking drumsticks you must make a cut, to the bone, all the way around the base of the thin end of the drumstick; this will allow the meat to shrink as it cooks, and the skin won't become so distended with steam that the drumstick explodes. To cook drumsticks only, arrange them spoke-fashion in a circular dish with the thick ends toward the outside of the dish, or alternate thin and thick ends if cooking them in a rectangular dish.

Times are for bone-in pieces. It is easier to bone chicken legs after they are cooked. Pieces may be skinned or not; it will make no difference to the timing. Legs seem to cook better with some liquid.

Whole legs, all thigh or all drumstick Cover tightly.

1 whole leg or 2 pieces with ¼ c. broth (6" round dish)	5 min. 7 min. 30 sec. (small oven)
1 whole leg with ¾ c. liquid and ½ c. vegetables (1-qt. soufflé)	12 min.
2 whole legs or 4 pieces with ¼ c. broth (11" × 6" rectangular dish)	7 min. 30 sec.
4 whole legs or 8 pieces with ¼ c. broth or coated with sauce (11" round dish)	12 min.
2 whole legs or 4 pieces with 2 tsp. butter, uncovered, turned once (9" square browning dish)	6 min.
4 whole legs or 8 pieces with 1 Tbs. butter, uncovered, turned once (10" square or round browning dish)	10 min. 30 sec.

COOKING TIMES FOR CHICKEN WINGS

Before cooking wings, cut off the wing tips and save them in your freezer until the next time you make broth. Divide wings at joint into 2 pieces. Six wings (12 pieces) make about 1 pound. The tips from 1 pound will give you 4 ounces to save. I can see no reason for ever cooking chicken wings without a sauce. All times below are with sauce, tightly covered.

Wings Remove tips; split in two; cover tightly.

6 wings, 12 pieces, with ⅓ c. sauce (9″ square pan or pie plate)	6 min.
6 wings as above	12 min. (small oven)
12 wings, 24 pieces, with ½ c. sauce (10″ × 8″ pan)	10 min.
24 wings, 48 pieces, with ⅔ c. sauce (14″ × 11″ dish)	14 min.

WHOLE BIRDS

Whole birds should be cut into parts. They cook better in the presence of liquid; this can be water, broth or ingredients for a sauce. Whole chickens are less expensive than the same weight of parts.

When cooking a whole chicken in pieces, arrange with thick part of drumsticks and thigh pieces toward the outside, and breast pieces and any other parts being cooked in the center, skin side down.

COOKING TIMES FOR WHOLE BIRDS

Cover tightly (2-quart soufflé or casserole).

2½-lb. bird with ¾ c. broth	15 min.
2½-lb. bird with 4 c. liquid and ¾ lb. vegetables	17 min.
3-lb. bird with ¼ c. to ¾ c. liquid	17 min.
4-lb. bird with 2 c. liquid, or 2 c. liquid and 1 lb. vegetables	22 min.

Yields

2 whole breasts	3 c. cooked meat in ½″ dice
4 drumsticks	1 c. cooked meat in pieces
4 thighs	1¼ c. cooked meat in pieces

CHICKEN BROTH This is one of the most useful basic preparations in the kitchen. In today's rushed world, I would venture to guess that it mainly comes out of a can in home kitchens—even mine—or that recipes calling for its use remain unmade. While I am sure that I will still resort to canned broth from time to time, I now have a good and rapid alternative. Since it can be unsalted, it is perfect for reduction in CHICKEN GLAZE or to make a more intense stock. I seldom make less than 4 cups, and I freeze what I don't use in 1-cup quantities for the future. See

Meat Broths. See also DEFROST-ING, homemade staples.

CHICKEN GLAZE A concentrate made from chicken broth, used to lend a strong chicken flavor to recipes where no extra liquid is needed. It may, for instance, be stirred into Beurre Blanc and served with chicken breasts. About 1 tablespoon glaze to each cup of sauce or stew is a good rule of thumb. See Meat Glazes.

CHICKEN LIVER Chicken livers are little dividends inside every whole chicken bought at the market. Don't throw them out. If you don't have immediate use for them, put them in a freezer container, cover with milk and freeze. As you acquire more livers, add them to the container and cover with more milk. Defrost when you want to make a pâté.

This is one of the few ingredients that can genuinely be sautéed and browned in a browning dish. They will also cook gently in the microwave oven in hot fat without toughening as long as they are not overcooked. Always heat the fat—chicken or butter—for 3 to 5 minutes (depending on the quantity) before adding the livers. If browning, heat the browning dish for 4 minutes at 100% before adding butter.

All livers should be cleaned of connective membranes, veins and fat before cooking.

DEFROSTING TIMES FOR CHICKEN LIVERS

Frozen in 1 cup milk Cook, uncovered, at 100%. Drain after cooking.

½ lb.	7 min. (stir after 5 min.)
1 lb.	9 min. (stir after 5 min.)

COOKING TIMES FOR CHICKEN LIVERS

Halved Cook in a single layer, uncovered.

½ lb. with 1 Tbs. butter, turned once (9″ square browning dish)	2 min.
1 lb. with 2 Tbs. butter, turned once (10″ square or round browning dish)	3 min.

Yields

½ lb. livers	1 c.
1 lb. livers	2 c.

CHICK-PEA Widely used in all the countries bordering the Mediterranean, they are available canned but have a slightly mushy texture. Like dried favas and unlike most beans, chickpeas have a skin that must be removed before final cooking or eating. For some reason microwave soaking makes the skins easier to slip off. Soak as for dried beans and legumes (see BEANS). Let the cooked chickpeas cool, covered, in their cooking liquid.

COOKING TIMES FOR CHICK-PEAS

Presoaked chick-peas Remove the skins; drain, rinse and return to 2-qt. soufflé; cover tightly.

1 c. chick-peas with 4 c. water	35 min.
2 c. chick-peas with 6 c. water	45 min.

Yields

1 c. chick-peas, dried	2½ c., cooked
2½ c., cooked	2 c. purée

CHIFFONADE A technique of thinly slicing leafy greens across the veins. (The heavy veins of spinach, sorrel, basil and other green leaves often make the cooked vegetable stringy.) Neatly line up the leaves in stacks for easy slicing.

CHILI Spicy pod peppers, both fresh and dry, red and green. The name also refers to the dishes made from them, in their native Mexico, the southwestern United States and Thailand, China and Hungary (with paprika), which have avidly adopted them as their own. See SOAKING, dried chilies.

Scads of sauces, differing in intensity, to shake and spoon, can be made following the method in Red Pepper Purée. They are much better than the bottled sauces. Make them when the chilies are in season; jar and refrigerate or can.

I dearly love Southwestern chili dishes, which can be varied practically ad infinitum. You can substitute venison, chicken, turkey, rabbit or pork for the beef, and vary the mix of seasonings, the amount of tomato, the presence or absence of chocolate. To invent your own, use Chunky Beef Chili and respect the proportion of liquid to solid. I have not found any advantage when cooking in the microwave oven to first cooking the peppers in fat, as is usual in most top-of-the-stove recipes. Again, if you really feel the need to brown the meat, do it first on top of the stove.

CHINESE BLACK BEAN See BLACK BEAN.

CHIPOTLE Peppers, often jalapeños, dried by smoking, that give a special flavor to many Southwestern dishes. See SOAKING, dried chilies. Canned chipotles are already soaked and can be used as is.

CHIVE Although these thin, tubular herbs—each a separate tiny plant even though they grow in clumps—are available dried and freeze-dried, I think they are only worth using fresh. When cutting, don't take the tips off of an entire clump or you will kill all the plants in it. Instead, cut off entire individual leaves. Either snip with scissors or slice with a sharp knife; do not attempt to chop—too messy. If chopping with other herbs or ingredients in a food processor, cut into 1-inch lengths first, or the long leaves will wrap themselves around the spindle. When fresh chives are not available, substitute thinly sliced scallion greens.

CHOCOLATE Chocolate is at once an everyday American delight and an arcane subject for specialists, who navigate their way amid warnings about the difficulties of tempering, scorching and seizing up. As an instinctive rather than a scientific cook, I was always rather intimidated by this. Imagine my delight when I found out how liberating it is to work with chocolate in the microwave oven: Properly handled, it becomes hassle-free. See Chocolate Glaze.

Remember that as chocolate cools, it acts as a thickening agent. Add, as in chili, for the last 3 minutes of cooking time, or it gets too hot and separates. Bitter chocolate is good as a background to spicy flavors.

When melting chocolate alone, do so on a plate, either in the paper in which it comes wrapped or unwrapped. Uncoated metal interiors of convection-microwave ovens will melt chocolate more quickly. When adding to a hot mixture, chop or grate first. Chocolate melted at 100%, covered, will not lose its temper. Usually, when chocolate is melted for candy or other coating, it is put through a complex series of controlled heatings and coolings called tempering so it stays

shiny and smooth. Temper in the microwave oven by melting half the chocolate; stir in remainder, grated.

MELTING TIMES FOR
CHOCOLATE

Break into ½- to 1-oz. pieces. Heat at 100%; cover tightly.

1 oz.	*45 sec.*
1 oz.	*2 min. (small oven)*
1½ oz.	*1 min*
1½ oz.	*2 min. 30 sec. (small oven)*
2 oz.	*2 min*
2 oz.	*1 min. 15 sec. (convection-microwave oven)*
4 oz.	*2 min.*
4 oz.	*3 min. (small oven)*
4 oz.	*1 min. 30 sec. (convection-microwave oven)*
8 oz.	*3 min. 30 sec.*
8 oz.	*2 min. to 2 min. 30 sec. (convection-microwave oven)*

CHOP To cut up into even but not regular (that would be diced) pieces that are fairly small but not really tiny (that would be minced). Chop with a knife, or in the food processor with short pulses.

CHRISTOPHINE See CHAYOTE.

CHUB In the U.S., used for a wide variety of fish. Before you buy, find out what fish you are actually getting and proceed accordingly. These tend to be soft-fleshed bony fish without much fat on them. You may want them filleted before cooking, and can substitute them in recipes with richly flavored sauces. For cooking times, see FISH.

CHUNKS These are irregular pieces of food that are not even on all sides. They are larger than cubes and thicker than slices.

CHUTNEY I love this kind of chunky, spicy fruit preserve. Almost any kind of fruit or non-leafy vegetable may be used; the mango version is often served as an accompaniment to curries. It is also a wonderful (if less classic) friend to simple grilled or roasted fish, birds and meat. Unfortunately, the bottled chutneys that I used to chop up and spread on bread with cream cheese or use with thinly sliced tomatoes as a sandwich have gotten more liquid (less fruit) over the years. Now that I have the handy, rapid microwave oven, I make my own. Try putting chutney in a grilled cheese sandwich. See Fresh Mango Chutney and Peach Chutney. You can easily substitute firm pears or apples for mangoes and add nuts.

CILANTRO See CORIANDER.

CINNAMON The inner bark of a tree, it comes in tight, dry rolls called sticks or quills. The best comes from Ceylon; ask for it. It is available ground,

too. Use the quills when infusing liquids; the dry powder will separate out.

CLAMS American varieties are available in a wide range of sizes, with hard as well as soft shells (those with soft shells are commonly called steamers). Littlenecks, the smallest hard-shell clams, are young and ideally should be no more than 1½ inches across, but you will find them up to 2 inches. Save the very smallest to eat raw—they are too good to cook. The medium-size, middle-aged cherry stones are about 3 inches across. The granddaddy quahogs are over 3½ inches across and are often called chowder clams. Hard-shell clams need only vigorous scrubbing and a check to make sure that all shells are tightly closed before cooking; discard any that seem the least bit open. Soft-shell clams have a protruding neck and, once the clams are cooked, clam-eaters will have to pull the black skin off the necks as they go along.

Littlenecks are usually served raw, on the half-shell; but they and their larger relatives are terrific contributions to seafood dishes and are good cooked on their own. Soft-shell clams are almost always eaten simply steamed, with the steaming liquid, lemon and melted butter on the side. Quahogs are usually cooked, chopped and added to soup or chowder. When cooking clams, if not using the broth they yield, save it, frozen, for use later in chowders and substitute for FISH BROTH See New England Clam Chowder and Clams Casino. See illustration page 63.

COOKING TIMES FOR CLAMS

Cook clams in a single layer, set on hinge ends and fit into a dish 2 inches deep; cover tightly. Clams are cooked as soon as they open; they don't have to gape.

Steamers 12 per lb.

14 clams with 2 Tbs. butter in a ramekin	*6 min. (small oven)*
18 clams with 2 Tbs. butter in a ramekin	*4 min.*
36 clams	*6 min.*
36 clams divided among 2 dishes	*8 min.*

Littlenecks 8 to 10 per lb.

6 clams	*2 min. 30 sec. to 3 min. 30 sec. (depending on size of clam)*
6 clams	*4 min. (small oven)*
12 clams (1½ lb.)	*4 min.*
24 clams (3 lb.)	*7 min.*
48 clams	*11 min.*

Cherrystones 3 per lb.

15 clams	*9 min.*

Quahogs 2 per lb.

16 (8 lb.) clams (14" × 11" × 2" dish)	*20 min.*

Yields Chopped meat.

3 lb. littlenecks	*½ c.*
5 lb. cherrystones	*1 c.*
8 lb. quahogs	*2½ c.*

CLAM BROTH This is not the medicinal stuff that comes in bottles, but the liquid from cooked clams. As clams vary in juiciness, yields may be different. Save any clam juice that you are not going to use in the dish under preparation; it can be used instead of fish broth to make Fish Velouté or as a base for soups, and can be frozen for later use. See DEFROSTING, homemade staples.

Yields

1½ lb. steamers	*⅓ to ½ c.*
3 lb. little-necks	*¾ c.*
5 lb. cherry-stones	*1¾ c.*
8 lb. qua-hogs	*3¾ to 5½ c.*

CLARIFYING *CLARIFYING BUTTER* is very simple and safe in the microwave oven—you won't get burned when the water in the butter spits as it is driven away. See BUTTER, clarified.

CLARIFYING BROTHS AND SAUCES to make them absolutely transparent—important for aspics and consommés—is a tedious chore on top of the stove and always a little suspenseful: Will it work? The microwave oven lets you breathe easy. Its strange effect of rubberizing egg whites is consummately useful and good here.

To clarify 4 cups of broth: Place broth in an 8-cup glass measure. Beat 5 egg whites until stiff, and stir them, with their shells, into broth with ½ pound very lean beef or other appropriate, coarsely ground meat. Let these solids collect on surface of liquid. Cook, uncovered, at 100% for 6 minutes. Wet a clean dish towel with warm water, wring it out and line a sieve with it. Place over large bowl. With a slotted spoon scoop egg whites and shells and meat into sieve. Slowly pour over hot broth. It should come through crystal clear; if not, repeat clarifying with 5 freshly beaten egg whites.

Broth can also be clarified by omitting meat; proceed exactly as above, omitting the ground meat. The broth will be more subtle and not quite as intense.

CLEMENTINE Small, almost seedless tangerines, the best of which come from Morocco, they are a recent and delicious addition to our winter fruits. The peel can be dried and makes an excellent seasoning. See DRYING, zest.

CLOVE Usually means the nail-shaped spice, really the dried, unopened flower bud of the clove tree. Always use carefully; the flavor is strong. It is available whole and ground. If you don't use it often, buy whole cloves and grind them as

needed; they will be more pungent. Ground cloves are always used in baking. Whole cloves are stuck into a ham before glazing.

One of the nicest ways of using this spice in microwave cooking is the old-fashioned trick of sticking a clove into a fruit or vegetable so that it can be readily located and, if necessary, extracted so that no one bites down on a still-hard stick. In microwave cooking, there is the added benefit that the clove flavor gently permeates the food into which it is stuck. See Light Poached Pears and Braised Onions. See also GRINDING.

Cloves have historically been a very dear spice. Do not confuse them with their inexpensive imitator, oil of clove, which is made from the bark of an American tree and used as a flavoring, anesthetic and breath freshener.

COCOA BUTTER Cocoa beans bare fatty little devils, almost one half fat. In the chocolate-making process the cocoa butter is pressed out of the beans. At a later point some of the cocoa butter is put back. The surplus cocoa butter is a valuable commodity for cooking, a rich fat that stays solid at higher temperatures than butter or oil. It used to be much more called for in the kitchen than it is today. Consequently, the only way I have been able to buy it recently is at old-fashioned drugstores where it is sold in sticks for use on the skin. If you want to buy some for the kitchen, make sure nothing in the way of scent or preservatives has been added. See Praline Paste.

COCONUT Most of us will cheat and buy this shredded or flaked and canned or sealed in airtight bags. The important thing is to check whether it is sweetened; sweetened may be all right for some baking, but you don't want to find it in your curry. The microwave oven can be of great help in opening your coconut. See the following recipes: Coconut Milk, Coconut Cream, Shredded Coconut and Toasted Coconut.

COCONUT MILK OR CREAM This is not the natural juice of the coconut, but a liquid made by cooking shredded coconut in milk and then straining. It is a basic ingredient of spicy dishes from India, Thailand, Indonesia, the Philippines and the Caribbean, all areas where the coconut grows lavishly; see, for example, Chicken Curry. Coconut milk also is essential to a piña colada. Fresh is better than canned, although canned may be used. Be careful not to buy sweetened coconut milk or cream if it is to be used in curry. See Coconut Milk.

COD Europe and Boston's most popular fish for centuries, either fresh or dried (even in countries such as Portugal, where fresh fish is plentiful). Small, young cod are called scrod. Cod is white-fleshed, tends to flake when cooked and is medium-firm. It falls apart if overcooked. Fresh cod can be cooked in steaks, fillets and medallions; for cooking times, see FISH. Salt (dried) cod must be soaked before use. The simple microwave way of soaking salt cod is a delight—it takes only 20 minutes—while the conventional way takes a couple of days and endless streams of cold running water.

SOAKING AND DESALTING
SALT COD

Skinned salt cod fillet, ½ lb. Rinse 2 min. under cold running water. Place in 10″ × 3″ round dish with 3 c. cold water. Cover tightly. Cook at 100% for 5 min. Uncover; drain. Rinse under cold water. Repeat twice.

COGNAC By most people's standards, this is the best of grape brandies coming from the Cognac region in France's Charente. See ALCOHOL.

COLLARDS One of the most primitive members of the cabbage family. Collards are typically used in the South's mess of greens or POT GREENS.

CONCASSÉ A French term for a simple tomato preparation often used in the making of sauces, or lightly seasoned and used as a sauce on its own.

There is a dispute as to whether it consists of tomatoes that have been peeled (see PEELING, tomatoes), cut in half across the fat part, gently squeezed to remove juice and seeds, and cleaned of remaining seeds with the flick of a finger or spoon before being chopped up, or whether it is also lightly cooked to dry it slightly and concentrate the flavors. (It is not cooked long enough to make a true sauce.) I favor the second, slightly cooked version; see Lightly Cooked Crushed Tomatoes. One advantage of this kind is that it can be frozen and used as needed.

CONCH This large, baroque shell provides something wonderful to eat only when it is exquisitely fresh. Then, the long fibrous muscle is best sliced thinly and eaten raw in a seviche. If you want to make conch chowder, prepare the chowder mixture (see Manhattan or New England Clam Chowder) and substitute thinly sliced raw conch for the clams; stir in while the mixture is still hot; cover tightly and cook at 100% for 1 minute 30 seconds. Substitute any fish broth for the clam juice.

CORIANDER This plant yields both an aromatic, tender, green-leaved herb (cilantro in Spanish-speaking countries, Chinese parsley in Oriental recipes) and a dry spice that is the light, small, brown seed of the

same plant. It has an earthy, pungent fragrance that people either love or loathe. See DRYING, herbs and GRINDING.

CORN Corn silk is easier to remove once the ear of corn is cooked. If you wish to serve corn in the husk without silk, tear the husk down far enough to strip away the silk, then pull husks back up.

COOKING TIMES FOR CORN ON THE COB

Ears with silk and husk intact 2 to 3 ears per lb. Place in a single layer on carousel or a platter, uncovered.

1 ear	2 min.
1 ear	3 min. (small oven)
2 ears	5 min.
2 ears	8 min. (small oven)
4 ears	9 min.
6 ears	14 min.

Yield

1 ear	½ c. kernels

CORNISH GAME HEN These American-bred birds of diminutive size and large breast make a perfect meal for one or two. When cooking them in the microwave oven, have the butcher split them in two. They will cook more evenly and will be easier for people to eat. Remember that these hens will brown only if stuffed under the skin.

COOKING TIMES FOR HENS

Split, backbone removed 1¾
lb. each. Spread flat in dish;
cover tightly.

1 hen with 1 c. grapes and ¼ c. liquid (10" × 4" × 4" oval dish)	7 min.
1 hen as above	16 min. (small oven, turn once)
2 hens with 2 c. fruit or vegetables cut small and ½ c. liquid (2-qt. soufflé)	12 min.
3 hens with 3 c. fruit or vegetables cut small and ¾ c. liquid (14" × 11" × 2" dish)	15 min.

CORNMEAL This great
American grain makes wonderful polenta in the microwave
oven. The Italian dish is usually
made with a coarsely ground
meal, although standard American white or yellow cornmeal
works perfectly well. See PO-
LENTA and Soft Polenta, Firm
Polenta and Fried Polenta. If
hot cereal for breakfast makes
a comeback, the microwave
oven combined with cornmeal
could star.

CORNSTARCH The most
satisfactory last-minute thickening to use in the microwave

oven. Generally, it is added in
a slurry of 2 parts water to 1
part cornstarch; 2 tablespoons
water with 1 tablespoon cornstarch thickens 1 cup of thin
sauce. Use less if the sauce is
already thick. When adding
cornstarch, leave the cooking
dish in the oven. Uncover carefully and quickly stir in the
cornstarch slurry; cover tightly
with fresh microwave plastic
wrap. (See illustration page
21.) At 100%, the sauce will
take about 2 minutes to thicken
if you have moved like lightning and up to 4 minutes if you
have been poking around. It
will have a nice silky texture.

Cornstarch also stars in microwave baking, where its abilities to hold things together
without problem-causing gluten
is invaluable; see Cakes and
Cookies.

COUSCOUS A form of miniature pasta and the dish made
with it, prevalent in the countries bordering the southern
Mediterranean, particularly
Morbocco, and in Sicily and
Spain. The authentic dish is
made by steaming the couscous
over a spicy stew. However, a
nonauthentic version that I find
a delicious adjunct to roast lamb
or chicken is Couscous made in
the style of risotto.

COVERING Lids, paper,
plastic wrap and so forth—this
is a large and important subject
in microwave cooking since it
truly is a major determinant of

the speed and manner in which foods cook. See pages 20–22 for a full discussion.

CRAB American waters yield a vast variety of crabs. The two most frequently cooked are soft-shells and the hard-shell Maryland blues. Sauté the soft-shells on top of the stove. Hard-shell crabs can be cooked in the microwave oven. Follow the recipe for Crab Boil or the even simpler Steamed Crabs.

Picked crabmeat, easier by far to use than whole crabs, comes both pasteurized and simply refrigerated. The refrigerated is infinitely better. Remember that this kind of crabmeat is already cooked. When preparing it in the microwave oven, make your sauce separately (Mornay, for instance), combine it with the crabmeat that you have picked over (to remove any cartilage) and reheat briefly in the microwave oven or brown under a broiler.

COOKING TIMES FOR CRABS

Whole hard-shell crabs 3 to 4 per lb. In a tightly sealed microwave-safe plastic bag.

6 crabs with dry seasonings (2 Tbs.)	*9 min.*
12 crabs with dry seasonings (4 Tbs.)	*15 min.*
24 crabs with dry seasonings (8 Tbs.)	*25 min.*

CRACKLINGS See REN-DERING.

CRANBERRY These bog berries are now available, frozen, year-round. Many relishes are best made with raw cranberries. However cooked, they also make wonderful sauces and jellies.

CREAM Is there anything more voluptuous than the really rich, heavy, sweet cream sometimes called whipping cream? I doubt it. If possible, find cream that has not been ultrapasteurized. If you are using a large amount of cream in the microwave oven, be sure to use a large, deep container—it has a nasty tendency to boil over.

CREAM CHEESE See SOFT-ENING, cream cheese. An 8-ounce package is 1 cup.

CREAM OF TARTAR Baking powder or a component of anonymous baking powders. You do little baking with wheat flour in the microwave oven; it is fairly irrelevant here.

CUBE Meats, peeled vegetables and peeled fruits are frequently cut into even, 6-sided cubes before cooking. Unless a size is given in a recipe, this normally means that each side of the cube is around $\frac{1}{2}'' \times \frac{1}{2}''$. A dice is smaller than a cube.

CUMIN This warm-tasting spice is one of my favorites. In the United States, it often crops up in prepared chili powders (though you can get chili powder made just with chili and add as much cumin as you want). Cumin is wonderful in a host of other dishes and is best ground fresh from the seeds. See GRINDING.

CURRANT These tiny jewellike berries come in red, black and gold but are not as available as they used to be. They were believed to carry white pine blister rust, so large stands of them were ripped out all over the country in an effort to preserve the pines. Gradually, the currants are being replanted. If you grow or can otherwise find them, you can make some of the world's best Currant Jelly, tart and sweet. Dried currants are often used in fruit cakes, honey buns and pound cakes. See SOAKING, dried fruit.

CURRY A blend of several spices, usually including dried hot peppers, turmeric, cardamom, cumin, ginger and coriander. (There is a rarely used Indian leaf herb whose name sounds, to Occidental ears at any rate, like "curry" and thus that name has been given to both the spice powder and the dishes made with that leaf.) "Curry" powders are commercially available in various qualities. Some Indian recipes call for particular blends, for which the spices are often toasted first. See TOASTING, whole spices, Chicken Curry and Green Curry of Summer Squash.

CUTTLEFISH See SQUID.

D

DAB See SOLE. For cooking times, see FISH.

DANDELION GREENS In early spring, these greens can be picked out of any lawn. Never pick from a lawn or roadside that has recently been sprayed with weed killer. Always pick the smallest leaves.

Today, dandelion is commercially grown. The leaves you buy in the store will be considerably larger than those you would pick. The French use dandelion leaves in a salad typically sprinkled with lardoons

and dressed with their rendered fat. In the American South, dandelion greens are often popped into spring Pot Greens. For purposes of cooking time, consider them soft greens.

Yields

1 bunch dandelion	½ lb., with stems
½ lb., with stems	⅓ lb., cleaned and stemmed
⅓ lb., stemmed and tightly packed	3½ c. raw, cut into 2" pieces

DAUBE There are many different explanations for the derivation of the word daube, the French name for a dish made by the long, moist cooking of meat that has not been previously browned. The explanation I favor takes into account the numerous countries that have similar dishes with seemingly related names and techniques: the various adobos of the Spanish-speaking countries, the Italian addobbo and even the English nonculinary "daub." The similar words all relate to a root word meaning "to whiten" (used also to describe the whitewashing of walls and thence to the covering materials of the walls, adobe—the same kind of earthenware from which pots are made).

In different regions of France there developed, over the centuries, earthenware pots of particular shapes specifically suited to the preparation of specific sorts of dishes. A daubière is taller than it is wide, with a bulbous bottom and a narrower neck. In later evolution, but before the universal appearance of ovens, the daubière lid was hollowed to hold hot coals, providing for top as well as bottom heat. This pot gave its name to a group of dishes in which meat is tightly covered and slowly cooked to a rich flavor, tasting slightly of the earthenware pot. The lack of browning and the tight sealing are perfect for the microwave oven. See Sliced Beef Casserole.

DEFROSTING One of my greatest pleasures in writing about microwave cooking is the feeling that I will be helping people to once again eat delicious fresh food. It really takes no more time to make food fresh in the microwave oven than to defrost it. Fresh tastes much better.

How you wrap and prepare foods for FREEZING determines how well and quickly you can defrost them.

Preprogramming. If you have an oven with a preprogrammed defrost cycle that you trust, use it. I tried seven different programs from different manufacturers. No two were the same. I also did not find their programs gave a better result than defrosting at 100% for a shorter time. Large blocks of food such as roasts and family-size quantities of soup got hot, slightly cooked or recooked, no matter what method was used.

Pack food for freezing in smallish quantities so as not to risk ruining it in the defrosting. Small quantities can either be defrosted or cooked, no matter what methods are used. In most cases, small quantities of frozen, raw foods (such as a single fish fillet or skinned and boned breast of chicken) are best cooked frozen, often in broth or sauce. See FREEZING.

Large quantities, such as roasts, sometimes defrost better at 30%. This may be difficult to locate on your oven due to manufacturer paranoia. (It is as if stove manufacturers refused to tell you what temperature the settings on their ovens mean.) The most usual euphemisms are "low defrost," "medium low," "simmer," "3," and "low," or "defrost" where there are fewer settings.

HOMEMADE STAPLES

Broths, tomato purées and the like, glazes, reductions, for Beurre Blanc, Duxelles, Sauce Espagnole, fruit sauces, and purées are the exceptions to the basic rule of fresh. These should be frozen in small quantities. Since you use modest quantities at a time, this will prevent you from having to defrost too much at once, which takes too long and wastes food. Defrosting these foods in the microwave oven does not leave them cold, as they would be if defrosted in the refrigerator, but the degree of recooking is not critical here.

Some generalizations can be made. Very small quantities, the kinds that are used to enrich a sauce or accompany a single portion of fish or chicken, will take the same time no matter what food is involved. Large and medium oven times should be roughly equal; in a small oven, allow 30 seconds more.

DEFROSTING TIMES FOR LIQUIDS, SMALL AMOUNTS

Frozen cube Put in a ramekin or small soufflé dish; cover tightly; defrost at 100%.

1 Tbs.	45 sec. to 1 min.
2 Tbs. (1 oz.)	1 min. to 1 min. 30 sec.
¼ c. (2 oz.)	1 min. 30 sec. to 2 min.

In larger quantities, a judgment has to be made as to the density of the liquid, or the solidity and butteriness of the purée. Take the lid off the freezer container. If the container is microwave-safe, cover it with microwave plastic wrap; if not, empty the contents into a suitable bowl or measure.

DEFROSTING TIMES FOR THIN LIQUIDS

Broths, juices and light sauces such as tomato Cover tightly; defrost at 100%.

½ c.	2 min. to 2 min. 30 sec.
1 c.	4 to 5 min.
1½ c.	6 min. to 6 min. 30 sec.
2 c.	8 min.
3¼ c.	15 min.

DEFROSTING TIMES FOR MEDIUM-WEIGHT LIQUIDS

Purées and sauces with some fat (such as Espagnole, Béchamel, Duxelles and Sorrel) Cover tightly; defrost at 100%.

½ c.	4 min. 30 sec.
⅔ c.	5 min.
1 c.	9 min.
1¼ c.	10 min.

DEFROSTING TIMES FOR THICK LIQUIDS

Thick sauces and heavy purées (such as potato and broccoli) Cover tightly; defrost at 100%.

½ c.	2 min.
1 c.	3 min. 30 sec.
2 c.	5 min.

For defrosting prepared *PASTA DISHES*, see Macaroni and Cheese.

RAW INGREDIENTS

Raw ingredients are occasionally acceptable when frozen and defrosted. Sometimes they are a necessity. What is bought frozen should be kept frozen until it is time to defrost and cook it. Food should be cooked as soon after defrosting as possible. Single-portion quantities of raw ingredients—vegetables, skinned and boned chicken breasts and filleted fish or fish steaks—should be cooked from the frozen, not thawed first. Roasts over 7 or 8 pounds should not be defrosted in the microwave oven; flat legs of lamb and loins of pork defrost most successfully.

MEAT

Beef roasts (braising cuts) 3½ lb. When buying, ask butcher to cover roast with fatback. This helps protect the surface. Place frozen, unwrapped meat in microwave-safe plastic bag. Knot to close. Heat at 30% for 25 min. Turn over; heat 20 min. at 30%. Season and roast or cook as desired.

Beef, steak Don't do it.

Lamb, short leg (spring lamb) About 4 lb., in a 14″ × 9″ × 2″ dish. Shield shanks with aluminum foil. Cook, uncovered, at 100% for 15 min. Remove foil and continue cooking for 6 min. Then season and cook for 20 min. in 500° F. oven for medium rare. Serves 6. See Roast Leg of Baby New Zealand Lamb.

Lamb, whole leg About 7 lb., in a 14″ × 11″ × 2″ dish. Shield shanks with aluminum foil. Cover tightly with microwave plastic wrap. Cook at 100% for 14 min. Uncover, remove foil. Re-cover and cook at 100% for 14 min. more. Then season and cook for 20 min. in 500° F. oven for medium rare. Serves 10.

Lamb chops Don't do it.

Pork loin Boned and rolled, 3 to 4 lb., wrapped in microwave-safe plastic bag or wrap, 20 min. at 30%. Let sit 5 min. after taking from oven. Roast normally.

Pork chops To defrost chops to be cooked in sauce in the microwave oven, lengthen the cooking time in the sauce.

4 thin chops in sauce	add 2 min.
4 thick	covered at

chops with	100% for 20
1 c. tomato	min.
sauce	

Spareribs, individual racks
Do not defrost. Cook frozen in sauce. Cook 30 min. for each frozen rack.

Bacon To soften and separate, see BACON.

FOWL

CHICKEN PIECES are best defrosted in their cooking liquid. To arrange, see page 29. For skinned, boned and halved breasts:

2 Half chicken breasts (1 whole breast split) In ½ c. liquid (and ¼ to ½ c. vegetables, if desired) in an 8½″ × 6½″ × 2″ dish, tightly covered. Cook at 100% for 5 min., turn over, re-cover tightly, and cook 3 min. longer.

4 Half chicken breasts (2 whole breasts, split) In 2 c. broth or light sauce (and ½ to 1 c. vegetables, if desired) in an 11″ × 8″ × 2″ dish, tightly covered. Cook at 100% for 5 min.; turn over, re-cover tightly, and cook 4 min. longer.

DUCK is often bought frozen. Remove from plastic package. Place at end of large microwave-safe plastic bag. Knot bag so as to contain bird moderately tightly. Defrost 20 minutes at 30%. Turn over and defrost another 20 minutes at 30%. Remove bird from bag to roasting pan. Carefully pry open tail end (it will still be

slightly frozen). Remove pockets of fat. With your hand, wiggle the package of neck and innards stored inside the bird until you can free and remove it (it may take a minute or two). Roast as is, or cut up for microwave cooking. See DUCK.

QUAIL is available frozen, in packages of four. Unwrap and defrost at 30% for 5 minutes, turning over once.

FISH AND SEAFOOD

FILLETS Individual fish fillets are better wrapped and frozen in individual serving portions, 5 to 8 ounces. Defrost in the cooking sauce where feasible. Directions here are for individual fillets wrapped tightly in microwave plastic wrap and defrosted without sauce. Cook afterward. This technique is good for dieters who want to keep portion-controlled pieces of fish on hand.

1-lb. fillet (4″ wide), tightly wrapped	7 min. at 30%
Small fillets (6 to 8 oz.), 1 on a small plate	1 min. at 100%, turn over, 30 sec. at 100%, rest wrapped 1 min.
	1 min. 30 sec. at 100%, turn over, 1 min. at 100%, rest wrapped 1 min. (small oven)

2 on a dinner plate	*1 min. 30 sec. at 100%, turn over, 1 min. 30 sec. at 100%, rest wrapped 1 min. 2 min. at 100%, turn over, rest wrapped 2 min. (small oven)*
4 on a platter	*1 min. 30 sec. at 100%, turn over, 2 min. at 100%, rest wrapped 2 min. Do not do in small oven.*

Boned or unboned steaks Defrost at 100% in microwave plastic wrap.

8-oz. steak (1" thick)	*1 min. 30 sec., turn over, 30 sec.; cook.*

WHOLE FISH Remove the head and tail if the fish is too long to fit in the oven. Wrap tightly in microwave plastic wrap. Shield (see page 12) 2 inches to 3 inches of tail end and around cut where head was removed in doubled aluminum foil. Place fish diagonally on the glass tray of the oven. For fish over 3 pounds, or without head and tail, start with a defrosting time of 25 minutes at

30%. Add 5 minutes for each pound over 3 pounds. Turn over once during cooking time. Remove foil for final one third of cooking time.

Small fish Defrost at 100%; turn over once. Wrap whole fish tightly in microwave plastic wrap.

1 fish, 14 to 16 oz.	*2 min.*
2 fish, 14 to 16 oz. each	*3 min. 30 sec.*

Large, thick fish Defrost at 30%; turn over twice. See illustration page 12 to shield fish.

8-lb fish, 6¼ lb. without head and tail	*45 min.; remove foil after 30 min.*
7½-lb. fish, 5¾ lb. without head and tail	*35 min.; remove foil after 30 min.*
4-lb. fish, 3½-lb. without head and tail	*30 min.; remove foil after 20 min.*
3¼-lb. fish with head and tail	*25 min.; remove foil after 15 min.*

Tiny shrimp To cook, 1½ min. longer.

½-lb. package	*2 min. at 100%*

Lobster tail Cover each tightly.

3 to 4-oz. tail	*30 sec.*

5 to 6-oz. tail	50 sec.
7 to 8-oz. tail	1 min. 45 sec.
9 to 12-oz. tail	2 min. 30 sec.

VEGETABLES

Even though I prefer fresh vegetables, I often cook frozen ones because I have a garden and I know no way of growing exactly the right amount. There are only two commercially prepared frozen vegetables that I use with any frequency—honest. They are the tiny little peas, often better than fresh, and the small lima beans, almost always better than fresh. These vegetables should be considered blanched, not raw. Sometimes I use peeled and frozen pearl onions to save myself work.

HOME-FROZEN VEGETABLES Asparagus and other whole vegetables frozen without prior blanching should be cooked directly from the frozen. Add 30 seconds to the cooking time for every ½ pound of frozen asparagus.

Small vegetables such as peas, baby limas, all kinds of fresh beans and sliced vegetables should be taken out of their wrapping and placed in a sieve. Run warm, not hot, tap water over them so that the pieces can be separated. Drain and cook immediately as if fresh. If vegetables are allowed to defrost fully before cooking, reduce cooking time by one quarter.

Treat vegetables that have been cooked in butter or sauce or have been made into purée before freezing like homemade staples (heavy purées).

COMMERCIALLY PREPARED FROZEN FOOD Such foods come with package instructions. If, even with this book in hand, you want to defrost commercially prepared frozen food, you don't need my help except for two warnings: (1) Even if the instructions don't tell you to, put the package on a plate or in a bowl. Some of the contents will invariably spill over and mess up the oven. Also, the plastic pouches are hard to handle when hot. It's easier to take a plate out of the oven. (2) Wait a minute or two after taking a plastic pouch of food out of the oven before opening it. Even if you have pricked the pouch as instructed, there will still be enough steam in the bag to give you a nasty burn. Unless you let it cool slightly, it is hard to avoid the steam because the plastic bag flops as you open it.

HOMEMADE FROZEN PREPARED FOOD In my house these are the result of miscalculation: too much prepared for the number of people or the appetites. I do not cook and freeze ahead now that I have a microwave oven except for homemade staples and vegetables. If I have leftovers and cannot bear to throw them out now rather than later, I pack them up in 1-cup quantities, or what is reasonable for one or two people, in order to freeze. Larger quantities, especially if there are chunks of meat in them, will take too long to defrost. This is not just defrosting, but defrosting and REHEATING in one operation. Increase the defrosting times for homemade staples (heavy purées) by one third.

DICE Fruits, vegetables and meats are sometimes cut into even 6-sided shapes before cooking. Unless a specific size is given in the recipe, they are to be ¼″ × ¼″ on each side.

DILL The feathery leaves and small, flat, oval seeds of this plant are one of Russia's gifts (along with rhubarb, sour cream and yogurt) to the culinary world. The seeds and dried flowers are normally used in pickling. The seeds are also good in salads. Fresh dillweed is wonderful in cucumber salad, chicken soup and summer squashes. Many preparations that call for mint are equally successful with dill.

I never used dried dill in the past because it was such an ugly color. With microwave-oven DRYING, dillweed stays green, wonderful for those with plentiful fresh dill in the summer and none in the winter. Use a teaspoon of dried dillweed to substitute for each tablespoon of fresh.

DRYING Before freezers and refrigerators, food that wasn't canned (preserved) was often dried. Even today, some foods such as herbs, apricots, prunes, raisins and seeds are routinely dried. Still other foods that used to be dried for preserving have become expensive and sought-after specialties because of their particularly good flavor, different from that of their fresh progenitors. Examples would be sun-dried tomatoes from Italy, dried mushrooms from many parts of the world, and salted and dried cod.

Some foods can be dried satisfactorily in the microwave oven. Others cannot, particularly those that have a high ratio of water to solid matter. I tried for weeks to create the equivalent of sun-dried tomatoes, to no effect. True Boletus edulis, or CEPE, dries very successfully. Its slimier, wetter cousins don't.

Most dried foods need to be soaked in olive oil, water or broth before they are used in a dish. There are some exceptions to this when cooking in the microwave oven. When included in soups and stews, dried mushrooms, other than MORELS, do not need to be presoaked; see Mushroom Barley Soup. Morels need to be presoaked to remove grit and sand. There may be dishes, such as sautés, for which you want to presoak other dried mushrooms. See SOAKING.

To dry *coconut*, see page 354.

DRYING HERBS

Microwave drying is standard practice for me. The color and

fragrance are the next best thing to fresh. Scatter 2 cups of loosely packed, washed and dried herb leaves or sprigs in an even layer on a 1-sheet double layer of paper toweling. Do not cover. Cook for 4 minutes at 100%. Keep tightly covered.

DRYING MUSHROOMS

Fairy rings, chanterelles, lactarii and cèpes all dry successfully. After wiping clean or washing only with a damp paper towel, dry mushrooms thoroughly. Slice cèpes ⅛ inch thick through the stem. Leave fairy rings whole. Cut chanterelles into quarters from top to bottom, or sixths if very large. Halve lactarii. Cover a doubled layer of paper toweling, 1 sheet large, with a single layer of mushrooms. Cook, uncovered, at 100% for 3 minutes. Turn mushroom slices over onto fresh toweling and cook 2 minutes at 100%. If the mushrooms are not light and perfectly dry, leave on a dry sheet of paper overnight. When perfectly dry, store in a tightly closed glass bottle.

DRYING ZEST

Oranges, lemons and tangerines are not usually dried at home, but the zests are a nice ingredient to have available to season stews or add, pulverized, to baked foods. Peel oranges and lemons very thinly with a potato peeler, taking none of the bitter white pith. Cut zest into strips about ¼ inch wide. Peel tangerines; turn peel orange side down and scrape off the white pith (using the edge of a silver spoon, if possible). Cut zest as above.

The zest of 1 orange or 2 lemons spread out on a double sheet of paper toweling and covered with a single sheet will dry in 2 minutes 30 seconds at 100%, to make 3 tablespoons.

The zest of 1 tangerine, 1 large clementine or 2 small clementines will take 2 minutes at 100% and make 2 tablespoons.

DUCK Properly cooked, duck takes advantage of the microwave oven's differential cooking properties (fat cooks more quickly than meat) more than almost any other food. Duck's plentiful extra fat also renders magnificently in the microwave oven. I am as pleased by the recipes for duck as anything I have done in the oven, and it is gratifying that this technique makes it reasonable to cook duck for only one or two people. See Crispiest Duck for timings on duck; see Duck Confit for this very special dish, so fashionable today in salads but traditionally used in cassoulet (see Paula Wolfert's *The Cooking of Southwest France*) or simply broiled to serve with potatoes cooked in the duck fat. See also RENDERING.

Ducks make wonderful broth and glaze. Duck livers are large and may be substituted by weight for other livers in recipes for pâtés. They also make very special creamy mousses on their own. The other innards can be made into a confit. If you are cooking one of today's numerous recipes for skinned and boned duck breast (magret), save the bones for broth and render the skin in flat pieces and use on a salad.

DUCK BROTH See Meat Broths. See also CLARIFYING, broths and sauces.

DUCK GLAZE See Meat Glazes.

E

EGGS All recipes in this book use U.S. Grade A Large eggs. These kitchen staples have idiosyncracies in microwave cooking: To wit, never try to cook an egg in its shell, as it will explode. In fact, even a whole egg yolk will explode unless pricked once or twice with the tip of a sharp knife before cooking. Strangely enough, this doesn't result in a gooey mess, and the yolk keeps its shape very well. In Eggplant, Tomato and Fennel with eggs or Baked Eggs, simply break the eggs where you want them; quickly prick each yolk a couple of times, and continue to cook according to the recipe. I hope this will bring back all the delicious baked egg dishes of the classic repertoire.

BINDING WITH EGG YOLKS

This presents few problems. A sauce will curdle if the yolks get too hot or aren't stirred thoroughly or frequently enough. Follow recipes exactly. Allow

1 yolk for each ½ cup of sauce. See Chicken Fricassee for technique. *CUSTARDS* work on the same principle; see Crème Brûlée. The classic French dessert sauce Crème Anglaise and the indispensable tart ingredient, Pastry Cream, are thinner versions of the custard.

QUICHE is made with a custard. I do not find crusts satisfactory in the microwave oven. If you are willing to settle for a quiche without a crust, see page 152 for a very successful recipe. You can bake the crust in a traditional oven, then fill and bake in the microwave oven.

EGG WHITE–RAISED DISHES

Soufflés are a disaster. When I first tried a soufflé in the oven and peeked through the glass door, I was ecstatic; I thought we were all going to be making the highest, best soufflés the world has ever seen. As this soufflé finished its rising act and continued to cook in order to set, my beautiful dome collapsed into a sad pancake. No fiddling with soufflé recipes worked. I have tried every recipe in every book that claims to be for soufflés for the microwave oven. Not one of them is worth making.

Prepare your soufflé bases in the microwave oven, then bake the soufflé conventionally; Basic Béchamel and virtually any vegetable, fruit or fish purée will make a good soufflé base. However, the fallen-soufflé technique is the basis of many of the cakes in this book.

Now, as for my own idiosyncracies as opposed to those of eggs themselves: There are those who prepare *SCRAMBLED EGGS* and *OMELETS* (which they don't seem to differentiate sharply) in the microwave oven. I don't like the texture (too fluffy), and I don't like constantly opening the door during a short cooking period. Make your omelets and scrambled eggs on top of the stove.

EGGPLANT This vegetable comes into its own in the microwave oven. Now, it is true that you will not get a charred taste cooking it this way, nor can you fry it in the microwave oven, but you will get a lightness of taste and lack of bitterness. Skins on whole eggplants—pricked a few times so the vegetables don't explode while cooking—have a nicer color than those of eggplants cooked any other way. The flesh stays a lovely pale green that is attractive for dips. See Classic Eggplant Appetizer and Eggplant Appetizer with Oriental Seasonings.

LARGE PURPLE EGGPLANT

COOKING TIMES FOR LARGE WHOLE PURPLE EGGPLANT

Prick several times with a fork; set on 2 layers of paper toweling, uncovered.

½ lb.	8 min.
1 lb.	12 min.
1 lb.	16 min. *(small oven)*
2 lb.	18 to 20 min.

SMALL PURPLE EGGPLANT

Alternatively called Japanese eggplant, these are miniature versions of the large eggplant. The best are 3″ to 4″ long. They are attractive halved and stuffed (see page 73). They are also excellent as part of a mixed vegetable dish.

COOKING TIMES FOR SMALL PURPLE EGGPLANT

Halved and stuffed 4″ long; cover tightly.

6 eggplants; stuff after 3 min. (9″ pie plate)	7 min.

CHINESE EGGPLANT

These are the long thin eggplants in various colors that are so often pictured in Chinese paintings.

COOKING TIMES FOR WHOLE CHINESE EGGPLANT

Prick several times with a fork; cook in a dish just large enough to hold them; cover tightly.

½ lb.	*10 to 12 min.*
1 lb.	*15 min.*

MINIATURE EGGPLANT

These are about 2 inches long and under 1 inch in diameter; they are usually preserved in oil or pickled.

EMULSIFICATION   The binding together of a fat (oil or butter) and an acid (such as vinegar) or a protein (such as egg yolks). An emulsion is a uniform suspension of minuscule fat droplets throughout a liquid, achieved either by rapid beating and/or warming to form a stable mixture. Mayonnaise, and the infamous Hollandaise are emulsions.

Emulsions such as egg-bound sauces and custards that involve stirring and the heat of actual boiling do splendidly in the microwave oven. (See EGGS.) It seems foolish to me to open the microwave oven every 15 seconds, as readers are often directed, to stir something like a Hollandaise. Be content

to use the microwave oven to melt the butter for Hollandaise; make the sauce itself on top of the stove.

Other sauces are thickened in other ways. See Savory Sauces and Sweet Sauces, and CORN-STARCH.

ENDIVE   The pale second growth of Belgian chicory, best known in this country as a salad leaf. In Europe, it is more often braised. You can vary the ingredients in the braising liquid (keep quantities and times the same).

COOKING TIMES FOR ENDIVE

Whole endive Braised in a dish just large enough to hold them; cover tightly.

2 heads with *⅓ c. liquid*	*8 min.*
2 heads as *above*	*12 min. (small* *oven)*
8 heads with *1 c. liquid*	*16 min.*

EVAPORATION   The liquid in foods or added to them partially evaporates in microwave cooking unless tightly covered. Sometimes evaporation is desirable, as in Risotto and in RE-DUCTIONS.

F

FATS   One of the nice things about cooking in a microwave oven, particularly for those of us on a perpetual diet, is that

very little fat is needed since foods do not stick to the cooking pan (and we cannot really sauté). Except for recipes where the food is cooked entirely in fat, a sort of melting procedure (see treatment of onions in risotto recipes, pages 117–119), think of fats primarily as flavorings when cooking in the microwave oven.

Many different kinds are used in cooking: animal fats such as bacon, butter, chicken, duck, fatback, lard and suet; vegetable oils such as corn and soy; fruit oils such as olive; and the seeming infinity of seed and nut oils such as coconut, hazelnut, sesame, walnut, sunflower, cottonseed (used mainly in margarine), peanut, safflower, almond and even mustard. Each has its own taste.

The flavor of a fat changes with heating. Some of the expensive oils, such as almond, walnut and hazelnut, taste much better cold and should rarely be heated (and then only slightly, as for a warm salad dressing). The flavor of other fats changes very noticeably when they are heated enough to brown, like butter and bacon, but the browned taste is often desirable. Some fats, like sesame oil, have an entirely different flavor when the seed or nut is toasted before the oil is extracted. (Oriental sesame oil is made from seeds toasted first and so is brown in color, rather than pale gold-to-clear.)

Fats can go rancid if kept too long in too warm an environment. Peanut oil, a neutral oil to start with, quickly develops an "off" taste, especially if kept in a clear bottle in a well-lighted place. While animal fats freeze well, the oils don't. Even refrigerating an oil such as olive (containing some fruit pulp and acid) may be enough to make it cloud and separate. Other oils, such as nut oils, that contain tiny solid particles separate when refrigerated.

Fats have different melting and burning temperatures. For melting techniques for animal fats, see BUTTER and RENDERING. If you respect the cooking times and quantities in the recipes, you will have no problem with fat burning.

DEEP-FAT FRYING

Deep-fat cooking, or frying, has traditionally been discouraged in the microwave oven. I have discovered, contrary to current misconception, that smallish amounts of foods fried at a time cook delightfully, and you have the added advantages of not heating up the entire kitchen or spattering the stove. For deep-fat frying, neutral-flavor oils such as corn, safflower and peanut tend to be most satisfactory. However, the Italians deep-fry in olive oil. See FRYING and Beignets, Tempura and Croutons.

Deep-fat frying in the microwave oven is not an all-purpose method of deep-frying. When it comes to deep-fat frying at a high temperature, you can use a saturated or unsaturated fat, because the heat will convert unsaturated fat molecules into saturated ones. The same is true for margarines. For use in salad dressings, on bread or when the fat isn't subjected to heat, saturated fats probably are not as good for you as either polyunsaturated or mono-unsaturated fats, particularly if you have a tendency to coronary artery disease or high cholesterol. Mono-unsaturated fats used to be thought less good for you than polyunsaturated; but in the fast-moving world of nutritional information, it has now been found that there are actually some health advantages to mono-unsaturated fats like olive oil. They certainly have more taste.

FATBACK Solid, unmelted pork fat without meat streaks. This also comes salted. The fatback used in pâtés and to line pâté molds must always be the unsalted kind. (Have the butcher slice the fat for lining; it will save much time and effort.) Be careful when getting a verbal recipe from Southerners. They may mean salt pork, not fatback. See SALT PORK.

FAVA BEAN A broad bean often used dried. It does not cook brilliantly in the microwave oven, but the microwave oven can subdue its difficult nature enough to make removing its tough skin child's play. See BEANS.

FENNEL There are two different, but related, plants called fennel. One is a weed that can be cultivated; it grows along the shores of the Mediterranean and in California. Its feathery tops, which look a lot like dill, are used in fish dishes, and its dried stalks are used as fuel for fires over which fish is grilled.

The other is Florence fennel, a root vegetable that looks sort of like a bulbous celery. It is terrific raw, thinly sliced, in salads with a lemony dressing. It also makes a good and unusual cooked vegetable, and this is where the microwave oven comes in. It cooks the vegetable quickly without leaving it fibrous or turning it mushy. I have added fennel to vegetable dishes (see Eggplant, Tomato and Fennel) and have served it on its own (see Fresh Fennel). If you can't find fennel, try substituting celery hearts or celery root.

COOKING TIMES FOR
FENNEL

Large bulb fennel 3″ diameter, about ½ lb. each. Trim and cut into 6 wedges each; wrap tightly.

1 bulb fennel	3 min. 30 sec., rest 2 min.
2 bulbs fennel	5 min., rest 2 min.

FENNEL SEED The seed of the weed fennel is used as a spice, whole or ground. See GRINDING. The flavor is something halfway between dill seed and anise, slightly licorice.

FIGS Fresh, fully ripe figs are one of the world's great pleasures, and they require no cooking. However, there are times when they are less than radiant but would be a welcome change as a dessert. They can be poached. See SOAKING, dried fruit.

COOKING TIMES FOR
WHOLE FRESH FIGS

With ½ cup liquid per dozen figs; cover tightly.

3 figs (2-c. ramekin)	*1 min. 30 sec. to 2 min.*
6 figs (8" ring mold)	*3 min.*
12 figs (10" ring mold)	*5 min.*

FILBERT See HAZELNUT.

FISH All fish cook magnificently in the microwave oven except for those that are simply too large; double-check size, especially if you have a carousel. Also, pieces more than 4 inches thick will not cook terribly evenly (but they don't in a fish kettle or the oven either). Fish stays moist without any hardening of its surface. When in doubt, undercook. You can always put it back for a few more minutes.

Fish cook with relative uniformity from type to type. Cooking time depends on the shape, thickness and quantity of bone. There are a couple of exceptions: monkfish and paupiettes (fillets rolled around a stuffing). Fish timings are based on the use of an oven with a carousel or the use of a separate carousel. *If you are not using a carousel*, all cooking times over 5 minutes should be interrupted at the halfway point and the cooking dish rotated 45 degrees. If the total cooking time is more than 15 minutes, rotate 45 degrees after each third of cooking time. All fish cooking times are based on tight covering with microwave plastic wrap. For additional information about arranging fish in a cooking dish, see page 29. All cooking times given here are for large or medium-size ovens, unless otherwise indicated.

To cook more than 1 plate of fish at a time, see page 158. To cook fish with seafood, see Scrod with Clams Livornese.

See also individual varieties, especially MONKFISH, TROUT and TUNA; DEFROSTING, fish and seafood; and SEAFOOD COMBINATIONS.

FILLETS

I am defining these as halves or quarters of fish removed lengthwise from the bones. Cooking times are the same whether they are skinned or not. If the skin is on, slash it across the width so the fillet does not curl. Line up fillets, in a single layer if possible, in a rectangular pan (it need not be greased). Season and cover tightly with microwave plastic wrap. Added liquid is not necessary; it will lengthen the cooking time and should be kept to a minimum (in any case, it need not cover the fillet). If adding liquid, about ¼ cup per ⅓ pound fillet is adequate. Each ½ cup will extend the cooking time 30 seconds.

COOKING TIMES FOR FILLETS

½″ thick fillets, 4 oz. each Steamed; cover tightly on a plate just large enough to hold them.

1 piece	*1 min.*
1 piece	*1 min. 30 sec. (small oven)*

½″ thick fillets, 6 to 8 oz. each Steamed; cover tightly.

1 piece	*2 min.*
1 piece	*3 min. 30 sec. (small oven)*
2 pieces	*2 min. 30 sec.*
4 pieces	*5 min.*
6 pieces	*7 min.*

1″ thick fillets, 6 to 8 oz. each Steamed; cover tightly.

1 piece	*3 min.*
1 piece	*4 min. 30 sec. (small oven)*
2 pieces	*4 min. 30 sec. 6 min. (small oven)*
4 pieces	*6 min.*
6 pieces, about 3 lb.	*8 min. to 8 min. 30 sec.*

PAUPIETTES

These are individual fillets split lengthwise down the center. Any bones and membrane are rolled individually, starting with the head end. Sometimes a stuffing is placed inside the roll. Add 15 seconds to the cooking time for each stuffed paupiette. Cover tightly with microwave plastic wrap.

COOKING TIMES FOR PAUPIETTES

Unstuffed Steamed; cover tightly.

1 piece	*45 sec.*
2 pieces	*1 min. 30 sec.*
4 pieces	*2 min.*
8 pieces	*3 min.*

PAPILLOTES

Portions of fish cook exceptionally well when enclosed in their own little packages of microwave plastic wrap or parchment paper. (Aluminum foil cannot be used, and waxed paper becomes soggy and unattractive.) Place individual fillet flat on a rather large square of microwave plastic wrap, parallel to and 2 inches from one side of square. Proceed to roll as vine leaves (page 37), keeping fillet flat.

COOKING TIMES FOR PAPILLOTES

½″ thick fillets Steamed; cover tightly.

1 piece	*45 sec. to 1 min.*
2 pieces	*1 min. 30 sec.*
More than 2 pieces	*Oven usually too small*

STEAKS

These are defined as cuts across the fish with or without bone and are usually cut from larger fish. They will cook for the same amount of time either way. Time variations for added liquid are as for fillets. Steaks, if on the bone, should be arranged in a circle with the thin belly-flap pieces toward the middle. Cover tightly with microwave plastic wrap. If you wish to add flavor to these thicker cuts, marinating works very well. Serve immediately.

COOKING TIMES FOR STEAKS

¾ thick boneless steaks 8 to 9 oz. each. Steamed; cover tightly.

1 piece	3 min.
1 piece	4 min. 30 sec. to 5 min. (small oven)
2 pieces	4 to 5 min.
2 pieces	6 to 7 min. (small oven)
4 pieces	8 min.

1″ thick boneless steaks 6 oz. each. Steamed; cover tightly.

1 piece	3 min.
1 piece	4 min. (small oven)
2 pieces	4 min. 30 sec.
4 pieces	6 min.
6 pieces	8 min. to 8 min. 30 sec.

MEDALLIONS

These are really variants of steaks. I cut them from 1½-inch-thick steaks or fillets using a stainless-steel cookie cutter 2 inches in diameter. They are best arranged in a ring, allowing ½ inch between medallions, ½ inch from the edge of the cooking dish. Vegetables may be placed in the center of the ring. Cover tightly with microwave plastic wrap. Serve immediately. Medallions cook particularly well because of their dimensions and look attractive on the plate. Save any trimmings for fish burgers, Paupiettes with Provençal Fish Sauce, Swordfish Quenelles and fish pâtés.

COOKING TIMES FOR MEDALLIONS

1½″ thick medallions Steamed; cover tightly.

2 pieces	1 min. 30 sec.
2 pieces	4 min. (small oven)
4 pieces	2 min. 30 sec. to 3 min.
6 pieces	4 min.
12 pieces	6 min.

WHOLE FISH

Gutted, with or without head and tail. The skin does not have to be slashed since the bones will hold the fish straight. More liquid is generally used so as to slow the surface cooking time. Cover tightly with microwave plastic wrap. Let whole fish rest, covered, after cooking.

To cook more than 1 fish: If fish are very small (sardines, for example), arrange spoke-fashion with tails toward the center; arrange 2 larger fish head to tail; continue this arrangement for more fish.

COOKING TIMES FOR WHOLE FISH

8-oz. fish Poached; cover tightly.

1 fish with ½ c. onions and ¾ c. liquid	4 min.
4 fish with 1 c. onions and 1½ c. liquid	10 min., rest 2 min.

8-oz. to 12-oz. fish Poached; cover tightly.

1 fish with 1 c. liquid	4 to 5 min.
2 fish with 1½ c. liquid	5 min.
4 fish with 2¼ c. liquid	6 min.

12-oz. fish Steamed with 2 Tbs. fat or liquid; cover tightly.

1 fish	2 min.
2 fish	3 min. to 3 min. 30 sec.
4 fish	5 to 6 min.

16-oz. fish Poached; cover tightly.

1 fish with 1 c. liquid	4 to 5 min., turn over once
2 fish with 1½ c. liquid	6 min., turn over once
4 fish with 2¼ c. liquid	10 to 11 min., turn over once

2-lb to 3-lb. fish Poached; cover tightly.

1 fish	10 to 11 min.

Larger, defrosted whole fish Steamed; cover tightly. See DEFROSTING.

1½-lb. fish, with head and tail	8 min. (large oven), 12 min. (small oven)
2-lb. fish, with head and tail	11 min. (large oven), 14 min. (small oven)
2½-lb. fish, with head and tail	14 min.
6-lb. fish, head removed: weight 4½ lb.	18 min.
8-lb. fish, head removed: weight 6 lb.	22 min.

FISH BROTH This wonderful gelatinous broth can be made from the head and/or bones of any white-fleshed fish (except the flatfish) that have been thoroughly washed to remove any blood—remove gills also—and cut into smallish pieces. Broth made with flatfish—sole, flounder and the like—turns bitter on top of the stove in about 20 minutes; in the microwave oven the same thing happens in 5 minutes. Use bass, rockfish, snapper and cod and you will have better, richer broths with more gelatin. Do not use the bones of fatty fish, such as salmon, mackerel, sturgeon and herring unless the broth is to be used with those fish; the taste will be too particular.

Fish broths are wonderful bases for any number of fish soups or sauces for fish. CLAM BROTH can be substituted for fish broth or used as a portion of the liquid in making fish broth; it will give a more intense flavor.

When buying fillets, ask for the bones and freeze them if you don't have time to make broth. See DEFROSTING, thin liquids, for defrosting times. See also CLARIFYING, broths and sauces; clarified fish broth is used primarily for Aspic or for cold jelled summer soups.

FISH GLAZE   Like the other glazes, this is a luxury to have on hand when fitting classic sauces to fish or seafood dishes. See Beurre Blanc. It can also be added to the sauce of a quick-cooking fish recipe if the flavor seems a little faded.

FIVE-SPICE POWDER   This Chinese seasoning has a strong licorice taste thanks to star anise. It is available, bottled, in the spice section of grocery stores and supermarkets. A smaller amount of star anise may be substituted.

FLAGEOLET   For cooking times, see BEANS.

FLOUNDER   One of the most readily available fish in fillet form. Sometimes it is sold under the name of its fancier cousin, sole. Individual flounder fillets make perfect dinners for one or two, depending on the size. See SOLE. For cooking times, see FISH.

FLOUR   Flour has been made not only from almost every grain known to man (wheat, rice, oats) but from nuts (acorn and chestnut), starchy fruits (cassava) and roots (arrowroot) as well. Those flours with a substantial amount of gluten, such as hard-wheat flours, behave disastrously in the microwave oven and should be avoided wherever possible except for very special cases (see Roux). This is why there are few conventional baking recipes in the microwave repertoire.

Every recipe in this book works. The ones you won't find here (French bread, for example) are absent not on a whim, but because there was no way I could get a result that I considered good. The raising of yeast doughs can be aided substantially by the microwave oven. See RAISING.

FREEZING   Just a few general notes: Mark your containers with a waxy marker or a label; later you will know what you have. Make sure frozen foods exclude air or are covered with a layer of liquid to avoid freezer burn. See DEFROSTING.

WRAPPING

For whole foods or fillets such as fish, pork roast, and skinned and boned chicken breasts, first wrap separately and tightly in microwave plastic before wrapping in aluminum foil or freezer paper. Wrap singly for even defrosting.

For cut-up birds, wrap parts separately so that you can make as many servings as you wish.

For meat cut up for stew, drape a large piece of microwave plastic wrap on a flat plate. Place the pieces of meat on it in a single layer. Fold wrap over meat. Freeze on plate. Remove plate when frozen. This will help the meat to defrost evenly in the cooking liquid.

LIQUID OR SEMILIQUID FOODS

Divide into reasonably small quantities among microwave-safe plastic containers. A pint (2-cup quantity) defrosts much more rapidly than a quart; 2 separate pints will go more quickly and evenly than 1 quart. Use containers that can be put directly in the microwave oven—containers larger than needed for the amount to be frozen, since liquids expand in freezing and tend to boil over when being defrosted. Remember that the lids of such containers are almost never meant for the microwave oven; remove them and cover the container with microwave plastic wrap. Flimsy plastic containers will get dangerously soft when

heated. Do not freeze in paper containers, as they may disintegrate by the time defrosting is accomplished.

Very small quantities of sauces and reductions, from 1 tablespoon to 2 ounces, can be frozen in plastic ice cube trays. When thoroughly frozen, store cubes of an equal size in a plastic bag.

FOODS TO BE REHEATED IN A SPECIAL CONTAINER

Macaroni and Cheese, for instance, should be placed, once cooked, in the serving dish of choice, lined with a large piece of microwave plastic wrap. Fold plastic over food to seal completely. Place in freezer. When food is frozen, remove plastic-wrapped package from container—now free for use—and double-wrap frozen food package before returning it to freezer. To serve, when reheating, unwrap food and place in serving dish. Place dish on a plate to avoid spills. See illustration page 151.

Vegetables are best frozen lightly blanched in the size pieces you wish to cook them in (see BLANCHING). Freeze in microwave-safe plastic bags.

FRUIT All the fruits and berries cook brilliantly in the microwave oven. Refer to specific entries in this Dictionary.

FRYING Some oven manufacturers say not to fry. Don't prejudice your warranty. However, small quantities fry well. I would not do chicken or large quantities in it. It is perfect for hors d'oeuvres, desserts and tempura. The advantages are a reduction of smell, mess and the risk of burned, bad-tasting oil. Always follow instructions exactly. Do not cook in plastic or in any chipped, cracked, mended or crazed container.

Don't remove fat from oven to put foods in it. Once fat is heated, open oven door and drop food in fat as quickly as possible. When the food is sufficiently fried, open oven door and remove with a slotted spoon or skimmer. Close door and bring fat back to temperature for the next batch. Repeat as needed.

While in recipes we have said not to attempt deep-fat frying in anything other than a full-size oven, you actually can deep-fry in a medium oven if it is configured in such a way that there is sufficient headroom between the top of the measure and the oven roof to permit putting in and removing the food. See also FATS.

HEATING TIMES FOR FAT
FOR DEEP-FAT FRYING

3 c. fat Heat at 100% in a 2-quart non-plastic container measuring at least 3¼ inches high, uncovered.

Large oven	15 min., heat 5 min. between batches
Medium oven	20 min., heat 10 min. between batches
Small oven	Do not attempt

G

GAME It used to be that any animal that appeared naturally in a habitat and raised itself in the wild was considered game, from fish to venison. A hare was game, some rabbits were game. These days, the lines of definition are blurring. Most of the venison and pheasant served in this country are farm-raised, often in countries far from our own. Today, game seems to mean animals that used to be caught wild, whether they actually are now or not.

Generally, game cannot be roasted in the microwave oven. Cook game birds and rabbit as you would CHICKEN, adjusting the seasonings. Cook red-meat game as you would lean BEEF, as it has almost no fat.

GARLIC Yes, I love it. Yes, many people do not. Most of us know that garlic cooked for a serious amount of time changes character. It becomes soft and sweet and tends to thicken the liquid in which it cooks. This sometimes desirable effect occurs (except to elephant garlic) with miraculous rapidity in the microwave oven. Almost any quantity of cloves, smashed, peeled and covered with 1 to 1½ cups of broth and tightly covered, will cook to that wonderful stage in about 8 minutes. This means that in long-cooking dishes you will need a much larger quantity of garlic than you might imagine. It also means that if you want a sharp garlic taste, add the garlic 3 minutes before the end of cooking, or after removing the food from the oven.

Recipes in the book call for garlic cloves to be "smashed and peeled." Garlic is a living thing, like a flower bulb. When you cut it, it gives off a bitter odor and flavor. Smashing the bulb first will prevent this from happening, and will also make it easier to peel. If you discover that the clove has a green center (or "germ"), fish out and discard the green part, as it tends to be bitter and tough.

Whole heads of cooked garlic make a wonderful garnish for people who love garlic and don't mind using their hands. Serve a whole head to each person; encourage eaters to remove 1 clove at a time and pull the pulp out between their teeth. (Give them a place to discard the garlic skins). See Roasted Garlic.

GELATIN A natural component of animal bones and certain plants (some seaweeds, mosses and fruits). Tapioca, for example, is made from the root of the cassava. Those neat little envelopes of commercial gelatin are made from gelatin ex-

tracted from bones, purified and powdered. One packet of gelatin used to weigh 15 grams (1 ounce) and measure out at 1 tablespoon. Now something is happening: incredible shrinking gelatin. Nevertheless, you can still figure that 1 packet of gelatin will gel 2 cups of liquid if it's not very acid (grapefruit juice, lemon juice and white wine all require half again as much gelatin) and does not contain pineapple, papaya, kiwi or fig (all of which contain an enzyme that will dissolve the gelatin).

One packet of gelatin sprinkled on ¼ cup cold water in a 1-cup glass measure (or 2 packets sprinkled on ½ cup water in a 2-cup glass measure), allowed to "soak" or absorb water for 2 minutes, can then be dissolved, tightly covered, at 100% in 30 seconds. Remove from oven and stir. Continue with recipe.

Agar-agar is a seaweed gelatin used in vegetarian recipes. Unlike bone-derived gelatin, agar-agar sets at room temperature. When it is being used to coat and layer a mold for an aspic, it may get too hard to work with. To remedy this, simply cover the aspic and stick it back in the microwave oven for 30 seconds.

GHEE A form of clarified butter, allowed to cool before it is used. In some parts of India it is aged until it acquires what is to a Western palate a distinctly high taste. Julie Sahni in her brilliant book *Classic Indian Vegetarian and Grain Cooking*, says of ghee that it is "... made by heating butter long enough to allow the moisture present in the milk solids, which causes spoilage, to evaporate. The slow heating and cooking process gives the clarified butter a gentle nutty aroma, a pale yellow color when cool, and a distinctly grainy texture. The unmistakable taste of authentic usli ghee is due to the lactic flavor present in the butter." See BUTTER, clarified.

GINGER This is a rhizome (such as irises grow from). Fresh ginger should be thin-skinned, light in color and juicy. It is also available dried and ground for use in baking. If fresh ginger is to be used as a flavoring only—in stir-frying, for example—and will not be eaten, it need not be peeled. Never add it before prolonged cooking; it will only give the dish a hot flavor without any fruity, acid freshness. Five minutes or so in the microwave oven is plenty. A few slices tucked under a fish fillet while cooking perfumes the entire fish.

A trick when fresh ginger is to be eaten is to grate it. A Japanese bamboo wasabi grater is ideal for eliminating strings.

GLAZE (GLACE DE VIANDE) In cooking, there are basically three types of glazes: thick glazes, such as a barbecue sauce, which give color and flavor to meats as they cook or after they cook (they do not substitute for true roasting); sweet glazes of chocolate, sugar or fruit purée to seal or ice cake layers and pastry; and savory glazes, made by reducing a broth (see Meat Glazes). Commercially, savory glazes are sometimes called concentrates. See Index for glaze recipes.

GOAT CHEESE Goat cheese is made in abundance, and only partially for its distinctive flavor. Mainly, it is made because goats can feed on much poorer and higher land than cows can. The cheese comes from many countries and may have very different textures and flavors; most are rather crumbly. In recent years, the United States has begun making it. Fresh, young, chalk-white cheeses are an interesting ingredient. See Goat Cheese Croutons.

GOOSE These wonderful, fat birds are always Christmas, Scrooge and Tiny Tim to me. For this purpose, roast in a conventional oven and enjoy with sage stuffing. Goose, like duck, can be made into a confit; cut up the goose so that the pieces and weights match that of the duck in Duck Confit and proceed as for duck.

GOOSEBERRY These fat members of the currant family come in several different varieties, including the romantically named cloudberries. Most gooseberries are a pale acid green or a soft pinky-mauve. Gooseberry jelly can be made as is Currant Jelly.

GORGONZOLA Creamy blue cheese from Italy. I often prefer Gorgonzola to Roquefort, which has, in this country at least, an enormous quantity of salt. My favorite kind, dolce di latte, is made from cream-rich summer milk.

GRAINS The seeds of grasses, used ground as flour. Some, such as wild rice, are cooked whole for a side dish, in desserts or as a cereal. See specific grains in this Dictionary.

GRATING Cheese and chocolate can be grated in a food processor fitted with a grating disc, in a small, rotary hand-held cheese grater or on a four-sided grater. Grate firm vegetables such as carrots, potatoes and even cabbage on a four-sided grater or in a food processor.

GREEN BEAN Fresh green beans and their pale look-alikes, wax beans, are a pleasure to cook in the microwave oven. No pots of water, no salt unless you choose, and bright colors, lots of vitamins and a perfect crisp but cooked texture.

See BEANS for cooking times. A portion of green beans placed on a plate around a piece of fish or a chicken breast will up the combined cooking time by only 20 seconds (1 minute for HARICOTS VERTS). If you really must salt the beans (they have enough flavor and cook better without it), add it to the water with which you sprinkle the beans. If you wish to cook the beans in tomato sauce or other liquid, add 1 minute for each ½ cup.

GREEN PEA Unfortunately, most peas available in markets are not very good. This is one case where I often counsel frozen. I use the tiny green peas. Unwrap frozen peas; place in sieve; run warm tap water over the peas until they separate. One box will then heat, tightly covered, with or without 1 tablespoon of butter, at 100% in 2 minutes. (To heat in a small oven, prepare as for a large oven and cook for 4 min. 30 sec.) When adding to recipes, remember that frozen peas are basically cooked; you are adding them just for the length of time it takes them to heat.

When tender, fresh peas are available, cook, with or without butter, salt, and a few fresh mint leaves, tightly covered.

COOKING TIMES FOR
FRESH GREEN PEAS

Large winter peas Cover tightly.

*1 c. with 1 tsp. butter   4 min.
(2-c. measure)*

Tiny new peas Cover tightly.

| 2 c. (4-c. measure) | 3 to 4 min. |

Yields

| 1½ lb. peas, unshelled | ½ lb. peas, shelled |
| ½ lb. peas, raw | 2 c., raw |

GRINDING Grinding of nuts and seeds, including spices, can be done with a mortar and pestle, but that is work.

Small quantities of nuts and all spices are best ground in a simple electric coffee mill reserved for that purpose; use it to grind allspice, anise, caraway, cardamom, cloves, coriander, cumin, fennel, etc. The quantity of seed that you can grind at home depends to an extent on the size of your machine, but a good rule of thumb is 2 to 3 tablespoons.

Large quantities of nuts can be ground in the food processor. (Seeds and coffee beans cannot; they are too light and fly around so madly that many of them entirely escape the blades.) Here again, the quantity you can grind at one time depends on the capacity of your machine. Don't fill the workbowl more than halfway full; in order to bring all the unchopped nuts down from the top, you'd have to overprocess the nuts closest to the blades. Grind nuts with pulses rather than a continuous, butter-producing whir. If the recipe contains sugar, it is safer to grind the nuts with the sugar.

GRITS In the American South, where grits for breakfast, lunch and dinner is epidemic, the plural noun takes the always singular verb. Grits is made from corn kernels soaked in lye to puff them up and remove the skins; this gives you hominy. The hominy is dried and ground, which is grits. Instant grits is available, but it is not as good as ordinary grits; and given the rapidity with which good grits cooks in the microwave oven, there seems to be no point in instant. The very best grits is black-heart grits, with the germ.

If you want grits for breakfast, try making them in half milk, half water. Use a very large container; milk tends to boil over. Stir in a lump of butter and salt or sugar. Serve with more butter and cream. Serve plain Grits instead of mashed potatoes, with fried chicken and a really Southern cream gravy. To go for a high-in-the-instep dish, try cooking grits in broth with a clove or two of garlic and 1 dried hot pepper. When cooked, stir in butter and grated Cheddar cheese.

COOKING TIMES FOR GRITS

Regular (not quick-cooking) grits Cover tightly.

| 3 Tbs. with 1 c. water (cereal bowl) | 4 min. (large oven) |

3 Tbs. as above	6 min. (small oven)
1 c. with 5 c. water (8-cup measure)	15 min. (large oven)
1 c. as above	25 min. (small oven)

Yields

3 Tbs. grits, dry	⅔ c. grits, cooked
1 c. grits, dry	4 c. grits, cooked

GROATS A term that can mean any hulled and cracked grain, including even grits, served to humans. In Scotland, it usually means OATMEAL; in England, BULGUR (cracked wheat).

GROUPER A family of fish from southern waters (North Carolina and down) related to the more northern sea bass. All fish in this group tend to be large; consequently, we generally cook filleted pieces. American grouper is better than French merou. It has a somewhat bland taste, and while not mushy like tilefish, it is not a very firm-fleshed fish. Try lemony or herbal sauces such as Hollandaise or Beurre Blanc. For cooking times, see FISH. If in doubt, undercook.

GUAVA These semitropical fruits come in a wide variety of colors, from yellow to red to purple. They are fairly hard (even when ripe), difficult to peel, full of seeds and are almost never eaten raw. Sounds unappealing; but cooked guavas are a delicacy. The most succulent preparation is a firm, if slightly gritty, jelly paste eaten as a dessert in South American countries along with cream cheese. Prepare in the same way as Quince Paste

H

HADDOCK A white-fleshed fish often used interchangeably with cod. There is a vigorous debate as to which is better. Haddock is often smoked. Those from near Aberdeen were called Finnan haddock (after a fishing village), which led to the dish "finnan haddie." See FISH for cooking times. See also COD for soaking.

HAKE This white-fleshed fish is cooked in ways similar to haddock and cod. In Spain, where it is vastly popular, it is called by the more melodious name of merluza. In Portugal, where it is the most widely used fresh fish, it is called pescada. Whiting is a rather soft member of the hake family; a favorite preparation is Whiting with Parsley Sauce. See FISH for cooking times.

HALIBUT The largest member of the flatfish family, a cousin to sole and flounder. Some halibut grow to be 6 feet long, which explains why they are usually cooked as filleted steaks rather than whole or as single whole fillets. For this reason halibut tends to get cooked more like hake, haddock and flounder than like the other flatfishes, although it may be steamed and served with Almond Butter Sauce or Browned Butter Sauce with Capers. See FISH for cooking times.

HAM It is many things to many different people. To a pig, it is its thigh. A fresh ham is raw. Things are confused because the Corsicans, among others, make hams that are neither meant to be cooked nor are they smoked. Such hams are called "raw" in the various languages of their countries; they are salted either in brine or by having salt rubbed into the meat, after which they are hung in a cool, dry, airy place to age and loose excess water. Then they are scrubbed with fresh water. The most famous of these raw hams is probably prosciutto crudo from Parma, also called Parma ham. Jambon de Toulouse is a sort of unsmoked Bayonne ham (an elegant, mildly smoked French ham meant to be eaten without further cooking). France has many other country hams meant to be eaten raw (*cru*). The Spanish version is jamón serrano ("mountain ham").

Almost every country and region of the United States smokes hams with its own particular combination of woods. The non-American hams are largely unavailable in this country due to American health laws.

A whole American smoked ham should not be cooked in the microwave oven, but lovingly tended at length in traditional ways. Be satisfied with preparing the accompanying vegetables in the microwave oven.

HARICOT VERT These French green beans take a little longer to cook than regular green beans and are usually undercooked in this country. They must be cooked sufficiently to develop their flavor. For cooking times, see BEANS; the same times apply as well to yard-long beans (known also as long beans and Philippine beans).

HAZELNUT These lovely shiny, brown-shelled nuts are also called filberts. While tons are eaten plain, they are used all over Europe in cakes, pastries and ice creams. Nocciole, the Italian ice cream, is one of my favorites. In Spain and in France the nut is ground to thicken savory sauces. For blanching and toasting, see NUTS. Like almonds, they make excellent Pralines.

HERBS This is one of the largest groups of food seasonings. See specific herbs in this Dictionary. A great pleasure of the microwave oven is its ability to dry fresh herbs better than any other method I know. See DRYING, herbs.

HERRING A large and, to me, confusing family of fish. Along with sardines and anchovies, which are relatives, it accounts for most of the fish eaten worldwide. Since such fish swarm in large schools, they are easy to net. Over the centuries their plenitude has been preserved by smoking, salting—both dry and in brine—and pickling. Salt herrings need to be desalted before they can be prepared; follow the directions for soaking and desalting COD. For cooking times, see FISH.

HOMINY Hominy is available canned (moist) or dried. If you like canned hominy, reheat the contents of a can, tightly covered, at 100% for 3 minutes. Dried hominy is most often used to make the Mexican and Southwestern soup-stew posole, which takes forever to cook. For preparation from raw corn, see Grits.

HONEY Long before man knew how to extract sugar from beets or cane, his sweet tooth led him to discover the extremely efficient factories of the bees. Today honeys from all over the world are sold here, each with its own distinctive taste, often based on the particular nectar of the flowers that have fed the bees. Honey is usually slathered on breakfast toast; don't forget that you can cook with it. When substituting honey for sugar in a recipe, remember that it is significantly sweeter than the equivalent measure of sugar.

To reconstitute honey or jam. Cook 1 cup in jar, top removed, covered tightly with microwave plastic wrap for 1 minute 30 seconds.

HORSERADISH An herb grown for its pungent, eye-watering, sharp root. Peel; grate in a food processor to avoid skinned knuckles and tears; prepare raw. Horseradish quickly loses its authority when cooked. A little stirred at the last minute into a sauce for kidneys, along with some mellowing cream, is very nice.

HOT RED-PEPPER SAUCE See RED-PEPPER SAUCE, HOT.

HUBBARD SQUASH These are large, warty, tough-skinned winter squashes that can be grayish-green or orange and keep well. They are so large that it is difficult to use up a whole one.

To cook, hack (these are tough-skinned) in half. Pressing firmly with the edge of a spoon, scoop out the seeds and fibers in the cavity. Cut the meat and skin into 3″ × 4″ pieces. Weigh out the amount of squash you want, allowing ½ pound per person. Place pieces on a pie dish, skin side down, cover tightly, and cook at 100%. For cooking times, see SQUASH, winter.

I

ICE CREAM So-called French ice cream is made with a custard base such as Crème Anglaise. It may be flavored either by adding crushed fruit or by flavoring the cream with which the custard is made; for example, steep coffee beans in the cream, tightly covered, for 4 minutes at 100%. After custard is made, cool; make ice cream.

J

JALAPEÑO These dark green, ovoid hot pod peppers, about 3 inches long, are frequently used in the Southwest. See CHILI.

JAM AND JELLY See PRESERVING.

JÍCAMA A large brown root with crisp, white, slightly starchy flesh. It can be cooked, but I see no reason for it; it is at its best raw, thinly sliced or cut in juliennes. To cook jícama, at the most cut it up to inexpensively replace water chestnuts in stir-fried dishes.

JULIENNE Meats and vegetables, raw and cooked, are often cut into even strips to be used raw or before cooking. Unless the specific size is given in the Dictionary, julienne size is $1/8'' \times 1/8'' \times 2''$. Lardoons, before cooking, are normally fatter and shorter, $1/4'' \times 1/4'' \times 1''$.

JUNIPER BERRY The taste of gin, predominantly flavored by these round, dried black berries, can be added to any dish. Simply crush a few into it while it cooks. This flavor adds a nice note to cabbage, fish and poached pineapple or Light Poached Pears. Use 3 berries per person; crush with fingertips before adding.

K

KALE Another strong-tasting green for POT GREENS, though some people prefer it on its own. If the leaves have very pronounced ribs, separate the ribs from the leafy parts. Kale may also be cooked as BOK CHOY.

COOKING TIMES FOR KALE

As a component of Pot Greens Cook in a $14'' \times 11'' \times 2''$ dish; cover tightly.

2 lb. kale with 3 c. water and	30 min.; uncover for last 5 min. of

Kale (cont.)

¼ lb. fat-back	cooking time

Yields

1 bunch with stems	1¼ lb., raw
1¼ lb., raw, stemmed	1 lb., raw
1 lb., raw	10 c. raw, cut into 2" pieces, tightly packed
2 lb. mixed greens, raw	6 c. Pot Greens, cooked

KEY LIME Almost no Key limes grow any longer in the Florida Keys. Certainly, none are grown commercially. You can bet that most of the Key Lime Pie made in this country today is made with the larger, ordinary limes. Key limes are grown commercially in Mexico; they are worth searching for with their strong perfume, slightly bitter taste and dark green and (when ripe) plentiful juice (which freezes well). When you find them, buy lots.

KIDNEY BEAN Dark red, dried beans that often pop up in chili. They are also used to make delicious Refried Beans. For cooking times, see BEANS.

KINGFISH See WAHOO.

KIWI This public relations success fruit originally comes from New Zealand and is now being grown in California. Much of its popularity is due to the brilliant green of the flesh, in which small black seeds make decorative patterns. The taste is similar to bananas. It is not a fruit to cook, but good sorbet can be made with its purée. See SIMPLE SYRUP.

KOHLRABI A cool, pale green relative of broccoli, it is round like a root vegetable, but the knob is a swelling in the stem from which its leaves grow. When you buy it, the leaves will have been, or should be, snapped off, leaving rather Turkish-looking arched points on the outside. When precooking kohlrabi to slice or mash and stir with butter, it is easier to peel it after it is cooked. Of course, Stuffed Kohlrabi must be peeled before cooking. This neglected vegetable should return to popularity with the benefits of microwave cooking: It cooks quickly, stays green and does not get watery.

COOKING TIMES FOR
KOHLRABI

Small kohlrabi 8 to 10 per lb. Cook ½-lb. quantities in tightly sealed microwave-safe plastic bags.

½ lb.	4 to 5 min.
1 lb.	6 min.

Large kohlrabi 4 per lb.; cook in a tightly sealed microwave-safe plastic bag.

2 kohlrabi	4 to 5 min.

Small, stuffed kohlrabi Each kohlrabi with 2 Tbs. stuffing; cover tightly.

2 kohlrabi with 1 tsp. water (serving plate)	3 to 4 min.
8 kohlrabi with 1 Tbs. water (9" pie plate)	7 min.

KOSHER SALT All of my recipes use kosher salt. I prefer the taste since it is pure salt without any added chemicals such as bitter-tasting iodine. If substituting table salt, use 1 teaspoon for every tablespoon called for, as kosher salt is much more coarsely ground. There are coarser and finer grades of kosher salt. Coarser is better.

L

LAMB As with beef, leave the chops and roasts to the skillet, broiler and grill. The one time when roasting comes into the picture at all is when you have a frozen leg stashed in the freezer for last-minute company or when you buy a frozen leg. It can be rapidly defrosted and cooked immediately. See DE-FROSTING, lamb, or Roast Leg of Lamb. Other than that, use the microwave oven to make Lamb Shanks, Irish Stew and Moroccan Stuffing. Before cooking lamb shanks, make a cut to the bone, all the way around the thin end of each shank. This will permit the meat to cook evenly.

COOKING TIMES FOR LAMB

Stewing lamb, bone in Cook in a 2½-qt. soufflé dish; cover tightly.

2 lb. lamb with 3 c. liquid and 1 lb. vegetables (2½-qt. soufflé)	18 min.
2 lb. lamb with 1½ c. liquid and 2 lb. vegetables (2-qt. soufflé)	25 min.

Lamb shanks Cook in a 12" × 10" dish; cover tightly.

4 shanks (8 pieces) about 1½ lb. each, each shank cut in half crosswise	22 min.
4 shanks about ¾ lb. each, with 6 lb. spinach	30 min.

LAMB BROTH A lot of flavor for very little work comes from lamb broth. Try substituting this broth and cubed lamb in Mushroom-Barley Soup. See Meat Broth and CLARIFYING, broths and sauces.

LARDOON See BACON, lardoons.

LEEK I love leeks, tiny whole ones for grilling and big fat ones for braising, leeks in soups and sauces, and to make meltingly good nests for fish, seafood and chicken. Before cooking leeks, it is important to clean them very well. They are kept white and tender at the bottom by being planted in a trough. As they grow, dirt is shoveled into the trough to hide the root end from chlorophyll-producing light. To clean them, first cut off the roots, being careful not to cut them off so high that the leaves fall apart. Slit the green leaves on either side down to the white part. If the leeks are very wide, take the tip of a sharp knife and cut a cross into the root end. Soak them in cold water, rinse and dry.

If you've never tried leeks on their own as a vegetable, try Braised Leeks. I like these so much I eat them as a first course, hot or cool. Leeks are also a lovely ingredient in other dishes (see Leek and Potato Soup). Melt them in butter or oil; place a spoonful of melted leeks in the shell under an opened oyster; top with Sauce Suprême or Mornay made with the oyster liquid and dry white wine or vermouth; slip under the broiler for an elegant first course. Two tablespoons under a fish fillet adds splendid flavor. Stir some into a Sauce Suprême made with chicken broth to serve with quickly cooked chicken breasts.

COOKING TIMES FOR LEEKS

Whole medium leeks Braise in a dish just large enough to hold them in a single layer; half-cover with broth; cover tightly.

½ lb.	20 min.
1 lb.	30 min.
2 lb.	40 min.

Sliced ⅛″ thick or into juliennes Melted, with 2 tbsp. butter per lb., uncovered.

½ lb. leeks (8″ round dish)	4 min.
1 lb. leeks (1-qt. soufflé)	6 min. 15 sec.

Yields

2 medium leeks	½ lb., untrimmed
½ lb., untrimmed and sliced ⅛″ thick	1¼ c., trimmed
1¼ c. raw, sliced	½ c., cooked

LEGUMES The dried seeds (pulses) of these plants are what the rest of the world had instead of dried beans before America was discovered. In season, many of them, such as fava beans, peas and chick-peas, are cooked fresh; many more are usually dried and later boiled. Many also have skins on the individual pulses that must be removed for palatability whether cooked fresh or dried. See individual legumes: BROAD BEAN (fava), CHICK-PEA, LENTIL, and SPLIT PEA. For peanuts, see NUTS. See also BEANS for soaking times.

LEMON Another of my favorite tastes is that of lemon

juice. I always mean freshly squeezed juice, never bottled or frozen. Except where it is used in a marinade, as in some of the fish dishes, lemon should be added at the end of cooking or after the dish comes from the oven. Lemon quickly loses its aromatic freshness when cooked.

I find its quantity one of the most difficult to specify in a recipe. The juice of 1 lemon makes no sense. We have all had the experience of straining at a stony lemon that after much effort gives us only a teaspoon or so of juice. There are also gushers, lemons that produce a quarter cup or more of impeccable juice. Why not then just give quantities? I do; but I always feel guilty. Lemon juice varies so much in acidity that one time you may need very little and at others much more.

Recipes that read "salt to taste"—an instruction I like since we all have different salt tolerances and palates—add more problems. The tastes of salt and acid make each other stronger. When adding them both to a recipe, alternate them and taste as you go along, so you don't have any nasty surprises. Many such dishes, when cooked in the microwave oven, should be seasoned at the end.

Lemon zest, the yellow part of the skin, is a nice addition to fish and fruit cooked in the microwave oven. It doesn't need to be blanched first. It may also be dried to add to fruit desserts, but it is not quite as good as orange or tangerine zest. See DRYING, zest.

LEMON BALM This lovely perennial herb is only good fresh. Do not bother to dry it.

LEMON GRASS An inedible seasoning (too tough), much used in Thai and Vietnamese cooking, it is available fresh, dried, and dried and powdered (usually as sereh powder). It is a delightful addition to chicken soup. The fresh herb should be bruised by smacking with a heavy knife or pot before being added to the soup. The dried herb is better off with a little microwave oven-intensified soaking. See SOAKING, herbs.

LEMON SOLE See SOLE. For cooking times, see FISH.

LENTIL One of the staples of cooking from India through Europe, this pulse (legume) is available in many colors: red, yellow, orange, brown and greenish. Sadly, the brilliant little discs all turn muddy when cooked. Lentils are available in normal and quick-cooking varieties; I find it really makes little difference which you use when cooking in the microwave oven. Lentils make terrific winter soups and mushes, usually served with sausage in Italy, Hungary and Germany. See Green Lentil Soup. They have an intense enough flavor to be a worthy mainstay of vegetarian cooking. In India, where they are cooked as dhal, they are a component of almost every meal. Their protein combines with that of rice to make a rich nutritional complex.

As with other dried legumes and beans, lentils are sometimes very old and dry when you buy them. If they are not sufficiently cooked at the end of the resting time, re-cover and cook at 100% for another 5 minutes. When you cook them, cover them with a double layer of microwave plastic wrap; cook at 100%.

COOKING TIMES FOR LENTILS

Green or brown lentils Cook in a 2½-qt. soufflé; cover tightly; rest, covered, for 20 min.

1 c. lentils with 4 c. water	*35 min.*
2 c. lentils with 6 c. water	*35 min.*

Red, yellow or orange lentils Cook in a 2½-qt. soufflé; cover tightly; rest, covered, for 20 min.

1 c. lentils with 4 c. water	*10 min.*
2 c. lentils with 6 c. water	*10 min.*

Yields

1 c. lentils, dry	*2¼ c., cooked*
2 c. lentils, dry	*4½ c., cooked*

LETTUCE A large family of leafy greens usually used in salads, lettuce cooks well—try whole heads as a light vegetable to serve with fish (see Braised Lettuce) or cooked shredded with green peas. It is not an old wives' tale: Lettuce is a natural calmative.

LIAISON See EMULSIFICATION and THICKENING, sauces.

LIMA BEAN These beans are never cooked in the pod. They are cooked fresh, frozen and dried. The microwave oven does not do a spectacular job of cooking dried lima beans, but it does make soaking them to remove their tough outer skins easy work. See BEANS.

Frozen baby lima beans are a modern triumph. Defrost as GREEN PEAS. Cook 1 defrosted package, tightly covered, in a 4-cup glass measure, with or without butter and seasonings, at 100% for 4 minutes. One tablespoon of butter and 2 teaspoons of fresh, chopped summer savory or sage (or ½ teaspoon dried), along with salt and pepper, turns lima beans into a lovely vegetable to go with broiled lamb chops or a simple fish.

LIME Aside from their pairing with tonic and appearance in Bloody Marys in the last ten years, these smallish, green citrus fruits are used mainly for their juice. Seviche relies on it. See also KEY LIME.

LIQUEURS (CORDIALS) These alcoholic drinks, often

sweet, are made with fruit (orange or pear, for example), nut (almond, hazelnut), herb (angelica) and spice (anise, caraway) flavorings. Many of the most famous originated in monasteries as restoratives or cordials. See ALCOHOL for advice on cooking with liqueurs in the microwave oven.

LIVER See BEEF LIVER, CALF'S LIVER, CHICKEN LIVER and DUCK LIVER; see Pâté in Index.

LOBSTER Two different animals are sold as lobster in American markets: one with claws and the other without. The kind with claws comes from North Atlantic waters. The clawless kind comes from southern waters and is also called rock lobster, spiny lobster and crawfish. Frozen lobster tails come from the clawless lobsters, often from a somewhat different variety shipped in from Australia. (See DEFROSTING, lobster tail, for timing.) Fresh (live) lobsters should be boiled or steamed on top of the stove.

LOUP See STRIPED BASS.

M

MACADAMIA These expensive Hawaiian nuts can be used in cooking, but it seems a shame, as they are so delicious on their own. You can use them, toasted and ground, for an especially rich dusting on baked goods and other sweets. See NUTS, toasting and GRINDING.

MACE Available dried and ground, this spice tastes a lot like nutmeg, which is hardly surprising since it is made from the nutmeg husk. It is less expensive, and also less aromatic. If substituting for nutmeg, increase the quantity to taste. While you do not need both spices in the kitchen, their slightly different flavors make for an interesting comparison.

MACERATING See SOAKING.

MACKEREL Of all the fish that swim in the sea, many are mackerel. All mackerel are oily. They make good soups and stews with pungent greens such as kale. Otherwise, they are usually cooked in acid liquids, such as white wine or tomato sauce, to balance the oil. Depending on the variety and size, they can be cooked whole, filleted or as steaks. See FISH for cooking times. See also Bluefish with Fennel and substitute mackerel.

MANDOLINE An excellent French tool that predates the food processor. It is much like an old-fashioned cabbage slicer except that it is metal and can be adjusted for different thicknesses of slicing and julienning. Use it when perfectly even cutting is important. It is the ideal substitute for a good sharp knife or a food processor with assorted slicing discs.

MANGO There are many different varieties of this fruit. The most delicious are flattened ovals with skin that is green when picked, yellow when the mango is ripe. The flesh is golden apricot in color. The only trouble with the mango is freeing the delectable flesh from skin and pit. It is easier to extract the flesh of underripe mangoes than ripe ones; this is no help when you wish to enjoy one raw, but it is nice to know for those times you want to make chutney or curry. See Fresh Mango Chutney.

MAPLE SYRUP Sweeter than cane sugar, maple syrup and honey were the staple sweeteners in Colonial days until molasses, rum and sugar were traded with the Caribbean countries. Syrup made from the first run of sap is the best, though mildest in flavor and palest in color. Different states and Canada have different designations for the various grades of syrup. It is a shame to squander Fancy, Grade AA, Pale or whatever the first-run designation might be on cooking, where its elegant flavor will be lost. Use a medium-grade syrup if it is going to be cooked at all;

it will have a distinct maple flavor, though not as overpowering as that of a dark maple syrup.

MARJORAM This annual version of oregano is somewhat milder in flavor. It is used extensively in Italian cooking. See DRYING, herbs.

MARROW Though a British name for summer squash, it usually refers to the soft center of bones. The best animal marrow for cooking is that found in the leg bones of veal; it is one of the things that makes Ossobuco so succulent. Many classic French recipes call for marrow that has been removed from the bone and sliced on top of steaks or into sauce (see Marchand du Vin).

Cooking marrow is one of the chores that the microwave oven performs superbly, better and more reliably than other ways. Be sure you really have veal bones. If the veal is superannuated, really an overgrown, milk-fed calf, it will have bloody, stringy marrow. Make sure the marrow you buy is white to pale pink and uniform in color. Have the bones cut into 2-inch to 3-inch lengths with marrow showing at both ends; soak in heavily salted water—¼ cup salt to each cup of cold water—for an hour. Rinse in clear water and dry. Stand the pieces up, not touching, in a soufflé dish deep enough to hold them. Cover tightly with microwave plastic wrap. After cooking at 100% for the recommended time, pierce the plastic wrap; let the bones cool just until you can handle them. Free the marrow with a thin sharp knife by running the blade all around between the marrow and the bone at each end of the bone. Gently shake out the marrow.

COOKING TIMES FOR MARROW BONES

Cut into 2″ to 3″ lengths and soak as above Stand in a dish just large enough to hold them without touching; add 2 Tbs. water per bone; cover tightly.

2 pieces bone, about 4 oz.	1 min.
4 pieces bone, about 8 oz.	2 min.
8 pieces bone, about 1 lb.	4 min.

MAYONNAISE A cold emulsion of oil and egg yolk flavored with vinegar or lemon juice, it is a very useful uncooked sauce (see page 382). It may be colored and flavored with green herbs or Lightly Cooked Crushed Tomatoes. Serve with cooked fish, seafood or fowl to make a salad.

MELLOWING A way of reheating to improve meat stew flavors. See page 235.

MILK When heating or cooking milk in a microwave oven as for New England Clam Chowder or Basic Béchamel, be sure to use a large container. Milk boils up easily, making a mess. One nice thing about cooking it in a microwave oven rather than on top of the stove is that you are much less likely to scorch the milk (and will not have a nasty pot to clean).

SCALDING TIMES FOR MILK

Cook in a 4-cup glass measure; cover tightly.

1 c. milk	1 min. 30 sec.
2 c. milk	3 min.

MILLET One of the world's oldest grains. It is still used in Russian cooking, and before corn hit Italy, Italians made their polenta with it. To cook millet, substitute it for couscous in Risotto of Couscous. You can vary the liquid and the seasonings as you wish. Millet is a nice change from potatoes.

COOKING TIMES FOR MILLET

2 c. millet with 4 c. liquid (14″ × 11″ × 2″ dish)	10 min., uncovered

MINCE While mince is an English holiday specialty I have never appreciated, it also means to chop really finely into even bits.

MINT An herb of which there are many different kinds. They freeze terribly but dry well, retaining green color and much of their flavor. Dried mint makes an agreeable tea. It is an ingredient essential to many Moroccan dishes. See DRYING, herbs.

MIRIN This Japanese sweetened wine is a component of many sauces, giving them what Westerners may think of as their characteristic Japanese flavor. Mirin can be a nice addition to the repertoire of Western seasonings; see Pâté with Chinese Black Beans. Mirin is now available in all kinds of markets

MIRLITON The New Orleans name for CHAYOTE.

MOLASSES A by-product of sugar refining. The best grade has some sugar left in it; the darker the molasses, the less sweet it is. It was a popular sweetener in America in the nineteenth century. Recipes using molasses usually call for baking soda to neutralize its acid.

MONKFISH Newly popular in America (although long esteemed in France as lotte), this firm, white-fleshed fish is generally sold as a skinned, boneless tail. It requires longer cooking than most fish. Braising is ideal. See Monkfish in Green Sauce.

COOKING TIMES FOR
MONKFISH

5-oz. fillets Cover tightly.

2 fillets with ½ c. liquid, 3 Tbs. oil and ¾ c. vegetables (9" pie plate)	5 min.
6 fillets with ½ c. liquid, ¼ c. oil and 1¾ c. vegetables (11" × 8" oval dish)	8 min.

MOREL One of the most expensive mushrooms, it is usually available dried since it is hard to locate—you don't even tell your best friend where your patch is—and has a short season. The dried reconstitute beautifully and quickly in the microwave oven. See SOAKING, dried mushrooms.

MULLET The king of this fish family is the famed French Mediterranean rouget. For cooking times, see FISH.

MUSHROOM In this, as in most American cookbooks, "mushrooms" without a modifying adjective means commercially grown agaricus mushrooms, with white caps and pinkish-brown gills. Scores of other mushrooms are great delicacies. A few are cultivated; many more are picked wild. They are available fresh and dried. See individual varieties: CEPE, CHANTERELLE, MOREL, and SHIITAKE. See DRYING, mushrooms, and SOAKING, dried mushrooms. See also Duxelles.

COOKING TIMES FOR MUSHROOMS

Sliced With 1 tsp. fresh lemon juice per ½ lb.; cover tightly.

½ lb. (11″ × 8″ oval dish)	3 min.
½ lb. as above	4 min. 30 sec. (small oven)
1 lb. (11″ × 8″ oval dish)	3 min.
2 lb. (14″ × 11″ × 2″ dish)	6 min.

Whole caps With 1 tsp. oil per ½ lb.; cover tightly.

½ lb. (11″ × 8″ oval dish)	8 min.
1 lb. (11″ × 8″ oval dish)	12 min.
2 lb. (14″ × 11″ × 2″ dish)	15 min.

Yields

32 medium mushrooms	1 lb.
¼ lb. sliced, raw	1 c. raw, sliced
½ lb. sliced, raw	1 c., cooked, plus 3 Tbs. mushroom liquid
1 lb. sliced, raw	2 c., cooked, plus ½ c. mushroom liquid
2 lb. sliced, raw	5 c., cooked, plus 1 c. mushroom liquid
½ lb. caps, raw	1½ c., cooked, plus ¼ c. mushroom liquid
1 lb. caps, raw	2 c., cooked, plus ⅓ c. mushroom liquid
2 lb. caps, raw	4 c., cooked, plus ½ c. mushroom liquid

MUSSELS The shells of most varieties are blue-black, but there is also a brown-shelled Venetian kind and a startlingly green-shelled New Zealand variety. Size tells you nothing about quality. Often the smallest shells have particularly nutty and delicious meat inside while the large shells have flabby meat; and sometimes the biggest are succulent. The most important thing is to get mussels that have been growing in clear, cold seawater on rocks or on special "mussel farm" constructions.

The only tricky part about cooking mussels is cleaning them. The "farm" mussels from Maine have no beards and require virtually no cleaning. For other mussels, scrape off the beard with a sharp knife, then scrub under cold water with a plastic scouring pad. If you want to store cleaned mussels before cooking, refrigerate in a clean plastic bag; do not keep in water or they will become watery. In the microwave oven, they may be cooked, tightly covered with microwave plastic wrap, with or without added liquid. They are done when they begin to open.

Save the liquid given off as

you cook mussels for adding to soups. Mussels make a nice addition to fish cooked on a plate and barely affect cooking time. See Scrod with Mussels Livornese.

COOKING TIMES FOR MUSSELS

16 to 18 per lb. Cook in a 2-qt. soufflé dish standing up, hinge end down; cover tightly.

1 lb.	3 min. 30 sec.
1 lb.	5 min. (small oven)
2 lb.	6 min.
2 lb. with about ¾ c. liquid	8 min.
4 lb.; cook 2 dishes of 36 mussels each simultaneously, using microwave	15 min.

oven rack. Reverse positions after 8 min.

Yields

36 mussels	1 c. mussel liquid
	1½ c. chopped meat

MUSTARD The tiny seeds that are ground to make prepared mustard grow almost all over the world. Toasted mustard seed is used in many Indian dishes. Mustard powder usually has some flour added to it. Mustard powder and prepared mustard both act as thickening agents when cooked with milk or cream as in Dijon Snails. See TOASTING, small seeds.

MUSTARD GREENS See POT GREENS.

N

NAPA CABBAGE This used to be known by its Cantonese name, bok choy. Today, BOK CHOY is used as a Mandarin word for another kind of cabbage. Napa cabbage is elongated oval heads of pale green, tightly packed, crinkly leaves.

COOKING TIMES FOR NAPA CABBAGE

Cut across into 2-inch lengths Cover tightly.

4 c. with 2 Tbs. butter (11" × 8½" × 2" dish)	4 min. 30 sec. (large oven)
4 c. as above	8 min. 30 sec. (small oven)
8 c. with 4 Tbs. butter (11" × 8" × 3" oval dish)	7 min.

Yields

1 large cabbage	2½ lb.
2½ lb.	2¼ lb., trimmed
2¼ lb., trimmed	18 to 20 c., 2" pieces
8 c., raw	2¼ c., cooked

NAVY BEAN   See BEANS for cooking times for this small dried bean.

NUOC NAM   This salty liquid sauce made by fermenting fish is a staple of Indonesian, Cambodian, Vietnamese, Laotian, Thai and other Malaysian cuisines. Adjust quantities as for SALT.

NUTMEG   A large hard seed, dried and ground as a spice. A little bit goes a long way, whether sprinkled on punches or into spinach or cake and cookie dough. Nutmeg has a tendency to be overpowering, and the microwave oven will bring out every bit of nutmeg flavor you put in.

NUTS   See varieties in Dictionary. See also GRINDING.

To *blanch nuts*, put them in a flat container in a single layer. Add water and cook at 100%. Rub off the skins with your hands or between layers of toweling.

BLANCHING TIMES FOR NUTS

Arrange in a single layer in a shallow dish. Add ½ c. water per lb. nuts; cover tightly.

4 oz. (⅔ c.)	1 min. 30 sec.
8 oz. (1⅓ c.)	3 min.
1 lb. (2 c.)	6 min.

Yields

4 oz., raw	3¾ oz., blanched
8 oz., raw	7½ oz., blanched
1 lb., raw	15 oz., blanched

Toasting times for nuts vary with their different amounts of oil.

TOASTING TIMES FOR NUTS

Arrange in a single layer in a shallow dish; cook at 100%, uncovered.

Almonds

6 oz. (1 c.)	5 min.

Macadamia nuts

⅓ lb. (1 c.)	4 min.

Peanuts

½ lb.	3 min.
1 lb.	4 min.

Pine nuts

½ lb. (1 c.)	8 to 10 min. (stir twice during cooking)

Walnuts or pecans

⅓ lb. (1¼ c.)	4 min. 30 sec.

Yield

⅓ lb. (about 1 c.)	1¼ c., ground

SPICING NUTS

Generally speaking, you can spice just about any nut there

is. And you can make sweet spiced nuts or piquant spiced nuts.

Spiced mixed nuts: Heat 1 teaspoon vegetable oil, uncovered in a 10-inch quiche dish at 100% for 2 minutes. Add 1 tablespoon chili powder, 4 drops hot red-pepper sauce and 1 teaspoon kosher salt. Cook, un-covered, at 100% for 1 minute. Add 12 ounces unsalted nuts and stir to coat. Cook, uncov-ered, at 100% for 5 minutes, stirring once. Vary seasonings.

To *salt nuts*, proceed as for Spiced Mixed Nuts, substitut-ing kosher salt for the chili powder and omitting the pepper sauce.

O

OATMEAL Oatmeal is used mainly in cookies and breakfast cereal; except perhaps in Scotland, it is much less used than it once was. Cereal com-panies have responded by mak-ing quicker-cooking oats. Use large cooking dishes or meas-uring cups; oatmeal tends to boil over.

COOKING TIMES FOR OATMEAL

Irish (coarse-cut) oatmeal Cover tightly.

¼ c. with 1 c. water; uncover after 4 min. 30 sec. (8-c. measure)	*9 min. 30 sec. to 10 min. 30 sec.*
½ c. with 2 c. water; uncover after 5 min. (8-c. measure)	*13 to 14 min.*

Old-fashioned (not quick-cooking) oatmeal Cover tightly.

⅓ c. with ¾ c. water (2-c. mea-sure)	*2 min. 30 sec., stand 1 min.*
⅓ c. as above	*4 min. (small oven), stand 30 sec.*
⅔ c. with 1½ c. water (4-c. measure)	*3 min. 30 sec., stand 1 min.*

OATS Grain from which oat-meal is made. Oats au naturel are horse feed.

OCTOPUS See SQUID.

OFFAL Animal innards are selectively eaten in our rich country. I remember when sweetbreads were cheap; they have become a costly specialty. Tongue gets made into sand-wiches with relatively little fuss. Brains, kidney, heart, lung and intestine are commonly avoided—I think, in part, because offal requires cooking procedures different from those we perform all the time, and that makes us nervous. The microwave oven vastly simplifies and improves this kind of cooking. See BRAINS, SWEETBREADS and TONGUE.

OIL See FATS.

OKRA When trimming this vegetable for stewing, it is important not to remove the entire stem end or cut into the okra pod itself; if you do, you'll find that every slimy tale you've heard about it is true. If you trim carefully, though, your efforts will be rewarded with succulent, well-behaved okra. On the other hand, if you are using it in a gumbo to act as a thickener, you will have to slice it across to let the viscous thickener out.

COOKING TIMES FOR OKRA

Stewed whole okra Trim stems; cook in a 9″ square dish, uncovered.

½ lb. okra (add 2 c. thick liquid and cover tightly)	3 min. in ¼ c. oil

Fried whole okra Trim stems; cook in a 2-quart nonplastic container measuring at least 3¼ inches high, uncovered.

8 to 10 coated okra pods in 3 c. hot oil	1 min. in ¼ c. oil

Yields

40 to 50 okra pods	1 lb. whole okra, raw
1 lb.	5 c. whole okra, raw
½ lb., raw	3 c., stewed with 2 c. tomatoes

OLIVE OIL Now that it's been discovered that mono-unsaturated fats are actually good for you or, in the most pessimistic rendering, no worse for you than polyunsaturated, we can all enjoy the wonderful olive oils with glee. Italy, France, Spain, Portugal, Greece and California all produce a wide variety of qualities and tastes. I generally buy small quantities of unfamiliar oils until I determine what I think each will be best for.

Apart from deep-fat frying, olive oil is used mainly as a flavoring in microwave cooking. It seldom gets so hot that it loses its essential flavor, which is why I use good, fruity oils but not ones so heavy that their flavor will overwhelm everything cooked in them. Your own palate is the only reliable guide for you. See FATS and FRYING.

ONION This large vegetable family, with its relatives the LEEK, SHALLOT, GARLIC and CHIVE, is a cooking staple, as much a flavoring as a major ingredient. Flavor depends on the onion variety and the soil it grows in and, in the case of Maui, Walla Walla and Vidalia onions, on their age as well.

When cooking, taste a little bit of the onion you have; if it is very sharp, reduce the quantity in the recipe. (If slicing an onion makes you cry more than usual, it probably is quite sharp.)

The sweeter the onion, the more likely it is to brown well with microwave cooking, except for red onions, which never brown well, no matter how they are cooked. Unfortunately, browning onions takes a long time even in the microwave oven. The advantage is you don't have to stand and stir and worry about scorching.

Since onions vary so wildly in size and weight, I have tried in these recipes to give you the size of the onion being used, or the weight, or the quantities of chopped onion.

Pearl onions seem delightful, until you realize you have to peel them. The microwave oven makes this easy: Trim the root ends; blanch onions. If they are very young, reduce the cooking time by about 15 seconds. When cool enough to handle, simply pop them out of their skins.

BLANCHING TIMES FOR PEARL ONIONS

Arrange in a single layer. Cook in an 11″ × 8½″ × 2″ oval dish, uncovered.

½ lb. onions with 1 Tbs. water	1 min.
1 lb. onions with 2 Tbs. water	2 min.

COOKING TIMES FOR ONIONS

Pearl onions, blanched Peel; cook in a 1-qt soufflé dish; cover tightly.

½ lb. onions with 6 to 8 Tbs. liquid	8 min.
½ lb. onions with about ½ to 1 c. liquid	10 min.
1 lb. onions with about 1 to 2 c. liquid; stir once	15 min.

Whole small white onions 12 per lb.; peel; cook in a 10″ quiche dish; cover tightly.

2 lb. onions with 2 c. sauce	10 min.

Whole Italian flat onions 2½″ × 3¼″ × ½″; peel and trim; cook in a 14″ × 11″ × 2″ dish, cover tightly.

1½ lb. with 1¾ c. sauce; uncover last 10 min. cooking time	25 min.

Sliced onions To caramelize, cook, sliced, uncovered.

2 c. with 4 Tbs. butter (1-qt. soufflé)	30 min.
4 c. with 8 Tbs. butter (14″ × 11″ × 2″ dish)	40 to 50 min.

Minced onions Cook in a shallow dish with fat previously heated for 2 min., uncovered.

¼ c. onions with 2 Tbs. fat (8″ square dish)	2 min.

¼ c. as above	3 min. (small oven)
⅓ c. onions with 4 Tbs. fat (10" quiche dish)	2 min.
½ c. onions with 4 Tbs. fat (10" quiche dish)	4 min.
½ c. as above	5 min. (small oven)
⅔ c. onions with 8 Tbs. fat (14" × 11" × 2" dish)	3 min.
1 c. onions with 8 Tbs. fat (14" × 11" × 2" dish)	3 min.

Yields

1 small onion	1 c., sliced
⅛ lb.	¼ c, chopped
¼ lb. onions, raw	1 c., coarsely chopped
1 c. chopped, raw	¼ c., cooked
1 lb. onions	2 c., sliced
2 lb. onions	4 c., sliced

ORANGE As with all citrus, oranges should be fresh wherever possible. When juice or zest is included in a recipe, it should be cooked for a minimum of time. The microwave oven does a good job of drying zests. See DRYING, zest.

OREGANO Often confused with marjoram, this perennial herb and its edible flowers have a strong, robust taste. Too often it dominates pasta sauces, pizza and chili; use with discretion. When using fresh in the microwave oven, slightly increase the quantity over the usual amounts, and decrease the quantity when using dry. See DRYING, herbs.

OSSOBUCO Thick cuts through the veal shank in a rich and unctuous Italian sauce cook wonderfully in the microwave oven. The center round of bone and marrow acts like a magnet for the microwaves. Suddenly, it is feasible to cook veal shank for one or two people—consider that 4 pieces of shank cook in 16 minutes at 100%! See recipe for Ossobuco or devise your own using the same times and proportions of liquid.

COOKING TIMES FOR SLICED VEAL SHANK (OSSOBUCO)

Veal shanks 2½"-thick slices, about ¾ lb. each. Brown on top of the stove for 10 min.; cover tightly.

2 shanks with ¼ c. liquid and ¼ lb. vegetables (8" × 6" oval dish)	12 min.
4 shanks with ½ c. liquid and ½ lb. vegetables (11" × 8" × 2" dish)	16 min.
6 shanks with ⅔ c. liquid and ⅔ lb. vegetables (14" × 11" × 2" dish)	22 min.

OYSTERS I eat oysters raw. No reasonable amount of cooking is going to turn a bad oyster safe, so I might as well eat them raw. There are times when it is nice to slip a few faintly cooked oysters into a sauce, or even to turn them into a dish like Oysters Rockefeller or Oysters Florentine.

You can open the scrubbed oysters for cooking in the microwave oven. Remove them from their shells; twist off the top shell and discard.

OPENING TIMES FOR
OYSTERS

Cook in a single layer in a shallow dish, hinge down, 6 per pound. Cover tightly.

6 oysters	2 min.
12 oysters	4 min.
24 oysters	9 min.

Yields

12 oysters	2 lb.
2 lb., in the shell	⅔ c. meat
	½ c. oyster liquid

P

PAPAYA A delightful fruit —almost as good as a mango, but a lot easier to peel and seed—that has a slightly orange-yellow skin when ripe. All too often it is available only green, and I seldom have the wit to think enough ahead to buy it and ripen it for a special meal. Fortunately, there are dishes that use underripe papaya to advantage: Chicken Curry, Papaya and Cumin Sauce and Steamed Papaya Pudding. There is even microwave help at hand for green papayas; ripen as you would AVOCADO. The easiest way to deal with papaya is to cut it in half lengthwise, scoop out the seeds, then scoop out the flesh.

PAPRIKA I have an aunt, a rather difficult lady, who used to admonish her daughter to be very careful: "Once a girl gets a bad name . . ." The sentence would trail off with dire implications. Well, paprika did some awful things, almost as bad as parsley. It ended up flaunting itself all over fish and chicken and even boiled potatoes until nobody wanted it anymore. If paprika promises to be good and show up only where it has something to offer, like in Chicken Paprikás, I think we can consider being seen in its company again.

Paprika is the name the Hungarians gave to American pod peppers when they turned them into a seasoning. It is available both as a powder and as a paste in different degrees of pungency (see Pepper Purées to make your own). Paprika adds no flavor to food if simply sprinkled over it dry; it needs to be cooked, which it already is in paste form.

PARMESAN More bad cheese —indeed, I am tempted to say sawdust—has been sold masquerading as the real Italian cheese from Parma. Buy Parmesan in bulk. Look for aged cheese. Grate it yourself as you need it (see GRATING) since it rapidly fades in taste once grated. It keeps well, tightly wrapped, in a chunk. Then when you add it to foods such as Risotto, you will really enjoy it. Also consider eating it on its own with a pear instead of dessert, or scatter slivers of it on

PARSLEY A Victorian tale: "The Green Menace, or Virtue Reclaimed," edifyingly told in three parts, being parsley, its dangers; parsley addiction; and parsley, redemption through restraint. When I first began my green temperance league, the signs of parsley abuse were already widespread. Sprigs showed up in the strangest places. I feared the day a cooking student would proudly show me a chocolate cake luridly wreathed in parsley, "for a little color." As cooks have become more aware of the possibilities inherent in contrasts and arrangements of food on the plate, this danger has faded. Abstinence is not the solution. Remember that parsley is a wonderful herb with very good flavor, an important seasoning in its own right.

There are two principal kinds of parsley, common curly parsley and Italian flat-leaf parsley and Italian flat-leaf parsley. Both are delicious. Contrary to popular supposition, curly parsley is stronger-tasting than flat-leaf. Young parsley of either kind will be better and more delicate than the older, tougher sprigs and may need to be increased in quantity. For maximum flavor, parsley needs to be cooked; this is particularly nice in the microwave oven, since it will keep its color. See Parsley Sauce. The stems can be saved for soup whenever you find only the leaves are called for. I dislike the quantity "a bunch of parsley" (though I'm guilty of the mistake myself); no two bunches are ever the same. See DRYING, herbs, and advice on quantities, page 524.

PARSNIP A delightfully old-fashioned vegetable that used to turn up in every greengrocer's soup bunch, the parsnip and its sweet, nutty flavor deserve to be reintroduced to common use. Add some cooked, puréed parsnips to mashed potatoes, or stir them into a winter vegetable soup or, cooked and cubed, into a winter version of Chicken Fricassee. Parsnips are unexpectedly elegant in Parsnip Flan.

COOKING TIMES FOR
PARSNIPS

Cut into 1½" chunks; cover tightly.

*½ lb. parsnips   5 min.
with ½ c. liquid
(4-c. measure)*

½ lb. parsnips with ½ c. liquid (4-c. measure)	9 min. (small oven)
1 lb. parsnips with 1 c. liquid (8-c. measure)	8 min.
2 lb. parsnips with 1½ c. liquid (1-qt. soufflé)	11 min.

Yields

1 lb. cooked, trimmed parsnips with 1 c. liquid	2 c. purée

PARTRIDGE Perfect, plump partridges should be roasted or grilled; should an older one fall your lot, it could be happily substituted in the Mini-Chartreuse. Serve roasted, pleasant with Braised Red Cabbage, Parsnip Flan or one of the vegetable purées, page 288–301.

PASTA I love pasta, but almost never cook it in the microwave oven. It's too slow, due to the relatively huge quantity of water. It is better cooked on top of the stove and then combined with a soup or sauce that has been prepared separately in the microwave oven.

Do remember to allow enough time for boiling your water, as well as for cooking your pasta, so that the microwave part of the recipe is not done far ahead of the pasta.

It's tricky to gauge just how much pasta to cook. You can figure that 1 cup of dry elbow macaroni, about ⅓ pound, will give you 1⅓ cups, cooked; 1

pound, dry (about 3 cups), will give you 7 cups, cooked.

PEA Here I am talking about green peas, both shelled and with edible pods, those glories of the early-summer kitchen. When fresh peas are not good, the best alternative is frozen tiny (petit) peas. Simply place frozen peas in a sieve and separate under warm running water; use as designated in your recipe, or combine in a glass measuring cup with 1 tablespoon of butter, a handful of shredded Boston lettuce, ¼ teaspoon salt and any other desired seasonings (such as 1 teaspoon dried mint; see DRYING, herbs). Cover tightly with microwave plastic wrap and cook at 100% for 2 minutes. See BEANS for black-eyed peas; see also SPLIT PEA.

COOKING TIMES FOR FRESH SHELLED PEAS

Large winter peas Cover tightly.

1 c. with 1 Tbs. butter 4 min. (2-c. measure)

Tiny new peas Cover tightly.

2 c. with 1 Tbs. water 3 to 4 (4-c. measure) min.

Yields

1½ lb., unshelled	½ lb., shelled
½ lb., shelled	2 c., raw

PEACH One of the many fruits that poach perfectly in the microwave oven. You can also make delicious Peach Butter.

COOKING TIMES FOR PEACHES

Whole, small peaches About 2½ oz. each. Prick each with a fork; cover tightly.

2¼ lb. peaches in 2 c. syrup (8-c. measure)	5 min.

Quartered and stoned for Peach Butter Cover tightly.

1½ lb. peaches with ½ c. liquid and ½ c. sugar (2-qt. soufflé)	15 min.
3 lb. peaches with 1 c. liquid and ½ c. sugar (14" × 11" × 2" dish)	22 min. 30 sec.

PEANUTS See Peanut Brittle. See also NUTS, toasting.

PEAR Today, pears are often better for a longer season than apples, since they must always be picked underripe and allowed to ripen off the tree, or they will be mushy. Storing the underripe fruit in the refrigerator keeps them in good shape for a pretty long time. This underripeness is actually an asset when cooking pears for a dessert; use firm varieties such as Bosc. Pears cooked in a microwave oven do not need any additional sugar, and they will cook evenly.

COOKING TIMES FOR BOSC PEARS

Whole Peel and core; wrap individually and set on carousel or on a plate.

1 pear	3 min.
1 pear	4 min. 30 sec. (small oven)
2 pears	4 min. 30 sec.
2 pears	8 min. (small oven, with carousel)
4 pears	7 min.
6 pears	8 min.

Halved Peel and core; arrange (see page 388) in a single layer; cover tightly.

1 pear in 1 c. syrup (small dish at least 2½" deep)	7 min.
2 pears in 2 c. syrup (8½" × 7" × 2½" dish)	12 min.
4 pears in 4 c. syrup (12" × 11" × 2½" oval dish)	17 min.

PEARL ONION These small, generally white onions no bigger than ½ inch in diameter used to be a highlight of mid-summer. Now they are being specially grown and are available almost year-round.

Rather than peeling them raw, it is easier to cut off the stem end, blanch them and then pop the skins right off. See ON-IONS. While they can be butter-glazed or mixed with Bécha-mel, they are most spectacular à la Grecque or Monégasque.

PECAN see NUTS, toasting.

PECTIN This is the other element, besides sugar, that makes jams and jellies set. Fruits that are rich in pectin, such as quince, are often added to low-pectin fruits like apples to make a jelly set. (Pectin is also available in bottles.) I don't like jellies that are too firm; none of the recipes in this book calls for added pectin, and I think you will find them sat-isfactory.

PEELING The peeling of hard fruits and vegetables is best done with a potato peeler.

Tomatoes, when really ripe, need no special treatment. Run the back of a knife blade firmly along the tomato to loosen the skin, then peel. Tomatoes that are not ripe can be cooked for 30 seconds in boiling water, then peeled and cored. Results in the microwave oven are too uneven.

Peaches can be treated as to-matoes. To peel the brown skin from nuts, see NUTS, blanch-ing. For help with peeling chestnuts, see CHESTNUT.

PEPPER, BELL Large sweet pod peppers, now available in a dizzying variety of colors. They make wonderful sauces

(see Red Pepper Purée), con-tribute color and flavor to veg-etable dishes, and are terrific stuffed either hot or cold as a first course or as a main course.

COOKING TIMES FOR
BELL PEPPERS

Whole Core and seed; cook in a tightly closed microwave-safe plastic bag.

½ lb.	4 to 5 min.
½ lb.	6 to 7 min. *(small oven)*
1 lb.	6 min.

Whole, as a stuffed vege-table Stuff; stand in a 10″ × 8″ dish; cover tightly.

4 large peppers, about 2 lb., with ½ c. liquid	20 min., stand 5 min.

PEPPER, BLACK There is no sense in using black pep-percorns whole; you're just wasting pepper. Pepper is one of the trickiest ingredients to use in microwave cooking; fol-lowing quantities in standard recipes will give wildly over-peppered results. It isn't so much that the pepper gets acrid, as it will with prolonged con-ventional cooking; but the briefer, more intense micro-wave cooking seems to elicit every last bit of pepper flavor from the spice. Begin by cutting your usual pepper quantities to one quarter, until you get a feel for it, or add pepper when foods come out of the microwave oven and are still warm.

PEPPER, CHILI see CHILI and JALAPEÑO.

PEPPERMINT See MINT.

PEPPER, WHITE This ground pepper is stronger in taste than black and, like it, should be used sparingly in microwave cooking. It is used primarily in elegant white sauces where black flecks would be a distraction. See PEPPER, BLACK.

PERCH Many fish are disguised under the name of perch. There are several different kinds of true perch; they live in fresh water and are generally small. Freshly caught, they are at their best pan-fried. They can be poached whole, like TROUT. For cooking times, see FISH.

PETRALE SOLE See SOLE.

PHEASANT See GAME.

COOKING TIMES FOR PHEASANT

Whole bird Cook in a shallow 12″ oval dish, uncovered.

2¼ to 2½-lb. bird 15 min. with ½ lb. fruit or vegetables

PIGNOLI See PINE NUT.

PIKE These long, thin, freshwater fish are often hard to come by. If you can order one, or if you know a friendly fisherman, try the classic Quenelle with pike; while other fish and seafood, such as scallops, can be cooked this way, the firm, fine, somewhat neutral flesh of pike is ideal. If you have filleted pike left over, see FISH for cooking times.

PINEAPPLE The symbol of hospitality, most pineapples used to come exclusively from Hawaii. Today, they come from Puerto Rico and other Caribbean islands, and some far-flung areas as well. There are different varieties coming onto the market. Some of the most sweetly ripe and aromatic are the small, reddish-skinned fruits from the Caribbean. The old test for ripeness—tugging on a leaf to see if it comes out easily—is not as reliable as it used to be. To examine for ripeness, gently press the bottom; it should give slightly, without feeling soft or mushy—signs that it may be overripe, have brown spots and be fermented. When you have one that feels right, smell it. It should give off the aroma of fresh, sweet pineapple.

Most fresh pineapple is eaten raw. There is one very nice way of preparing it that works well in the microwave oven: Cut the top from the pineapple; quarter. Trim and discard the strip of core; cut the meat from the skin. Replace the meat on the skin and slice it, crosswise, into bite-size pieces. Arrange quarters spoke-fashion on a plate, leaf ends toward the center. Cover tightly with microwave plastic wrap. Cook as for "boats" and serve warm with vanilla ice cream.

COOKING TIMES FOR
FRESH PINEAPPLE

4-lb. pineapple for compote Trim, peel, quarter and core; cook in a 10″ × 8″ × 2″ dish; cover tightly.

4 quarters pineapple 8 min.

4-lb. pineapple to serve as "boats" Trim, quarter and core; skin, slice across and arrange on skin; cover tightly.

4 quarters pineapple 10 min. (2 dishes 12″ × 10″ × 2″); cook simultaneously on a microwave rack

Yield

4-lb. pine-apple	4 c. pineapple chunks, cooked ½ c. juice

PINE NUT The seeds that are shaken out of certain pine cones when they are ripe. Pine nuts are often used in Italian food, and are called pignolis. In pesto, no prior cooking is needed. To top ice cream or some stews, they are nice toasted. See NUTS, toasting.

PINK BEAN For cooking times, see BEANS.

PINTO BEAN For cooking times, see BEANS.

PISTACHIO A bowlful of these little nuts in their natural beige or dyed red shells can cause an addiction and a room littered with shells. As you open them, you will notice that they have a thin, papery skin over their softish green flesh; remove before making into ice cream or adding (about ¼ cup) to Veal Pâté. Blanch as peanuts; see NUTS, blanching.

PITA Heats and puffs in the microwave oven at 100% for 1 minute.

PLUM "A plum ripe for the picking" tells us the high esteem in which plums have been held. There are countless varieties, from the tiny mirabelles that the orchard man in Vermont calls "little yaller plums" to huge greengages. There are pointy purple prune plums, and red plums with golden flesh that can be as small as mirabelles and almost as large as greengages.

Because of their high sugar content, plums have been used throughout Europe to prepare brandies, which are frequently named after the type of plum from which they are made.

All plum varieties poach well, and most make good jam. Watch out for those little yaller ones, though; they will turn to alcohol practically while you look at them.

Prunes are dried plums. They can be cooked with almost no liquid, their skins pricked once or twice with a fork, and tightly covered with microwave plastic wrap, to put in a compote or eat alone. They can also be poached in a syrup with or without wine. Small prunes can be pitted; little prunes should be left whole.

COOKING TIMES FOR PLUMS

Whole plums About 6 per lb. Poach in a 2-qt. soufflé dish in 2 c. syrup (see SIMPLE SYRUP); cover tightly.

6 plums	*8 min.*
10 plums	*10 min.*
16 plums	*Cook in 2 batches as above, reusing syrup*

POACHING Cooking food in a large quantity of liquid, often liquid to cover, at a temperature below boiling. Unless you want to poach in a sugar syrup (see Figs in Red Wine) or other flavored liquid, poaching is inefficient in the microwave oven. It is preferable to steam the food with a minimal amount of added liquid.

POIRE The French word for pear, usually used to describe a delicious, nonsweet, white brandy (alcool blanc) made from pears. Most poire is made in Switzerland. My favorites are made in the Haute Savoie of France and come in slim, long-necked bottles like Alsatian wine bottles. True poire is expensive. Drink very cold in small quantities at the end of a meal. Splash a little on a fruit salad or add to a fruit dessert. When using in a cooked dish, add as close to the end of the cooking time as possible to preserve flavor. Watch out for pear

liqueurs that are sweetened, as they are never as freshly fruity. See ALCOHOL.

POKEWEED Only the young shoots of this wild green are edible. Popular from Pennsylvania Dutch country down through the South, it is either blanched and pickled, or cooked as part of POT GREENS.

POLENTA The Italian name for cornmeal and cornmeal mush. Before the arrival of corn in Italy, various grains and pulses were cooked in similar fashion to make those diet staples, porridges. See CORNMEAL.

POMPANO A flat, silvery fish that looks as if it had been designed by an early exponent of streamlining. Pompano comes out of the waters around Florida and Louisiana in neat individual or two-person servings; each fish weighs from 1½ to 2 pounds. While they are often grilled whole or butterflied and filleted, I find that a gentler kind of cooking with milder flavors lets the delicate but firm flesh star more prominently. See FISH for cooking times.

PORGY Every Gershwin fan must realize that porgy is a Southern fish. It is related to the world-famous dentice (sea bream) of the Adriatic and the tai of Japan. Close, but no cigar: Porgies are very good fish, not great fish. Depending on the size—you don't want to cook a piece more than 1½ inches thick—you may be dealing with a whole fish or a fillet; steaks don't work too well. Whole fish should be slashed through the skin and rubbed with olive oil, lemon juice, salt and pepper. A few garlic cloves can be tucked inside. Then it should be grilled, preferably outdoors. Fillets cook rapidly in their own juices or prepared as for the grilled, whole porgy. See FISH for cooking times.

PORK Here again, I do not believe that the microwave oven roasts. However, a good compromise is achieved in Smothered Pork Roast. I see no reason for us all to waste money attempting to panbroil or broil pork in the microwave oven, particularly today's leaner pork. It can be stewed in chunks, or ground, or enjoyed in chops as an entire dish or as part of a robust pasta sauce.

New guidelines for cooking pork indicate that it is safe to eat once it reaches a uniform internal temperature of 140° F. I realize that pork can be cooked as concerns taste and texture in the microwave oven without reaching the requisite internal temperature, and I have developed recipes that are unquestionably safe. If you have any doubts when following or adapting recipes, use a little instant-reading thermometer. See also DEFROSTING, meat.

COOKING TIMES FOR PORK

Thin pork chops Cut ½" to ¾" thick. Cover tightly.

1 chop about ⅓ lb., with ¼ c. sauce (6" round dish)	*4 min.*
6 chops about 2 lb., with 1 c. sauce (12" square dish)	*8 min.*

Thick pork chops Cut 1" to 1½" thick. Cover tightly.

4 chops, about 2 lb., with 3½ lb. vegetables (14" × 11" × 2" dish)	*16 min.*

Spareribs Cover tightly.

3½ lb. ribs brushed with sauce (14" × 11" × 2" dish)	*20 min., then grill 4 min.*

Loin pork roast Cover tightly.

3½-lb. roast with 1½ lb. vegetables; uncover for last 15 min. of cooking time (11" × 8" × 2" dish)	*cook 35 min. at 100%, then broil as desired*

Sausage Cut into 2" lengths, uncovered.

2 lb. sausage, last 7 min. of cooking time with ½ c. sauce and 1½ lb.	*17 min.*

*vegetables; cover
tightly (11" × 8"
× 2" dish)*

POTATO I am going to get myself in real trouble discussing potatoes, since one of the first things that everybody tries and marvels at is "baking" potatoes in the microwave oven. I have given the cooking times for baked potatoes here because I think that potatoes so cooked are useful in myriad preparations, such as mashed potatoes and purées. I do not think that a baking potato cooked in the microwave oven is a baked potato as I understand it: with a crisp skin and light, mealy flesh. Of course, if you've been baking potatoes wrapped in foil in a regular oven, you won't see the difference. Baking potatoes cooked for a good hour in a 500° F. oven are real baked potatoes.

Potatoes in general do something funny in the microwave oven. When they are fully cooked, they will still have a somewhat firm, waxy texture. This is an asset when making soups or stews, where you want them to retain their shape rather than fall apart, but is less wonderful if you want to make potatoes Lyonnaise or baked potatoes. When the potatoes have cooked in the microwave oven, take them out immediately and, holding them in a doubled cloth, squeeze each potato gently, making a lighter potato but not entirely solving the

problem. Oddly, letting them cool and then reheating for about 2 minutes helps.

On the other hand, it's hard to beat the rapidity of the microwave timings, especially when you remember you don't need to wait for the oven to heat or for water to come to a boil. Potatoes cooked in fat do better (probably because nobody expects them to be mealy). Under the proper circumstances (see Potato Galette), they will even brown. If you are cooking larger quantities than those given below, you are better off cooking them on top of the stove or in a conventional oven.

COOKING TIMES FOR POTATOES

Times are the same for large and medium ovens. For 9-ounce to 10-ounce Idaho potatoes, add 1 minute to cooking times in large and medium ovens.

Whole Idaho potatoes 7 oz. to 8 oz. each. Prick twice with a fork; place 1 potato in center; arrange more potatoes spoke-fashion; do not cover.

1 potato	*7 min.*
1 potato	*10 min.*
	(small oven)
2 potatoes	*11 min.*
2 potatoes	*18 min.*
	(small oven)
3 potatoes	*16 min.*
4 potatoes	*20 min.*

Whole new potatoes Cover tightly.

½ lb. potatoes with ½ Tbs. butter; stir once (1-qt. soufflé)	*8 min.*
1 lb. potatoes with 3 Tbs. oil; stir once (1½-qt. soufflé)	*10 to 15 min.*
1 lb. potatoes in circle on dinner plate with 2 Tbs. water	*10 min.*
4 lb. potatoes with ¾ c. oil; stir once (14" × 11" × 2" dish)	*20 min.*

Sliced Cover tightly.

½ lb. with ½ Tbs. butter (1-qt. soufflé)	*4 to 5 min.*
1 lb. with 1 Tbs. butter (2-qt. soufflé)	*4 to 5 min.*

Peeled and cubed ½" all-purpose potatoes, boiled Cover tightly.

½ lb. with 1 c. water (4-c. measure)	*8 min.*
1 lb. with 2 c. water (8-c. measure)	*15 min. 30 sec.*

POT GREENS Tossed into a pot with fatback and a little water, these may include beet tops, collards, dandelion greens, mustard greens, pokeweed, kale, rape, creasy greens (land cress) and turnip greens —in short, whatever's on hand.

If this sounds like Greek to you, you're not from the South. Pot Greens as a dish is sometimes known as mess of greens.

There are long-cooking greens and short-cooking, softer greens. Greens taste better all mixed up, several varieties together, than all of one kind. If preparing long-cooking and short-cooking greens together, follow the time rule for long-cooking ones. If you like your greens with Ham Hocks, cook the hocks first. Use 1 ham hock along with its cooking liquid to cook each 2 pounds of greens, omitting the fatback. To cook any of the softer greens at their simplest, cook as for SPINACH.

Long-cooking greens: beet greens, collard greens, creasy greens, kale, mustard greens, pokeweed and turnip greens (large).

Short-cooking greens: dandelion greens (young), rape, watercress, spinach and turnip greens (very young).

COOKING TIMES FOR POT GREENS

Cook with 1 cup liquid and ¼ pound fatback in a 14" × 11" × 2" dish.

½ lb. short-cooking greens, uncovered	*8 min.*
1 lb. short-cooking greens, uncovered	*10 min.*
2 lb. long-cooking greens, covered tightly; uncover for last 5 min.	*30 min.*

Yield

2 lb. greens,   6 c., cooked raw

PRALINE   See ALMOND.

PREHEATING They say microwave ovens don't heat up. Well, they do. The air and moisture in the oven warms, and that shortens already short cooking times. See, for example, the cookies on pages 423–431. This heating effect can be useful in creating a warm, protected environment for something like RAISING.

PRESERVING   Usually means making jams and jellies. In a larger sense, it means storing things so that they will not spoil and includes DRYING, FREEZING, salting and smoking.

Jams, jellies and fruit butters can be made in the microwave oven; see pages 450–463. Since I am not a frontier farm wife putting things by for a long, hard winter, I find making them in small batches in the microwave oven ideal. I usually don't want to pick more than that quantity of fruit anyhow. The process is so controllable that I always get a gel.

Jars and lids for putting up preserves are best sterilized on top of the stove. If the jam or jelly is boiling hot, it can be placed immediately in the sterile jars and sealed with paraffin (which must be melted on top of the stove—it is impervious to microwaves). It can also be hot-sealed in a water bath on top of the stove. If you have any qualms, refrigerate your production.

PRUNES   see PLUMS.

Q

QUAIL Good as these small birds are (2 ounces each), I have some hesitation about serving them at fancy parties, especially when I don't know the guests very well. It is very hard to eat quail without using your fingers. They are good quartered and deep-fried as finger food for a cocktail party. See Deep-Fried Quail. Quail are delicious split and broiled or sautéed. One especially succulent recipe for quail cooked in the microwave oven is Mini-Chartreuse. Quail are now widely available frozen. See DEFROSTING, fowl.

QUATRE-ÉPICES   This classic French seasoning is made up of 1 part each ground ginger, nutmeg and clove, and 3 parts freshly ground black pepper. See Smooth Country Pâté.

QUINCE There exist both quince bushes and quince trees. The trees have pink and white blooms on dark bare branches in the spring; they are beautiful and fragrant. The bushes have red blooms and thorns, and attract hummingbirds. The fruits are fuzzy, knobby, yellow-green and hard to peel. I know of no one who eats them raw, but they are good in compotes and a boon beyond belief to the world of jam- and jelly-making. Quinces are rich in natural pectin, and for that reason are often combined with fruits like apples, whose jelly is more difficult to set; in cases such as these, usually one quarter of the total fruit weight is quince. (See PECTIN.) There is one oddity about cooking quince in the microwave oven. Ordinarily, cooked quince turns a pale pinkish-orange; in the microwave oven it stays yellow-gold.

The Austrians make a Quince Paste (Quittenkäse) that is a delicious dessert or sweet snack when thinly sliced.

R

RABBIT Increasingly, rabbit is available frozen in supermarkets. It can be cooked in the same ways and for the same times as comparable weights of chicken. Hare is a wild rabbit, somewhat larger and stronger-tasting. Defrost as in Rabbit in Mustard Cream. See also DEFROSTING.

RADICCHIO There is much to be said about the large family of red chicories. Some, like endive, are second growths, forced in a cold (slightly above freezing), dark environment to intensify the red coloration. Other species of radicchio are field-grown. All are early-spring or late-fall-to-winter vegetables due to their need for cold weather. The kind most commonly available in this country, Rosso da Verona, looks like an undernourished red cabbage except that it is softer and costs more.

Other heads of radicchio are more oval in form. Some are quite loose; some are splotched like cranberry beans or red on green; some have pointed leaves. All radicchio are natives of the Veneto around Venice; there they are so varied and important (grown for cooking as vegetables more than for use in salad) that whole cookbooks have been written about them. The most desirable radicchio for cooking is Treviso.

When radicchio is cooked, it generally loses its beautiful red color. It retains more of it when cooked in the microwave oven. I have developed two classic Italian recipes into microwave oven recipes, with some improvement: See Risotto with Radicchio and Red Vermouth, and Radicchio Gratin.

COOKING TIMES FOR WHOLE RADICCHIO

Cook in a tightly sealed microwave-safe plastic bag.

1 lb. radicchio	*5 min.*
2 lb. radicchio	*8 min.*

RAISIN To plump or macerate, see SOAKING, dried fruit.

RAISING I don't usually use the microwave oven to raise my doughs. Firstly, it is frequently in use for something else. Secondly, I prefer doughs to be cold-raised for a longer length of time; I think they develop more flavor. Nevertheless, there are times when I am in a hurry.

Prepare dough and place in a bowl to rise as usual. Cover with a damp sheet of paper toweling. Set bowl in a dish 3 inches deep and add water to almost fill the dish. Heat at 100% for 1 minute, and leave oven door closed for 15 minutes. Now rotate the bowl one-quarter turn, and heat again for 1 minute. Let stand again for 15 minutes more. Dough should be doubled in bulk.

RAPE See POT GREENS or, for the Italian version, BROCCOLI DI RAPE.

RASPBERRY See Raspberry Jam. See also PRESERVING.

RECIPES Expanding or reducing them in quantity is one of the trickiest problems when working or playing with the microwave oven.

To adjust microwave recipes: Look up the major ingredient in your recipe in this Dictionary. See if you can find a formula that resembles the proportions in your recipe and is for the quantity you want, and follow that. Do not change the proportions of liquid to solid. If, for instance, you have a recipe for beef stew that calls for 1 pound of meat and you want to cook 2 pounds, look up BEEF. Locate beef, 2 pounds. Multiply your liquid ingredients and your vegetables by 2. Adjust those quantities so that they conform to the formula, and cook as indicated.

RED BEANS These large dried beans are widely used in Mexican cooking. See BEANS for cooking times. They are delicious in Refried Beans.

RED CABBAGE This dark, almost purple cabbage with a winy taste is not good in salads, where it often shows up "for color." It is very special in sweet and sour soups like Winter Borscht, and as a vegetable, Sweet and Sour Red Cabbage. These wonderful traditional dishes had left my repertoire because red cabbage normally takes a long time to cook. The microwave oven has returned them to frequent use.

COOKING TIMES FOR
RED CABBAGE

Shredded Cover tightly.

9 c. cabbage with 2 Tbs. fat and ¾ c. liquid added after 8 min. (12" × 10" × 3" dish)	*18 min.*

Yield

2½ lb., cored	*9 c., shredded*

Red Cabbage (cont.)
9 c., shred-   5½ c., cooked
ded

REDFISH A really meaning-
less name on both the East and
West coasts since it is used to
refer to various groups of fish.
In the Northwest it generally refers to one of the ROCKFISH. For
cooking times see FISH.

RED-PEPPER SAUCE, HOT
This is available as a commercially bottled hot sauce. I prefer
the fresher-tasting ones that you
make in the microwave oven.
See Pepper Purées.

RED SNAPPER Along with
pompano, probably the most
highly esteemed of America's
southern Atlantic coastal fish.
Red·snapper is a member of a
big family. While they may be
very large, the most common
sizes in the market range from
a fish to feed two to eight-
pounders that will feed a
small horde. The rose-red scal-
loped skin stays red during
cooking, which has put the fillets in demand in restaurants
with nouvelle cuisine and new
American cooking.
    Generally, the fish is cooked
whole or in fillets, rarely in
steaks. When buying or cooking a whole fish, remember that
because the snapper has a big
head and heavy bones, more
than one third of its weight will
not be edible. It has very white
flesh, a medium flake and is
medium firm. See FISH for
cooking times.

REDUCTION When cooked
uncovered, liquids evaporate
quickly in the microwave oven.
Do not reduce salted liquids or
vegetable mixtures. If you have
cooked something and are left
with too much water that you
cannot drain—a purée, for instance—place it for a short
time, uncovered, in the microwave oven at 100%. The microwave is also efficient for
other kinds of reduction, where
you are intentionally intensifying the taste or texture of a liquid. See Beurre Blanc or
Béarnaise to make a reduction
of aromatic vegetables and liquid. This may take too long in
low-powered (small and medium) ovens to make it worthwhile. Where feasible, reduce
in a glass measuring cup so that
you know precisely what your
result is.

REDUCTION TIMES FOR
BROTH TO GLAZE

Cook uncovered at 100%.

6 Tbs. liquid	8 min.
(1-c. mea-	
sure)	
Yields 1½	
Tbs.	
1 c. liquid	12 to 15 min.
(2-c. mea-	
sure)	
Yields	¼ c.

REDUCTION TIMES FOR
BROTH TO DOUBLE
STRENGTH

Cook uncovered at 100%.

| 4 c. liquid (14" × 11" × 2" dish) | 30 min. |
| 6 c. liquid (14" × 11" × 2" dish) | 40 min. |

REHEATING It takes so little time to make things fresh in the microwave oven that, by and large, it is better not to reheat. When planning to reheat, shorten cooking time slightly. If you want to work ahead, make your sauces, purées, caramels and other components. Arrange your vegetables for cooking. Set up your seafood and fish dishes ready for cooking. Cover them both tightly with microwave plastic wrap. When the time comes, cook them.

Meat stews may actually profit from reheating. I call that mellowing; see page 234 for times. To make risotto and other rice dishes ahead, or to reheat, see page 119. I'm not mad for bread reheating in the microwave oven. The choice seems to be between dry bread and soggy crusts. Wrap bread in a triple layer of microwave-safe paper toweling and reheat at 100% for 2 minutes. See also DEFROSTING.

TO REHEAT SAUCES, BROTHS, PURÉES

To bring from refrigerated to boiling, cover tightly; cook at 100%.

½ c.	4 min.
1 c.	5 min.
2 c.	4 min., stir, 2 min.
4 c.	4 min., stir, 4 min.

RENDERING When a solid fat or almost pure fat (bacon, chicken fat, duck fat, pork fat) is cooked, the fat liquefies, and the solid matter can be skimmed out as cracklings or lardoons—particularly rapid and painless in the microwave oven. See BACON for rendering lardoons. Lardoons are good tossed with a salad of chicory and a dressing made with 2 parts of the warm bacon fat, 1 part vinegar, salt and pepper. The rendered fat keeps indefinitely refrigerated and is used for cooking.

FOWL FAT

To render *duck fat*, remove the solid fat from the inside of ducks and trim it from skin flaps as well. Using scissors, cut fat into ½-inch square pieces. Cook in batches of 2½ cups each: Place in a 2-quart soufflé dish and cover with a sheet of paper toweling; cook at 100% for 25 minutes. Remove cracklings to drain fat. You can include duck skin cut into strips as part of the measured fat.

To render *chicken fat* (*schmaltz*), proceed as for duck, above, using both skin and fat. Some people add a peeled, quartered onion or 5 whole garlic cloves as fat renders.

Yield of fat from:

| 5 to 5½-lb. duck | 2 to 3½ c. rendered fat ½ c. or more cracklings |
| 4-lb. chicken | 1 c. rendered fat |

SUET

Cut it into chunks and process until coarsely ground. Cook as duck fat.

CRACKLINGS

Solids left when fat is rendered. Store, tightly covered, in the refrigerator for up to 2 weeks. Heat in a single layer on a sheet of paper toweling at 100% for 30 seconds. Serve instead of nuts; sprinkle with kosher salt or on salads or mashed potatoes.

RHUBARB Early in chilly northern springs, one of the most decorative of perennial food plants pushes up year after year. Its pink-to-red stalks and dark-green leaves are inviting indeed. Originally a Russian plant, it has been used all over Europe and North America to make spring tonics—a wise move in earlier times, since it is rich in vitamins that would have been lacking all through the dark winter. Be careful, though, of the leaves; they contain too much oxalic acid to be human fodder. Incidentally, if someone in the family is prone to the insult of kidney stones, you might omit rhubarb from the menu.

Vitamin C in pill form and the winter arrival of warm-climate citrus have vitiated the need for rhubarb, but it still merits a place in garden and kitchen for its taste. Fibrous, like celery, it is best cooked by first being cut across the stalk into ¼-inch diagonal slices. Then it can be cooked rapidly, retaining more color and flavor than when cooked traditionally for a longer time. Add it to early strawberries for jam and pie. See Rhubarb Strawberry Jam.

Rhubarb freezes beautifully if it is first blanched: Cook each cup of cut stems for 1 minute in 1½ cups of "1 to 1" SIMPLE SYRUP. Freeze in half-pint microwave-safe plastic containers. To defrost, uncover container; cover tightly with microwave plastic wrap. Cook at 100% for 4 minutes. Allow to sit until completely defrosted. Use as fresh rhubarb.

COOKING TIMES FOR RHUBARB

Fresh rhubarb as a side dish Scrub, trim and slice ⅛″ thick; cover tightly.

2 c. rhubarb with ¼ c. sugar (4-c. measure)	3 min. 30 sec.

RICE One of the most adaptable grains, or starches, it is the staple food of over half of the population of the world. Different regions and culinary cultures have developed countless rice varieties. The major descriptive categories have to do with the shape (round or oval), width (in India, superfine, fine or coarse) and length (long, medium or short), whether its brown (bran) layer under the husk has been removed, and whether it is raw or processed (precooked, converted and so forth). Some varieties of rice are even described by their scent as well as their color. Often the most useful way to describe a rice is by the dish in which it is most commonly used. No matter what the kind of rice, the best grade has unbroken grains.

It is difficult to give an exact amount of liquid for cooking rice as it will vary with the age of the grain. Old rice, like all old grains, takes considerably more cooking liquid than does "new" rice. In India, the home of the pilaf method, rice is often specially aged to be cooked in this way.

In many instances you are better off cooking rice as a side dish on top of the stove; while the rice is cooking, the main business of meal preparation can go on in the microwave oven. As in timing all starches, just be sure your calculations include time for the water to come to a boil, or your microwave-cooked main course may be ready before your rice.

Some special rice preparations become joyously easy in the microwave oven.

Imagine a risotto that can be cooked in the microwave oven while you busy yourself with other things—no standing over the stove dribbling in broth and stirring.

Rice pilaf (also known as pilaff, pilaw, pilau) has many pseudonyms because it is a basic preparation common to an enormous part of the rice-eating world, from Bulgaria and Greece through most of the Middle East, and throughout India. It is normally differentiated from risotto in two ways: first, by the long grain used (see RICE, basmati, and RICE, patna); second, by the fact that after the rice is initially cooked in oil, the liquid is added all at once rather than a little at a time. (In the Near East, the procedure is a little different and entails endless soakings of the rice. I don't find it works any better.) The rice is then cooked covered. In microwave cooking, the liquid is added all at once to both preparations, and it is the variety of rice type and the covering that make the difference.

RICE, AMBRA This other northern Italian rice is slightly longer and more pointed than its cousin, arborio, and makes a somewhat less glutinous risotto. Italians often prefer seafood risottos with ambra, in part for its pale-gold color.

RICE, ARBORIO (Sometimes called avorio.) A short (though not as short as the Oriental rices) oval grain with an opaque white spot near the midpoint, grown in the Po Valley north of Venice. It suits risotto as it stays firm, yet releases a fair amount of starch, giving the dish its creamy texture. See also RICE, AMBRA, and Risotto.

RICE, BASMATI Julie Sahni, in *Classic Indian Vegetarian and Grain Cooking*, translates basmati as "queen of fragrance." It is a highly esteemed Indian and Pakistani rice: long, thin, white and expensive. It has a delicate warm smell, somewhere between nuts and tea. It is usually cooked pilaf-fashion.

RICE, BROWN Rice that has not had its external germ removed. Because it is more nutritious than rice that has (e.g., white rice), it has become extremely popular in this country in recent years. Any kind of rice can be prepared in this way; but the most commonly available are Carolina-type rices, sometimes converted, and Oriental rices, notably in macrobiotic diets. All brown rice takes longer to cook than the comparable white grain. Cook it on top of the stove; it doesn't do as well in the microwave oven.

RICE, CAROLINA Unless I specify a special rice in a recipe, I am talking about Carolina rice. Up until the Civil War, the Carolinas were a prolific rice-growing area, exporting to the world at large. A long-grain rice, rounded in profile, was developed there, and it became the American standard. Even though little rice is grown in the Carolinas today, that type is called Carolina rice. It is of a medium hardness and can be used in most recipes, though it will not make a true risotto (it is not starchy enough and gets soft too quickly) or a true pilaf (the grains do not stay separate enough as it cooks). However, you can cook it in either of those fashions (see pages 118–119, 128–129) for very good flavor.

RICE, "CONVERTED" See RICE, PARBOILED.

RICE, GLUTINOUS See RICE, STICKY.

RICE, INSTANT See RICE, PARBOILED.

RICE, LONG-GRAIN This should only be a physical description of rice that tends to cook up with individual fluffy grains rather than in a "sticky" or risottolike fashion. There are many different kinds of long-grain rice from various regions, with different degrees of fluffiness when cooked. In the United States it usually means CAROLINA RICE.

RICE, ORIENTAL (SHORT-GRAIN) Where chopsticks or hands are the eating tools and rice the staple food (eaten in conjunction with almost every meal), it is desirable that the rice cook in such a way that it more or less sticks together, so that it can be easily picked up. This is the rice of sushi; the Japanese-grown version has a smallish oval grain and, instead of arborio's central white mark, it has a central dark mark.

RICE, PARBOILED There are two kinds, quick-cooking rice (which I have nothing to do with) and a rice that is really power-steamed rather than boiled. The latter, which is excellent, has a brand name, converted rice, in this country. It takes a little longer to cook than other American long-grain rices, and it holds its shape well. It can be substituted for patna and basmati rices in pilafs and for arborio rice in risotto.

RICE, PATNA Originally referring to a very fine-quality, long-grain Indian rice, the name now indicates only rice grown from a patna-type seed and suitable for cooking pilaf. You can substitute basmati rice or converted rice.

RICE, STICKY A short-grain, almost round rice that is sticky when cooked. Also call glutinous rice and Oriental round short-grain rice.

RICE, SWEET This is usually used in sweet Oriental dishes. It is sometimes also called glutinous or sticky—very confusing.

RICE, WILD The microwave oven cooks wild rice better than any other method I have tried. One has to fuss very little, and the results are remarkably consistent. This dark-brown native American grain is not rice at all, but rather a grain shaped like rice. These days it is often not wild. The best-quality wild rice is longish, fat and glossy, with no loose husks and an herby, tealike fragrance. The object of its preparation is to swell it and expose the more tender inner meat.

COOKING TIMES FOR WILD RICE

Cover tightly. Let stand 15 minutes after cooking with microwave plastic wrap lightly pierced by a knife tip.

½ c. rice with 1 c. water (4-c. measure)	7 min.; stand; drain
½ c. rice as above	12 min.; stand; uncover, cook 12 min. (small oven)
1 c. rice with 2 c. water (8-c. measure)	12 min.; stand; drain (large oven)
1 c. rice as above	20 min.; stand; uncover, cook 10 min. (small oven)
1½ c. rice with 3 c. water (11″ × 8½″ × 3″ dish)	18 min.; stand; uncover, cook 10 min.

Yields

½ c. raw rice	1 c., cooked
1 c. raw rice	2 c., cooked
1½ c. raw rice	3 c., cooked

RICE WINE A light, clear, marginally sweet wine used by the Japanese for cooking. It is available in specialty food sections. One kind is MIRIN.

RIPENING See BANANA or AVOCADO.

ROASTING No, never, not in the microwave oven. Painting food with colored glazes doesn't mean that they have browned on their own. By the time such browning takes place, the food is cooked to death. You have a regular oven. Use it. The results will be much better.

ROCKFISH Occasionally, this term is used, erroneously, for striped bass (see BASS) in the Baltimore area. It is actually the name for a large group of fish caught off the coasts of California, Oregon and Washington, where it is sold as rock cod, black sea bass and even, heaven help us, snapper. One of the best species of true rockfish is yellowtail, much used for sushi (not to be confused with the south Atlantic yellowtail or with yellow-fin tuna, also used for sushi and sashimi).

Rockfish has white, fairly firm flesh that tends to flake like cod when cooked (though the flakes are smaller). Small fish are best cooked whole. Large fish should be cooked in steaks and portion-size filleted pieces, medallions or squares. The bones and head are excellent for

Fish Broth. See FISH for cooking times.

ROSEMARY This richly aromatic herb often associated with lamb can be found in several varieties. Some look like small pine trees, and in the south of France are trimmed into hedges. Others are hanging and crawling plants grown on stone walls and used as ground cover. In northern climes, plants need to be transferred to pots and brought indoors in the winter.

This is one herb where the fresh and dried are fairly close in flavor and quantity used. Of course, fresh is still preferable. See DRYING, herbs. See also page 34 for amounts to use in the microwave oven.

ROTATING Moving food in a flat circular motion. I think much less of this needs to be done than is called for in most books. If your oven has a carousel, or if you have purchased a separate one (see page 10), you don't need to worry about rotating. Additionally, the tight wrapping you do with microwave plastic wrap creates a mini-environment that helps even out the cooking. If you will be unhappy unless you rotate the food, see page 10.

RUTABAGA As a child, I thought this was a root-er-baker. It is a large, waxy yellow turnip with a sharper taste than a regular turnip. If it is to be puréed or steamed, it requires longer cooking than a regular turnip. On the other hand, julienned and quickly blanched, it can be used instead of celery root in a mustard vinaigrette or mayonnaise for a first-course salad.

COOKING TIME FOR RUTABAGA

Cut into ½" cubes; cover tightly.

1½ lb. rutabaga with ½ c. water (8-c. measure)	*15 min.*

Yield

1½ lb. raw	*1¾ c. purée*

RYE A widely used grain for bread in cold climates, for whiskey in warm ones. Sadly, due to the problems with bread and gluten-based baking, rye is not of much use in the microwave oven.

S

SAFFRON These tiny pistils from a special fall-blooming crocus are available whole or ground. The same weight of saffron will be much smaller when ground. It is always very expensive, which is why I don't use it very much, and it has the most beautiful color, the color of Tibetan monks' robes. The flavor is slightly musky, a background taste. It is much used in Indian cooking, usually with rice. In Milan, it is used in the risotto that accompanies veal shanks (ossobuco). See Saffron Risotto.

SAGE A perennial herb with many varieties such as pineapple, variegated and red. Fresh sage is frequently used in Italian and other Mediterranean cooking with green beans and in stews. Dried, it is used in holiday stuffings and in meat loaf.

Sage flowers are edible. See DRYING, herbs. See also page 34 for adjusting herb quantities when cooking in the microwave oven.

SALMON One of the great fish families. Its rich fat even turns out to be good for us. The Atlantic, Pacific, farm, ocean and spring-run river varieties all have different colors and tastes, but they cook the same way. See FISH for cooking times.

SALMON TROUT Occasionally, this name is misapplied, particularly in the South, to WEAKFISH in an attempt to class them up. Properly, these are the brown trout (see TROUT) that were introduced into American streams and, in many cases, won territorial disputes with the native trout. The salmon trout usually is larger and has taken to the sea. It is called "salmon" because it eats the same food as the salmon, and its flesh turns a paler version of the same color. The flesh itself is firm, but with a smaller flake and less fat than salmon. It is usually cooked whole or in fillets. Cook as salmon; use the less seasoned sauces. See FISH for cooking times.

SALT In this book salt is always kosher salt. It has no added chemicals and is coarsely ground. If substituting table salt, divide salt quantity by 3. Pickling salt may be substituted; it is also additive-free, though a little less evenly ground. Use half the quantity of kosher salt.

SALT COD See COD.

SALTING See NUTS, salting.

SALT PORK Known as fatback in the South, where it is also sometimes called side meat. It is frequently used in POT GREENS, and can also be rendered into salty nuggets: Cut into 1-inch cubes and cook as lardoons (see BACON, lardoons). Don't confuse it with fatback in non-Southern recipes.

SAND DAB A member of the seemingly endless group of flatfish, the flounders and soles. They tend to be small, with a firm texture, although not as firm as Dover sole or pompano. They are delicious cooked as fillets and paupiettes. See SOLE for more general information. See FISH for cooking times.

SARDINE Many of us have never seen these excellent little fish except in cans. Sardines, baby pilchards, have become virtually extinct in Pacific waters. When they are available fresh in this country, they are almost always imported. It should be noted that baby herrings of species other than pilchards are often substituted.

Fresh sardines are at their absolute best sprinkled with salt and grilled out-of-doors. Second best is still good enough for me. Sardines that are cooked and then marinated are highly esteemed in Venice; see Marinated Sardines. Arrange many in a single layer, spoke-fashion, heads out, tails to the middle. See FISH for cooking times.

SAUCE Different from a gravy in that it is made apart from the food on which it is to be served. Some sauces use the pan juices or a broth made with a similar principal ingredient. See Savory Sauces for meats, vegetables, fish and the like. See also Dessert Sauces.

SAUTÉING You can cook in fat in the microwave oven, but you cannot truly stir-fry or sauté, as it is impossible to keep the food moving. The positive side of this is that you can cook without the fat called for in sautéing.

SAVORY, SUMMER An annual herb that grows in a somewhat disorderly fashion, it is good with HARICOTS VERTS, in egg dishes and as part of an herb mixture to season eggs. When using it fresh in the microwave oven, increase standard quantities by one third. I often grow more than I need; then I dry it in the microwave oven; see DRYING, herbs.

SAVORY, WINTER This perennial herb grows as a small round bush. Most varieties have delicate, edible, attractive white flowers. A strong-tasting herb, it is best used in stews and wild mushroom dishes; it accompanies pork with brio. Try adding ¼ teaspoon dried to each cup of cannellini beans before cooking them (see BEANS). Use slightly less dried winter savory than usual when cooking in the microwave oven. This is another herb that, like rosemary, is almost the same dried and fresh. See DRYING, herbs.

SAVOY CABBAGE The most tender of the cabbages, it has a largish firm head and pale-green, crinkly leaves. If you can find it, use it.

COOKING TIMES FOR
SAVOY CABBAGE

Shredded Cook in a 4-c. glass measure; cover tightly.

2 c. cabbage	*4 min.*

Yield

½ lb. raw	*2 c., shredded, raw*

SCALLION Until fairly recently, scallions were not generally available. Today I find them in all parts of the country in all seasons. Both the green part and the white part, sliced, are frequent inclusions in Oriental recipes. Young scallion greens can be substituted, very thinly sliced, for the less available fresh chives, even though they have a slightly different flavor. Scallions also make an attractive vegetable when braised; see Scallions à la Grecque. See also SPRING ONION and LEEK.

Yields

1 bunch scallions	*6 to 7 scallions*
6 to 7 scallions	*¼ lb.*
¼ lb., trimmed	*3 oz.*
3 oz.	*⅔ c., cut into 1" lengths, or ½ c., cut into ¼" slices*

SCALLOP Gourmets the world over are all scallop-lovers. Aphrodite, goddess of love, beauty and fertility, rose from the sea and rode it on a scallop shell, which was not inappropriate as the scallop is one of the most beautiful of shells. Scallop shells were worn as pendants by her worshipers at Knidos. St. James the Apostle wore the scallop as his emblem, and it became the emblem of the many thousands of pilgrims in the Middle Ages who flocked across Europe to Compostela, Spain, where his principal shrine was located. The French name for scallops and the many dishes made with them is coquille ("shell") Saint-Jacques ("St. James"). Concha ("shell") de peregrino ("pilgrim") is its Spanish name.

The most edible parts of the scallop are its large, white, central muscle and its *roe*, a delightful reddish-orange quarter moon found in many varieties. Unfortunately, in America the roe was generally discarded. Now it is beginning to be available. If you are lucky enough to find scallops with the roe attached, cook as for sea scallops.

Scallops come in many sizes. Generally, different sizes indicate different species. A *bay scallop* is not an immature *sea scallop*, but rather one that is small at maturity.

Scallops vary in quality. The best have a white, semitranslucent flesh that is medium firm. Less fortunate scallops growing in less favored waters have flesh that is more ivory in color, more opaque and considerably firmer. All scallops must be carefully cooked so that their considerable liquid content is not lost and they become dry. The darker-colored ones will be drier and less tender in any case.

Judging freshness is a little problematic. They do not begin to smell fishy with age. Instead, their natural sweetness becomes more intense, and they begin to spew liquid. Sometimes they get mushy.

In my opinion, the expensive bay scallops are overused in this country. They are best wiped dry and sautéed very briefly in butter with fresh herbs and perhaps a shallot or two. Do not salt until removing from pan. They are almost as good briefly cooked in the microwave oven. See Sauté of Bay Scallops.

Sea scallops cook perfectly and without fat in the microwave oven. Simply arrange on a plate or in a cooking dish in a single layer; use a dish with a lip or some depth to it, to hold the liquid the scallops give off. If a small number is being cooked, arrange in a circle toward the outer edge of the dish. Cover tightly with microwave plastic wrap. They are fully cooked when they just turn white and opaque. Any extra cooked juices may be saved to add to fish sauces or broths.

COOKING TIMES FOR SCALLOPS

Bay scallops   In butter.

½ lb. with 1 Tbs. butter (9" browning dish, uncovered)	2 min. (small oven)
½ lb. (dinner plate, cover tightly)	4 min. (small oven)

¾ lb. with 1 Tbs. butter (9" browning dish, uncovered)	1 min. 30 sec.
1½ lb. with 2 Tbs. butter (10" browning dish, uncovered)	2 min.

Sea scallops Steamed; cover tightly.

½ lb. (dinner plate)	2 min. 4 min. (small oven)
½ lb. with 1 c. vegetables (dinner plate)	3 min.
1 lb. (2-qt. soufflé)	3 min.
1 lb. with 1⅓ c. vegetables (2-qt. soufflé)	7 min.
1½ lb. (11" × 8½" × 2" dish)	5 to 7 min.
2 lb. (14" × 11" × 2" dish)	9 to 10 min.
2 lb. with 2⅔ c. vegetables (14" × 11" × 2" dish)	11 min

Yields

¾ lb. scallops	1½ c.
1½ lb. scallops	3 c.

SCHMALTZ The Yiddish word for rendered chicken fat. It is more important in kosher cooking than in other kinds, since butter may not be used with meat. Seasoning varies from cook to cook. For some, an onion must be cut into the fat as it renders; for others some garlic, to achieve the flavor they desire. See RENDERING, chicken fat.

Schmaltz is also descriptive of a kind of particularly fat herring.

SCROD The young, small cod, much prized in Boston; see COD. For cooking times, see FISH.

SEA BASS An ocean-dwelling bass species. Cook it as you would cook salmon. See FISH for cooking times.

SEA BASS, BLACK These delicious Atlantic fish live off the American coast. They have relatively large heads. Allow about one third more poundage per person than you might with other fish. Very popular with Chinese-Americans, their white flesh shows to advantage when deep-fried whole. Use the microwave oven as if it were a steamer and cook whole, small black bass on a plate or platter. See FISH for cooking times.

SEAFOOD COMBINATIONS Putting clams, oysters, mussels together or with fish raises the problem that it may take longer for some shells to open than others, or longer than the fish to cook. Arrangement helps (see page 29) by keeping the clams, for example, to the faster-cooking plate edge and putting the fish in the center. For model recipes, see Scrod with Clams Livornese or Simple Fish Stew.

SERRANO A small hot chili pepper. See CHILI.

SESAME OIL The oil pressed from these seeds is available in two ways, colorless and tasteless, or brownish in color because the seeds have been toasted before pressing. This brownish oil, also called Oriental sesame oil, is the one used in this book.

SESAME SEED See TOASTING, small seeds.

SHAD, SHAD ROE These twin delights are harbingers of spring, living in rivers that go to the sea. Like salmon, they should not be eaten in summer; all that rushing upstream and then spawning exhausts them.

Never buy shad with the bones in; there are endless quantities of hard-to-extract bones. Fillets are no problem. Whole fish, filleted, seem to have as many folds and flaps as paper origami fish; these pockets are a good place to poke extra bits of butter and seasonings. Filleted shad weigh about 2 pounds, are rich in flavor, dark in color, have a melting texture and will serve three to four of all but the most ardent appetites. Sorrel is the traditional accompaniment. See Shad Fillet.

Shad roe is a delicacy in its own right and is often served without any accompanying fish. While many people broil it, sometimes with slices of bacon, I find that this toughens it. It is best poached in water or, more extravagantly, in melted butter. A pair of roe weighs anywhere from 7 to 8 ounces.

COOKING TIMES FOR SHAD

Shad fillets Cover tightly.

1½ lb. fillet with 2 Tbs. fat and 2 Tbs. lemon juice (14" × 11" oval dish)	4 min.
2 lb. with 2 Tbs. fat and 2 Tbs. lemon juice (14" × 11" oval dish)	6 min.

COOKING TIMES FOR SHAD ROE

Shad roe Cover tightly.

1 pair with ¾ c. liquid (9" × 5" × 3" dish)	2 min. 45 sec.
1 pair as above	5 min. (small oven)
2 pairs with 1½ c. liquid (9" × 5" × 3" dish)	7 min.
3 pairs with 3 c. liquid (14" × 11" × 2" dish)	9 min.

SHALLOT Another member of the onion (allium) family. Shallots with red-brown skins are milder than those with bluish-gray ones. They seem to have grown larger and easier to peel than they used to be; but they are still small and persnickety, and you can't bang them first as you do garlic. They are essential for Beurre Blanc, and are excellent pickled like onions.

SHERRY A fortified wine (alcohol is added) from Spain, it comes in many different varieties, from bone dry to rich, sweetish and creamy. When sherry is called for in a recipe, it is usually a medium sherry of modest quality, but never "cooking" sherry, which is a disaster. A bottle of sherry, recorked, keeps practically indefinitely. As with all alcohols, if adding it to a recipe to be cooked in the microwave oven longer than 7 or 8 minutes, double the quantity.

SHIITAKE Mushrooms with dark-brown tops and pale-beige gills used in Oriental cooking are mainly available in this country dried, listed in cookbooks as dried Chinese mushrooms. They are available fresh; sometimes called golden oak mushrooms. If dried mushrooms are called for, do not substitute fresh; it changes the flavor of the dish. Break into pieces dry without stems into stews, sauces and other dishes with at least ¼ cup liquid and at least 3 minutes or more cooking time. For use in stir-fry, see SOAKING, dried mushrooms.

SHRIMP Despite all the brouhaha about fish and seafood, this is still America's favorite. There was a time when all shrimp were born equal. Today, increasing sophistication and the demands of a growing market have introduced us to many unfamiliar kinds of shrimp. Some of them we can even find unfrozen. (Usually the shrimp you find reposing on ice in the market have been frozen on the boat and defrosted in the store.)

Other shrimp to look for are the giant red Spanish shrimp—grill, don't boil them—Texas Gulf shrimp with hard shells to boil in beer, Monterey shrimp and Hawaiian blue prawns.

See Shrimp Pâté, Shrimp Butter and Shrimp Cream.

COOKING TIMES FOR
SHRIMP

Times are the same for large and medium ovens. Shrimp are "medium" shrimp, about 24 per pound. When cooking shrimp en masse, not arranged on a plate in a single layer, shake the cooking dish about halfway through the cooking time to redistribute them for even cooking.

Shrimp in the shell Cover tightly.

¼ lb. (dinner plate)	45 to 55 sec.
½ lb. (9" pie plate)	2 to 3 min.
¾ lb. (1½-qt. soufflé)	3 min. to 3 min. 30 sec.
1 lb. (2-qt. soufflé)	3 to 4 min.

Shelled shrimp Cover tightly.

¼ lb. (dinner plate)	1 to 2 min. 1 min. 30 sec. (small oven)

Shelled shrimp (cont.)

½ lb. (9″ pie plate)	2 to 3 min.
¾ lb. (1½-qt. soufflé)	2 to 3 min.
2 lb. (14″ × 11″ × 2″ dish)	7 to 8 min. (stir once)

Butterflied shrimp Cover tightly.

¼ lb. (dinner plate)	25 to 30 sec. 45 sec. (small oven)
½ lb. (9″ pie plate)	1 min. to 1 min. 30 sec.
¾ lb. (1½-qt. soufflé)	2 to 3 min.

SIMPLE SYRUP This is a preparation with unlimited usefulness. It is what you use to sweeten anything in which undissolved sugar granules would be unwelcome. Anyone who has drained a glass of lemonade to find a wad of wet sugar at the bottom knows what I'm talking about.

Simple syrup is just that: simple. It is made by boiling sugar and water together. There are two syrups: "1 to 1" and "2 to 1," referring to the proportions of sugar to water. The sweetness will be determined by the percentage of sugar. The density, viscosity and thickness will be determined by the percentage of sugar and the length and heat of cooking time. See also CARAMEL.

Simple syrups can be flavored by replacing the water, or part of it, with wine or juices and by adding spices. See Index for Fruit, poached.

Simple syrup can be kept refrigerated for a long time, which is nice during the hot days when you will want lemonade and iced tea. It is very important to cover the cooking dish tightly with microwave plastic wrap. This causes the steam to wash down the sides of the container and avoids the formation of crystals. Use a large cooking dish so that the hot sugar mixture doesn't get near the plastic wrap. When opening the plastic wrap to stir, do so by pulling it away from the side of the dish to let the steam escape without your getting burned. See page 21 for illustration.

"1 to 1" simple syrup Combine 2 cups sugar and 2 cups water in a 2-quart soufflé dish. Cook, uncovered, at 100% for 3 minutes. Stir. Cover tightly with microwave plastic wrap. Cook at 100% for 6 minutes more. (Use it for fruits that will not be cooked, such as lemons for sorbet.)

"2 to 1" simple syrup Combine 2 cups sugar and 1 cup water in an 8-cup glass measure. Cover tightly with microwave plastic wrap. Cook at 100% for 15 minutes, stirring twice during cooking time; be sure to reseal tightly after stirring. (Use it to cook fruit. The liquid from the fruit will dilute the syrup.)

SLICE To cut a piece of food lengthwise, or across, into even strips that are broader than they are thick and the same length or longer than they are broad. Meats should generally be sliced with a long, thin slicing knife and cut across the grain. Breads, very juicy fruits and vegetables such as tomatoes and oranges are usually better cut across with a serrated knife between the stem and bloom end. Slice sizes are generally given in the recipes.

SLURRY Equal amounts of a starch, in this book usually cornstarch, and water stirred together until smooth, can be added to a hot mixture without caking.

SMELT These small fish—6 to 8 inches long, 10 to 12 to the pound—live primarily in salt water, running up rivers only in the spring. Even so, some of America's best are landlocked in lakes, where they are fished through the ice. True aficionados eat them head and bone. The more timid may want to remove the heads before cooking; then they can pick them up and nibble around the backbone.

The very freshest smelts taste best dusted with seasoned flour and quickly fried, an ideal fisherman's breakfast. Frozen smelts can be cooked in Saor like sardines, page 196, or steamed on a bed of sliced celery and served with boiled potatoes. Be careful not to get the sauce too messy as most people eat smelts with their fingers. See FISH for cooking times.

SNAILS For all intents and purposes, these denizens of vineyards come in cans and have been cooked. All we do when we cook them is to reheat them in a flavoring. See Snail Butter and Dijon Snails.

SNOW PEA The thin, edible pod peas so much seen in Chinese restaurants. If you are adding them to a stew or Chinese-style dish, lay on food, tightly covered, for the final 1 minute 30 seconds cooking time.

Snow peas really should not be cooked in much water. One cup will feed at least two people. To cook as a separate vegetable in the microwave oven, string; heat 2 teaspoons butter or water for each 1 cup of peas for 2 minutes, uncovered, at 100%; stir in snow peas; cook as on page 564. SUGAR SNAP PEAS cook as for snow peas.

COOKING TIMES FOR SNOW PEAS

Snow peas Cover tightly.

¼ lb. (4-c. measure)	2 min.
¼ lb. as above	3 min. (small oven)
½ lb. (14" × 11" × 2" dish)	3 min.

Yields

½ lb.	3 c., loosely packed, raw
3 c., raw	1¼ c., cooked

SOAKING To soak *dried beans* and *legumes,* see BEANS.

DRIED FRUIT

To soften, a minimum of liquid is needed. (The soaking of fruit is called macerating, whether for the purpose of reconstituting or flavoring.) Place fruit in a single layer on a plate; sprinkle with water; cover tightly with microwave plastic wrap; cook at 100% for the times below. Sometimes you may want to use more water to soften the fruit for purée. Today, many dried fruits are vacuum-packed, which keeps them from drying out until you open the package. If they dry out once the package is opened and you want to eat them, soak as below. Flavor can be added at the same time the fruits soak by using wine or fortified wine (see SHERRY) as the soaking liquid and adding seasonings.

SOAKING TIMES FOR
DRIED FRUIT

Apricots   Arrange "belly" side up; cover tightly.

6 to 10 apricots (small plate)	30 sec.
24 apricots with 1 Tbs. water	1 min.
8 oz. (1½ cups) with 1½ c. water (4-c. measure)	2 min.

Currants   Cover tightly.

½ c. currants with 1 Tbs. water (2-c. measure)	1 min.

Raisins   Cover tightly.

1 c. raisins (6 oz.) with 2 Tbs. water (2-c. measure)	1 min. 30 sec.

DRIED PEPPERS (CHILIES)

Do not presoak for use in sauces. Cook in sauce—at least 4 minutes. Reconstitute dried chilies to make them into the freshest-tasting of chili pastes. Put 1 cup dried chili peppers, about 2 ounces, in a 4-cup glass measure with 1 cup water. Cover tightly with microwave plastic wrap. Cook at 100% for 8 minutes.

DRIED MUSHROOMS

Dried mushrooms, particularly slices, do not need to be presoaked if they are being cooked for more than 3 minutes in a dish that contains liquid, such as soup, sauce or stew. When using dried shiitake in such a dish, break into pieces and discard the stem and the hard place where the stem attaches to the cap. Morels must always be presoaked because they tend to contain lots of sand. Save the soaking liquid; put it through a dampened cloth in a sieve and use the liquid either in your dish or in other soups and stews.

SOAKING TIMES FOR
MORELS

Place in measuring cup with water; cover tightly with microwave plastic wrap and heat at 100%.

2 Tbs. mushrooms (1 oz.) with ¼ c. water	3 min.
2 Tbs. as above	4 min. 30 sec. (small oven)
¼ c. mushrooms (2 oz.) with ½ c. water	5 min.
½ c. mushrooms (4 oz.) with ¾ c. water	7 min.

SOAKING TIMES FOR CAPS

Discard stems of cèpes (porcini) or whole shiitake. Swish briskly in cold water to rinse off grit. Arrange bottoms up in a single layer on an 8″ plate with 1 Tbs. water; cover tightly; cook at 100%; let stand, covered, 4 min.

4 large caps	4 min. (small oven)
20 small caps	2 min.
8 large caps	4 min.

DRIED HERBS

Dried herbs to be used in non-microwave cooking benefit from being briefly soaked in a small container with cooking liquid or water to cover. Cover tightly. Cook at 100% for 2 minutes.

SOFTENING *To soften brown sugar:* Set the opened bag on the microwave carousel. Place a mug of water next to it. Heat at 100% for 2 minutes, and check to see if the sugar is soft enough to use. If not, heat for 1 minute more.

To soften cold butter: Cut 1 stick of butter into 4 pieces. Put in a glass measuring cup and heat, uncovered, at 100% for 30 seconds. Remove from oven and whisk; the butter will have the consistency of whipped butter.

To soften or eliminate crystals from jam, preserves, jelly or honey, see HONEY.

SOFTENING TIMES FOR CREAM CHEESE

Set on a plate; cover tightly.

3 oz.	30 sec.
8 oz.	1 min.

SOLE Part of the large world of bottom-dwelling flatfish, along with flounder, plaice, dabs and turbot. It is distinguished in the culinary world by having hundreds of classic preparations assigned to it. Pride of place is usually given to Dover sole, caught in the English Channel (though there are Venetians who would make a strong argument for their sfoglia, the same species but tending to be smaller and more delicate).

Unless they buy imported fish, Americans are never cooking or eating true sole. Some of these look-alikes are very good. The so-called petrale (puh-trá-lay) sole of California (truly a flounder), its slightly smaller California cousin the rex sole and the larger lemon sole (truly a winter flounder) are all excellent. (To confuse matters yet further, there is a European lemon sole that is different from the American kind, although it, too, is a flounder.) Good as these fish are, it is important to recognize the difference. They have cooking characteristics different from those of real sole, and attempts to follow French and English recipes will lead to less than satisfactory results.

The true and the false sole all have 2 fillets. They divide easily down a prominent central line into 2 half-fillets. Larger fish should always be divided into the 4 pieces. For microwave cooking, arrange the thicker, center edge of the half-fillets toward the edge of the dish. Half-fillets are used for making paupiettes (see FISH). Some eaters may want a whole fish—2 fillets, 4 half-fillets—for themselves as a main dish, or 1 fillet—2 half-fillets—as a first course. Others may be satisfied with half the quantity.

True sole is firm-fleshed and is never meant to flake in cooking. I prefer it cooked whole, grilled or sautéed briefly so that the flesh doesn't harden. Melted butter and a little lemon are all it needs. Forget the fancy sauces that just mask the flavor.

The American soles—small flounder species in masquerade—have a medium-firm flesh and are better cooked in fillets, as their tough skins will make it hard to cook the subtle flesh evenly. They can be cooked in butter or poached. They like the protection of a goodish amount of liquid and should not be vigorously sautéed. This makes them perfect candidates for microwave cooking. They may be substituted in any recipe calling for fish fillets; such fillets are often sold anonymously, frozen, defrosted or fresh. Do not buy block-frozen fillets; they will lose too much of their natural juice while defrosting. Cook individual frozen fillets directly from frozen, adding 1 minute of cooking time for each whole fillet (30 seconds for a half). See FISH for cooking times.

Sole are responsible for one important culinary confusion. In many French cookbooks (and in the books that use them as a source, without too much reflection), we are told never to cook fish stock for more than 20 to 30 minutes. This was a warning that used to puzzle me, an avid maker of fish soups that used long-cooked fish stocks, until I began to work in restaurant kitchens. There I discovered that the bones most commonly used for broths were sole and other flatfish frames. So much "sole" is sold filleted and used in restaurant dishes that the bones are in plentiful supply. These bones do indeed turn bitter when cooked longer than 20 minutes. So, yes, if using sole bones for broth, keep the cooking brief, 5 minutes in a microwave oven. For other broths, cook away.

SORREL The thought of sorrel soup has sustained me through many hot weeding sessions. I prefer the small wild sorrel to the larger leaves of French sorrel, a garden perennial. Both have what are called shield or lance-shaped leaves. They look rather like arrowheads to me. All sorrels need to be thoroughly washed, dried and the leaves piled up going in the same direction so that they can be thinly sliced, into strips ⅛ inch wide, across the central vein (so they won't be stringy). This is called chiffonade. Never cook sorrel in an aluminum or coated aluminum pot. The sorrel will look and taste nasty due to the interaction of its considerable acids with the aluminum.

Sorrel makes the classic sauce for shad, page 192. The sauce can be easily thinned to make a cold soup that is one of the delights of spring and summer.

COOKING TIMES FOR SORREL

Cut into chiffonade; cover tightly.

⅛ lb. sorrel with 1 Tbs. butter (4-c. measure)	2 min.
½ lb. sorrel with 4 Tbs. butter (2-qt. soufflé)	3 min.

Yields

1 bunch sorrel	¼ lb., stemmed
¼ lb.	2 c., lightly packed chiffonade, raw
1 c., raw	3 Tbs., cooked
2 c., raw	¼ c., cooked
4 c., raw	½ c., cooked
¾ c., cooked	6 frozen 1-oz. cubes, for sauce

SOUR CREAM When called for in this book, commercially soured cream, preferably unstabilized (read the label), is intended. Sour cream is much used in Hungarian and Russian recipes. Unfortunately, it is just as fattening as heavy cream. It also tends to separate when cooked at too high a heat. The best method is to add it toward the very end of the cooking time. See Pork Chops with Sauerkraut.

SOY These legumes are among the most nutritious and widely grown of foods and are rich in an oil that has extensive commercial use. I like them neither as a vegetable nor as an oil. Processed, turned into soy sauce (shoyu) and bean curd, they are one of the Orient's greatest gifts to cooking, appreciated particularly by vegetarians whose diet might otherwise be poor in protein.

The *soy sauce* called for in the recipes in this book is the commercial brand most commonly available. It should be noted that it is an authentic soy sauce of no known country, but an acceptable compromise. I prefer tamari soy, which is authentically fermented and has a richer taste. It may be substituted in all recipes in this book, to their benefit. I do not recommend low-sodium soy because it has a thin taste. Those on salt-restricted diets would be better off substituting the similarly rich taste of balsamic vinegar, though it is slightly more expensive (see VINEGAR). True Chinese and Japanese soy sauces, usually marketed as shoyu, have a variety of distinct tastes; you may want to try them and substitute according to your results. One caution: Chinese soy sauce is often very salty.

Bean curd (tofu) is sold in many stores in two main forms: pillows $3'' \times 2'' \times 2''$, and cubes. The pillows are firmer and drier. Both are usually sold packed in water. When you get them home, rinse them off and re-cover with cold water to store. Three quarters of a cup of tofu per person, cut into 1-inch squares, may be stirred into any of the vegetable stews or casseroles before cooking. Add 30 seconds of cooking time to the recipe for each portion of tofu added. This will make nutritious vegetarian dishes.

SPAGHETTI SQUASH

Cooking spaghetti squash takes approximately the same amount of time in the microwave oven as in regular cooking. I would cook the squash conventionally and make the sauce in the microwave oven.

COOKING TIMES FOR SPAGHETTI SQUASH

Halve lengthwise; wrap each half tightly.

1 squash,	*20 min.*
4¾ lb.	

Yield

1 squash,	*4 c. cooked,*
4½ lb.	*separated into shreds*

SPICE Buy spices in small quantities and unground if possible; ground spices quickly lose the valuable flavor you have paid for. Most of these seeds and nuts need grinding before cooking. Exceptions are mustard seed, anise, caraway and other spices that are either used as is or toasted before use. See GRINDING; see also TOASTING, whole spices.

If spices are in glass bottles, they should be stored in a dark place away from the heat of the stove. Both light and heat affect them adversely. Read about spices and learn what makes for good ones. Pay a little more for the best; it makes a big difference in the food.

Microwave cooking tends to accentuate spices' effect, extracting all the volatile flavors. In most recipes, you can decrease spice quantities by one third. In long-cooking recipes, more than 15 minutes in the oven, you may want to return to something nearer standard quantities. For more specific information about quantities, see page 34.

For specific information, see ANISEED, CARAWAY, CARDAMOM, CAYENNE, CELERY SEED, CHILI, CLOVE, CUMIN, CURRY, DILL, GINGER, JUNIPER BERRY, MACE, NUTMEG and PAPRIKA. See also Spice Powders.

SPINACH Cooking spinach, either plain (no water needed) or in melted butter, takes the same brief time in the microwave oven. It is not only quick and clean, but also produces unusually bright green spinach, a joy in Creamed Spinach. The flavor is so intense you may very well not need any salt. If you find it is too strong for you, try cooking it uncovered.

COOKING TIMES FOR SPINACH

Stemmed

¼ lb. spinach (11" × 8½" × 2" dish, uncovered)	4 min. (small oven)
½ lb. spinach (14" × 11" × 2" dish, uncovered)	4 min.
2 lb. spinach (tightly sealed microwave-safe plastic bag)	5 min. 30 sec.

Yields

½ lb., stemmed	2 c., raw
2 c., raw	⅓ c. cooked
2 lb., stemmed	8 c., raw
8 c., raw	1½ c., cooked

SPLIT PEA I went to a progressive school where all the children learned how to cook—a fairly radical notion at the time. I made pea soup and was proud of myself. I went home and insisted on cooking it for my parents. What I prepared for them with so much fanfare was a thick, green, unappetizing sludge; that ended my split pea soup efforts. As I was creating recipes for this book, I realized that split peas must be tested. To my surprise, this rapid, controllable cooking method made my peace with both the peas and the soup.

It is inefficient to cook split peas in the microwave oven with all the liquid you will want for soup. Presoak and cook as you would large dried beans (see BEANS). Purée, then make one of the soups on page 106. The joy of this method is that, having no evaporation, you don't risk scorching, making library paste or leaving uncooked peas in the pot.

Consider using the purée as a vegetable with roast pork or Oriental Glazed Duck. If desired, stir some room-temperature butter and salt into the split peas after cooking. Yellow and green split peas cook exactly the same way. The taste isn't wildly different, either. The choice depends on the history of a dish and the colors on your plate.

Yield

1 c. dry   2 c. purée
peas

SPRING ONIONS Though
often confused with scallions,
spring onions have a distinct
round bulb at the bottom. They
may be cooked as are scallions.
The tops are almost never used
as a separate ingredient. See
SCALLION.

SQUAB Two kinds of small
birds strut under the name of
squab: pigeons, the better and
more expensive, and 1-pound
chickens, called poussin in
France. Pigeon has a deeper
taste and can take stronger seasoning. Along with small Cornish hens and quail, these are the
only birds that cook well whole
in the microwave oven: The in-
terior cavities are not so large
that timing becomes odd and
cooking uneven. While the
birds do not roast, a flavored
butter stuffing under the skin
not only improves the flavor, it
also causes the skin to turn an
attractive color. Allow 1 bird
per person. See Squab Seasoned with Butter Under the
Skin.

COOKING TIMES FOR SQUAB

Whole squab Stuff butter under skin, uncovered:

1 squab with   4 min.
2 Tbs. but-
ter (dinner
plate)

1 squab as   5 min. 30 sec.
above   (small oven)
2 squab with   6 min.
4 Tbs. but-
ter (serving
plate)

SQUASH The many varieties
of squash fall into either of two
categories: winter squash or
summer squash; thick-skinned
and thin-skinned, respectively.
For cooking times of winter varieties (acorn, butternut or hubbard), see SQUASH, winter. For
cooking times of summer varieties (zucchini and yellow or
summer squash), see SQUASH,
summer. See SPAGHETTI
SQUASH for that vegetable's
own particular cooking times.
Occasionally you may find, at
high prices, tiny baby vegetables in the store. They are more
beautiful than good-tasting. Remember that of the normally
sized squash, particularly the
summer varieties, smaller—
say 3 to 4 inches long—is better. If you must cook the baby
squash, steam whole at times
below.

SUMMER SQUASH

COOKING TIMES FOR
SUMMER SQUASH

Trim ends and wash well.
Times are the same for large
and medium ovens. For small
ovens, add 1 minute to cooking
times.

Quartered lengthwise Arrange in a dish just large
enough to hold squash in no

more than 2 layers; cover tightly.

¼ lb.	8 min.
½ lb.	8 to 9 min.
1 lb.	10 min.
2 lb.	12 to 14 min.

¼" crosswise slices or ¼" juliennes. Arrange as above; cover tightly.

¼ lb.	2 min. 30 sec.
½ lb.	3 min. 30 sec.
1 lb.	5 min.
2 lb.	8 min. 30 sec.

Yields

1 small zucchini	4 to 5 oz.
4 to 5 oz.	1 c. juliennes or ¼" slices, raw
1 c., raw	½ c., cooked

WINTER SQUASH

Varieties include acorn, butternut and hubbard squashes. Acorn squash is a marvelous vegetable on its own, unseasoned. *To make Seasoned Squash:* Sprinkle flesh of each cleaned squash half with salt and pepper and a little ground ginger or nutmeg, and place a 1-tablespoon lump of butter in the cavity before wrapping. *To make Glazed Squash:* For each half combine 1 tablespoon maple syrup with 1 teaspoon lemon juice, a pinch each of salt, pepper and cumin; swirl over flesh, letting any excess glaze pool in the cavity, or top after cooking with maple syrup or brown sugar and glaze under the broiler. Each half makes a single serving, either as is or scooped out and puréed with butter. See Acorn Squash Purée.

Cooked acorn squash can be a wonderful component of soups, purées and even desserts. See Acorn Squash Soup and Thanksgiving Pudding.

Cooking times for acorn squash apply to butternut squash and hubbard squash as well. To cook hubbard squash, cut it into pieces approximately 4" × 5". Arrange pieces skin side up in a ring and cover tightly with microwave plastic wrap; see illustration, page 296.

COOKING TIMES FOR WINTER SQUASH

Halve winter squash. Remove seeds and fibers. (Wash seeds and toast in conventional oven.) For acorn and butternut, wrap each seeded half tightly in microwave plastic wrap. For hubbard, cut the seeded halves into 3" × 4" pieces; arrange in a dish just large enough to hold the pieces, nubbly side down, in a single layer; cover tightly.

½ lb.	5 min.
1 lb.	7 min
1 lb.	10 min. (small oven)
2 lb.	15 min.
3 lb.	20 min.

Yields

1 acorn squash	1 lb.
1 lb. squash	1 c. purée

SQUID A member of a many-legged family of ink-bearing undersea animals whose large heads are also their bodies. Familiar as calamari fritti (fried rings and curly legs) in Italian restaurants. They are available fresh and frozen and can be cooked in other ways, notably stuffed. Their longish funnel-shaped body seems made for stuffing once the legs and innards, including the quill that contains the ink, have been removed. The legs can be chopped to add to the stuffing. While the ink can be a pleasant addition to a sauce, it is not copious enough to make really dark black risottos and pastas; for that you need cuttlefish. Most books say you should peel the thin speckled membrane from the body of the squid. I find it unnecessary. See Stuffed Squid. Briefly cooked, squid are a fine salad component; see Calamari Salad. The main thing is never to overcook them, or they will toughen.

Cuttlefish (seppie in Italian) is more round-oval than the elongated-oval squid and generally much larger. Its most prominent virtue is the generous quantities of ink in its sac; it also contains a second sac with a yellow fluid that is used in stews. Instead of a quill it has a large bone inside, the kind that canaries have in their cages for pecking. They are available frozen. See defrosting times on page 521.

To clean a cuttlefish, hold it over a bowl and tug gently on the legs. All the innards may come out at the same time. If not, reach into the head-body and pull out any remaining structures. Try not to break the ink sac. If the sac has broken, pour the ink through a coarse sieve. If the sac is intact, hold the tip of one end with your fingers, gently squeeze the sac with the thumb and forefinger of your other hand and slide them away from the first hand. It is much like squeezing the last toothpaste out of the tube. Wash your hands. In similar fashion, remove the liquid from the yellowish sac into another bowl. Cut the legs and tentacles free, in one piece. Discard remnants and bone. Wash the now-empty head. Do not bother to peel. Cut into strips as required by the recipe.

Cuttlefish are generally stewed to take advantage of their ink and other fluids. The ink is added to the cooking liquid for the last few minutes to warm and thicken. If cooked too long at too high a heat, it will coagulate, giving an unpleasantly grainy texture. When the ink is added to risotto to make Black Risotto, it must be measured. The broth quantity is then reduced by the amount of ink, and the ink is stirred in 3 minutes before the risotto is done. The squid body is sliced into rings and gently, briefly cooked in olive oil or butter with garlic and parsley, salt and pepper, if desired. The white squid is then arrayed dramatically on top of the dark risotto.

Allow 1 small cuttlefish for each cup of cooked risotto.

Occasionally, another smaller variety of cuttlefish, no more than 1 to 1½ inches long measured all the way to the tippy-toe end, comes on the market. It is best fried whole, dusted with flour or not. If flour-coated, do not fry in the microwave oven. For frying times, see Tempura. Elegant cooks will have the quill and ink sac fished out before cooking. I cook them intact and just watch for the quill when eating. Serve with lemons to squeeze over them. Truly, these are extraordinary. It is also the proper pre-preparation for paella.

The last member of the family to get much culinary attention is the *octopus*—not the giant creature from the deep seen in late-night movies, but a smaller relative. There are no octopus recipes in this book; I just don't have the patience or energy for octopus, which must be repeatedly clubbed or slammed on rocks to tenderize it before cooking. I have seen fishermen in Greece work on an octopus for half an hour at a time. Then the pieces are charcoal-grilled and are delicious.

COOKING TIMES FOR SQUID

Rings Tentacles separated, body cut into rings; cover tightly.

¾ lb. squid with 1 c. vegetables (1-qt. soufflé) — 2 min. 30 sec.

Stuffed Cook with 2 Tbs. stuffing per squid, uncovered.

1½ lb. squid with ½ c. sauce (12" round dish) — 5 min.

DEFROSTING TIMES FOR CUTTLEFISH

1½-lb. cuttlefish, covered tightly (2-qt. soufflé) — 40 min. at 30%

STEAMING Many foods are best steamed in the microwave oven, rather than poached or boiled. Fish, chicken and vegetables require little or no added liquid as they are very liquid themselves. To get the foods to steam, it is very important to cover them tightly with microwave plastic wrap (see page 20). Some of the advantages of steaming are the lack of a need for fat, the evenness and rapidity of cooking, the bright color and retained vitamins of vegetables.

STEWING The leisurely cooking of meats, vegetables and seafoods, and fruit, alone or in combination, in seasoned liquids. It works very well in the microwave oven. Due to the tight sealing, which eliminates evaporation and assures evenness of cooking, you must use less liquid than called for in standard recipes.

STOCK See CHICKEN BROTH and Meat Broths. See also CLARIFYING, broths and sauces, and DEFROSTING, homemade staples.

STRAIN This can mean two different things: to place something that has been cooked in a liquid in a sieve to remove the liquid (usually "strain in"), or to force a soft, generally cooked food through a sieve in order to purée it and remove any hard particles (usually "strain through"). Read your recipe to make the meaning clear. Straining to purée can be done in a food mill (page 25). It cannot be done in a food processor or blender because it will not remove pits, seeds, skin, etc. When this kind of straining is done through a sieve, you will have to push on the sieve firmly with a wooden spoon to push as much through as possible. It is easier if the sieve fits firmly on the bowl into which your purée or sauce will pass.

STRAWBERRY These wonderful red fruits—both the small, pointy Alpine (European) variety from everbearing plants and the large, roundish, originally American variety propagated by runners from their plants—are at their best fresh and in season. I really don't like what happens to strawberries when they are cooked or frozen: They get fuzzy. The one great exception is Strawberry Jam. If you do want to freeze a bumper crop in syrup rather than berry by berry (to save room), make SIMPLE SYRUP ("2 to 1"): 1 quart (4

cups) syrup to an equal amount of berries. Allow syrup to cool 4 minutes, uncovered, after it comes out of the microwave oven. Stir in washed, hulled and dried (sliced if you wish) berries. Place in freezer containers and freeze immediately.

Yields

16 large berries	1 pt.
1 pt.	3/4 lb.
3/4 lb.	2 c., cored, sliced 1/4"

STRING BEAN Green bean. See BEANS, fresh.

STRIPED BASS This North American Atlantic coastal fish often goes upriver for the winter to spawn. It is the best of the white-fleshed fish from this area, and I think it is one of the best fish in the world—certainly equal to, if not better than, the famous French Mediterranean loup de mer. The flesh is firm without being extra firm. It has enough fat to keep it moist when grilled or steamed without ever getting oily. Depending on the size, it is cooked whole, in fillets, or steaks. See FISH for cooking times.

STURGEON I find it confusing that a fish that brings a premium price when smoked, and whose eggs sold as caviar bring very high prices, itself sells at very modest prices. This is no doubt because people don't know how to cook it. In Russia, it is a highly desired prime ingredient for fish soup, solianka.

Sturgeon has exceedingly firm flesh with a color like that of veal, to which it is often compared. Although it is a fat fish, it is not self-basting due to its firmness, so it is not a candidate for grilling. It also toughens if boiled or poached whole. The best results are obtained by filleting the fish, then cutting it into crosswise slices and cooking it like veal or tuna. See Index for tuna recipes. See FISH for cooking times.

Incidentally, in the realm of little-known facts, the cartilaginous spinal marrow of sturgeon is in great demand in Russian recipes as a thickening, in Coulibiac and other delicacies. It is sold dried and called vesiga. When you cook the broth for solianka, you can easily remove it from the spine. Use as is, or dry—cut in 2-inch lengths—on a sheet of paper toweling, uncovered, for 3 minutes at 100%. Store tightly covered and refrigerated.

SUET Hard, white animal fat, the best of which cushions beef, veal and mutton kidneys (leaf lard). It can be used raw and flaked or ground up for pie crusts, or melted to make a superior (in terms of taste if not nutrition) frying fat. See RENDERING.

SUGAR Sugar is one of those surprises in microwave cooking. While it dissolves fairly slowly in water and needs to be stirred, on its own it cooks very quickly, acting almost as a magnet for the microwaves. Heavily sugared mixtures will cook more quickly. It is impossible to create a true caramelized glaze on top of a cooked mixture in the microwave oven; sugar mixtures, however, will increase in density and caramelize rapidly in the microwave oven. Caramelizing in this way is a delight: no untoward crystals, no burned and hard-to-clean pots, perfect control. Always uncover sugar mixtures carefully to avoid the hot steam. See CARAMEL and SIMPLE SYRUP; see also Pralines.

BROWN SUGAR

Brown sugar, dark or light, is sugar with some of the molasses left in or added. Due to its high moisture content, it tends to coalesce into a solid block once the package is opened. It can be easily softened in the microwave oven; see SOFTENING.

SUGAR SNAP PEA An edible pod pea with fully formed peas inside, this has been touted as a recent innovation, but nineteenth-century strains existed. Sugar snap peas must be strung, from both ends. They are at their best flung on top of stew to steam for the last 2 minutes of cooking time in the microwave oven. Do not overcook, or the pods become mushy. Cook as for SNOW PEA.

SUNFLOWER SEED A few large sunflowers will cheer up a vegetable garden. Their heads will provide enough seeds for a long winter by the fire. When the petals begin to go, cut off the flowers and bring indoors. Turn flowers upside down on a clean piece of paper. The seeds will drop out by themselves; after a few days you can shake the flower to hasten the dropping of the seeds. Toast in a conventional oven.

SWEATING In French cooking, vegetables are sometimes diced, then slowly cooked in a little fat to evaporate some of their water and intensify their taste. This can be done rapidly in the microwave oven by tossing the vegetables with melted butter and cooking, uncovered, at 100% for 2 to 3 minutes.

SWEETBREADS Cooked almost exclusively—and often incorrectly—in restaurants, sweetbreads become easy to cook with the microwave oven. The result is better than by any other method: less cleaning, blanching, firming and so forth, and better texture at the end. Suddenly, sweetbreads are easy, and there is no longer a reason to have to omit them in sneaky guilt from classic preparations such as financière. See Summer Pâté with Veal, Sweetbreads and Spinach.

COOKING TIMES FOR
SWEETBREADS

Trimmed; cover tightly.

1¼ lb. sweetbreads   5 min
  with ½ c. vegetables
  and 1 c. liquid (2-qt.
  soufflé)

SWEET POTATO Both yellow and white, these starchy tubers are often confused with yams. White sweet potatoes are sweeter than the yellow and take about 3 minutes longer to cook. Both do well in purée, a use to which they are frequently put in the Caribbean, but will take much more butter and cream to come smooth than white potatoes. Cook for following times for purée or pie.

COOKING TIMES FOR
SWEET POTATOES

Whole Prick and set on paper toweling, uncovered.

2 lb. yellow pota-   13 to 15
  toes (about 2   min.
  large)

SWORDFISH This large game fish produces marvelous boneless steaks for grilling. They are also very good cooked in the microwave oven. Medallions and cubes for specific recipes are easily cut from thick steaks. A healthy fat content keeps the tightly grained and firm flesh moist. Do not overcook. See FISH for cooking times.

T

TAMARI See SOY.

TAPIOCA I hated this when I was a child; but it cooks so thoroughly in the microwave oven that it is a treat. Use for dessert or, as in older French recipes, to thicken soups. Cooked in the microwave oven, there is no stirring during the cooking, no first bringing the liquid to a boil. The quick-cooking tapioca available in stores today is preferable.

COOKING TIMES FOR QUICK-COOKING TAPIOCA

For dessert Makes 2½ cups. Cover tightly.

*3 Tbs. tapioca with   10 min.
  2 c. milk, 1 egg and
  3 Tbs. sugar (8-c.
  measure)*

To thicken soup Cover tightly.

*1 Tbs. tapioca with   10 min.
  2 c. broth (4-c.
  measure)*

TARRAGON Russian tarragon is not worth growing. French tarragon with its leaves tasting slightly of licorice is a delight. Tarragon should never be cooked for a long time. Its leaves, whole or chopped, may be added to stews like Chicken Fricassee and Veal Fricassee or to sauces like Sauce Suprême and Sauce Espagnole a few minutes before serving. Use about 1 tablespoon fresh leaves to each cup of sauce or every 2 cups of stew. Normally, I don't like dried tarragon. It tastes like bad tea. Microwave-oven-dried tarragon is far superior in color and flavor. If you don't have the space to freeze tarragon (in whole branches, then stored loosely wrapped in a plastic bag), try drying it. See DRYING, herbs.

TEMPERING Usually done to chocolate that is melted for glazing or dipping to keep it shiny and stable. It does not need to be done when chocolate is melted in the microwave oven; it will not lose its temper if melted exactly as described. See CHOCOLATE, melting.

THICKENING Many soups, sauces and purées need to be thickened at the end of their cooking times. See CORNSTARCH and EMULSIFICATION. See also ROUX.

THYME There are two major forms of this herb, bush and creeping. There are many varieties of each of these forms: different colors of leaves and flowers and different nuances to the taste (lemon, for one). It is the bush kind that is generally used as part of a bouquet garni and in meat and mushroom preparations. It has a strong flavor. It dries magnificently. Reduce quantities for use in microwave cooking by about half for both fresh and dried. See DRYING, herbs. See page 34 for adjusting quantities when cooking in the microwave oven.

TILEFISH A white-fleshed fish whose plenitude and inexpensiveness have recently made it popular along the eastern seaboard. It tends to get quite mushy, as it has soft flesh. For this reason, I find it better cooked quickly in fillets. Since it lacks a defined taste, it is better cooked in dishes with other seafoods or with tomato sauces. Substitute in recipes like Scrod with Clams Livornese or Cod Mexican. See FISH for cooking times.

TIMING It is not only that almost everything cooks more quickly in the microwave oven. Remember, too, that you do not have to allow time for water to come to a boil; that time is included in the recipe. To time a meal, or the proper preparation of courses in a meal, see Microwave Basics (pages 23–34).

TOASTING The browning of the sugary part of a usually dry food in the presence of heat. Do not attempt to make breakfast toast in the microwave oven. The toast dries out before it browns, and it will brown unevenly. Many other foods are often toasted before using in a recipe. Many of them will do well in the microwave oven.

To toast *croutons*, see page 355.

To toast *nuts*, see NUTS, toasting.

To toast *coconut*, see page 354. You can toast coconut that has already been used in the making of coconut milk or cream.

To toast *whole spices and small seeds* (such as mustard, caraway or sesame), spread a quantity, up to ¼ cup, in a shallow layer in a flat dish. Cook, uncovered, at 100% for 6 minutes. This is particularly desirable before making curry powder. See Spice Powders, page 345. It also can rescue herb seeds that are a little old. Large raw seeds such as sunflower toast better in the conventional oven.

TOMALLEY The greenish liver of lobsters, crayfish and shrimp should never be thrown away. Tomalley is a flavorful addition to Mayonnaise to be served with cold lobster or to other fish sauces. Try whisking it into a fish broth-based Sauce Suprême or a Sauce Américaine. It adds creamy texture and a mysterious richness of background flavor.

TOMATILLO The tomatillo is not a tomato, even if its name means small tomato and it is sometimes called husk tomato or green tomato. Related to the ground cherry and cape gooseberry, it originally comes from South America, and is most used in Mexican and southwestern American cooking. It grows in a papery husk that has to be removed before cooking; after removing it, you'll find the tomatillo is sticky to the touch and should be washed.

Despite common wisdom that says tomatillos should be slightly cooked to bring out their flavor, I prefer green salsa to be based on raw, chopped tomatillos. Tomatillos have a pleasant acidity, and substituting them for part of the chopped tomatoes in chili is a nice touch. Add them later than the tomatoes, 5 minutes before the end of cooking, so they retain some texture. See Caribbean Fish Stew.

TOMATO I love tomatoes. To my mind, one of the best reasons to put in the work of planting a vegetable garden and maintaining it all season long is to have sunwarm, vine-ripened tomatoes of a broad range of colors, sizes, textures and flavors available in one sense-startling glut, and the joy of putting them up in so many guises for winter-long pleasure! There is a deadening uniformity in an increasingly lower standard of commercial tomatoes. Do not despair. I enjoy them within their limits: I use commercially canned tomatoes, packed whole, in juice or paste, Italian plum or American; tomatoes canned as juice, paste (better in tubes), purée, crushed, commercial pasta sauce and even ketchup.

Microwave cooking can help us with many of the pedestrian tasks involved in cooking tomatoes. It helps us make sauces and pastes quickly enough so that some of the acid freshness of the tomato remains. In addition, it is a joy to cook stuffed tomatoes in the microwave oven; they retain their shape and color, cooking without collapsing.

Despite prevailing snobbery, I tend to use American-style tomatoes rather than the Italian, except when making Italian-style pasta sauces. American tomatoes, to me, have a fresher, more acid taste.

While tomatoes are used frequently in this book, I have restrained myself. Wanting this book to be as usable as possible with commonly available ingredients, I do not call for glorious reddish-gold tomatoes or firm, green tomatoes, nor for those wonderful little Italian tomatoes that dry and sweeten as they hang from drying racks. I use all of these and recommend that you try them when you can get them. In early fall, when the acrid smell of late tomatoes is in the air and they can be bought by the inexpensive bushel, do at least consider putting up some for winter use; with the microwave oven, it is easy.

Most of the basic tomato recipes are better made in the microwave oven. See Lightly Cooked Crushed Tomatoes and Chunky Tomato Sauce.

TONGUE Fresh tongue does not cook as well in the microwave oven as on top of the stove; but smoked tongue does very well, and in 20 minutes becomes a valid quick dinner for a crowd.

TROUT How confusing: Many native American trout are really Arctic char. Most of the trout caught in this country are brown trout that were introduced from Europe and took over. Rainbow (speckled) trout is a true trout and a true American, although it has been naturalized in Europe. Almost all the trout we get to eat is farm-raised. The highly esteemed wild brook trout is protected from being eaten as an object of sport in most American waters (it also comes from a totally different family from the rest of the trout). Some varieties go to sea and acquire different names there; they also appear in larger forms in lakes, where they acquire yet a third set of names. If I were you, I would let your fisherman be responsible for the name of the fish. What you buy in the store will probably be a rainbow weighing about 14 ounces.

If I could make one reform in trout cookery in America, it would be to get anglers and fish stores alike to gut the trout through the gills rather than slitting the stomach. Trout have very thin flesh on the stomach flaps, and it dries out when the fish are gutted by slitting. This becomes particularly important when cooking Blue Trout (au bleu), my favorite way.

Normally, trout can only be cooked au bleu when freshly caught with their natural, protective slime intact. With the aid of the microwave oven, I can get a creditable result with store trout, even with trout that have been frozen. See Blue Trout. For defrosting times see DEFROSTING, fish and seafood.

TRUFFLE This precious underground growth, black or white, is highly esteemed by eaters and cooks. The white Italian truffle should not be washed or cooked. It should be brushed with a soft toothbrush to remove sand and grit, then thinly shaved over hot risotto or egg pasta in a cream sauce. If you have the truffles or the money, try it. Black truffles really need to be cooked to bring out all their potential. Again, if you have some, stud the French Pâté with them and watch it all come together.

These expensive delights are echoed in name, shape and color by Chocolate Truffles, made, basically, of cream and chocolate.

TUNA Different varieties are found in salt waters in most parts of the world where the water is not gelid. The American white meat (for canning purposes) albacore tuna is light-fleshed throughout. Most tuna are whiter where they are fatter, in the belly; this belly meat is called ventresca in Italy and toro in Japan, where it is the most highly esteemed cut for sashimi.

There are many different sizes and kinds of tuna, each with its own name in different parts of the world. Mahi-mahi and ahi, which have turned up recently on American menus, are not new fish, merely different tunas called by their Hawaiian names.

I am a great defender of canned tuna and the tuna fish sandwich. When it comes to fresh tuna, my favorite way of eating it is raw. That does not mean that I don't also adore it grilled, steamed and stewed. Cooked tuna seems to be a different fish altogether. It develops its characteristic smell, darkens in color and becomes firmer. Although liberally supplied with fat, it will dry out if overcooked.

Tuna is generally sold in filleted steaks. At this point it can be cut into medallions, cubes or other portions for cooking. See FISH for cooking times.

TURBOT The most highly esteemed of the European flatfish, with firm, gelatinous white flesh and a nice fat layer under the skin. In the Pacific, some flounder go around masquerading as their betters. Recently, in Canada a small "almost turbot" has been farm-bred. For the best, buy imports. Turbot is almost always poached or steamed plain and served with a little melted butter or Hollandaise to let its delicate flavor and texture shine. This makes it a perfect candidate for microwave cooking, where the oven can serve as that odd-shaped pot, the turbotière. If it will fit in the oven, wrap the whole fish tightly in microwave plastic wrap. Cook at 100%. Turbot cooks well in steaks and fillets, as long as they're not too small. See FISH for cooking times.

TURKEY Once more, the microwave oven does not roast. When you want a glorious, festive, crisply browned bird, light up the regular oven.

If you want to cook individual portions of turkey, or enough for salad, cook as CHICKEN by weight without bone.

TURKEY BROTH While your turkey is roasting, place giblets and neck (no liver!), 1 small peeled and quartered onion and 1 stalk of celery in an 8-cup glass measure with 3 cups of water or Chicken Broth. Cover tightly. Cook for 20 to 40 minutes at 100%. Slice gizzard and heart; remove meat from neck. Use meat and broth to make gravy. After your guests have demolished the turkey, reclaim the bones. Rinse them off and cut them up; proceed as for Chicken Broth with Vegetables.

TURNIP Here, I mean all-white or white and purple turnips. They are peeled before cooking. See RUTABAGA for yellow turnips.

COOKING TIMES FOR
TURNIPS

Diced Cover tightly.

4 turnips (4-c. measure)	6 min.
4 turnips as above	10 min. (small oven)

Yields

4 turnips	1 lb.
1 lb.	¾ lb., trimmed and peeled
¾ lb., raw	3 c. diced, raw
3 c., raw	2½ c., cooked

TURNIP GREENS See POT GREENS.

V

VANILLA This is one of the only ugly orchids, but it has the advantage of being the only one with a usable seed. The whole pod is long and thin and dark brown. For the purposes of cooking, vanilla is available as an essence in an alcohol base, as a powder and as whole beans. Watch out for vanillin: It is an artificial substitute with a disagreeable aftertaste. Vanilla is often thought of either in ice cream or in combination with chocolate. It is good both ways; it is also a taste that goes with seafood sauces.

I have only recently learned that the French trick of storing vanilla beans in granulated sugar is not the ideal way. They are supposed to be stored in the refrigerator in a tightly closed glass jar or tube. I may go on storing an odd bean in sugar; I like the way the sugar tastes and smells, particularly in a cup of tea. I have found, however, that for this purpose I can rinse off and use a piece of bean that has given the first blush of its youth to a custard or a fruit-poaching syrup.

Where feasible (not in cookies), beans are always preferable to extract. This is particularly true in microwave cooking. You will get unexpectedly vivid flavors from the bean, while the extract will tend to dissipate and more will be required (see ALCOHOL). A 2-inch piece of vanilla bean split lengthwise equals 1 teaspoon vanilla extract.

VEAL This is expensive meat, and very often what we buy doesn't fulfill the promises of young and tender. One has only to see the huge legs masquerading as veal to know that it is simply food-starved baby beef. Real veal, small, young and gelatinous, is delicious. Reluctantly, I give recipes based on commercially available veal; if smaller veal comes your way, substitute the cooking times below.

While it is true that the microwave oven will not roast, it

is less important in the case of veal than beef. Veal is easily dried out and toughened by dry-heat cooking. The moist method available in the microwave oven will produce superior results. Think of the texture of the best Vitello Tonnato and you will get the idea.

One of my favorite tricks of the microwave oven is its ability to cook Ossobuco in short order, even ossobuco for one or two—unthinkably silly by any other method. Two other star turns are the cooking of MARROW and the extraction of gelatin from bone to make broth. See Meat Broths.

Carefully time when braised and stewed veal will be ready. It should be served instantaneously, or it will toughen. Do not overcook.

COOKING TIMES FOR VEAL

Stewing veal Cut into 2″ cubes; cover tightly.

2 lb. veal with 2¾ c. liquid and 1 lb. vegetables (2-qt. soufflé)	15 min., stand 10 min., then 4 min.
2 lb. veal with 1½ c. liquid (2-qt. soufflé)	10 min., stand 10 min.

Veal shank Cut across the bone, 2½″ thick; cover tightly.

1½ lb. (2 shank pieces) with ⅜ c. liquid and ¼ c. vegetables (8″ × 6″ dish)	12 min, stand 15 min.
3 lb. (4 shank pieces) with ¾ c. liquid and ½ c. vegetables (11″ × 8″ × 2″ oval dish)	16 min., stand 15 min.
4½ lb. (6 shank pieces) with 1 c. liquid and 1½ c. vegetables (14″ × 11″ × 2″ dish)	22 min., stand 15 min.

Loin Boned; cover tightly.

1½ lb. with ½ c. liquid (9″ × 5″ × 3″ dish)	6 min.

VEAL BROTH See Meat Broths. See also DEFROSTING, homemade staples, and CLARIFYING, broths and sauces.

VEAL GLAZE See Meat Glazes.

VEGETABLE OIL By this I do not mean olive oil, Oriental sesame oil, walnut or hazelnut oil. I mean the neutral-tasting oils made from various seeds and grains. They are cold- or hot-pressed. Aside from that, the vegetable oils can be used interchangeably.

VEGETABLE PEAR See CHAYOTE.

VEGETABLES Vegetables cook brilliantly in the microwave oven. When cooking a variety of them at once, make sure that they cook evenly by arranging slow-cooking vegetables toward the outside of the dish and quick-cooking vegetables in the center. See Pasta Primavera (pages 146–147).

SLOW-COOKING VEGETABLES: broccoli, carrots, cauliflower, cherry tomatoes, green beans, peas, red cabbage, sugar snap peas.

QUICK-COOKING VEGETABLES: asparagus, bell peppers, mushrooms, red onion slices, scallions, yellow summer squash, zucchini.

VERMOUTH A fortified red or white wine (alcohol is added) made with various herbs and spices. It may be aged or not, dry or not. While some may be sweet, I generally call for the stronger, more bitter-tasting ones in my recipes. A little dry white vermouth can be used in sauces for fish instead of white wine. If you have these wines in the house, experiment with them. A deep-red aged vermouth would be very good as part of the wine in Pears in Red Wine.

VINEGAR After one set of yeasts has produced wine from fruits or grains, another set comes along and turns the wine into vinegar—not something you want to have happen to your best bottles, but a lovely fate for apple juice and lesser wines. Vinegar retains some flavor from its starting liquid and can acquire more from the way it is aged or from having things steeped in it.

For instance, the best raspberry vinegar is made from raspberries that are fermented; however, most, even the fancy imports, are made by adding a raspberry syrup to a plain wine vinegar. There is still another way of making raspberry vinegar that I prefer to the syrup method. Fresh raspberries are macerated in white vinegar. If enough raspberries are used, this gives a fresh fruity taste and nose. The syrup kind smells and tastes like candy.

Special vinegars are aged over a long period of time in a succession of casks of decreasing size in different woods. Balsamic, for example, acquires a rich, sweetish, complex taste that is very attractive. Even though it is quite high in acid, due to its flavor balance, it tastes less acidic than plain white American vinegar. Balsamic vinegar is a good substitute for soy sauce for those who must diminish their salt intake. If a recipe calls for both vinegar and soy, substitute two thirds as much balsamic vinegar.

Other special vinegars include Japanese rice vinegar—clear, with a hint of yellow and a light, pleasant flavor. Sherry vinegar from Spain has a nutty flavor and does well in salads made with nut oils and even actual nuts in the dressing. Malt vinegar has a medium depth of flavor and is favored by the British for sprinkling on fish and chips.

W

WAHOO (KINGFISH) An excellent game fish, it is unfortunately not generally available in stores. If your personal deep-sea fisherman brings some home, remember that it is a firm fish with a definite, but not oily, taste. Preparations similar to those for swordfish and tuna will do very well. See FISH for cooking times.

WALNUT Available in the shell and shelled, whole, in pieces and halves, they are lovely seasoned and toasted (see NUTS, toasting). Walnuts are less oily and firmer than pecans, and hence easier to grind (see GRINDING). Walnut oil is very full-tasting, but it goes rancid quickly and can even get a rancid taste when cooked. I prefer to use it cold in salad dressings.

WARMING See REHEATING.

WATER The presence of water is very important in the microwave oven, since much of the cooking is done by generated steam. Since the oven will generate steam from the liquid already in most foods, quantities of additional water are not generally needed. However, water takes a relatively long time to heat, so it is important to minimize water and liquids containing water in recipes for the microwave oven.

When cooking recipes in this book, it is important not to increase the proportion of liquid. When making your own recipes, look first for a similar one already adapted for the microwave oven and be guided by it. An advantage of little water usage is that you don't throw the vitamins out with the cooking water.

WATERCRESS Watercress risks falling into parsley's trap: overuse as decoration (see PARSLEY). Remember that watercress is a green with a sharp, peppery taste and should be used to take advantage of this, not used just for decoration. It needs cooking to set its color; in the microwave oven, the color will be radiant. Consider substituting watercress for part of the spinach in soups and purées, and don't season with pepper until the cooking is done. See Watercress Sauce.

WATERLESS COOKING Most foods have a high water or fat content, they really don't need added liquid to cook well in the microwave oven as long as they are tightly wrapped. See STEAMING.

WAX BEAN See BEANS.

WHEAT See FLOUR.

WHISK A handle with thin wires attached to it, used to beat sauces and other mixtures in order to smooth out lumps. It is sometimes used to beat in air, as for egg whites and cream. Some mixers have whisk attachments.

WHITE BEAN See BEANS, dried.

WHITEBAIT Tiny fish, a gaggle of which are usually fried whole and eaten like chips. They should be cooked in a deep-fat fryer, since they need to be lightly dusted with flour before frying.

WHITEFISH Landlocked lake fish, with white flaky flesh and a good amount of fat. Do not overcook; cook in fillets. They are a traditional ingredient of Gefilte Fish and are also often served smoked.

WHITING A white-fleshed fish of the hake family, with rather soft flesh. Its fillets can be substituted for hake, but will not be quite as good. See Whiting with Parsley Sauce. See FISH for cooking times. See illustration, page 200.

WINE See ALCOHOL.

WORCESTERSHIRE SAUCE A quick way to get color and flavor into sauces such as Red Barbecue Sauce, page 377.

Y

YAM Cooking times (except for white yams, which take forever) are the same as for SWEET POTATO.

YARD-LONG BEAN Known also as Philippine bean and long bean. See BEANS, fresh, for cooking times.

YEAST Yeast doughs can be given a boost in rising with the microwave oven. See RAISING.

YELLOW SQUASH Known also as summer squash. The distinction between straightneck and crookneck varieties is made in gardening, but seldom in cooking. For cooking times, see SQUASH, summer.

YOGURT This is not the fountain of youth. It is a delightful, acid-tasting ingredient for cooking. All yogurt called for in this book is unsweetened and unflavored. Lowfat yogurt will cut down on calories. Yogurt, like sour cream, tends to separate with heat; it should be stirred in at the end of the cooking time. See Cold Curried Tomato Soup with Yogurt and Lamb Shanks with Spinach.

Z

ZEST   The thin outer rind of citrus fruits, widely used in cooking and baking. It should have no pith—the white, bitter, inner rind—clinging to it. The easiest way to remove zest is to peel it off in strips from whole fruits using a potato peeler. Some recipes may call for these strips to be cut lengthwise into thin sliverlike strips.

When zest is being used as decoration rather than cooked as an ingredient, it is often blanched. Place strips of zest in a single layer on a plate; sprinkle with 2 tablespoons water. Cover tightly; cook at 100% for 1 minute. See DRYING.

ZUCCHINI   For cooking times, see SQUASH, summer.

INDEX

This index is a list by food and category. If you are looking for kosher, vegetarian or hors d'oeuvre foods, you will find them listed under those headings as well. Page numbers in italics refer to illustrations.